ENGLISH LITERATURE IN THE
SIXTEENTH CENTURY
EXCLUDING DRAMA

ENGLISH LITERATURE
IN THE
SIXTEENTH CENTURY
EXCLUDING DRAMA

BY

C. S. LEWIS

The Completion of
THE CLARK LECTURES
Trinity College, Cambridge
1944

OXFORD UNIVERSITY PRESS
LONDON   OXFORD   NEW YORK

Oxford University Press

OXFORD LONDON NEW YORK

GLASGOW TORONTO MELBOURNE WELLINGTON

CAPE TOWN IBADAN NAIROBI DAR ES SALAAM LUSAKA ADDIS ABABA

DELHI BOMBAY CALCUTTA MADRAS KARACHI LAHORE DACCA

KUALA LUMPUR SINGAPORE HONG KONG TOKYO

First published 1954
First issued as an
Oxford University Press paperback 1973

Printed in Great Britain
at the University Press, Oxford
by Vivian Ridler
Printer to the University

PUBLISHER'S NOTE

THE cloth-bound edition of this book forms vol. III of The Oxford History of English Literature, edited originally by F. P. Wilson and Bonamy Dobrée, and now by Kenneth Allott and Norman Davis. That edition contains a detailed Chronological Table and an extensive Bibliography (referred to in the Author's Preface) which, to make the main text more cheaply available, have been omitted from this paperback.

PREFACE

WHEN I began this book I had the idea—perhaps most literary historians have—of giving each author space in proportion to the value I set on him; but I found it would not do. Things need to be treated at length not in so far as they are great but in so far as they are complicated. Good books which are remote from modern sympathy need to be treated at greater length than good books which everyone already knows and loves. Bad books may be of importance for the history of taste and if they are passed over too briefly the student's picture of a period may be distorted. Finally, if I had worked strictly to scale I should have been forced either to leave out many minor authors altogether (as roads and small rivers could not be made visible in maps unless their width were exaggerated) or else to say more on some great authors not because more needed to be said but for the sake of proportion.

Where I have quoted from neo-Latin authors I have tried to translate them into sixteenth-century English, not simply for the fun of it but to guard the reader from a false impression he might otherwise receive. When passages from Calvin, Scaliger, or Erasmus in modern English jostle passages from vernacular writers with all the flavour of their period about them, it is fatally easy to get the feeling that the Latinists are somehow more enlightened, less remote, less limited by their age, than those who wrote English. It seemed worth some pains to try to remove so serious and so latent a misconception.

As I write 'French' not *Français*, I have also written 'Scotch' not *Scottish*; aware that these great nations do not so call themselves, but claiming the freedom of 'my ain vulgaire'.

It is the rule of this series that the titles of books (with certain exceptions) should be modernized in the text but given exactly in the Bibliography.

I have to thank the Master and Fellows of Trinity College, Cambridge, for allowing me to use this book, in an embryonic state, as the Clark Lectures (1944); Professor F. P. Wilson for such painstaking and skilled help as few authors have ever had from their friends; Mr. Dowling for much help with my Bibliography, and Professor Douglas Bush for submitting to certain petty pilferings from his; Mr. R. E. Alton for guidance through the labyrinth of our Faculty library; Dr. J. A. W. Bennett and Mr. H. V. D. Dyson for advice and criticism; and Miss Joy Davidman for help with the proofs.

C. S. L.

MAGDALEN COLLEGE
    OXFORD
   7 *October* 1953

CONTENTS

INTRODUCTION
New Learning and New Ignorance

THE rough outline of our literary history in the sixteenth century is not very difficult to grasp. At the beginning we find a literature still medieval in form and spirit. In Scotland it shows the highest level of technical brilliance: in England it has for many years been dull, feeble, and incompetent. As the century proceeds, new influences arise: changes in our knowledge of antiquity, new poetry from Italy and France, new theology, new movements in philosophy or science. As these increase, though not necessarily because of them, the Scotch literature is almost completely destroyed. In England the characteristic disease of late medieval poetry, its metrical disorder, is healed: but replaced, for the most part, by a lifeless and laboured regularity to which some ears might prefer the vagaries of Lydgate. There is hardly any sign of a new inspiration. Except for the songs of Wyatt, whose deepest roots are medieval, and the prose of the Prayer Book, which is mostly translation, authors seem to have forgotten the lessons which had been mastered in the Middle Ages and learned little in their stead. Their prose is clumsy, monotonous, garrulous; their verse either astonishingly tame and cold or, if it attempts to rise, the coarsest fustian. In both mediums we come to dread a certain ruthless emphasis; bludgeon-work. Nothing is light, or tender, or fresh. All the authors write like elderly men. The mid-century is an earnest, heavy-handed, commonplace age: a drab age. Then, in the last quarter of the century, the unpredictable happens. With startling suddenness we ascend. Fantasy, conceit, paradox, colour, incantation return. Youth returns. The fine frenzies of ideal love and ideal war are readmitted. Sidney, Spenser, Shakespeare, Hooker—even, in a way, Lyly—display what is almost a new culture: that culture which was to last through most of the seventeenth century and to enrich the very meanings of the words *England* and *Aristocracy*. Nothing in the earlier history of our period would have enabled the sharpest observer to foresee this transformation.

Some have believed, or assumed, that it resulted from what

seemed at the time to be a resurrection, rejuvenescence, or
renascentia[1]—the recovery of Greek and the substitution of Augustan for medieval Latin. It is, of course, true that the rich vernacular literature of the eighties used the fruits of that event, as
it used the Middle Ages and everything else it could lay its
hands on. It is also true that many movements of thought which
affected our literature would have been impossible without the
recovery of Greek. But if there is any closer connexion than that
between the *renascentia* and the late sixteenth-century efflorescence of English literature, I must confess that it has escaped
me. The more we look into the question, the harder we shall
find it to believe that humanism had any power of encouraging,
or any wish to encourage, the literature that actually arose.
And it may be as well to confess immediately that I have no
alternative 'explanation' to offer. I do not claim to know why
there were many men of genius at that time. The Elizabethans
themselves would have attributed it to Constellation. I must
be content with trying to sketch some of the intellectual and
imaginative conditions under which they wrote.

It comes naturally to a modern to suppose that the new
astronomy made a profound impression on men's minds; but
when we look into the literary texts we find it rarely mentioned.
The idea that it produced a shock comparable to that which
Darwin gave to the Victorians or Freud to our own age is certainly mistaken. Nor are the reasons hard to find. In the first
place it must be remembered that the *De Revolutionibus* (1543)
of Copernicus put forward only a theory: verification, at the
hands of Kepler and Galileo, came only at the end of our period,
and general acceptance later still. And secondly, humanism,
dominant in mid-sixteenth-century England, tended to be on
the whole indifferent, if not hostile, to science. It is an English
humanist, a classical pedant, who in Bruno's *Cena delle Cenere*
(1584) still thinks that Copernicus can be dismissed with an
airy gibe from the *Adagia* of Erasmus. Even where the new
theory was accepted, the change which it produced was not of
such emotional or imaginative importance as is sometimes supposed. For ages men had believed the earth to be a sphere. For

[1] 'Revertuntur…graeca et latina lingua seu renascuntur verius' (Vives, *De Causis
Corruptarum Artium*, 1). '(Poesis) tametsi rediviva novam sub Petrarcha pueritiam
inchoasse' (Scaliger, *Poet.*, VI. i). 'In veterum lucubrationibus restituendis laborant
et ceu a mortuis revocant' (Huldrichus Coccius, *Ep. Ded.* to *Opera Vivis*. Basel,
1555).

ages, as we see in Vincent of Beauvais or Dante or 'John Mandeville', men had realized that movement towards the centre of the earth from whatever direction was downward movement. For ages men had known, and poets had emphasized, the truth that earth, in relation to the universe, is infinitesimally small: to be treated, said Ptolemy, as a mathematical point (*Almagest*, I. v). Nor was it generally felt that earth, or Man, would lose dignity by being shifted from the cosmic centre. The central position had not implied pre-eminence. On the contrary, it had implied, as Montaigne says (*Essais*, II. xii), 'the worst and deadest part of the universe', 'the lowest story of the house', the point at which all the light, heat, and movement descending from the nobler spheres finally died out into darkness, coldness, and passivity. The position which was locally central was dynamically marginal: the rim of being, farthest from the hub. Hence, when any excitement was shown at the new theory, it might be exhilaration. The divine Cusanus (1401–64), who was an early believer (for his own, metaphysical, reasons) in earth's movement, rejoiced in 1440 to find that she also is 'a noble star' with her own light, heat, and influence (*De Docta Ignorantia*, II. xii).

What proved important (and that slowly) about the new astronomy was not the mere alteration in our map of space but the methodological revolution which verified it. This is not sufficiently described as a change from dogmatism to empiricism. Mere empiricists like Telesius or Bacon achieved nothing. What was fruitful in the thought of the new scientists was the bold use of mathematics in the construction of hypotheses, tested not by observation simply but by controlled observation of phenomena that could be precisely measured. On the practical side it was this that delivered Nature into our hands. And on our thoughts and emotions (which concern a literary historian more) it was destined to have profound effects. By reducing Nature to her mathematical elements it substituted a mechanical for a genial or animistic conception of the universe. The world was emptied, first of her indwelling spirits, then of her occult sympathies and antipathies, finally of her colours, smells, and tastes. (Kepler at the beginning of his career explained the motion of the planets by their *animae motrices*; before he died, he explained it mechanically.) The result was dualism rather than materialism. The mind, on whose ideal constructions the whole method depended, stood over against its object in ever sharper dissimilarity. Man with his new powers became rich like Midas but all that he touched had gone dead and cold. This process, slowly working, ensured during the next century the loss of the old mythical imagination: the conceit, and later the personified abstraction, takes its place. Later still, as a desperate attempt to bridge a gulf which begins to be found intolerable, we have the Nature poetry of the Romantics.

But it must be very clearly understood that these consequences were not felt nor foreseen in the sixteenth century. Behind all the literature studied in this volume lies the older conception of Nature. Davies's *Orchestra* gives us the right picture of the Elizabethan or Henrician universe; tingling with anthropomorphic life, dancing, ceremonial, a festival not a machine. It is very important to grasp this at the outset. If we do not, we shall constantly misread our poets by taking for highly conceited metaphor expressions which are still hardly metaphorical at all. The 'prophetic soul of the wide world' is not a mere personification: it is the veritable *anima mundi*. The 'teeming earth' can almost literally be 'pinch'd' with a kind of colic, as in *Henry IV*, Part I, for is she not a huge animal breathing out *per montium crateres ceu os et nares*? (Fromondus, *Meteor*, IV. iv).[1] Even when hills are praised for not despising lowly plains we have still hardly reached the realm of metaphor pure and simple; the natural and civil hierarchies were felt to be—somehow or other —continuous. There is, of course, in sixteenth-century poetry, as in most poetry, a use of the pathetic fallacy; but it is less than a modern reader is likely at first to suppose.[2]

Historians of science or philosophy, and especially if they hold some theory of progress, are naturally interested in seizing those elements of sixteenth-century thought which were later to alter Man's whole picture of reality. Those other elements which were destined to disappear they tend to treat as mere 'survivals' from some earlier and darker age. The literary historian, on the other hand, is concerned not with those ideas in his period which have since proved fruitful, but with those which seemed

[1] The doctrine is set out more fully in Kepler, *Harmonices*, IV. vii.

[2] Some evidence suggests that the belief in a 'genial universe' was strong enough to produce actual hallucination. Machiavelli (*De Republica*, I. lvi) cannot deny that men see warriors fighting in the clouds. Chapman (*Hero and Leander*, vi. 157) says that people 'sometimes' think they see a face in the sun.

important at the time. He must even try to forget his knowledge of what comes after, and see the egg as if he did not know it was going to become a bird. From his point of view it is misleading to call the animistic or genial cosmology of the sixteenth century a 'survival'. For one thing, that word hardly does justice to the fact that it seems to be rather more lively and emphatic at this time than it had been before. For another, it carries the dangerous suggestion that this cosmology was now something alien and intrusive, no longer characteristic of the age. It teaches us to divide the men of that period into two camps, the conservatively superstitious and the progressive or enlightened: even, possibly, to suppose that they would have agreed with our dichotomy. In reality it would leave nearly every one of them a border-line case. The groupings of which they were conscious were quite different from those which our modern conceptions of superstition or enlightenment would impose on them.

Pico della Mirandola (1463–94) attacked astrology. This would seem to be a good reason for placing him among the enlightened. But then Pico also defends both the reality and the lawfulness of magic. It is true that, when attacked, he will distinguish *magia* from *goeteia* and describe the former in terms which make it sound as innocent as chemistry, being an art which 'doth not so much worke wonders as obeyeth Nature in her working of the same' (*Apology*). But he is being disingenuous. Look back at his *Conclusiones Magicae* (especially 15, 19, 22, and 24) and you will find the magical ideal expressed in its sharpest contrast to the scientific.

Pomponatius (1462–1524) is a determinist who attributes all religions to the operation of cosmic laws: including Christianity which, he thinks, has nearly had its day (*De Naturalium Effectuum Causis*, pp. 251–86). This may be called enlightenment if you wish. But the reason why Pomponatius thinks in this way is that he is an astrologer: the determinism he believes in is that of Constellation.

This conflict between the magician and the astrologer seems very surprising to those who want to impose our modern grouping on the men of the past; for by our grouping magic and astrology go together as 'superstitions'. But the moment we drop our grouping (which is from the historical point of view irrelevant and accidental) and try to see these two arts as they appeared to their exponents, the thing becomes perfectly simple.

Magic and astrology, though of course often mixed in practice, are in tendency opposed. The magician asserts human omnipotence; the astrologer, human impotence. The common emotion (whether of repulsion or whimsical curiosity) which unites them in our minds is modern: something on the lens of the glass we look through, not something in the historical object. The thorough-going astrologer is a determinist. He holds the creed (in William James's words) of the 'tough-minded'. He shatters the illusions and despises the exciting hopes of the magician. Those temperaments that are attracted by modern forms of determinism in our own day would have been attracted by astrological determinism in the sixteenth century.

Telesius (1509–88) opens his *De Rerum Natura* with an attack on those 'who trusted ouer much in their owne witte and forgat to looke vpon the things themselues' (*Prooemium*). He means chiefly Aristotle, of whose physics and cosmology he is a stern critic. All knowledge, he insists, must be grounded in the senses. Even the human soul, whatever we accept about her from the Christian faith, as actually known to us is *corporea quadantenus* (v. xl). It is a passage to delight an historian of progress: here, surely, is the road to enlightenment beginning. But in Campanella (1568–1639), who develops the sensationalism of Telesius, the road takes a most unexpected turn. In his *De Rerum Sensu et Magia* he maintains that the senses are more certain than any intellectual knowledge (II. xxx). But then, striving after monism, he argues that sense, which we share with the brutes, cannot have come *ex nihilo*. It must unite us with the whole universe. We must conclude that 'the elements and all things' are sentient. But if so, it must be possible to awake their sleeping sense (*sopitus sensus*) by *magia divina*. If we and Nature are all one, there must be some nearer way of controlling her than by mechanics; some direct way, 'as when one man commandeth another who is in his power' (IV. ii).

This last example, in which we see new empiricism leading to a new conception of magic, should make it clear how inadequate the term 'medieval survival' is for all that we count superstitious in the sixteenth century. We might reasonably call eighteenth-century magic, if there is any, a 'survival' from the seventeenth century: but to talk in that way about the sixteenth is to antedate the real change and to misconceive the period we are studying. A vigorous efflorescence of forbidden or phantasmal

arts is not an anomaly in that period, but one of its characteristic traits: quite as characteristic as exploration, Ciceronianism, or the birth of secular drama. Nor did they appear simply
as the prolongation of a movement whose impulse was derived
from the medieval past. On the contrary, they appeared to
themselves to be striking new roots, to be having, like Latinity,
their own *renascentia*. They are in fact the extreme exemplifica-
tion of a common tendency, or a common mood, which can be
traced in many other departments of sixteenth-century life.

By magic I do not here mean mere witchcraft—traditional,
perhaps Satanistic, rites practised by the poor, the ignorant, or
the perverted. When I first approached this part of my subject
I was tempted to regard the witch scare, beginning roughly, I
thought, with the publication of the *Malleus Maleficarum* in 1497,
as a useful confirmation of the view forced on me by the other
evidence. Two considerations deter me from doing so now. In
the first place M. Brouette (in *Satan*) has raised a doubt lest the
witch-trials appear more numerous between certain dates only
because they are better recorded. And secondly, it appears to
me impossible to be sure that much witchcraft—I had almost
said that any—was really going on. Most of the evidence was
gossip: nearly all the confessions were made in answer to leading
questions and under torture. Judges who examine in that way
will infallibly find confirmation of whatever theory the prosecu-
tion was holding before the trial began. The witch scare, therefore, concerns us at the moment, if at all, not as evidence of the
things practised by common people but as evidence of the views,
and (implicitly) the whole world picture, accepted by learned
and respectable people in positions of authority. And with that
I drop the subject of witchcraft altogether: and I must ask the
reader to dismiss from his mind Gilles de Retz, Black Mass,
Hieronymus Bosch, and Mr. Crowley. My concern is with high
magic: not concealed but avowed and vindicated by eloquent
scholars who draw much of their strength from the New Learning. Of course in this high magic there is no Satanism and no
Faustian compact. Equally, of course, critics of the high magic
(like King James in his *Demonology* of 1597) maintained that it
was all a snare and would lead you into the goetic sort in the
end. Whether it was as dangerous to the soul as King James
(and probably most contemporaries) thought, is not for me to
judge: but there seems reasonable ground for thinking that it

affected the general imagination more strongly and widely than medieval magic had done.

Only an obstinate prejudice about this period (which I will presently try to account for) could blind us to a certain change which comes over the merely literary texts as we pass from the Middle Ages to the sixteenth century. In medieval story there is, in one sense, plenty of 'magic'. Merlin does this or that 'by his subtilty', Bercilak resumes his severed head. But all these passages have unmistakably the note of 'faerie' about them. They could arouse a practical or quasi-scientific interest in no reader's mind. To ask *how* they were done would show a misunderstanding of literary kinds. And when magic occurs in the more realistic setting of the *Franklin's Tale*, it is quite clearly an art of mere illusion which does not change Nature but only makes her appear changed 'to mannes sighte' (F. 1158), in 'an apparence' (1265) so that people will 'wene and seiye' (1267) what is not true. But in Spenser, Marlowe, Chapman, and Shakespeare the subject is treated quite differently. 'He to his studie goes'; books are opened, terrible words pronounced, souls imperilled. The medieval author seems to write for a public to whom magic, like knight-errantry, is part of the furniture of romance: the Elizabethan, for a public who feel that it might be going on in the next street. Neglect of this has produced strange readings of the *Tempest*, which is in reality no fantasy (like the *Midsummer Night's Dream*) and no allegory, but Shakespeare's play on *magia* as *Macbeth* is his play on *goeteia* or the *Merchant* on usury. Shakespeare's audience believed (and the burden of proof lies on those who say Shakespeare disbelieved) that magicians not very unlike Prospero might exist. His speech of renunciation, sometimes taken as an autobiographical confidence by the poet, was to them necessary in order that the ending might be unambiguously happy. The epilogue, cunningly written so that it suits equally the penitent magician and the actor whose part is ended, underlined the point. Nor could anyone at that date hear the soft and timely 'I'll drown my book' without remembering that earlier magician who had screamed too late 'I'll burn my books'. All the difference between fire and water is there.

This high magic can be studied in Pico, Ficino (1433–99), Paracelsus (1493–1541), Agrippa (1486–1535), or our own Dr. Dee. It can even be studied in the *Philosophical Works* of

Henry More which appeared as late as 1662: a book to which
Dr. Johnson referred Boswell. This supposedly 'medieval
survival' in fact survived the Elizabethan type of lyric, the
Elizabethan type of play, the Elizabethan type of monarchy,
and the older English music. Its exponents quite clearly regard
themselves not as continuing an existing movement but as
reviving something that had been lost during the ignorant
Middle Ages. 'Once,' says Agrippa, 'by the iudgment of all
olde philosophers Magick held the hyest place of honour',
but from the first days of the Church (*a principio nascentis ecclesiae
catholice*) it has been forbidden and denounced: most unjustly,
for it is 'a hye holy learning', *sublimis sacraque disciplina* (*De
Occulta Philosophia, Ep. Ded.*). Medieval contributions to the
subject he tosses aside as frivolous: authors like Roger Bacon
and Arnold of the New Town wrote *deliramenta* and *superstitiones*
(ibid.). What permits his own magic to be 'high' (I have not
found the term 'white' till later) is the belief that there are many
potent spirits besides the angels and devils of Christianity. As no
one doubts (and anyway Psellus had told us) that evil spirits
can be called to us by profane arts, so by proper means the
mundana numina can be called: or at the very least the daemons
(not demons) who are their attendants. But not, of course, the
angels (*supercelestes*), not even the inferior sorts: only the aereals
(*aëreos daemones*). Trismegistus is quoted in support (ibid. 1.
xxxix). But there seems to be another road to power which
carries you farther. The Arabs say that men can rise above their
corporeal and their sensitive powers and in that state receive
into themselves 'the perfection of heaven and of the diuine in-
telligences', for 'all spirits do obey perfected souls'. That way
even the resuscitation of the dead may be possible (ibid. 1. liii).

The points to notice here are, first, the link with Greek and
the New Learning (and indeed Agrippa mentions Pliny, the
Hermetica, the Orphic books, and 'the Platonists' among his
authorities); secondly, the belief that the invisible population of
the universe includes a whole crowd of beings who might almost
be called theologically neutral. Both these connect the high
magic with the 'Platonic theology' of the Florentines Pico and
Ficino, which is, in a sense, the characteristic 'philosophy' of
the time.

This Platonic theology, under the name of Platonism, is too
often treated only in relation to its effect on love poetry. From

that point of view its importance has possibly been overstressed. At first sight we feel that it ought to have been immensely fruitful. Centuries of courtly love had prepared a place for lofty erotic mysticism: it might be supposed that Plato's doctrine, which in its own day had found no better soil than Greek pederasty, would now find the very soil it required. But on a deeper level this is not so. The thought of the *Symposium*, like all Plato's thought, is ruthless, and the more fervid, the more ruthless. The lowest rung of his ladder is perversion; the intermediate rungs are increasing degrees of asceticism and scientific clarity; the topmost rung is mystical contemplation. A man who reaches it has, by hypothesis, left behind for ever the original human object of desire and affection. Any preference for one beautiful person over others was among the earliest obstacles he overcame in his ascent. There is no possibility of adapting this scheme in its full rigour to a heterosexual love which promises fidelity and perhaps even hopes to be blessed by marriage. Hence the so-called Platonism of the love poets often amounts to little more than an admission that the lady's soul is even more beautiful than her person and that both are images of the First Fair.

But however the value of this erotic Platonism is assessed, it was not of this that an Englishman of that period thought exclusively, or even thought first, when Platonism was mentioned. If he had, he would have been puzzled when Drayton said (*Polyolbion*, v. 178) that he would not 'play the humorous Platonist' by maintaining that Merlin's father was an *incubus daemon*: for the loves of such a creature are by definition not 'Platonic'. Drayton writes thus, as the following lines make clear, because Platonism primarily means to him the doctrine that the region between earth and moon is crowded with airy creatures who are capable of fertile unions with our own species. Platonism, in fact, is for him a system of daemonology. And Drayton's view, though incomplete, is not very far wrong.

I have called this system, as Ficino himself calls it, 'Platonic theology', to distinguish it from the Platonism on which lectures are given in a modern university. It is not sufficiently distinguished even by the term 'neo-Platonism'. It is a deliberate syncretism based on the conviction that all the sages of antiquity shared a common wisdom and that this wisdom can be reconciled with Christianity. If Plato alone had been in question the Florentines would in fact have been attempting to 'baptise' him as Aquinas had 'baptised' Aristotle. But since for them Plato was merely the greatest and most eloquent of the consenting sages, since Pythagoras, the Hermetic Books, the Sibylline Books, the Orphic Books, Apuleius, Plotinus, Psellus, Iamblichus, and the Cabbala all meant the same, their task was hardly distinguishable from that of reconciling paganism, Judaism, and Christianity in general. It is significant that Ficino hazarded the suggestion that the diversity of religions might have been ordained by God as conducive to 'a certain beauty', *decorem quendam*; assuming, as such men do, that the main difference between religions is in their ritual, *ritus adorationis* (*De Christiana Religione*, iv).

Hence, paradoxically, it comes about that though the Florentine Platonists were wholly pious in intention, their work deserves the epithet *pagan* more than any other movement in that age. That their conscious purpose was Christian we need not doubt. Ficino, at a sign from heaven, burnt his commentary on Lucretius: he was a priest, and apparently a good one, for the last twenty-four years of his life; all his doctrines were submitted to the judgement of the Church. So, indeed, were those of Agrippa (*De Occult. Phil.* I. i). Yet the actual trend of Ficino's thought is always away from the centre of Christianity. One has the suspicion that though he and Pico doubtless believed Christianity to be true, they valued it even more for being lofty, edifying, and useful. They have the air of men rallying the forces of 'religion' or even of 'idealism' in general against the danger of naturalistic philosophies that deprive man of his dignity and freedom; a danger represented for them not by the new real sciences but by astrological determinism. The title of Pico's *De Dignitate Hominis* would really have served as the title for all their works. In their readiness to accept from whatever source all that seemed to them elevated, or spiritual, or even exciting, we sometimes seem to catch the first faint suggestion of what came, centuries later, to be called 'higher thought'.

In their task of defending what they thought a spiritual cosmology they raked together all that the late pagan sources (some of which they believed to be not late but primeval) could tell them about the invisible population of the universe. They re-admitted all those 'middle spirits . . . betwixt th' Angelical and Human kinde', which St. Augustine is labouring to expel all through the eighth and ninth books of the *De Civitate Dei*. Even in the Middle Ages some tradition of them had trickled down from Apuleius into Bernardus Sylvestris and Geoffrey of Monmouth: thence into Layamon. But our unambiguous friends and foes, ministering angels and seducing devils, occupied the centre of the stage. Now the imagination is filled with spirits 'of another sort': the *aërii homines* with whom Cardan's father conversed, Prospero's Ariel, the amiable though intolerably tedious being whom Dr. Dee evoked—for the tragi-comical human story in his *True Relation* has to be picked out from reams of stuff as fatuous as is reported from any modern *séance*. Pico even allows the use of evil spirits when enslaved by *magia* and not given dominion over us by *goeteia*. Paracelsus is, I think, less grounded in ancient daemonology. The pleasing little tract *De Nymphis* mainly gives a pseudo-scientific form to local and contemporary folk-lore, mostly of a very innocent sort. I am glad to know that undines desire marriage with men not only (as we all learned from De La Motte Fouqué) because they thus acquire an immortal soul, but also for the more prosaic reason that their own species suffers from a grave surplus of females. (We may notice in passing that Spenser's Mammon, though in the canto only a personified vice, is in the versicle a Paracelsian 'gnome' ripening his gold by solar influence.)

This mass of mysterious but not necessarily evil spirits creates the possibility of an innocent traffic with the unseen and therefore of high magic or *magia*. That, at any rate, is its external and possibly accidental condition. But to grasp the real psychology of the magicians, the megalomania or (to revive a word) anthropolatry which lies at the back of the whole movement, we must look a little deeper. In this densely populated universe a very peculiar position was allotted to Man. Cassirer has traced how the time-honoured truism that Man is a microcosm who has in him a bit of everything now underwent a strange transformation. Christians had always held that a man was a composite creature, *animal rationale*, and that it lay in his own choice to be governed by his reason or his animality. But that choice could produce order or disorder only within the limits assigned to him by the hierarchy of being. He could become a saint but not an angel: a swinish man but not a pig. The Florentines, on the other hand, sometimes appear to think that Man can become any kind of creature he pleases. In a passage that oddly anticipates Sartre, Pico suggests that Man has no specific nature at all but creates his own nature by his acts. 'To thee, O Adam' are the words he puts into God's mouth, 'We haue giuen no certain habitation nor countenance of thine owne neither anie peculiar office, so that what habitation or countenance or office soeuer thou dost choose for thyselfe, the same thou shalt enioye and posses at thine owne proper will and election—We haue made thee neither a thing celestial nor a thing terrestrial, neither mortal nor immortal, so that being thine owne fashioner and artificer of thyselfe, thou maist make thyselfe after what likenes thou dost most affecte' (*De Dignitate*, para. 3). No impassable barrier, then, cuts us off even from the highest spirits. I have already noticed that though Agrippa in one place limits the power of our ceremonial to calling up the *mundana numina* or even their inferior daemons, in another he hints a more direct access to 'the perfection of heaven'. Ficino seems to think the same. We are akin not only to the aereal daemons but to the highest orders of created beings. No one, seeing us as we now appear, would suspect our almost limitless powers. But that is because souls in earthly bodies 'are wondrously abated of their proper dignity', *longissime a sua dignitate discedunt*. We have come into these bodies not by fate nor as a punishment, but of our own free will, drawn to them because we loved them. The power we now have over them we once had over all Nature. But if, now incarnate, the soul once again conquers her partiality for this individual organism, why should she not recover her original dominion over the whole created universe? And in fact such recoveries have occurred. Pythagoras and Apollonius of Tyana are cited as examples (*Theologia Platonica*, XIII. iv).

This glance at a forgotten, but influential, philosophy will help, I hope, to get rid of the false groupings which our *ex post facto* judgements of 'enlightenment' and 'superstition' urge us to impose on the past. Freed from those, we can see that the new *magia*, far from being an anomaly in that age, falls into its place among the other dreams of power which then haunted the European mind. Most obviously it falls into place beside the thought of Bacon. His endeavour is no doubt contrasted in our minds with that of the magicians: but contrasted only in the light of the event, only because we know that science succeeded and magic failed. That event was then still uncertain. Stripping off our knowledge of it, we see at once that Bacon and the magicians have the closest possible affinity. Both seek knowledge for the sake of power (in Bacon's words, as 'a spouse for fruit' not a 'curtesan for pleasure'), both move in a grandiose dream of days when Man shall have been raised to the performance of 'all things possible'. That means, doubtless, all things that do not involve contradiction: no higher omnipotence was claimed for God. Nor would Bacon himself deny the affinity: he thought the aim of the magicians was 'noble'. The theory of poetry shared by Scaliger (1484–1588), Sidney, and Bacon (which I reserve for a later chapter) depends on the belief that the soul 'is in proportion superior to the world'; and if it errs, it errs with the same megalomania. Even Machiavelli's dream of a political power absolute, mysterious, protected by unremitting force and fraud, may be regarded as bearing the same stamp. Against the Wellsian or Shavian immensity of these aspirations the consistent astrologer (but of course most were inconsistent) came with the cold assurance that Man's destiny did not depend on his own efforts but on stellar movements which he could never resist or placate: that the little creatures who dreamed of controlling the winds and raising the dead were in reality only the stars' tennis-balls. If I were asked what was common to both attitudes I would hazard the guess that it is something negative. Both have abandoned an earlier doctrine of Man. That doctrine had guaranteed him, on his own rung of the hierarchical ladder, his own limited freedom and efficacy: now, both the limit and the guarantee become uncertain—perhaps Man can do everything, perhaps he can do nothing. But, once more, there is no question of two strictly defined camps. Both views can be found in the same writer. In his *De Imaginibus* (cap. xii) Paracelsus tells us that 'man conteineth in himself the stars and heauen, they lie hidden in his minde . . . if we rightly knew our owne spirite no thing at all would be impossible to vs on earth'. In his *Liber Paragranum* (*Tract*. i) he says that Man is related to the elements as the image in a mirror is related to a real object: is in fact, as we should now say, a mere epipheno-menon, and can know no more of himself or his sources than a mirror image knows.

The new geography excited much more interest than the new astronomy, especially, as was natural, among merchants and politicians: but the literary texts suggest that it did not stimulate the imagination so much as we might have expected. The aim of the explorers was mercantile: to cut out the Turk and the Venetian by finding a direct route to the east. In this the Portuguese had succeeded by circumnavigating Africa and crossing the Indian Ocean; Vasco da Gama reached Malabar in 1498. Columbus, a man of lofty mind, with missionary and scientific interests, had the original idea of acting on the age-old doctrine of the earth's rotundity and sailing west to find the east. Lands which no one had dreamed of barred his way. Though we all know, we often forget, that the existence of America was one of the greatest disappointments in the history of Europe. Plans laid and hardships borne in the hope of reaching Cathay, merely ushered in a period during which we became to America what the Huns had been to us. Foiled of Cathay, the Spaniards fell back on exploiting the mineral wealth of the new continent. The English, coming later and denied even this, had to content themselves with colonization, which they conceived chiefly as a social sewerage system, a vent for 'needy people who now trouble the commonwealth' and are 'daily consumed with the gallows' (Humphrey Gilbert's *Discourse*, cap. 10). Of course the dream of Cathay died hard. We hoped that each new stretch of the American coast was the shore of one more island and that each new bay was the mouth of the channel that led through into the Pacific or 'South Sea'. In comparison with that perpetually disappointed hope the delectable things we really found seemed unimportant. In Virginia there was 'shole water wher we smelt so sweet and so strong a smell as if we had beene in the midst of some delicate garden'; a land 'so full of grapes as the very beating and surge of the sea ouerflowed them'; a king 'very iust of his promise'; a people 'as manerly and ciuill as any of Europe', most 'gentle, louing and faithfull, voide of all guile and treason', living 'after the maner of the golden age'. But that was all rather beside the point; nothing but 'a good Mine or a passage to the South Sea' could ever 'bring this Countrey in request to be inhabited by our nation' (Hakluyt, vii. 298–331). Hence the desperate attempts of Pert (1517), Hore (1536), Willoughby (1553), and Frobisher (1576–8) to find either a North-West or a North-East passage. Judged in the light of later events the history of English exploration in the sixteenth century may appear to modern Americans and modern Englishmen a very *Aeneid*: but judged by the aims and wishes of its own time it was on the whole a record of failures and second bests. Nor was the failure relieved by any high ideal motives. Missionary designs are sometimes paraded in the prospectus of a new venture: but the actual record of early Protestantism in this field seems to be 'blank as death'.

The poetic charm with which these voyages appear in the pages of Charles Kingsley or Professor Raleigh is partly conditioned by later romanticism and later imperialism. Wild Nature—plains without palaces and rivers without nymphs—made little appeal to men who valued travel almost wholly as a means of coming, like Ulysses, to know the cities and manners of men. And the best European consciences had still to undergo a long training before they reached the untroubled nineteenth-century acquiescence in imperialism. Go back even as far as Burke or Johnson and you will find a very different view: 'in the same year, in a year hitherto disastrous to mankind', America and the sea-passage to India were discovered (*Taxation No Tyranny*). Go back farther, to Buchanan (1506–82), and you read that the great explorer, the true discoverer of all these new lands, was Avarice (*De Sphaera*, 1. 182 et seq.). The best European minds were ashamed of Europe's exploits in America. Montaigne passionately asks why so noble a discovery could not have fallen to the Ancients who might have spread civility where we have spread only corruption (*Essais*, III. vi). Even on the utilitarian level the benefits of the whole thing were not always obvious to home-dwellers. Our merchants, observes William Harrison in 1577, now go to Cathay, Muscovy, and Tartary, 'whence, as they saie, they bring home great commodities. But alas I see not by all their trauell that the prices are anie whit abated . . . in time past when the strange bottoms were suffered to come in we had sugar for fourpence the pound that now is worth half a crowne' (*Description of England*, II. v).

We must not therefore be surprised if the wonder and glory of exploration, though sometimes expressed by Hakluyt and the voyagers themselves, was seldom the theme of imaginative writers. Something of it is felt in the *Utopia*, and there are casual references in Spenser, Shakespeare, Donne, and others. As the great age of the voyages receded it was perhaps more valued. I think Drayton cared more about it than Shakespeare, and Milton more than Drayton. In the sixteenth century imagination still turns more readily to ancient Greece and Rome, to Italy, Arcadia, to English history or legend. Lodge writing a romance about Arden while he sails to the Azores is typical.

There is, however, one respect in which America may have affected not only imaginative but even philosophical thought. If it did not create, it impressed on our minds more strongly, the image of the Savage, or Natural Man. A place had, of course, been prepared for him. Christians had depicted the naked Adam, Stoics, the state of Nature, poets, the reign of Saturn. But in America it might seem that you could catch glimpses of some such thing actually going on. The 'Natural Man' is, of course, an ambivalent image. He may be conceived as ideally innocent. From that conception descend Montaigne's essay on cannibals, Gonzalo's commonwealth in the *Tempest*, the good 'Salvage' in the *Faerie Queene* (vi. iv, v, vi), Pope's 'reign of God', and the primeval classless society of the Marxists. It is one of the great myths. On the other hand, he might be conceived as brutal, sub-human: thence Caliban, the bad 'Salvages' of the *Faerie Queene* (vi. viii), the state of nature as pictured by Hobbes, and the 'Cave Man' of popular modern imagination. That is another great myth. The very overtones which the word 'primitive' now has for most speakers (it had quite different ones in the sixteenth century) are evidence of its potency; though other causes, such as evolutionary biology, have here contributed.

If the new astronomy and the new geography did not seem at the time quite so important as we should have expected, the same cannot be said of either humanism or puritanism, and to these I now turn. But I must immediately guard against a possible misunderstanding. Both words have so changed their sense that *puritan* now means little more than 'rigorist' or 'ascetic' and *humanist* little more than 'the opposite of puritan'. The more completely we can banish these modern senses from our minds while studying the sixteenth century the better we shall understand it. By a puritan the Elizabethans meant one who wished to abolish episcopacy and remodel the Church of England on the lines which Calvin had laid down for Geneva. The puritan party were not separatists or (in the modern sense) dissenters. They usually remained in the Establishment and desired reform from within. There were therefore degrees of puritanism and it is difficult to draw a hard and fast line. I shall use the word to mean 'advanced' or 'radical' Protestantism: the marks of a puritan, in my sense, are a strong emphasis on justification by faith, an insistence on preaching as an indispensable, almost the only, means of grace, and an attitude towards bishops which varies from reluctant toleration to implacable hostility. Humanism, in the only sense I shall give to the word, is more easily defined. By a humanist I mean one who taught, or learned, or at least strongly favoured, Greek and the new kind of Latin; and by humanism, the critical principles and critical outlook which ordinarily went with these studies. Humanism is in fact the first form of classicism. It is evident that if we use the words in this way we shall not see our period in terms of a conflict between humanists and puritans. That is another false grouping: one that is much encouraged by using both the terms in their loose, modern sense. If they are used in that sense, if in fact each is defined almost by its opposition to the other, then, to be sure, the sixteenth century, or any other period, is bound to appear as a conflict between puritans and humanists. But if we give the words their older meaning we shall get quite different, and more useful, results. In reality the puritans and the humanists were quite often the same people. Even when they were not, they were united by strong common antipathies and by certain affinities of temper. 'Humanists' in the modern sense hardly existed. As for 'puritans' in the modern sense, every shade of Christian belief whatever (and there is no evidence for any considerable body of unbelievers) then had traits which would now be called 'puritanical'. It is clear that More and Fisher had these traits in a much higher degree than most Protestants. As for paganism (unless we use this word, absurdly, to mean debauchery) the most pagan school of thought at this time was that of the Florentine Platonists whose moral teaching was severe and ascetic.

The humanists did two things, for one of which we are their endless debtors. They recovered, edited, and expounded a great many ancient texts in Latin, Greek, and Hebrew. We must, indeed, remember that many Latin authors had never been lost; Virgil, Ovid, Lucan, Statius, Claudian, Boethius, and many others were as familiar to Dante and Chaucer as they were to Ronsard and Jonson. We must also remember, as modern scholars have shown, that a real knowledge of the ancients was not nearly so common among sixteenth-century authors as their

writings would at first lead us to suppose. Quotations are often
at second or third hand. But it remains true that we owe nearly
all our Greeks, and many of our Latins, to the humanists: also,
a prodigious advance in philology and textual criticism.

If this had been all, their name would have been a blessing.
But they also initiated that temper and those critical principles
which have since come to be called 'classicism'. It is not unusual
to make a distinction that is almost a contrast between humanism and the 'neo-classical' school. I believe that the difference
has been very much exaggerated, under the influence of that
same obstinate prejudice which I have alluded to before (and
must still postpone my account of). There are, no doubt, modifications as we pass from the fifteenth- and sixteenth-century
humanists to critics like Rymer and Boileau: but the neo-
classics are the humanists' lawful heirs. The worst of all neo-
classical errors, that which turned Aristotle's observations on
Greek tragedy into arbitrary 'rules' and even foisted on him
'rules' for which his text furnishes no pretext at all, began not
with Richelieu nor Chapelain but in 1570 with Castelvetro
(*Poetica d'Aristotele*, IV. ii). Scaliger's critique of Homer (*Poetices*,
v. ii, iii) is very like Rymer's of Shakespeare. Swift's contempt
for natural science in *Laputa*, Johnson's in his critique of Milton's
educational theory, Chesterfield's request that Stanhope should
stick to useful books and avoid 'jimcrack natural history of
fossils, minerals, plants, &c.', are all in the spirit of Vives and
Erasmus. If Dryden departs from Aristotle to make 'admiration'
the 'delight of serious plays', Minturno had led the way (*De
Poeta*, II). The *Poetica* of Vida (1490–1566) is still a central
book for Johnson and Pope. The differences between the humanists and the neo-classics have to be sought for by minute study:
the similarities leap to the eye. We have no warrant for regarding our Elizabethan literature as the progeny of the one and
our 'Augustan' as the progeny of the other. I shall notice in a
later chapter the one point at which humanism, in the person
of Scaliger, here following Plotinus, may have given to the
Elizabethans something they could really use. Apart from that,
all the facts seem consistent with the view that the great literature of the fifteen-eighties and nineties was something which
humanism, with its unities and *Gorboducs* and English hexameters, would have prevented if it could, but failed to prevent
because the high tide of native talent was then too strong for it.

Later, when we were weaker, it had its way and our pseudo-classical period set in.

The difficulty of assessing this new temper which the humanists introduced lies in the fact that our educational system descends from them and, therefore, the very terms we use embody humanistic conceptions. Unless we take care, our language will beg every question in their favour. We say, for example, that they substituted 'classical' for 'medieval' Latin. But the very idea of the 'medieval' is a humanistic invention. (According to Lehmann it is in 1469 that the expression *media tempestas* first occurs.) And what can *media* imply except that a thousand years of theology, metaphysics, jurisprudence, courtesy, poetry, and architecture are to be regarded as a mere gap, or chasm, or *entre-acte*? Such a preposterous conception can be accepted only if you swallow the whole creed of humanism at the same time. We may change our terms and say that what the humanists ousted was not 'medieval' Latin but 'barbarous' Latin. That will do very well if we take our ideas of this rejected Latinity from the *Epistolae Obscurorum Virorum*—that is, from an amusing humanist satire in which imaginary people use a Latin not to be found in the great medieval writers in order to say things which would be silly in any language whatever. But if, turning from the satire, we look at the facts, we shall soon ask ourselves in what sense the word *barbarous* can be applied to the growing, sensitive, supple language of Bede, Aquinas, the great hymns, or the *Carmina Burana*. And the answer will be obvious: we can call that Latin *barbarous* only if we choose to adopt humanistic standards and so make the humanists judges of their own cause. If we took for our criterion the implicit (as distinct from the expressed) judgement of posterity, we should arrive at a startlingly different result. The medieval philosophy is still read as philosophy, the history as history, the songs as songs: the hymns are still in use. The 'barbarous' books have survived in the only sense that really matters: they are used as their authors meant them to be used. It would be hard to think of one single text in humanists' Latin, except the *Utopia*, of which we can say the same. Petrarch's Latin poetry, Politian, Buchanan, even sweet Sannazarus, even Erasmus himself, are hardly ever opened except for an historical purpose. We read the humanists, in fact, only to learn about humanism; we read the 'barbarous' authors in order to be instructed or delighted about any theme they choose to handle. Once we cease to let the humanists' own language beg the question, is it not clear that in this context the 'barbarous' is the living and the 'classical' the still-born?

It could hardly have been anything but still-born. It is largely to the humanists that we owe the curious conception of the 'classical' period in a language, the correct or normative period before which all was immature or archaic and after which all was decadent. Thus Scaliger tells us that Latin was 'rude' in Plautus, 'ripe' from Terence to Virgil, decadent in Martial and Juvenal, senile in Ausonius (*Poetices*, VI. i). Vives says much the same (*De Tradendis Disciplinis*, IV). Vida, more wildly, makes all Greek poetry after Homer a decline (*Poeticorum*, I. 139). When once this superstition was established it led naturally to the belief that good writing in the fifteenth or sixteenth century meant writing which aped as closely as possible that of the chosen period in the past. All real development of Latin to meet the changing needs of new talent and new subject-matter was thus precluded; with one blow of 'his Mace petrific' the classical spirit ended the history of the Latin tongue. This was not what the humanists intended. They had hoped to retain Latin as the living esperanto of Europe while putting back the great clock of linguistic change to the age of Cicero. From that point of view humanism is a great archaizing movement parallel to that which Latin had already undergone at the hands of authors like Apuleius and Fronto. But this time it was too thorough. They succeeded in killing the medieval Latin: but not in keeping alive the schoolroom severities of their restored Augustanism. Before they had ceased talking of a rebirth it became evident that they had really built a tomb. Fantastic pains and skill went to its building. Bembo's friend Longolius bound himself by oath to abstain not only from every word but from every number and case of a word that could not be found in Cicero. A negative conception of excellence arose: it was better to omit a beauty than to leave in anything that might have the shadow of an offence (Scaliger, *Poetices*, v. ii). Men vied with one another in smelling out and condemning 'unclassical' words, so that the permitted language grew steadily poorer (Vives, *De Causis*, II). The energy of neo-Latin poets was wasted on a copying of the ancients so close as to approach forgery or conjuring. The results often please, but only as a solved puzzle pleases: we admire the ingenuity with which ancient parallels are found for modern situations, just as we admire the opposite process in Pope's or Johnson's imitations of Horace or Juvenal. Only rarely (for genius is sometimes unconquerable) does real poetry force its way through the doubled and trebled artifice of the masquerade; as in Sannazarus' *Quae voces? Charitum* (*Epigr.* I. xxxvii) or his fine ode on homesickness (IV) which perhaps suggested or provoked Du Bellay's finer sonnet.

All this was destined to have a serious, and mostly mischievous, effect on vernacular poetry. A time was coming when English poets would bring to their work habits formed by

> the trade in classic niceties,
> The dangerous craft of culling term and phrase
> From languages that want the living voice.

School training in Latin elegiacs of the rigid Ovidian type lies behind the stopped couplet of our 'Augustans'. Dryden significantly takes it for granted (Epistle to the *Rival Ladies*) that you must not do in English things which you were whipped at school for doing in Latin. But this effect was delayed and is hardly yet to be found in sixteenth-century England, though Du Bellay's specimens of Antonomasia in the *Défense et Illustration* (ix) show its early stages in France. For the moment, and in our own country, what was more important was the change which humanism produced in our conception of the ancient writers themselves.

The humanists and the men of the Middle Ages both saw the ancients, of course, through the medium of their own taste and temper. We, no doubt, do the same. Until recently it has been assumed without discussion that the medieval distortion was far greater than the humanistic. This was natural, since the humanists themselves assured us that such was the case and it was from them and their heirs that we learned our Greek and Latin. But the moment we use our own eyes instead of looking through our masters', it is almost impossible not to agree with Burckhardt that medieval poems like *De Phyllide et Flora* and *Cum Diane Vitrea* are very much closer to the spirit of ancient literature than most of the humanistic pieces that sedulously ape its form. This inevitably raises a doubt whether the humanists may not have misread the ancients as seriously in some directions as the medievals had done in others.

Such misreading was perhaps inherent in the humanistic temper; and the first step towards understanding that temper is to recognize quite clearly what it was not. It was not a surrender to the sensuousness or to the spiritual suggestions of the Greek imagination: it was not even a delight in the myths as good 'yarns'. Myth interested these early classicists much less than it had interested Dante or Guillaume de Lorris or Chaucer. We must be careful here to distinguish humanism as it originally was from humanism in its last English phase after it had been modified by the Romantic Movement. Two quotations will make the point clear. Mackail in his *Latin Literature* says that even Valerius Flaccus, though a bad poet, 'cannot wholly destroy the charm of the story of the Golden Fleece'; Vives (*De Tradendis*, III), speaking of Apollonius Rhodius' *Argonautica*, blames it for 'vaynnesse of matter', *argumenti levitas*. The same theme which, for the later humanist, almost saves a bad poem, for his predecessor almost damns a good one. Scaliger's attitude is the same. He scolds Homer for his 'old wives' tales', *nugae anicularum (Poetices, v. iii)*.

For the humanists the attraction of ancient literature lay in quite a different direction. It is nowhere more clearly revealed than in Vives' praise of the Latin language. And it is perfectly fair to concentrate on his view of Latin, for no one would now deny that, despite the recovery of Greek, humanistic culture was overwhelmingly Latin. There were many reasons—the greater difficulty of Greek, the demand for Latin secretaries, orators, and official historians, the utility of Latin as an international language, and the patriotism of Italians who regarded the speech of Dante as a 'Gothic tongue' (*Gethica lingua*) and felt they were reviving their native language. But the preference for Latin had an even deeper and more temperamental root. As Vives says (*De Tradendis*, III): 'It is copious by reason of the great multitude of excellent Wits that have labour'd in the manuring and augmentation thereof, and hath moreouer a sweetnesse in the sound meddled with a certeyn weighte and grauitie, not as in some tongues brutish and rusticall (*ferinae et agrestis*) but liuelie expressing the image of a right prudent and valiant man born and nurtured in a well order'd commonwealth.' Gravity, prudence, the well ordered *civitas*; on the other hand, boorishness and rusticity—these are the clues. Whatever else humanism is, it is emphatically not a movement towards freedom and expansion. It is the impulse of men who feel themselves simple, rustic, and immature, towards sophistication, urbanity, and ripeness. In a word, it is the most complete opposite we can find to the Romantic desire for the primitive and the spontaneous. The metaphor of 'broken fetters' which some have used to describe the revival of learning is emotionally misleading. The desire was for order and discipline, weight, and decorum; and men rightly felt that these qualities were to be learned from the Romans rather than the Greeks. Thus Aeneas Sylvius, praising Alphonsus of Aragon, says that he is as much greater than Socrates as a Roman is graver (*gravior*) than a Greek (*In Libros Antonii Panormitae Prooemium. Lib.* I). Politian, forced to concede with Quintilian that the Latins 'limp' in comedy, gives the reason; *gravitas Romana repugnat* (*Nutricia* 682). 'The Romane grauitie relucteth.'

This desire to be very 'adult', as we now say, had some unfortunate consequences. The qualities which the humanists admired are, of course, to be found in Latin literature, even if less exclusively and continuously than they supposed. But few qualities are less suitable for imitation. Elevation and gravity of language are admirable, or even tolerable, only when they grow from elevation and gravity of thought. To imitate them directly is to manufacture a symptom. The trouble is not that such manufacture is impossible. It is only too possible: even now any clever boy can be taught to write Ciceronian prose. The gestures and accents of magnanimity, laboriously reproduced by little men, clever, meticulous, primed with the *gradus* or the phrase-book, nervously avoiding what is 'low', make an ugly spectacle. That was how the humanists came to create a new literary quality—vulgarity. It is hard to point to any medieval work that is vulgar. When medieval literature is bad, it is bad by honest, downright incompetence: dull, prolix, or incoherent. But the varnish and stucco of some neo-Latin work, the badness which no man could incur by sheer defect of talent but only by 'endless labour to be wrong' is a new thing. Vida's *Christiad* is the supreme example. It polishes up the lowness of the gospel story as Virgil, in Scaliger's opinion, polished up the lowness of Homer. One changeless and unmeaning glossiness spreads over every episode; Lazarus, we are told,

haud procul hinc Bethanes regna tenebat
Dives opum, clarus, genus alto a sanguine regum (I. 102),[1]

---

[1] Not far from thence sate in his royal Throne
 Bethanian, rich in gold and fame, his blood
 Deriv'd from kings illustrious.

and the room where the Last Supper was held becomes

Tectum auratum, ingens, pictisque insigne columnis (II. 546).[1]

The influence of such poetry was deadly. It must, no doubt, be confessed that where the grand manner of the real classics met with an answering magnanimity in the modern disciple, a greatness was produced which might not otherwise have been attainable. But instances of this are very rare. Racine and Milton are perhaps the only poets who thoroughly followed out the humanistic ideal of style and were not destroyed by it; and even in *Paradise Regained* we are sometimes disquietingly reminded of Vida.

Such a taste naturally disposed men to find the classics a good deal more 'classical' than they really are; or sometimes, with clearer insight, to blame them for not being 'classical' enough. This is the real ground of Scaliger's preference for Virgil over Homer. Homer is 'low'. In words hard to forgive he says that Andromache's lament for Hector 'smacketh not so moche of a noble lady as of som butterwife', *plebeiam mulierculam* (*Poetices*, v. ii). In the same place he complains, of one of the loveliest mythical scenes in all poetry, *Achilles flet apud matrem*. Let Dryden translate it: 'Achilles went roaring along the salt seashore . . . like a booby . . . complaining to his mother' (*Dedication of the Aeneis*). It is, indeed, in Dryden, and especially in his translations, that we find the essential vices of humanistic taste carried to their final absurdity. Virgil writes

Quare agite, o iuvenes, tectis succedite nostris.

Douglas, working in the medieval tradition, renders it

Therefore have done, gallandis, cum on your way,
Enter within our lugeing, we you pray.

Dryden has

Enter, my noble guest, and you shall find,
If not a costly welcome, yet a kind.

Even now the humanistic or pseudo-classical virus is strong enough, I suspect, to make some think for a moment that Dryden is more Virgilian. But only for a moment. *Juvenes* must have sounded to a Roman reader almost exactly as *gallandis* did to a sixteenth-century Scot. *Have done* and *cum on* are very

---

[1] Flaming with gold, with pictur'd columns bright,
A vasty Hall.

close to the encouraging alacrity of *quare agite*. And, of course, Virgil has no 'noble guest' and is free from the genteel mock-modesty of Dryden's second line.

The humanists, then, brought to their reading of the ancients certain damaging preconceptions; and, as we shall see in a moment, they retained the worst of all medieval literary habits, that of allegorical interpretation. What they lost was the power, apparently common in the Middle Ages, of continuing, despite such interpretation, to respond to the central, obvious appeal of a great work. The medieval reader's interests were often far closer than the humanists' to those of the ancients themselves. Dante, accepting Virgil as his guide through hell and acclaiming him as the poet of that Italy for which Camilla died, had read Virgil as Virgil wished to be read. But to Stanyhurst the literal sense of the *Aeneid* is merely 'a Canterbury tale' (*Epistle to the First Four Books*): to Dryden the poem is a *roman à clef*, and 'those who lost the prizes' in Book V were people who 'had disobliged the poet or were in disgrace with Augustus' (*Dedication to the Aeneis*). In the same spirit Mantuan picks out of the *Bucolics* precisely what is least pastoral and helps to distort men's conception of that kind for over a century. There are plentiful indications that if the medievals had known Homer they would have gone straight to the heart of his poetry as no humanist ever did. W. P. Ker in his *Dark Ages* remarks that the author of *Waltharius* has apparently read Virgil and seen in him 'nothing but Homer'; heroic legend, *sóp and sárlic*. This is an inadequate but not a perverse reading of Virgil, for the 'Homer' is really there. It is difficult not to conclude that this poet, at second hand, came nearer to the *Iliad* than Chapman who found in it 'all learning, gouernment and wisdom' (the Zodiac, too, on Achilles' shield) and thought its style best preserved in a hothouse full of conceits. Is not Lydgate, making his *Troy-Book* as an 'historial' thing and assuming that Homer (apart from his regrettable Greek sympathies) had worked in the same spirit, far more truly classical than Ronsard who thought that Homer had made the whole thing up *voulant s'insinuer en la faveur et bonne grâce des Aeacides* (Preface to *Franciade*, 1572)?

In the fourth chapter of *Eothen* Kinglake draws a contrast between a child reading Homer (in Pope's version) and a 'learned commentator'. The child, he says, is 'nearer by twenty centuries to the old Greeks' because he is 'not grubbing for

beauties but pressing the siege'. In some ways this is a parallel
to the difference between the medieval and the humanistic
reader. The latter never really cares about the siege: he is too
interested in literature, literature conceived almost exclusively
as style, and style valued chiefly as a model for imitation. This
'literariness' was destined to introduce a serious change in
our whole attitude to great writers. The difference between
Chaucer's *Hous* and Pope's *Temple* of Fame is evidence of it.
In Pope the great poets have the place we should expect: they
are present because they are famous. But in Chaucer it is not
the poets but their subjects that have the fame. Statius is present
to bear up the fame of Thebes, Homer to bear up the fame
of Troy, and so forth. Poets are, for Chaucer, not people
who receive fame but people who give it. To read Virgil sets
you thinking not about Virgil but about Aeneas, Dido, and
Mezentius.

Humanistic culture, as I have already said, was overwhelmingly Latin. A real understanding of humanist taste shows that
this was inevitable. Greek was given abundance of 'mouth
honour', but only the minor Greek authors (Plutarch, Heliodorus, Achilles Tatius, the Anthology) were really relished.
Greek will not take the hard, high polish which was what the
humanists principally cared for: it is too supple, sensitive, and
intimate. You can hardly be marmoreal in Greek. The Romans
—or rather selected Romans—were more congenial. It would
be quite a mistake to think of the sixteenth century as a period
in which we were much influenced by the spirit or form of
Greek literature. Plato's influence was one of doctrine not of
form: he affected philosophers and philosophizing poets. Chapman's Homer might almost have been written to show that the
real Homer was in that age impossible for us to assimilate. The
great age of Greek influence is not the sixteenth century but
the nineteenth. Shelley, Landor, Browning, Tennyson, Arnold,
Ruskin, and even Morris, were all, in their different ways,
more receptive of the Greek spirit than any Elizabethan. No
doubt they saw the Greeks with a romantic distortion of their
own, but that is a trifle compared with the humanistic distortion. Much misunderstanding on this point exists at present.
Whether Professor Murray's version of Euripides is good or bad
literature, I need not here decide; but to blame it simply for
being romantic, on the supposition that there are no romantic

passages in the original, is absurd. How can a man translate 'Εσπερίδων δ' ἐπὶ μηλόσπορον ἀκτὰν or Ἱκοίμαν ποτὶ Κύπρον without sounding romantic? For the truth is that a very large area of sensibility is common to the ancient, the medieval, and the romantic mind, and that humanism stands outside that area. Until the fog of classicism has lifted, the greater classics are invisible.

So far we have been considering the positive characteristics of humanism; its chief negative characteristic was a hatred of the Middle Ages. I have kept this till the last because it is this that unites the humanist with (our next subject) the puritan. As I have already noted, there was one most unfortunate exception to the humanists' rejection of the Middle Ages. The new criticism took over from them the idea that every great poem is an allegory and an encyclopedia. Vives, who in one place protests against the method, himself allegorizes Virgil (*In Allegorias Bucolicorum*) as fantastically as Fulgentius had done, and Scaliger thinks that he makes Jove send down Iris as a messenger in order to teach us that the planets determine events by their influence, not by descending bodily (*Poetices*, III. xxv). Burckhardt quotes from Codrus Urceius the promise that Homer will teach you grammar, rhetoric, medicine, astrology, history, philosophy, strategy, cookery, and architecture. The reason which Vives gives for applying to the *Bucolics* the method which, in general, he had sense enough to distrust is very illuminating: 'if naught more hidden lay beneath, the work had scarce bene worthy those three yeares that Maro laboured in perfecting the same'. This chimes with the passage quoted above in which Stanyhurst dismisses the literal story of the *Aeneid* as a 'Canterbury tale'. The humanists could not really bring themselves to believe that the poet cared about the shepherds, lovers, warriors, voyages, and battles. They must be only a disguise for something more 'adult'. Medieval readers had been equally ready to believe in a poet's hidden wisdom: but then, perhaps because they had been taught that the multiple meanings of Scripture never abrogated the literal sense, they did not allow the hidden wisdom to obscure the fact that the text before them was 'a noble and joyous history'. They pressed the siege, wept with the heroines, and shuddered at the monsters.

Having thus preserved from the Middle Ages what least

merited preservation, the humanists rejected (with contumely)
everything else. The two especial objects of their aversion were
chivalrous romance and scholastic philosophy.

Ascham's attack on the Arthurian stories is sometimes called
a puritan attack; but Ascham the humanist would have made
it whether he were a puritan or not. The only difference in this
matter between a Roman and a Protestant humanist was that
the former had to be content with calling the romances barbarous and silly while the latter could add 'And popish too'.
Both beat the same dog, but the Protestant had an extra stick.
The military methods of More's Utopians are mischievously
devised to flout the chivalric code at every turn; they think it
shame to win in plain battle, exult in overreaching by guile,
and bribe enemy subjects to assassinate their leaders (*Utopia*,
II. viii). Erasmus would forbid a young prince to read 'Arthurs
and Lancelots' which 'smacke of tyrannie and are moreouer
rude (*ineruditi*), foolishe and anile' (*Inst. Principis Christiani*, ii).
Montaigne congratulates himself on an education which had
made Ovid his nursery book and kept him from hearing even
the names of Amadis, Huon, and such trumpery (I. xxv). Vives
condemns books 'such as are Amadis and Florisand in Spain
or Lancelot and the Round Table in France, the which were
made and compiled of idle fellowes (*hominibus otiosis*) and stuffed
fulle of leasings' (*De Causis*, II). As for women, it were better
they had their eyes put out than used them for reading such
stuff (*De Christiana Femina*, I).

So far as the common reader was concerned, the humanists'
attack on romances was not, in the sixteenth century, very
successful; their attack on medieval philosophy had more
serious consequences. Here again we must beware of false
simplifications. We must not picture a straight fight in which
humanism, with the new science as its ally, rebelled against
'the tyranny of Aristotle'. Humanists were seldom, even by
accident, allied with scientists: scientists did not always despise
scholasticism; Aristotle and scholasticism are sometimes in
opposition. In reality the humanists' revolt against medieval
philosophy was not a philosophical revolt. What it really was
can best be gauged by the language it used. Your philosophers,
says Vives (*De Causis*, I), are straw-splitters, makers of unnecessary difficulties, and if you call their jargon Latin, why then
we must find some other name for the speech of Cicero. 'The

more filthie barbarisme they haue in their style (*si quam maxime barbare spurceque loquantur*) the greater theologians they doe account themselues', says Erasmus (*Moriae Encomium*, cf. also Letter 64). 'Calle ye Thomas Aquinas a doctor?' said Johan Wessel, 'He knew no tongue but the Latin and barely that!' We are invited to admire the Utopians because they could never understand the Second Intentions (*Utopia*, ii. vi). 'Second Intentions', says Rabelais in effect, 'ask whether a chimaera buzzing in a void can eat them. There'd be a proper question for a schoolman' (*Pantagruel*, vii). These are not the terms in which a new philosophy attacks an old one: they are, unmistakably, the terms in which at all times the merely literary man, the bellettrist, attacks philosophy itself. No humanist is now remembered as a philosopher. They jeer and do not refute. The schoolman advanced, and supported, propositions about things: the humanist replied that his words were inelegant. Of the scholastic terminology as an instrument of thought—that instrument which, according to Condorcet, has created *une précision d'idées inconnue aux anciens*—no reasoned criticism was usually vouchsafed. Words like *realitas* and *identificatio* were condemned not because they had no use but because Cicero had not used them. Sometimes comically enough, you can catch a humanist using such words himself and thinking to counteract this testimony to their value by branding them with a futile note of infamy: as when Scaliger writes *quae nostri barbari circumstantias appellarunt* 'what those barbarous fellows have called *circumstances*' (*Poetices*, iii. ii), or Gabriel Harvey apologizes for speaking *Thomae Dunsique more* to place Tully *in transcendentibus* (*Ciceronianus*).

The war between the humanists and the schoolmen was not a war between ideas: it was, on the humanists' side, a war against ideas. It is a manifestation of the humanistic tendency to make eloquence the sole test of learning; embittered (if not partly caused) by the fact that in the universities of that age the teachers of eloquence usually had less secure and lucrative posts than their enemies. As far as England is concerned, humanism, here linked with puritanism, won the victory in 1550 at Oxford. It was then that the works of the scholastics were 'cast out of college libraries' and 'those most noble authors', as Anthony Wood says, condemned for 'barbarism, ignorance of Scripture, and much deceit' and publicly burned, along with mathematical books, which were suspected of being 'Popish or diabolical' (*History and Antiquities of Oxford*). As a result, he adds, there was soon nothing to be heard in the University but 'poetry, grammar, idle songs and frivolous stuff'. Bruno describes England in 1584 as a country 'widowed of good learning in philosophy and the mathematics . . . all their doctors be doctors of grammar, full of obstinate ignorance, pedantry, presumption, and boorish inciuilitie'. It should be noted, however, that this rejection of scholasticism did not necessarily involve a rejection of Aristotle. It might mean a return to his original text 'purged' of Popish, Ramistic, or inelegant interpretations. Thus in 1585 bachelors and undergraduates at Oxford were ordered to lay aside 'authors that caused dissensions and strifes in the schools' and 'only follow Aristotle and those that defend him'.

In the field of philosophy humanism must be regarded, quite frankly, as a Philistine movement: even an obscurantist movement. In that sense the New Learning created the New Ignorance. Perhaps every new learning makes room for itself by creating a new ignorance. In our own age we have seen the sciences beating back the humanities as humanism once beat back metaphysics. Man's power of attention seems to be limited; one nail drives out another.

In the passages from which I have already quoted, Anthony Wood tells us that the burning of the books in 1550 was carried out 'to the sorrow of many as well of the Protestant as of the other party'. This warns us against another falsely simple grouping to which we might be tempted. Men of the Old Religion, if they were humanists, might despise scholasticism; men of the New, if they were philosophers, might revere it. Thus we find Hooker strongly impregnated with Thomism, and More and Erasmus among the mockers of the schoolmen.

I am unwilling to end this short account of the humanists on a note of condemnation. Despite the immense harm they did, despite their narrowness, their boasting, and their ferocity —for it is a strange delusion that represents them as gentle, amiable, and (in that sense) 'humane'—our debt to them can never be cancelled. If we must now judge that, in the very act of discovering some classics, they introduced a subtle falsity of approach to them from which we took centuries to recover, yet we so judge only from a reading of texts which the humanists themselves first gave us. If their manners were often like those of giants, so were their labours.

Puritanism, as I have defined it, splits off from general Protestantism in the second half of the sixteenth century. Stow traces the word *puritan* to about the year 1567.[1] Originally coined by certain Anabaptists to describe themselves, it came to be used as a hostile term (though they sometimes accepted it) for those Protestants who believed that the Elizabethan Church was insufficiently reformed and wished to make her more like the Protestant churches on the continent; especially like that of Geneva. The puritans were so called because they claimed to be purists or purifiers in ecclesiastical polity: not because they laid more emphasis than other Christians on 'purity' in the sense of chastity. Their quarrel with the Church of England was at first rather ecclesiastical than theological. In Hooker Anglicanism is, indeed, already beginning to be marked off from other species of Protestantism by its greater respect for human reason and for tradition. But the specifically Anglican faith defined itself less rapidly and neatly than the puritan and chiefly under the pressure of puritan attacks. Neither can be understood apart from the original Protestant experience in which both were rooted, though puritanism more exclusively. To that experience I must now turn. The very word *experience* perhaps makes clear the angle at which I approach it. Some social or economic historians treat the Reformation solely from the point of view of their own disciplines, regarding its spiritual and even its intellectual side as mere epiphenomena; perhaps as 'rationalizations' by which men explained to themselves behaviour whose real causes were of quite a different kind. Fortunately there is no need to discuss the correctness of this view: for even if it were wholly correct it would not much concern the historian of literature. His business is with the past not as it 'really' was (whatever 'really' may mean in such a context) but with the past as it seemed to be to those who lived in it: for of course men felt and thought and wrote about what seemed to be happening to them. The economic or social historian's 'appearances' may be the literary historian's 'facts'. We want, above all, to know what it felt like to be an early Protestant.

[1] John Poynet in his *Short Treatise of Politic Power* (1556) had spoken of 'Catharistes and newe Puristes'.

One thing is certain. It felt very unlike being a 'puritan' such as we meet in nineteenth-century fiction. Dickens's Mrs. Clennam, trying to expiate her early sin by a long life of voluntary gloom, was doing exactly what the first Protestants would have forbidden her to do. They would have thought her whole conception of expiation papistical. On the Protestant view one could not, and by God's mercy need not, expiate one's sins. Theologically, Protestantism was either a recovery, or a development, or an exaggeration (it is not for the literary historian to say which) of Pauline theology. Hence in Buchanan's *Franciscanus ad Fratres* the Friars' prophylactic against it is to keep clear of the 'old man from Tarsus' (*Tarsensis fuge scripta senis*). In the mind of a Tyndale or Luther, as in the mind of St. Paul himself, this theology was by no means an intellectual construction made in the interests of speculative thought. It springs directly out of a highly specialized religious experience; and all its affirmations, when separated from that context, become meaningless or else mean the opposite of what was intended. Propositions originally framed with the sole purpose of praising the Divine compassion as boundless, hardly credible, and utterly gratuitous, build up, when extrapolated and systematized, into something that sounds not unlike devil-worship. The experience is that of catastrophic conversion. The man who has passed through it feels like one who has waked from nightmare into ecstasy. Like an accepted lover, he feels that he has done nothing, and never could have done anything, to deserve such astonishing happiness. Never again can he 'crow from the dung-hill of desert'. All the initiative has been on God's side; all has been free, unbounded grace. And all will continue to be free, unbounded grace. His own puny and ridiculous efforts would be as helpless to retain the joy as they would have been to achieve it in the first place. Fortunately they need not. Bliss is not for sale, cannot be earned. 'Works' have no 'merit', though of course faith, inevitably, even unconsciously, flows out into works of love at once. He is not saved because he does works of love: he does works of love because he is saved. It is faith alone that has saved him: faith bestowed by sheer gift. From this buoyant humility, this farewell to the self with all its good resolutions, anxiety, scruples, and motive-scratchings, all the Protestant doctrines originally sprang.

For it must be clearly understood that they were at first

doctrines not of terror but of joy and hope: indeed, more than hope, fruition, for as Tyndale says, the converted man is already tasting eternal life. The doctrine of predestination, says the XVIIth Article, is 'full of sweet, pleasant and unspeakable comfort to godly persons'. But what of ungodly persons? Inside the original experience no such question arises. There are no generalizations. We are not building a system. When we begin to do so, very troublesome problems and very dark solutions will appear. But these horrors, so familiar to the modern reader (and especially to the modern reader of fiction), are only by-products of the new theology. They are astonishingly absent from the thought of the first Protestants.[1] Relief and buoyancy are the characteristic notes. In a single sentence of the *Tischreden* Luther tosses the question aside for ever. Do you doubt whether you are elected to salvation? Then say your prayers, man, and you may conclude that you are. It is as easy as that.

It follows that nearly every association which now clings to the word *puritan* has to be eliminated when we are thinking of the early Protestants. Whatever they were, they were not sour, gloomy, or severe; nor did their enemies bring any such charge against them. On the contrary, Harpsfield (in his *Life of More*) describes their doctrines as 'easie, short, pleasant lessons' which lulled their unwary victim in 'so sweete a sleepe as he was euer after loth to wake from it'. For More, a Protestant was one 'dronke of the new must of lewd lightnes of minde and vayne gladnesse of harte' (*Dialogue*, III. ii). Luther, he said, had made converts precisely because 'he spiced al the poison' with 'liber-tee' (ibid. III. vii). Protestantism was not too grim, but too glad, to be true; 'I could for my part be verie wel content that sin and pain all were as shortlye gone as Tyndale telleth us' (*Con-futation*). Protestants are not ascetics but sensualists. They will not fast (*Dialogue*, IV. i). They teach and use 'more sensual and licentious liuing then euer did Makomet' (ibid. IV. ix). And it is certainly true that in their own writings we find a strong bias against asceticism. Even when we pass on from the first Pro-testants to Calvin himself we shall find an explicit rejection of 'that vnciuile and froward philosophy' which 'alloweth vs in

---

[1] I am speaking, of course, about initial doubts of election. Despair after apostasy (see *A Notable and marvellous Epistle of Dr. Mathewe Gribaldi*, translated by E. A(glionby), 1550) is another matter and was no Protestant novelty. When Judas hanged himself he had not been reading Calvin.

no vse of the creatures saue that which is needful, and going about (as it were in enuie) to take from vs the lawful enioyment of God's blessings, yet can neuer speede vnless it should stoppe vp all a man's senses and make him a verie block'. When God created food, 'He intended not only the supplying of our necessities but delight and merriment' (*hilaritas*). Clothes serve not only for need but also for 'comelinesse and honesty'; herbs, trees, and fruits, 'beside their manifold commodity', for 'goodlinesse, brauery, and sweete smelling sauour'. A comparison of the whole passage (*Institutio*, III. x. 2) with, say, the sermons of Fisher, will correct many misapprehensions. When Newman in his *Letter to X Y* professed an 'abstract belief in the latent sensuality of Protestantism', he was, in my opinion, dreadfully mistaken; but at least, like More and Harpsfield, he was making the right mistake, the mistake that is worth discussing. The popular modern view of the matter does not reach that level. To be sure, there are standards by which the early Protestants could be called 'puritanical'; they held adultery, fornication, and perversion for deadly sins. But then so did the Pope. If that is puritanism, all Christendom was then puritanical together. So far as there was any difference about sexual morality, the Old Religion was the more austere. The exaltation of virginity is a Roman, that of marriage, a Protestant, trait.

Another false impression is that Protestantism discouraged, or even forbade, the giving of alms: and it is countenanced by the close connexion which a great scholar has seen between the New Religion and the 'New Economics'. But in the earliest period of English Protestantism, if there is any such connexion, it is entirely hidden from the Protestants themselves. Outcries against new forms of economic cruelty come equally from both sides. I shall show in a later chapter that the social ethics of Tyndale were thoroughly medieval and almost indistinguishable from those of More. When we come on to Calvin, the situation is admittedly different, and we find a real attempt to re-interpret Christian ethics in relation to a society which is no longer medieval. It must, however, be remembered that Calvin's sanction of moderate usury failed to win the approval of many Protestant divines. On the duty of alms-giving, and even on the subtle corruptions of alms-giving, few men have written better than Calvin himself. The limit of giving is to be the limit of our ability to give. We must not consider ourselves free to refuse because those who ask us are undeserving, 'for Scripture here cometh to our aide with this excellent reason, that we respect not what men merit of themselues but looke only vpon God's image which they bear'. We must guard against that subtle insolence which often poisons the gift. Even 'a merry countenance and courteous wordes' accompanying it are not enough. A Christian must not give 'as though he would binde his brother vnto him by the benefit'. When I use my hands to heal some other part of my body I lay the body under no obligation to the hands: and since we are all members of one another, we similarly lay no obligation on the poor when we relieve them (*Institutio*, III. vii. 6, 7).

It was, of course, maintained that giving alms had no 'merit'. You could not thus purchase salvation nor gain a bargaining power against God. The same was true of chastity or martyrdom. But this doctrine no more excused you from giving alms than it excused you for committing adultery or turning apostate under persecution. I am speaking so far of the doctrine as it was intended by its first exponents. How such teaching might be travestied by their critics or misapplied by their own baser adherents is another matter. We shall not be surprised to find that both abuses took place. The Pauline doctrine, on St. Paul's own showing, seems to have suffered in the same way. What might possibly come of the doctrine, and what was certainly believed to come of it, may be gathered from the literary texts. The denial of 'merit' interests a surprising number of Shakespearian characters. 'See, see, my beauty will be saved by Merit! O heresy', says the princess in *Love's Labour's Lost*. If men were to be saved by merit, what hole in hell were hot enough for Gadshill? (*Henry IV*, Part I). King John sneers at the 'corrupted pardon' which can be bought by the 'Merit of vile gold' (III. i. 164). But it was not exactly on theological grounds that this matter interested the poets. Two further quotations show its real bearing. Spenser writes of Envy:

> He hated all good workes and vertuous deeds,
> And him no lesse that any like did vse;
> And who with gratious bread the hungry feeds,
> His almes for want of faith he doth accuse.

> (*F.Q.* I. iv. 32.)

And in *As You Like It* Corin tells us that his churlish employer (significantly a sheep farmer)

little recks to find the way to heaven
By doing deeds of hospitality (II. iv. 80),

is, in fact, wholly free from the heresy of trusting to works. The real reason why any reference to faith and works (or merit) is sure of a response in the theatre is that this topic touches men's pockets: one of the seats of laughter. The best works are those of charity. Hence he who cries up merit (a mendicant friar or the Pope himself for instance) is probably going to ask for money: that is the sort of thing King John has in mind. And he who cries up faith (a close-fisted landlord, perhaps) is probably going to refuse money: that is Corin's point of view. Shakespeare uses either jibe impartially.

The process whereby 'faith and works' become a stock gag in the commercial theatre is characteristic of that whole tragic farce which we call the history of the Reformation. The theological questions really at issue have no significance except on a certain level, a high level, of the spiritual life; they could have been fruitfully debated only between mature and saintly disputants in close privacy and at boundless leisure. Under those conditions formulae might possibly have been found which did justice to the Protestant—I had almost said the Pauline—assertions without compromising other elements of the Christian faith. In fact, however, these questions were raised at a moment when they immediately became embittered and entangled with a whole complex of matters theologically irrelevant, and therefore attracted the fatal attention both of government and the mob. When once this had happened, Europe's chance to come through unscathed was lost. It was as if men were set to conduct a metaphysical argument at a fair, in competition or (worse still) forced collaboration with the cheapjacks and the round-abouts, under the eyes of an armed and vigilant police force who frequently changed sides. Each party increasingly misunderstood the other and triumphed in refuting positions which their opponents did not hold: Protestants misrepresenting Romans as Pelagians or Romans misrepresenting Protestants as Antinomians.

Thus in Germany the new theology led into a quarrel about indulgences and thence into a quarrel about the nature of the Church. Whether it need have done so if Leo X had not wanted money, or if Tetzel (backed by the great house of Fugger) had not applied to the indulgences grotesquely profane and vulgar methods of salesmanship, may be doubted. In England, Henry VIII, wanting Anne Boleyn and therefore wanting his previous marriage annulled, quarrels with the Pope; caring nothing for Protestant doctrine but accidentally creating a situation in which Protestantism, sometimes exploited and sometimes repressed by government, can become important in England. Not till the reign of Edward VI was there a seriously Protestant government. It went too far for the people and provoked a strong reaction. Mary availed herself of that reaction but grossly misjudged what it would bear. Then came the accession of Elizabeth, the new settlement, and the return of Protestant refugees from the Continent.

During this series of ecclesiastical revolutions and counter-revolutions England as a whole somehow changed her religion. 'The general acquiescence' in this process has been described by Sir Maurice Powicke as 'one of the most mysterious things in our history'. Of course acquiescence is here a very relative term. There were resistances and rebellions; on both sides there were heroic martyrs, cruel persecutors, prudent time-servers. If literary texts reflect little of this, their silence can be explained by the well-grounded fears of authors and their printers. But when all allowances have been made, some may still think that the great change was carried through with less of an upheaval than we should have expected. I do not believe this is to be explained by the hypothesis that most sixteenth-century Englishmen had no religion at all and therefore trotted to and fro unconcernedly at the bidding of government. It is hard to believe that a people so indifferent as that under Henry could have become so religious, in a sense, as we find it to have been under Elizabeth. I have said 'in a sense' because this ubiquitous piety was clearly, in Johnson's phrase, 'not very theological'. It is, indeed, best seen in the writers who are not dealing with religion; in Tusser, the chroniclers, Shakespeare, or Hakluyt's voyagers. In all these we find the assumption, unemphasized because it is unquestioned, that every event, every natural fact, and every institution, is rooted in the supernatural. Every change of wind at sea, every change of dynasty at home, all prosperity and all adversity, is unhesitatingly referred to God. The writers do not argue about it; they know. It is probable that the actual religion of most Englishmen in the earlier part of the century was of a similar kind. If so, its centre did not lie where the controversial divines teach us to look. It is significant that changes in ritual seem to have provoked more opposition than changes in doctrine. English instead of Latin at the altar made church a different kind of place and was therefore resented. A marriageable clergy changed the pattern of village life and was also resented. Such things could offend thousands to whom the question of the ecclesiastical Supremacy might appear a far-off quarrel among one's betters. Elizabeth's own willingness to go much farther in doctrinal change than in changes of order may, after all, have been grounded not on deep policy but on a temperament which she shared with most of her people.

We must, at all events, take care not to assume that a six-teenth-century man who lived through these changes had necessarily felt himself, at any stage, confronted with the clear issue which would face a modern in the same circumstances. A modern, ordered to profess or recant a religious belief under pain of death, knows that he is being tempted and that the government which so tempts him is a government of villains. But this background was lacking when the period of religious revolution began. No man claimed for himself or allowed to another the right of believing as he chose. All parties inherited from the Middle Ages the assumption that Christian man could live only in a theocratic polity which had both the right and the duty of enforcing true religion by persecution. Those who resisted its authority did so not because they thought it had no right to impose doctrines but because they thought it was imposing the wrong ones. Those who were burned as heretics were often (and, on their premisses, logically) eager to burn others on the same charge. When Calvin led the attack on Servetus which ended in his being burnt at Geneva, he was acting on accepted medieval principles. A man's beliefs, like his actions, were to be ruled by his Betters. What began in Henry VIII's time was not an encroachment by these Betters on a sphere hitherto free, but a quarrel among the Betters themselves. And all Betters, whether secular or spiritual, had an authority of divine origin: disobedience was sin as well as crime. What we should now call 'Church' and 'State' were (by our standards) deeply confused. Even western Christendom as a whole had never achieved an agreed definition of the relations between pope and emperor; Henry's England, as it split off, inevitably retained the dual nature of the parent mass. Thus Henry's claim to the Supreme Headship of the English Church first came before the ordinary layman in a very curious form. Up till 1534 you could be burnt by your mayor or sheriff on the findings of an ecclesiastical court: by the act of that year your burning required the king's writ as well. It is rather hard to demand that even the pious layman should have leaped to arms in defence of his right to be burnt without royal permission. He was, in any case, well used to quarrels between his masters. They had always been at it, Pope against anti-Pope, Papalists against imperialists, clergy against laity (*semper clericis infesti*, as Convocation noted in 1487), secular clergy against friars, English clergy against interference by foreigners from Italy. The common man might have—I think he had—a conscience and a religion; a conscience much burdened by his own unchastity, profanity, or deficiency in alms-giving, and a religion deeply concerned with the state of the crops and the possibility of making a good end when his time came. But the great controversies were too hard for him. And he was not directly faced either with pope or king; squire and parson, parents and neighbours, an itinerant preacher on one or the other side, were the immediate factors in his problem. We may well believe that such a man, though baptized in the Old Religion and dying in the New, did not feel that he had, in any clear sense, either committed apostasy or undergone a conversion. He had only tried to do what he was told in a world where doing what he was told had been, according to all his Betters, the thing mainly demanded of him.

It is, of course, true that even in the sixteenth century some individuals deplored persecution. Erasmus, writing to George of Saxony in 1524, pronounced it 'very harsh' (*non aequum*) 'that anie error be punished with the fire vnlesse there bee ioyned to it sedition or som other fact that the lawes do vse to punish with death'. This, it will be seen, is only a plea for mercy, not for religious liberty. The Frenchman Bellus (or Castellion) in his *De Haereticis* (1554) and the Italian Acontius in his *Stratagemata Satanae* (1564) go farther. But the work of Bellus remained unpublished till 1612, and Acontius most unfortunately bases his position on the view that fewer opinions than we suppose are certainly erroneous, and fewer errors than we suppose certainly damnable. Such an argument is useless because it leaves untouched those who believe they are suppressing real, and really damnable, errors: and these, after all, are the people most likely to persecute. It is also dangerous, because it tends to confirm them in their suspicion that every tolerationist is a sceptic in disguise. Far stronger were certain isolated voices in the English House of Commons; one Atkinson, who in 1562 argued against the imposition of the Oath of Supremacy that 'if any were rebellious before, now will his heart be more rebellious for that he is forced to perjury', or Aglionby, who in 1571 declared the 'conscience of man' to be 'eternal, invisible, and not in the power of the greatest monarchy of the world in any limits to be straitened, in any bounds to be contained, nor with any policy of man if once decayed, to be again raised'. Best of all, since they find a religious ground for not enforcing religion, are the words of Robert Browne; to compel religion 'belongeth not' to the magistrate, for 'the Lords people is of the willing sort, they shall come into Zion and enquire the way into Ierusalem not by force or compulsion but with their faces turned thitherward' (*A Book which sheweth, etc.*, 1582). With Browne we may class the anonymous author of the beautiful *Temporis Filia Veritas* (1589) who would tolerate all 'so they loue God and desyer to liue vnder obedience to the king', because 'the trueth itself' cannot be formulated by flesh and blood but is 'the louely lyfe or being of God'. But the chief importance of such utterances is to remind us, after all our talk of 'periods', that in every age nearly every conceivable opinion is held by somebody: 'there have always', says Sir Maurice Powicke, 'been civilised men.' The exceptions must not be allowed to obscure the general picture. Throughout the sixteenth century the great mass of those who seemed at the time to be sane, normal, practical men, ignored the few who spoke for liberty. The Church of Rome and the new churches retained the principle of theocracy. Jewel makes it a point in favour of the Church of England that she persecutes; Cardinal Allen makes it a point against her that she does not.[1] Martyrs on both sides would have been horrified if they had thought that their sufferings were going to encourage freedom of conscience. Search in the most capacious mind of that age for any echo of Browne's wisdom and you will hear only the thin gaggle of Sir Andrew, 'I had as lief be a Brownist as a politician'.

---

[1] 'You haue purposely repealed ... all former laws of the Realme for burning heretiques, which smelleth of something I need not here expresse' (*True Sincere and Modest Defence*, cap. 3).

With the accession of Elizabeth English Protestantism enters on a new phase. The refugees who had fled to the Continent from Mary's persecution now began to return. They returned to an England embittered by that persecution, and their own minds had in exile been not only embittered but, as they thought, clarified. Opinion is now increasingly dominated by thorough, consistent, continental ideas, hostile to English compromise and haziness. Many surrendered to, all were influenced by, the dazzling figure of Calvin. It ought to be easier for us than for the nineteenth century to understand his attraction. He was a man born to be the idol of revolutionary intellectuals; an unhesitating doctrinaire, ruthless and efficient in putting his doctrine into practice. Though bred as a lawyer, he found time before he was thirty to produce the first text of the *Institutio* (1536) and never made any serious modification of its theory. By 1537 he was already at Geneva and the citizens were being paraded before him in bodies of ten to swear to a system of doctrine. Sumptuary legislation and the banishment of the dissentient Caroli made it plain that here was the man of the new order who really meant business. He was driven out of Geneva but returned to new triumphs in 1540, successfully maintaining his theocracy both against civil magistrates who wished to govern a little more, and private citizens who wished to be governed a good deal less, than Calvin would permit. The banishment of Bolsec (1551) and the burning of Servetus (1553) were among its achievements. The moral severity of his rule laid the foundations of the meaning which the word 'puritan' has since acquired. But this severity did not mean that his theology was, in the last resort, more ascetic than that of Rome. It sprang from his refusal to allow the Roman distinction between the life of 'religion' and the life of the world, between the Counsels and the Commandments. Calvin's picture of the fully Christian life was less hostile to pleasure and to the body than Fisher's; but then Calvin demanded that every man should be made to live the fully Christian life. In academic jargon, he lowered the honours standard and abolished the pass degree.

Modern parallels are always to some extent misleading. Yet, for a moment only, and to guard against worse misconceptions, it may be useful to compare the influence of Calvin on that age with the influence of Marx on our own; or even of Marx and Lenin in one, for Calvin had both expounded the new system in theory and set it going in practice. This will at least serve to eliminate the absurd idea that Elizabethan Calvinists were somehow grotesque, elderly people, standing outside the main forward current of life. In their own day they were, of course, the very latest thing. Unless we can imagine the freshness, the audacity, and (soon) the fashionableness of Calvinism, we shall get our whole picture wrong. It was the creed of progressives, even of revolutionaries. It appealed strongly to those tempers that would have been Marxist in the nineteen-thirties. The fierce young don, the learned lady, the courtier with intellectual leanings, were likely to be Calvinists. When hard rocks of Predestination outcrop in the flowery soil of the *Arcadia* or the *Faerie Queene*, we are apt to think them anomalous, but we are wrong. The Calvinism is as modish as the shepherds and goddesses. The wicked Bishop in *Diotrephes* complains that at the universities 'puritans start up every day'. Cartwright had got all the fellows of St. John's out of their surplices before he was thirty, Travers wrote his *Explicatio* when he was twenty-six, Penry and John Udall were twenty-eight when the one brought out his *Treatise to the Queen* and the other his *Diotrephes*. Youth is the taunt commonly brought against the puritan leaders by their opponents: youth and cocksureness. As we recognize the type we begin, perhaps, to wonder less that such a work as the *Institutio* should have been so eagerly welcomed. In it Calvin goes on from the original Protestant experience to build a system, to extrapolate, to raise all the dark questions and give without flinching the dark answers. It is, however, a masterpiece of literary form; and we may suspect that those who read it with most approval were troubled by the fate of predestined vessels of wrath just about as much as young Marxists in our own age are troubled by the approaching liquidation of the *bourgeoisie*. Had the word 'sentimentality' been known to them, Elizabethan Calvinists would certainly have used it of any who attacked the *Institutio* as morally repulsive.

Of course not all Calvinists were puritans. Nor am I suggesting that the great fighting puritans who risked ruin and torture in their attack on the bishops were merely conforming to a fashion. We must distinguish a hard core of puritans and a much wider circle of those who were, at varying levels, affected by Calvinism. But a certain severity (however seriously we may take it) was diffused even through that wider circle, in the sense

that denunciation of vice became part of the stock-in-trade of
fashionable and even frivolous writers. Perhaps nothing in our
period is so surprising to a modern as the readiness with which
a Lyly, a Nashe, or even a Greene, will at any moment launch
out into moral diatribe of the most uncompromising ferocity.
All our lifetime the current has been setting towards licence.
In Elizabeth's reign it was the opposite. Nothing seems to have
been more saleable, more *comme il faut*, than the censorious. We
are overwhelmed by floods of morality from very young, very
ignorant, and not very moral men. The glib harshness is to us
a little repulsive: but it won applause then as easily as attacks
on Victorianism, romanticism, or nostalgia have won it in
our own century. The gentleness and candour of Shakespeare's
mind has impressed all his readers. But it impresses us still more
the more we study the general tone of sixteenth-century literature. He is gloriously anomalous.

The puritan party, properly so called, insisted on Calvin's
system of church government as well as on his general theology.
They themselves would not have admitted a distinction between
the two. They taught that a system—as they called it, a *platfourme*—of church government could be found in the New
Testament and was binding on all believers till the end of the
world. To a modern reader, examining the texts on which they
based this theory, it appears one of the strangest mirages which
have ever deceived the human mind: only explicable, if at all,
by the strong enchantment of the master's exploits at Geneva.
They demanded that such a 'godly discipline' should be instantly
set up in England. In Scotland Knox was prepared to establish
it by armed revolution. The English puritans were at first
milder: but Udall in his *Demonstration* (1588) is already saying
that, since peaceful methods have failed, 'if it come in by that
meanes which wil make all your heartes ake, blame yourselues'.

The psychology of the puritan proper is not so easily determined as that of the merely Calvinist fringe: just as, in our own
age, we know pretty well what sorts of people will be fashionably
Leftist, but not who will be real Communists. In all deep conviction there is something that cuts across the ordinary divisions
of age, sex, class, and culture. One kind of puritan, drawn by
the hostile pen of Lodge in *Wit's Misery* (1596), is recognizable
enough: a 'malecontent', lately returned from abroad, hating
his own country and always muttering that 'good Wits' get

better 'entertainment' on the Continent. But there were many other types: saints, no doubt, and cranks, a rag-tag and bobtail of mere anticlericals, but also 'great friends', wealthy land-owners, and even courtiers.

The position of these 'great friends' is somewhat ambiguous. There seems to be little doubt about the fact. Elizabeth, address-ing Whitgift in 1583, attributed the disorders of the Church partly to 'the power of some noblemen'. Leicester, Walsingham, Huntingdon, and Norfolk all seem to have had puritan sym-pathies. Even more significantly, Martin Marprelate in his *Epistle* (1588) scolds Whitgift for refusing a request made to him by the Earl of Warwick and adds an unmistakable hint that the nobility will not stand such independent bishops much longer. The critics of the puritans accounted for their 'great vpholders' by a very cynical hypothesis. 'English Pasquil' in his *Returne* (1589) says that these upholders are men 'as readie' as Martin himself 'to rob the Church'. Thomas Cooper in his *Admonition* (also 1589) says that 'an infinit number of Epicures and Atheistes' share the puritans' hatred for bishops because bishops 'staye from them that spoyle and praye which now for a fewe yeeres with great hope they haue gaped after'. The charge is not unplausible. No one had forgotten how profitable the spoliation of the monasteries had been to some eminent lay-men: if the revenues of the bishops were similarly taken from them, might there not be similar pickings? Of course such a charge was certain to be made whether it was true or not; but then the very reason why it was certain to be made was that it has some probability. Fortunately a literary historian need come to no conclusion on such a point. It is perhaps worth noting that Kirkrapine (*Faerie Queene*, I. iii. 16 et seq.) is prob-ably an allegory of the puritan conceived as a church-robber. Like Martin, he works in darkness. Like the puritans, he strips 'churches of their ornaments'. When Kirkrapine 'spoild the Priests of their habiliments' he was doing what the puritans wanted to do in their controversy against the surplice. 'The holy Saints' whom he stripped 'of their rich vestiments' cannot be robed images of saints, which would have been an abomina-tion to Spenser. They are either the same as 'the priests' or else some section of the clergy especially revered by the poet whether for their personal character or for their episcopal office. Kirk-rapine's partnership with Abessa allegorizes the charge, made also in *An Almond for a Parrot* (1590), that puritanism, by disturbing the Protestant Church in England, was really playing into the hands of the common enemy. Throughout these controversies between Anglican and puritan, naturally enough, each accused the other of being the Pope's best friend.

What has been said above about the intellectual character of puritanism is quite consistent with the fact that an extreme puritan could reach a position which left hardly any room for secular learning or human reason. It is a paradox which meets us more than once in the history of thought; intellectual extremists are sometimes led to distrust of intellect. But in its earlier stages puritanism went well enough with rigid logic and with humanism. Humanist and puritan both felt themselves to be in the vanguard, both hated the Middle Ages, and both demanded a 'clean sweep'. The same youthful intransigence characterized both. The eagerness to smell out and condemn vestiges of popery in the Church and the eagerness to smell out and condemn vestiges of 'barbarism' in one's neighbour's Latin had, psychologically, much in common.

Both these movements were militant and obtrusive, inclined rather to emphasize than to belittle their own novelty. The change in political thought—or at least in political sentiment—which was beginning in the sixteenth century was stealthier. It has left its mark on some purely literary texts. In Malory Sir Mador says to Arthur, 'Though ye be our king in that degree, yet ye are but a knight as we are' (xviii. iv). The slaying of a bad king like Mark excites nobody's disapproval (xix. xi). Lancelot spares Arthur in battle, not because he is a king simply, but because he is 'that most noble king that made me knight' (xx. xiii). In Jacobean drama we find a very different tone. Amintor, on learning that the man who has injured him is the king, says that that very name 'wipes away all thoughts revengefull', and has in it a terror which paralyses mortal arms (*Maid's Tragedy*, ii. i). Camillo cannot find in all history a single instance of a man who has struck an anointed king 'and flourished after' (*Winter's Tale*, i. ii. 358). No doubt allowance should be made for court patronage in these dramatic examples, and for the French origin in Malory. But there is no question that in these quotations we hear the echo of a very important change in men's attitude to the royal power. The doctrine of Divine Right has risen above the horizon. During the following century it will reach its full blaze of paradox in Filmer's *Patriarchia*, Hobbes's *Leviathan*, and Bossuet's *Politique tirée de l'Escriture Sainte*.

It would, however, be easy to exaggerate the adherence to this doctrine in sixteenth-century England. Emphasis on the sacred authority of the 'Prince' does not necessarily mean that the Crown is being exalted against Parliament or the Common Law. 'Prince' could often be translated 'government' or 'State'. It would also be easy to miss the true and permanent significance of what was happening if we overstressed its connexion with one particular form of government, the monarchical. That connexion (as Hobbes knew) was temporary and largely accidental. The Divine Right of Kings is best understood as the first form of something which has continued to affect our lives ever since— the modern theory of sovereignty. It is often called Austinian, but might just as well be called Johnsonian, for it is very clearly stated in *Taxation No Tyranny*; 'all government is ultimately and essentially absolute'. On this view, total freedom to make what laws it pleases, superiority to law because it is the source of law, is the characteristic of every state; of democratic states no less than of monarchical. That doctrine has proved so popular that it now seems to many a mere tautology. We conceive with difficulty that it was ever new because we imagine with difficulty how political life can ever have gone on without it. We take it for granted that the highest power in the State, whether that power is a despot or a democratically elected assembly, will be wholly free to legislate and incessantly engaged in legislation.

It seems, however, quite certain that many ages (not barbarous) believed nothing of the sort. Aristotle (*Politics*, 1282[b]) explicitly ruled that the highest power should hardly legislate at all. Its function was to administer a pre-existing law. Any legislation there was should be directed to supplementing and particularizing that law where its necessary generality failed to meet some concrete situation. The main outlines of the law must be preserved. It creates, and is not created by, the State. I do not know that Aristotle ever tells us where this original and immutable law came from; but, whether derived from our ancestors or from a philosophical constitution-maker, it must be accepted by the State as a *datum*. There is no sovereign in the Johnsonian sense. Roman practice and Roman jurisprudence took a very different view, but the Middle Ages (at first uncon-

sciously) reverted to Aristotle. Two factors worked against the
emergence of a theory of sovereignty. One was the actual dominance of custom in medieval communities. 'England', says Bracton, 'uses unwritten law and custom' (*De Legibus*, I. i)—speaking
truly about England, though wrongly thinking that this was
peculiar to her. A. J. Carlyle quotes coronation oaths (not English) in which the king swears to keep *les ancienes costumes*. Pleas
are to be decided *selonc les costumes*: custom is to be determined
either by the previous decision of a court, or, significantly, by
the fact that no one can remember when it was not so. This law
or custom is the real sovereign. 'The King is under the Law for
it is the Law that maketh him a King' (Bracton, I. viii). It is
true that Bracton often exalts the power of the king, but he is
thinking of it as an executive power. The other factor was the
doctrine of Natural Law. God, as we know from Scripture (Rom.
i. 15), has written the law of just and reasonable behaviour in
the human heart. The civil law of this or that community is
derived from the natural 'by way of particular determination'
(Aquinas, *Summa Theol.* I³. 2ᵃᵉ. xcv. iv). If it is not, if it contains
anything contrary to Natural Law, then it is unjust and we are
not, in principle, obliged to obey it (ibid. 2ᵃ. 2ᵃᵉ. lx. v). Sedition
is, of course, a sin; but then the *perturbatio* of a tyrant (defined,
from Aristotle, as one who rules in his own interest) is not sedition, for his rule is unjust (ibid. 2ᵃ. 2ᵃᵉ xlii. ii). Thus for Aquinas,
as for Bracton, political power (whether assigned to king, barons,
or the people) is never free and never originates. Its business is
to enforce something that is already there, something given in
the divine reason or in the existing custom. By its fidelity in reproducing that model it is to be judged. If it tries to be original,
to produce new wrongs and rights in independence of the
archetype, it becomes unjust and forfeits its claim to obedience.

It would be quite impossible here to suggest the causes, or
even to trace the process, of the change which introduced the
concept of sovereignty. Wycliffe, a pioneer of the new theory,
was exceptional in his own age. The years 1445 and 1446 are
important: in the first the Cortes of Olmedo announced that it
was contrary to divine law to touch the Lord's Anointed, and
the second saw the publication of Aeneas Sylvius' *De Ortu
Imperii Romani* in which he declares the emperor to be *legibus
solutus*. Nor can I here deal with works which attacked the
novelty. Its naturalization in England may be seen in Tyndale's

Obedience of a Christian Man (1528), where we are told that 'The King is in this world without lawe and may at his owne lust do right and wrong and shall give accounts to God only.' It is true that this quotation gives (by itself) a false impression of Tyndale's character and of that strange treatise in which he flings such appalling power to Henry VIII almost scornfully, like a bone to a dog; but it is a fair illustration of Tyndale's political theory. The *First Book of Homilies*[1] (1547) substantially agrees with him: rebellion is in all circumstances sinful.

We must not suppose that the medieval conception of Natural Law vanished overnight. On the contrary, as not infrequently happens to systems of thought, it reached its fullest and most beautiful expression when the tide of history had turned against it. In the first book of Hooker we find that God Himself, though the author, is also the voluntary subject, of law. 'They err who think that of the will of God to do this or that there is no reason besides his will' (I. i. 5). God does nothing except in pursuance of that 'constant Order and Law' of goodness which He has appointed to Himself. Nowhere outside the minds of devils and bad men is there a *sic volo, sic jubeo*. The universe itself is a constitutional monarchy. The Almighty Himself repudiates the sort of sovereignty that Tyndale thinks fit for Henry VIII. Only one further step was left to be taken, and Grotius took it in the *De Jure Belli ac Pacis* (1625). There he asserts that the Law of Nature, actually derived from God, would be equally binding even if we supposed that no God existed. It is another way of saying that good would still be good if stripped of all power. It is the extreme opposite of the Calvinist view which comes near to saying that omnipotence must be worshipped even if it is evil, that power is venerable when stripped of all good; and it is no doubt incomparably less dangerous to theism. But Calvin was more in tune with the spirit of his age: everyone can see that the difference between Hooker's God and Calvin's is very like that between Bracton's king and Aeneas Sylvius' emperor. It may even be not too fanciful to connect these changes, theological and political, with a tendency in this period which I noticed above. In the magician and the astrologer we saw a readiness either to exaggerate or to minimize the power and dignity of Man. Calvinism perhaps satisfies both inclinations by plunging the unregenerate man as deep as the astrologers and exalting

---

[1] Or, to give it its true title, *Certain Sermons or Homilies.*

the elect as highly as the magicians. Similarly the new polities embody limitless power and freedom in the prince, and make the subjects his (as they were the stars') tennis balls.

Few of those who accepted, or even of those who promoted, this change quite saw what they were about. Men continued to hope that the prince would, of his own virtue, obey the Law of Nature. His rule on earth, reproducing God's rule in the universe, even seemed a lovely example of that law, of hierarchy imitated from Nature herself. It was, indeed, Henry VII who emphasized the natural hierarchy in a whimsical form by ordering the death of some dogs that had baited a lion, their 'kindly' king (Harrison's *Description of England*, III. vii). Poets so attached to the new order as Spenser and Shakespeare continue to pour out tranquil, golden poetry about the great chain of concord and the beauty of degree. They did not dream that the concept of the State as something *legibus soluta* would presently sever all connexion between political life and 'Nature' as they understood that word—the divine, anthropomorphic harmony. Hobbes knew better. A Law of Nature such that it furnished, even *in foro interno*, a court of appeal against the State was inimical to a fully developed theory of sovereignty; he therefore abolished the concept while astutely retaining the name. The new theory makes political power something inventive, creative. Its seat is transferred from the reason which humbly and patiently discerns what is right to the will which decrees what shall be right. And this means that we are already heading, via Rousseau, Hegel, and his twin offspring of the Left and the Right, for the view that each society is totally free to create its own 'ideology' and that its members, receiving all their moral standards from it, can of course assert no moral claim against it. The subtle and far-reaching effects of the change, which are still proceeding, may be gauged by the implications of the fact that those who were once called a nation's *rulers* are now almost universally called its *leaders*.

Though Tyndale was an early and vigorous spokesman of the new theory, it must not be supposed that Protestants necessarily agreed with him. Hooker, as we have seen did not: and Poynet's *Shorte Treatise of Politic Power* (1556), written in exile and against Mary, is a resounding defence of Natural Law. Aeneas Sylvius, afterwards Pope, is closer to Tyndale. Once again, no neat grouping into 'old' and 'new' is possible.

It would be unreasonable in this context to pass over in silence the *Prince* (1513) of Machiavelli, for there the repudiation of medieval principles goes farthest. But for that very reason Machiavelli is not very important. He went too far. Everyone answered him, everyone disagreed with him. The book's success was a success of scandal. To readers who seriously sought instruction in the art of tyranny he could, after all, reveal only the secrets which all men knew. Not to be, but to seem, virtuous—it is a formula whose utility we all discovered in the nursery. But Machiavelli may have some importance for literature. I will not repeat the time-honoured statement that our Elizabethans mistook him, reading as devilish advice what was in fact coolly objective political science; such a view will hardly survive a re-reading of the *Prince*. It is (implicitly) written in the imperative mood throughout, and Machiavelli had no more notion of the amoral as distinct from the immoral than of the steam-engine. He thought himself immoral: 'if it be lawful', he says, 'to speake wel of euil' (viii). The Elizabethans, I believe, understood him much better than the subtle moderns. But the question need not concern us. Machiavelli is important to the historian of literature only as a possible father of the 'Machiavellian villain'.

The new type of villain which we meet in Elizabethan drama is an image of some interest. I say 'new type' because we must all deprecate the tendency to use the words 'Machiavellian villain' when we mean merely a great or ruthless villain. By a 'Machiavellian' villain we ought to mean one who circumvents his victims by cunning and hypocrisy—like Machiavelli's ideal prince. Thus Kyd's Lorenzo and Shakespeare's Iago are Machiavellian; Tamburlaine is not. The cunning villain is so useful to dramatists and has so long been part of their stock-in-trade that we tend to take him for granted. But the typical villains of medieval literature are not often cunning. They are seldom cleverer than the good characters. Herod is not a politician, but something between a buffoon and an ogre. Ganelon is a traitor and Mordred a tale-bearer but neither is particularly subtle. The devil himself is usually 'an ass': Marlowe's and Milton's are new. The archetype in the medieval mind seems to have been a story like Jack the Giant Killer, in which the good, clever people (with all the odds against them) beat the strong, stupid, 'outrageous' ones. The situation between Lancelot and Meliagrance (Malory, xix, vii), where the hero's very goodness makes him gullible, is not typical. On the Elizabethan stage it is. Machiavelli may have helped to make it so, but the exigencies of plot may have had more to do with it. Side by side with the new villain a far more disquieting, but temporary, novelty appeared. The older type of villain starts up as hero. Tamburlaine is Grendel, Herod, and Giant Blunderbore all in one, but the author seems to me to be on his side.[1] The play is a hideous moral spoonerism: Giant the Jack Killer.

It is difficult to decide how far the new villain represents a real change in outlook and how far he springs from dramatic convenience. But the theatre reveals another novelty about which I think we can be more certain. In ancient and medieval literature, as in ancient and medieval life, there is no inhibition about tears. Achilles wept, Aeneas wept, the Roman legionaries wept, Hrothgar wept, Roland wept *cum chevaler gentil*, and Lancelot, to his lasting glory, wept like a beaten child at the healing of Sir Urre (Malory, xix. xii). In Shakespeare a male character seldom weeps without apologizing for it: 'his eyes will tell tales of him', 'nature her custom holds, let shame say what it will', he 'had not so much of man in him' as to restrain his tears. Something, of course, must be allowed for the needs of the stage: because the actor cannot really weep at will, he must say something to let the audience know that he is supposed to be weeping. But that is not the whole explanation. Puttenham expects 'highminded' persons (the adjective is significant) to turn away their faces when they weep (*Art of English Poesy*, iii. xxxiv). Milton half apologizes for Adam's tears (*P.L.* xi. 494 et seq.). And the change about tears is only symptomatic of something larger.

It could hardly be called a philosophy but it was the nearest approach to a philosophy which humanism achieved, for Florentine Platonism, though dependent on the recovery of Greek, was alien to the humanist temper and indeed attacked it (see Pico's Letter to Hermolaus Barbarus in 1485). The mode of feeling (for it was hardly a mode of thought) which I am referring to was closely connected with the spirit shown in Vives' praise of the Latin language. It was the humanist response to the moral philosophy of the ancients. In one sense, and that the most profound, it must be admitted that the true subtlety and sagacity of Aristotle's *Ethics*, which had been preserved by

[1] Some critics think otherwise.

Aquinas, were now being lost again. But on a more superficial level we may speak of a revival of ancient moral philosophy. The new theology by its insistence on the distinction between faith and works, between the regenerate and the merely virtuous life, helped to disengage the concept of morality as such, morality as something other than religion. Hence Donne (Sermon LXXV) speaks of 'Philosophy and morall constancy' as a 'Meteor that hangs between two worlds', above the carnal and below the spiritual life. At the same time the humanists, disinclined for prolonged and serious thought, yet anxious for 'wisdom' if it could be had at an easier rate, turned naturally to that kind of 'philosophy' or 'moral constancy' which embodies itself in striking attitudes, anecdotes, and epigrams. In the ancients, and especially in Plutarch and Diogenes Laertius (the *Golden Legend* of paganism) they found materials for building up their picture of high, antique virtue and the heroically moral man. The word *philosopher*, without losing its old meanings, comes also to mean one who can 'endure the toothache patiently'.

The best elements in Aristotle's ethical thought contributed to this picture comparatively little. The doctrine of the Mean was dully and dutifully allegorized by Spenser in *Faerie Queene*, II. ii. But what proved far more attractive was Aristotle's Magnanimous Man: the man who both had, and was entitled to have, a high opinion of his own worth. Hence, I believe, comes that astonishing absence of humility which separates Sidney's and Spenser's heroes so widely from those of Malory. 'This secret assurance of his own worthinesse', says Sidney, 'always liues in the worthiest minds' (*Arcadia*, 1593, v). 'Oft times nothing profits more', says Milton, 'Then self-esteem grounded on just and right' (*P.L.* VIII. 571)—a beautifully exact account of Aristotle's Magnanimity. The contrast between the medieval and this 'philosophical' ideal comes out almost comically if we lay two passages side by side. In *Gawain and the Green Knight* the hero, travelling alone,

> had no fere but his fole bi frithes and downes
> And no gome but God bi gate with to karp (695).

Spenser's Guyon in the same situation

> ever more himselfe with comfort feedes
> Of his own vertues and praise-worthie deedes (II. vii. 2).

I fear there was no hint of a smile on Spenser's face as he described this windy diet.

But, for many sixteenth-century men, as for the Stoics, Aristotle's Magnanimity was not magnanimous enough, 'for he saith', complains Vives, 'that magnanimitie goeth about to seeke honours . . . but Plato, Cicero, Seneca and other place it rather in despising them' (*De Causis*, VI). They desired something far loftier, something as highly exalted as the magician, the prince, or the elect, the 'right prudent and valiant man', not only above tears (that, of course) but above all dependence on fortune. Thus the Stoic *sapiens*, far more than the Aristotelian μεγαλόψυχος, is the image really potent in Elizabethan, and in much later, literature. He is (like Chapman's Clermont) 'gladly obedient' to anything 'the high and general cause' may lay on him; he regards the world (like more than one Shakespearian character) merely as a stage; he is content (like Guyon) with what Nature needs; a king over himself (like Milton's Christ and Dryden's Almanzor); undazzled by worldly splendours (like Dryden's Leonidas); indifferent (like Addison's Cato) to the success or failure of his own actions. Far from desiring fame, he rather prefers obloquy. Coriolanus (II. iii. 53) would prefer the rabble to forget him: Milton's Christ regards the vulgar as judges 'of whom to be disprais'd were no small praise' (*P.R.* III. 56). He is indifferent to death. He lacks no divine attribute (once more, like Coriolanus) save eternity; and that is one which really does not matter. His mind (like Satan's) is its own place. He is as free as Nature first made man. He is more an antique Roman than a Dane.

All these attitudes can be paralleled from ancient texts, Stoic or Cynical (Seneca's Epistles are at least as important to the student of the sixteenth century as his tragedies). They yield an image which influenced the English poetic mind very deeply. This unmoved, unconquerable, 'mortal god' (as Henry More calls him), if modified in one direction gives us Milton's Christ: if in another, his Satan. Let him talk enough, and he is a Chapman hero; coarsen him in the Cynic direction, and he will supply traits both to Wycherley's Manly and to Pope's self-portrait in the *Epilogue to the Satires*. Inflate him without discretion, and he is Almanzor. He was perhaps hardly displaced until, in the eighteenth century, tears became fashionable again and the Man of Feeling succeeded him.

It may or may not have been noticed that the word *Renaissance* has not yet occurred in this book. I hope that this abstinence, which is forced on me by necessity, will not have been attributed to affectation. The word has sometimes been used merely to mean the 'revival of learning', the recovery of Greek, and the 'classicizing' of Latin. If it still bore that clear and useful sense, I should of course have employed it. Unfortunately it has, for many years, been widening its meaning, till now 'the Renaissance' can hardly be defined except as 'an imaginary entity responsible for everything the speaker likes in the fifteenth and sixteenth centuries'. If it were merely a chronological label, like 'pre-Dynastic' or 'Caroline' it might be harmless. But words, said Bacon, shoot back upon the understandings of the mightiest. Where we have a noun we tend to imagine a thing. The word *Renaissance* helps to impose a factitious unity on all the untidy and heterogeneous events which were going on in those centuries as in any others. Thus the 'imaginary entity' creeps in. *Renaissance* becomes the name for some character or quality supposed to be immanent in all the events, and collects very serious emotional overtones in the process. Then, as every attempt to define this mysterious character or quality turns out to cover all sorts of things that were there before the chosen period, a curious procedure is adopted. Instead of admitting that our definition has broken down, we adopt the desperate expedient of saying that 'the Renaissance' must have begun earlier than we had thought. Thus Chaucer, Dante, and presently St. Francis of Assisi, became 'Renaissance' men. A word of such wide and fluctuating meaning is of no value. Meanwhile, it has been ruined for its proper purpose. No one can now use the word *Renaissance* to mean the recovery of Greek and the classicizing of Latin with any assurance that his hearers will understand him. Bad money drives out good.

It should also be remembered that the word *Renaissance* is in a curiously different position from the general run of historical terms. Most of these, when not merely chronological, designate periods in the past by characteristics which we have come, in the course of our historical studies, to think distinctive or at least convenient. The ancients were not ancient, nor the men of the Middle Ages middle, from their own point of view. Gothic architecture was not 'Gothic' at the time, it was merely architecture. No one thought of himself as a Bronze Age man. But the humanists were very conscious of living in a *renascentia*. They claimed vociferously to be restoring all good learning, liberating the world from barbarism, and breaking with the past. Our legend of the Renaissance is a Renaissance legend. We have not arrived at this conception as a result of our studies but simply inherited it from the very people we were studying. If the earlier modern scholars had not themselves been bred in the humanist tradition it may be doubted whether they would ever have chosen so lofty a name as 'rebirth' to describe the humanist achievement. The event, objectively seen, would perhaps have appeared not quite so important nor so wholly beneficent. But, once established, this glowing term inevitably linked itself in the minds of English scholars with those two other processes which they highly approved in the sixteenth century—the birth of Protestantism and the birth of the physical sciences. Hence arose, as it seems to me, that strong prejudice, already more than once alluded to, which predisposed our fathers to see in this period almost nothing but liberation and enlightenment: hence, too, by reaction, and among scholars of anti-Protestant sympathies, the opposite tendency to see in it little else than the destruction of a humane and Christian culture by kill-joys and capitalists. Both views perhaps exaggerate the breach with the past; both are too simple and diagrammatic. Both thrust into the background things which were, at the time, important.

Thus far we have been concerned with ideas, and ideas have an effect on literature which can be traced, often with great probability, and sometimes with certainty. When we turn to social, political, and economic conditions, we are in a very different situation. No one doubts that these things affect a man's writing at least as much as his ideas can do: but the influence is very much harder to identify. Everything looks as if authors of talent had considerable freedom in working up the material which their experience offers to them. Attempts to connect men's circumstances too closely with their literary productions are usually, I believe, unsuccessful.

In this age the class of middling landowners and greater tenants were becoming richer and the peasantry poorer, but both processes had been going on before the Reformation, or the century, began. The same is true of enclosures, sheep-farming, eviction, depopulation, and distress. These things had been increasing long before More wrote his famous protest. Genuinely feudal relations between peasant and landlord had long since decayed.

The word *upstart* was noted as a neologism in 1555 by the anonymous author of the *Institution of a Gentleman*. But the thing itself was not new, save in so far as the *novi homines* of any period are likely to differ from those of another. Langland had complained of 'sopers' who rise to be knights. It is interesting, however, that our anonymous author distinguishes 'honest' from dishonest means of rising. Those who have risen by being employed in the public service he approves; but there is another sort who have not fairly earned their promotion, and these, he says, 'have chefely florished since the puttyng down of Abais'. He means, of course, those who have successfully speculated in land stolen from the Church.

In the spiritual sphere this spoliation was, no doubt, a catastrophic event. While it was being carried out, government amused the public with talk of many fine ecclesiastical and educational projects on which the money was to be employed. But when the time came government threw most of the land on the market and the projects were heard of no more. Skilful buyers profited by the crisis and several new landed families came into existence. But new landed families had often done so before. On that side the Dissolution produced only a temporary acceleration of a normal process.

The individual monks were on the whole fairly liberally provided for. What their disappearance, as landlords and dispensers of hospitality, counted for in the life of the country is a question very hard to answer. Testimonies conflict and come from the most unexpected sources. The Protestant Brinkelow in his *Complaint* (1545?), while approving the Dissolution on theological grounds, says, 'it had been more profytable, no dowte, for the comon welth' to have left the monks alone: they were better landlords than their successors. On the other hand, More in the *Utopia* expressly chooses an Abbot as his specimen of those bad, sheep-farming landlords who 'enclose all into pastures, throw down houses, pluck up villages'. (Dr. Rowse in *The England of Elizabeth* shows us an abbey at just such work in Leicestershire.) Perhaps it is safe to conclude that the monks were neither so bad as they seemed while we had them nor so good as they seemed in retrospect. Our quotations may at least serve as one more warning against too symmetrical alignments. The 'new' economics did not necessarily go with the new religion. The keenest diagnosis I have read of that impersonality which is held to have characterized the new order comes in the Puritan Crowley's *Way to Welth* (1550), where he speaks of 'men that haue no name because they are doers in al things'.

It is not always remembered that the bishoprics probably, and the colleges certainly, came near to sharing the fate of the monasteries. For the colleges, as Harrison says (*Description*, ii. iii), 'greedie gripers did gape wide'. Brinkelow ought to have learned his lesson from the fate of the monastic lands: in his simplicity he had really believed that government would spend its booty on 'social services', and had been bitterly disappointed by the event. But experience beats in vain upon a congenital progressive. He urged the spoliation of the colleges in the firm hope that this time—that mystical 'this time' which is always going to be so different—government, having sucked in, would give out.

It is tempting to connect the increasing prosperity of the smaller gentry and the greater yeomen with a change which comes over our poetry in the second half of the century. To a medieval poet (unless outlaws are his subject) the typically pleasant place out of doors is a garden, usually a garden well walled or hedged. In Elizabethan poetry the country appears. Philisides lies by a river side in flowery field, sweet woods take on 'the delight of solitarinesse', Zephyrus breathes on fairest mountain tops, the shepherd pipes 'besides a crystal fountain in shadow of a green oak tree', Lodge invokes 'fair enriched meads', 'sacred woods', 'sweet fields', and 'rising mountains'. Fairies (no longer august or dreadful) begin to people the woods; a nymph rises from every water. In Shakespeare 'Alexander Iden, a Kentish gentleman' paces the 'quiet walks' of his 'small inheritance', delighting to 'send the poor well pleased from his gate', and wonders how anyone could prefer to live 'turmoiled in the court'. In all this there may be much from Theocritus, Virgil, Sannazaro, Tasso, or Guarini. It is never safe to attribute a man's imaginations too directly to his experience. Yet it would not be unnatural to suppose that the pleasures of country life now began to be celebrated because they now began to be enjoyed. It is doubtful if the medieval noble or the medieval peasant felt them. The Elizabethan gentleman had every reason to do so. He was a richer man than his father, and counted for more in the scheme of things. He was a Justice of the Peace. His house and household stuff were better: his garden (if we may trust Harrison) incomparably better. Beyond the garden might lie the beautiful, if deleterious, sheep pastures and the even more beautiful, if more deleterious, park. Aesthetically, I suspect, the new landscape was a great improvement on the old. Space, neatness, privacy had come in. In such conditions, if not as their result, there arose that rural poetry which, descending from the Elizabethans into Milton, Vaughan, and Herrick and then, through poets like Thomson and Cowper, into the Romantics, was never quenched till the nineteen-thirties. A great deal of English poetry has been read by small squires.

This class—which is not very like even the smallest nobility of other countries—was coming into existence in the late sixteenth century: not without a cost. It is indeed true that the world has often paid, and will pay again, a heavier price for the creation of leisured classes far smaller, coarser, and less humane. During the long period of their happiness, our debt in every department of life to our petty gentry is enormous. But all was not well. Alexander Iden (whom we must take for an Elizabethan, though he is feigned to be living under Henry VI) charms us; but we have an uneasy suspicion that his 'small inheritance' includes a ruined abbey and that the very conditions he lives in may have helped to create the poor whom he relieves. The prosperity of his class depended, after all, on rising rents. The larger tenants could pay them and still be richer than their fathers. The small men sank and swelled the ranks of those who were 'daily consumed with the gallows', or disappeared, says Harrison (*Description*, II. x) to 'Fraunce, Germanie, Barbarie, India, Muscouia and verie Calecut'. Hence the increase of what we call tramps: whose punishment was slavery; whom it was criminal to feed or lodge. The reality behind Autolycus is not a merry one: yet he and his fellow wretches frequent our literature chiefly in a comic capacity. Whole books of roguery are devoted to them. The comedy comes in because the books expose their tricks and knaveries. It is not such genial comedy as some accounts would suggest. These are books written to soothe the consciences of the wealthy: 'easy speeches that comfort cruel men'. Some of the anecdotes can still win their laugh, but I find in none of them the sympathy of Burns's *Jolly Beggars*.

The sixteenth century saw the completion, or almost the completion, of a process whereby education had long been spreading, not down, but up, the social scale. In the high Middle Ages the presumption had been that a layman, and especially a noble layman, would not be a clerk. By Tudor times the idea that an aristocrat should be illiterate has disappeared in England, though Ascham and Castiglione both suggest that it lingered in France. Education, by Elizabeth's time, had come to include the highest classes but was not yet peculiar to them. The exclusion of the poor was, however, beginning. Harrison, Humphrey Gilbert (in his *Queen Elizabethes Achademy*) and others complain that in some grammar schools 'poore mens children are commonlie shut out', that in some colleges it is hard for a poor man to get a fellowship, that the 'youth of nobility and gentlemen' by taking up scholarships and fellowships 'do disapointe the poore of their liuinges and auauncementes'. In this way also new learning (for one class) meant new ignorance (for another). But the process was far from complete. Boys of many different social classes might still meet at school: a learned sixteenth-century divine was often a yeoman's son. If some schools were destroyed during this period, some were also founded.

'Classical' Latin, taught with a view to conversation as well as to reading, was the staple of education, though many masters used it as a means of teaching 'copiousness' and 'eloquence' in English as well. There were different degrees of Ciceronianism and a *bellum Ciceronianum* as fierce as the war of the frogs and mice. Greek long continued to be, as Johnson said, 'like lace'. Vives reserves it for the better pupils and thought it fortunate that Attic contained most of what really deserved study, the other dialects being mainly used by lyric poets 'whom it importeth lesse to know' (*De Tradendis*, III). Burton cites his Greek authors in Latin translations. Shakespeare's blundering statement that Aristotle forbade young men to study moral philosophy is endorsed by Bacon and derived from Erasmus. Few sixteenth-century Englishmen—I suspect, none—would have had a chance of a classical scholarship in a nineteenth-century university.

While Tudor education differed by its humanism from that of the Middle Ages, it differed far more widely from ours. Law and rhetoric were the chief sources of the difference. Young men of fortune commonly passed from the university to one of the inns of court. In respect of the students' ages, the life lived, the temptations, and the intellectual stimulus, the inn of court was to them very much what the university is to their successors: the university was more like one's public school. Rhetoric is the greatest barrier between us and our ancestors. If the Middle Ages had erred in their devotion to that art, the *renascentia*, far from curing, confirmed the error. In rhetoric, more than in anything else, the continuity of the old European tradition was embodied. Older than the Church, older than Roman Law, older than all Latin literature, it descends from the age of the Greek Sophists. Like the Church and the law it survives the fall of the empire, rides the *renascentia* and the Reformation like waves, and penetrates far into the eighteenth century; through all these ages not the tyrant, but the darling of humanity, *soavissima*, as Dante says, 'the sweetest of all the other sciences'. Nearly all our older poetry was written and read by men to whom the distinction between poetry and rhetoric, in its modern form, would have been meaningless. The 'beauties' which they chiefly regarded in every composition were those which we either dislike or simply do not notice. This change of taste makes an invisible wall between us and them. Probably all our literary histories, certainly that on which I am engaged, are vitiated by our lack of sympathy on this point. If ever the passion for formal rhetoric returns, the whole story will have to be rewritten and many judgements may be reversed. In the meantime we must reconcile ourselves to the fact that of the praise and censure which we allot to medieval and Elizabethan poets only the smallest part would have seemed relevant to those poets themselves.

We must picture them growing up from boyhood in a world of 'prettie epanorthosis', paranomasia, *isocolon*, and *similiter cadentia*. Nor were these, like many subjects in a modern school, things dear to the masters but mocked or languidly regarded by the parents. Your father, your grown-up brother, your admired elder schoolfellow all loved rhetoric. Therefore you loved it too. You adored sweet Tully and were as concerned about asyndeton and chiasmus as a modern schoolboy is about county cricketers or types of aeroplane. But against what seems to us this fantastic artificiality in their education we must set the fact that every boy, out of school, without noticing it, then acquired a range of knowledge such as no boy has today; farriery, forestry, archery, hawking, sowing, ditching, thatching, brewing, baking, weaving, and practical astronomy. This concrete knowledge, mixed with their law, rhetoric, theology, and mythology, bred an outlook very different from our own. High abstractions and rarified artifices jostled the earthiest particulars. They would have found it very hard to understand the modern educated man who, though 'interested in astronomy', knows neither who the Pleiades were nor where to look for them in the sky. They talked more readily than we about large universals such as death, change, fortune, friendship, or salvation; but also about pigs, loaves, boots, and boats. The mind darted more easily to and fro between that mental heaven and earth: the cloud of middle generalizations, hanging between the two, was then much smaller. Hence, as it seems to us, both the naïvety and the energy of their writing. Much of their literary strength (when at the end of the century they became strong) is bound up with this. They talk something like angels and something like sailors and stable-boys; never like civil servants or writers of leading articles.

During this century the professional author in the modern sense, the man who writes for the booksellers, was coming into existence. When printing was invented, government of course wished to control what was printed. In 1557 the Stationers' Company, whose history can be traced back to 1403, was incorporated by Royal Charter and became the principal organ by which this control was exercised. This concerns literature because copy, duly entered in the company's register, became the property of the bookseller who entered it. As a result booksellers were now prepared to buy copy from authors. By the end of the century, according to Nashe, they were glad to pay Greene 'deare' for the 'very dregs of his wit'; early in the seventeenth century, forty shillings is mentioned as a poor price for a pamphlet. Authors who wished to be regarded as gentlemen, however, usually disdained, or concealed, such payment. Many looked for reward to the patron rather than to the open market: hence the innumerable dedications to noble persons. These might be rewarded only by 'hearty thanks with commendations'; by a present; or by employment—a tutorship in the patron's household, as fell to Daniel, or a permanent post in the Civil Service such as Spenser got. It is not easy to determine how these conditions affected the quality of literature. I have found no evidence that the taste of the Court was particularly good. I am inclined to think that the practice of writing to sell in the open market did more good than harm. The most frankly commercial type of literature, the drama of Marlowe, Shakespeare, and the rest, includes much of the greatest work. A commercial success must have some sort of merit, though in certain periods it need only be merit of the lowest kind: a *succès d'estime* may, now and then, have none at all. The coarse, indifferent public cannot be made to believe that you are entertaining unless you entertain them, but a *côterie* or a patron can possibly be induced to think you 'important' when you have effected nothing.

The picture which I have tried to draw in this introduction is no model of neatness; but we may be sure that, along with all its other faults, it is too neat, too diagrammatic, for the facts. A man who wants to get the feel of that age must not be deceived by the tranquil harmonies of the great Italian painters; the amazing hodge-podge or rag-bag which we find in Montaigne or Burton is far more characteristic. He must beware of schematizing. He must not impose either on the old things that were dying out (not all old things were) nor on the new things that were coming in (not all of them to stay) a spurious unity. He must constantly remind himself that a Protestant may be Thomistic, a humanist may be a Papist, a scientist may be a magician, a sceptic may be an astrologer. He must recognize, side by side with what certainly seems to be a quality of adventurousness and expansion, a growing restriction and loss of liberty: Calvinism and Constellation both threatening free will, sovereignty threatening political freedom, humanism imposing new prohibitions on vocabulary and spontaneous emotion. The tight, starched ruff in an Elizabethan portrait, combined with the heroic or villainous energy of the face that rises above it, is no bad symbol. Some think it the historian's business to penetrate beyond this apparent confusion and heterogeneity, and to grasp in a single intuition the 'spirit' or 'meaning' of his period. With some hesitation, and with much respect for the great men who have thought otherwise, I submit that this is exactly what we must refrain from doing. I cannot convince myself that such 'spirits' or 'meanings' have much more reality than the pictures we see in the fire. Whether the actual content of the past or (less plausibly) of some artificially isolated period in the past has a significance is a question that need not here be raised. The point is that we can never know that content. The greater part of the life actually lived in any century, any week, or any day consists of minute particulars and uncommunicated, even incommunicable, experiences which escape all record. What survives, survives largely by chance. On such a basis it seems to me impossible to reach the sort of knowledge which is implied in the very idea of a 'philosophy' of history. There is also this to be said of all the 'spirits', 'meanings', or 'qualities' attributed to historical periods; they are always most visible in the periods we have studied least. The 'canals' on Mars vanished when we got stronger lenses.

But though 'periods' are a mischievous conception they are a methodological necessity. The mass of literature which I attempt to study in this book must be divided up somehow. I have accordingly divided it into what I call the Late Medieval, the Drab Age, and the 'Golden' Age. They overlap and cannot be precisely dated, and the divisions between them do not apply to prose nearly so well as to verse. The Late Medieval extends very roughly to the end of Edward VI's reign. The most obvious mark of Late Medieval poetry in England is its metrical irregularity; other marks, common to England and Scotland, are allegory and the predominance of rhyme royal. There is some aureation. Prose is usually simple and unartificial. The Drab Age begins before the Late Medieval has ended, towards the end of Henry VIII's reign, and lasts into the late seventies. *Drab* is not used as a dyslogistic term. It marks a period in which, for good or ill, poetry has little richness either of sound or images. The good work is neat and temperate, the bad flat and dry. There is more bad than good. Tottel's *Miscellany*, 'Sternhold and Hopkins', and *The Mirror for Magistrates* are typical Drab Age works. Prose is now more artificial in some writers, more cumbersome in others. The Golden Age is what we usually think of first when 'the great Elizabethans' are mentioned: it is largely responsible, in England, for the emotional overtones of the word *Renaissance*. The epithet *golden* is not eulogistic. By *golden* poetry I mean not simply good poetry, but poetry which is, so to speak, innocent or ingenuous. In a Golden Age the right thing to do is obvious: 'good is as visible as green'. The great age of Greek sculpture was similarly 'golden'. Men had at last attained the power of making a block of stone look really like a human body, and after that, for a few years, the artist's task was obvious. He had only to find the most beautiful models, pose them in the most graceful attitudes, and get to work. Only later, when the ingenuous taste has been satisfied, will it become necessary to seek for novelty, to set oneself difficult tasks, to make beauty out of violence. It was the same in the Golden period of Elizabethan poetry. Men have at last learned how to write; for a few years nothing more is needed than to play out again and again the strong, simple music of the uncontorted line and to load one's poem with all that is naturally delightful—with flowers and swans, with ladies' hair, hands, lips, breasts, and eyes, with silver and gold, woods and waters, the stars, the moon and the sun. Prose does not become Golden so suddenly as verse; many of its Golden triumphs were in the following century. It is, of course, neither possible nor desirable that a Golden Age should last long. Honey cloys and men seek for drier and more piquant flavours. At the end of the century this is already beginning to happen. The whole process of poetry from its Golden to its more sophisticated condition could be exemplified from Shakespeare's work alone. The growing difficulty, the decreasing obviousness, of his style is usually (and, of course, rightly) treated in connexion with his dramatic progress. But it also illustrates a movement which is almost dictated by the occurrence of a Golden Age.

BOOK I
Late Medieval

I

THE CLOSE OF THE MIDDLE AGES IN SCOTLAND

I

IN 1488, raised by the rebellion which dethroned and killed his father and of which he repented his own share, wearing an iron girdle while he lived, James IV was crowned at Scone. Though patrons cannot create poets, and though James was no great patron, it is deeply appropriate that the court poetry which will mainly concern us in this chapter should have been written under such a king; for in him and in it alike, as also in the dress and architecture of the period, all that is bright, reckless, and fantastical in the late medieval tradition finds superb expression. He was primarily a knight, only secondarily and disastrously a king; 'not a good captain' notes the Spanish ambassador, 'for he begins to fight before he has given his orders' and is 'more courageous than a prince should be'. 'He luvid nothing so weill', says Pitscottie, 'as able men and guid hors and used great jousting', so that the fame of his tournaments drew knights-errant from all Europe. At the same time he shared with the poets a hearty relish for low life and loved to 'ludge in poore mens houses' unattended and disguised. His very vices were chivalrous; no avarice, no countenance shown to 'pick-thanks', but a weakness for loving *par amors*. He was mercurial, wilful, restless, and inquisitive; much like Arthur himself (in *Gawain and the Green Knight*), who hated to be still for long—'so busied him his young blood and his brain wild'. The price was Flodden, and if he half killed Scotland he did it in character. A 'lufe letter' from the Queen of France containing a ring and a claim on his services as her true knight helped to speed him on that last journey, and the very act whereby he made defeat certain was a repetition of Byrhtnoth's heroic folly at Maldon.

His master-gunner had the English at his mercy while they were crossing the bridge and begged on his knees to be allowed to open fire. 'I sall hang thee', replied the king, 'if thou shoot ane shot this day, for I am determinate to have them all before me on ane plain field and essay them what they can do'; and so it came about that in later times men could point to no great house in Scotland that had not a grave on Brankstone Moor.

But during much of his reign there had been (by Scotch standards) 'guid peace and rest'. Sumptuary laws, as early as 1458, show that some at least of the commons had become sufficiently prosperous to ape the dress of their betters. At his accession the university of St. Andrews had already existed for seventy-four years and that of Glasgow for thirty-seven. In his reign Aberdeen was founded and an important enactment obliged all freeholders to put their sons to grammar school until they had 'perfect Latin'. The printing press of Chepman and Myllar dates from 1507. James himself has been pronounced illiterate by Buchanan, but the humanist probably means only that his Latin was not Ciceronian. In reality the king was something of an intellectual, 'weill lernit in the art of medicine' and proficient in several languages which included not only Latin but even 'the speech of the savages who live in some parts of Scotland and on the islands'. The new forces of humanism and Protestantism had not yet much altered the medieval character of Scotch civilization in his time. Lollardry had made itself felt, but James had shown in 1494 that he was no persecutor; Boece was a humanist, Major a scholastic. During the reign an effective Scotch navy was being built up, and the names of such captains as Sir Andrew Wood and Sir Andrew Barton were famous; the battleship and broadside which figure so unexpectedly in the *Golden Targe* were topical. Interest in scientific experiment is represented in 1507 at Stirling when Abbot Damian of Tungland attempted to fly with artificial wings before a large audience. Since he risked (and almost lost) his life we may assume that he was sincere, and the mockery lavished upon his failure is perhaps unworthy; if he had succeeded in finding the pernicious secret he sought he would have received ample praise from the historians of progress.

Such is the contemporary background of the brilliant poetry written by Douglas and Dunbar; a word about its 'background' in a different sense will not be amiss. When they began their work Scotch poetry had already a considerable achievement behind it and was by no means a local or provincial department of English poetry. Its history belongs to an earlier volume of the present series, and it will here be enough to remind the reader of the principal strands of which that history is woven. I distinguish five.

I. The forthright narrative in octosyllabic couplets as in Barbour's *Bruce*.

This is of Norman and Anglo-Norman origin, but becomes tougher and harder when written by poets of Germanic blood and speech. It is used for many purposes which have now been abandoned to prose, but in epic and metrical romance can achieve some of the highest qualities of poetry. Blind Harry's *Wallace*, which falls outside my period, has substituted decasyllabics for octosyllabics but belongs on the whole to this kind. A purer example is the anonymous *History of Sir Eger, Sir Gryme, and Sir Gray-Steel*. We possess this only in very late texts (one in the Percy Folio and one printed at Aberdeen in 1711), but it goes back in some form to the fifteenth century; in April 1497 'twa fithelaris' received a payment of nine shillings for singing it at court. It may be much older, and, again, it may in 1497 have been very different from the texts we have. But it is not likely to have been inferior to them, and in them it is far too good to be bandied to and fro from volume to volume of this series and described in none—as may easily happen to a text whose historical position is uncertain. Percy has called it 'a well invented tale of chivalry scarce inferior to any of Ariosto's'. This is true; not, of course, that its poetical character is at all like that of the *Orlando Furioso*, but that its 'well invented' plot or fable would have suited Ariosto in one of his graver and less fanciful moods. Its poetry is at the opposite pole from his; hard, plain, vivid, and economical in manner, effortlessly and unobtrusively noble in sentiment. The adventures are as palpable as those in Homer. I never realized what fighting an enemy who wore full armour would be like until I read in this poem:

> I strake him while that I might stand,
> While *there came blood through the steel*;
> He wants some teeth I wote right weel.

Equally convincing is Eger's account of his recovering consciousness after being defeated and left for dead:

> Beside me ran a river strand,
> And there I crap on feet and hand,
> And from mine eyes I washt the blood
> And drank while that I thought it good.

The Romantic idea of steadfast devotion amidst strange perils has never been better summed up than in Grime's words to the lady:

> And ever I had mind of you
> The Land of Doubt when I rode through.

It is, of course, a poetry with strict limitations; what we admire is the perfection of taste (as if vulgarity had not yet been invented) and the sureness of touch within those limitations. It will also be noticed that it does faultlessly what poetry soon after became incapable of doing at all. From this sort of heroic narrative we were to descend into fustian about Mars and Bellona. The 'Renaissance' involved great losses as well as great gains.

II. A fairly large body of poems which combine rhyme and alliteration in various patterns and which, whether the connexions can still be traced or no, must be fairly closely related to the north-west midland poetry of the English fourteenth century. This is a sophisticated kind with a developed poetic diction in marked contrast to the plainness of the octosyllabic narratives. In *Golagros and Gawain* it achieves great nobility. But the impulse is almost spent by the time we reach the sixteenth century and the form is henceforward used chiefly for comic purposes. This brings us to the next of the five strands I am distinguishing.

III. Our knowledge of comic poetry, like our knowledge of the lyric, in this period depends mainly on the praiseworthy taste of some sixteenth-century Scotchmen for compiling anthologies. The three which most concern us are the Bannatyne MS. (1568), the Maitland Folio MS. (1580), and the Maitland Quarto MS. (1586). The poems which these contain are of all sorts—devotional, moral, political, amatory, and sportive. Some are by famous hands—Henryson, Douglas, or Dunbar—some bear the names of authors who cannot be certainly identified, and most are anonymous. Only a minority of them can be dated. But one at least of the comic pieces, *Cowkelbie Sow*, is earlier than 1501, when it is mentioned in Douglas's *Palice of Honour*; 'The Gyre Garling' was an established nursery tale in the childhood of James V, say by 1519; and a number of others show the peculiar Scotch taste in such matters so fully developed that it is reasonable to regard the *genre* as one of the things which Dunbar found ready to his hand.

This comic poetry has often been misunderstood by English critics, for memories of Chaucer and Dickens are here almost a hindrance. Edward Lear and Lewis Carroll would be a far better introduction to it; Rabelais, Aristophanes, and Lucian better still. Bannatyne No. CCXXX is a good specimen to begin with. It relates (in rough four-beat couplets) the creation of the first Highlander. God and St. Peter were out for a walk in Argyll one day when St. Peter, observing a certain unsavoury object on the path, jokingly suggested that God might like to create something from it. One stir of the almighty 'Pykit staff' and 'vp start a helandman, blak as ony draff'. Questioned about his plans, the new creature announced that he would be a cattle-thief. God laughed heartily, but even while He was doing so (it is like Mercury and Apollo in Horace's ode) the Highlander had contrived to steal His pen-knife. All the characteristics of the *genre* are present here. It is primarily nonsense poetry, and in the interests of nonsense makes free use of blasphemy and indecency. The blasphemy is not intended to move ironical smiles, nor the indecency to move prurient titters; what both want from the audience is a hearty guffaw. And there is no human comedy; the joke lies in the extravagance, the nonsensicality. 'The Gyre Carling' (or 'Giant Quean', Bannatyne CXCIX) tells us how 'North Berwick law' came into existence by a physical accident which befell a giantess in an over-hearty fit of laughter. This is in rhyming alliterative stanzas followed by 'wheels'. So is 'Kynd Kittok' (Bannatyne CXCVII). This poem, anonymous in the manuscript, and in the old print, has been attributed by many to Dunbar; but there is an indulgent twinkle of the eye in it, a gentleness amid its fantasy, which seems to me foreign to his temper. The disreputable 'guddame', Kynd Kittok, 'died of thirst and made a good end', stopped at an ale house near Heaven for the night, arrived at the gate next morning something the worse for wear, and managed to steal in without St. Peter's notice; which was the worse for him since, during her seven years' residence as Our Lady's hen-wife, she 'held him in strife'. The end of the poem leaves her once more outside the gate and permanently established at that same neighbouring ale house, where future travellers, we are told, will find it worth their while to call on her. In this poem, as in the 'First Highlander', we are allowed to hear God laugh, and His laughter is very different from that of *Paradise Lost*. At Kynd Kittok's surreptitious entry into Heaven, 'God lukit and saw her lattin in and lewch His hairt sair'.[1] It is a note rarely struck in later Scotch literature. In other places the comic super-naturalism is drawn not from Christianity but from northern superstition. In 'The Gyre Carling' we have 'the King of Fary... with elffis mony ane'. The same 'eldritch' material, as they would have called it, is used in 'The Laying of Lord Fergus Gaist' (Bannatyne CLXXVI). Here, in lines which hop and dance (as the ghost itself is said to do) between octosyllabics and the rhythm of Skelton, a formidable battery of spells is prescribed for laying the least formidable of all recorded ghosts; a timid yet merry spirit, almost as big as a gnat, which will fall in a swoon 'cryand mercy petously' at your conjurations, but which is also an expert thief—God, Abraham, and the Man in the Moon have all been among its victims. One is relieved that the poem should have a happy ending in which the ghost marries 'the littil spenzie fle' and becomes the father of 'Orpheus king and Elpha quene'. Wilder and more 'eldritch' even than this is the *Dreme* of 'Lichtoun Monicus' (Bannatyne CLXV); a dream which has, for once, no allegorical significance. In *Cowkelbie Sow* (Bannatyne CCCCI) the element of extravagance is supplied not so much by the events as by the preposterous connexions between them. A sow is sold for three pennies. One of the pennies is lost. The finder spends it on a pig and decides to give a party (here follows a list of the guests). When they set about killing the pig it flees with a yell which brings all the pigs of the neighbour-hood to its rescue (here follows a list of pigs). This roused the owners of the auxiliary pigs ... here follows a list of owners ... and so on. The humour of the thing depends on the real in-consequence and apparent logic with which each new catalogue and each new story branches out of what has gone before. I am speaking of *Pars Prima*, which, I would willingly believe, was

---

[1] *Lukit*, looked. *lattin*, let. *lewch*, laughed.

originally the whole poem. But in Bannatyne it is preceded by a prologue in wretched shambling couplets reminiscent of Heywood and followed by two moral tales (of no value) which relate the adventures of the two remaining pennies. *Pars Prima* is in rough trimeters of Skeltonic type.

In some of these poems a satiric element no doubt occurs; a poet who liked Highlanders would not have written Bannatyne CCXXX. But it would, in my opinion, be quite misleading to describe them as satires. They are satiric, when at all, only incidentally, and to concentrate our attention on that side of them is to miss the real point—the northern wildness, the grotesque invention, the eldritch audacity which likes to play with ideas that would ordinarily excite fear or reverence. The comic *diablerie* of Burns's *Tam-o-Shanter* is the nearest parallel in later Scotch literature.

IV. Of the pure lyric before Dunbar we have few certain specimens. We may have more than we know; the very numerous pieces in the three anthologies which we tend to label 'school of Dunbar' may include work by his masters as well as by his imitators, for dawn and evening are hard to distinguish. However that may be, I think we can infer from the finished perfection of his poems, and of certain other poems not very like his, a considerable lyric activity in fifteenth-century Scotland. Of those that look to me early work, Bannatyne CCLXIX ('In May in a morning I movit me one') is neither better nor worse than most of its kind; Bannatyne CCLXXIII ('Flowr of all fair heid') is perhaps richer. Far beyond these in restraint and vitality is 'Tayis Bank' (Bannatyne CCLXXVIII) in which some like to discover an allusion to Margaret Drummond, one of James IV's mistresses, poisoned in 1501. The poem is in eights and sixes and uses alliteration not merely as ornament but as part of its structure. *Pearl*, or poetry of the same kind as *Pearl*, is close behind it:

> This myld meik mensuet Margrite
> This perle polist most quhyt,[1]
> Dame Natouris deir dochter discreit,
> The dyamant of delyt.

But the marvel is how freely the poet moves in this heavy armour and how fresh and spontaneous the song sounds. The

[1] *Mensueit*, courteous. *Quhyt*, white.

building of the poem is simplicity itself; a May morning, a pleasant landscape, the appearance of a beautiful lady, and then her withdrawal. No words pass between the lady and the poet, nor does he suggest that he is her lover. When she has gone he remains as before, sitting on the hillside and listening to the birds' song.

> Quhair Tay ran doun with stremis stout
> Full strecht under Stobschaw.

The absence of comment, or even of apparent emotion, is the making of the poem. The setting, and the lady, seem to exist in their own right; we have simply been shown something. Quite different is 'The Murning Maidin' (Maitland Folio CXXX). Here, in a more complex stanza, we have a tale of false love and misery turned by a second and truer love to a happy issue. The pathos of the Mourning Maiden herself, deserted, starving, and armed as a huntress yet unable to shoot the deer because she 'may not se thame bleid' is not subtle, but it is strong; and because it has engaged our feelings the conclusion is deeply satisfactory.

Some poems in the anthologies bear names which occur in Dunbar's list of dead poets; if we can trust the ascriptions and if an identity of name means (as it need not) an identity of person, then, since the 'Lament for the Makaris' was printed in 1508, we can date some lyrics earlier than that. Patrick Johnston, since we have his christian as well as his surname, may with some confidence be taken for the same man as Dunbar's 'Patrik Johnestown'. His single surviving poem, 'The Thre Deid Pollis' (Bannatyne LXVI), is a charnel house morality in which three death's-heads warn us that we shall shortly resemble them. The *macabre* element is submerged under the moral instead of strengthening it as it would have done in the hands of Dunbar. Sir John Roule's 'Cursing' (Bannatyne CLXVIII and Maitland Folio XLVI) is one of the duller specimens of eldritch humour. Shaw is another poet who lives for us in one poem only (Maitland Folio CXLVI), but this one is well worth remembering. It is built on a comparison between the dangers of court life and those of navigation, and this conceit, commonplace enough in itself, comes to life because Shaw has apparently really sailed a ship. I do not indeed understand his technicalities, and have no notion how to *huke hail* a *bolyn*, and only a vague one of the 'bubbis ye not suspek', or the *flaggis* to be looked for at 'Sanct Tabbis Heid and Buchan Ness'. But the note of well-informed urgency catches our imagination. Clerk—who may or may not be Dunbar's Clerk—is most memorable for his two comic pieces, 'In Secreit Place' and 'Robin's Jock come to wow our Jynny' (Bannatyne CLXVII and CCI). They are human and realistic and quite distinct from the eldritch class, depending on the pleasure (not all unkindly) which the gentles took in laughing at the manners of the peasantry. In the first the poet overhears a rustic assignation; much of the humour turns on the language, in which exaggerated dialectalism and terms of endearment border on nonsense:

> Quoth he 'My claver, my curledoddy,
> My hony soppis, my sweit possoddy,
> Be not o'er bustious to your billie'.

The indecencies which lurk behind some of the strange words are also part of the joke; they cannot perhaps be defended against the charge of prurience so confidently as the equal indecencies of the eldritch style. As for the second piece, the very title 'Robin's Jock come to wow our Jynny' indicates the sort of humour (and a very good sort too) which we are invited to enjoy. Clerk had other moods, represented by Bannatyne CCCXXXI, which is either a dim anticipation or a poor copy of Dunbar, and by Bannatyne XXXVI, a poem on the Passion, mostly lifeless, but containing one line that any sacred poet might envy. It is put into the mouth of the Saviour,

> My Fader said, 'Go to thy deid,[1] my deir'.

The four pieces (three in Bannatyne and one in Maitland Folio) attributed to Kennedy are in Dunbar's sententious manner. Mersar, by mere reiteration, attains a certain weight in 'Eird apone Eird' (Maitland Folio CLXIII), but the rest of his work, where it is not diluted Dunbar (as in the pleasant ballade, Bannatyne CCCLX) is of little merit; it is mostly heavy erotic advice in the halting metre of Lydgate. It is no injustice to the comparative literary civilization of the two countries at this period to say that Mersar writes like an Englishman.

V. Finally, we have the full-blown high style, from which I am anxious, if I can, to remove the epithet 'Chaucerian'.

---

[1] Death.

Admittedly, the man who introduced it into Scotland—James I —was influenced almost exclusively by Chaucer. But even in the *King's Quair*, and still more in Henryson, new elements begin to appear. The most obvious of these is what the critics call aureation, that is, the use of polysyllabic coinages from Latin (*celsitude, jocundity, lachrymable*, &c.) as an ornament to style. It is possible that this was an element in Chaucer's own style though it is no longer observable there by the modern reader who, of course, notices as aureate only those words which have not been incorporated into modern English. It may well happen that what is now a common word began its English life as an 'aureate term'. It is, therefore, conceivable that readers who came to Chaucer's verse from that of *Havelok* and *Handlyng Synne* felt it to be more rich and exotic in vocabulary than we ever can. But when all allowance has been made for that possibility, it remains certain that aureation was not a major characteristic in Chaucer. After Chaucer it becomes a major characteristic in British and French poetry alike. Lydgate, Hoccleve, and Skelton all practise it; and so do those contemporary French poets who are called the *grands rhétoriqueurs*. It is, in fact, one of those literary phenomena (like the 'conceit') which spring up over an area far wider than a nation and for which no simple cause is usually to be found. It is this widely diffused Anglo-French school to which the so-called 'Chaucerians' of Scotland really belong; a school whose allegorical method descends not from Chaucer but, along with Chaucer, from Guillaume de Lorris, Machault, Deschamps, and the like, and in which Chaucer is, for British poets, an early and distinguished practitioner; in whom, however, the characteristic style is still undeveloped. The poetry of this school does not naturally and immediately appeal to a modern reader, but the taste for it can be recovered. In its weaker disciples aureation, I grant, becomes less a kind of poetry than a substitute for poetry; but of what literary fashion could this not be said? In the good poets the aureation can be enjoyed. The long, surprising words are to be savoured slowly on the tongue and pronounced with deliberate pomp. Their effect is one of costliness; 'far fetched'—

> mádma fela
> Of feorwegum frætwa gelǽded—

must be felt as an adjective of praise. They are in language what the gorgeous armours of tournament were in life; the proper expression for a vision of brightness, largesse, ceremony, exhilaration. And we must continually remind ourselves, naïve though the reminder be, that the *rhétoriqueurs* did not know that they were at the end of the medieval tradition. No shadow of a Reformation, or Machiavelli, or an omnicompetent state, fell (for them) across the sunny heraldic scene. They looked forward to a long succession of still more splendid feudal courts, more famous tournaments, fairer ladies, more generous princes, poems yet richer and more enamelled, and wrote as men who 'think warm days will never cease'.

Of these five kinds of poetry let it be noticed that none is 'popular' in the negative sense of being confined to the lower classes. Any poet may write in them all; nearly all poets write in more than one. It is their familiarity with many different, and equally reputable, *kinds*, and, as its result, their sharpened awareness of each, which separates the Scotch 'Makers' from Chaucer. We have no evidence that Chaucer felt before him any choice between diverse kinds; ever regarded alliterative verse or tail-rhyme stanzas (save for parody) as real and equal alternatives to the kind of verse he wrote himself. In that sense he was probably a less conscious and sophisticated artist, less of a professional, than Douglas and Dunbar. As with kinds, so with language. Chaucer uses dialects other than his own for dramatic and comic effect. But the Scotch poets recognize dialectal differences (almost in the Greek way) as being proper to different species of composition. Thus in alliterative metre, or on eldritch or bawdy matter, they become broadly and exaggeratedly Scotch; for moral lyric they use what I take to be the language they spoke; in courtly allegory or panegyric they are aureate. Poetry is for them a complex instrument and there are clear rules for using it. For good or ill they are professional to the finger tips; *docti poetae*. To approach them with the expectation that (because Edinburgh is not now in all senses a capital) their poetry will be rugged or simple is to ensure total misunderstanding.

Our century opens with the appearance (1501) of the *Palice of Honour* by Gavin Douglas,[1] a young churchman of a great house,

---

[1] Son of Archibald Bell-the-Cat. b. about 1475. Matriculated St. Andrews, 1489. M.A., 1494. About 1501 became Provost of St. Giles's, Edinburgh. After 1513 a close counsellor of the Queen Dowager, a member of the Anglophil faction, and

almost exactly the same age as the king. The problem of the poem 'Where does true Honour lie?' was one that probably had more than literary interest for the poet; and if his own political career after Flodden does not suggest that he solved it very well in practice, we need not thence assume that he did not ask it in good faith. It was perhaps not very easy during the regency of the Queen Dowager to see where Honour lay. Not, certainly, a modern will reply, in those intrigues with England (he almost begs Henry VIII to invade) of which Douglas stands convicted by his own letters. But even that was not quite obvious. The intrigues were family intrigues, the ambitions family ambitions. 'Your blood is maid for ever' was the bait the tempter, Adam Williamson, held out to him. External greatness for one's house —that certainly was one of the things that Honour meant in 1514. The word was ambiguous; it wavered before men's eyes with the same dazzle as (in later ages) 'Nature' or 'Wit' or 'Democracy'. But there is no denying that Douglas was wiser about it in 1501 than he was twelve years later; for when it comes to virtue, experience, as Kant tells us, is the mother of illusion.

The poem is substantially an original work and owes little to the *Séjour d'Honneur* of Octovien de St. Gelais. In the dream which it relates the various paths to Honour are represented by various processions or courts on progress. Sapience and her court pass by and 'To the Palice of Honour all thay go'. That may be the true path—nay, that certainly is *one* of the paths—to Honour; the way of intelligence, whether practical like Ulysses', or contemplative like Pythagoras'. One might become a great philosopher or a great statesman; only in the latter event—this is where Douglas's youthful vision was clearer than his mature vision—one must distinguish very carefully between true wis-

supporter of the queen's marriage to his nephew, Archibald, the new Earl of Angus (1514). 'All the court was rewlit by the Erle of Angus, Mr. Gavin Douglass, and the Drummonds, but nocht weill' (quoted by Small from a contemporary diarist). Becomes Chancellor, 1514. Correspondence with Adam Williamson. Appointed Bishop of Dunkeld, 1515. In same year Albany returns from France and assumes the Regency. Intrigues which had led to his bishopric, and treasonable correspondence, brought to light. Douglas imprisoned. Liberated, 1516, and consecrated Bishop of Dunkeld. On embassy to France, 1517. Present at the preliminaries of the 'Clean-the-Causeway' fight between the Angus and Hamilton faction, 1520. (The Archbishop Beaton having sworn on his conscience and struck his breast, the mail hidden under his vestments rang. Douglas replied 'My Lord, methinks your conscience clatters'.) Second visit of Albany to Scotland, 1521; Douglas sent by Angus to London to negotiate with Wolsey for English support. Deprived of his bishopric. Ob. 1522 in London.

dom and 'craftynes, deceyt, and wit abused'. Sinon and Achi-
tophel follow Sapience in vain on her journey to the Palice; 'our
horsis oft, or we be thair, will founder'. Then there is, of course,
the way of virginity (the court of Diane goes by). Women and
men too have won immortal Honour by the triumph over the
flesh. 'Bot few I saw with Diane haunt', says the poet. The truth
is, he is in haste to describe the court of Venus which next rode
by; the dazzling glory of courtly love and (no doubt) of a poetical
career spent in its celebration. He spends stanza after stanza on
it; and yet perhaps he likes even better the court that follows
next. This is the 'court rethoricall':—

> Yone is the court of plesand steidfastnes,
> Yone is the court of constant merrines,
> Yone is the court of joyous discipline.

Joyous discipline, the gay science, is poetry—and rhetoric too,
for our modern distinction would have been unintelligible to
the writer. When he represents this court as rescuing him from
the anger of Venus, and when he follows it through the whole
world to the Palice, he is in his own fashion saying like Keats
and many another young poet:

> Oh, for ten years that I may overwhelm
> Myself in poesy!

But, like Keats again, he recognizes that there is a stage beyond
that, and when we reach the Palice we find that it is founded on
the craggy rocks of moral virtue, that the officers of true Honour
have such names as Charity, Conscience, and Justice, and that
Honour himself, seen only for a moment through 'a boir', a key-
hole, and, in that moment blinding the seer's eyes, is God.

All this is, in my opinion, very well contrived and is, on the
emotional level at least, a real resolution of the conflict with
which the poet started; not a mere 'moral' stuck on as an after-
thought. But to say only this is to leave out most of the quality
of the work. That quality is prodigality; its vice is excess. The
poet is still too delighted with the whole world of poetry, as he
understood it, to control his delight. He is happily overwhelmed,
like a surf-bather. All his reading, too often in the form of mere
catalogue, pours into his poem. Everything that can be either
gorgeously or terrifyingly described is introduced—May morning, desolate wilderness, journey, the pleasant plain by Hippo-
crene, stormy sea, late Gothic palace with 'Pinnakillis, fyelles,

turnpekkis mony one', a magic mirror full of 'excelland schaddouis gracious', and the final presence chamber blazing with birds, flowers, and curious knots of burnished ivory and enamelled gold. He has chosen for his work—inevitably—the most difficult metre he can think of; the nine-lined stanza which has only two rhymes, and even this varied at certain points in Parts I and II by the almost impossible addition of a tenth line and in Part III by a different nine-lined form which gives a concluding couplet. Aureation with its indefinite licence of coinage makes such verse possible. It may also be supposed that the dullness of mere lists of names was concealed from the writer by the pleasure he took in fitting them in. One may call such ingenuity perverse, but one must not call it affected—unless the very young cyclist is affected when he first revels in the discovery that he can ride with his hands off the handle bars; and amidst all this virtuosity the imagination of the poet is alert and sensitive. In his opening lines Dawn has a 'russat mantill' (Horatio yet unborn), 'Eous' lifting his head from the sea restores 'the new collour that all the nicht lay deid', sweating horses shine as if they had been oiled, streams chattering over stones make a 'sober' noise in contrast to the 'birdis sang and sounding of the beis', and the sea-nymphs sit on the rocks 'dryand thair yallow hair'. Nor is the inner world neglected. Where the dream passes into nightmare and Douglas is alone in the frightful wilderness, his feelings are brought before us by the statement that, at this moment, the mere squeak of an unseen mouse would have been to him 'mair ugsum than the hell'. But then, later, and just as it ought to be in a dream, all his fear vanished, 'bot yit I wist not quhy'. Best of all is the passage in which, fearing that Venus may transform him into a beast (for angry goddesses have been known to do such things), he keeps on passing his hand over his face to make sure that it is still human.

It is worth noticing that these deliberate contrasts between scenes of beauty and scenes of terror are much helped by a variation in the language—a variation which would hardly have been possible to Chaucer and which depends on the fact, noticed above, that Scotch poetry had become a bow with more than one string. You rendered beauty by aureation; for terror (as for bawdy or invective) you became 'boisteous' and native. Thus in a stanza from the Prologue describing the May morning the rhyming words run *lamentabill, sabill, circumstance, honora-*

bill, amiabill, observance, plesance, amiabill, varyance; but in a stanza from Part I describing the 'laithlie flude' the list is *routit, schoutid, fordeifit, doutit, sproutit, unleifit, leifit, moutit, reifit.* Douglas could have learned this from Henryson, in whose *Swallow and Other Birds* the stanzas on the seasons undergo a similar change as we reach winter. The young student will soon discover that in the 'Makers' the hard words which send him to the glossary tend to bunch at particular places. This is not an accident; just as the increase of Doric forms in the lyric parts of a Greek play is not an accident.

We can date the *Palice of Honour* from Douglas's own reference to it at the end of his Virgil. The lost works cannot be dated. Bale's *Index Britanniae Scriptorum* credits him with 'golden stories' (*aureas narrationes*); Tanner's *Bibliotheca* adds *De Rebus Scoticis, Comoedias aliquot*, and a version of Ovid's *Remedium Amoris*. The punning poem 'Conscience', which survives, is of no importance. *King Hart* is, but we have no conclusive evidence that Douglas wrote it. The ascription to him in the Maitland Folio is in a much later hand; there is no mention of it in Douglas's admitted works, nor in Bale, nor in Tanner. Lyndsay in his *Papyngo* refers to Douglas's works as 'mo than fyve', but we can still reach that number without including *King Hart*. Internal evidence, while in no way excluding the traditional ascription, does not in any way support it. Our best reason, when all's said, for supposing it to be his is that it is the work of a very considerable poet who was obviously not Dunbar nor Lyndsay, and no other candidate for its authorship has stronger claims than Douglas.

It is an allegory as different as possible from the *Palice of Honour*. It is in a simpler stanza, classically free from irrelevancies, and as stern as the *Palice* was luxuriant. Its theme is mortality, the inevitable shipwreck of all merely human hopes and pleasures, and this is enforced by images of great, sometimes of disquieting, potency. King Hart (the human soul) at home in his own castle and in his youth is 'so fair, so fresche, so liklie to endure'. But from the very first:

> About the wal thair ran ane water void,
> Blak, stinkand, sowr, and salt as is the sey,
> That on the wallis wiskit, gre by gre,
> Boldning to ryis the castell to confound.[1]

---

[1] *Wiskit on,* swept or washed against. *boldning,* swelling.

All his middle life is passed away from home, imprisoned by love in the house of the Lady Pleasaunce; and when at long last he is set free from that slavery it is only to find that life has slipped through his fingers and death is at the door. There is nothing new in this morality; nor nothing that can ever be old.

The plan of translating the *Aeneid* had been in Douglas's mind ever since 1501, for in the *Palice* Venus commissions him to perform that work. He finished it in 1513, having spent only eighteen months on the actual translation; but it bears in almost every line the impress of a mind so long steeped in Virgil that when he set pen to paper he knew exactly what had to be done and many of his problems (we may suppose) had been sub-consciously solved. If I speak of this great work at some length I trust the reader will bear with me. Its greatness easily escapes modern eyes. The public for which it was intended no longer exists; the language in which it was written now awakes false associations or none; its very original has been obscured first by classicism and then by the decay of classicism. An effort is re-quired of us.

The *XIII Bukes of the Eneados*, as Douglas called his version, were undertaken partly as a correction of Caxton's *Eneydos* (1490) which Douglas claims to have read 'with harmes at his hert', and he piques himself on the fidelity of his own version and even hopes that it will be fit for use in the schoolroom:

> a neidfull wark
> To thame wald Virgill to childryng expone;
> For quha list note my versis one by one
> Sall fynd tharin hys sentens every deill
> And almaiste word by word.
> *(Dyrectioun of his Buik.)*

The modern reader, whose Latin is likely to be better than his Scots, will test this claim most easily in the reverse manner— that is by keeping an open Virgil on his knees for glossary and comment while he is reading Douglas. He will find that *almaiste word by word* is an exaggeration: Douglas expands freely both for literary effect and also for the inclusion of explanations, and himself, in another place, has reminded us that Saint Gregory 'forbiddis ws to translait word eftir word'. But if he often inserts, he never omits; and the two texts are generally so close that a glance at one serves to elucidate anything that is difficult in the other. At worst, Douglas is a very honest translator and always lets you see how he is taking the Latin; his mistakes—for some he makes—are never sheltered by the vagueness of Dryden or Pope. His Virgil differed from the received text of our own days. In it the division between Books I and II came thirteen lines later than in ours. It had the reading *de collo fistula pendet*, which modern editors reject, at iii. 661, and *campus* for *campos* at vi. 640, and *lectisque* for *tectisque* at vii. 12. I suspect that it also gave *patriae* for *patrios* at vii. 636; and at ii. 737 and vi. 203 it had readings I am unable to identify.

Poetically, the first impression which Douglas's version makes on a modern English reader is one of quaintness. I am glad that the question of quaintness should cross our path so early in this book; let us get it out of the way once and for all. To the boor all that is alien to his own suburb and his 'specious present' (of about five years) is quaint. Until that reaction has been corrected all study of old books is unprofitable. To allow for that general quaintness which mere distance bestows and thus to be able to distinguish between authors who were really quaint in their own day and authors who seem quaint to us solely by the accident of our position—this is the very *pons asinorum* of literary history. An easy and obvious instance would be Milton's 'city or suburban' in *Paradise Regained*. Everyone sees that Milton could not have foretold the associations that those words now have. In the same way, when Douglas speaks of the Salii 'hoppand and singand wonder merely' in their 'toppit hattis' it is easy to remember that 'top hats', in our sense, were unknown to him. But it is not so easy to see aright the real qualities of his Scots language in general. Since his time it has become a *patois*, redolent (for those reared in Scotland) of the nursery and the Kailyard, and (for the rest of us) recalling Burns and the dialectal parts of the Waverley novels. Hence the laughter to which some readers will be moved when Douglas calls Leucaspis a 'skippair', or Priam 'the auld gray', or Vulcan the 'gudeman' of Venus; when *comes* becomes 'trew marrow' and Styx, like Yarrow, has 'braes', when the Trojans 'kecklit all' (*risere*) at the man thrown overboard in the boat race, or, newly landed in Latium, regaled themselves with 'scones'. For we see the language that Douglas wrote 'through the wrong end of the long telescope of time'. We forget that in his day it was a courtly and literary language,

> not made for village churls
> But for high dames and mighty earls.

Until we have trained ourselves to feel that 'gudeman' is no more rustic or homely than 'husband' we are no judges of Douglas as a translator of Virgil. If we fail in the training, then it is we and not the poet who are provincials.

About this first mental adjustment there can be no dispute; but there is another adjustment which I think necessary and which may not be so easily agreed to. Virgil describes Aeneas, on hearing Turnus's challenge, as *laetitia exsultans*; Douglas says 'he hoppit up for joy, he was so glad'. To get over the low associations of the verb 'hop' in modern English is the first adjustment. But even when this has been done, there remains something—a certain cheerful briskness—in Douglas which may seem to us very un-Virgilian. Here is another example; Virgil writes:

> Quamvis increpitent socii et vi cursus in altum
> Vela vocet, possisque sinus implere secundos. (iii. 454.)

Douglas translates:

> Ya, thocht thi fallowis cry out, Hillir haill!
> On burd! ane fair wind blawis betwix twa schetis![1]

It is admirably vivid; but it sounds very unlike the Virgil we knew at school. Let us suspend judgement and try another passage.

> lumenque juventae
> Purpureum et laetos oculis adflarat honores. (i. 590.)

Douglas says that Aeneas' mother made him 'Lyk till ane yonkeir with twa lauchand ene'.[2] The picture is fresh and attractive; yet somehow unlike the Aeneas of our imagination. But is that because Virgil has never said anything about the beauty of Aeneas, both here and in other places? On the contrary, Virgil quite clearly has told us that his hero was of godlike beauty. There has been something in our minds, but not in the mind of Douglas, which dimmed the picture; our idea of the great king and warrior and founder apparently shrinks (as Virgil's and Douglas's did not) from the delighted vision of male beauty. Douglas shocks us by being closer to Virgil than we. Once a

---

[1] *Hillir haill*, nautical cry. *On burd*, aboard.
[2] *Lauchand ene*, laughing eyes.

man's eyes have been opened to this, he will find instances everywhere. *Rosea cervice refulsit*: 'her nek schane like unto the rois in May'. Do you prefer Dryden's 'she turned and made appear Her neck refulgent'? But *refulsit* cannot possibly have had for a Roman ear the 'classical' quality which 'refulgent' has for an English. It must have felt much more like 'schane'. And *rosea* has disappeared altogether in Dryden's version—and with it half the sensuous vitality of the image. Thus, again, Douglas translates *omnibus in templis matrum chorus* by 'in caroling the lusty ladeis went'. If this seems altogether too merry and too medieval, turn to Dryden again, and you will find that Dryden has flatly refused to translate those five words at all. And that brings us to the real point.

It is hard to blame Dryden for suppressing *matrum chorus*. In the style which he is using it simply cannot be translated. As long as we are under the spell of schoolroom 'classicality' we can do nothing; 'women', 'wives', 'matrons' are all equally fatal. But it will go at once and delightfully into the medieval line about ladies 'caroling.' And the reason is that at this point there is a real affinity between the ancient and the medieval world, and a real separation between both of them and the modern. And as soon as we become aware of this we realize what it is that has made so many things in Douglas seem to us strangely un-Virgilian. It is not the real Virgil; it is that fatal 'classical' misconception of all ancient poets which the humanists have fastened upon our education—the spectral solemnity, the gradus epithets, the dictionary language, the decorum which avoids every contact with the senses and the soil. (Dryden tells us that though he knew *mollis amaracus* was sweet marjoram, he did not so translate it, for fear 'those village words' should give the reader 'a mean idea of the thing'.) Time after time Douglas is nearer to the original than any version could be which kept within the limits of later classicism. And that is almost another way of saying that the real Virgil is very much less 'classical' than we had supposed. To read the Latin again with Douglas's version fresh in our minds is like seeing a favourite picture after it has been cleaned. Half the 'richness' and 'sobriety' which we have been taught to admire turns out to have been only dirt; the 'brown trees' disappear and where the sponge has passed the glowing reds, the purples, and the transparent blues leap into life.

I must not be taken to mean that Douglas attends only to the more vivid and sensuous elements in his original, that he fails to respond to its grandeur. He has indeed his own theory of the style which a great poem demands from its translator, and develops it in his Ninth Prologue. He calls it the 'knychtlike stile' in which we 'carp of vassalage'. This goes back to the doctrine of the three styles as we find it in Johannes de Garlandia; it has left its mark on Dante's *De Vulgari Eloquentia*. It must be admitted that when Douglas says that the 'knychtlike' style should, among trees, prefer the laurel, the cedar, and the palm, to broom and heather, we seem to be heading for something as false as Dryden's feeling about 'village words'; yet the theory, at worst, is based not on the superstition of 'the Classical', but on some dim perception of social and psychological facts. In practice it means that 'thar suld na knyght reid bot a knychtly tale' and that horses, hounds, and hawks will naturally interest such a reader more than goats. More important than his theory is his practice. He is not always great in the great passages; but he has often rendered the sublimity of Virgil in lines that no translator, and not many original poets, have surpassed:

> The langsum luife drinkand inwart full cauld. (i. 749.)
>
> Wet in the mindless flude of Hell, Lethe. (v. 854.)
>
> Mychtfull in hevin and dym dungeon of helle. (vi. 247.)
>
> And the paill furowr of Tysiphonee
> Walkis wod wroth amydwart the melee. (x. 761.)

He has even done more than this. One of the things that test a translator's quality is that mass of small additions which metre inevitably demands. In Douglas what is added is often so Virgilian that when we turn back to the Latin we are surprised not to find it there. Thus *caeco marte resistunt* becomes 'Quhen blind-lingis in the battell fey thai fycht'; or Creusa cries 'Quham to sall we be left *in this waist hous*'; or the single word *fessum* (iii. 710) gives the line 'Wery and irkit in ane fremmyt land'. The words themselves are not in Virgil, but they are so true to the dominant emotion of the Third Book that it is, in a sense, from Virgil that Douglas is getting them. Even when, in the Tenth, there is really nothing at all to correspond to

> Than thus fra deid to deid, from pane to pane,
> Be catchit on and euery day be slane.[1] (x. 60.)

[1] *Deid*, death. *catchit*, chased.

I find it impossible not to forgive lines which so pierce to the very heart of the *Aeneid*.

He is not, of course, a perfect translator. He does not succeed with *lacrimae rerum* nor *possunt quia posse videntur*. He knew much more than Virgil about ships; hence while his landfalls are as good as Virgil's (they could not be better) his storms and embarkations are almost too good—in the sense that his poem as a whole smells much more strongly of salt water than the original; Palinurus becomes almost a character. He puts into his text explanations that a modern translator would relegate to the notes—stopping to tell us that nymphs and fauns are 'fair-folkis' and 'elvis' or that the 'gammis Circenses' were what we call 'justing or than turnament'. At times these interpolated explanations are wildly wrong. Where Pallas, falling, bites the earth in Book X, Douglas says this was done on purpose 'as was the gys' in order that a warrior might not cry out in his death pains. Surely this is a happy error?

These faults—for so, I suppose, we must call them—are part and parcel of the general medievalization to which he subjects the *Aeneid*. The whole Virgilian underworld is mapped out in circles and limbos on the Christian pattern, the gods become planets, the Aegis is blazed like a 'coat', Mercury has a 'fedrame' like Volund, and Camilla a Turkish bow. *Suos patimur manes* is rendered 'Ilkane of us his ganand Purgatory Maun suffir', the Sibyl is a 'holy religious woman clene', and Chloreus 'ane spiritual man'. In other words, Douglas pays for his freedom from the specific blindness of the *renascentia* by a specifically medieval blindness of his own. But the price is not really a very heavy one. The fact, noted above, that the medieval world and the ancient world (still more, the imagined prehistoric Italy of Virgil) have so much in common goes far to palliate the anachronism. *Phrygios leones* loses very little by becoming 'The lionis that the Phrygiane armis bene'. *Fulvo nutricis tegmine laetus* and 'Cleid in his nureis talbart glaid and gay' belong to the same world of legendary emblem and symbolic costume. Only once, if I remember rightly, does Douglas foist upon Virgil the confidential manner of a medieval poet and pull him up from a digression with a 'bot to our purpos'. At the very worst, I am convinced that even where Douglas is out, he is no further out in one direction than many Virgilians are out in the other. To the present day a reading of his version is the best possible preparation for a re-reading of the Latin. Douglas gives us new eyes—unless, of course, we approach him with the assumption that wherever medieval Virgilianism differed from humanistic, the medieval must have been simply wrong.

An account of Douglas's *Aeneid* which confined itself to his version of the text would be very incomplete. His work contains, in addition, Prologues to every book, a Thirteenth Book, an epilogue, a note between the Sixth and Seventh Books, and a Commentary, most unluckily incomplete and covering only part of the First. The Thirteenth Book is translated from the work of Maffeo Vegio, an Italian humanist of the fifteenth century who appears to have been dissatisfied with the abrupt ending of Virgil's poem—and very un-Homerically abrupt it is —and had the audacity to continue it, working out the happy ending in full. He concludes foolishly enough, but his earlier scenes, at least if you read them in Douglas, are far from contemptible; it is a little odd that he refuses, as resolutely as Virgil himself, to make a character of Lavinia. The book which Douglas has given us is, therefore, a composite work, and it ought to be read as a whole. The mere presence of the Thirteenth Book and the Prologues shows no lack of respect for Virgil; but it shows a lack of that particular species of respect which came in with the *renascentia*. The sacrosanctity of the epic form and of the number twelve mean nothing to Douglas. He is ready to interrupt his master with comic, familiar, or devotional poetry of his own at the beginning of every book. The resulting volume is thus the fine flower of medieval Virgilianism.

The Prologues have a threefold interest, as poems, as criticism, and as familiar self-portraits of the artist. His habits both in winter and summer, his reading, his difficulties as a translator, his haunting consciousness that a man is not made a bishop in order to translate Virgil, and the excuses which he makes to himself, are here all faithfully set out. His delight in his own work, wrestling and successfully wrestling with his modesty, is expressed with humorous frankness:

> Yit by myself I fynd this proverb perfyte,
> 'The blak craw thinkis hir awin byrdis quhite'
> Sa faris with me, bew Schirris, will ye hark,
> Can nocht persaue a falt in all my wark. (Prol. ix.)

His criticism is to be found chiefly in the First, Fifth, Sixth, and

Ninth Prologues. Much of it is simply a good statement of the ordinary medieval opinion of Virgil. He is a heathen poet and all his work, in a sense, is *fenyeit*; but under the *derk poetrye* lies *great wisdome*. He has described the *stait of man baith life and deid* and it is wonderful how often he is substantially right even about *mysteris fell* which we have learned by revelation. Augustine quoted him freely, we must remember, and Ascencius in modern times has gone so far as to call him a *hie theolog sentencious*. Presumably this wisdom was learned by Virgil from *Sibillis sawis*. On the moral plane, his story is plainly full of *nobilitie*, and Aeneas a mirror of *wirschap* and *manheid*. Douglas defends his desertion of Dido (in the First Prologue), rejecting the opinion of Chaucer who *was ever, God wait, wemenis frend* and showing a much better understanding of Book IV than many modern critics. Douglas, in fact, regards the *Aeneid* much as Malory and Caxton regarded the *Morte*:

> Weill auchtin eldris exemplis ws to steyr[1]
> Tyll hie curage, all honour till ensew. (Prol. xi.)

and while *churlish wychtis* are simply to be told that his translation is correct, *nobillis* are invited to *amend* it.[2] This choice of nobles rather than scholars is significant.

For sheer poetry his best Prologues are the Seventh, Twelfth, and Thirteenth—three nature poems of such discriminating sensibility and effortless technical power that they set us wondering why (in that field) we ever needed a romantic revival, just as Douglas's translation makes us wonder why we needed a *renascentia*. The history of literature is very far from being one of simple progress. The least good of these (the Seventh, on winter) leaves nothing to be improved, and much to be corrupted, by Thomson. Douglas himself in the midst of the scenes he describes —Douglas baking himself by the fire, and creeping into bed under *claythis thrinfauld*, Douglas watching the bitter moonlight shining in his room all night, Douglas next morning opening the window *a lytill on char*[3] and hastily shutting it after a glance that prints the landscape indelibly on our imaginations—all this saves the poem from the flatness of mere description. Some-

---

[1] *Auchtin*, ought. *eldris*, ancestors. *steyr*. incite.
[2] 'Ane Exclamatioun' (appended to Bk. XIII).
[3] *On char*, ajar.

times a single line evokes not only the momentary scene, but the sensation of many winter days on end:

> The wind made wayfe the reid weyd on the dyk.[1]

But the Twelfth and Thirteenth are better. The former is as hackneyed in subject as any medieval poem could be—a description of spring—but after we have read it, Chaucer and the Elizabethans in this kind seem tepid. It begins with a regular salvo of mythology and personification; but the shining figures which Douglas makes move across his sky are no more conventional or merely ornamental than the similar figures in Botticelli. Saturn draws off into dim distances *behind the circulat warld of Jupiter*—Aurora opens the windows of her hall—crystalline gates are unfolded—the great assault is ready and marches forward with banners spread,

> Persand the sabill barmkyn nocturnall.[2]

This is not simply a better or worse way of describing what we *see*. It is a way of making us see for always what we have sometimes felt, a vision of natural law in its angelic grandeur, a reminder of something that Chaucer ignores—of the pomp and majesty mingled even in the sweetest and most gracious of Nature's workings. It is a true spiritualization (true, at least, to our experience) of the visible object; Douglas here reaches out in one direction to Wordsworth or even Blake, and in another to the Homeric hymns. The greatness of the opening, contrasted with the humbler sweetness that follows, enables Douglas to hit off to a nicety the experience of any man who wakes early and walks out on such a morning; for the intimate pleasures of the lanes and woods, once reached, as the dew begins to ascend, do thus decline from the more august splendours of the dawn— decline so amiably that we welcome the declining. Throughout this part of the poem his observation is admirable; his attention to shadows and his use of shadows to tell us about the light could hardly be bettered. The Thirteenth Prologue is gentler. It records a visionary meeting with *Mapheus Vegius* which the poet feigns as his excuse of the Thirteenth Book. The angry humanist appears *Lyke to sum poet of the auld fassoune*—for Douglas has been reading Henryson—and the interview is described with considerable humour. But the real value of the Prologue lies in

---

[1] Made wave the red weed on the ditch.
[2] *Persand*, piercing. *barmkyn*, rampart.

the setting—a northern summer night, described in full, from its late twilight to its early dawn. The best lines (where nearly all are good) have been quoted, I doubt not, by many others; but they are so characteristic of the whole that I cannot help giving them again:

> Yondyr dovn dwynis the evin sky away,
> And vpspryngis the brycht dawing of day
> Intill ane other place nocht far in sundir,
> That to behald was pleasans and half wondir.[1]

About Douglas as a translator there may be two opinions; about his *Aeneid* (Prologues and all) as an English book there can be only one. Here a great story is greatly told and set off with original embellishments which are all good—all either delightful or interesting—in their diverse ways. The couplet in which most of the book is written seems very rough if we read ten lines. It seems less so after ten pages. When we have finished a volume we find it an admirable medium for narrative—a happy mean between the severity of Pope and the rambling of Keats. Often it has the ring and energy of Dryden; I would particularly recommend to the reader's attention the twenty-four lines entitled *Conclusioune of this Buik* as an example of Douglas's skill in bringing out the proper powers of this metre.

After the publication of his *Aeneid* (unless *King Hart* is later) Douglas concerns us no more. He is the queen's man and flies from Scotland at Albany's return, to live on an English pension and die of an English plague at London in 1522.

The poetical career of his older contemporary, William Dunbar,[2] probably began earlier and ended later than his. Only some of Dunbar's poems can be dated. The piece called 'Learning Vain without guid Lyfe', in virtue of its rather gratuitous subtitle 'Written at Oxinfurde', may be connected with a mission to England in 1501, and the panegyric on London was probably composed at the same time. *The Thrissill and the Rois* and the 'Welcome to Queen Margaret' date themselves by James's marriage in 1503. 'Against Treason' ('In vice most

---

[1] *Dwinis*, dwines, dwindles.   *dawing*, dawning.
[2] Born *c.* 1460. B.A., St. Andrews, 1477; M.A., 1479. In France, 1491. Payments to him in Treasurer's Accounts, 1500–13. Probably on embassy to London, 1501 (on this see *London thou art the Flowre*, C. F. Bühler, *R.E.S.*, vol. xiii, Jan. 1937). Date of death unknown (−1522). The rest of Dunbar's biography must be based on inferences of varying probability from his poems.

vicius') comes from 1506 when Donald Owre was captured. The 'Fenyeit Freir of Tungland' and 'Birth of Antichrist', since both refer to Abbot Damian's aeronautical experiment, cannot be earlier and are unlikely to be later than 1507; 'Of Ane Blak-Moir' concerns a tournament held in the same year. *The Twa Mariit Wemen*, the 'Flyting', *The Goldyn Targe*, the 'Lament for the Makaris', the 'Testament of Mr. Andro Kennedy', and the poem on Lord Bernard Stewart are all earlier than 1508 when Chepman and Myllar printed them. The elegy on Lord Bernard Stewart dates from June in that year, 'Blyth Aberdeen' records the queen's visit to that city in 1511. 'To the Quene Dowager' is, of course, later than Flodden, and Albany's departure to France in 1517 gives us the date of 'Ane Orisoun'. If we try to get more chronology than this we are thrown back on inferences from internal evidence which usually involve hazardous assumptions; as, for example, that men write more religiously in age than in youth or that poems on the amours of James IV must be earlier than the marriage of that chivalrous prince. Nor can I trace clearly any technical development in Dunbar's work; when he first comes before us he is already fully armed and master of his weapon.

He himself would not have understood our desire to arrange his poems in a chronological order. They were not written to 'unlock his heart'. He would have thought it more reasonable to group them (as poems are grouped in the Bannatyne MS.) by their kinds, and I am content to follow this method.

Firstly, then, we have the court poems in the high style, the fine flower of the composite tradition which descends from the Rose, with Chaucer, and with the *rhétoriqueurs* of France. In 1503, as we have already noted, he celebrated the King's marriage in *The Thrissill and the Rois*, a triumph of fruitful obedience to conventions. By one convention the political match becomes an instance of *l'amour courtois*, and this, by another convention, becomes of course a May morning dream. By a third convention, that of heraldry, we bid farewell to men and women and talk instead about a lion, an eagle, a thistle, and a rose; and the goddess Natura, out of Alanus, Chaucer, and others, as the patroness of flowers, beasts, and lovers alike, interlocks the whole. This minuet of conventions—which were felt not as arbitrary necessities but as the delightful accomplishments of the gay science—enables the poem to remain recognizably occasional and yet at the same time to become almost 'pure' poetry. We celebrate the royal wedding, as our duty obliges us to do; yet equally, we wander in a world of beautiful forms and colours where our dream wishes are gratified by seeing a lion lay its humbled head on a lady's lap. This is what comes of having an art with rules and, therefore, a good understanding between the artist and his audience. Very similar in quality is the *Goldyn Targe*. Its simple allegory (that the poet is temporarily defended from love by reason) is little more than a peg, but an adequate peg, on which to hang its poetry—a poetry even more elaborate than that of *The Thrissill and the Rois*. The stanza is more complicated and the aureation is carried further. Every kind of delight, and one shock, is provided for the senses; a white sail like a hawthorn branch against the sky, reflected light cast up by water on the underside of leaves, singing birds, and finally a broadside from a battleship that went near to crack the rainbow with its loudness. The chief weakness of this brilliant poem is the multiplication of allegorical persons who remain (as in bad eighteenth-century poetry) mere names. Yet elsewhere no one knows better than Dunbar how to touch a personification into life; witness the poem 'Quhome to sall I compleine' where

> Flattry weiris ane furrit goun,
> And Falsett with the lordis dois roun,
> And Trewth standis barrit at the dure,[1]

or that quiet and sinister line 'and than sayis Age, "My freind, cum neir",' from the 'Meditatioun in Wyntir'.

Apart from these two allegorical pageants Dunbar's tributes to the god of Love are few. 'Bewtie and the Prisoneir' is a neat but slightly frigid psychomachy; 'To a Ladye' ('Sweit Rois') is neither better nor worse than the innumerable sonnets which were soon to drive its kind out of fashion; and another poem 'To a Ladye' bears the significant subtitle 'Quhen he list to feyne'. Dunbar is in fact no lover and it is to his credit that, despite its literary popularity, he so seldom assumes that character. The 'Merle and Nychtingaill', in which (as in 'Quha will behold') he rejects love, is as full of colour and music as anything he ever wrote. No attempt is made to give the debate between the two birds a dramatic turn, the merle being suddenly and inexplicably converted. Dunbar's interest is not in the morality

---

[1] *Weiris*, wears. *furrit goun*, furred gown.   *roun*, whisper.

but, once more, in the world of ear and eye, in morning sunlight on running water and in the nightingale's singing whose
'sound went with the rever as it ran'.

A large number of Dunbar's poems may be classified as peti-
tionary. He was primarily the queen's man and found it hard
to get money out of James. Poems of this sort can easily become
disagreeable and most unpoetically pathetic; in Dunbar's we
admire the almost unfailing skill and taste by which they become little works of art capable of existing in their own right.
Thus in the 'Birth of Antichrist' the appeal for preferment is
twisted into another joke at poor Abbot Damian. In 'Solistaris
in Court' the statement of his own 'sympilnes' and dependence
on the king is made to appear merely the climax (and structurally it is a good one) to a vivid satirical account of the other
suitors. The poem 'To my lordis of Chacker' wins us at once by
a certain merry impudence. In another, Dunbar, being sure of
the queen's favour, tells the king that he is praying for 'your
Grace, baith nicht and day'; but what he prays is that the king
should become 'John Thomosunis man' (i.e. a hen-pecked husband). In the 'Complaint to the King' we have, what is hackneyed in itself, the unsuccessful suitor's protest that unworthy
rivals are winning the promotion which he lacks; but the whole
poem is touched into life by the rollicking gusto with which
Dunbar abuses these rivals, these drivelling, shuffling, puff-
cheeked, club-faced hashbalds, haggar-balds, and mandrakes.
Burton could not have done it better. In the 'Remonstrance' a
deeper note is struck; there is a manlier assertion of his poetic
dignity and a more serious indignation. Of all the poems which
he wrote in this (at first sight) unattractive *genre* hardly one lacks
some outstanding excellence.

A third group of his poems is comic; if you will, satiric,
though 'abusive' would be a better word. I am not certain that
they often have any very serious satirical intention. Many are
mere topical squibs on some episode that had amused the court
for a day—on a burlesque tournament where a negress was
made Queen of Beauty, on a 'rag' in the queen's apartments
which seemed funny to the participants though its humours
have long since faded, on a detected amour of the king's, on the
death of the cheery old reprobate Andrew Kennedy, whose
testament in shameless, reeling, goliardic vein does a man's
heart good to the present day. In reading many of these comic

pieces we have to make a readjustment. We must sever the
modern association which connects extreme indecency with
technical coarseness of form and with low social rank, and must
think ourselves back into a world where great professional poets,
for the entertainment of great lords and ladies, lavished their
skill on humours now confined to the preparatory school or the
barrack-room. In this prevailing atmosphere of horseplay it is
difficult to distinguish a lampoon that is really hostile from one
that is merely a joke. The 'Flyting' is clearly in the latter class;
but whether Dunbar had any serious quarrel with James Doig
I cannot be certain. The most celebrated of all his so-called
satires, *The Twa Mariit Wemen and the Wedo*, is almost a flyting.
Comparisons with the Wife of Bath's prologue are here, to my
way of thinking, wide of the mark. Chaucer creates a richly
human personality; I do not think Dunbar is trying to do anything of the sort. He is playing a practical joke on his audience.
That is the point of the beautiful idyllic opening which contains
not the slightest hint of what is to follow. You are to picture the
audience at its first recitation, and especially the ladies in that
audience (for manners have changed), settling themselves to enjoy a serious allegory or a serious romance full of the 'honour
of love', and then to imagine with what shattering detonation
the main body of the poem burst upon them. The almost un-
paralleled grossness of the things the three women say is not
there for the sake of character drawing. The fun lies in its sheer
preposterousness and in the virtuosity with which the poet goes
on piling audacity on audacity—and on the ludicrous contrast
between this and their appearance. It is no nearer to real 'satire
on women' than the impossibly red nose of an old-fashioned
comedian is to real satire on drunkenness. If any one of the
three women became even for a moment a live character like
Alison of Bath or Doll Tearsheet the poem would be destroyed.
If you cannot relish a romp you had best leave this extravaganza
alone; for it offers you no other kind of pleasure.

In claiming that the *Twa Mariit Wemen* is mainly 'Dunbar's
fun', I do not mean to deny that his fun is of a ferocious kind.
Rather, that is the point I would stress; that in him, as in so
many Scotch poems of the period, and in him more than in any
other, the comic overlaps with the demoniac and the terrifying.
He also is of the 'eldritch' school; the wild whoop of his noisiest
laughter has, and is meant to have, something sinister in it. By

way of *diablerie* his comic poetry shades off into one of his kinds of religious poetry. In the 'Visitation of St. Francis' ('This nicht befoir the dawing cleir') St. Francis appears to Dunbar urging him to be a friar. On Dunbar's replying that he would rather be a bishop, the apparent St. Francis, who was really a devil, vanishes 'with stink and fyrie smoke'. This, of course, is comic; even, if you please, a 'satire on friars'. But can we be certain that it was quite so purely comic then as it is now—then, when no man doubted the existence of devils and few would have been surprised to find them disguised as friars? So in 'The Dance of the Seven Deadly Sins'. There can, on the one hand, be no question that these 'sweir bumbard belly huddrouns' and these highlanders whose clatter deeves the devil himself are intended to make us laugh. But notice, on the other hand, that we are laughing at torture. The grotesque figures skip through fire, jag each other with knives, and are constantly spewing out molten gold with which they are constantly refilled 'up to the thrott'. Dunbar and his contemporaries seriously believed that such entertainment awaited in the next world those who had practised (without repentance) the seven deadly sins in this. They believed and (doubtless) trembled; yet they also laughed. The mixture of farce and terror would be incredible if we did not remember that boys joked most about flogging under Keate, and men joked most about gallows under the old penal code. It is apparently when terrors are over that they become too terrible to laugh at; while they are regnant they are too terrible to be taken with unrelieved gravity. There is nothing funny about Hitler *now*.

Some of Dunbar's finest work was done in religious poetry of a more ordinary kind. He does not deal much in solitary devotional feeling, like the Metaphysicals or the Victorians; he is public and liturgical. His two supreme achievements in this vein are his poems on the Nativity and on the Resurrection. The first of these (*Rorate celi desuper*) might almost claim to be in one sense the most lyrical of all English poems—that is, the hardest of all English poems simply to *read*, the hardest not to sing. We read it alone and at night—and are almost shocked, on laying the book down, to find that the choir and organ existed only in our imagination. It has none of the modern— the German or Dickensian—attributes of Christmas. It breathes rather the intoxication of universal spring and summons all Nature to salute 'the cleir sone quhome no clud devouris':

> Sing Hevin imperiall most of hicht,
> Regions of air mak armony,
> All fishe in flud and foull of flicht
> Be myrthfull and mak melody;
> All *gloria in excelsis* cry,
> Hevin, erd,[1] se, man, bird and best;—
> He that is crownit abone the sky
> *Pro nobis Puer natus est.*

I would hesitate to read Milton's Hymn on the same evening with this. The 'Resurrection' is equally, but differently, excellent. It is speech rather than song, but speech of unanswerable and thundering greatness. From the first line ('Done is a battell on the Dragon blak') to the last (*Surrexit Dominus de sepulchro*) it vibrates with exultant energy. It defies the powers of evil and has the ring of a steel gauntlet flung down.

The most widely remembered of his poems come in the class which he himself would probably have called 'moral'. There is a real affinity between these and the *Odes* of Horace. Both poets keep strictly within the range of thought and feeling which will be familiar to all their readers and make commonplaces into poetry by the accurate weight of their strokes. The difference is that where Horace relies on the artful, yet seemingly chancy, development of the thought, Dunbar relies on mere songfulness. He does not, like Horace, progress, but he does wonders with the poignancy of repetition. Hence the metre and, above all, the refrain, are usually the making of the poem. His refrains are, indeed, among the best in the world; *Quod tu in cinerem reverteris*, 'Best to be blyth', 'All erdly joy returnis in pain', *Timor mortis conturbat me*.

To pick and choose among these gnomic lyrics, where nearly all are good, will perhaps only reveal the idiosyncrasies of the critic. 'Learning Vain without guid Lyfe' and 'O Wreche be war' seem to me to excel in eloquence; the 'Meditatioun in Wyntir' bites deep and has a pleasantly unexpected turn at the end; 'Of the Changes of Lyfe' gives us (what is rare in Dunbar) a glimpse of weather; and 'None may Assure' achieves grandeur in the stanzas on Domesday:

> Quhat help is thair in lordschippis sevin
> Quhen na houss is bot Hell and Hevin?

---

[1] *Erd*, earth.

In the 'Lament for the Makaris' I myself would have thought there was too much catalogue; but 'the common reader' has taken it to his heart.

Like most writers of 'moral' lyric, Dunbar finds that stern and sombre thoughts suit the medium best. Yet he has also, at times, another philosophy and valiant maxims, 'Best to be blyth' or

> Be mirry, Man, and tak nocht far in mynde
> The wauering of this wrechit world of sorrow,

or again, with more infectious nonchalance:

> Man, pleis[1] thy Makar and be mirry,
> And sett nocht by this warld a chirry.

The strain is manly, yet has in it perhaps a deeper pathos than the laments.

If I see Dunbar at all correctly, such nicknames as 'Scotch Chaucer' or 'Scotch Skelton' are inept. He lacks what is best in Chaucer and Chaucer lacks what is best in him. He is not a story-teller nor a delineator of character, and his wild whoops of laughter have little in common with Chaucer's human comedy. He has nothing of Chaucer's confiding informality—we never see him in literary undress. On the other hand, he has at his command a resonant singing voice (a voice to lift a roof with) and a goblin energy which Chaucer has not. As for Skelton, though I can imagine a man, and not a foolish man, who preferred him to Dunbar, yet it must be insisted that, beside Dunbar, Skelton is not a *writer* at all. In a poem by Skelton anything may happen, and Skelton has no more notion than you what it will be. That is his charm; the charm of the amateur. But Dunbar is professional through and through; the accomplished master of one tradition that goes back to *Beowulf* and of another that goes back to the Troubadours. All his effects are calculated and nearly all are successful; the last line of each poem was in view before he wrote the first. His harsh and poignant sense of mortality—'Deth followis lyfe with gaipand mowth'—he shares with many late medieval lyrists, notably with Villon, but Villon, so far as I know or remember, lacks his gay splendour. Horace (as I have suggested) and perhaps Dryden are the poets that seem to me to resemble him most, in the sense that all three are men of strongly masculine genius, professional to the point of

[1] Please.

virtuosity, and much in love with the languages they write. But, of course, Dunbar is very unlike them in his eldritch quality, and no two sorts of indecency could be more different than his and Dryden's. He is likely to be underrated rather than overrated in our own age. He seems to tell us much about himself—his headache, his lean purse, his pretence that he has other reasons than poverty for not going with his friends to the tavern—but his poems are not 'human documents'. We remain his audience, not his confidants, cut off from him (as it were) by the footlights; and though he can describe real Nature when he chooses, he prefers to transform her, giving his nightingale 'angell fedderis', making his animals heraldic, and turning even lawns and hedges into a kind of jewelry. For both reasons he will in our time be more often admired than loved; a reaction with which he would have been quite content. But he was a very great man. When you are in the mood for it, his poetry has a sweep and volume of sound and an assured virility which (while the mood lasts) makes most other poets seem a little faint and tentative and half-hearted. If you like half-tones and nuances you will not enjoy Dunbar; he will deafen you.

I have already suggested that some of the poems in the anthologies which resemble Dunbar may be by his predecessors; but it is reasonable to assume that many of them are by his imitators. If so, the anthologies provide some indication of his power and value as a model. Six pieces adopt, in varying degrees, the manner of his sacred macaronics. Two of these (Bannatyne XXI and Maitland Folio LVI) are unremarkable; but Bannatyne XXIV ('Cum Haly Spreit moist superne') and XXXIII ('We that ar bocht with Chrystis blude') are superior—for what such superiority is worth—to most modern hymns. 'Jerusalem reioys for joy' (Bannatyne XXXI) is in a different class; it might well be by Dunbar himself, and is full of colour and clangour and exultation. The comical eldritch vein is seen in 'The Droichis Pairt of the Play' (Bannatyne CLXXXII and Asloan). The 'play' was no doubt an interlude but the 'Dwarf's part' is of little interest for the historians of drama. The dwarf represents *Welth*, not in the narrower modern sense, though there is a reference to merchants, but in the sense of plenty; he has come from strange lands in the east, where he has lived long with 'the fary', to banish *Dearth* from Scotland. Thus for the modern reader, though hardly perhaps for contemporaries, a primordial connexion between buffoonery and fertility rituals is recalled. I am not sure whether the part of the dwarf was performed by a real dwarf or by a man of gigantic stature; if the former, the joke lay in attributing to him an ancestry of giants (Hercules, Fin MaCowl, and Gog Magog); if the latter, the joke lay in his explanation that he had now become 'for eild' a mere dwarf (by the standards of his family) —'This littill as ye may sie'. Either way, the humour is that of monstrosity—comic effects wrought out of nursery terrors by a Rabelaisian insistence on the magnified human body. Giants, in this kind of literature, are chronically flatulent; yet the extravagance gives the coarse jokes a quality they would not have without it and even a sort of crazy poetry:

> He wold apoun his tais vp stand
> And tak the starnis down with his hand
> And sett thame in a gold garland
> Aboif his wyvis hair.[1]

From the opening words 'Hiry, hary, hubbilschow' the whole thing goes with an infectious zest which makes it a masterpiece of its kind. If anyone chooses to believe that it is by Dunbar, the internal evidence will not be against him. The *Freiris of Berwick*, on the other hand (Maitland Folio XLII), will seem like Dunbar only to those who think Dunbar like Chaucer. This excellent *fabliau*, in decasyllabic couplets, is by a real Chaucerian and ranks above all other attempts to continue the tradition of the comic Canterbury Tales.

The two poems by Clapperton (Maitland Folio LXXIX and LXXX) are also like Dunbar; but for all we know may be derived less from him than along with him from the old Provençal stock. The first of them, a song of the *mal mariée* with the refrain 'Wa worth maryage for evermair', is done with great spirit. The anonymous Christmas song and the complaint 'Auld kyndnes is quyt forgett' (Maitland Folio LXXIV and Bannatyne CXXVI) represent the school of Dunbar at its best; Maitland Folio LXXIII—with the all too true refrain 'Thus wait I nocht quhairof to wryt'—at its worst.

But it must not be supposed that Dunbar dominates the minor poets completely. In the beautiful lyric by 'Fethe' or Fethy (Bannatyne CCCIX) the poignancy of the refrain, 'Cauld, cauld culis the lufe that kendillis our het',[2] depends on a quality

---

[1] *Tais*, toes. *starnis*, stars.   [2] *Our het*, too hot.

of rhythm which is quite unlike Dunbar's; and so does the beauty of

> The flesche is fawin, wes umquhile brawin,[1] I list nocht for to pley,
> The medowss mawin, the claith is drawin, the grace is said away.
> (Bannatyne CCCXXXV.)

When King James was at his prayers in Linlithgow on the eve of his fatal expedition, there thrust into his presence a strange man 'clade in ane blew gowne' who warned him to beware of this journey and of women. Pitscottie vouches for the story on the evidence of two 'young men and spetiall serwandis to the kingis grace' who were standing by. One of these men was David Lyndsay (1486-1555)[2] afterwards Lyon King of Arms, the last major poet of the old Scotch tradition.

His works are a beautiful example of the 'single talent well employed'. The *Satyre of the Thrie Estaitis*, which holds an important place among our scanty materials for a history of the allegorical drama in Scotland, will be dealt with in another volume of this series; here it will be enough to say that this long morality stands apart from the rest of Lyndsay's output by the looseness of the metre and the general popularity of the style, and that it is rich in pathos and low humour. In his remaining works he everywhere keeps well within the lines marked out for him by his great predecessors; there is no novelty in them, and he usually lacks the originality of Henryson and the brilliance of Dunbar and Douglas. But what there is of him is good all through.

His earliest poem, the *Dreme* (not before 1528), has grown as logically as the circles made by a pebble thrown in a pond. The centre is a vision of John Commonwealth 'all raggit, revin, and rent, With visage leyne as he had fastit Lent' hastening for

---

[1] The flesh that once was muscle is fallen away.

[2] Born *c.* 1486. Acted in a play before James IV, 1511. Became usher to the child James V, 1513. Married one Janet Douglas, 1522. Received grant of the lands of the Mount 1524. Temporarily dismissed the king's service, 1524 (?) –1528, during the ascendancy of the Angus faction. A herald by 1530. On embassy to the emperor, 1531; to France, 1532, 1534; to England, 1535; to France, 1535, 1536, 1537. Composed a masque (now lost) to welcome Marie of Lorraine as the king's bride at St. Andrews, 1538. First version of his *Satyre* produced at Linlithgow, 1540. Was a knight and Lyon King of Arms by 1542. Embassy to England, 1543. May (or may not) be the David Lyndsay recorded as M.P. for Cupar, 1541-6. Embassy to Denmark, 1548. Death of Wm. Meldrum, 1550. Second version of his *Satyre* produced at Cupar, 1552. Dead by 1555.

the border to leave a Scotland which has no place for him. In order that the poverty of Scotland may be shown as the fault not of nature but of corruption, this is set in a picture of the country as a whole, and the country then set in a complete picture of the earth, earth among the planets, and all in the heavens. Hell is also described, and the total vision, which has thus become a humble relative of the *Somnium Scipionis* and the *Divine Comedy*, is enclosed in a dream and prefaced with a pleasingly realistic account of a winter morning's walk on the sea-shore. It is readable work in a good, though familiar, tradition. The modern reader, no doubt, has to acquire the taste for such things, but the acquisition is easy and worth making. There is a more obvious appeal in the dedicatory epistle where the poet reminds the king how he carried him in his arms as a child, played games with him on the nursery floor, and told him stories about Thomas the Rymer, the *reid etin*, and the *gyir carlyng*. The stanzas on purgatory contain the first indication of Lyndsay's Protestant sympathies.

The 'Complaynt to the King', written in octosyllabics that have the spring of Burns or Scott, is a begging poem which shares many of the merits of Dunbar's efforts in the same kind. Like Dunbar, and perhaps in imitation of him, Lyndsay gets great fun out of 'Flyting' the king's evil counsellors; and he knew these lines were good, for he used them over again in the *Thrie Estaitis*. But the poem as a whole is gentler than Dunbar would have made it. The repetition of Lyndsay's services to the infant king, which might so easily have reminded us of Mime's *Starenlied* in the opera, is full of humour and affection. The conclusion is graceful in the highest degree. After jokingly asking for a loan, to be repaid

> Quhen kirkmen yairnis[1] no dignitie
> Nor wyffis no soveranitie,

the poet rises into a more serious vein and hopes, in lines which recall the close of *Il Penseroso*, that, if the king after all prove unkind, God will grant him in his *Latter aige* such contentment on his small ancestral estate as Diogenes enjoyed in his tub.

In 1530 came the *Testament and Complaynt of the Papyngo*, an account in rhyme royal of the death and last words of the king's parrot. Its *complaynt* is a sermon to its fellow-courtiers and to the

---

[1] *Yairnis*, yearn for.

king on mutability, with special reference to Scotch history of which the bird displays an extensive knowledge; its *testament* is made in the unwelcome presence of certain birds of prey who turn out to be monks and friars of the feathered world. The dying parrot inveighs against their hypocrisy and avarice, with the usual references to Constantine's unfortunate liberality, while they vigorously defend themselves by throwing the blame on the secular clergy. So far, the satire has been ordinary enough; but we find real satiric invention, and even a strange beauty, when the popinjay, having provided for the poor by leaving her gay coat to the owl, her eyes to the bat, and her voice to the cuckoo, and for herself by committing her spirit to the *Quene of Farie*, is torn in pieces by her carrion executors the moment the breath is out of her body—*hir angell fedderis fleying in the air*. The poem is of historical interest for the list of Scotch poets in the prologue.

The years between 1533 and 1542 saw the production of several occasional poems—a 'Flyting', a 'Complaynt' for Bagsche the king's dog (in which the supposed caninity of the speaker is never lost sight of amid the author's moral and political opinions), an attack on the female fashion of *syde taillis*, and a burlesque 'Justing' on the lines of Dunbar's 'Tailyeour and Sowtar'. The 'Deploratioun of the Deith of Quene Magdalene' (1537), which begins dully enough, deserves to be remembered for an excellent concluding stanza and for a stirring picture of the pageantry which would have celebrated the queen's coronation. 'Kitteis Confessioun' (1542) is an attack on the confessional in which the serious part—that is, the bulk of the poem—tends to be read with some disappointment because the opening has led us to expect a comic treatment. The first forty lines are not unworthy of Prior.

The killing of Cardinal Beaton in 1546 was the occasion of Lyndsay's dullest poem, a *Tragedie of the Cardinall* in the tradition of Boccaccio's *De Casibus*; but who could delay on this when we are already in sight of his masterpiece? *Squire Meldrum* (after 1550) ought to be in everyone's hands; a lightly modernized and heavily glossed text at a reasonable price is greatly to be desired. This wholly delightful poem stands, as it were, at the triple frontier where the novel, the romance, and the biography all march together. The ideals of love and war are those of romance, but the hero is an historical person whom the author has known, a skilled physician and good footballer as well as a warrior and a lover, whose exploits are kept within the bounds of possibility—though, to be sure, when the enemy are English we may be told that 'The Sutheron wes ay fyve for ane'. The circumstances of Meldrum's battle with the English champion in France might have come straight out of Malory, but there is no leaping up from fallen horses and 'foining like boars' for hours on foot—only the long series of courses with the lance which may actually have occurred and which are described as lovingly as a modern writer of school-stories describes a cricket match. The sea-fight and the mêlée in the streets of a French town, more easily enjoyed by such laymen as ourselves, are among the very best things of their kind. They are in the hammer-like octosyllabics of the *Bruce* and almost any couplet taken from them at random would make the rhetorical battle poetry of Spenser and Drayton look like a tailor's sword beside the sword of a trooper. The strange idea that the poem is a burlesque, unless it is based on the first fifty lines or so, may come from the love scenes where much chivalry, good sense, and wholesome sensuality are mixed with much humour. But the humour is not burlesque; in English medieval romance homely realism thus often blends with courtly love, and *Risus*, *Jocus*, and *Petulantia* are, at all times, the natural attendants of Venus. The hero's *Testament* in rhyme royal, which follows the story in octosyllabics, would show, in real life, a levity not very suitable to a death-bed; as a purely poetical fanfare to round off a knightly tale, it is excellent. After committing his soul to God, Meldrum asks for a procession a thousand *hagbutteris in gude ordour* instead of monks and friars; no black for mourning but red for Mars, green for Venus, and blue for Mercury; and instead of requiems *Alleluya with melodie and game* and *cannounis crak*, 'I will that day be heard no hevines'. His farewell to the *sterne of Stratherne, my ladie Soveraine*, whom he had loved *par amors* (with every intention, poor man, of marrying her in the end, but both found it *greit vexatioun to tarrie upon dispensatioun*) almost concludes his speech, but he has time to say quickly at the last 'Sir Curat, gif me incontinent my crysme'. In short, while we are given to understand that he made a good end, we see him with our own eyes die game. It is a fitting conclusion to this unambitious but noble poem. We have greater stories in verse; perhaps none, even in Chaucer, more completely successful.

The *Dialog betwix Experience and ane Courteour* (1553?), more familiarly known as the *Monarche*, is the last of his poems, and the most medieval in form and spirit, though it refers to Erasmus and to Diodorus Siculus whom Lyndsay had read in one of the early editions of Poggio's Latin version. It opens with a May morning's dream in rhyme royal where Lyndsay attempts, not very successfully, to rival the brilliant colouring of Dunbar and Douglas; it goes on to an octosyllabic history of the five great empires (the papacy being the fifth) preceded by an account of the creation and followed by an account of the Day of Judgement, and relieved from time to time by complaints and apostrophes in decasyllabic stanzas. The presence of these suggests that poets could no longer count on that unjaded appetite in their readers for which the *Cursor Mundi* was written, but the work is substantially true to that old tradition. Nothing is made of the dialogue form; and if the papacy is treated from the point of view of a Reformer, this does not modify the medieval character of the poem. It is a metrical homily on world history, based largely on Orosius, Josephus, and Diodorus. In poems of this type we do not look for 'jewels five words long' nor for any great originality of conception. Their attraction lies in the perennial interest of the matter and in those local variations which it elicits from authors happily ignorant of archaeology and therefore compelled to see the past as if it were part of their own present. They are very seldom dull. From Lyndsay's I gather much that has made it, for me, worth reading. I learn (in answer to a question often raised) that our first parents loved *par amors* in Eden, delighting in each *utheris bodeis soft and quhyte*, and no wonder, says the poet, *consyderyng thare gret bewte*; that in the antediluvian world

> The watter was so strang and yne
> Thay wald nocht laubour to mak wyne;

that the Mediterranean and all other inland seas are relics of the flood; and that when the building of the tower of Babel was abandoned the *schaddow of that hidduous strenth* was already six miles long. It will be seen that Lyndsay usually has his eye on the object. The style of the *Monarche* does not rise to very great heights except in some of the lyrical interludes; but he must be a dull reader who finds it dull.

Warton—still our most reliable critic on much later medieval poetry—praises some of Lyndsay's lines as 'nervous, terse, and polished' and claims that they need only a modernized spelling to recommend them to the taste of his own age. This affinity between Lyndsay and the eighteenth century is naturally best seen in the ease and mastery of his lighter octosyllabic pieces; but even where his artistic formulas are most widely removed from those of the Augustans, he might be called a *medieval* Augustan. Decorum, discipline, a perfect understanding of his aim and of the means to that aim—these are his characteristics.

Lyndsay, as I have said, is the last of the major medieval poets in Scotland, but the anthologies display a vigorous undergrowth which is still to be examined. Comic poetry, of the 'kale-yard' rather than the 'eldritch' kind, is represented by several pieces whose date and authorship are uncertain. The two most famous of these, *Christis Kirk on the Green* (Bannatyne CLXIV and Maitland Folio XLIII) and *Peblis to the Play* (Maitland Folio XLIX), have both been attributed to James I. His claim to *Christs Kirk* rests on the attribution in Bannatyne, but some would there read *fift* for *first* and the philologists do not encourage us to date the language of the poem within James I's lifetime. His claim to *Peblis to the Play* rests on a passage in Major where he is said to have composed the *jucundum cantum* 'At Beltayn'—which certainly is the opening of the extant *Peblis to the Play*; but then Major spoils everything by adding *quem alii . . . mutare studuerunt*. The words ('they busied themselves to change it') suggest either that the poem was much imitated or that it got abroad in very corrupt texts. The extant *Peblis to the Play* is certainly earlier than *Christis Kirk*, in which it is mentioned. Both poems deal with the humours of what we should now call 'a bank holiday crowd'. The bustle of early morning preparation, the giggling and squealing coyness of the women, the refreshments in packed eating houses, the quarrels and finally the riots in which the extreme pugnacity of both sexes is neutralized by their lack of skill and courage, the tumbles and wrangles and perspiration of a 'fire-hot day', are all rendered with great spirit. *Christis Kirk* is the more violent and, I think, the less amusing of the two. In subject-matter they are not unlike some of the work of Skelton; the difference lies in the art. These are poems about confusion and vulgarity, not confused and vulgar poems. The poet—or poets—have perfect command both of their material and of their stanzas, and let us see pretty clearly that they had poetry of a very different sort at their disposal if they had wished to use it. The lyric quality peeps out in

> Bot yallow yallow was hir heid
> And sche of luif so sillie,
> Thocht all hir kin suld haue bein deid
> Sche wald have bot sweit Willie
> > Allane
> At Chrystis Kirk of the grein.

or even in

> All the wenchis of the West
> War up or the cok crew.

'The Wife of Auchtermuchty' (Bannatyne CLXXXIII), attributed, but in a later hand, to 'Mofat', is of the same kind and tells the common story of the man and wife who exchanged work for one day with disastrous results. It is more decorous than the German version which Ritson first discovered in the *Silva Sermonum* of 1568; from which, perhaps, we may infer that the Scotch poet had never heard the German version. 'The Dumb Wife' (Maitland Folio XXXV, in an imperfect text) tells amusingly enough how a husband by means of a spell learned from 'ane greit grim man' cured his dumb wife and how bitterly he regretted it. Two drinking songs (Bannatyne CLXIX and CLXXIV) are also worth mentioning. The note at the end of the former 'q(uod) allane matsonis suddartis' means, I believe, 'Thus say Allen Ma(l)tson's subjects'—i.e. the subjects of King Beer. 'Sym and his Bruder' (Bannatyne CCXVII) on the comic adventures of two palmers, and Maitland Folio LXXVII on Football, are lively. I am inclined to think that Arbuthnot's poem in praise of women (Maitland Quarto XXXV) is ironical and therefore intended to be comic. But if so, it has failed, and for a curious reason—it is too musical, too lyrically turned. This was a source of failure which most English poets of the period did not need to guard against.

When we turn to the minor poets whose names and dates happen to be known we soon learn the hopelessness of trying to date the anonymous pieces by internal evidence. This, indeed, is one of the most useful lessons which the anthologies have to teach us. 'Periods' are largely an invention of the historians. The poets themselves are not conscious of living in any period and refuse to conform to the scheme. Thus Stewart, who was writing 'daylie' when Lyndsay composed the *Complaynt of the Papyngo* in 1530, will write aureate stanzas (Bannatyne CCXLVII) whose poetics would not surprise us in the age of Henryson. Equally medieval, but far superior, is his song 'Thir lenterne dayis' (Bannatyne CCCXXV). But of course he may not be Lyndsay's Stewart. We are more certain of Bellenden who was a new poet ('now of lait starte up') in the *Papyngo* and whose *Proheme* to his Chronicle (Bannatyne IV) is pure stanzaic aureate morality in the old style. It must date from 1536. His *Benner of Peetie* (Bannatyne III) deals with the Four Daughters of God in the same style. Sir Richard Maitland, who lived ninety years (1496–1586) is a more interesting poet. Most of his poems are very like Dunbar and by no means contemptible. Three stand out: 'Thocht I be auld' (Maitland Quarto XX) for its cheerful resolution; Bannatyne VI, a lyric narrative of the Fall, for its music; and 'Quhen I haue done consider' (Maitland Quarto XXXI), for both; the moral that a merry heart is best leaps cheerily to the tune of

> It will not be our sorrow
> That will stope Goddis hand
> To stryike baith evin and morrow
> Bayth on the sie and land.

Alexander Scott (1525?–1584?) is more independent. There is in some of his poems a new music, lighter than Dunbar's, and often suggestive of Burns. There are also poems (notably Bannatyne CCCXV and CCCXXIV) in short lines and plain language which remind us of Wyatt. But then again there are poems which, so far as their literary quality is concerned, might have been written a hundred years earlier—Remedies of Love like Bannatyne CLXXXV, or aureate stanzas like CLII. It would be delightful if we could arrange his work in chronological order so as to show a picture of the young poet slowly 'escaping' from the Middle Ages, but the most medieval of all his pieces—'Welcum illustrat Ladye and oure Quene' (Bannatyne CLII)—bears on its face the date 1562. Scott is using a certain style not because he is 'still' medieval but because he considers it appropriate to the kind of poem he wants to make. In his best work, and even in his second-best work, melody is his great virtue; that, I suppose, is why Pinkerton called him 'the Anacreon of old Scottish poetry'. He does not, like Anacreon, excel in gaiety, but rather in pathos:

> Scho wait my wo
> That is ago
> Scho wait my weilfair and remeid;
> Scho wait also
> I lufe no mo
> Bot hir, the well of womanheid.
> Scho wait withouttin faill
> I am hir luvar laill
> Scho hes my hairt alhaill[1]
> Till I be deid. (Bannatyne CCXCII),

or again:

> To luve unluvit is ane pane,
> For scho that is my soverane
> Sum wantoun man so he hes set hir
> That I can get no lufe agane,
> Bot brekis my hairt and nocht the bettir. (Ibid. CCCXXXIV.)

Anacreon's melody is much simpler than this; nor could Anacreon conceivably have written such a line as (from the first of these two poems) 'The quyet secreitis of my harte'.[2] But our opinion of Scott is not raised when we read his work as a whole; music seldom fails him, but he is often empty and in some of his more medieval poems there are very dull conceits.

Even now—such are the riches of Scotch poetry—there remain many anonymous pieces which I cannot bring myself to pass over in silence; the pretty *nequitiae* of 'I met my lady weil arrayit' (Bannatyne CCIX), the 'jolly woe' and 'lusty sorrow' of 'Quhen Flora had ourfret the firth' (CCLI), or the delightful poem on Old Age:

> As schadow in the sonnis beme
> Or primrois in the winter showr.
> So all my dayis is bot ane dreme
> And half the sleiping of ane howr . . .
> Ane nap is nowrissand eftir none,
> Ane fyre is fosterand for my feit,
> With dowbill sokkis for my schone
> And mittanis for my handis meit.
>
> (Maitland Folio LIX.)

Perhaps best of all is the poem (Maitland Quarto LXXXVIII)

---

[1] *Wait*, knows. *laill*, loyal. *alhaill*, entirely.
[2] But time has improved this. As readers of Pitscottie know, *quyet* meant very little more than 'secret' or 'stealthy'. Cf. mod. 'on the quiet'.

entitled—and the title is part of its beauty—'The Reed in the Loch says'.

But every good order, in poetry as in commonwealths, draws to an end. In Maitland Quarto XXXVIII a vague and confused echo of the Italian *canzone* can be heard. The confusion of what we call 'Periods' is particularly apparent in XL from the same manuscript. It sets off in the style of *Pearl*:

> O blissid bird brichtest of all
> O flour of femenein . . . ,

suddenly darts forward into something like the Cavalier lyric:

> So Nature has ordanit wyislie
> That in all kynde of thing
> Perfyite the unperfyite supplie
> And to perfectioun bring . . . ,

and then retracts to what, but for the language, we should call pure Elizabethan:

> Your goldin hair lyik Phoebus schein
> Quhaireuer ye go dois glance.

Here we see different kinds of good poetry contending together. In Maitland Quarto XLVIII ('Declair ye bankis of Helicon') the Elizabethan manner is superbly victorious. Elsewhere—in XLVII, LXXVI, LXXVII, LXXVIII, and LXXXVIII—we see the simple conquest of the worse over the better. The very draff and scum of contemporary English poetry, the lumbering Poulter's Measure creeps in. It is a sign that the Scotch medieval literature is doomed. 'Newfangleness' and the power of foreign fashion must have become strong indeed before men nurtured on the great 'makaris' could welcome such alien imbecility. We are very near the day when Scotch poets will cease to write in their own rich and perfected tongue and Scotch poetry will become, for centuries, a backwater.

The representative poet of this transitional period is Alexander Montgomerie (1545?–1611?), a friend and probably a distant relative of James VI and I who quotes him for a specimen of versification in his *Rewlis and Cautelis* (1584). Montgomerie's implication in a popish plot to establish a Spanish garrison on Ailsa Craig afterwards led to his disgrace and banishment. He had commenced poet before 1568, for he appears in the Bannatyne MS. His most celebrated work, *The Cherrie and the Slae*, existed in some form before 1597 (the textual problems are rather complicated) and his *Flyting* against Polwart before 1584. His posthumous reputation in Scotland was very great and twenty-two editions of the *Cherrie* are recorded before 1792.

The new elements in Montgomerie's work are very obvious. He is, to begin with, a sonneteer, and as such indebted to Constable and Ronsard. His seventy sonnets are not, perhaps, opened once in a hundred years by those who read for pleasure. Yet they cannot exactly be called bad; they are careful, dignified work from which here and there a good line could be picked out. The miscellaneous poems are on the whole more interesting than the sonnets. In those which are of the new school Montgomerie sometimes has just a hint of that stateliness which comes in when the classic model of the ode begins to mix with the native song in men's conception of lyric poetry. The *Solsequium* is perhaps the best, or else the *Address to the Sun*, beginning:

> Quhill[1] as with whyt and nimble hand
> My maistres gathring flowrs doth stand.

He would have enjoyed, though he would never have learned to imitate, Ben Jonson's lyrics. Elsewhere he can be flat enough; he admired Tottel's poets.

But the old elements are equally important. Side by side with the *Solsequium* we find ordinary medieval moralizing stanzas, occasional aureation, and poems in the manner of Dunbar. The best poem he ever wrote belongs to no particular age:

> Hay! Nou the day dawis,
> The jolie cok crawis,
> Nou shroudis the shawis[2]
> Throu Natur anone.

But here he had an old tune to keep him right. The most medieval of all his works, the *Flyting*, is arguably (at least in places) his best. The *genre* is indeed dead; but then so are his sonnets, and the 'Flyting' sounds as if it had once been alive. I, at any rate, find the opening irresistible:

> Polwart, ye peip like a mouse amongst thornes;
> Na cunning ye keip; Polwart, ye peip.
> Ye luik like a sheipe and ye had two hornes;
> Polwart, ye peip like a mouse amongst thornes.[3]

---

[1] *Quhill*, while.
[2] The woods clothe (themselves with green)? Cf. Chaucer *Rom. Rose*, 55.
[3] *Peip*, squeak. *and*, if.

Surely this is better, unless we are very fond of novelty, than 'Bright amorous ee where Love in ambush lyis' and its kind.

In *The Cherrie and the Slae* Montgomerie pours very old wine into (comparatively) new bottles. The matter of the poem is purely medieval—a May morning, a river, a hesitation whether to pluck the accessible sloe or climb for the more delicious cherry, and a 'psychomachy' in the form of an interminable debate between Hope, Courage, Will, Dread, Danger, Skill, Experience, Reason, and Wit. A thirteenth-century poet would have done it in octosyllabic couplets, a Tottelian in octosyllabic quatrains. Montgomerie's very unhappy innovation consists in a more lyrical stanza. It is a very delightful stanza in itself; the same that we find in Sir Richard Maitland's poem on the Fall, with the ending movement of:

> Sum creiping, sum fleiting
> Sum fleing in the air,
> So heichtly, so lichtly
> In moving heir and thair.
> (Bannatyne VI.)

But this tumble-home is unendurable in a prolonged narrative, and still more in a prolonged debate. The long-continued popularity of the *Cherrie* among Montgomerie's countrymen is something of a puzzle. Perhaps men liked it because it is so quotable —stanza after stanza consists almost entirely of proverbs (or sentences capable of becoming proverbs) which are certainly stitched into the verse with great dexterity. Perhaps, too, a patriotic desire to read Scotch poetry coupled with a decreasing knowledge of Middle Scots may have had something to do with it. But Pinkerton was not deceived; 'the allegory', he said, 'is weak and wire-drawn, and the whole poem beneath contempt. Let it then sleep.' If for 'the whole poem' we read 'four-fifths of the poem' this is about right.

The rest of Montgomerie's certain output is made up of religious poetry; he fails, like his betters, as a translator of psalms. Some poems in the Laing MS. are suspected of being his. One of these, though its ending is ugly enough, begins delightfully:

> Glade am I! Glade am I!
> My mother is gone to Henislie. . . .

In so far as Montgomerie writes his own mother tongue, you may if you like call him the 'last of the makaris'. If you prefer,

you can call him for his sonnets the precursor of Drummond.
But unless you are a student you will not read him in either
capacity.

What remains of Scotch poetry in this century may, for our
purposes, be briefly gathered up. John Rolland published his
Sevin Seages in 1560 and his *Court of Venus* in 1575. The former is
a versification of the prose version printed by Wynkyn de Worde
in 1515; the latter an erotic allegory strangely encumbered by
the author's legal interests, and almost (but not quite) without
merit. Much more important is the collection of Protestant
hymns, compiled and largely composed by the Wedderburn
brothers, which is known under many names; *A Compendious
Book of Godly and Spiritual Songs*, the *Gude and Godlie Ballatis*, the
Psalms of Dundee, and the *Psalms of Wedderburn*. There are several
editions. Hymnody is an extreme case of literature as an applied
art. Its products can be judged only when we have heard them
used for their proper purpose. To the literary critic, judging in
his library, the *Gude and Godlie Ballatis* will appear very uneven,
ranging from the bathos of

> He is the Lord Christ, God and Man;
> He will do for you what He can,

to the excellent lyric 'All my lufe leif me not'. The latter belongs
to a large class which are either certainly or probably 'anti-
parodies' (if I may coin a most necessary word)—the conversion
of popular and secular songs to devout purposes; as in:

> Hey, now the day dallis,[1]
> Now Christ on us callis,
> Now welth in our wallis
> Apperis anone.

One of the most vigorous pieces is the 'Flyting' of the Pope
('that Pagan full of pride') with its refrain 'Hay trix, tryme go
trix, under the greenwood tree', familiar to every reader of *The
Abbot*. In Alexander Hume's *Hymnes or Sacred Songs* (published
in 1598 but composed, Hume tells us, 'in my youth') we reach
religious poetry proper as distinct from hymnody; and we also
reach the point at which Scotch poetry is ceasing to be very
noticeably Scots. Hume's modest statement that he is making
'rude Scottish and hask [i.e. harsh] verses' is significant; it was
for his 'Inglis' words that Douglas had apologized. There is also

[1] *Dallis*, dawns.

a plentiful crop of controversial and satirical ballads, mostly on the Protestant side. The authors are usually anonymous, but the name of Robert Sempill (ob. 1595), famous for his coarseness, survives. And with that we are at an end. We enter upon a period in which historians of Scotch literature can fill their chapters only by dwelling on writers who in happier lands and ages would hardly secure a mention. One sonnet by Boyd (ob. 1601) is remembered. And of course there is always Drummond. But Drummond himself, when all's said, is a Scotchman only 'out of school'.

It is impossible not to wonder at this sudden extinction of a poetical literature which, for its technical brilliance, its vigour and variety, its equal mastery over homely fact and high imagination, seemed 'so fair, so fresshe, so liklie to endure'. Historians whose sympathies are Roman attribute the catastrophe to the Reformation. But if the cause lies in that quarter at all it must be sought in some peculiarity of the Scotch Reformation; for in England the old religion had no such poetical glories to show and the new had many. Perhaps the Scotch poetry was essentially court poetry and could not live without a court. But however we explain the phenomenon, it forces on our minds a truth which the incurably evolutionary or developmental character of modern thought is always urging us to forget. What is vital and healthy does not necessarily survive. Higher organisms are often conquered by lower ones. Arts as well as men are subject to accident and violent death. The philosophy of history outlined by Keats's Oceanus is not true. We ask too often why cultures perish and too seldom why they survive; as though their conservation were the normal and obvious fact and their death the abnormality for which special causes must be found. It is not so. An art, a whole civilization, may at any time slip through men's fingers in a very few years and be gone beyond recovery. If we are alive when such a thing is happening we shall hardly notice it until too late; and it is most unlikely that we shall know its causes.

II

Prose is a plant not easily brought to perfection north of the Tweed; even when, in a later age, it became plentiful and vigorous, it seldom flowered, so that to the present day it is difficult to point to any Scotch authors except Hume and Stevenson whose fame depends much on their style. In the two great glories of medieval prose—the Romance and the devotional treatise—Scotland seems to have had no share. No Scotch Malory or Berners, no Scotch Hilton or Lady Julian, has come down to us.

In the sixteenth century the crop is more plentiful and some of it can be classified as medieval. The controversial literature arising out of the Reformation will be treated in a later chapter, except for one work which is at once so early and so unimportant that we may as well dispose of it here. This is *The Richt Vay to the Kingdome of Hevine* (1533) by John Gau (or Gaw, or Gall). The author spent much of his life at Malmö in Sweden, where he married. His book is a translation of Christiern Pedersen's *Den Rette Vey till Hiemmerigis Rige* (1531) which is itself mainly a translation from the German of Urbanus Rhegius. Gau was a Protestant and his book is a modest little commentary on the Ten Commandments, the Apostles' Creed, and the Lord's Prayer. The style is lucid and no other merit was attempted. The *Richt Vay* has the distinction of being the first specimen of Protestant theology in Scots; otherwise it counts for little in the history of thought and for less in the history of literature.

One of the most remarkable works of the century is the *Complaynt of Scotlande*, composed, as the author tells us (cap. v), in 1549. The compiler of the Harleian Catalogue may have had evidence which has since been lost when he attributed it to 'Vedderburn'; but it is certainly not by any Wedderburne who had a hand in the *Gude and Godlie Ballatis*, and must here be treated as an anonymous work. It is based chiefly on Alain Chartier's *Quadrilogue Invectif* (1422)—an appeal to the defeated and dissentient 'estates' of France made in the terrible years after Agincourt, and taking the form of an allegorical dream in which France personified addresses her children (peasant, knight, and churchman), and they try unsuccessfully to throw the blame on one another. The Scotch author, writing in the years that followed Pinkie, finds it easy to substitute Scotia for France and bring the work up to date. To that extent his book may be called medieval. But the moment we start reading it we find that Chartier has been metamorphosed. Between the prologue and the vision proper there comes in (page after page of it) a 'Monologue Recreative' in which, after some dazzling landscape, we are introduced to a number of wholly idealized shepherds, one of whom lectures on cosmography till silenced by his wife. Tales, songs, and dances succeed; and the list of their names will always give the *Complaynt* a place in the memory of antiquarians. The names of the tales are especially alluring and everyone would wish to know more about that 'Volfe' (some would read 'Velle') 'of the varldis ende' which struck so fortunately on the ears of William Morris. Before this, in the dedicatory epistle to the queen, and in varying degrees throughout the book, we are deluged with ink horn terms; 'magnanime avancing', 'prochane enemies', and 'sempiternall Olymp'. In aureate verse Scotchmen had done this sort of thing before; the inundation of prose was a novelty. Everywhere, too, the author lets loose on us a flood of anecdote and authority, unknown to Chartier, from Sallust, Seneca, Livy, Plutarch, Aristotle, Thucydides, and who not? The flavour is unmistakable. Here, unforetold, unsucceeded, unexplained, tricked out in all its heterogeneous ornaments as in jewels 'that were the spoils of provinces', what we call the 'Renaissance' has come dancing, shouting, posturing, nay as it were sweating, into Scots prose. It comes, for a moment. This author looks as if he were to be the first of many such; but no more came. There was to be no Scotch Lyly, no Scotch *Arcadia*, no Scotch Rabelais or Nashe. The author himself hoped that it would be merely his first book and looked forward to his 'next verkis'. It would be idle to deny this 'Renaissance' quality on the ground that the *Complaynt* is deeply medieval, its form a dream allegory, its landscape painting indebted almost certainly to Dunbar and probably to Alanus ab Insulis. The *Courtyer*, the *Faerie Queene*, the *Furioso*, and Petrarch's *Rime* all have such medieval roots. What baffles the modern reader is the union of a wholly serious purpose in this book with great extravagance of manner. The author is in tragic earnest about the miseries of Scotland, the fatal tendency of its nobles to disunion, treachery, and neutrality in the face of their 'ald enemies' the English. He is also in earnest about the corruptions of the Church in which he finds the true cause of 'Heresy' (he is a papist), and which, while they remain, make persecution useless. He can express in words that still move us the 'curses not loud but deep' of the hopeless peasants. It stretches our modern sensibilities to reconcile this with his jackdaw-like collections of classical tags, the glittering artificiality of his style, and his own hearty enjoyment of that artificiality. Yet when we have got into the mood we can even now see that there is a certain crazy beauty about the thing; and mere copiousness was regarded as a merit by our ancestors, if not by us.

The historians are more to our taste. They are also interesting because in them we see the art of history itself at the moment of an important transition. Behind the vernacular historians lie the Latin historians, Hector Boethius (or Boece; 1465?–1536) and Johannes Major (1479–1550), who represent the humanistic and the medieval conceptions of historical writing respectively. Major is not, indeed, nearly good enough to be taken as the type of the older school and we shall have a much better example in a moment; but all that there is of him is medieval through and through. His *Historia Majoris Britanniae tam Angliae quam Scotiae* is dry and annalistic in narrative, and when he discusses a problem (read what he says of Merlin's birth in II. iv) he sets it out like a disputation in the schools. Boece, on the other hand, writes classical Latin, keeps his eye on Livy, and is never so happy as when he can set his characters making speeches. The gain, if there be a gain, is not one in historical accuracy. Much of his *Historia Scotorum* (1527) is as fabulous as Geoffrey of Monmouth, but not, I think, so interesting, though we must thank him for supplying to Shakespeare (through Holinshed) the story of Macbeth.

Vernacular history begins by translation, and proceeds by continuation, of Boece. In 1536 John Bellenden, whom we have met before as a very minor poet and who had already in 1533 translated part of Livy, published his version of the *Historia Scotorum*. He is not one of the great translators and does not quite succeed in getting rid of the idiom of the original. Tell-tale absolute constructions, historic presents, and excessive linking of sentences abound.

John Lesley (1526–96), Bishop of Ross, is a sounder historian than Boece and a better writer than Bellenden. His unpublished *History of Scotland from 1437 to 1561* was dedicated to Queen Mary in 1570. It was written during his residence in England and arose from his reading of Polydore Vergil, Bede, Froissart, Fabian, Stow, and others in whom he found 'sundry thingis sett furth of the daedis and proceedingis betwix Scotland and England far contrair to our annals, registeris, and trew proceedingis'. Where Lesley is on his mettle, as in his dedicatory epistle, he shows himself to be a writer of the new school, and in that kind very good. His builded periods are those of a judicious classicist. This manner is, however, hardly maintained after he gets to business; his narrative is free from rhetoric and not very typical either of the medieval or the humanist kind of history. The truth is that he writes primarily as a man of affairs; he has read too many state papers and sat on too many committees to be either affected or racy. If the word had not been spoiled by ironical usage, 'respectable' would be the right adjective for his style. His history in Scots was first printed for the Bannatyne Club in 1830. But in 1579, while in exile at Rome, he had turned it into Latin under the title *De Origine, Moribus et Rebus Scotorum*, and this Latin text was retranslated into Scots in 1596 by a certain Father Dalrymple, apparently an exile for his religion at Ratisbon. Father Dalrymple's work is not of much literary importance. He was not very good at Latin, yet his Scots is too Latin by half.

Lesley's great opposite on the Protestant side, Robert Lindsay of Pitscottie (1532–92), had a somewhat similar fate, in so far as his *Historie and Cronikles of Scotland* was never printed till the eighteenth century. It was, however, certainly intended for publication. In his dedicatory verses (he was a poor poet) he expresses a wish that its 'fame' should not be 'sprong as yit' and gives the reason. The book 'mells' with present authority and could not be safely published while Morton—or any Douglas for that matter—was in power. From internal evidence it is clear that at least a large part of it was composed before 1577 and that none of it can be later than 1579. It is in Pitscottie that we find a worthier specimen than Major of that old school of chronicling which the rhetorical histories of the humanists displaced; the kind of history which is still saga, full of the sharp sayings and tragic deaths of great men, and which can boast Herodotus, Snorri, the *Gesta Francorum*, and Froissart among its glories. Pitscottie himself is quite unaware of the difference. He feels himself to be merely continuing Boece and his First Book is a translation of Boece's Eighteenth—that Eighteenth which did not appear in the 1527 text of the *Historia* but which Ferrerius published in 1574. This arrangement, however, serves to bring out all the more clearly the classicism of Boece and the medievalism of Pitscottie. I do not mean that we notice an abrupt change as we pass from Pitscottie the translator to

Pitscottie the original writer. But we gradually become aware, as his story takes hold of him, that we have entered a different world. The point can be illustrated by quotation. Here is a speech from Book I:

Gif transgressiounis of the lawis and statutis of the realm hopit for nane other thing of Kingis' and Princes' handis haveand the rule and governament of otheris, bot that quhilk the lawis decernis (Maist mightie Prince) I see na place left to me this day for remissioun of my cryme; yeit notwithstanding, Reason itself persuadis me, &c.,

Here is a speech from the real Pitscottie:

God forbid that the Queen's artaillyie be left in danger or yeit brekin for fear of Inglischemen. I had liever fight to deid in keeping of the Queen's artaillyie nor flie with shame and leave it behind me. I vow to God and by St. Bryde I sall put it free in the Castell of Dunbar or ellis die for it . . .[1]

Or again,

I vow to God they sall not take seisin of my lands bot I sall bear thame witness gif I may and help to make thair instrumentis with langer pens and redder ink nor thay bring with thame.

Some will prefer the one manner, some the other; but the examples will at any rate make plain in what sense I classify Pitscottie as a medieval, not a Renaissance, historian. In the class to which he belongs he is not one of the finest—not to be compared with Snorri or Froissart. But in great scenes he can be great. The murder of Cochran, the escape of Albany, the heroic humours of Lord David Lindsay of the Byres, Bishop Forman's *faux pas* at the papal banquet, the death-bed of James V, and the whole battle of Ancrum, are admirable in their varied merits of vividness, dry fun, or pathos. He writes frankly on the Protestant side but he was not, as things went in that fierce age, an embittered partisan and can praise merit in a Popish Churchman when he sees it; but he hates a persecutor, and a Douglas. His Scots is pure and racy (so pure, indeed, that de la Bastie becomes, delightfully, 'Tillabatie') and though his prose is not very artful it answers all the demands he makes upon it. In his history, for the first and last time, Scots prose of medieval character achieves permanent value.

A consideration of the *Complaynt*, of Lesley, and Pitscottie might serve as a warning against any simple and over-schematic

[1] *Artaillyie*, artillery. *deid*, death.

picture of the sixteenth century. The Papist bishop, when he chooses, writes classically. The most purely medieval of the three is a Protestant continuing the work of a humanist. And the most floridly Renaissance book has the deepest roots in the literature of the Middle Ages.

THE CLOSE OF THE MIDDLE AGES IN ENGLAND

I

IN a fifteenth-century book of devotions, a vernacular 'Primer'
as men called it, we find a hymn that goes like this;

> The Wisdom of the Father, The truethe of the high king,
> God and Man, was taken In the morening.

In a similar book dating from 1535 we also have a hymn;

> Holy Mary pray to thy son
> The weak in sprete[1] to encorage
> To socore the miserable in their affliction
> To comfort the sorrowful their sorrows to assuage.

The contrast between these two pieces of anonymous verse—
the graceful movement and firmness of line in the former, and
the doggerel rigmarole of the latter—epitomizes the history of
later medieval poetry in England. From the varied excellence
of the fourteenth century to the work of the early sixteenth it is
a history of decay; so that in turning from the Scotch poetry of
that age to the English we pass from civilization to barbarism.
In certain other respects, of course, it might be called a transition from barbarism to civilization. We pass from a Scotland
perpetually torn by feudal wars, in which neither life nor property is secure for a moment, to an England where Henry VII's
triumph at Bosworth (1485) had at least begun the restoration
of national unity, where the New Learning was already beginning to spread, and where the new king's mythical connexion
with Arthur (after whom he named his son) might be expected
to give a poetic sanction to men's not ill-grounded hopes of a
new era of prosperity, splendour, and power. All the conditions
—or what we naturally suppose to be the conditions—of a
great literature seem to be present in early Tudor England.
If that great literature had been written, can we doubt that
most historians would confidently point to those conditions as its
cause? In Scotland they are all lacking. But it is Scotland which
has the literature.

[1] *Sprete*, spirit.

We shall even find that the transition from poetical mastery to poetical imbecility as we come southward is a gradual one. On the border we still have ballads (treated in another volume), and some of them excellent. In Cheshire we shall find an alliterative poem which, if not at the top of its own class, can still be read with continuous pleasure. It is when we reach London that the really bad work meets us.

The alliterative poem is *Scotish Feilde*, a miniature epic in two 'fyttes' celebrating (in general) Henry VIII's French campaign and the victory of Flodden, and (in particular) the house of Stanley. This partial and local loyalty may perhaps explain both why the poem is so completely medieval and why poetry of the old sort languishes in the south. It is the little court that is favourable to heroic poetry: organization, centralization, bigness, and all the other necessary evils of a complex society, are not. The poem has not greatly pleased most modern critics. They complain that it is a mosaic of stock phrases; but so is the *Iliad*. It must be allowed, indeed, that the author of the *Scotish Feilde* does not always use them with discretion. The tag 'saddest (i.e. staunchest, most reliable) of all other' is contradictorily used of two different earls within ten lines. But even that offends a reader much more than a listener, for whom, I suppose, the poem was intended; and in general the traditional character of the language, if it throws no light on the poet's personal sensibility, does throw light (where, for my part, I much prefer to have it) on the bills and bows, the moors and the banners. What has been used often before is none the less useful here: it works, just as 'Savage, his sister's son' may be true even though it also carries the mind back to many a *swuster sunu* at Maldon and before. The descriptions of morning ('damped with dew' and birds singing that it 'was solace to heare') which precede two of the battles may, as the editors tell us, be commonplaces: but in their context they give us just the right sense of expectation and alacrity. The 'gaping gunns', the thirst and hunger of the English army ('Water was a worthy drinke; win it who might!'), the 'clowdes cast up cleerlye like castles ful hie', the beautiful terror of the trumpets before the action begins ('Heavenly was their melody'), the Scotch dead—

Beside Brinstone in a bridge breathless they lyen
gaping against the moon—

E

all seem to me admirably vivid. If the poet was not really at the battle his convincing use of the first person ('Then we seen our enemies, were moving over the mountains') is all the more to his poetical credit; but perhaps he was. Hales and Furnivall concluded that he was not, because 'he is far from accurate in the details', but that is the argument of a civilian; what a man sees, still more what he remembers, of an engagement seldom agrees with the official histories. One pleasing feature of his poem is its treatment of enemies. He dismisses Richard III (for its narrative starts at Bosworth) without reviling in the words

> He fought full freshlie his foemen among . . .
> I will min(d)e him no more,
> But let Droughten[1] deale with all as him deare liketh,

and though he thinks the Scots fell and treacherous he does not jeer at them nor exult shrilly. We are ready to believe him when he tells us 'He was a gentleman by Jesu that this geste made'; and compared with the *geste*, Skelton's 'Against the Scots' is like a guttersnipe putting out his tongue. The poem is not great: there is nothing in it like Roland's last moments, or the speech of Byrhtwold, or 'Norway from thy hand, oh King'; but it is incomparably better battle poetry than England was to produce for many centuries. It must have been written after 1515.

From the same region, at Chester, we find Henry Bradshaw's *Lyfe of St. Werburge*, completed in 1513, the year of its author's death. He had also, according to Anthony Wood, written a Latin *De Antiquitate et Magnificentia Chestriae*. From the *Lyfe*, which is between five and six thousand lines long, in rhyme-royal stanzas, some pleasure may be gleaned, if not always the kind of pleasure the author hoped to give. The penitent wild geese summoned before St. Werburge for destroying the crops remind us of the Jackdaw of Rheims:

> Dredfully darynge comen now they be,
> Theyr winges traylynge, entred into the hall;
> For great confusion, after theyr kynde and propryte
> Mourninge in theyr maner.[2]

It is pleasant to record that the charitable lady pardoned them all (even restoring to life one who had been stolen by a servant with a weakness for roast goose) and dismissed them with

---

[1] *Droughten*, the Lord.
[2] *Dredfully*, timidly. *darynge*, cowering. *propryte*, property.

advice on their religious duties (*benedicite volucres celi domino*). The scene (i. 932 et seq.) in which Werburge's mother, though herself a saint, becomes a very human *grande dame* to put her daughter's upstart suitor in his place is amusing. Amusement is not the end that Bradshaw had in view: yet our pleasure is not merely an accident. The passage is funny because it is true to nature, and it is true to nature because Bradshaw keeps his eye on the object. He knows too, as authors of his kind did not always know, that poetry must please: all is written for 'our doctryne', admittedly, but also for our 'endeles pleasure' (ii. 9) and 'to augment our solas' (i. 2714). I cannot discover in him the Homeric qualities which his editor Carl Horstmann claimed for the *Lyfe* in 1887, but he is not quite contemptible. In a sense, but a sense creditable to the Middle Ages, his work shows how bad medieval narrative poetry could be. It could be as bad as this and no worse: that is, it could be dull and feeble, but not odious or perverse. Its badness is always an honest, innocent kind of badness: and at any moment there may come a gleam of imagination. The same can be said of the stanzaic romance *Generydes* which, on internal evidence, need not perhaps be dated earlier than 1500.

The lines which I have just quoted from *St. Werburge* introduce us to the most perplexing and repellent feature of late medieval poetry in England, its metre. The popular theory is that Hoccleve, Barclay, and Hawes were trying to write Chaucerian decasyllabics and failed because they were confused by the loss of final -e. To the best of my knowledge Mr. Fitzroy Pyle and myself have gone farthest in our disbelief of this theory. There are indeed some poems, a very few, which look as if their metre could have been arrived at in that way. The verse of *Generydes* is roughly what might be expected from a man who had the true lilt of the decasyllable in his head but ignored some changes of pronunciation and perhaps had a negligent scribe. But if we turn to the *Assembly of Gods* or Barclay's *Egloges* or Hawes, we find something very different. The test lies in the ear, exercised not for a stanza or two but day after day over thousands of lines. The man who reads *Generydes* straight through for the story (and a man may do many worse things) will have the general impression that he has been moving, if a little jerkily, to the five-beat rhythm. From Hawes or Barclay he will get no such impression. The lines which are 'normal' by that standard come so rarely that the ear rejects them as accidents. Mr. Pyle and I think the poets were not trying to write Chaucer's metre.[1] To explain their departures from it by the loss of final -e is to presuppose the metrical ignorance which this theory attempts to explain. If men understand metre, that understanding itself reveals to them that pronunciation has changed. If a boy does not see from the metre that Marlowe pronounced *Mahomet* differently from ourselves, that is because the boy cannot scan. Accordingly Mr. Pyle and I advanced theories as to the metre that the early Tudor poets were really writing. But I have not heard that anyone agreed with either of us: and it must be confessed that almost any piece of English, whether in prose or verse, could be squeezed into the metres we suggested. Nor, even if his theory or mine were accepted, would it much help the fame of these poets; for neither of our hypothetical metres is at all good. If we are both rejected, then the true state of the case is that early sixteenth-century England witnessed a poetical barbarism in which rhyme itself became the only constant characteristic of verse (a fact very relevant to the rise of the Skeltonic), and that the causes of this barbarism are unknown. It must be remembered that no art lives by *nature*, only by acts of voluntary attention on the part of human individuals. When these are not made it ceases to exist.

When Erasmus paid his first visit to England in 1499, Grocyn was close on sixty years of age, Skelton and Linacre nearly forty, Barclay and Colet (like Erasmus himself) in their thirties, and Thomas More twenty-one. The age of Stephen Hawes we do not know. The first Greek scholars had come to England nearly a hundred years before. Five Greek books were presented to Oxford in 1443. Between 1489 and 1500 a Greek called John Serbopoulos copied several Greek manuscripts at Reading. At court the new Latin, the 'pure' Latin as humanists called it, was already favoured for diplomacy and historiography, and foreign scholars such as Bernardus Andreas of Toulouse and Polydore Vergil were patronized by Henry VII. Before 1493 Grocyn had given those lectures on pseudo-Dionysius which, by exploding the traditional authorship of the *Celestial Hierar-*

[1] It seems to be certain, at any rate, that these poets regarded the line as two half-lines. A verse tract of Robert Crowley's (1550) so prints them. Even after the decasyllabic has been mastered, Barnaby Googe prints it as two lines, and Churchyard nearly always puts after the fourth syllable a comma which, since it ignores syntax, is to be regarded as a metrical point.

chies, ushered in that period of critical scholarship in which we are still living. In the year of Erasmus's own visit Colet was lecturing on the Pauline Epistles. He worked, indeed, only from the Vulgate, not from the original: but his historical approach and his rejection of the allegorical senses gave the lectures a sufficiently revolutionary character.

That is one side of the picture; we seem to see humanism steadily eating its way into the public mind. If, on the other hand, we glance at the list of Caxton's publications we get at first quite a different impression. The seventy-odd books which he printed between 1475 and his death in 1491 are all directed to satisfying medieval needs or medieval tastes; they are either service books, books of devotion, 'morality', and 'nurture', or else allegories and 'historiall' romances. It has been disputed whether Caxton followed his private taste, or that of a public, or that of his noble patrons. The last seems the most probable: his own prefaces often tell us at whose instance a book was printed, and usually translated as well. This, however, might not disqualify him as a witness to public taste; noble personages often reflect it with great accuracy. What disqualifies him much more is the fact that an English printer could not then, nor long after, compete with the continental presses in printing Greek or Latin. Caxton had to rely on English as his sole *specialité de maison*. The absence of Sallusts and Plutarchs from his list does not therefore prove that no one wanted them: any who did would get them from abroad.

The extent to which humanism had penetrated beyond the court and beyond specially cultured circles such as that in which More grew up (the universities were not pioneers in this matter) is thus not very easy to determine. But oddly enough the question does not matter nearly as much as might be expected to an historian of English literature, or at least of English poetry. For the truth is that at this period northern humanism still carried with it few or no implications about a man's taste in vernacular verse. It did imply a hatred of Romance and of scholastic philosophy: if men like More had been able to control English printing we should have lost our Malory. But there is little trace of that demand for classical form in the vernacular which was later to produce *Gorboduc*. Men who were Ciceronian in Latin might still be almost wholly medieval when they wrote or read poetry in their mother tongue.

A characteristic work of that age was the 'literature of folly' inaugurated in 1494 by the *Narrenschiff* of Brantius or Sebastian Brant; a germinal work, if ever there was one. It budded into translations in Latin, French, and English, translations some of them so very free that they are almost new growths and therefore bear all the stronger witness to the vitality of the parent stem. Most of the comic literature which will meet us later in the present chapter is influenced by it: *Jill of Brentford* and the *Highway to the Spittle House* are essentially new frameworks for catalogues of fools. The modern scholar who has most right to speak on the subject, Father Pompen, has warned us not to exaggerate the warmth of the humanistic reception given to this work: but there is certainly little sign that its amorphous prolixity and total lack of invention displeased the humanists. Erasmus and Reuchlin both praise it; Trithemius calls it a *divina satira*; Locher's Latin version is humanistic. Yet it has no merits which could please a taste really formed upon the ancients: it has, without the medieval virtues, all the medieval vices. Many readers have doubtless been led by the title to expect some real comic construction, some satiric story about a ship full of fools gloriously embarked for a Rabelaisian Land of Folly. In reality, the ship is a mere figure of speech, dismissed in the opening lines, and the body of the poem consists of disconnected pieces in each of which some particular type of fool is either made to expose himself in soliloquy or (more often) directly belaboured by the author. Irony is little employed: flat denunciation of the obviously indefensible, reiterated statements that black is black, make the bill of fare. It is difficult to think oneself back into a taste which could have enjoyed such writing. Some of the enjoyment, no doubt, was due to the woodcuts. These have a remarkable, even a frightful, energy and they, or cuts clearly derived from them, appear in the Latin, French, and English texts. The flaying of 'Marcia' (Marsyas) is especially memorable. Notice (in Jamieson's text) the absorbed enjoyment on the face of the bearded spectator, the smiling lady who looks down on the execution from her window, and the 'culinary coolness' of the nearer executioner. What is more to our purpose, many of these pictures are enigmatic without the letterpress—they lure a man to read on and find what they are about. But this is not the whole explanation of Brant's enormous vogue. There is abundant evidence for the satiric bent (not the satiric power) of that age in several countries. In their crowded cities and among a flourishing burgher class, as confident as need be of their own good sense and often, perhaps, in conscious revolt against the more ideal elements of medieval culture, there arose a critical impulse which, far out-running any satiric skill then available, seems to have produced an unwearied appetite for bold delineations, or even mere catalogues, of squalor, roguery, and folly. In the comic parts of Sir Thomas More's work we see it transformed by a real genius for drollery. Skelton and Heywood are better representatives, though Skelton at his best is too good to be typical. It is a different thing from the Scotch ribaldry of the same period—the work of heavier men, men who take a long time to get tired either of a moral platitude or a slap-stick joke. A steamy smell as of large dinners seems to pervade it all; if worse smells sometimes intrude, that is part of the joke. Humanism did not create the taste, but most humanists seem to have shared it.

It is therefore not possible in the late years of the fifteenth and the early years of the sixteenth century to distinguish a medieval and a humanist strain in English poetry. In the work of Hawes and Barclay, of the young Thomas More, and of Skelton wherever Skelton is not simply *sui generis*, all the medieval characteristics survive—the seven-lined stanzas, the love of allegory, the commonplaces. Yet More was among the greatest of all English humanists: Barclay was certainly, Skelton arguably, tinged with humanism. It makes no difference to their poetry. It does not, so far as we can see, arouse in them any effort to heal the disease of which English verse had been slowly dying for a century—the disease of bad metre. This alone would remove the work of Hawes and Barclay, and some of Skelton, from serious critical consideration: but it is not their only defect. Their language is undistinguished, their sentences untrussed, their thought commonplace and indistinct. They are as far below Lydgate as Lydgate is below Chaucer; for their workmanship is at least as coarse as his and, with the possible exception of Hawes, they lack the fineness and tenderness of temper which alleviates his tediousness. This is the real mid-winter of our poetry; all smudge, blur, and scribble without a firm line or a clear colour anywhere.

In an amusing passage of the *Moriae Encomium* Erasmus

describes the salient characteristics of the European nations. Germans are tall and good at magic (it was the fashionable form for the dream of power): Scotchmen are argumentative and related to the royal family: Spaniards are the best soldiers. To the English he allots three things—bodily beauty, an elegant table (*lautas mensas*), and music. On the first Holbein's portraits are our best comment. The second and third help to correct a false impression of that age which we should have if we considered its poetry alone. Music and architecture show that it had artistic impulses, though poetry was not, for the moment, the channel in which they flowed. Conversely, the acknowledged supremacy of English poetry in some other ages has been accompanied by extreme penury in the remaining arts. The splendour of London in the early sixteenth century astonished the Venetian ambassador, and Erasmus was delighted with the society he found there.

Of the bad poets who wrote at this time I shall first mention Stephen Hawes, not because he is necessarily the oldest (his dates are uncertain) but because he is the most completely medieval. He was groom of the chamber to Henry VII and his life, according to Bale, was an 'ensaumple of vertue' (*virtutis exemplum*). Appropriately, he wrote *The Example of Virtue* (1504), *The Pastime of Pleasure* (1505), a *Joyful Meditation* on the accession of Henry VIII (1509), and a *Conversion of Swerers* and *Comfort of Lovers*. The *Pastime* and the *Example* have a not unimportant place in the history of English allegory, and it is probable that Spenser had read the *Pastime*. Hawes knows he is writing an old-fashioned kind of poetry and complains that men nowadays 'fayne no fables pleasaunt and coverte', but he sticks to what he prefers. Mrs. Browning claimed for him 'true poetic faculty', but 'faculty' seems to me exactly the wrong word. Faculty was what he lacked; there was more and better poetry in him than he could express. The adventurousness, the wonder, and the devout solemnity of his allegorical stories gleam fitfully through his broken-backed metre and dull excursions into the seven liberal arts. There was a certain genuinely medieval fineness and simplicity about his mind if not about his art. He is not, like Barclay, a man contentedly making fifth-rate translations of second-rate originals, but a man grasping at really good things beyond his reach. Accordingly, his failure excites sympathy rather than contempt—if indeed sympathy is needed for a man who lived in such a happy dream of love, chivalry, and wandering.

With Alexander Barclay (1475?–1552), Chaplain of St. Mary's College at Ottery in Devonshire, Monk of Ely, and, after the Dissolution, Vicar of Much Baddow in Essex, we touch rock bottom. Barclay is influenced by humanism. He imitated Mantuan and translated Sallust's *Jugurtha*. This, in vigorous and dignified prose, is incomparably his best work. His *Introductory to Wryte and Pronounce French* (1521), though a less favourable specimen of his prose style, is of greater historical interest as an early instance of those efforts towards a decorated prose (*Kunstprosa*) in the vernacular which will engage our attention in a later chapter. The following passage from his Prologue shows the 'ink-horn' terms already in operation:

Many and dyuers lettred men experte in sondry scyences have done theyr deuoyr to inclere the dulnesse and wylfull ignoraunce of theyr countrees natyfe; and to brynge this theyr entrepryse to effect some haue wryten in solute language maternall of our englyshe tonge, some in the same language hath coarted theyr style in meter. . . .

But his poetry has no intrinsic value. It is disputed whether the *Castell of Labour* (1503) is by him or no: but if it is not by Barclay it is by someone equally bad. The opening exhortation, 'Subdue you to payne to rede this tretyse' is fully justified. The original by Pierre Gringoire, published in 1499, is not absolutely without merit. It is a prosaic allegory in which the economic anxieties of the usual Dreamer are, at the advice of Reason, allayed by the sound, if not very original, scheme of working for his living. There is some humour in the idea of making the Dreamer's wife sleep soundly all night while he sustains a very unpleasing conversation with such visitors as Necessity, Distress, and Poverty. But the translator is a bungler. He turns the elaborate decasyllabic stanza of Gringoire into rhyme royal and when Gringoire later changes to octosyllabics he at first continues with his long lines. Then gradually he becomes aware that the original has somehow changed and begins to shorten his line: sometimes (but almost certainly by accident) hitting true octosyllables. It is as if he were working in his sleep.

Even worse, in so far as it is longer, is the *Ship of Fools* (1509). It is almost shocking to find that the same year saw the publication of another English version of Brant, by one Watson:

concerning which all but specialists will probably be content
with Father Pompen's hair-raising assurance that it is inferior
to Barclay's. Barclay works chiefly from Locher's Latin though
he also makes use of the French text of Rivière: he would have
us believe that he knew German but that seems to be a lie.
He admits to being no strict translator of any text, 'some tyme
addynge some tyme detractynge'. Two or four lines of Locher
will usually be muffled up in a whole stanza. He introduces
much local colouring, substituting praise of Henry VIII for
praise of the emperor, interpolating a compliment to James IV
(some traditions make Barclay a Scot), lampooning one Man-
sell of Ottery, or attacking Skelton with the very true boast

> It longeth not to my scyence nor cunnynge
> For Phylyp the Sparowe the Dirige to synge.

In such a huge mass of verse it is inevitable that many passages,
worthless in themselves, should have an accidental interest for
a modern reader, and it is these (with the woodcuts) that make
the reading of it tolerable. It is pleasant to meet in that distant
age the book collector who loves his volumes

> Full goodly bound in pleasant coverture
> Of domas,[1] satyn, or els of velvet pure,

but never reads them. The piece on 'Unprofitable Study' is
humanistic in its attack on scholasticism. A revolution in
medicine is brought vividly home to us when we read of patients
who 'followeth Ryot' by 'receyuynge colde water' when the
doctors have strictly ordered them to limit themselves to ale and
wine. 'Of them that make Noyse in the Chirche' shows us a scene
that would startle our own less pious age: hawks and even
cuckoos are brought to Mass, young gallants stroll to and fro
before the altar, dogs are everywhere, and the gossiping does not
cease even at the consecration. Witches, unexpectedly for a
modern, differ from true physicians in neglecting the astrological
side of medicine: in their empiric ignorance they demand 'What
nedes it note the synes or firmament?' The new discoveries in
geography are astonishingly used—and this also may be a
humanist touch—as a proof that geography is a folly: 'Ferdi-
nandus that late was Kynge of Spayne' has found out 'plenty
and store' of countries that no geographer had ever heard of—
which just shows how silly it is to study geography. The Turkish

[1] Damask.

peril (a background to 'Renaissance' Europe which we too easily forget) is stressed and a new crusade called for. The interest of such things as these often wins for an old text unmerited praise. But they owe nothing to art: if the matters touched on were modern they would be nothing. As poetry Barclay's translation is nothing. Out of these thousands of lines one alone clings to the memory: that about hanged men 'Wauynge with the wether whyle their necke wyll holde'. Yet even there the image may owe as much to popular speech as to Barclay; hanged men 'wauer with the wynde' in 'The Nut Broun Maid' and elsewhere.

In 1523 came the *Mirrour of Good Maners*, translated from a dull poem *De Quatuor Virtutibus* in elegiacs by Dominicus Mancinus. It is a little, a very little, better than the *Ship of Fools*, the four-beat anapaestic rhythm occurring so often that I am almost inclined to think it may have been, in some dim and fitful fashion, intended. But the assurance at the beginning of the poem is a pretty accurate statement of its merits:

> The sad and wyse husband this treatise may recite
> Vnto his wyfe, not hurtynge her courage with delite.

With the *Egloges* we come to the unmistakable impact of the *renascentia*: these are pastorals *en règle*, dialogues between Cornix, Minalcas, and the like, with satire on current abuses, and an elegy. It will be noticed, however, that while the presence of the elegy conforms to classical example, the elegy itself is a pure specimen of medieval allegory in its last decay. For the rest of his matter Barclay draws on two sources. One of them is the *Courtiers' Miseries* (*Miseriae Curialium*) of Aeneas Sylvius, a bitter prose satire on life at the imperial court. To a modern this does not seem very suitable for treatment in the manner of Theocritus or the *Bucolics*; but Barclay's other source was Mantuan and that, properly understood, explains the mystery.

The Eclogues of Baptista Mantuanus, first printed in 1498, mark the final stage of a perversion in the pastoral which had been begun by Virgil himself. In him a real imaginative vision of idealized, yet not excessively idealized, rusticity is ever present, but allegorical and even polemical elements play a considerable part. These elements were unfortunately emphasized till in Mantuan we have the extraordinary spectacle of a literary impulse almost exactly like that of Juvenal expressing itself through a medium originally devised for the purposes of refreshment and escape. That 'dread voice' in *Lycidas* to which Johnson objected is not a foolish novelty of Milton's but rather his glorious transfiguration of a well-established, and singularly unhappy, tradition—just as the exquisite idealism of Drayton is a triumphant escape from it. Mantuan was immensely popular, and can still be enjoyed: but the enjoyment has nothing to do with Arcadia or Sicily. It has three sources. Firstly, we enjoy the success with which, every now and then for a few lines, he imitates the externals of Virgil:

> Vos quibus est res ampla domi, quibus ubera vaccae
> Plena ferunt, quibus alba greges mulctralia complent.

Secondly, we enjoy the pointed dialogue, the repartee. And thirdly, we enjoy the invective. These pleasures came in the humanistic age to pass for the proper pleasures of pastoral poetry. And thus it comes about that many a medieval poet who had never read the *Bucolics* nor ever heard of eclogues might—in a 'Robyn and Makyn', a 'Nut Brown Maid', or a ballad—be far nearer to Theocritus in spirit than a scholar of the *renascentia* who was steeped in Mantuan. It is another instance of that fatal flaw in humanism which draws a veil over Greek literature in the very act of discovering it; that urban and bookish limitation which sees in an ancient text everything rather than the radical, obvious, and universal pleasures which it was intended to give.

Barclay's *Egloges* are, like the rest of Barclay, bad. Some homely pictures, as that of the old shepherd with his hair starting through his torn hood and a wooden spoon in his hat, must have given some pleasure even in his own day, and naturally give more now. There are many lines which would sound well in quotation; but when you replace them in their context and see with what rubble they are surrounded you must conclude that their merits were due to chance. The real importance of the book is that it shows how a work which is humanistic in design may remain completely medieval in manner, and also how little tendency the humanism of that time had to kindle poetic imagination or mend poetic art. It may also be suspected that Barclay's hard words—*frowise*, *quacham*, and *kempes*—have some responsibility for the odd language in the *Shepherds Calendar*.

All Barclay's works are outweighed in value by the few poems which Thomas More wrote in his youth. These are quite free from traces of humanism. The 'Merry Jest' about a sergeant disguised as a friar is written correctly enough in a jerky dimeter and begins in true medieval fashion with nine successive variations on the proverb *ex sutore medicus*. It is a dull trifle and has none of that superb mastery of comic anecdote which More was later to reveal in his prose. But the lamentation on the death of Queen Elizabeth (1503) is of real value, and the next piece, the verses for the *Book of Fortune*, is perhaps better. Here, on a characteristically medieval theme, and in firmer metre, we have something like an anticipation of Spenser's court of Philotime in the underworld, and allegorical figures which are not much below Sackville's. Few things even about More are more impressive than the merit of these two poems. They are quite off his own beat: they owe nothing to his humour or to his classical scholarship; they succeed not by anticipating any new conception of poetry but by momentarily restoring the medieval kind to something of its former value.

But when all's said John Skelton[1] (1464?–1529) is the only poet of that age who is still read for pleasure. Skelton was a translator, a laureate of more than one university, tutor to Henry VIII, the satirist and later the client of Wolsey, and a jest-book hero in Elizabethan tradition. Pope's epithet of 'beastly' is warranted by nothing that ought either to attract or repel an adult; Skelton is neither more nor less coarse than dozens of our older comic writers. His humanism is a little more important than his supposed beastliness, but it did not amount to much. It led him to translate 'Tully's Familiars' and (from Poggio's Latin version) Diodorus Siculus, at some date before 1490. These translations, which still remain in manu-

---

[1] b. 1460?–1464? Laureated at Oxford before 1490; at Cambridge, 1493; Holy Orders, 1498; already at court and tutor to P. Henry in 1499 when he met Erasmus; Rector of Diss by 1502: after 1511 not traceable at Diss with certainty (i.e. unless *chorus de Diss* in his Latin poem on Flodden be taken to prove residence); begins to describe himself as *orator regius* in 1512; possibly accompanied the king to France in 1513 (see evidence produced by W. Nelson, *John Skelton, Humanist*, pp. 128 et seq.); lampooned Wolsey, 1521–2; driven to seek sanctuary from his anger in Westminster, but the evidence that he died in sanctuary is not strong; in 1523 and 1528 made, or tried to make, his peace with the cardinal by flattering dedications; about 1523 apparently patronized by Countess of Surrey; ob. 1529. Some believe that fragments of true biography can be found in the *Merry Tales of Skelton* (1567).

script, are said to abound in neologisms, often successful, and it is plain from such scraps of Skelton's prose as are accessible in print that he was a lover of ink-horn terms. But his human-ism extended only to Latin and he was one of those who opposed the study of Greek at the university and called themselves 'Trojans'. One of his objections to Greek learning is of great historical interest. He complains that those who learn Greek cannot use it in conversation, cannot say in Greek

How hosteler fetche my hors a botell of hay.   (*Speeke Parot*, 150.)

This shows that the very conception of a *dead* language, so familiar to us, was to Skelton a ridiculous novelty. The process of classicization which was finally to kill Latin seemed to him merely the improvement of a living tongue.

If the list of his own works which Skelton gives in the *Garland of Laurel* is accurate he must have been one of our most prolific authors, and his lost books must have outweighed in volume those which have survived; indeed his *Of Man's Life the Pere-grination*, if it was really a version and a complete version of Deguileville's *Pèlerinage*, would have done so by itself. But it is hard to believe that so busy and erratic a genius ever completed such a task. In what follows I must naturally base my judge-ment on the extant works; but it should be remembered that we know Skelton only in part and the part we do know is by no means homogeneous. We cannot be sure that the recovery of the lost works might not seriously modify our idea of him.

In his earliest surviving pieces Skelton appears as a typical poet of the late Middle Ages: a poet no better than Barclay and, in my judgement, inferior to Hawes. His elegies on Edward IV (1483) and on the Earl of Northumberland (1489) reveal nothing of his later quality. We may probably assign to the same period (and certainly relegate to the same oblivion) three heavily aureate poems addressed to the Persons of the Trinity, a poem on Time, and an amatory 'Go Piteous Heart'. The only effect of all these is to set us thinking how much better they did such things in Scotland.

With the *Bouge*[1] *of Court* (probably written in 1498 or 1499) we reach work which is of real value, but we do not reach the fully 'Skeltonic' Skelton. The *Bouge* is just as characteristic of the late Middle Ages as the previous poems; the difference is

---

[1] Rations, allowance of food.

that it is good. There is no novelty, though there is great merit, in its satiric and realistic use of the dream allegory. The form had been used satirically by Jean de Meung and Chaucer and had always admitted realistic detail; in the *Flower and the Leaf* and the *Assembly of Ladies* it had offered almost nothing else. The merit of Skelton lies not in innovation but in using well an established tradition for a purpose to which it is excellently suited. The subject is a perennial one—the bewilderment, and finally the terror, of a man at his first introduction to what theologians call 'the World' and others 'the racket' or 'real life'. Things overheard, things misunderstood, a general and steadily growing sense of being out of one's depth, fill the poem with a Kafka-like uneasiness. As was natural in Tudor times the particular 'world' or 'racket' described is the court; but almost any man in any profession can recognize most of the encounters —the direct, unprovoked snub from Danger ('She asked me if ever I drank of sauces cup'), the effusive welcome of Favell, the confidential warnings of Suspect, the apparently light-hearted good fellowship of Harvy Hafter (but the very sight of him sets your purse shivering), and the downright bullying of Disdain. It ends in nightmare with the hero leaping over the ship's side: his name, which is *Drede*, gives the keynote to the whole dream. The metre is chaotic, but the poem almost succeeds in spite of it.

So far, if my chronology is correct, we have seen Skelton working along the lines marked out for him by his immediate predecessors. He was to do so again in the Flyting 'Against Garnesche' (1513–14), in *The Garland of Laurel* (1523), and in the huge morality play of *Magnificence* (1515–16) which I surrender to the historians of drama. But in the next group of poems which we must consider we are confronted with a different and almost wholly unexpected Skelton. The pieces in this group cannot be accurately dated. *Philip Sparrow* was certainly written before 1509. 'Ware the Hawk' was obviously written while Skelton was resident at Diss, and therefore probably between 1502 and 1511. The 'Epitaphe' (on 'two knaves sometime of Diss') cannot be earlier than 1506 when the will of one of the 'knaves' was proved. The 'Ballad of the Scottish King' and its revised version 'Against the Scots' must have been composed in the year of Flodden (1513). The *Tunning* I cannot date, for the fact that the real Alianora Romyng was in trouble for excessive prices and small measures in 1525 does not much help us.

The most obvious characteristic of all the poems in this group is the so-called Skeltonic metre; 'so-called', for by some standards it is hardly a metre at all. The number of beats in the line varies from two ('Tell you I chill') to five ('To anger the Scots and Irish keterings with all') with a preference for three. The rhyme is hardly ever crossed and any given rhyme may be repeated as long as the resources of the language hold out. In other words there is neither metre nor rhyme scheme in the strict sense; the only constant characteristic is the fact of rhyming. Scholars have shown much learning in their attempts to find a source for this extraordinary kind of composition. Short lines with irregular rhyme have been found in medieval Latin verse, but they do not show the Skeltonic irregularity of rhythm. More recently attention has been drawn to the rhyming passages in later medieval Latin prose; and in an earlier chapter we have noticed something faintly like Skeltonics in such Scotch poems as *Cowkelbie Sow* and 'Lord Fergus' Gaist'. This is not the only affinity between Skelton and his Scotch contemporaries; his 'Lullay, Lullay' (not to be confused with the noble carol) and his 'Jolly Rutterkin' may be regarded as poor relations of the comic lyric about low life which we find in the Scotch anthologies. Skelton himself would rise from the grave to bespatter us with new Skeltonics if we suggested that he had learned his art from a Scotchman: but these affinities may suggest (they certainly do not prove) some common tradition whose documents are now lost but from which the lower types of early sixteenth-century poetry, both Scotch and English, have descended. But whatever view is finally taken it remains true that there is nothing really very like Skeltonics before Skelton, and that his practice alone gives them any importance. Hints and vague anticipations there may have been, but I suspect that he was the real inventor.

The problem about the source of Skeltonics sinks into insignificance beside the critical problem. A form whose only constant attribute is rhyme ought to be intolerable: it is indeed the form used by every clown scribbling on the wall in an inn yard. How then does Skelton please? It is, no doubt, true to say that he sometimes does not. Where the poem is bad on other grounds the Skeltonics make it worse. In the 'Ballad of the

Scottish King' the rodomontade of the non-combatant, the government scribbler's cheap valiancy, is beneath contempt, and qualifies the poet for the epithet 'beastly' far more than *Elinor Rumming*; and in the revised version the sinister hint that those who disliked the 'Ballad' must be no true friends of the king adds the last touch of degradation. Here the looseness of the form does not help matters: it aggravates the vulgarity. This can be seen by turning to the similar poem on 'The Doughty Duke of Albany' (1523) where the *Envoy*, by dint of its strict trimeter quatrains, is much more tolerable than the main body of the poem. Where thought grovels, form must be severe: satire that is merely abusive is most tolerable in stopped couplets. But, of course, there would be no problem if all Skelton's Skeltonic poems had been on this level. The real question is about *Elinor Rumming* and *Philip Sparrow*. I am not at all sure that we can find the answer, but we may at least eliminate one false trail. They certainly do not please by the poet's 'facility in rhyme' considered as virtuosity. On Skelton's terms any man can rhyme as long as he pleases.

In modern language the kind to which *Philip Sparrow* belongs may roughly be called the mock-heroic, though the term must here be stretched to cover the mock-religious as well. Requiem is sung for the pet bird. At the appropriate place in the poem, as in *Lycidas*, the mourner remembers that 'her sorrow is not dead' and asks

> But where unto shuld I
> Lenger morne or crye?

Solemn execration is pronounced on Gib our cat (mountain mantichores are to eat his brain) and on the whole nation of cats. She calls on the great moralists of antiquity to teach her how to moderate her passion. Thus, superficially, the humour is of the same kind as in the *Rape of the Lock*: much ado about nothing. But Pope's intention was ostensibly corrective; if Skelton had any such intention it got lost early in the process of composition. It may indeed be thought that something of the same kind happened to Pope, that he loved, if not Belinda, yet her toilet, and the tea-cups, and the 'shining altars of Japan', and would have been very little pleased with any 'reform of manners' which interfered with them. But if such love for the thing he mocks was one element in Pope's attitude, it is the whole of Skelton's. *Philip Sparrow* is our first great poem of childhood. The lady who is lamenting her bird may not really have been a child—Skelton's roguish reference to the beauties hidden beneath her kirtle (itself a medieval commonplace) may seem to suggest the reverse. But it is as a child she is imagined in the poem—a little girl to whom the bird's death is a tragedy and who, though well read in romances, finds Lydgate beyond her and has 'little skill in Ovid or Virgil'. We seem to hear her small reed-like voice throughout, and to move in a demure, dainty, luxurious, in-door world. Skelton is not (as Blake might have done) suggesting that such 'sorrows small' may be real tragedies from within; nor is he, in any hostile sense, ridiculing them. He is at once tender and mocking—like an affectionate bachelor uncle or even a grandfather. Of course, he is not consistently dramatic and by no means confines himself to things that the supposed speaker could really have said: a good deal of his own learning is allowed to creep in. The mood of the poem is too light to require strict consistency. It is indeed the lightest—the most like a bubble—of all the poems I know. It would break at a touch: but hold your breath, watch it, and it is almost perfect. The Skeltonics are essential to its perfection. Their prattling and hopping and their inconsequence, so bird-like and so childlike, are the best possible embodiment of the theme. We should not, I think, refuse to call this poem great; perfection in light poetry, perfect smallness, is among the rarest of literary achievements.

In the *Tunning of Elinor Rumming* the metre has a more obvious and, I think, less fruitful appropriateness to the subject. Skelton here lets himself loose on the humours of an inn presided over by a dirty old ale wife. Her customers are all women, confirmed drinkers, who mostly pay for their beer in kind—one brings a rabbit, another her shoes, another her husband's hood, one her wedding ring. We have noisome details about Elinor's methods of brewing, and there are foul words, foul breath, and foul sights in plenty. The merit of the thing lies in its speed: guests are arriving hotfoot, ordering, quarrelling, succumbing to the liquor, every moment. We get a vivid impression of riotous bustle, chatter, and crazy disorder. All is ugly, but all is alive. The poem has thus a good deal in common with *Peblis to the Play* or *Christis Kirk on the Green*: what it lacks is their melody and gaiety. The poet, and we, may laugh, but we hardly enter into the enjoyment of his 'sort of foul drabs'. It is here that the metre most fully justifies Mr. Graves's description of Skelton as 'helter-skelter John'. The shapeless volley of rhymes does really suggest the helter-skelter arrival of all these thirsty old trots. But there is much less invention in it than in *Philip Sparrow*. The technique is much more crudely related to the matter; disorder in life rendered by disorder in art. This is in poetry what 'programme music' is in music; the thing is legitimate, it works, but we cannot forget that the art has much better cards in its hand.

If I see these two poems at all correctly, we may now hazard a guess at the answer to our critical problem. The Skeltonic, which defies all the rules of art, pleases (on a certain class of subjects) because—and when—this helter-skelter artlessness symbolizes something in the theme. Childishness, dipsomania, and a bird are the themes on which we have found it successful. When it attempts to treat something fully human and adult —as in the Flodden poem—it fails; as it does also, to my mind, in 'The Duke of Albany' (1523) and the unpleasant 'Replicacioun' (1528). The other poems in which Skelton has used it most successfully are *Colin Clout* and *Why Come Ye Not to Court?* (1522).

All right minded readers start these two lampoons with a prejudice in favour of the poet: however he writes, the man who defies all but omnipotent government cannot be contemptible. But these poems have a real, and very curious, merit. I would describe it as anonymity. The technique, to be sure, is highly personal; but the effect produced is that of listening to the voice of the people itself. A vast muttering and growling of rumours fills our ears; 'Lay men say' . . . 'Men say' . . . 'the temporality say' . . . 'I tell you as men say' . . . 'they crye and they yelle' . . . 'I here the people talke' . . . 'What newes? What newes?' . . . 'What here ye of Lancashire?' . . . 'What here ye of the Lord Dacres?' . . . 'is Maister Meautis dede?' Thus to hand over responsibility to a vague *on dit* is no doubt a common trick of satirists: but thus repeated, thus with cumulative effect accompanying Skelton's almost endless denunciations, it acquires a strange and disquieting potency. It may be the truth that Wolsey needed to care for Skelton no more than Bishop Blougram for Gigadibs, and that the forgiveness for which the poet paid heavily in flattery was the forgiveness of tranquil contempt. But our imaginative experience in reading the poems ignores this possibility. In them Skelton has ceased to be a man and become a mob: we hear thousands of him murmuring and finally thundering at the gates of Hampton Court. And here once again the Skeltonics help him. Their shapeless garrulity, their lack of steady progression are (for this purpose) no defect. But he is very near the borders of art. He is saved by the skin of his teeth. No one wishes the poems longer, and a few more in the same vein would be intolerable.

But Skelton's abusive vein was not confined to Skeltonics. In the astonishing *Speke Parot* (1521) he had returned to rhyme royal. This poem exists in two widely divergent texts; in the Harleian MS. it is mainly an attack on Wolsey, in the early print, mainly an attack on Greek studies; both are put into the mouth of the Parrot and both are almost wholly unintelligible. The obscurity is doubtless denser now than it was in 1521, but it was there from the beginning and is certainly intentional. Modern scholars have laboured with great diligence, and not without success, to dissipate it, but a critical judgement on the poem cannot be made with any confidence; not that we have no literary experiences while we read, but that we have no assurance whether they are at all like those the poet intended to give us. The very first lines have for me their own whimsical charm.

> My name is Parot, a byrde of Paradyse
> By nature deuysed of a wondrous kynde,
> Deyntilye dyeted with dyuers delycat spyse
> Till Euphrates that flode dryueth me into Inde ...

His curiously carven cage, his mirror for him to 'toot in', the maidens strewing the cage with fresh flowers and saying 'Speak, parrot', the utter inconsequence (as it seems to us) of the statement 'In Poperynge grew paires when Parot was an egge'—all this delights us scarcely less than the voyage of the Owl and the Pussycat or the Hunting of the Snark. The same crazy sort of pleasure can be derived from lines like

> For Ierichoe and Ierseye shall mete together as sone
> As he to exployte the man out of the mone

or

> To brynge all the sea to a chirrystone pytte.

This raises in some minds the question whether we are reading the first of the nonsense poets, or whether Skelton is anticipating the moderns and deliberately launching poetry on 'the stream of consciousness'. I believe not. I fear the poem was not meant to be nonsense: it is nonsense to us because it is a cryptogram of which we have lost the key. Our pleasure in it may be almost wholly foreign to Skelton's purpose and to his actual achievement in 1521; almost, not quite, because unless his mind had been stocked with curious images, even the disorder into which they necessarily fall for us who know too little of the real links between them, would not affect us as it does. His modern admirers are thus really in touch with a certain level of Skelton's mind, but probably not of his art, when they enjoy *Speke Parot*.

In the *Garland of Laurel* (1523) Skelton returns, as far as the main body of the poem is concerned, to the broad highway of medieval poetry. The occasion of the poem was a desire to compliment the Countess of Surrey and certain other ladies: its form, stanzaic allegory: its characters, Skelton as dreamer, Pallas, Fame, Gower, Chaucer, and Lydgate. The catalogue of 'laureate' poets is enlivened by a refrain about Bacchus which has a hearty ring, but the only other good passage (that where Daphne, though already tree, quivers at Apollo's touch) is from Ovid. All that is of value in this production is contained in the seven lyric addresses to ladies which are inserted at the end. Only one of these ('Gertrude Statham') is exactly Skeltonic, though 'Margaret Hussey' comes near to being so. 'Jane Blennerhasset' and 'Isabel Pennell' have the short, irregular lines, but there is in both a real rhyme-scheme. 'Margery Wentworth', 'Margaret Tylney', and 'Isabel Knight' are in stanzas. Some of these are very good indeed: what astonishes one is the simplicity of the resources from which the effect has been produced. In 'Margery Wentworth', which is twenty lines long, the same four lines are thrice repeated. Of the eight lines which remain to be filled up by a fresh effort of imagination, one is wasted (and in so tiny a poem) on rubble like 'Plainly I cannot glose'. Yet the thing succeeds—apparently by talking about flowers and sounding kind. 'Isabel Pennell' captures us at once by the opening lines, which sound as if the 'baby' (whether she was really an infant matters nothing) had been shown to him that moment for the first time and the song had burst out *ex tempore*. After that, the flowers, the April shower, the bird, and

'star of the morrow gray' (only slightly improved by the fact
that *morrow* is now an archaism) do the rest. 'Margaret Hussey'
lives only by the opening quatrain: just as that very different
lyric 'Mannerly Margery Milk and Ale' (which Cornish set)
lives almost entirely on the line which makes its title.

The tenderness, though not the playfulness, of these little
pieces is found also in 'Now sing we', and also, with much more
elaborate art, in the fine devotional lyric 'Woefully Arrayed'.
If this is by Skelton it is the only piece in which he does not
appear to be artless.

It may naturally be asked whether this artlessness in Skelton
is real or apparent: and, if apparent, whether it is not the highest
art. I myself think that it is real. The result is good only when he
is either playful or violently abusive, when the shaping power
which we ordinarily demand of a poet is either admittedly on
holiday or may be supposed to be suspended by rage. In either
of these two veins, but especially in the playful, his lack of all
real control and development is suitable to the work in hand.
In *Philip Sparrow* or 'Margery Wentworth' he 'prattles out of
fashion' but that is just what is required. We are disarmed; we
feel that to criticize such poetry is like trying to make a child
discontented with a toy which Skelton has given it. That is one
of the paradoxes of Skelton: in speaking of his own work he is
arrogant (though perhaps even then with a twinkle in his eye),
but the work itself, at its best, dances round or through our
critical defences by its extreme unpretentiousness—an unpretentiousness quite without parallel in our literature. But I think
there is more nature than art in this happy result. Skelton does
not know the peculiar powers and limitations of his own manner, and does not reserve it, as an artist would have done, for
treating immature or disorganized states of consciousness. When
he happens to apply it to such states, we may get delightful
poetry: when to others, verbiage. There is no building in his
work, no planning, no reason why any piece should stop just
where it does (sometimes his repeated *envoys* make us wonder if
it is going to stop at all), and no kind of assurance that any of
his poems is exactly the poem he intended to write. Hence his
intimacy. He is always in undress. Hence his charm, the charm
of the really gifted amateur (a very different person from the
hard working inferior artist). I am not unaware that some
modern poets would put Skelton higher than this. But I think

that when they do so they are being poets, not critics. The things that Mr. Graves gets out of Skelton's work are much better than anything that Skelton put in. That is what we should expect: achievement has a finality about it, where the unfinished work of a rich, fanciful mind, full of possibilities just because it is unfinished, may be the strongest stimulant to the reader when that reader is a true poet. Mr. Graves, Mr. Auden, and others receive from Skelton principally what they give and in their life, if not alone, yet eminently, does Skelton live. Yet no student of the early sixteenth century comes away from Skelton uncheered. He has no real predecessors and no important disciples; he stands out of the streamy historical process, an unmistakable individual, a man we have met.

Whatever Skelton's limitations may be, our respect for him will be increased when we turn to the minor comic and satirical poets of his age. The anonymous *Cock Lorell's Boat*, which may belong to the first decade of the century, survives only in a fragment. What we have begins with the embarkation of a crew of choice knaves under Cock Lorell, referred to in 1610 as 'the most notorious knave that ever lived'. A tale told by a pardoner has gleams of humour and the appearance of 'Slingthrifty Fleshmonger' encourages us with the promise of at least some good names: this promise, however, is not kept. The greater part of the work is mere catalogue and the rhyme scheme with which it opens (a a b c c b) is soon forgotten and replaced by couplets. It can hardly be said to have metre and I cannot find the 'spirit' and 'humour' for which one of its editors praised it. The Protestant pamphlet *Read me and be not Wroth*, printed in Strasbourg, 1528, is perhaps a little worse in so far as its attempts to set off serious polemical matter with an appearance of mirth are more pitiable than the *Boat's* simple buffoonery. Thus a song will begin 'In the ioyfull moneth of ioly June' only to continue

> Fyrst to begynne at the spretualtie
> Whose lyvynge shulde be example of grace.

When the sugar coating is as thin as this, we feel that we should get on better without it. Another Protestant satire which dates from this period is the pseudo-Chaucerian *Pilgrim's Tale*. The part in rhyme royal (ll. 449–550) is wholly unmetrical: but the couplets furnish the nearest parallel we have to the rhythm of Spenser's *Februarie* eclogue and may have been its model. Robert Copland's *High Way to the Spyttall House* (1536) in couplets that stagger between four and five beats is a little more interesting. It is based on a French prose original, *Le Chemin de l'Ospital* by Robert de Balzac: but such merits as it has owe more to Copland than to him. The author feigns that on a night when 'it had snowen and frozen verie strong' he took shelter in the porch of a hospital (possibly St. Bartholomew's) and learned a great deal from the porter about beggars and their impostures. There is some real humour in the lines

> I saw the beggar pull out xi pens
> sayeing to his felowes 'Se what here is!
> Many a knave have I called Mayster for this,'

but as the poem proceeds, the fatal tendency to catalogue takes possession of it. The language is, however, redeemed from dull-ness by its slangy vitality. Jail-birds are 'nightingales of New-gate'; hanged men are 'buryed aloft in the ayre': beggars who insist on wheaten bread, though bread of any sort is a minor element in their diet, are said to want 'Whyte thread to sewe good ale'. There is also a rich sprinkling of cant or thieves' English, especially in lines 900 to 971. The whole poem would have been a world to George Borrow. *Jyl of Braintfords Testa-ment*, also by Robert Copland, has a promising theme. Jyl is making her will and leaving to several classes of people that same airy legacy which the goodman left the friar in Chaucer: for example to him

> that goeth to a fray at the begynnyng
> And to a good meal at the latter endyng.

The story of Jyl herself is merely a frame for these types, of which it was easy to extend the list almost endlessly: the dog-gerel metre and mean knowingness of the one I have quoted is a fair specimen. The main interest of the *Testament*, as of all these pieces, is that it shows the roots (roots may be excused for being grubby) out of which grew the lower elements of comedy in More's prose and, later, in the dramatists.

Coverdale's *Goostly Psalmes and Spirituall Songs* (before 1539) is on the border line between the Late Medieval or the Drab. It is nearly regular in metre; perhaps because Coverdale knows what he would be at, but perhaps only because he sticks mainly to octosyllables and they had never been so completely ruined as the longer line. In other respects he is prosaic and of no literary importance. A more interesting transitional poet is John Heywood (1497–1578). Ignoring his dramatic works, which are reserved for another hand, we can distinguish two distinct strains in Heywood's verse. At times he is, quite unmistakably, a Drab Age poet;

> The virtue of her looks
> Excels the precious stone;
> Ye need none other books
> To read or look upon.

All the marks of good Drab are there, the regularity, the short lines, the simple diction, the quietness. On the other hand, he can write:

> Beggars should be no choosers: but yet they will.
> Who can bring a beggar from choice to beg still?

It might have come from almost any poet dealt with in this chapter. And the interesting thing is that Heywood's work does not appear to have begun by being Late Medieval and then to have become Drab in obedience to the general movement of the age. On the contrary, my first example comes from a 'Description of a Most Noble Lady' probably written in 1534. We are thus led to conclude that Heywood understood regular syllabic scansion from a very early period in his career but continued to the end to prefer the old shambling line for comic and satiric poetry—that is, for the great part of his work. And this incidentally gives some support to the belief, suggested above, that the Late Medieval line is never, or seldom, an unsuccessful attempt at a decasyllable. It is not on that account better; it is only bad for different reasons.

The Drab Age poet in Heywood is represented by a small and not very important body of poems. The 'Description', already quoted, has a curious metrical pattern; two stanzas in trimeters to one of eights and sixes, as it were in triads, all through.[1] The clumsiness so common in Drab appears in a line like 'Whose face yours all blank shall'. The 'Ballad against Slander and Detraction' is equally regular and as wooden and gnomic as any minor Tottelian could desire. The *Ballad* on the marriage of Philip and 'bloody' Mary, with its slight irregularities, its symbolic

---

[1] Tottel's text of this poem (No. 199 in Rollins's edition) corrupts it into normal metre and omits some lines.

beasts, and its alliterations, reads like a very feeble attempt to imitate Dunbar.

His more characteristic output consists of the *Dialogue containing the Number of Proverbs* (1546), the various 'Hundreds' of *Epigrams* and *Epigrams upon Proverbs* issued in 1555, 1556, and 1560, and *The Spider and the Fly* (1556). The *Dialogue* (on marriage) is merely a peg on which to hang proverbs. The *Epigrams upon Proverbs* consisted of proverbs either combated, as in the quotation about beggars above, or pointed with a satirical application to some imaginary hearer. The *Epigrams* may be almost anything, fables, funny stories, cautionary tales, or maxims. All these works use chiefly the cacophonous, irregular couplet, though we sometimes find octosyllabics or trimeters. The anecdotes are sometimes good anecdotes and may have come from More's lips in conversation; one would like to think that this was the truth behind Gabriel Harvey's and Anthony Wood's belief that More had assisted Heywood. But it is not every man who can carry a *bon mot*. Heywood's verse does not help the tales; and where verse does not do good it does harm. In general these vast collections are filled up with stuff that might just win a smile if it were rhymed *ex tempore* in a merry hour when beards wagged all: served cold in print, and in such quantity, they are (at least to my taste) unendurable. Their value to those interested in the history of the proverb will, however, long keep them from oblivion.

The Spider and the Fly, in rhyme royal, was already in its own century condemned for obscurity. 'Neither he himself that made it', says Harrison, 'neither anie one that readeth it can reach vnto the meaning thereof.' In recent years it has attracted the attention, not unfavourable, of more than one scholar. We must be especially thankful to those who by abstracts and judicious quotation have enabled us to see that the plot is not without spirit. But what abstracts necessarily leave out is the actual quality of the writing, the shambling rhythms (though you can find here and there a whole stanza that scans) and the unrelieved dullness of the language. Against execution like this all beauties of conception contend in vain; to ask us to admire them is like asking us to admire the fine features of a face covered with a loathsome disease of the skin. Though Heywood the poet cannot be recommended, what we know of the man deserves respect, and he made on his death-bed (then long an exile for his religion) a better joke than he ever put in a book. His kindly old confessor (*bonus quidam sacerdos*) answered, when he deplored his sins, that the flesh is frail, *carnem esse fragilem*, and again and again *carnem esse fragilem*, till at last 'Marry, Father,' said the old man, 'it will go hard but you shall prove that God should a made me a fish' (*Deum arguere videris quod me non fecerit piscem*). That is Heywood's best title to fame; that, and the refrain (if he made it)

> All a green willow, willow,
> All a green willow is my garland.

II

The reader has already been warned that our 'periods' do not apply to the history of prose so clearly as to that of verse: if for no other reason, because the staggering metre which clearly marks out the Late Medieval work in the one art naturally does not occur in the other. In this section I shall mention a few works in prose which are medieval by almost any standard: but the list could easily have been made longer by including authors whom I have in fact reserved for a later chapter.

Vernacular prose history at this period is just beginning to branch off from the records of the city of London. The folio of 1502 under its traditional name of 'Arnold's Chronicle' has probably led many a young student on a wild goose chase which he would have been spared had he known the real title: *The Names of the Baylifs Custos Mairs and Sherefs of the Cite of London*. The volume can hardly be classified as a literary text. A little history is worked into its interstices, but it is in fact a miscellany containing lists of city officers, the articles of 'the charter and liberties' of London, the 'ordinaunce for the assise and weight of bred', various forms of oaths, an article on 'the lawes and beleve of the Sarasyns', some recipes, and amidst all this, like a gold ring found lying in an old drawer full of odds and ends, the text of the 'Nut Brown Maid'.

In Fabyan's *Cronycle* (1516) we still find what seems to us a disproportionate attention to the city offices and to city ceremonials, especially as Fabyan (who was an alderman) draws nearer to his own age, but the greater part of the book consists of genuine chronicle. It well illustrates the different fates of prose and verse at the time. It has poetical prologues which might be the work of an infant, but its prose can be read, at least for an hour or so, with pleasure. It is below Pitscottie and perhaps about as good as Major. Here is a specimen on the character of Henry V:

> Thys man before the deth of hys father applyed hym vnto all vyce and insolency and drewe vnto hym all riottours and wyldly dysposed persones. But after he was admytted to the rule of the lande, anon and sodainly he became a new man and tourned all that rage and wyldnes into sobernes and sadnes and the vyce into constant vertue. And for he would continewe the vertue and not to be reduced therevnto by the famylyarite of his olde nyse company, he therefore after rewardes to them gyuen charged them vpon payne of theyr lyues that none of them were so hardy to come wythin x myle of such place as he were lodged.

'To be reduced therevnto' does not quite work, but it is on the whole a tolerable way of writing. As an historian Fabyan is not quite uncritical. He usually tells us his authorities—'the englysshe cronycle', 'Beda', 'Policronyca', 'Vincent Historiall', 'another wryter called John Froysarde'. He rejects Arthur's continental victories because neither French nor Latin historians make any mention of them. But he begins, as was then the custom, with Brut and does not reach Hengest till chapter 83. His philosophy of history is a simple Providentialism which leaves him completely agnostic about second causes; the Norman Conquest happened because 'God of his vnknowen iudgementes to man and by his hygh and hyd counsayle wolde suffer this duke to conquer so noble a lande'. It is a method which saves minor historians from writing a great deal of nonsense and compels them to get on with the story.

Comic prose is represented by two works of very different merit, the *Hundred Merry Tales* of 1526 and the *Howleglass* whose date has been disputed. The latter, a version of the German *Eulenspiegel* (which in 1567 attained the dignity of a Latin rendering, *Noctuae Speculum*) is a collection of practical jokes. The hero is hardly a character and it is a little over-solemn to inquire into his motives. The author's motive is to make readers laugh and the hero is his obedient puppet. The jokes are hoaxes and over-reachings, usually coprophilous and sometimes macabre, for Tyll Howleglass continues to provide (or solicit) laughter even on his bier and in his coffin. Hence a modern reader might even find the book sinister. But there was nothing sinister in the author's intention, and it is pleasant to find that some of Howle-glass's victims—such as the Bishop of Bremen, though it cost him thirty 'gildens'—thoroughly appreciate the joke against them-selves. No moral question is involved in our liking or loathing for this book: it depends on how strong a man's stomach is and how long he can go on enjoying stories whose point is always per-fectly visible four or five hundred words ahead. My own judge-ment would be that whatever you can get from *Howleglass* you can get better from Deloney. But it was popular in its day.

With the *Hundred Merry Tales* we enter a different world. It smells of Thomas More's circle with which, of course, John Rastell its printer was connected. One of its stories occurs also in Heywood who has been suggested as a possible author. It is indeed far better than any of Heywood's known works, but that superior-ity might be sufficiently accounted for by the difference between bad verse and a good plain prose. It is not original save as a good anthology is original: most of its tales can be found elsewhere. One, 'The Dumb Wife', we met in the previous chapter. But in any story which one happens not to have read before, the point comes like a thunderclap, and even such a drudge as a literary historian, reading on a hard chair in a library, will probably laugh aloud. The manner is just what it should be: imperturb-ably grave and droll with feigned simplicity. A moral is ap-pended to each story and may be the funniest part of all. A woman is told that a cuckold's hat is a good charm against some disease that is attacking the pigs; her efforts to borrow one from her neighbours naturally lead to various rebuffs; she resolves to have one of her own by next year and thus be out of her gossips' 'danger' (as we should say 'be under no obligation to any one'). Moral: 'it is more wysdome for a man to trust more to his owne store than to his neyghbours gentylnes.'

But no prose writer of that period has deserved nearly so well of posterity as Sir John Bourchier, Lord Berners;[1] at least in one of his literary capacities, for he is two-sided. All of his work that is still read with delight shows him as the last of the great medieval translators. The originals which he chooses are chival-

---

[1] b. *c.* 1469. Perhaps at Balliol College. Succeeded his grandfather as Lord Berners, 1474. Knighted, 1477. Involved in plot to place Richmond on the throne: flies to Brittany. In service of Henry VII, 1492. Serves in suppression of Cornish rebellion, 1497. In the king's train to Calais, 1513. Chancellor of the Exchequer, 1516. On diplomatic mission to Spain, 1518. Present at the Field of the Cloth of Gold. Becomes Deputy of Calais, 1520. Ob. 1533.

rous romance and chivalrous chronicle and his professed motives are the characteristically medieval ones, to eschew 'ydelnesse' which is 'the moder of all vices' and lest the 'chyvalrous feates and marciall prowesses' of 'tymes past' should be 'had clene out of remembraunce'. He has a power, not inferior to Malory's, of transmitting the valiant and gentle old French prose into English without loss. His apology for not (thank Heaven) presuming to 'reduce' it into 'fresshe ornate polysshed Englysshe' because he lacks 'the facondyous arte of rethoryke' is equally medieval. But that is not the whole story. In his prefaces he attempts the facundious art. Their chief ornament is the multiplication of synonyms: thus in the preface to Froissart he recommends histories because they 'shewe, open, manifest and declare to the reader by example of olde antiquite what we should enquere, desire, and followe, and also what we should eschewe, auoyde, and vtterly flee'. If this love of rhetoric had found expression only in his prefaces it would almost be forgotten now. But it is the bright day brings forth the adder. Towards the end of his life and in what modern taste must regard as an evil hour, his nephew Sir Francis Bryan put into his hands Bertaut's 1531 French version of Antonio de Guevara's *Libro del Emperador Marco Aurelio* with a request that he would translate it. The Spanish original was, by our standards, an impudent forgery, purporting to be a contemporary life of the great emperor discovered in Cosimo de Medici's library: the real *Meditations* being then, and till 1558, safely unknown. The interest turned on the morality, the countless 'ensaumples', and the rhetorical style. Guevara said he had sweated to collect 'sentences' (that is *sententiæ*, gnomes) and also to place words and connect syllables. He combined a humanistic faith in the ethical superiority of the ancients with an optimistic belief that we had improved on them in style: 'so hygh sentences are not founde at this present tyme nor so hygh a style they of tyme past neuer atteyned vnto'. Berners was ready to oblige Bryan; he liked the 'high and sweete style'. His translation ran into fifteen editions within the century and must share with North's later version the responsibility of introducing a very questionable model into English literature. The extent and quality of its influence have been matters of controversy. Landmann's theory that Guevara is the origin of euphuism has been severely, and I think rightly, criticized. It is more the origin of *Euphues*—that is, not of Lyly's language but of the floods of facile moralizing. The love of antithesis is common to euphuism and Guevara, but also to many other styles, Hebrew, Latin, and Anglo-Saxon. Full-blown euphuism I take to be a genuinely English variation of 'Renaissance' rhetoric: but more of this in a later chapter. Perhaps Marco Aurelio's healthiest offspring in English is the elder Mr. Shandy.

Berners's excursion into this rhetorical territory should probably not be regarded either as senile decay or as 'movement with the times'. He had always had his own modest ambitions in that direction: fortunately he liked other things as well. We know that he left at his death a library of eighty books. He was probably omnivorous, and his taste was excellent as long as he did not think about it. To the present day one meets men, great readers, who write admirably until the fatal moment when they remember that they are writing.

The chronology of his works is obscure and does not perhaps matter very much. Of the two romances which he translated, *Arthur of Little Britain* is not among the best of its kind. Its chivalry is mainly an affair of heraldry and etiquette: there is little real fineness of feeling. The pleasure depends on the pictures offered to the imagination. These often fail because marvels are multiplied till we grow weary, and in this kind of fiction, more than in any other, the half is greater than the whole. But there is a real impressiveness in the voice that cries through the enchanted castle of Porte Noyr, 'Behold, now the ende': and a much more spiritual magic in the occult sympathy whereby when the image of Florence in the garden leans forward and lays a chaplet on Arthur's head, the real lady, leagues away in her father's palace, begins, she knows not why, to love. The achievement of this adventure is all the better because it has been foretold:

And so on a fayre grene benche she sette her doune betwene the bysshop and Maister Steven and so passed the tyme with many goodli sportes. And than it began to waxe late and the evenynge was very clere and the sterres shone full bryght. Than Maister Steven dyd beholde them a grete space and at the laste he said, Madame, for certayne I know by the course of the planettes that there is a Knyght comynge, &c.

But there are no characters and we have a feeling that the author has taken his work either too seriously or else not seriously enough. In a grave romance there should be more restraint; or conversely, such reckless use of all the ingredients needed a touch

of Boiardo's humour. *Huon of Bordeux* is on a much higher level.
We do not feel that it is simply being made up out of the author's
head. It has those roots in legend and folk-lore without which it
is hard for romance to have the necessary solidity. Oberon is a
noble invention. He is, in reality, a good being but only Huon's
courtesy reveals the fact: worldly wisdom, in the person of
Gerames, had warned him against the 'crokyd shuldryd' dwarf
with the 'aungelyke vysage' in the fifteen leagues' forest by
Babylon. Huon's faith is rewarded by Oberon's favour and ines-
timable gifts: but Huon, light-minded and full of young blood,
disobeys every command laid upon him by his elven patron. The
execution here is faulty: Huon's disobediences are crowded too
closely together and instead of feeling pity for human frailty we
lose patience. So in the end does Oberon. Huon lies bound and
starving in the Isle Noysaunt and the fairy is now his enemy;
only relenting when one of his own elven knights, Malabrun,
offers to suffer Oberon's wrath in his stead and saves him in the
form of a beast. Most wisely this is not elaborated into full-blown
allegory: you must not say that Oberon 'is' God the Father,
Malabrun Christ, and Huon *humanum genus*. It haunts the recesses
of the story as a mere suggestion and makes the story more
serious—thus incidentally enabling it at pleasure to be genuinely
comic. Our own age is, almost beyond example, hostile to
romance: and we may have to wait long before 'The circular
turn shall have ripened alteration' so far that men can
enjoy *Huon* again. Even now there are things in both romances
that must give pleasure. One is the phrasing: the swamp
so deep that it seemed to go down to 'the abysme and
swalowe of the earth'; in the castle of Porte Noyr the 'halles of
vehement adventures'; an army on march whose 'noise seemed
to be a new world'; or Huon's resolution that on a certain adventure 'None shall go with me but myself and Jesu Christ'. Another
is that admirable blend of fantasy in large things with homely and
realistic detail in small ones, which produces such whimsically
convincing effects. Thus in the *Arthur* when a magic whirlwind
falls upon the pavilions of a great king's camp 'there was blowen
up into the ayre streamers, towels, and other cloths so high that
the sight of them was clean lost'; in *Huon* after we have been
driven on the Isle of Adamant and crashed through the thick
fringe of rotted shipping by which its coast is of course surrounded, we descend into a cave and find 'ten fayre yonge men

all of the Fayry' engaged in baking bread, and then 'they all ceased of their laboure and busyness and beheld Huon *and rubbed off the paste and meal off their hands and fingers*'. It is an art that almost every medieval romancer knew but it was soon to be lost for many a year.

If Berners had translated *Huon* alone, he would have stood immediately below Malory: the two volumes of his Froissart (1524 and 1525) make him Malory's equal. His translation, if scrutinized closely, will not, indeed, be found to be perfect. He sometimes misunderstands and sometimes makes injudicious abridgements. But taken as a whole it fits the original like a glove. Froissart shares with much old French prose the great virtues of being quite effortless and unflagging. It is the sort of writing which, as W. P. Ker said, is 'free from any anxiety or curiosity about rules of good taste because it had good taste to begin with'. The temptation is to describe it negatively, to say that it is never clumsy, never affected, never strident, and thus to produce the very false impression that it must be like the style of Defoe. In reality it has none of Defoe's workday quality. Its smoothness resembles his as little as the smoothness of springy turf resembles that of a well-laid wooden floor. It is half-way to poetry: full of the author's relish for bright colours, his never-wearying admiration for noble deeds, and his spontaneous tenderness. It is, in one sense, like conversation; but like a conversation in which both tears and smiles may occur and in which there is no check on enthusiasm because it is taken for granted that we all understand one another and that no boorish persons are present. It is this enthusiasm which gives to the book as a whole, however grave or painful the matter may sometimes be, its quality of gaiety and youthfulness.

The world which Froissart presents is in many ways a shocking one. In the twenties when we all cherished pacific hopes, his outlook might have been condemned as a crying example of that 'false glamour' which had too long concealed, and yet not quite concealed, the real miseries of war. Now, when we have discovered that the scheme of 'outlawing war' has made war more like an outlaw without making it less frequent and that to banish the knight does not alleviate the suffering of the peasant, we may be disposed to give Froissart a humbler hearing. He does not conceal the atrocities which, then as now, occurred; the rape of the nuns at Origny Saint Benoiste, the Scotch massacre at

F

Durham, the English soldiers running amuck at Caen, and the Christian barbarities against the Turks at Comette. On the English murder of their prisoners at Aljubarrota his comment is surprisingly, even comically, cold-blooded: 'Lo, beholde the great yuell aduenture that fell thate Saturday, for they slewe as many good prisoners as wolde well have been worthe, one with another, foure hundred thousande frankes.' But his disapprovals are not always so strictly economic. Scott's Claverhouse was not quite truthful when he represented Froissart as wholly indifferent to the fate of harmless and ungentle civilians. 'God haue mercy on their soules, for I trowe they were martyrs.' But such things are not his main concern.

His theme is chivalry—the life of the romances reproduced as nearly as possible in the real world—chivalry in all its hardness, all its softness, and all its fantasticality. The hardness has perhaps never been better expressed than in the last words of the Douglas at Otterburn, when Sir John Sinclair 'demaunded of the erle how he dyd. Right yuell, cosyn, quoth the erle, but thanked be God there hath been but a fewe of myne auncytours that hath dyed in their beddes.' The softer side, the honour of ladies, is a recurrent accompaniment to the story, like the sound of a brook beside a road. 'Howsoeuer they blamed or counsailed hym, the gentle knyght wolde neuer chaunge his purpose but sayd he hadde but one dethe to dye, the whiche was in the wyll of God: and also sayd that all knyghts ought to ayd to their powers all ladyes and damosels chased out of theyr owne countreys.' The garrison in a castle held against the Scots by Sir William Montague were so fortunate as to have with them the Countess of Salisbury, the sagest and fairest lady of all England 'for by the regarde of such a lady and by her swete comforting a man ought to be worthe two men at nede'. But ladies were not always content only to inspire valiant feats: real life drew closer to the romances than we usually think, and a Britomart or Bradamante had her counterpart at the sea fight off Guernsey when 'the countesse that day was worth a man; she had the harte of a lyon and had in her hande a sharp glayue wherewith she fought feersly'. As for the fantastical, Cyrano himself could not have overgone the 'young bachelars' in the English army who 'had eche of them one of their eyen closed with a peace of silk. It was sayd how they had made a vowe among the ladyes of their countrey that they wolde nat se but with one eye tyll they had done some dedes of armes in Fraunce.'

These bachelors were young, and I have already mentioned youthfulness as a characteristic of Froissart and Froissart's world. We misread all medieval romance and chronicle if we miss this quality. Whatever age the knights and ladies may actually be, they all behave as if, like Sidney's shepherd boy, 'they should never be old'. The folly, the pathos, and the generosity of youth meet us everywhere: in the 'damoselles freshly apparayled, redy to have daunced if they might haue leue'; in the crazy wager ('youthe and lybertie of corage made them to do it') which sent the French king and the Duke of Touraine riding off a hundred and fifty leagues from Montpellier to Paris; above all in the gay absurdity whereby Ernaulton of Spain, on a frosty day, carried a live and loaded donkey on his back upstairs into hall. Modern historians may trace all these wars to grey, impersonal causes, political or economic. They may thus find truth, but surely not the whole truth; the other half is known to Froissart, as it were, from within—'the Kyng was as than but in the floure of his youth, desyring nothyng so moche as to haue dedes of armes'. This freshness is not even confined to love and war. It leaps out in Froissart's conversation with the squire about the enchantment of Sir Peter of Bearn, which came by killing a bear 'and it might be so that this bere was before some knight chasyng in the forest of Bisquay and peraduenture displeased in that time some god or goddes, whereby he was transformed vnto a bere to do there his penaunce, as aunciently Acteon was chaunged vnto an hart. Acteon, quod the squyer, I pray you shewe me that storie. I wolde fayne here it.' Note the unspoiled appetite for myth; there was no humanist meddler to tell them that Acteon was 'classical'.

While Froissart's temper is thus youthful, his art is mature. The temper can be found again in later writers: indeed there is no better comment on his attitude to war than Montaigne's praise of a soldier's life (III. xiii) which delights him by its variety, its free and unceremonious conversation, and the crowd of 'brisk, young, and noble men' which it brings together. But the art died. In French medieval romance and chronicle there is a perfect adaptation of means to ends and a perfect understanding between the author and those for whom he wrote, which we hardly find again. In later ages prose as plain as this tends to be a little jejune, and prose as tender and sappy as this tends to be rhetorical. It was the misfortune of medieval England to have achieved no original work of this kind; our debt to Berners and Malory (and let us add, to Caxton, who improved Malory) is all the greater. They made these things ours just in time. To have snatched these ripe fruits of the Middle Ages when the Middle Ages were already over may even have carried a certain advantage with it. They were still fresh in men's minds at a moment when new forms and new modes of sentiment might otherwise have swept us off our feet; their popularity may have helped to save us from a too complete break with the past. As it was, we started going back to the Middle Ages almost before we had emerged from them. Hence in English literature it is hard to distinguish the last medieval writers from the earliest medievalists, the survival from the revival. Already in Malory there are elements of medievalism: and in Spenser there are still elements really medieval. The humanist repudiation was short-lived. This slowness to abandon, or readiness to reinstate, the old traditions of courtesy and honour may partly explain the speed and success with which the new aristocracy 'gentled their condition'.

BOOK II

'Drab'

I

DRAB AGE PROSE—RELIGIOUS CONTROVERSY AND TRANSLATION

I

IN England, as elsewhere, the Reformation was a process that occurred on three planes: firstly in the thought and conscience of the individual, secondly in the intertangled realms of ecclesiastical and political activity, and thirdly on the printed page. All are connected but only the third is our direct concern. We are to consider what men wrote, and our judgement on it must, of course, attempt to be literary, not theological. This does not mean that we are to confine ourselves rigidly to questions of style. Though we must not judge our authors' doctrine as doctrine, we must certainly attempt to disengage the spirit and temper of their writings to see what particular insights or insensibilities went with the varying beliefs, what kinds of sentiment and imagination they unwittingly encouraged. It will not be easy to do so without giving offence: I ask my readers to believe that I have at least intended to be impartial. Unfortunately the very names we have to use in describing this controversy are themselves controversial. To call the one party Catholics implicitly grants their claim; to call them Roman Catholics implicitly denies it. I shall therefore call them Papists: the word, I believe, is not now used dyslogistically except in Ulster, and it is certainly not so intended here. 'Reformation' is a term equally ambiguous. Reform of the Church, in some sense or other, was desired by innumerable laymen and many clergy of all parties. The controversy was fought about 'Reformation' in a different, almost a technical sense: about certain changes in doctrine and order. To call these changes 'reformation' again begs the question: but the word is now so deeply entrenched in historical usage that I shall continue to employ it—as a mere label, intending no *petitio*.

Thus no man could be, in one sense, more of a 'reformer' than Dean Colet (1467?–1519), more given to exposing ecclesiastical abuses and to demanding amendment. His celebrated sermon to Convocation in 1511 lashes the vices of the clergy as fiercely as any Protestant could desire. But he has no wish for any alteration in the doctrine or structure of the Church. 'The waye whereby the churche may be reformed into better facion' (I quote from the almost contemporary translation of the sermon) 'is not for to make newe lawis For there be lawes many inowe.' Colet is, in fact, a declamatory moralist. By calling him declamatory I do not at all mean that he is insincere, but that his methods are those of the declamation; repetition, hyperbole, and a liberal use of emotional adjectives. The morality he wishes to enforce is harsh and ascetic. He maintains the very questionable though popular belief that all the evil in man arises from his animal nature—'omne malum homini ei suboritur ex inferiori sua parte quae animal et hominis bestia potest vocitari' (*Enarratio in Ep. ad Romanos*, vii). In his lectures on First Corinthians he strongly reaffirms the doctrine that marriage is merely a concession to human infirmity—'infirmitas ab indulgenti Deo exegit nuptias' (*Enarratio in Ep. I ad Corinthios*, vii). Everyone should wish to be able to do without it. It is true that if we all did, the human race would cease to live on this earth and survive only in heaven: but what consummation is more devoutly to be wished, *quis aut magis opportunus aut magis optatus finis*? In the meantime, marriage has to be tolerated, but 'no step further downward is allowed' (*ultra quem gradum descensus non conceditur*), as though lechery were not a different kind of thing from marriage but simply a further move in the same direction. This is not a new doctrine but a return to earlier severity. And there is likewise, I suggest, no real novelty in Colet's communism. The crucial passage comes in the fourth chapter of his *Expositio* (not to be confused with his *Enarratio*) on *Romans* where we are told that the law of corrupt or fallen nature first introduced *meum* and *tuum*: unspoiled Nature would have all things in common. Modern readers are apt to misunderstand this if they forget that medieval thought had inherited from both the Bible and the Stoics a sharp contrast between a lost, prehistoric state of innocence and the world as we actually know it, and that things like slavery and private property were normally attributed to the latter. This did not usually imply a belief that they could or should be abolished as the world now is. Though contrary to pure Nature, they have a sort of justification, as necessities, or even as punishments, for the nature man now has. Though they can, in some degree, be judged by the standard of perfection with which they are contrasted, there is no direct route back to Eden. The doctrine has been abundantly illustrated by A. J. Carlyle and should be remembered when we come to consider the *Utopia*. Colet was no communist. He is very ready to declaim against avarice but he has no notion of encouraging a revolution.

The truth is that Colet is a Platonist at heart and has really little interest in the temporal and mutable world below the moon. The sooner it comes to an end the better. Till then it is his business to thunder against it from the platform of his perfectionism, without perhaps considering very carefully how all his lessons are to be applied in detail. This helps to explain what might otherwise seem a not very creditable episode in his career. On Good Friday 1513, at the outset of the war with France, he preached a sermon before the king which appears to have come within measurable distance of what we now call 'pacifism'. He was immediately summoned to Greenwich, had a conversation with Henry in the garden, came away, and shortly afterwards preached a sermon so different that it is said to have filled all who heard it with martial ardour. But we need not assume that he had been either bought, or flattered, or frightened into subservience. A cloistered perfectionist, who happens to be also a rhetorician, often says, not exactly more than he means, but more than he understands. He leaves out the reservations: he has really no idea of the crudely literal applications which will be made. He forgets that his audience are much less serious than he about the fallen and perishable and makeshift character of all earthly institutions alike, and much more serious than he about the difference between one war and another or one king and another.

Colet has two other characters besides that of the moralist; he has an important place in the history of Biblical studies and he is the most virulent of the humanists. In the first capacity he is one of those who helped to banish the old allegorical methods of interpretation, at least as regards the New Testament, and made some attempt to see the Pauline epistles in their real historical setting. In the *Epistolae ad Radulphum* he himself allegorizes freely on the opening chapters of *Genesis*, as St. Augustine had done before him, but he is seeking a scientific or philosophical, rather than a moral or spiritual sense. It is one among many attempts made in this century to reconcile the Mosaic account of the creation with the cosmological ideas of the day. In this difference between Colet's treatment of St. Paul and his treatment of *Genesis* there is inherent the recognition that the Bible contains books very different in kind. It was not exactly new— St. Jerome had allowed what we should now call the 'mythical' element in *Genesis*—but it was timely and useful. In his capacity of humanist we see Colet at his worst. Two ideas were uncomfortably united in his mind. On the one hand, he shared, to excess, the humanistic belief in the virtues of 'classical' Latin; his feeling about medieval Latin was one not so much of critical disapproval as of rankling, personal animosity. On the other hand, he had a distrust of pagan literature which carries us back to the earliest ages of the Church. The spirit of the classical writers was to be avoided like the plague and their form to be imposed as an indispensable law. When Colet founded St. Paul's School this extraordinary position was embodied in its statutes. The boys were to be guarded from every word that did not occur in Virgil or Cicero, and equally from every idea that did. As an inevitable result, their fare was to be Lactantius, Prudentius, Sedulius, Mantuan, and Erasmus. No more deadly and irrational scheme could have been propounded—deadly, because it cuts the boys off from nearly all the best literature that existed in Latin, and irrational because it puts an arbitrary value on certain formal elements dissociated from the spirit which begot them and for whose sake they existed. To Colet, however, this seemed a small price to pay for excluding 'all barbary, all corrupcion, all laten adulterate which ignorant blynde folis brought into this world'; and later (even in a statute he cannot contain himself) 'that ffylthinesse', that 'abusyon' which 'more rayther may be called blotterature thenne litterature'. Thus Bernard and the *Summa*, Alanus and *Pange lingua* are kicked out by the one door; Virgil, Horace, Ovid, and Catullus by the other.

Colet's claims to be regarded as an English writer are tenuous —a possibility that he is the translator of his own Latin sermon to Convocation, a modest little work of practical divinity called *A Ryght fruitful monicion*, and the *Proheme* to his Latin grammar. The *Monicion* appears to have been popular; it is the sort of book that is given to godchildren. The *Proheme*, encouraging the 'lytel babys', the 'lytel chyldren' with the hope that they may 'come at the last to be gret clarkes', and bidding them 'lyfte up their lytel whyte handes' to pray for their founder, has (for adults with no children of their own) a certain prettiness: I am afraid the real boys may have pulled snooks at it in private—especially if they knew that the dean had by statute forever forbidden all 'remedies', that is, all holidays.

The same strongly ascetic strain is to be found in John Fisher[1] (1459–1535) the Bishop of Rochester. I have put Fisher in this chapter partly because I did not wish to separate him from the other martyrs and partly because he preached against Luther; but on literary grounds he might equally well have been dealt with in the last. He is almost a purely medieval writer, though scraps of what may be classified as humanistic learning appear in his work—a reference to 'the Georgycke' (that is, the *Gorgias*) of Plato, to the virtue of 'epicheia' (ἐπιείκεια), to the Platonic desire for philosophic kings (Henry VIII's book against Luther, it is suggested, almost admits him to the class), and a sympathetic mention of the Cabala. His vernacular works include devotional treatises—a *Consolation* to his sister and *The Ways to Perfect Religion*—and sermons; a series on the Penitential Psalms, funeral orations for Henry VII, and for the Countess of Richmond, and the famous sermon against Luther in 1521.

Fisher's style is grave and a little diffuse, never comic (though the pulpit then admitted that excellence), mildly rhetorical, and at times really eloquent. The apostrophe to the corpse in the funeral sermon, 'A kynge Henry, Kynge Henry, yf thou wert on lyve agayne many one that is here present now wolde pretende a full grete pite and tendernesse vpon thee' has been rightly praised

---

[1] b. 1459 at Beverley, Yorkshire. Educated at Cathedral School, Rochester, and Michaelhouse, Cambridge. B.A., 1487. Fellow. M.A., 1490. Senior Proctor, 1494. Master, 1497. Patronized by Margaret, the Queen Mother; becomes her confessor. Vice-Chancellor of Cambridge, 1501. Professor of Divinity, 1503. Chancellor of Cambridge, 1504: repeatedly re-elected to this office and finally given it for life: Bishop of Rochester. Offers to resign Chancellorship in favour of Wolsey, 1513. Criticizes Wolsey. Instrumental in bringing Erasmus to Cambridge. Begins to learn Greek. Accuses the House of Commons of 'lack of faith'. Appears in Legate's Court and speaks strongly against the Divorce, 1529. An attempt is made to poison him, 1530. Opposes the Royal Supremacy and secures some modification of the form in which it is presented to Convocation, 1531. Supports the Nun of Kent. Refuses Oath of Supremacy: beheaded, 1535.

by critics. The address of the soul to the body in the *Consolation* ('Now my wretched body thy bewtie is faded', &c.) is as good; the passage on the beauty of Christ in *Perfect Religion* ('Behold the Rose, the Lillie, the Vyolet, beholde the Pecocke') perhaps better. Many of his comparisons, such as that of the Blessed Virgin to morning in the sermon on Psalm xxxviii or of faith and works to the sunbeams in the sermon on Luther, are ingeniously beautiful and, if compressed and versified, would be exactly what we call 'metaphysical' poetry. His chief weakness is that he is too leisurely: he is in no hurry to end a sentence or to let an idea go. His translations from the Vulgate enlarge on the original and pass imperceptibly into glosses. How beautiful such floral elaboration can be we know from Taylor, but Fisher's style, though sometimes sweet, is not great enough to carry it off. At times his love of elaboration leads him into something like absurdity. In the *Perfect Religion*, the Nun is very properly encouraged to be thankful that God created her in a Christian society: this is well. She is also to be thankful that He created her at all; it is still well and orthodox, but troublesome questions are drawing near. She is to be especially grateful to God for making her a human being when He might have made her a stone or a toad. Made *whom* or *what* a stone or a toad? Finally, she is to be grateful because God created her instead of all the other people whom He might have created and who might have been better than she is if they had existed (ibid., *The first consideration*). The fate of the virtuous heathen is problem enough: it is too much to be saddled with the potentially virtuous non-existent. He would be a bold man who blamed Fisher for not solving these questions; the trouble is that he does not seem to know that he is raising them. His sincerity is undoubted; but while his heart is earnest, his intellect is perhaps not so hard at work as he supposes.

Some of the medieval sweetness and richness still hangs about the prose of Fisher as it hangs about the verse of Hawes; but for our present purpose he matters less as a literary figure than as a convenient representative of the religion in possession at the very beginning of the English Reformation. He was a bishop and died for his faith: in him we ought to find what men like Tyndale were attacking. It was not in all respects what they imagined it to be. The Pelagianism of which they implicitly accused the Roman Church is, like the antinomianism of which the Papists accused them, a figment of controversy. Some of Fisher's statements seem, at least to a layman, to be very close to Tyndale's own, as when Fisher writes:

From the eyen of almyghty God whiche may be called his grace shyneth forth a meruaylous bryghtnes lyke as the beme that cometh from the sonne. And that lyght of grace stereth and setteth forthwarde the soules to brynge forth the fruyte of good werkes. (Sermon on Psalm xxxii.)

And again, on Psalm li, 'no creature of himselfe hath power to do good werkes without the grace and help of God'. What Tyndale would have regarded as the cloven hoof appears chiefly when Fisher is talking of penance. By penance, on his view, sinners can 'make due satysfacion' so as to be 'clene out of dette' (*Sermon on Psalm xxxii*), and so 'iustyfyed by the sacrament of penaunce' that 'God can ask no more of them' (ibid.). It was this suggestion of balancing an account that the Protestants felt to be so repulsive and illusory. They would have also been repelled by that type of asceticism with its deep distrust of the body, which Fisher shares with Colet. Tyndale, almost in his first work, takes over from Luther the important recognition that 'flesh' in St. Paul does not mean primarily the sins of appetite; how could it, since such eminently spiritual sins as envy and magic are among the works of the flesh? Fisher, on the other hand, takes it for granted that 'synne is caused and cometh of the vnlawfull pleasures of the body' (*Sermon on Psalm vi*), that 'dyrtie corruption', that 'sachell full of dunge' (*Consolation*), and calls the deed of kind, here making no distinction between marriage and promiscuity, 'the foule and fylthy pleasure'. He thinks it unwholesome, too, and produces medical opinion to the effect that that 'effusyon' does more harm than to lose ten times the amount of blood (*Sermon on Psalm xxviii*). Even more important, if we are to understand why the Reformers, whether rightly or wrongly, felt that they were escaping from a prison, is Fisher's conception of purgatory. A modern tends to see purgatory through the eyes of Dante: so seen, the doctrine is profoundly religious. That purification must, in its own nature, be painful, we hardly dare to dispute. But in Fisher the pain seems to have no intrinsic connexion with the purification at all: it is a pain which, while it lasts, separates us from God. Since even in this life pain 'will not suffre the soul to remember itselfe, moche lesse therefore it shall haue any remembraunce abydynge in tourmentes, for cause also the paynes of purgatory be moche more than the paynes of this worlde, who may remember God as he ought to do, beynge in that paynfull place? Therefore the prophet sayth *quoniam non est in morte qui memor fit tui*?' (*Sermon on Psalm vi.*) Thus the pains which in Dante were genuinely purgative have become, it would seem, merely retributive. Tyndale's reaction to such a doctrine can be gathered from a sentence in his answer to More, 'To punish a man that has forsaken sin of his own accord is not to purge him but to satisfy the lust of a tyrant'. Perhaps Fisher might not mean exactly what he said: or, meaning it, might not do justice to the doctrine of his own church. That is not here our concern. We want to know how people in England felt; we shall not succeed if Dante's picture dominates our minds.

One merit, very unusual in that age, Fisher can claim: he is hardly at all scurrilous. His attack on Luther is not, indeed, masked under those forms of politeness which are usual between theological (though not between political) opponents today. But there is hardly any real abuse; compared with More, or even with Tyndale, Fisher is almost courteous.

We must now turn to those two less courteous, but far greater figures, the opposed martyrs Thomas More and William Tyndale; and though they were deeply divided by temper as well as by doctrine, it is important to realize at the outset that they also had a great deal in common. They must not, except in theology, be contrasted as the representatives respectively of an old and a new order. Intellectually they both belonged to the new: both were Grecians (Tyndale a Hebraist as well) and both were arrogantly, perhaps ignorantly, contemptuous of the Middle Ages. And if the view be accepted (it is said to be very doubtful) that a feudal world was at this time being replaced by something harsher in the social and economic sphere, then More and Tyndale both belonged to the old. Both inveighed against enclosure and sheep-farming and demanded that the desires of the 'economic man' should be completely subordinated to traditional Christian ethics. Both disapproved of the annulment of the king's marriage. To the men themselves what they had in common doubtless seemed a mere 'highest common factor': but it was enough, had the world followed that only, to have altered the whole course of our history. Nor is it, perhaps, irrelevant to add that they were alike in their fate; even curiously alike, since both risked death by torture and both were mercifully disappointed, for More was only beheaded (not disembowelled alive) and they strangled Tyndale at the stake before they lit the fire.

Thomas More[1] (1478–1535) who held his place in our older critical tradition on the precarious tenure of one Latin work, has in recent years been restored to his rightful place as a major English author. Of his poems I have spoken already. His remaining works fall into three classes; first those of 'pure' or comparatively 'pure' literature, secondly the controversies, and thirdly the moral and devotional treatises.

His Latin prose, with the exception of the *Utopia*, may be ignored in a history of English literature, the more so because its chief glory, the *Historia Ricardi Tertii*,[2] can be read in his own

---

[1] b. 1478. Educated at St. Anthony's School, London. Page to Cardinal Morton, 1490–2. Canterbury College, Oxford, 1492–4. New Inn (London), 1494. Lincoln's Inn, 1496. Meets Erasmus, 1499. Contributes epigrams to John Holt's *Lac Puerorum* (before 1500). About this time 'gave himself to devotion and prayer in the Charterhouse of London . . . without vow'. Studies Greek under Grocyn, 1501. His father disapproves of this. Enters Parliament and leads successful opposition to financial demand by Henry VII, 1504. Writes Latin epigrams and English poems about this time. Translates the Life of Pico della Mirandola, *c.* 1505. Marries eldest daughter of John Colt, though he prefers the younger, because 'it would be both great grief and some shame also to the eldest to see her younger sister in marriage preferred', *c.* 1505. Refuses John Colt's advice that he should beat her. Translates some of Lucian in collaboration with Erasmus. Visits Paris and Louvain, 1508. Visited by Erasmus who writes the *Moriae Encomium* in his house, 1509. Appointed an Under Sheriff of the City, 1510, His first wife dies, 1511. Marries Alice Middleton, 1511. Writes *Historia Ricardi III*, 1513–14; *Utopia*, Book II, 1514–15, Book I, 1516. On embassy to Flanders, 1515. Erasmus's last visit to England, 1517. More's distinguished conduct during the riots of 'Evil May Day', 1517. Enters the service of Henry VIII, 1517. Member of the King's Council by 1518. Present at the Field of the Cloth of Gold, 1520. His daughter Margaret m. to William Roper, 1521. More knighted; appointed Under Treasurer, 1521. Advises Henry on composition of the *Assertio VII Sacramentorum*. Becomes Speaker of the House of Commons, 1523. Resists Wolsey's attempt to interrogate the House, 1523. Becomes Chancellor of the Duchy of Lancaster, 1525. Meets Holbein, 1527. Consulted by Henry about the 'Divorce', 1527. Accompanies Wolsey on embassy to France, 1527. Licensed by Bishop of London to have and read heretical books, 1528. Again on embassy to France, 1529. Becomes Lord Chancellor, 1529. Attacks Wolsey. Reports to both Houses the learned opinions obtained by the king on his marriage out refuses to give his own, 1531. Henry allowed the title of Supreme Head, 1531. Act against payment of Annates to Rome. Commons' supplication against the Clergy. Submission of the Clergy. More's resignation, 1532. Accused of misprision of treason for having had a conversation with the 'Holy Maid of Kent', the charge withdrawn, 1534. Refuses oath on the supremacy and succession: executed for treason, 1535.

[2] More's authorship of the *Life of Richard III* has been questioned on the grounds of external and internal evidence. The external evidence is Sir John Harington's statement that it was 'written as I have heard by Morton but as most suppose by

unfinished English version. It is an ambitious undertaking modelled on the ancient historians, and in it the long set speeches dear to Thucydides and Livy claim the lion's share. Although their dramatic function is not neglected the author is more interested in them as rhetoric, and Queen Elizabeth pleading for her child's right to sanctuary is not really much less 'facundious' and forensic than Buckingham addressing the citizens in the Guildhall. More, who had been so purely medieval in his poetry, is here medieval and humanistic at once; he writes for an audience in whom the medieval love of fine talk had been slightly redirected and heavily reinforced by classical example. He expects us to share the enjoyment of the citizens when Buckingham 'rehersed them the same matter again in other order and other wordes, so wel and ornately and natheles so euidently and plaine, with voice, gesture and countenance so cumly and so conuenient, that every man much meruailed that herd him'. More is also a lawyer writing for an audience whose education had for the most part a legal twist, and law is the worst influence on his style. He sets out for a whole column the proclamation of Hastings's treasons and probably regards its conveyancing prolixity as an ornament rather than a blemish to his page. The character sketches, pithy and sententious and much indebted to the ancient models, will be more congenial to a modern taste. The portrait of Hastings would not disgrace Tacitus, and that of Jane Shore is a beautiful example of the author's mingled charity and severity. The book now pleases best in those passages which are most intimate—Hastings chatting with his namesake, Richard calling for the mess of strawberries, Richard with his eyes 'whirling' and his hand on his dagger 'like one always ready to strike again', or the lively picture of a queen moving house with 'heavinesse, rumble, haste and businesse ... chestes, coffers, packes, fardelles, trusses ... some lading, some going, some discharging, some coming for more'. It is not an economical style, but it lives. We

Sir Thomas More' (*Metamorphosis of Ajax*, 1596). The internal evidence, as estimated by C. Whibley (*C.H.E.L.* iii. 334), is its 'asperity of tone' and 'eager partisanship' which 'belong more obviously to Morton than to the humane author of *Utopia*'. To the first it may be answered that Rastell's attribution is of more weight than Harington's much later, and confessedly hearsay, statement. To the second, those who have read More's controversial writings will, I expect, reply that we find no degree of asperity in the *Life* which is not equalled, and surpassed, in his undisputed works. For full discussion see E. V. Hitchcock and R. W. Chambers, *Harpsfield's Life of More*, E.E.T.S., London, 1932, pp. 336 et seq.

must not, however, represent a sixteenth-century book as a modern one by over-emphasizing merits which are really subordinate. More is not an early Strachey nor even an early Macaulay. The *Historia* in its entirety will succeed only with readers who can enjoy the classical sort of history—history as a grave and lofty Kind, the prose sister of epic, rhetorical in expression and moral in purpose. If read in the right spirit, More's performance will seem remarkable. He brings to his work a great knowledge of affairs, a sufficient measure of impartiality, a sense of tragedy, and a sense of humour. He makes an attempt, something more than half-hearted, to sift fact from tradition; and to his dramatic moulding of the story Shakespeare's close discipleship is sufficient testimony. He produces a much more interesting example of the new kind of history than Boece.

In 1516 came the *Utopia* which, though it was written in Latin, is so good and has given rise to so many controversies that I should hardly be forgiven if I passed it over in silence. All seem to be agreed that it is a great book, but hardly any two agree as to its real significance: we approach it through a cloud of contradictory eulogies. In such a state of affairs a good, though not a certain, clue is the opinion of those who lived nearer the author's time than we. Our starting-point is that Erasmus speaks of it as if it were primarily a comic book; Tyndale despises it as 'poetry'; for Harpsfield it is a 'iollye inuention', 'pleasantly' set forth; More himself in later life classes it and the *Praise of Folly* together as books fitter to be burned than translated in an age prone to misconstruction; Thomas Wilson, fifty years later, mentions it for praise among 'feined narrations and wittie invented matters (as though they were true indeed)'. This is not the language in which friend or enemy or author (when the author is so honest a man as More) refer to a serious philosophical treatise. It all sounds as if we had to do with a book whose real place is not in the history of political thought so much as in that of fiction and satire. It is, of course, possible that More's sixteenth-century readers, and More himself, were mistaken. But it is at least equally possible that the mistake lies with those modern readers who take the book *au grand sérieux*. There is a cause specially predisposing them to error in such a matter. They live in a revolutionary age, an age in which modern weapons and the modern revolutionary technique have made it only too easy to produce in the real world states recognizably like those we invent on paper: writing Utopias is now a serious matter. In More's time, or Campanella's, or Bacon's, there was no real hope or fear that the paper states could be 'drawn into practice': the man engaged in blowing such bubbles did not need to talk as if he were on his oath. And here we have to do with one who, as the Messenger told him in the *Dialogue*, 'used to look so sadly' when he jested that many were deceived.

The *Utopia* has its serious, even its tragic, elements. It is, as its translator Robinson says, 'fruteful and profitable'. But it is not a consistently serious philosophical treatise, and all attempts to treat it as such break down sooner or later. The interpretation which breaks down soonest is the 'liberal' interpretation. There is nothing in the book on which the later More, the heretic-hunter, need have turned his back. There is no freedom of speech in Utopia. There is nothing liberal in Utopia. From it, as from all other imaginary states, liberty is more successfully banished than the real world, even at its worst, allows. The very charm of these paper citizens is that they cannot in any way resist their author: every man is a dictator in his own book. It is not love of liberty that makes men write Utopias. Nor does the *Utopia* give any colour to Tyndale's view that More 'knew the truth' of Protestantism and forsook it: the religious orders of the Utopians and their very temples are modelled on the old religion. On the other hand, it is not a defence of that old order against current criticisms; it supports those criticisms by choosing an abbot as its specimen of the bad landlord and making a friar its most contemptible character. R. W. Chambers, with whom died so much that was sweetest and strongest in English scholarship, advanced a much more plausible view. According to him the Utopians represent the natural virtues working at their ideal best in isolation from the theological; it will be remembered that they hold their Natural Religion only provisionally 'onles any godlier be inspired into man from heuen'. Yet even this leaves some features unaccounted for. It is doubtful whether More would have regarded euthanasia for incurables and the assassination of hostile princes as things contained in the Law of Nature. And it is very strange that he should make Hedonism the philosophy of the Utopians. Epicurus was not regarded by most Christians as the highest example of the natural light. The truth surely is that as long as we take the *Utopia* for a philosophical treatise it will 'give' wherever we lean our weight. It is, to begin with, a dialogue: and we cannot be certain which of the speakers, if any, represents More's considered opinion. When Hythloday explains why his philosophy would be useless in the courts of kings More replies that there is 'another philosophy more ciuil' and expounds this less intransigent wisdom so sympathetically that we think we have caught the very More at last; but when I have read Hythloday's retort I am all at sea again. It is even very doubtful what More thought of communism as a practical proposal. We have already had to remind ourselves, when considering Colet, that the traditional admission of communism as the law of uncorrupted Nature need carry with it no consequences in the world of practical sociology. It is certain that in the *Confutation* (1532) More had come to include communism among the 'horrible heresies' of the Anabaptists and in the *Dialogue of Comfort* he defends private riches. Those who think of More as a 'lost leader' may discount these later utterances. Yet even at the end of the *Utopia* he rejects the Utopian economics as a thing 'founded of no good reason'. The magnificent rebuke of all existing societies which precedes this may suggest that the rejection is ironical. On the other hand, it may mean that the whole book is only a satiric glass to reveal our own avarice by contrast and is not meant to give us directly practical advice.

These puzzles may give the impression that the *Utopia* is a confused book: and if it were intended as a serious treatise it would be very confused indeed. On my view, however, it appears confused only so long as we are trying to get out of it what it never intended to give. It becomes intelligible and delightful as soon as we take it for what it is—a holiday work, a spontaneous overflow of intellectual high spirits, a revel of debate, paradox, comedy and (above all) of invention, which starts many hares and kills none. It is written by More the translator of Lucian and friend of Erasmus, not More the chancellor or the ascetic. Its place on our shelves is close to *Gulliver* and *Erewhon*, within reasonable distance of Rabelais, a long way from the *Republic* or *New Worlds for Old*. The invention (the 'poetry' of which More was accused) is quite as important as the merits of the polity described, and different parts of that polity are on very different levels of seriousness.

Not to recognize this is to do More grave injustice. Thus the suggestion that the acquisitive impulse should be mortified by using gold for purposes of dishonour is infantile if we take it as a practical proposal. If gold in Utopia were plentiful enough to be so used, gold in Utopia would not be a precious metal. But if it is taken simply as satiric invention leading up to the story of the child and the ambassadors, it is delicious. The slow beginning of the tale, luring us on from London to Bruges, from Bruges to Antwerp, and thence by reported speech to fabulous lands beyond the line, has no place in the history of political philosophy: in the history of prose fiction it has a very high place indeed. Hythloday himself, as we first see him, has something of the arresting quality of the Ancient Mariner. The dialogue is admirably managed. Mere conversation holds us contented for the first book and includes that analysis of the contemporary English situation which is the most serious and the most truly political part of the *Utopia*. In the second book More gives his imagination free rein. There is a thread of serious thought running through it, an abundance of daring suggestions, several back-handed blows at European institutions, and, finally, the magnificent peroration. But he does not keep our noses to the grindstone. He says many things for the fun of them, surrendering himself to the sheer pleasure of imagined geography, imagined language, and imagined institutions. That is what readers whose interests are rigidly political do not understand: but everyone who has ever made an imaginary map responds at once.

Tyndale's belief that More 'knew the truth and forsook it' is a crude form of the error which finds in the *Utopia* a liberalism inconsistent with More's later career. There is no inconsistency. More was from the first a very orthodox Papist, even an ascetic with a hankering for the monastic life. At the same time it is true that the *Utopia* stands apart from all his other works. Religiously and politically he was consistent: but this is not to say that he did not undergo a gradual and honourable change very like that which overtook Burke and Wordsworth and other friends of liberty as the Revolutionary age began to show its true features. The times altered; and things that would once have seemed to him permissible or even salutary audacities came to seem to him dangerous. That was why he would not then wish to see the *Utopia* translated. In the same way any of us might now make criticisms of democracy which we would not repeat in the hour of its danger. And from the literary point of view there is an even greater gulf between the *Utopia* and the works which followed. It is, to speak simply, beyond comparison better than they.

It is idle to expect that More's polemical writings, to which I now turn, should be as good in their own kind as the *Utopia* is in its. In the first place they are commissioned work, undertaken at the instance of the Bishop of London and conscientiously carried out not because More wants to write them but because, on his view, they must be written by someone. There is no evidence that he ever felt a literary and intellectual, as distinct from a religious, vocation to this kind of work. His weariness, until the task has become a habit, is apparent. 'Would God,' he says in the *Confutation*, 'after all my laboure done, so that the remembrance of their pestilent errours were araced out of Englishe mennes heartes and their abominable bookes burned up, myne owne were walked with them, and the name of these matters vtterly putte in oblivion.' In the second place More was limited by the very terms of his commission to write for the vulgar, *simplicibus et idiotis hominibus*. He was not allowed to fly very high in theology: how high he could have flown if free, I am not qualified to judge. Hooker, writing many years later, gave it as his opinion (*Sermon on Justification*) that More, though a very learned man, had not fully understood the position that his own church was defending against the Lutherans.

One work in this group, the *Dialogue* of 1528, stands apart from the rest. It is the first and the iron has not yet entered into More's soul. The plan of it is good. More feigns a series of visits from a mysterious Messenger who puts forward the Lutheran positions with a disinterested air, disclaiming all belief in them but sometimes betraying it. Considerable dramatic humour results from this device. The discussion is brought to life in true Platonic style by notes of time and place, by interruptions, and by references to Lady More. Passages of hard dialectic are relieved by 'merry tales' and by lengthier speeches which aim at eloquence. As controversy it does not rank very high and perhaps in the circumstances could not: the main questions at issue hardly admit of so popular a treatment. It is easy to put the case for justification by faith as it appears to a text-hunting and ignorant fanatic, and easy to reply in terms of commonplace good sense and morality. But the real problem, set by the very nature of Christian experience, remains where it was. On saints' miracles More does better, and the marvellous story of the young couple of Walbrook is at once a piece of excellent comedy and an effective argument; but too many pages are wasted on that facile interchange of anecdotal credulity and anecdotal incredulity which you may hear in any casual conversation about spiritualism or flying saucers. A lawyer, we feel, ought to have had something more pertinent to say about the whole nature of evidence. But if this book is not great theology, it is great Platonic dialogue: perhaps the best specimen of that form ever produced in English. Berkeley is urbane and graceful and more profound, but his Hylas and Philonous are mere men of straw beside More and the Messenger. The latter is perhaps too stupidly obstinate and repeats himself too often. No doubt this is so because More wishes to depict the patience of the Papists, but he has not foreseen how severely he would also exercise the patience of his readers. But for the most part the thing is admirably alive. We watch with delight the slow, inevitable progress of the Messenger into snare after snare; and this, together with the richness of its colloquialisms and the wholly excellent humour of its funny stories, will always make the *Dialogue* worth reading.

One more work is worth separate mention before we reach the real slough. The *Supplication of Souls* (1529) is a defence of the doctrine of purgatory and More has chosen to put it into the mouth of the souls whom purgatory now contains. The first book, which is almost entirely factual and statistical, contains some of More's best and most muscular prose—for More is happiest when he is not trying to be eloquent. The second book, which has a peculiar literary merit of its own, illustrates a further stage in the degradation of the idea of purgatory. In Fisher the pain has been separated from any spiritual purification, but the torments had at least been inflicted by angels. In More this last link with heaven is severed. The attendants (if that is the right word) are now devils. 'Our keepers', say the imprisoned souls, 'are such as God kepe you from, cruell damned spirites, odious enemies and despitefull tormentours, and theyr companye more horrible and grieuous to vs than is the payn itself and the intollerable tourmente that they doo vs, wherewith from top to toe they cease not to teare vs'. The length of the sentence has thus become the sole

difference between purgatory and hell. Purgatory is a department of hell. And More's humour, continued even here, somehow increases the horror. Instead of the psalms and litanies
which resounded on the sunlit terraces of Dante's mountain
from souls 'contented in the flame', out of the black fire which
More has imagined, mixed with the howls of unambiguous
physical torture, come peals of harsh laughter. All is black, salt,
macabre. I make the point not to disgrace a man before whom
the best of us must stand uncovered, but because the age we
are studying cannot be understood without it. This sort of thing,
among others, was what the old religion had come to mean in
the popular imagination during the reign of Henry VIII: this
was one of the things a man left behind in becoming a Protestant. Nor, I think, is that its only relevance for the history of
taste. Has not the wildness of the 'eldritch' poetry in Scotland
a secret affinity with it? The thing cannot be proved: but I feel
that the burlesque heaven of *Kynd Kittok* springs from the same
mood as the serious, yet dreadfully comic, purgatory of the
Supplication.

Although we have now skimmed more than four hundred
columns of the 1557 folio, the greater part of More's controversial writings remains—the *Confutation of Tyndale's Answer* (1532
and 1553), the *Letter* (against Frith) (1532–3), the *Apology* (1533),
the *Debellation of Salem and Byzance* (1533), and the *Answer to the
Poisoned Book* (1533). The earliest criticism ever made on these
works is recorded by More himself ('The brethren cannot beare
that my writing is so long') and it cannot be seriously questioned.
There are indeed differences between them. The *Confutation* is
the longest, the harshest, and the dullest. The *Letter* is exceptional not only for its brevity but for its charitable and almost
fatherly tone. In the *Apology* we see More being drawn, as all
controversialists are drawn, away from the main issue into self-
defence. In the *Debellation* what was first undertaken as a duty
is only too plainly becoming a habit. More is at pains to excuse
himself for answering what in his own judgement needed no
answer, and tells us the illuminating fact that this huge treatise
was composed in a few days. A not unwelcome air of senility is
perceptible in the rambling pages with which it opens and there
is charm in the passage where the old lawyer pictures himself
once more a young man at a moot. In the *Answer to the Poisoned
Book* this loss of grip becomes even more noticeable and we

repeatedly escape from the matter in hand into digressions—on gluttony, on the Arian heresy, on the Annunciation, on Free Will, on Judas Iscariot. This twilight is welcome after the heat of such a day.

But in spite of these differences the controversial works, after the *Dialogue*, may well be criticized in the lump. Pure literature they do not aspire to be; and theologically More's commission confines him to stating the 'stock' case for orthodoxy in an entirely popular form. It only remains, therefore, to judge them as specimens of the art of controversy. That this art can produce masterpieces which outlive their occasion, no one who remembers Plato, Hooker, Burke, or Newman will deny. But More's controversies are not on that level. Apart from the deficiencies of his style (a point we must return to) he is hampered by two self-imposed principles which are fatal to the highest kind of success. In the first place he has decided that his case against the heretics should be in his books as the soul is in the body—*tota in toto et tota in qualibet parte*; that the reader, whatever page he lights upon, should find there all that he needs for refutation of the enemy. He is monotonously anxious to conquer and to conquer equally, at every moment: to show in every chapter that every heretical book is wrong about everything—wrong in history, in logic, in rhetoric, and in English grammar as well as in theology. And secondly his method of attacking a book is to go through it page by page like a schoolmaster correcting an exercise, so that the order and emphasis of the discussion are in fact dictated by his opponent. How to throw the grand arguments into bold relief and to condense the lesser, how to decline small points and to answer others while seeming to decline them, where to refresh the reader with some eloquent assault over the ruins of a lately demolished fortification—of all this More has no notion.

Yet even in these books his real talent sometimes appears. Wherever he allows himself to use the weapon of low comedy he is at once excellent. Even the faintest hint of it—as in the last book of the *Confutation* where he transfers the case against Barnes to two imaginary old women—is sufficient to refresh us; and the fully developed 'merry tales' will bear comparison with anything of the same kind in Chaucer or Shakespeare. It is true that the best of them all, the story of Richard Hunne, comes in the *Dialogue*: but even in the later works we have the goodwife of Culham, *Te igitur clementissime pater*, the lady who stopped her husband's lecture on astronomy, and the woman who talked in church. About these there can be only one opinion; but More has other devices bordering on the comic which do not seem to me so successful. He has the Arnoldian trick of catching up some phrase used by the enemy and ridiculing it by repetition. No instance of this is as good as 'Wragg is in custody', but it can be effective enough when the pilloried phrase has the rhythmic qualities that go to make a good refrain; like 'the great, brode, bottomless ocean sea of euils' in the *Supplication*. But at times it may descend to a kind of nagging or snarling which is unattractive—'I have not contended with Erasmus my derling because I founde no such malicious entente with Erasmus my derling as I fynde with Tyndall. For hadde I founde with Erasmus my derling the shrewde entente and purpose that I fynde in Tyndall, Erasmus my derling should be no more my derling', &c. What is this but the rhetoric of the preparatory school?

The mention of More's humour brings us to the question of his scurrility. From the moral point of view no very serious charge can be made; More is not much more scurrilous, only more amusingly scurrilous, than many of our older controversialists. Even if we judged his scurrility to be a fault it would be hard to wish away a fault so intertwined (or even identical) with what is the chief and often the only merit of these works: that is, the gusto of their hard-hitting, racy, street-corner abuse. It was More's business to appeal to the vulgar, to play to the gallery, and it suited one side of him extremely well. He is our first great cockney humorist, the literary ancestor of Martin Marprelate and Nashe. It would be a loss to his polemical writings if they were purged of their references to heretics who 'haue as much shame in their face as a shotten herring hath shrimps in her tail', to 'lowsy Luther' and his disciples' 'long babelary', to 'hammer-heads meete to make horse-shoon in helle'. If he would talk a little less about faggots and Smithfield and about Luther's 'abominable bichery', a theme that almost obsesses him, I for one should have no quarrel with his comic abuse. It is when he is being serious that his abusiveness becomes a literary fault. To rebuke magnificently is one of the duties of a great polemical writer. More often attempts it but he always fails. He loses himself in a wilderness of opprobrious adjectives.

He cannot denounce like a prophet; he can only scold and grumble like a father in an old fashioned comedy.

As we read these controversies we become aware that More the author was scarcely less a martyr to his religion than More the man. In obedience to his conscience he spent what might have been the best years of his literary life on work which demanded talents that he lacked and gave very limited scope to those he had. It may well have been no easy sacrifice.

I turn with relief to his devotional works. One of these, the meditation *De IV Novissimis* was early work and might on that account have been treated at the very beginning. I have preferred to place it here, side by side with the *Dialogue of Comfort*, in order to bring out the almost laughable, wholly beautiful, contrast between them. The late work written under the shadow of the scaffold, is full of comfort, courage, and humour; the early meditation is a piece of unrelieved gloom. Thus some men's religion fails at the pinch: that of others does not appear to pluck up heart until the pinch comes. The *De IV Novissimis* is, for its darkness, a pendant to the *Supplication*. It may justly be called a religious 'exercise' provided that we do not associate with that word any idea of insincerity. That is to say, it is not an outpouring of individual experience. The theme comes first and is selected for its intrinsic and objective importance; the business of the writer is to find reflections suitable to it. Self-improvement, not self-expression, is the purpose. More's scheme consisted in applying each of the four last things to each of the seven deadly sins in turn, and he gave it up in the middle of applying the first *Novissimum* (death) to the sixth sin (sloth), having thus completed five of the twenty-eight panels or niches intended. Of its value as a devotional work who dares consider himself a judge? If most of it now seems helpless either to encourage or to alarm, the fault may be ours: but not, I think, all ours. Almost everywhere it tries to prove too much. Gross exaggeration of the part played by gluttony in our diseases leaves the conscience undisturbed. The passage in which all life is compared to an illness shows some inability to distinguish between a conceit and an argument. The colours are too dark. In the true late medieval manner More forgets that to paint all black is much the same as not to paint at all. What was intended to be a rebuke of sin degenerates almost into a libel upon life and we are forced into incredulity. It is true that More once assures us that even in the natural order 'virtue bringeth his pleasure and vice is not without pain' but this little taper does not cast its beam very far in the general gloom. The real merits of the book are incidental. The medieval homiletic tradition wisely admitted the grotesque and the comic and where More avails himself of this licence he writes well. The picture of the glutton 'with his belly standing a strote like a taber and his noll totty with drink' is as good as that in the *Ancren Riwle*. We are reminded of Falstaff's death when we read of the dying man 'thy nose sharping, thy legges cooling, thy fingers fimbling'. Few pictures of the deathbed are more vivid than the following:

Haue ye not ere this in a sore sicknes felt it very grieuous to haue folk babble to you, and namely such thynges as ye sholde make aunswere to, whan it was a pain to speake? Thinke ye notnow that it wil be a gentle pleasure whan we lye dying, al our body in pain, al our mind in trouble, our soul in sorow, our hearte al in drede, while our life walketh awaiward, while our death draweth toward, while the deuil is busy about vs, while we lack stomak and strength to beare any one of so manifold heynous troubles, wil it not be as I was about to say, a pleasaunt thing to see before thine eyen and heare at thine eare a rable of fleshly frendes, or rather of flesh flies, skipping about thy bed and thy sicke body (now almost carreyn) crying to thee on euery side, What shal I haue, what shall I haue. . . . Than shall thyne executours ask for the kayes. . . .

But I have done the author a little more than justice by making one omission and by stopping where I did. More sows from the sack, not from the hand.

The *Dialogue of Comfort against Tribulation* (1534) is the noblest of all his vernacular writings. It was written in the Tower while More waited for death (for all he knew, death by torture, hanging, cutting down alive, and disembowelling). Its form is an imaginary conversation between two Hungarian gentlemen who foresee the possibility of martyrdom if the Turk comes much nearer. It is thus a fairly close parallel to Boethius' *De Consolatione* and the difference between them is interesting. In Boethius the thought that would be uppermost in any modern mind—that of physical pain—is hardly present at all; in More it is ubiquitous. We feel that we are reading the work of a man with nerves like our own, even of a man sensitive in such matters beyond the norm of his own coarse and courageous century. He discusses at length whether a man should envisage such horrors beforehand. To do so may clearly lead either to false confidence (reckoning with pain's image, not pain) or to despair (reckoning without the grace which will not perhaps be given before the need). His reply is that there is no choice. When once the matter has been raised we cannot refuse to think about it, and to advise us otherwise is 'as much reason as the medicine that I haue heard for the toothache, to go thrice about a church-yard and never think on a fox tayle'. He would therefore have everyone, of whatever sex or age, 'often to thinke thereupon'. We must do the best we can, meditating much on the Passion of Christ, never 'full out of feare of fallynge' but 'in good hope and full purpose' to stand. There is no attempt to disguise the situation; 'whan we remember the terrour of shamefull and painefull death, that poynt sodaynly putteth us in obliuion of all that shold be our comfort'. There is here a precision unusual in More. 'Whan we remember'—the mind is numb for hours even in a condemned cell, and then the terror rushes back: and 'sodaynly'. Worse even than this is the haunting fear that the pain itself might force a man 'to forsake our Saviour even in the myddes, and dye there with his synne, and so be damned for-euer'. Yet when all's said, a man must 'stand to his tackling' and any Christian would be very glad today to have so suffered yesterday.

The theme is almost the gravest that the human mind can entertain, but it must not be supposed that the book is a gloomy one. The *Dialogue of Comfort* justifies its title; it overflows with kindliness and humour and the beautiful self-mockery of old age aware of its own garrulity and its own limitations. The 'merry tales' are here in abundance, the old medieval jokes about women, so stale in themselves yet, after all, so amusingly handled, and so touching when we remember the hard road which they are now helping the author to travel. In a slightly different vein the longer story of a false alarm in war (ii. 12) is admirably told. But I would not quote much from this book: it is (or was) accessible in a cheap reprint and should be on everyone's shelves.

Of the *Treatise on the Passion* in its English form, we have only part from More's own hand; the rest, translated from his Latin by Margaret Roper's daughter. Those who turn to it expecting to find the beauties of the dialogue continued will be dis-appointed. It is as much exegetical as devotional and takes the form of a commentary on Gerson's *Monatesseron* (a gospel concordance made on a rather clumsy plan). As a Biblical commentator More is wholly medieval. Long ago in the *Supplication* he had used as a proof of the existence of purgatory the fact that Hezekiah wept when told that he must die; here he allegorizes in the old fashion on Our Lord's repetition of the word *Father*, on the name Simon, and on Malchus. From the literary point of view the most unfortunate feature of the book is the indiscretion with which More puts words into the mouth of Christ. It can be done successfully; witness the *Imitation*. But More seems wholly unaware of the dangers involved: it is indeed remarkable how one who had been, as a man, so attentive to the spirit of the Dominical utterances, could have remained, as a critic, so deaf to their style. Already in the *Answer to the Poisoned Book* this insensibility had led him to grotesque results ('For I am, as I dyuers times now haue told you, the very bread of life'); here it leads to the following:

Thys is the shorte whyle that is graunted yee and the libertie geuen vnto darknesse, that now ye maye in the night, which till this howre ye could neuer be suffered to bring to passe in the daye, like monstruous raueninge fowles, like skriche owles and hegges, like backes, howlettes, nighte crowes and byrdes of the hellye lake, goe aboute with your billes, your tallentes, your teeth and your shyrle shrychinge, outrageouslye, but all in vayne, thus in the darke to flee uppon me.

All this (and there is much more than I have quoted) is a gloss on the words 'This is your hour and the power of darkness'; and More cannot see that he is weakening them. It is true that the words quoted are his granddaughter's translation: but those who know More's English best will not say that the style is much inferior to his own, and those who look at the Latin will not find its *bubones striges* and *nycticoraces* much of an improvement on their vernacular equivalents. Yet these errors (of which there are plenty in the *Treatise*) are balanced by passages of exquisite pathos and insight. The following, also put into the mouth of Our Lord and explaining the final cause of the agony in the garden, is noteworthy—though more, I confess, for the matter than for the style.

Plucke up thy courage, faint heart, and dispaire never a deale. What though ye be fearefull, sory, and weary, and standest in great dread of most painful tormentry that is like to falle uppon thee, be of good comfort for all that. For I myself have vanquished the whole worlde, and yet felt I far more feare, sorowe, wearinesse, and much more inward anguish too, whan I considered my most bitter, painful passion to presse so fast uppon me. He that is strong harted may finde a thousand gloryous valiant martyrs whose ensample he may right joyfully follow. But thou, now, o temerous and weke sely shepe, thynke it sufficient for thee onely to walke after me.

Great claims have in modern times been made for More's English prose; I can accept them only with serious reservations. To compare it with that of the *Scale of Perfection* or the *Revelations* of Lady Julian will, in my opinion, only reveal its inferiority to them. The man who sits down and reads fairly through fifty pages of More will find many phrases to admire; but he will also find an invertebrate length of sentence, a fumbling multiplication of epithets, and an almost complete lack of rhythmical vitality. The length of sentence in More is quite different from the fullness of impassioned writers like Cicero or Burke or Ruskin, or from that of close thinkers like Hooker or Coleridge. It is not even the winning garrulity of Montaigne, or not often. Its chief cause is the fact that More never really rose from a legal to a literary conception of clarity and completeness. He multiplies words in a vain endeavour to stop up all possible chinks, where a better artist forces his conceptions on us by the light and heat of intellect and emotion in which they burn. He thus loses the advantages both of full writing and of concise writing. There are no lightning thrusts: and, on the other hand, no swelling tide of thought and feeling. The style is stodgy and dough-like. As for the good phrases, the reader will already have divined their nature. They come when More is in his homeliest vein: their race and pith and mere Englishry are the great redeeming feature of his prose. They ring in our ears like echoes of the London lanes and Kentish villages; 'whispered in hukermoker', 'damn us all to Dymmingesdale', 'the goose was ouer the moon', 'every finger shall be a thumb', 'fume, fret, frot, and foam', 'sauing for the worshipfull name of wine ichad as leue a drunken water'. They belong to the same world as his merry tales. Nearly all that is best in More is comic or close to comedy.

We think of More, and rightly, as a humanist and a saintly man. On the one hand, he is the writer of the *Utopia*, the friend of Erasmus, the man whose house became a sort of academy.

On the other, he is the man who wanted to be a Carthusian, who used a log of wood for his bolster and wore the hair, the martyr who by high example refused the wine offered him on his way to execution. The literary tragedy is that neither of these sides to his character found nearly such perfect expression in his writings as they deserved. The *Utopia* ought to have been only a beginning: his fertility of mind, his humour, and his genius for dialogue ought to have been embodied in some great work, some *colloquies* meatier than those of Erasmus, some satiric invention more gravely droll than Rabelais. As for his sanctity, to live and die like a saint is no doubt a better thing than to write like one, but it is not the same thing; and More does not write like a saint. 'Unction' (in the good sense of that word) is noticeably lacking in his work: the beauty of holiness, the fragrance of the *Imitation* or of St. François de Sales or of Herbert. What is actually expressed in most of his work is a third More, out of whom both the saint and the humanist have been made and with whom (that is both his glory and his limitation) they never lose touch—the Tudor Londoner of the citizen class. However high he rises he remains unmistakably rooted in a world of fat, burgher laughter, contentedly acclaiming well-seasoned jokes about shrewish wives or knavish servants, contemptuous of airs and graces and of what it thinks unnecessary subtleties; a world not lacking in shrewdness, courage, kindness, or honesty, but without fineness. No man even half so wise and good as Thomas More ever showed so little trace of the *cuor gentil*. There is nothing at all in him which, if further developed, could possibly lead on to the graces of Elizabethan and Jacobean literature. It might have led to things which some would prefer, but very different things.

Of Tyndale[1] (?–1536) as a Biblical translator something will

---

[1] b. before 1495 in Gloucestershire. Admitted Magdalen Hall, *c.* 1506. Goes to Cambridge, *c.* 1518. Tutor to children of Sir John Walsh at Little Sodbury, *c.* 1522. Appears before Chancellor of Diocese of Worcester on charge of heresy. Goes to London: attempts unsuccessfully to secure patronage of Bishop of London, 1523. Leaves for Hamburg, 1524. Apparently visits, and may have matriculated at, Wittenberg, 1524. At Cologne with William Roye begins publication of English New Testament: interrupted by Cochlaeus and flies to Worms, 1525. In house of Margaret von Emersen, Hamburg, 1529. (Residence at Marburg doubtful since Marburg colophons are false.) Offers to return to England if Henry will allow anyone whatever to publish a translation of the Bible, 1531. Trepanned by a government spy Henry Phillips: imprisoned by the emperor's Procuror General at Vilvorde, 1535. Strangled and burnt 1536.

be said in a later section: our present concern is with his theological works. To give a detailed account of these one by one would be tedious. Tyndale's message is always the same and a single abstract would serve for nearly all his books. This repetition is intentional, as appears from his *Prologue to Leviticus* where, repeating what he has said elsewhere of allegories, he adds 'though I haue spoken of them in another place, yet, lest the boke come not to all mens handes that shall read this, I will speake of them here also a woorde or twayne'. He never envisaged the modern critic sitting down to his Works in three volumes: he is like a man sending messages in war, and sending the same message often because it is a chance if any one runner will get through.

The early translation of Isocrates has not survived and presumably stood as much apart from his life's work as an academic thesis in our own days may stand apart from the mature work of a professional writer. His version of Erasmus's *Enchiridion* arose out of an argument when he was still an unknown private tutor in the house of Sir John Walsh. From these early and private controversies sprang the famous *béotword* 'if God spare my life, ere many years I will cause a boy that driveth the plough to know more of the scriptures than thou dost', and the fulfilment of that vaunt is the history of his life. The constancy of his purpose triumphed not only over perpetual danger, exile, poverty, and persecution, but even (which may be rarer) over all that was personal in the vaunt itself. In May 1531, speaking to one of the numerous spies whom Henry sent to entrap him, he offered that 'if it would stand with the king's most gracious pleasure to grant only a bare text of the scripture to be put forth among his people', he would in return write no more and would put himself in England at the king's mercy—thus throwing life and life-work together to the wolf. Every line he wrote was directly or indirectly devoted to the same purpose: to circulate the 'gospel'—not, on his view, to be identified with the Gospels—either by comment or translation.

The earliest work of the fully dedicated Tyndale is the prologue to the 1525 edition of his New Testament which Cochlaeus succeeded in strangling at birth. Of this edition only a few sheets are now known, but they contain the Prologue. It was later enlarged into *A Pathway into the Holy Scripture*. Next follows the beautiful *Prologue to Romans* (1526) which is mainly translated from Luther's *Praefatio in epistolam ad Romanos* (1523), and in 1528 the *Parable of the Wicked Mammon*, whose title is not much truer to its real contents than Montaigne's *Of Coaches*. In the same year the *Obedience of a Christian Man* was published; an ill-planned and digressive book on which, for various reasons, we had better pause.

When it is remembered that in the *Obedience* Tyndale makes his famous statement that 'the kyng is in thys worlde without lawe and may at his lust doe right or wrong and shall geue accomptes but to God onely', and also that the favour of Henry might have turned the whole situation in the Protestants' favour, it is easy to suspect that Tyndale is here deliberately using carnal policy to advance his cause. A reading of the *Obedience* dissipates the suspicion. The work has, indeed, a political occasion. The enemies have been saying that those who demand a vernacular Bible are a source of insurrection and even of communism. In answer to this Tyndale develops his real political philosophy. It is not one flattering to kings, though we are told that Henry read it with pleasure. They are, according to Tyndale, cradled into tyranny by bishops who murmur 'Your grace shall take your pleasure'. They are the dupes and puppets of the Pope who 'geueth to some a rose, to another a cappe of mayntenaunce: one is called Most Christen King, another Defender of the Fayth'. Lechery and pride are 'the common pestilence of all princes. Read the stories and see.' They must be obeyed— because it is better to suffer one tyrant than many and because by resistance we generally get something worse. We are not very far from Rousseau's epigram, 'Every King comes from God: so does every plague.' As we look deeper, and supplement the *Obedience* from Tyndale's other writings, we find ourselves in the presence of a political theory almost identical with Shakespeare's.

Tyndale asserts the doctrine of 'Degree' or natural hierarchy in its most uncompromising form. Of his parents a child is exhorted to think 'thou art theyr good and possession'. The marriage of children 'perteineth unto their elders'; without their elders' consent it is unlawful. As for husband and wife, 'Sara, before she was maried, was Abrahams sister and equall with him; but as soon as she was maried . . . became without comparison inferior.' Of kings Tyndale accepts (in the *Exposition on Matthew V, VI, and VII*, 1533) the medieval doctrine that their office is in some way ultimately derived from the people, but he expressly denies the conclusion that the people can therefore depose them. For in a sense 'God and not the common people chuseth the Prince though he chuse hym by them; for God commaundeth to chuse officers. Now hath God geuen no commaundement to put them downe agayne.' Therefore they must be suffered. Insurrection even against a heathen prince is forbidden to Christian subjects. And their temporal authority is not to be interfered with by a spiritual authority. That the Roman church had intolerably so interfered was, of course, common ground to all the Reformers. But Tyndale has, I think, no Calvin-like hankering to set up a new spiritual interference in its place. I can recall no passage in his writings that favours theocracy.

Such obedience to the temporal sovereign is, of course, an affair of this world. Sovereigns are 'to be obeyed onely as their commaundements repugne not against the commaundement of God: and then, Ho' (*Pathway*). After that, not rebellion, but martyrdom. Of such temporal subordination temporal welfare is the reward: hence the Turks who excel us in obedience also 'farre exceede vs Christen men in worldly prosperity'. Of all this, for Tyndale as for Shakespeare, the Wars of the Roses are an illustration drawn by the hand of God.

Let Englande look about them and marke what hath chaunced them since they slue their right kyng whom God had annointed ouer them, King Rycharde the Second. Their people, townes, and villages are minished by the third parte; and of their noble bloude remayneth not the third nor I beleue the sixte, yea, and if I durst be bolde, I wene I might safely sweare that their remaineth not the sixteneth part. Their owne sworde hath eaten them vp (*Exposition of Matthew*).

In two respects Tyndale carries Shakespeare's philosophy of history further than Shakespeare himself. Henry V's famous victories do not lead him to let sleep the question 'whether he were right heyre vnto England or held the land with the sworde as an heathen tyraunt agaynst all right.... And I ask whether his father slew not his leige King?' (*Answer to More*). He also traces the story a stage further back. As Britain's disregard of Gildas's preaching was punished by the Saxon invasion, so England's disregard of Wycliffe was punished by York and Lancaster's long wars (*Prologue to Jonas*).

In the *Practice of Prelates* (1530) Tyndale returns to politics and finds himself unexpectedly on the same side as Sir Thomas More and the Pope. His object is to dissuade Henry from the repudiation of Catherine of Aragon and his contention is that marriage with a deceased brother's wife is not unlawful. This leads him into an interesting discussion on the whole conception of incest. Like St. Augustine, he refuses to accept it as a mere taboo, and seeks for reasons. He finds them in his doctrine of hierarchy: the wife being inferior to the husband, a man may not marry any woman who is his natural superior—as aunts, for example, are. Hence marriage with one's foster-mother would be scarcely less objectionable than marriage with one's mother, and marriage of brother and sister might in certain circumstances be tolerated.

The same year saw the publication of his *Pentateuch*, enriched with prologues, and in the following year came the *Answer to More*, which suffers from the same structural defects as More's own polemical writings. The *Exposition upon Matthew V, VI, VII* (1533) comes nearest of all Tyndale's works to offering us a system of Christian ethics. *The Supper of the Lord*, also 1533, is attributed to him on internal evidence. Revisions of his earlier translations, new translations of *Jonas* and of the books from *Joshua* to *Second Chronicles* (left in manuscript), and a *Brief Declaration of Sacraments* occupied the rest of his life.

I have already explained why I do not propose to analyse these works separately: but what emerges from them all, taken in the mass, is so important for our understanding of the whole period that we must attempt to disengage it. I shall begin with the periphery of his thought and work gradually to the centre.

Mr. Gavin Bone, the deeply lamented Marcellus of our faculty at Oxford, gave it as his opinion that 'Tyndale hated literature'. It is too strong. Tyndale certainly dismissed 'Beuis of Hampton, Hercules, Hector, and Troylus' in the *Obedience* as 'fables of loue and wantonnes and of ribauldry, as filthy as hart can thinke', and oddly included Robin Hood in the same class. This is the ordinary attitude of the humanist to medieval story: it is very unlikely that More would have thought otherwise. He also repeatedly twits More with being a 'poet': but everyone knew that poets were feigners and under the rules that then governed controversy the jibe was almost inevitable. Even now a writer who has ventured on any imaginative work is likely to have the fact used against him when he turns to criticism or theology.

G

In the *Wicked Mammon* again Tyndale speaks with contempt of the 'railing rhymes' in *Rede me and Be not Wroth*: but they were really contemptible. What is true is that Tyndale thought very little about *belles lettres*, about literature for its own sake: he had matters in hand which seemed to him more important. He also speaks with great harshness (as More had spoken with droll mockery) of scholasticism, and, unlike More, extends his disapproval to the real Aristotle and the pagan philosophers in general. Near the end of the *Wicked Mammon* he attributes to Aristotle views which I do not think Aristotle held. But later, in the *Obedience*, it appears that Tyndale's objection is not to Aristotle as such but to Aristotle as a substitute for, and contamination of, the Biblical revelation. Let men be first grounded in scripture, and then 'if they goe abroad and walke by the fieldes and medowes of all maner doctors and philosophers, they could catch no harme: they should discerne the poyson from the hoonny and bring home nothyng but that which is holsome'. Modern critics do not perhaps always remember that where the premiss ('there has been a revelation') is accepted, some such conclusion is logically unavoidable.

On scripture Tyndale has naturally much to say. He has learned that Greek and Hebrew both go better than Latin into an English version, and even 'worde for worde', whereas, 'thou must seeke a compasse in the Latin and yet shalt haue much worke to translate it well fauouredly, so that it haue the same grace and sweetenesse'—not the words, surely, of a man who in all senses 'hated literature'. He thinks Deuteronomy 'the most excellent of all the books of Moses' and Romans 'the most principal and excellent part of the New Testament'. He leaves the real authorship of Hebrews an open question, and refuses to follow Luther in rejecting the Epistle of St. James. It need hardly be added that he departs entirely from the medieval method of interpreting the sacred text. 'Scripture', he says, 'speaketh after the most grossest maner: be diligent therefore that thou be not deceaued with curiousnes', and elsewhere more beautifully 'God is a spirit and all his wordes are spirituall. His literal sense is spirituall.' Parables are not to be tortured 'word by word' into detailed allegories; the meaning is in the whole story only. At the same time he shows real critical balance by allowing allegories in what he conceives to be their proper place. We may draw an allegory from scripture 'in the liberty of the

Spirit' provided we know what we are doing—provided that we know it is our own work and not the sense of the text, provided that we do not claim to prove anything by it and say nothing by it which cannot be proved from the literal sense of some other passage. The use of such allegories is not to prove but to impress, 'for a similitude doth printe a thing much deper in the wittes of a man than doth a plaine speakyng and leaueth behynd him as it were a stinge'.

The 'gospel', for whose sake everything else in Tyndale's work exists, is easy to misrepresent in quotation. When he says (in the *Wicked Mammon*) that the divine law 'damneth' us not for our refusal, but precisely for our inability, to obey it, or again (in the *Prologue to Genesis*) that in God's sight 'the deede is good because of the man and not the man because of his deede', we seem to be faced with a doctrine both irrational and repellent. In reality Tyndale is trying to express an obstinate fact which meets us long before we venture into the realm of theology; the fact that morality or duty (what he calls 'the Law') never yet made a man happy in himself or dear to others. It is shocking, but it is undeniable. We do not wish either to be, or to live among, people who are clean or honest or kind as a matter of duty: we want to be, and to associate with, people who like being clean and honest and kind. The mere suspicion that what seemed an act of spontaneous friendliness or generosity was really done as a duty subtly poisons it. In philosophical language, the ethical category is self-destructive; morality is healthy only when it is trying to abolish itself. In theological language, no man can be saved by works. The whole purpose of the 'gospel', for Tyndale, is to deliver us from morality. Thus, paradoxically, the 'puritan' of modern imagination—the cold, gloomy heart, doing as duty what happier and richer souls do without thinking of it—is precisely the enemy which historical Protestantism arose and smote. What really matters is not to obey moral rules but to be a creature of a certain kind. The wrong kind of creature is damned (here, as we know; hereafter, as Tyndale believes) not for what it does but for what it is. 'An adder is hated not for the euill it hath done but for the poyson that is in it.' 'We must first be euill ere we do euill, and good before we do good.' And we cannot change our own nature by any moral efforts.

Another way of putting it would be to say that Tyndale, as

regards the natural condition of humanity, is a psychological determinist. Action necessarily obeys the strongest impulse— 'the greatest appetite overcometh the less' (*Prologue to Romans*). Man is like a hound 'that cannot but folow his game when he seeth it before him if he be louse' (*Exposition on Matthew*). By nature we can 'do no good worke freely without respect of some profit either in this world or the world to come' (*Wicked Mammon*). That the profit should be located in another world makes, as Tyndale clearly sees, no difference. Theological hedonism is still hedonism. Whether the man is seeking heaven or a hundred pounds he can still 'but seeke himself' (*Prologue to Numbers*). Of freedom in the true sense—of spontaneity or disinterestedness—Nature knows nothing. And yet, by a terrible paradox, such disinterestedness is precisely what the moral law demands. The law requires not only that we should do thus and thus but that we should do it with 'a free, a willing, a lusty, and a louing hart'. Its beginning and end is that we should love God and our neighbours. It demands of us not only acts but new motives. This is what merely moral men—those who are now called 'puritans' though Tyndale, I am afraid, identified them with the Papists—never understand. The first step is to see the law as it really is, and despair. Real life does not begin till 'the cockatrice of thy poysoned nature hath beheld herselfe in the glasse of the righteous law of God' (*Brief Declaration*). For, when God 'buildeth he casteth all downe first. He is no patcher' (*Obedience*).

After the 'thunder' of the law comes the 'rain' of the gospel. Though Nature knows nothing of freedom, Supernature does. There is one will in existence which is really free and that will can join us to itself so that we share its freedom: 'as a woman though she be neuer so poore, yet when she is maried, is as rich as her husband.'

The transition comes by the gift of faith which immediately and almost by definition passes into love. We are confronted with the redemption which God performed 'to winne his enemye, to ouercomme him with loue, that he might see Loue and loue againe'. The essence of the change is that we now have power 'to loue that which before we could not but hate'. The 'fretting' voice of the law is now the will of the Beloved, already in principle (if not at every moment) our own will, and a man can 'be glad and laugh from the low bottome of his hart' (*Pathway*).

Here at the centre—miles inward from all the controversies about pardons and indulgences and relics and images—one sees how tragically narrow is the boundary between Tyndale and his opponents, how nearly he means by faith what they mean by charity. The idea that his doctrine of faith dispensed a man from works is a gross misunderstanding. They are not, for him, the cause of salvation, but they are its inseparable symptom. We are 'loosed from the law'—by fulfilling it. 'Deedes are the fruites of loue and loue is the fruit of fayth.' 'Whatsoeuer fayth has receaued . . . that same must loue shed out, euery whit, and bestow it.' This is indeed inevitable for 'as a man feeleth God in hymselfe, so is he to his neighbour' (*Wicked Mammon*). In Christ we are all one—'I am thou thyselfe and thou art I myselfe, and can be no nearer of kyn.' Where deeds of love—to enemies, to Turks, to 'the very beasts' (*Prologue to Exodus*)—do not follow what seemed to be faith, we may conclude with certainty that it was not faith but 'a dreame and an opinion'. Hence Tyndale's social ethics are exactly the same as those of More. 'To bye as good chepe as he can and to sell as deare as he can, to rayse the market'—all the deeds of Economic Man—are damned by God (*Wicked Mammon*). Not to give alms is 'murder and theft'. Rent-raising and enclosure are forbidden—'God gaue the earth to man to inhabit; and not unto sheep and wild deer' (*Obedience*).

A modern is tempted to say that if both parties were thus agreed about practice the difference between them must have been an idle subtlety. Is it not a little pedantic of Tyndale to insist so vehemently that all these works, however indispensable, could never *earn* the divine approval? But to answer Yes would be to overlook the gigantic effort which Tyndale's theology is making to leave room for disinterestedness and the desperate need for such an effort which then existed. Christianity is in constant danger of relapsing into theological hedonism. It had so relapsed in the eighteenth century when Boswell could say (without contradiction from Johnson) that the doctrine of future rewards and punishments was its very essence. And few, of any school, will deny that it had similarly relapsed in the later Middle Ages. Heaven, hell, and purgatory had been too long and too vividly presented. If in the resulting religion, with its fasts, pilgrimages, penances, and treasuries of 'merits', Tyndale could see nothing but a system of prudential bargaining,

I will not say that he was right: but he was not grossly, nor inexplicably, wrong. From all this spiritual commercialism—this system in which the natural and economic man could be as natural and economic about religion as about anything else—he had found freedom in his doctrine of faith. Here at last a man could do something without a business motive. Once the tree had been made good (by no merit of its own) of course it would bear good fruit, almost as a by-product—'naturally', 'of hys owne accorde', 'without commandment, even of his own nature', 'without looking after any reward'. Eternal life will of course follow good works in fact 'without seekyng . . . though no man thought thereon': nay 'we are in eternal life already'; no longer bribed, no longer acting like a baby 'for payne of the rod or for fear of bugges or pleasure of apples' (*Prologue to Exodus*).

In all this we may be very sure that what Tyndale is attacking is a mere travesty of what his best opponents held; as what they attack is also a travesty of his own view. In these controversies each party writes best when he is defending what (well considered and in a cool hour) the other did not really deny. But it is important for us as historians to see how the Roman system appeared to Tyndale and to numbers of Englishmen in that century. It seemed to them the religion of gloom and anxiety, the service of a hard taskmaster. 'If thou trust in thy workes, there is no rest. Thou shalt thinke, I haue not done inough. If thou trust in confession, then shalt thou thinke, haue I told all? Haue I told all the circumstances? Did I repent inough?' But, equally, it seemed to them the religion of self-righteousness. If the devout person thinks that his good works are done 'of his own natural strength and of the natural power of his free will' he must, according to Tyndale, draw the conclusion 'that euery man hath might euen so to do' and thence despise those who do not: they could if they liked. It reads more like an answer to Pelagius than to the Church of Rome: but Tyndale thought the Church of Rome Pelagian.

The questions left unanswered and the difficulties raised by Tyndale's gospel will be visible to all, but we are not here obliged to judge him as a theologian. What concerns us more as literary historians (seeking to get into men's minds, to taste tempers rather than to judge doctrines) is the beautiful, cheerful integration of Tyndale's world. He utterly denies the medieval distinction between *religion* and secular life. 'God's literal sense is spiritual.' Wiping shoes, washing dishes, nay, our humblest natural functions (he uses all these examples) are all equally 'good works', and the ascetic life wins 'no higher room in heaven' than 'a whore of the stews if she repent'. I do not know that many had exactly denied this, but it was usefully said. Pain and hardship sent by God or self-inflicted may be needed to tame the flesh. They had, Tyndale thought, no other value: therein differing from More who thought that God might have many other ways of taming yet chose pain 'for His godly delight in justice'. Finally, Tyndale said something long over-due, and set his heel on one of the ugliest tendencies in medieval thought, when he wrote:

Beware that thou get thee not a false fayned chastitie made with the vngodly persuasions of St. Hierome or of Ouid in his filthy booke of the remedy agaynst loue; lest, when throughe such imaginations thou hast vtterly despised, defied, and abhorred all womankynde, thou come into such case thoroughe the fierce wrath of God, that thou canst neither lyue chast nor finde in thy hart to mary (*Prologue to Numbers*).

If much that was holy and lovely in medieval ascetism was lost at this time, some genuinely vile and Manichaean elements were rejected also.

As a writer, Tyndale is almost inevitably compared with More. In one quality he is obviously inferior to his great antagonist: that is, in humour. He ventures on an occasional pun ('Nicholas de Lyra *delirat*'), and he has contemptuous coinages—*chopological* for *tropological* is the best. Nor would he be a man of his age if he could not sometimes fling out a happy violence, as when he speaks of a sickly stomach 'longing after slibbersauce and swash'. Only once does he venture on to More's own territory and then with a joke (to my thinking) so good that, however he detested the application, the Chancellor's lips must have twitched when he read it. Tyndale has been attacking the doctrine that we can profit by the superfluous merits of the religious orders; and ends with the advice 'If thy wife geue thee nine wordes for three, go to the Charterhouse and bye of their silence'. But it is only one flash against More's re-current summer lightning. In scurrility they are about equals; except that hard words sound less unlovely from the hunted than from the hunter. Digressions are a fault in both, not always from the same causes. Tyndale's is the digressiveness of a stretched mind, full of its theme and overflowing all bounds in its impetuous and happy prodigality: More's, sometimes, the rambling of a brooding, leisurely mind—a man talking, with the whole evening before him and the world full of interesting things. Where Tyndale is most continuously and obviously superior to More is in style. He is, beyond comparison, lighter, swifter, more economical. He is very unadorned (an occasional alliteration, some rhetorical repetitions, some asyndeton) but not at all jejune. The rhythm is excellent, the sort of rhythm which is always underlining the argument. In its sharpness of edge, its lucidity, and its power of driving the reader on, it has certain affinities (allowing for the difference of period) with the prose of Mr. Shaw's prefaces. What we miss in Tyndale is the many-sidedness, the elbow-room of More's mind; what we miss in More is the joyous, lyric quality of Tyndale. The sentences that stick to the mind from Tyndale's works are half way to poetry— 'Who taught the Egles to spy out their pray? euen so the children of God spy out their father'—'that they might see Loue and loue againe'—'where the Spirit is, there it is always summer' (though that last, we must confess, is borrowed from Luther). In More we feel all the 'smoke and stir' of London; the very plodding of his sentences is like horse traffic in the streets. In Tyndale we breathe mountain air. Amid all More's jokes I feel a melancholy in the background; amid all Tyndale's severities there is something like laughter, that laughter which he speaks of as coming 'from the low bottom of the heart'. But they should not be set up as rivals, their wars are over. Any sensible man will want both: they almost represent the two poles between which, here in England, the human mind exists— complementary as Johnson and Shelley or as Cobbett and Blake.

More and Tyndale easily make good their claim to the attention of the literary critic: among the lesser writers on either side the controversy gradually fades away into regions that concern us not much more than state papers. But there is one man of real genius still to be considered. Hugh Latimer's[1] character

---

[1] b. 1485?–1490? at Thurcaston, Leicestershire. Cambridge, 1506. Fellow of Clare Hall, 1510. Priest's Orders, 1524. Proceeds B.D. and pronounces oration against Melanchthon. Converted to Protestantism by Bolney and goes prison-visiting with him. Sermon before the Bishop of Ely arouses suspicion of heresy, 1525: Latimer summoned before Wolsey. Two sermons 'On the Card' at Cambridge, 1529. Is one of the divines mustered by Gardiner in favour of the king's divorce,

may be ambiguous or even repellent: his sermons, in their own kind, are resounding successes, 'though, to be sure, not very theological'. Latimer assents, indeed, to the doctrine of justification by faith, but he is no theologian; some of his apparent tergiversations may perhaps result from the bewilderment (even the impatience) of a 'plain man' entangled in matters above his capacity. Whatever he may say (when he remembers) about faith, he is really so exclusively interested in works that not only a Papist but a Pelagian or even a good pagan could read nine-tenths of his sermons without a qualm. Nor is he a humanist: *ego non calleo Graece*, he professed in his final examination. He is one of the purest examples in English of the 'popular' preacher in the fullest—if you will, the lowest—sense of that word. He boasts himself the son of an English yeoman and works in 'the uprightly, plain Dunstable way'. He is full of anecdotes, jibes, digression, and simple vituperation; he takes his hearers into his confidence, explains how this or that illustration came into his head, forgets himself and recalls himself: all sounds as if it were extemporaneous. We should probably be naïve if we took the style at its face value. An appearance of casualness ('I am no orator as Brutus is') is one of the rhetorician's weapons: and I suspect that everything which seems to fall by chance from Latimer's lips is consciously devised to hold the attention and undermine the resistance of the audience. He establishes intimacy with them in order to sway them. It is a

1530. Appointed to preach before the king at Windsor. One of the Commission to report on heretical books. Vicar of West Kingston, Wilts., 1532, cited before Convocation and finally confesses to error of doctrine. Attempts to persuade Bainham (then waiting in Newgate to be burnt) to submit; without success. Sermon at Bristol leads to fresh accusation, 1533. Apparently protected by favour of Anne Boleyn. Appointed to preach before the king every Wednesday in Lent, 1534. Becomes Bishop of Worcester, 1535. Collaborates with Cranmer and Shaxton in examining heretics. Protests against use of recently dissolved monasteries as royal stables. Sermon before Convocation, 1536. Argues against Purgatory in correspondence with the king, 1537. Examines John Forest, complains to Cromwell that his imprisonment is insufficiently rigorous, and preaches at his execution, 1538. Absents himself from Parliament during final debate on the Six Articles: resigns bishopric: attempts flight: caught and placed under arrest, 1539. Liberated, forbidden to preach and to visit London, Oxford, or Cambridge, 1540. Imprisoned in Tower as a supporter of Crome, 1546: released on accession of Edward VI. Sermon on 'Restitution' in king's garden, 1548. Seven Lenten sermons before the king, 1549. Serious illness, 1550: sermon at Stamford. Member of commission for correcting Anabaptists, 1551. After accession of Mary summoned to London, 1553: given chance of flight but refuses to take it; imprisoned in the Tower. Sent to dispute at Oxford and refuses to abjure, 1554. Burnt at Oxford, 1555.

well understood homiletic technique which descends to him from the Middle Ages (his method has affinities with that of Chaucer's Pardoner) and which has survived into our own days under the opprobrious names of 'straight talkism' or 'high pressure Christianity'. Some cannot endure it. They have a right to their taste, but they must not infer from the style that Latimer is a charlatan. The spiritual cheapjack and the sincere preacher both have equal, though different, motives for wishing to arrest and control a congregation and therefore may both (if they can) adopt a manner which will certainly achieve this end. 'Young feller', said General Booth to Kipling, 'if I thought I could win one more soul to the Lord by playing the tambourine with my toes, I'd—I'd learn how.' The only test which Latimer would admit as relevant for his sermons is their practical efficacy. And they were efficacious. We are told that when he preached on the duty of restitution it was not long before certain anonymous donations began to reach the king's treasury. That does not perhaps justify us in calling his work literature: but the mere strength and pith and urgency of his sentences, in that age so given to verbiage, is a literary virtue. He is as importunate as Hazlitt. He would have been a fine broadcaster.

Thomas Cranmer's[1] great achievements as a translator are sunk in the corporate anonymity of the *Book of Common Prayer*. As an original writer he is a much more shadowy figure than Latimer. That he had thought about the art we know from the very interesting annotations which he made on Henry VIII's corrections of the *Institution of a Christian Man* in 1538. The frankness of these comments does credit to both parties. Most are naturally doctrinal, but some are stylistic; 'These sentences, methinks, come not in aptly in some places as they be brought in but rather interrupt and let the course and phrase of the paraphrasis', or 'the sentence as it is printed runneth more euenly'. This is our only glimpse into Cranmer's workshop: the

[1] b. 1489. Taught by 'a marvellous severe and cruel schoolmaster'. Fellow of Jesus, Cambridge, 1511. Marries, forfeits fellowship, loses his wife and recovers fellowship. Ordained, 1523. His views on the divorce, expressed to Gardiner at a chance meeting, recommend him to the king. Ordered to write on this question. Archdeacon of Taunton, 1529. Sent to Rome on the same matter, 1530. Ambassador to the emperor, 1531. Re-marries, 1532. Archbishop of Canterbury, 1533. Member of the Council of Regency, 1547. Signs Edward VI's act devising the crown to Lady Jane Grey, 1553. On accession of Mary sent to the Tower. Removed to Oxford, 1554. Degraded and handed over to the civil power as a heretic; recants, recants his recantation, and is burnt, 1556.

finished product, except in the Prayer Book, is so severely utilitarian that we might not have suspected any conscious concern for style in the author. His preface to the Great Bible of 1539, after some preliminary flourishes which are a very faint anticipation of euphuism, consists mainly of translation, and very good translation too, from Chrysostom and Gregory Nazianzene. The three pieces certainly known to be his in *Certain Sermons or Homilies*[1] (1547) are those on salvation, on faith, and on good works. They aim neither at subtlety nor eloquence. Cranmer's only concern is to state an agreed doctrine with the least possibility of misunderstanding: the thing could hardly be done delightfully but it is done well. His *Defence of the True and Catholic Doctrine of the Sacrament* (1550), revised in 1551 as *An Answer to . . . Stephen Gardiner*, nowhere rises above the usual level of controversy in that age. In all these works Cranmer writes a prose with which it is difficult to find any fault, but it gives curiously little pleasure. It never drags and never hurries; it never disappoints the ear; and (*pace* John Foxe) there is hardly a single sentence that leaves us in doubt of its meaning. He could have taught More and even Tyndale some things about the art of English composition: but they can be loved and he cannot. This is partly because while avoiding their vices he lacks their virtues. He is not stodgy and verbose like More: but then he has neither humour nor pathos. He is not digressive like Tyndale, but then he lacks Tyndale's fire. The explanation is that Cranmer always writes in an official capacity. Everything he says has been threshed out in committee. We never see a thought growing: his business is to express the agreed point of view. Everyone who has tried to draw up a report knows how fatal such conditions are to good writing. Every phrase that really bites or flashes has to be crossed out in the end: it would offend one party, or be misunderstood by another, or unduly encourage a third. What remains when all the necessary erasures have been made is inevitably flat and grey. In Cranmer the wonder is that what remains is even so lively as it is. Compared with official publications either by Church or Civil Service in our own day, it is almost magnificent: but in such a book as this we are comparing it with real literature. By that standard it cannot rank high. It is praiseworthy: it is (if I may put it that way) devastatingly praiseworthy. What Cranmer might have

[1] i.e. the 'first Book of Homilies'.

written if the burden of responsibility had ever been lifted from his shoulders and he had made a book to please himself, we can only guess. He did his proper work and he did it very well, but I do not think I shall often re-read him. I had much rather hear Latimer thump his tub.

Four other controversialists may be briefly mentioned. Simon Fish's *Supplication for the Beggars* (1529) provoked More's *Supplication*. Fish writes more as a politician and economist than as a theologian: his rhetoric is monotonous and commonplace but not quite ineffective. John Rastell's *Book of Purgatory* (1530) on the opposite side is more happily conceived, under the influence of More. It is an imaginary dialogue between a Turk and a German which attempts to defend the doctrine of purgatory on philosophical grounds. It lacks More's humour and dramatic invention and Rastell does not understand his opponents well enough to be dangerous. John Frith whom they tied to a post in Newgate so that he could neither stand nor sit and who died at the stake praying for his enemies in 1533, looms larger as a man than as an author, though he is not contemptible even in the second capacity. His works include a *Disputation of Purgatory* (against Rastell, More, and Fisher), an *Antithesis* (of Christ and the Pope), a second book *Against Rastell*, a *Mirror to know thyself*, and treatises on Baptism and the Sacrament. Most of these were written in the Tower where he was forbidden books and writing materials and therefore 'when I heare the keyes ryng at the dore, strayte all must be conuayed out of the way; and then if any notable thing had been in my minde it was cleane lost'. His style, if a little wordy, is alive and he is fond of such rhetorical questions as are learned in conversation rather than in the schoolroom. He is not without humour. Robert Barnes (1495–1540) is in every way a lesser man. His tracts, which cover the usual topics, are all combined in John Day's folio with his *Supplication* to Henry VIII. His style is not good enough to enliven dull matter nor bad enough to spoil a plain tale; hence the account of his trial before the chapter of Westminster is still readable. Barnes, Frith, and Fish all share More's faults without his virtues, and all bring into the field the same undisciplined armies of adjectives. Rastell is more concise, but he is dry and jejune.

Before turning from the controversies to the translations it will be convenient to deal with two Scotch writers, Knox and

Winzet. They carry us beyond the proper chronological boundaries of the present chapter, but I deal with them here lest they should trouble us later when better game is before us.

The six volumes into which Laing collected the works of John Knox[1] (1505–72) are of absorbing interest to the historian; of less, I suspect, to the theologian who may find nothing in them which is not said better elsewhere. On the literary historian their claim, though by no means negligible, is smaller. One might assess it by saying that Knox is about as important a literary figure as More would have been if he had written neither the *Utopia* nor the *Comfort against Tribulation*.

If the *Vindication* (of the doctrine that the Mass is idolatry) represents exactly what Knox said before the Bishop of Durham in 1550, it must be almost his earliest work; but in it he has already reached his maturity. He writes a good, level prose, not notably Scotch, nor notably Ciceronian, nor even, despite the years that have passed, notably archaic. The humanist peeps out when he complains of the Canon that 'thairin is indigest, barbarous, fulische congestioun of wordis', but he attempts no classicisms.

At the accession of Mary, Knox, who had been preaching in England since 1549, fled to the Continent, and thence poured forth short pieces to his persecuted co-religionists at home. They are his most moving, though not necessarily his best, works. In the *Confession and Declaration of Prayers* he recalls his days in the French galleys, how he 'called to the Lord when not onlie the ungodlie but evin my own faithfull brether, yea and my own self (that is, all naturall understanding) judgeit my cause to be irremeadable. . . . I know the grudgeing and murmuring complayntes of the flesche: I know the angeir, wraith and indignatioun.' In the *Exposition upon the Sixth Psalm* his conscience seems to be troubled about his flight from England. 'Some will ask then, why did I flie? Assuredlie I can not tell: but of one thing

[1] b. at Gifford, East Lothian, 1505; at University of Glasgow, 1522; priest's orders, 1530; tutor to sons of Hugh Douglas, 1544; adherent of George Wishart, 1545; at surrender of St. Andrews castle treacherously handed over to the French as a galley slave, 1547; released, 1549, and appointed preacher at Berwick; defends his doctrine before the Bishop of Durham, 1550: appointed Chaplain to Edward VI, 1551; refuses bishopric of Rochester, 1552; on accession of Mary flies to Dieppe, Jan. 1554; accepts call from English congregation at Frankfort, Sept. 1554; at Geneva, and revisits Scotland, 1555: m. Marjorie Bowes and returns to Geneva, 1556; returns to Scotland, minister at Edinburgh, diplomatic mission to Berwick, 1559; loses his wife, 1560; remarries, 1564; paralytic stroke, 1570; ob. 1572.

I am sure, the feir of death was not the chief cause. . . .' He had learned, beyond his expectation, to love England as well as Scotland. The *Godly Letter to the Faithful in London* which begins by disclaiming oratory is in fact the most rhetorical pamphlet he had yet written. But it is the rhetoric of passion, not of affectation. The *Epistle to His Afflicted Brethren in England* is full of his exulting certainty that the persecutors will be punished in this life and in the next. It is impossible to suppress the uneasy remembrance (even though we dare make no judgement) that these fiery exhortations are uttered by a man in safety to men in horrible danger. The peak of violence was reached in the *Faithful Admonition*: 'that outrageous pamphlet' which as the English congregation at Frankfort protested to Calvin himself had 'added much oil to the flame of persecution in England'. Knox is already becoming the *enfant terrible* of Calvinism; and in the *Admonition* we see both why and how. He imagined that his error lay in just the opposite direction. He thought himself a timid temporizing, culpably gentle preacher. Others (inexplicably) accused him of 'rude plainness': he knew in his heart that he constantly sinned by not speaking out. He was 'not fervent and faithfull enough'; partly through cowardice, 'the blynd love that I did beare to this my wicked carcase', but partly for a reason which no man who had ever met him would have remotely suspected. 'My wicked nature desired the favours, the estimation, and the prayse of men . . . so prively and craftily dyd they enter into my breast that I could not perceive myself to be wounded tyl vainglory had almost gotten the upper hand.' One is tempted to say that no equal instance of self-ignorance is recorded until the moment at which Johnson pronounced himself 'a very polite man'.

In 1558, now once more in Geneva, excommunicated and burnt in effigy, he addressed an *Appellation* (that is, an appeal) from this ecclesiastical sentence to the *Nobility and Estates of Scotland*. It is at once an appeal against persecution and (in the long run) an appeal for counter-persecution: in a word, it develops the whole plan of Presbyterian theocracy. The civil magistrate is mistaken if he thinks it is not his concern to 'feed Christ's flock'. On the contrary, the 'ordering and reforming of religion' is his special business. Kings are told in scripture to serve the Lord; how can they do so unless they punish and 'by a godlie severity' forbid whatever is done against His command?

But perhaps a king may fail in this duty: then the nobles must 'correct and repress' him. For 'none provoking the people to idolatrie oght to be exempted from the punishment of death', and Moses laid the duty of inflicting this punishment not on kings only but on the whole people, even on every individual. 'To a carnal man', it is true, some of the Old Testament judgements on idolatrous cities may seem too rigid: so much the worse for the carnal man. This for the nobility: for the *Commonalty* he adds another letter explaining that if they do not accept their share of the duty it will not avail them in the day of wrath to say 'we were but simple subjects'. Knox, in fact, undisguisedly appeals to every section of the community to use instant violence for the establishment of a revolutionary theocracy. The writing is admirably lucid.

In the same year, though it was probably written earlier, appeared the most embarrassing of all his works, the *First Blast of the Trumpet against the Monstrous Regiment of Women*. It was embarrassing because in a certain sense nearly everyone (except regnant queens) agreed with Knox. Everyone knew that it was contrary to natural and divine law that women should rule men. But then a great many political arrangements as the world now is are equally contrary to Natural Law. We are fallen. It is no use trying to make a sudden return to the Golden Age: prescription, usage, municipal law, must all be respected. Spenser knew as well as Knox that the 'regiment' of women was 'monstruous'. The whole point of the story of Radigund is that women are 'borne to base humilitie'; but then Spenser, as a practical man and as the loyal citizen of a concrete state, adds the qualification 'Vnlesse the heauens them lift to lawfull soueraintie'. Calvin knew as well as Knox that the rule of women 'was a deviation from the original and proper order of nature' and 'to be ranked, no less than slavery, among the punishments of the fall of man'. But since 'by custom, public consent and long practice' certain principalities do descend to women by inheritance, it is unnecessary to raise the question, because it is 'unlawful to unsettle governments'. Bullinger thought the same. Of course, if you press it, women should be subject to men. But if positive laws have in fact placed the crown on a woman's head pious persons had better mind their own business and say nothing about it. St. Philip never told the Ethiopian eunuch to depose Candace. Knox had, in short, acted exactly like himself. No book more calculated to damage the Protestant cause could have been written—and all, as Calvin says, *ob inconsideratum unius hominis fastum*, because one conceited man would not think what he was doing. No one wanted the thing to be said, yet no conscientious doctor could answer it in the resounding style which alone would satisfy Queen Elizabeth. No woman likes to have her social position defended as one of the inevitable results of the Fall.

The *First Blast* was intended to be the first of three. But it was loud enough alone. Knox admits exceptions to the general principle, but they are not based on law or hereditary right. They are such women 'as God, by singular privilege . . . hath exempted from the common rank of women'. As for the rest ('women as nature and experience do this day declare them . . . weake, fraile, impacient, feble, and foolish') no merely human law can sanction their rule. It is not only in itself 'monstruous' but 'monstriferous'. St. Paul has said in so many words that he permits not a woman to bear rule over a man; therefore, 'Nowe let man and angell conspire against God, Let them pronounce their lawes and say, We will suffre women to beare authoritie, who then can depose them? Yet shall this one word of the eternal God spoken by the mouth of a weake man, thruste them everie one into hell.' He concludes by pronouncing it the duty 'as well of the Estates as of the People' to depose all sovereign queens and to kill all who defend them, previous oaths of allegiance notwithstanding. And he never to the end of his days seemed quite to understand why Elizabeth disliked this little book. He had advanced proofs from scripture; if they were invalid, let them be answered. If not, as he wrote to her in 1559, 'Quhy that youre grace be offendit at the authore of such ane worke, I can perceave no just occasion.'

The two works of Knox which come nearest to being books are the *History of the Reformation in Scotland* and the treatise on Predestination. The latter, printed in 1560, is *An Answer to a Great Number of Blasphemous Cavillations*; an answer, that is, to an otherwise unknown Anabaptist tract entitled *Careless by Necessity*. Its tone is harsh and vindictive. The burning of Servetus is applauded and Knox itches to use the sword of the civil magistrate against his opponents. But the tone of the Anabaptists and (in their brief moment of power) their action had been equally harsh. It was an age very like our own. Behind every system of sixteenth-century thought, however learnedly it is argued, lurks cruelty and Ogpu.

The four books of the *History of the Reformation of Religion within the Realm of Scotland* were composed between 1559 and 1566; the fifth book added in David Buchanan's edition of 1644, though of historical value, is not by Knox. From the literary point of view it may be said that too much scissors and paste went to the making of Knox's *History*: original documents, a popular poem, large passages from Foxe and other authors are inserted at length and spoil its narrative flow. There is some Latinism in the style, not in the long sentences but in the short, where historic presents and extreme conciseness at times give a faintly Tacitean effect. In the cast of his mind, too, there is something not unlike Tacitus' sombre pungency, though Knox's humour, as becomes a countryman of Dunbar, is more boisterous and ferocious. Sometimes, indeed, it is so ferocious that we should not recognize it at all if we were not told; as when after describing the murder of Cardinal Beaton down to the last grim detail of packing the corpse in salt ('the wether was hote') he proceeds, 'These thingis we wreat mearelie: but we wold that the reader should observe Goddis just judgementis'. He was apparently afraid lest the fun of the thing might lead us to forget that even an assassination may have its serious side. More to modern taste is the spirited farce of the following ecclesiastical rough and tumble:

Then begane no litill fray but yitt a meary game; for rockettis war rent, typpetis war torne, crounis war knapped, and syd gounis mycht haue been sein wantonly wag from the one wall to the other. Many of thame lacked beardis and that was the more pitie, and tharefore could not bukkill other by the byrse[1] as bold men wold haif doune.

Much alliterative verse lies behind such a passage. And though it is intended to make us laugh, it has also a very different function in the narrative where it occurs. Knox is working out an elaborate parallel between the passion of George Wishart (his most beautiful martyr) and the Passion of Christ. As the trial of Christ reconciled Herod and Pilate, so that of Wishart reconciled Cardinal Beaton and the Archbishop of Glasgow. To know why they needed reconciliation we must know how they quarrelled; and thus the comic story of the previous fray

[1] *bukkill other by the byrse*, grapple one another by the bristle.

between their attendants comes in. Elsewhere the comedy is unconscious, as in the whole account of Knox's dealings with Elizabeth. It was at the moment when English aid was all-important to the Scotch Protestants that he saw fit to write her the letter in which he protests that she has no reasonable cause to be offended at his *Monstrous Regiment*. He is, of course, not 'myndit to retract or call back' a word of it. Elizabeth, however, need not feel her withers wrung provided she recognizes herself as one of those rare exceptions to whom a special divine mercy has made lawful what is not naturally lawful to her sex, and does not show herself 'ungrate' by claiming anything on the grounds of inheritance. 'Forgeteth youre birth and all tytill which thairupoun doth hing'; and then, as a timely inducement to humility, 'consider deiplie how for feir of your lyef ye did decline from God and bow till idollatrie'. His relations with Mary Stuart make even better reading. In graver merits the history is not very rich. Except for Wishart, none of his martyrs is made lovely: usually brutal arrogance in the judge confronts brutal courage in the prisoner. His battles are harder to follow than those of Pitscottie; which does not at all prove that they are less accurate.

Although this survey has omitted several of Knox's works (notably the 'Familiar Epistles' in which we see him as a spiritual director) it is perhaps sufficient to give the reader some idea of his scope and quality. It might be supposed that to read a body of work so occasional, so little varied in subject-matter, and so fierce in temper, was a hard task. In reality, the surprising thing is that it is not harder. He has humour: in places he even has tenderness. But his chief merit is his style. Except for a few alliterative passages ('wyly Winchester, dreaming Duresme, and bloudy Bonner'—'glorious Gardener and treacherous Tunstall') and some apostrophes, it is very unadorned: and one's praise of it tends to be in negatives—a mere list of the faults that it avoids. But it is safe and dependable prose; a better prose than any (except Tyndale's) which we have met in this chapter. It is not the style that keeps readers away from John Knox.

Knox's chief opponent in the vernacular was Ninian Winzet (1518–92) who began his career as master of the Grammar School in Linlithgow and ended it in exile as Abbot of St. James's in Ratisbon. The Reformation ejected him from his mastership and he replied with *Certane Tractatis* in 1562. The 'tractates' are three: an address to Queen Mary, an open letter to John Knox, and what Winzet truly calls a 'declamation' on the suppression of Christian festivals. The *Last Blast of the Trompet*, which he tried to publish in the same year, was suppressed by government and only a few pages survive. He was soon driven from the country and his most important vernacular work, the *Buke of Four Scoir Thre Questions*, was printed at Antwerp in 1563. His earlier books, being written by one of the defeated party and not yet in exile, are distinguished from most polemical writings of that age by the absence of direct insult. They gain by it immensely: Winzet adopts an ironical (almost a demure) tone which is, to a modern taste, far more effective than scurrility. The schoolmaster is very clearly discernible. In the 'Third Tractat' he admits that his matter is such as he had often set to his pupils for original Latin composition and that he is now 'almaist for pastyme' working it up into a vernacular 'declamation'. As an account of his motive for writing this is, no doubt, ironical, but as an account of his method it is true enough. The artful *dispositio*, the opening paragraphs which begin far away from his real theme, and the long sentences, unmistakably though not grotesquely Latin in structure, all tell the same tale. In this respect, though in no other, his prose sometimes suggests that of a Scotch Milton. When he gets down to business in the *Buke of Questions* he is more idiomatic. The burden of his complaint is that for all his questions, challenges, and open letters he could never get an answer out of the 'Calvinians', except for a few inadequate words in a sermon by Knox. This seems to be true; whether that Knox feared his opponent or that Power was already beginning to learn the shabbiest *arcanum imperii*—'Never answer'. Abbot Ninian was a serious critic and well worth meeting, though his place in literary history is naturally a small one. One leaves this brave, clever man with regret. He must have been a pleasant dominie, for his memory recalls 'children of happy ingynis, mair able to leir than I wes to teche'. He writes a pure Scots and is disgusted, honest man, with Knox's anglified affectations—'Gif ye, throw curiositie of novationis hes foryet our auld plane Scottis quhilk your mother lerit you, I sall wryte to you my mynd in Latin, for I am nocht acquyntit with your Southeron.'

II

The English Bible and the *Book of Common Prayer* are achievements of much more lasting value than the original works of More and Tyndale. The Prayer Book is the one glory of the Drab Age; so glorious indeed that it would throw doubt on the justice of the epithet 'Drab' if we forgot that it was principally a work of translation. The qualities which raise it above its period are due, in the main, to its originals. The story of the English Bible might be denied a place in our account of the Drab Age on a different ground; that age saw only the beginnings of the work. But those beginnings coloured the entire process, and it will be convenient to treat the story as a whole in this section, even though we are thereby forced to run over its chronological boundaries.

There is no occasion for saying anything here about the Wycliffite versions of scripture. Tyndale tells us that he made no use of any English predecessor and we have no reason to doubt his word. He was making a fresh start. The new scholarship, even without the new theology, was sufficient to determine this; translators who knew only Latin were now out of date. The first Hebrew Psalter was printed in 1477, the Pentateuch at Bologna in 1482, the complete Soncino Bible in 1488. The Hebrew Grammar of Pellicanus Rubeaquensis (1503) had been followed in 1506 by the Grammar and Dictionary of Reuchlin. The years 1514 to 1517 produced two works of capital importance. At Alcala (the Latin Complutum) Cardinal Ximenes superintended the monumental Bible known as the *Complutensian Polyglot*, in which St. Jerome's Latin, the Vulgate, appeared flanked by Hebrew on the one side and Greek on the other, thus placed between the Synagogue and the Greek Church (as the cardinal pleasantly remarks) like Christ crucified between two thieves. The other great work was Erasmus's Greek text and new Latin version of the New Testament. He is said to have used manuscripts inferior to the cardinal's: he was working in haste, for his publishers were anxious to forestall the Polyglot. They won the race by getting his New Testament out in 1516: not, perhaps, to the lasting advantage of Biblical scholarship. In 1522 came Luther's New Testament, largely his independent work on the Greek. 'No fine words' was his avowed principle, and the tradition of homely simplicity passed from his work, through Tyn-

dale, to the English translators. During the years in which
Tyndale and Coverdale were at work (1525–40) new helps to
study were produced; Münster's Hebrew Grammar in 1525, the
great Zürich Bible (based on Luther but worked over by Zuin-
glius with several learned assistants) in 1529, the French versions
of Lefèvre (1534) and of Olivetan (1535). Most important of all
were the two Latin translations of the Old Testament by Sanctes
Pagninus (1528) and by Münster (1534–5). The English translators were taking part in a general European effort, which,
though predominantly, was not exclusively, Protestant.

In England itself the story is most easily disentangled if we
distinguish three streams, or groups. There is firstly what may be
called the central Protestant tradition, which starts with Tyndale and passes through Coverdale into those officially approved
translations the 'Great' Bibles and the 'Bishops' Bible. Secondly,
there are what may be called the Protestant irregulars—Taver-
ner, Sir John Cheke, Whittingham, and his collaborators in the
Geneva or 'Breeches' Bible. Thirdly, there are the popish versions, the Rheims New Testament and later the Douay. The
central Protestant group begins by being predominantly Lutheran but becomes less so as time goes on. The Geneva Bible is
the work of Calvinists. All three groups affect one another and
all affect the Authorized Version. Though there was little
charity between translators in rival camps they remained in
some degree united by the common humility of scholarship and
most of them recognized the principle *fas est et ab hoste doceri*. Thus
Tyndale accepts corrections of his work flung out in controversy
by More; the Jesuits who make the Rheims version draw upon
Coverdale's *Diglott* and Geneva; and it is pretty to see that some
phrases pass from Geneva through Rheims into the Authorized.
In spite of its divisions all western Christendom is involuntarily
collaborating: it is as if 'this rich thing' (like the Grail) 'went
about' among them of its own will.

I begin, then, with the central Protestant tradition. In 1525
the heretic-hunter Cochlaeus (or in the vernacular Dobneck; he
was not fortunate in names) discovered that Tyndale and an
assistant were seeing a translation of the New Testament through
the press at Cologne. He raised the hue and cry, and the cul-
prits fled up the Rhine to Worms, carrying the printed sheets
with them. By chance a single fragment survives of the quarto
whose printing was interrupted at Cologne: it goes as far as the

twenty-second of Matthew and is now in the British Museum. In 1526 the interrupted work was issued at Worms in octavo by Peter Schoeffer: two copies of it are known. In 1530 came Tyndale's version of the Pentateuch, in 1531 his Jonah; in 1534 revised editions both of his Genesis and his New Testament. A still further revision of the latter followed in 1535. He is also judged (on good evidence both external and internal) to have made the translation of the books from Joshua to 2 Chronicles which was included in the so-called Matthew's Bible of 1537.

Ever since his own day Tyndale's translation has been blamed for being tendentious. If we are thinking of his violent marginal glosses, this is fair enough; if of his peculiar renderings (*congregation* for ἐκκλησία, *senior* or *elder* for πρεσβύτερος, *favour* for χάρις, and the like), a little explanation seems to be needed. The business of a translator is to write down what he thinks the original meant. And Tyndale sincerely believed that the mighty theocracy with its cardinals, abbeys, pardons, inquisition, and treasury of grace which the word *Church* would undoubtedly have suggested to his readers was in its very essence not only distinct from, but antagonistic to, the thing that St. Paul had in mind whenever he used the word ἐκκλησία. You may of course disagree with his premiss: but his conclusion (that *Church* is a false rendering of ἐκκλησία) follows from it of necessity. Thomas More, on the other hand, believed with equal sincerity that the 'Church' of his own day was in essence the very same mystical body which St. Paul addressed; from his premiss it followed of course that *Church* was the only correct translation. Both renderings are equally tendentious in the sense that each presupposes a belief. In that sense all translations of scripture are tendentious: translation, by its very nature, is a continuous implicit commentary. It can become less tendentious only by becoming less of a translation. Hence when Bishop Gardiner in the Convocation of 1542 tried to stem the tide of Protestant translation he found himself driven by the logic of his position to demand that in all future versions nearly a hundred Latin words (his list included *Ecclesia, Penitentia, Pontifex, Sacramentum,* and *Gratia*) should be left Latin or only morphologically 'Englished'. This is not popish dishonesty, and Tyndale's renderings are not Protestant dishonesty: both follow from the nature of translation. It need hardly be added that the merely aesthetic or emotional grounds on which some moderns would prefer *church* to *congregation* would have disgusted More and Tyndale alike by their frivolity; souls were at stake.

As a scholar, Tyndale, while always retaining his independence, is deeply indebted to Erasmus's Latin version of the New Testament, to Luther, and to the Vulgate. He is also in full sympathy with Luther's conception of what Biblical translation should be—a homely, racy affair that can reach the heart and mind of a plough-boy. Partly for this reason, and partly because he is still steeped in the medieval blindness to anachronism, he naturalizes his originals in a way that will seem quaint to modern readers. Thus the gates of Lystra in Acts xiv become a 'churche porche', a centurion is an 'under-captain', there are 'shyre touns' in Palestine, and St. Paul 'sayled away from Philippos after the Ester holydayes' (Acts xx. 6). He uses at times more homely language than the Authorized Version wished to retain; 'when ye praye, bable not moche as the hethen do' at Matt. vi. 7, or 'choppe and change with the worde of God' at 2 Cor. ii. 17. Such, at least, is his general tendency, but there are times when he uses the foreign and harder word without need, so that in the first two chapters of Romans (i. 3, 8 and ii. 11) we find *perteyning*, *published*, and *parcialite*, where only Geneva follows him in the two first and none that I have seen in the third. He is a free translator and does not scruple to omit a noun where he thinks a pronoun will serve better or to interpolate a clause when he thinks the meaning would be difficult without it. He is, of course, sometimes astray: the details of St. Paul's shipwreck proved too much for him as for nearly all the early translators. All critics have rightly praised him for some of his coinages: *shewbread* (to which he was helped by Luther), *peacemaker*, *passover*, *long-suffering*, and *scapegoat*, and also for some unforgettable phrases such as 'Die the death', 'The Lord's Anointed', 'flowing with milk and honey', and 'filthy lucre'. He has also expressions less fortunate, such as the word *blessedfulness* in Romans. He established in English the form *Jehovah*, and was among the first who used the word *beautiful*.

Tyndale's immediate successor was Myles Coverdale (1488–1568) whom we have already met as a versifier. He claims the honour of having produced the first complete English Bible. It is almost certain that this was first printed at Zürich by Froschover in 1535 and the original title-page claimed that it was translated 'out of Douche and Latyn'. It will be noticed that there is no mention of Greek, still less of Hebrew: it is disputed whether Coverdale knew any Hebrew and agreed that he did not know much. 'Douche' of course means German: the title-page stamped Coverdale's work as Lutheran, dangerous therefore to the author. Whether because his fears increased or because the changing policy of governments soon encouraged him to hope for a permitted circulation in England, his work was reissued in the same year by James Nycholson at Southwark with a new title-page in which the words 'Douche and Latyn' were omitted. Only a part of this Bible was new. Coverdale used the Pentateuch, Jonah, and New Testament of Tyndale; the residue of the Old Testament he translated himself with help from the Vulgate, Pagninus, Luther, and the Zürich Bible. From this onward Coverdale becomes, in a sense, the official government translator, repeatedly employed on authorized revisions of his own and other men's work for the Matthew's Bible and the Great Bibles. The tendency of his revisions was influenced by the official policy of the moment. We need not accuse him of insincerity. He had not learning enough to have solid grounds of his own for choosing between the various interpreters who all lay together on his desk: ignorance, in a sense, left him free to be accommodating.

It may also be suspected that ignorance left him free to indulge aesthetic preferences, to follow this or that interpretation according as it agreed with his own, often exquisitely melodious, English style. But the suspicion must not be too readily accepted. Thanks to the labours of Mr. Clapton it is easy to compare his 1535 version of the Psalms with that which he made for Cromwell's Great Bible in 1539, and which survives in our prayer books today. Here we find change after change which so improves the rhythm that one might suppose it made for that purpose alone, but which in fact brings his rendering nearer to that of Münster, whom he somewhat overvalued. Thus in i. 4 'His leaves shall not fall off' becomes 'His leaf also shall not wither'; in ii. 1 'Why do the heathen grudge?' becomes 'Why do the heathen so furiously rage together?'; or 'How long?' in vi. 3 is expanded to 'How long wilt thou punish me?' All these alterations appear to be made in deference to Münster. There is also in the later version a tendency (I think) to move away from Luther and Zürich and certainly a tendency to make more use of the Gallican Psalter (that is, St. Jerome's earlier version from the Greek, not to be confused with his later version from the Hebrew). This is doubtless accounted for by the 'moderate' policy of the bishops for whom Coverdale was working in 1539. Yet much remains which seems to have its principal source in his own poetic impulse. We owe to him, and to some primers, the beautiful 'even', 'neither', and 'yea' to introduce a Hebrew parallelism. From nothing more than *oculus* in Jerome and *Gestalt* in Luther he produced 'my *beauty* is gone for very trouble' (vi. 7). He blended Jerome's earlier *patientia* with his later *expectatio* to get 'the patient abiding of such as be in trouble' (ix. 18), and likewise *in medio umbrae mortis* with *in valle mortis* to get 'the valley of the shadow of death' (xxiii. 4), and out of Münster's *in imagine pertransit* conjured his own 'walketh in a vain shadow' (xxxix. 4). 'Daughter of Babylon wasted with misery' (cxxxvii. 8) is compounded of *vastata* in the Gallican Psalter and *misera* in the later Jerome. In one sense his work is hardly translation at all, but a mixed production like Pope's Homer or Fitzgerald's *Rubaiyat*. Sometimes the misunderstood original sets his own imagination working with results that are not beautiful but ridiculous: as in Acts xxvii. 16, 17 where he gives 'We coulde scarce get a bote. Which they toke vp and vsed helpe, and bounde it under harde to the shippe.' Sometimes he can be unsuitably familiar, as when he begins Isa. v with the words 'Now well then I will synge my beloved frende a songe of his vyneyarde'. He can be misleading even where (I think) he understands the text, as at Rom. v. 7 where 'Now dyeth there scarce any man for the righteous' would be taken by most readers as a general reflection on the decay of charity and thus ruin the argument. But there are felicities everywhere. He is responsible for 'baptized into his death', for 'tender mercies', and for 'lovingkindness'; 'respect of persons' instead of 'parcialite' was also his. Compared with great divines and scholars like Ximenes, Erasmus, Tyndale, and those who made the Geneva, the Rheims, and the Authorized, Coverdale might perhaps be regarded as a mere hack: but he is often an inspired hack.

In 1537 while Nycholson was still reprinting Coverdale's first Bible, the curious production known as the Matthew's Bible was already in the press, probably at Antwerp. It professes to be 'truly and purely translated . . . by Thomas Matthew'. In reality it is mainly Tyndale (including his Joshua to 2 Chronicles) and Coverdale, corrected by one John Rogers, a pupil of

Tyndale's. It is doubted whether any real Thomas Matthew had a finger in it. The important thing is that it is 'set forth with the kinges most gracyous lycence', is at last an 'authorized' version. The shadowy Matthew is probably government's device to make it appear that they are producing a new thing and not merely sanctioning a *fait accompli*. In 1538 came Coverdale's *Diglott*, consisting of the Vulgate and a close English rendering. After this the Bibles of the central tradition are so related that nothing short of actual collation would much help the reader. In 1539 under the auspices of Cromwell came the Great Bible, a revision by Coverdale: in 1540 another Great Bible (with Cranmer's Prologue) which was a further revision by Coverdale. Its second edition in the same year claims to have been revised by the bishops of Durham and Rochester, but scholars have not discovered traces of their work. In 1542 the reaction began, and it was then that Bishop Gardiner produced his list of words that should never be translated. In 1543 it became illegal for all except the higher classes of society to read the Bible in English: in 1546 all subjects whatever were forbidden to 'have, take or keep' either Tyndale's or Coverdale's New Testament. By 1554, Mary being now on the throne, the mere painting of a text on a church wall became illegal. In 1559 Elizabeth's government ordered the Bible once more to be set up in the churches, but the central Protestant tradition did not produce a new one till the Bishops' Bible of 1568. It was based on the Great Bible from which the revisers were ordered not to 'recede' except where it was in manifest error. They were also, in accordance with Elizabeth's policy, forbidden 'bitter notes'. The chief novelty of principle in this version is that the revisers were instructed to see that 'all such wordes as soundeth to any offence of lightness or obscenitie be expressed with more convenient termes and phrases'; prudery had been as unknown to the earlier translators as to the originals. In other respects the Bishops' Bible is blamed by scholars for its conservatism, for neglecting real progress which had been made since the Great Bibles appeared.

Of the Protestant irregulars an account on this scale must confine itself to the Geneva Bible of 1560, for Cheke's work (mainly remarkable for his personal hobby horse about 'pure English') was not published till the nineteenth century and therefore had no influence on the tradition, and Whittingham's

1557 New Testament is eclipsed by his share in the Geneva itself. His collaborators were Anthony Gilby and Thomas Sampson. With this group we find ourselves at Geneva among the Marian exiles. Whittingham had married a sister of Calvin and Calvin contributed an epistle to his New Testament. What Coverdale had called 'the Douche' becomes less important; new influences are at work—Calvin himself, Beza, and the French translators. To the eye, the Bible now first takes on its familiar aspect, printed in Roman, using italics for words supplied by the translator (as Beza had done) and dividing the verses—an innovation which improved it as a book of reference but made sad work of narrative and argument. In translation it attempts, like Tyndale, to keep close to the Hebrew, and it has none of the Bishops' prudery. In many ways it marks a great advance. Of the versions I have seen Geneva first makes sense out of the nautical passage in Acts xxvii. Some of its most felicitous turns have gone into the Authorized—'smite them hip and thigh', 'vanity of vanities', 'except a man be born again'. It has its share of odd, and unnecessary, words such as 'guiltieship' (Rom. v. 16), and perhaps 'patron' for ναυκλήρῳ in Acts xxvii. 11 may be regarded as a Gallicism. One of its most familiar contributions to our text I find difficult to judge. At Isa. xl. 1 Coverdale first wrote 'Be of good cheer my people'. In Cranmer's Great Bible he changed this to 'comfort my people'. Geneva has 'Comfort ye, comfort ye my people', reproducing (I am told) the rhythm of the Hebrew but obscuring the construction. This illustrates the extreme uncertainty of our literary judgement on all the translators. What chance has Coverdale's second rendering with us against the familiarity of the Geneva adopted by Authorized and most unfairly backed by Handel? A man would need to unmake himself before he was an impartial critic on such a point. But on almost any view, Tyndale who inaugurated, and the Genevan translators who first seriously advanced, our tradition, tower head and shoulders above all others whom I have yet mentioned.

There remains the Roman tradition, represented within our century by one work, the New Testament printed by Fogny in 1582 and translated at the English College of Douay (temporarily housed at Rheims from which this version derives its name). The work was directed by Cardinal Allen and assisted by Richard Bristow; the actual translator was Gregory Martin,

Lecturer in Hebrew, and sometime a scholar of St. John's, Oxford. The Council of Trent in 1546 had pronounced the Vulgate to be the only authentic Latin version and Martin worked from it, not from the original. This, however, does not by any means remove his work from serious consideration; he had the Greek also before him, he used Geneva, and was himself used by the Authorized Version. The principles on which he proceeded are set out in the preface to the Rheims Testament: 'We presume not in hard places to mollifie the speches or phrases, but religiously kepe them word for word and point for point, for fear of missing or restraining the sense of the holy Ghost to our phantasie'. The results of this principle led to the Protestant criticism that Papists, when at last forced to translate the scriptures, took good care to make their translation unintelligible. It was an irresistible debating point, but it misses the real problem. All parties were agreed that the Bible was the oracles of God. But if so, are we entitled to worry out the sense of apparently meaningless passages as we would do in translating Thucydides? The real sense may be beyond our mortal capacity. Any concession to what we think the human author 'must have meant' may be 'restraining the Holy Ghost to our phantasie'. If this line of thought is followed far enough we shall be forced to abandon the design of writing down what (we think) the sacred text means, and merely write down the English of what it actually says, whether this makes sense or no. Translators who are agreed on the oracular character of the original are thus faced with a dilemma. If you follow the one alternative you may arrive at nominal 'translations of scripture' in which the originals are made to mean anything that the translator and his sect happen to believe. If you follow the other you may arrive at the idea of a magical text (like the hymn of the Salii) whose virtues are quite independent of meaning—at devotions to 'the blessed word Mesopotamia'. Fortunately none of our translators is at either extreme; but Tyndale is nearer to the first and Rheims to the second. This does not mean that Tyndale is dishonestly periphrastic or Rheims nonsensical: both are honest and skilful attempts to solve the problem. Thus Rheims leaves many words as near the Latin as it can, writing *veritie* instead of 'truth', *benignity* instead of 'kindness', *justice* instead of 'righteousness' (which is misleading) and *longanimity* instead of 'patience' (which can be very strongly defended). Sometimes it offends

quite unnecessarily against English idiom as in Rom. i. 22—
'saying themselves to be wise'. The medieval naturalizations of
the earlier translators are dropped; the 'under-captain' becomes
a 'centurion' and what Tyndale had called 'a flaw of wind out
of the Northeaste' becomes 'a tempestuous wind that is called
Euro Aquilo'. But to pick out such renderings gives a false impression. A great deal of Rheims is vigorous and genuine English, and there are even places in which it finds homelier renderings than its precursors; as in Acts xxvii. 3 where all other
versions say that Paul was allowed ashore to 'refresh himself',
but Rheims 'to take care of himself'. It has contributed some
beautiful turns to the Authorized. In Rom. vi. 1 where Tyndale
had 'that there may be abundance of grace', and Geneva 'that
grace may more abound', Rheims by omitting *more* produced
the rhythm which the Authorized took over: and in v. 9 it first
introduced the word 'dominion' (Geneva and the rest have
'power') which contributes so much to our own text's 'Christ
being raised from the dead, dieth no more: death hath no more
dominion over him'.

These examples illustrate the difficulty of making literary
judgements on the several translations. The variants are in-
dividually so small, the steps by which perfection is achieved so
gradual, that it is almost impossible to allot to each translator
his share of praise. We can seldom be sure that the changes
which seem to us to add beauty were made with that purpose.
I do not know whether Martin when he changed 'power' to
'dominion' was attentive to its phonetic superiority, or whether
he merely obeyed the same principle which led him to write
'verity' and 'benignity' instead of 'truth' and 'kindness'. I do
not know whether the Authorized translator, having accepted
'dominion' from Rheims, then retained 'being raised' from the
earlier English versions (as against Rheims' 'rising') because of
its rhythm, or to keep close to the Greek, or for theological
reasons. Even a few hours spent in actual collation will, I think,
leave the impression that the vast majority of variants result
neither from differences in doctrine nor from literary taste but
from the steady advance of scholarship.

The Authorized Version is treated, by a more learned pen
than mine, in a later volume, and little need be said of it here.
Some accounts of the subject do not, I think, sufficiently emphasize its debts to Geneva and Rheims. It is in a sense true that

Tyndale and Coverdale remain the base: but after Tyndale nearly all that is of real value was done by Geneva, Rheims, and Authorized. Our Bible is substantially Tyndale corrected and improved by that triad—almost in collaboration. The literary value and literary influence of the final result are singularly difficult to assess. The effect of any passage from it depends in so high a degree on the qualities of the original (which contributes the images and tropes as well as the matter) and on the qualities of an English that is to us archaic, and these in turn are both so overlaid with liturgical associations, that very little remains to be attributed to the translators and still less to the last translator in the long succession; and that small residuum is hard to isolate. Some endeavour to isolate it by concentrating on the book's rhythm: but I am not convinced that its rhythms (they are various) are very different from those of any good prose that is written for the most part in short sentences, nor that they would strike us as noticeably fine if divorced from their matter. 'After the cocktail, a soup—but the soup was not very nice— and after the soup a small, cold pie'. It is not a bad sentence: but it is very different from its rhythmical equivalent 'After the earthquake, a fire; but the Lord was not in the fire: and after the fire a still small voice' (1 Kings xix. 12). Is it not possible that critics whose philosophy forbids them to attach much value to the matter of scripture are tempted to attribute to rhythm, and indeed to style in general, more than its due—as Mr. Pickwick and his friends were agreed that whatever had so affected them at the party, it couldn't have been the wine? As for the influence of the Authorized Version, we must make a distinction. An influence (on thought and feeling) of ever present quotation, or half-quotation, or parody, recognized as such, is different from fully assimilated influence which has become unconscious. Obviously the Bible has plenty of the first. This reaches its peak in the nineteenth and early twentieth centuries: in writers like Swinburne, Trollope, and Kipling its use as a ready recipe for solemnity or irony becomes distressing. Of the second kind of influence it has, perhaps, less than we should have expected. I doubt if its style penetrates us so much as Dryden's. Fragments of it indeed are, or were, on everyone's lips—'the fear of the Lord', 'the fatted calf', 'whom the king delighted to honour', 'coals of fire', and the like. But they are always felt as quotations, or at least as archaisms, which stand out from the surrounding texture of the language and which (whether in reverence or derision) are valued for that very reason. It is indeed remarkable that so common a turn as 'it came to pass', after so many centuries, is never used except in this way, has never penetrated into the blood-stream of the language. The Authorized Version, in fact, haunts our prose not as Mr. Eliot haunts modern poetry or as Macaulay used to haunt journalists, but much more as Homer haunts the prose of Plato; that is, as something set apart, like plums in a cake or lace on a frock, not like wine mixing in water. As the metre and dialect set every scrap of Homer apart from the Plato in which it is embedded, so the archaism and sanctity tend to set apart the fragments of scripture embedded in English literature. I am not of course denying that it has some influence of the deeper and less obtrusive kind, but the wonder is that it has so little.

There is no such sharp break between the *Book of Common Prayer* (1549) and earlier liturgical prose as there is between Tyndale and the medieval translators of scripture. It is an anonymous and corporate work in which Cranmer bore the chief part, and it is almost wholly traditional in matter though some of the excellences of its style are new. It has two main sources. One of these is that form of the Latin service used during the Middle Ages in the diocese of Salisbury and known as the *Use of Sarum*. The other is the long series of books of devotion called *hours* or *primers* which had sometimes appeared in the fourteenth and fifteenth centuries in English as well as in Latin and which after a long interval are again found in English from 1534 onwards—reflecting, of course, many doctrinal changes. For the psalms, gospels, and epistles, Coverdale's revised version in the Great Bible of 1539 was used, with a few alterations. The litany made by Cranmer for the king's *Exhortation unto Prayer* in 1544 was taken over unchanged. Sometimes, but very sparingly, the compilers borrowed from the recent liturgical experiments of the continental Reformers. Some prayers they translated from the Greek; and some they added of their own, but these were closely modelled on scripture. They wished their book to be praised not for original genius but for catholicity and antiquity, and it is in fact the ripe fruit of centuries of worship.

From the vernacular primers we can see just how far writing of this kind had developed before the book was made. And in one respect, as I said in a previous chapter, the primers have a doleful story to tell. Their hymnody shows the ruin of our poetry. But prose (which, of course, fills far the greater part of them) is fairly steadily improving. In the medieval primer it is still awkward and enslaved to the Latin: 'Thee the preisable noumbre of prophetis, thee preiseth the whit oost of martris.' That rendering, indeed, seems to me to have, by chance, its own exotic beauty: but not so (from Psalm xcv) 'Before occupie we his face in knowleching', nor (in the *Te Deum*) 'Thee, endeles Fadir, every erthe worschipeth'. In the sixteenth-century primers, though all difficulties have not been overcome, we are already well on the way to the grace and freedom of the Prayer Book. The twelfth verse of Psalm li gives a good deal of trouble. A 1535 book printed by Byddell for Marshall does fairly well— 'and a stedfast right spirit make anew within me'; but John Gowghe's Latin–English Primer is reduced to 'strengthen me with a spiritual spirit' and a primer of 1539 reads 'with a principal heart'. On the other hand, the 1535 version of Psalm xix, whatever its value as translation, can vie with Coverdale as English literature; 'One day following another whetteth continually our thoughts, and one night following another increaseth our knowledge. . . . He hath fastened in them a tabernacle for the sun and he cometh forth of his clouds like a bridegroom; yea, like a fresh valiant knight to make his course.' This knight, especially to those who had seen the dazzling splendours of a Tudor tournament, is better than the 'giant' who has replaced him. A single petition in the litany well illustrates the same process. 'That thou vouchesaaf to give us fruits of the erthe', says the medieval book, plainly and perhaps not very idiomatically. In 1535 we have, 'That the fruits, Lord, on the erthe may give good increase and thou wilt conserve them'; and in 1539 'That thou vouchsafe to give and preserve the fruits of the earth'. Notice in the first of these the love of adjacent strong syllables (*fruits, Lord*) and in the second the coupling of *give and preserve*, which both anticipate the style of the Prayer Book. Then in 1544 we get the master's touch—'That it may please thee to give to our use the kindly fruits of the earth so as in due time we may enjoy them.'

In the vernacular books, then, the compilers of 1549 found worthy predecessors, and in the *Use of Sarum* they had an original which might tax the powers of any translator. The chief characteristic of its *orationes*, from which the book takes our collects, are three. In the first place they are what the Elizabethans called 'pithy': they condense in a few complex sentences matter which a more ejaculatory type of prayer would distribute over many petitions, and leave us much to chew on. Secondly, they show a distinct though restrained love of antithesis and epigram: this gives them an air of finality which only the polysyllabic character of Latin saves from being abrupt. And finally they rely for their musical effect on a great use of what scholars call the *cursus*, that is, on certain regular distributions of accent at the end of a sentence or clause, which are an accentual adaptation of the quantitative patterns used by classical prose writers.

The first great service which the compilers did us was to sweep away all the wretched attempts at hymnody which had made some primers ridiculous. They wanted very much to have hymns but had the good taste and humility to realize that they could not make them. 'Mine English verses', said Cranmer, 'want the grace and facility that I could wish they had'—a statement which in his age shows more loyalty to poetry than a wilderness of sonnets. But their great positive achievement is in translation. Their version of the collects is perhaps the supreme example of the virtues required for translating highly-wrought Latin. In the art of finding for Latin phrases free equivalents which, when found, will seem inevitable and carry no tang of alien speech about them, they set a standard which has hardly ever been equalled. In a sense, no doubt, their devices are obvious and prescribed by the very nature of the two languages; *securi videamus* (may with sure confidence behold him), *celestia simul et terrena* (all things in heaven and earth), *stella duce* (by the leading of a star), *presta in nobis religionis augmentum* (increase in us true religion). Yet any one of these could easily have gone wrong. The test is to start from the Latin at a place where you do not remember the English and see what your own rendering is like.

I have so far been considering passages where the book follows its originals closely. Its departures from them (when they are literary, not doctrinal) are equally interesting. Its most obvious difference from the Latin is its habit of coupling together synonymous or nearly synonymous words, so that *peccata* becomes 'sins and wickednesses', *mortifica* 'mortify and kill', *videant* 'perceive and know', *tradi* 'to be betrayed and given up'. It has sometimes been supposed that the second word is added in order to

H

explain the first to the unlearned, but this is a mistake. Six-teenth-century writers (including Cranmer himself in his *Homilies*) do sometimes add synonyms for this utilitarian pur-pose, but much more often they add them to adorn their style. In the example I have just quoted it is most improbable that 'betrayed' needed to be explained to anyone, and impossible that anyone either did not know the word 'sins' or would find it clarified by 'wickednesses'. It is worth noticing that 'acknow-ledge and confess' is matched by *agnoscimus et fatemur* in the *Liturgia Sacra* (1551) of the Flemish Protestant Pollanus. The truth is that the rule 'one idea, one word' is arbitrary and pedantic. To ring the changes, *wordum wrixlan*, was as natural a delight to the men of that age as it had been to Virgil or the Anglo-Saxon *scop*. The device can be abused, as Ascham knew, but the Prayer Book does not abuse it, and often derives from it, as from other expansions of the original, great rhythmical bene-fits. Thus in *que agenda sunt videant* (first after Epiphany), *que agenda sunt* by the mere nature of English has to become at least 'what they ought to do'. This, in obedience to the book's choice of a strongly supported rhythm, is made into 'what things they ought to do', and *videant* then has to be expanded to produce a balance: 'That they may both perceive and know what things they ought to do'. Similarly, on Ash Wednesday 'create and make' balances 'new and contrite'. The same motive which prompts pairs of synonyms also prompts additions. Thus in *vota humilium* (third in Lent) English forces us to have a noun with *humilium* so that we get 'thy humble servants'. It then seems to the translator's ear that *vota* also should have a satellite, and, selecting (for he is an Englishman) one that alliterates, he writes down 'the hearty desires of thy humble servants', where a medieval translator would probably have been content with 'vowes of us humble'. In addition to such rhythmical motives I suspect the influence of a feeling, and, I believe, a just feeling, that the resonant Latin words carry more not only to the ear but also to the heart and the imagination than their short English equivalents, so that 'faithfully to fill' is not an excessive allowance for *ad implenda* nor 'in the midst of so many and great dangers' for *in tantis periculis*.

Since the *cursus* of medieval Latin was, in comparatively recent times, rediscovered, many scholars have searched the Prayer Book to find how far the compilers endeavoured to reproduce in English this feature of their original. In my opinion some have found in it more specimens of the *cursus* than it contains and sometimes tortured the rhythm of the English to do so; but many of their claims may be just. There are four kinds of *cursus*; the *Planus*, as *nostris infunde* or 'help and defend us'; the *Planus* B, as *esse videatur* or 'written for our learning'; the *Tardus*, as *tradi nocentium* or 'them that be penitent'; and the *Velox* as *gloriam perducamur* or 'glorious resurrection'. Now it is obvious that such endings must often occur whether we intend them or not. Thus in the last paragraph but one, though I intended no such thing, I find that I have used three of them; 'highly-wrought Latin' (*Planus*), 'wilderness of sonnets' (*Planus* B), 'Primers ridiculous' (*Tardus*); and even 'achievement is in translation' might pass for a *Velox*. The question is whether they occur in the Prayer Book too often to be the work of chance. The reader must judge for himself. In the collects up to Trinity Sunday I count thirty-five: in a longish chapter of Caxton's Malory (vii. 16) three: in a page of the preface to *Crockford's Clerical Directory* containing thirty sentences I made out seven. Mathematically the results are not strikingly favourable; but we must take into account Cranmer's remarks to Henry on 'the course of the paraphrasis' and indeed the certainty that all the compilers were aware of the *cursus* in their Latin reading. It is therefore reasonable to suppose that some, at least, of the instances of it in the Prayer Book were intentional. But I am no less convinced that it does not hold the secret of the Prayer Book's music. It is very doubtful if these endings have the same value in English that they had in Latin: what English ear would find 'them that be penitent' (or 'higgledy piggledy') a *slow* movement? Anglo-Saxon verse is probably a better guide here than Latin prose. In English 'happen to the body' is essentially the rhythmical equivalent of 'hurt the soul', and its resemblance to *esse videatur* is probably quite unimportant. Certainly the compilers were fond of clashing strong syllables together in a manner that is purely native—'thy bright beams of light', 'borne of a pure virgin', 'all desires known'.

Such collisions of strong syllables are closely connected with what I have called the 'strongly supported' rhythms of the Prayer Book. A sentence may be regarded phonetically as a succession of peaks and valleys, the peaks being those syllables on which (at least) there is a full accent, and perhaps long quantity and emotional value as well. A strongly supported rhythm occurs when the peaks come close together and the valleys are short, and such rhythm is characteristic of the Prayer Book: as in 'our hearts may surely there be fixed where true joys are to be found', where at least six (possibly eight) out of the sixteen syllables are peaks. Where necessary this rhythm is kept up by insertions; by adding to *Son* the words *Jesus Christ* where the original had *filium* only or by using 'the same' where mere clarity does not demand it. It is chiefly this, I think, that gives to almost every sentence its aquiline movement—'upborne with indefatigable wings'. We find also, as in all good prose, a nice use of the principle *idem in alio*. Thus long monosyllables in one clause balance pairs of short syllables in the next, so that we 'cast away' the works of darkness but 'put upon us' the armour of light. Clauses which are co-ordinate, or in other respects similar, unexpectedly vary in length, so that we have a sudden sense of expansion and liberation at 'and from whom no secrets are hid' or 'by thy glorious resurrection and ascension'.

In tone, the differences between our Prayer Book and the *Use of Sarum* are not great but they are interesting. The translators tended to smooth out what was epigrammatic and to reject whatever might by the severest standards be thought exuberant. Sometimes they removed antitheses. *Te largiente regatur in corpore et te servante custodiatur in mente* became 'that by thy great goodness they may be governed and preserved evermore both in body and soul'. The Tacitean trenchancy of *quem nosse vivere cui servire regnare est* is abandoned; they are too wise to compete with Latin where Latin is supreme. And *regnare* is reduced to 'perfect freedom'. *Regnare* cannot have been thought unscriptural: but it is just on the far side of a line which the compilers do not willingly cross. Here, as elsewhere, we come on the affinity between the Drab Age and the eighteenth century. Of all things, the Prayer Book dreads excess. It has almost an Augustan shrinking, not from passion, but from what came to be called enthusiasm. Its preferences reveal themselves sometimes in tiny details. Where the Latin exhorts us on St. Stephen's day to pray 'even for our enemies', the English has simply 'for our enemies'. *Speciem tue celsitudinis*, tempting as it must have been in an age of ink-horn terms, is chastened into 'thy glorious godhead': *celesti pietate* becomes plain 'mercifully', *omnes celos*, 'thy kingdom in heaven', *omnis voluntas loquitur*, 'all desires known', and *crucis tormentum* and *crucis patibulum* both merely 'death of the cross'. The litany is made less exclamatory, the baptismal service less dramatic. And if we compare the book not with the *Use of Sarum* but with the primers we find a much sharper contrast. These, in the XV O's and elsewhere, strike a note utterly foreign to the Prayer Book—'Have mind, blessed Jesu, of all the great dreads, anguishes, and sorrows thou suffredest in thy tender flesh. . . . O Jesu, sweetness of hearts. . . . O bountiful Jesu, O sweet Jesu, the son of the pure virgin . . . the solatious comfort of all creatures. . . . O my sweet love and potential lord.' Our book is as sparing as the Gospels themselves of references to wounds, hearts, flames, blood, and tears.

The difference here does not exactly coincide with that between Roman and Anglican piety, though it comes near to doing so. It is partly the difference between private and public prayer; the tone of the XV O's is not so alien to our hymns as to our liturgy. It is partly, too, the difference between the freely emotional Middle Ages with their ready tears and boyish ardours and the graver, more deliberative period that was coming in. The book may even be said to owe something to the Drabness of the Age in which it was composed. Sobriety is the reverse side of Drabness. In the Prayer Book that earnest age, not itself rich either in passion or in beauty, is matched in a most fruitful opposition with overwhelming material and with originals all but over-ripe in their artistry. It arrests them, binds them in strong syllables, strengthens them even by limitations, as they in return erect and transfigure it. Out of that conflict the perfection springs. There are of course many good, and different, ways both of writing prose and of praying. Its temper may seem cold to those reared in other traditions but no one will deny that it is strong. It offers little and concedes little to merely natural feelings: even religious feelings it will not heighten till it has first sobered them; but at its greatest it shines with a white light hardly surpassed outside the pages of the New Testament itself.

DRAB AGE VERSE

THE 'new company of courtly makers' who came up, says
Puttenham, at 'the latter end' of Henry VIII's reign are
usually, and rightly, taken to constitute a decisive novelty
in the history of our literature. Yet they too had their precursors. During the later Middle Ages in England the lyric had
suffered less than any other form. The tune of the shorter line,
as anyone can see by comparing Lydgate's *Reason and Sensuality* with his *Troy Book*, had never been so completely lost as
that of the decasyllable; and in the lyric, which was nearly
always written to be sung, it was still further supported and
disciplined by the music. In the late fifteenth and early sixteenth
centuries we were a very musical nation. The art flourished at
the courts of Henry VI and Henry VIII, the names of Dunstable, Fairfax, and Cornish are still remembered by the historians of music, and Erasmus complimented us on our skill.
Most, perhaps all, the lyric poetry of that age is to be regarded as
words for music; hence purely literary judgement on it may be
as unfair as the study-criticisms we make about plays we never
saw acted.

The stanzas used by this poetry are mainly derived from those
of rhyming Latin. The rhyme schemes are never very complex,
the macaronic is often used, refrains are common. Short lines or
(what is the same thing to the ear) lines with internal rhymes
are favourites. The language is very plain. There is little
aureation, few metaphors, no stylized syntax, and none of the
sensuous imagery loved by the Elizabethans. One reason for
this plainness is that we are reading songs; richness and
deliciousness would be supplied by the air and the lute and
are therefore not wanted in the words. When they are read
merely as poems it produces results which were probably
unforeseen by the authors. It makes some pieces seem flat and
dull; others, admirably fresh and ingenuous. But those which
make dull poems need not have made dull songs. One that I
had thought very dry and colourless came dancing into life as
soon as a learned pupil (Mr. Norman Bradshaw) played me
the air on his recorder.

The best specimens of early Tudor lyric have long since won
their place in our anthologies. The 'Nut Brown Maid' may
be a little too long, but it has no other fault. 'Who shall have my
fair lady' is alive with chuckling gaiety. 'He bare him up he bare
him down' contrives, in homeliest language, to sound like news
from another world. 'My lady went to Canterbury' is among the
best nonsense poems in the language. The quatrain 'Western
Wind' need fear no rival in the Greek Anthology. There is
almost everything in it—weather, distance, longing, passion,
and sober home-felt reality. Many poets (not contemptible)
have said less in far longer pieces.

All that is best in Sir Thomas Wyatt (1503–42)[1] is rooted in
this poetry, such poetry as the song books have preserved. But
he cannot be regarded simply as the last of the early Tudor
lyrists. He modified the tradition by several new borrowings and
added something of his own.

He is, for one thing, the first of our Italianate poets, though
this element in his work may not have quite that importance
which the older critics claimed for it. In the first place, to
translate Petrarch was not necessarily to introduce a new note
into English poetry; it depended on the poems you chose and
on the quality of your rendering. Thus Wyatt's 'Myne olde dere
enmy my froward maister' is in fact a version of Petrarch's
canzone *Quel antiquo mio dolce*; but the canzone (an erotic allegory in the *Rose* tradition) is so medieval, and Wyatt's version
in stumbling rhyme royal is so like the rhyme royal of Hawes
or Skelton, that if the original had been lost and Wyatt were not
known to be the author, no one would dream of classifying the
poem as anything but late medieval. It is not a bad poem, but
it is written by a medieval Wyatt, who appears again in the
poem 'Like as the bird' (which is bad) and in the translation
from Boethius 'If thou wilt mighty be', which is good though

---

[1] b. at Allington Kent, 1503. As a boy fights a pet lion, 1515 or 1516. Enters
St. John's, Cambridge; M.A., and married Elizabeth Brooke, 1520. Clerk of the
King's Jewels, 1529: Christmas, 1525, one of the challengers in a tournament. Accom-
panies Sir Thomas Cheyne on embassy to France, 1526. On embassy to Italy, 1527.
Translates Plutarch's *Quyete of Mynde*, 1528. Marshal at Calais 1528–30; present
at coronation of Anne Boleyn, 1533. Imprisoned in the Fleet for a brawl, 1534.
Imprisoned in Tower, released, rusticated to Kent, knighted, made Sheriff of
Kent, 1536; on embassy in Spain, 1537. Corresponds with Cromwell, quarrel with
his fellow envoy Thomas Bonner; returns, 1538. On embassy, Paris and Flanders,
1539. Returns, 1540. Imprisoned in Tower on charges made by Bonner, 1541.
Trial; his *Oration*; acquitted. Ob. 1542.

not very lucid. And some medieval habits hang about him
elsewhere; tags like *without any fable* and *if Livy doth not lie*, and
doggerel that reminds us of Heywood. And, secondly, even
where the thing translated might be expected to impinge on
English poetry as a novelty, the translation may be so bad that
the impact is muffled: some of Wyatt's sonnets from the Italian
are so. No later sonneteer could learn anything from lines like

> Yet this trust I have of full great aperaunce
> Since that decept is aye retourneable
> Of very force it is aggreable
> And therewithal be done the recompense.

The rhyme scheme may be that of the sonnet: the poetics are
those of Barclay. To be sure, Wyatt wrote better sonnets than
this: the gap between his worst and best in this kind shows both
the difficulties he faced and the fine perseverance with which he
overcame them. Witness the liquid movement of

> Vnstable dreme according to the place
> Be stedfast ons; or else at leist be true:
> By tasted sweetenes make me not to rue
> The sudden losse of thy false fayned grace.

But it is not in these rare anticipations of the Elizabethan
sonnet that Wyatt's true importance lies. Knowledge of the
Italians, both directly and through their French disciples, was
to be so common in the Golden period that its poets had no
need of such scanty help as Wyatt's sonnets could give them.
The Elizabethan sonnet might not have been very different if
Wyatt had never lived.

His real place in the evolution of English poetry (as distinct
from his intrinsic value, his place of honour among English
poets) is really an unfortunate one. His own lyric gift he did not
bequeath to most of his successors; he did bequeath to them,
by his worst poems, the terrible poulter's measure[1] and the flat,
plodding style which almost inevitably goes with it. His 'Song
of Iopas' and 'Complaint of the Absence of his Love'[2] proved a
ruinous legacy. The latter, incidentally, shows how ambiguous
the expression 'Italian influence' may be. It is a translation of
Petrarch's *Si e debile il filo*; but not one drop, not one breath,

---

[1] A couplet consisting of an Alexandrine followed by a Fourteener.
[2] Sometimes called 'In Spayne'.

of the Petrarchan quality has gone into it. The thudding
verbiage of

> Thes new kyndes of plesurs wherein most men reioyse
> To me they do redowble still off stormye syghes the voyce,

raises a wonder why the man who thought Petrarch could be
translated so, also thought Petrarch worth translating. Historically considered, Wyatt is not the father of the Golden, but
of the Drab, Age.

His metre has lately become a controversial subject. A
majority of his lines scan according to the principles which
governed English verse from Spenser to the Edwardians: a
fairly large minority do not. The regular lines occur chiefly, not
exclusively, in his lyrics: the irregular, chiefly, not exclusively, in
what look like decasyllabic poems. The older critics took it for
granted that the irregular lines were due to the blundering of a
prentice poet who had not yet learned how to scan. Some modern
critics find in them extreme, and deliberate, subtleties of rhythm.
One critic thinks that this holds for some of the irregular lines,
but that others are mere blundering. In favour of the modern
view is the fact that some of the irregular lines give great
pleasure to our ear. Most of us like the reading of the Egerton
MS.

> Into a straunge fasshion of forsaking

better than Tottel's

> Into a bitter fashion of forsaking.

This, I allow, favours the modern view; but everything else
is against it. We have seen that Wyatt is often on a level with
Barclay. We have seen that, at the other end of the scale, in his
poulter's, he ticks out regular metre with the ruthless accuracy
of a metronome. Both phases are what we should expect in a
man who was escaping from the late medieval swamp; first,
his floundering, and then, after conversion, a painful regularity.
That both extremes should be absent from his lyrics is again
what we should expect, for the lyrical music had never been lost.
It is immensely improbable *a priori* that the same man at one
period of his career should have gone on, beyond the regularity,
to the subtlest departures from it. It is immensely improbable
that such departures could have had for him or for his contemporaries the beauty they have for a modern. To us the variation

is beautiful because we hear it against the background of the imagined norm: when the norm itself was a novelty to Wyatt (and a mystery to most of his hearers) the particular beauty which we feel could hardly have existed. Nothing, it seems, could incline us to the modern view except our reluctance to believe that melody can come by chance; and I am not sure whether it is a rational reluctance. Fortunately the question, though important for our verdict on Wyatt, is of no importance for the general history of our poetry. Even if Wyatt had such a subtle scheme as has been supposed, the secret of it had been lost before Tottel printed him, and had no influence on later poets.

Wyatt's work as a translator or adapter was not confined to sonnets and epigrams. His longer attempts are of very unequal merit. The *Penitential Psalms* are based on a prose version by Pietro Aretino set in a narrative framework, with help from Ioannes Campensis and from Zwinglius. The pictures of David entering the cave and of the sunbeam falling upon him are striking. The two opening lines of the Prologue,

> Love to gyue law vnto his subiect hertes
> Stode in the iyes of Barsabe the bryght,

show Wyatt in one of his rare Elizabethan moments. But the work as a whole is flat and sometimes cacophonous. Much better are the *Satires* based on Horace and Alamanni. From the latter he borrows *terza rima*. The excessive enjambment between the tercets which makes Wyatt's satires read almost like blank verse is not wholly due to the original; by comparing Alamanni's tenth satire with Wyatt's second we find that Alamanni has thirty-four stopped tercets out of a total of thirty-six, Wyatt twenty-four out of a total of thirty-four. It is more an imitation (in the eighteenth-century manner) than a version: as Juvenal's *graeculus esuriens* became Johnson's 'fasting monsieur', so Alamanni's *Provenza* becomes Wyatt's 'Kent'. Alamanni mentions winter to exult in the fact that, being now no courtier, he need not go out *quando agghiaccia e piove*; Wyatt sees in winter a chance of going out with a bow. The whole thing has a pleasantly English, country-house, atmosphere and reads like an original. The foreign model has here been thoroughly assimilated. In another piece the story of the town and country mouse is told with considerable spirit.

But Wyatt's permanent value is to be found in his lyrics. They are not, except in a very few places, precursors of the Elizabethan lyric. A single line such as 'The erth hath wept to here my heavines' or a whole poem like 'The answer that ye made to me my dere' may look forward; but essentially Wyatt is doing work of a different kind. His language is usually as plain as that of his English lyric predecessors; to a taste formed on the decorated tradition which runs through English poetry from Spenser to Tennyson it may even sound sub-poetical. The point can be brought out by comparing his refrains with those of other poets. From others we get refrains like Αἴλινον αἴλινον εἰπέ, τὸ δ᾽εὖ νικάτω,[1] and *cras amet qui numquam amavit quique amavit cras amet*[2] and *Mais où sont les neiges d'antan?* or 'Sweet Thames run softly till I end my song', or 'Put on perfection and a woman's name', or 'With hey-ho, the wind and the rain'. But Wyatt makes refrains out of words like 'ye old mule', 'Spite of thy hap, hap hath well happ'd', 'Disdain me not', 'Therefore take heed', 'It is impossible'. Clearly, we are not dealing with an incantatory or evocative poet. We are in fact dealing with a Drab poet—provided we remember always that 'Drab' is not a pejorative term. All Wyatt's weaknesses, and nearly all his strength, are connected with his unadorned style. When he is bad, he is flat, or even null. And when he is good he is hardly one of the irresistible poets. He has no splendours that dazzle you and no enchantments that disarm criticism. It is almost as though he said 'If you don't want to like me, you need not'. In order to appreciate Wyatt you must read with great attention and do your fair share of the work. He is not necessarily the worse on that account.

Here is a specimen of what I take to be bad Wyatt (though not Wyatt at his absolute worst)

> For cause yourself do wink
>   Ye iudge all other blinde;
> And secret it you think
>   Which euery man doth finde.
> In wast oft spend ye winde
>   Yourself in loue to quit;
> For agues of that kinde
>   Will show who hath the fit.

[1] 'Say alas alas, but let the good prevail.'
[2] 'Let him love tomorrow who never loved, and let him who loved love tomorrow.'

The thought and emotion are those of the dreariest wrangle, and the expression differs from that of prose only by being a little less flexible and lively. Compare with this,

> I promiside you
> > And you promisid me,
> To be as true
> > As I wolde bee.

It is, in one way, divided only by a hair's breadth from the previous example. It is no more adorned and certainly no more elevated. But the creaking inversions are gone; the rhythm exactly underlines an intonation that would occur in real speech; and yet the rhythm pleases. It is characteristic of Wyatt that his bad pieces are very like his worst. He is a miniaturist; one false stroke mars the work.

It is possible to cull from Wyatt, as from other poets, phrases or lines which remain beautiful when torn from their context. Dr. Tillyard has analysed with great accuracy the various ways in which the stanza 'Perchance thee lie withered and old' surpasses its Horatian counterpart (I do not say its Horatian original, for that would be hard to prove). Everyone remembers 'With naked fote stalking in my chambre' and

> for sodenly me thowght
> My hart was torne owte of hys place

and again

> But yet, alas, that loke all sowle
> That I do clayme of right to haue.

But such things do not necessarily come in the best pieces; it is not on them that Wyatt's success depends. It depends much more on the degree to which he has been able to give a whole poem a shape. His danger is that of being unprogressive, of writing poems that stop rather than end, poems that do not carry in themselves the reason for their length or for the order in which the stanzas come. Such are 'Farewell the heart' (or *rayn*) and 'I see that chance'. Each stanza might occur in a good lyric, but you cannot make a poem by simply stringing half a dozen such stanzas together. I think Wyatt himself was aware of the problem. In 'Marvel no more' he seems to have realized by the end of the third stanza that something must be done to make a capital for the column he was building and to have

attempted to supply it by some verbal wit on the word 'chance'.
In 'Disdain me not' the return to the original refrain in the last
stanza was probably made for the same reason. But these are
his unsuccessful pieces. In 'My Lute Awake' the whole poem is,
as it were, an ending, but it turns from this into another idea at
the fifth stanza and then resumes the main theme with an air
of great finality in the eighth. 'Perdie, I said it not' similarly
offers a new twist (a counter-attack) in the fifth, and after it a
real conclusion. 'What rage is this', in a stanza admirably
suited to the purpose, hurls line after line at us in a sullen monotony of passion for four stanzas and then rises to a curse. *In
eternum* is subtler. The refrain is given a slightly different meaning at each repetition. The last two lines do not in my opinion
mean that he has found a new mistress. They mean that another
thought, the thought of eternity, now occupies him; he is doing
his palinode, 'Leave me, oh love that reachest but to dust'.

Except for the form of the rondeau (and he did not make
much of that) Wyatt's debt to French poetry is small. If one
tried to reduce his lyrics under a recipe, one would have to say
'Petrarchan attitudes expressed in the traditional form of the
Tudor lyric'. But this would be most misleading. In a sense the
Petrarchan matter is all there, the ice and fire, the implacable
beauty. But when Wyatt handles them they all become different. Nothing could be more alien to him than the devout
Frauendienst, and the drugged or tranced melancholy of the
Rime. (Readers who do not know Italian will, by the way, learn
much more of that strange, great work from Synge's prose
version than from all the Elizabethans and all the Pléiade put
together.) His poems are full of resentment. Except in one
short, pleasant trifle about fingers, he does not praise ladies.
He never goes out of himself: how badly his mistress has treated
him, how well he deserves to be treated, how much more
fortunate he has been with other women, how sorry she will
be some day—such are his recurrent themes. Hence when we
read him in bulk, some of us find in him an atmosphere which
is from the first oppressive and finally suffocating. Poor Wyatt
seems to be always in love with women he dislikes. My sympathy
deserts my own sex: I feel how very disagreeable it must be for
a woman to have a lover like Wyatt. But I know this reaction
to be unjust; it comes from using the songs as they were not
meant to be used. Look at them again:

My days decaies, my grefe doeth gro
The cause thereof is in this place.

This was not intended to be read. It has little meaning until it is
sung in a room with many ladies present. The whole scene
comes before us. The poet did not write for those who would sit
down to *The Poetical Works of Wyatt*. We are having a little
music after supper. In that atmosphere all the confessional or
autobiographical tone of the songs falls away; and all the cumulative effect too. The song is still passionate: but the passion is
distanced and generalized by being sung. We may hear another
of Sir Thomas's inventions another night; but we are not going
to have ten or twenty on end. Each will be judged by itself;
they will never build up into the composite picture which the
modern student gets from the printed page. So taken, his best
pieces are very remarkable work indeed. They reach an intensity, and sometimes a dramatic quality which the English
lyric had hardly even attempted before. And they do this with
great economy, never going beyond the resources of Drab
poetry, using little sensuous imagery and no poetic diction. For
those who like their poetry lean and sinewy and a little sad, he
is a capital poet. His fame is in the ascendant.

Henry Howard, Earl of Surrey,[1] was in his twenties when
Wyatt died and there is no doubt that he greatly admired
Wyatt both as a poet and as a man. But the relation between
them was not exactly that of master and pupil. Surrey saw
Wyatt as one who had 'dayly' produced some famous work 'to
turne to Britains gayn' and 'taught what might be sayd in ryme'.
Though they come in a poetical elegy (where a man was not

---

[1] b. 1517. Said to have made good translations from Italian and Spanish as
a boy. Intimate with Henry, Duke of Richmond (bastard son of Henry VIII).
Married to Frances Vere, d. of Earl of Oxford, 1532. At French court with Rich-
mond, 1532. Begins to live with his wife and to borrow money, 1535. Present at
Anne Boleyn's trial; serves under his father against the Pilgrimage of Grace, 1536.
Suspected of sympathy with the rebels, strikes one who repeats this story and is
imprisoned at Windsor, 1537. In charge of anti-invasion defences in Norfolk, 1539.
Distinguishes himself in a tournament, 1540. Knight of the Garter, 1541. Attends
execution of Catherine Howard; imprisoned in Fleet, 1542. Again imprisoned in
Fleet for breaking Lent and breaking windows, 1543. Serves at siege of Landrecy,
1543. Employs Thomas Churchyard as page, serves at Montreuil, is wounded;
reprimanded for exposing himself to unnecessary danger, 1544. His dispatches
begin to displease government. He loses a battle at St. Étienne and is relieved of his
command. Later arrested on several charges of treason and beheaded, 1547. It is
hardly necessary to add that the picture of him given in Nashe's *Unfortunate Traveller* (1594) is of no biographical value.

expected to be precisely critical) these words, as it happens, define pretty well what Wyatt meant to Surrey. He was not so much the technical master as the man who had suggested new possibilities, who had claimed, and partly shown, that the new-fashioned continental poetry could be naturalized in England. In that sense, he inspired Surrey. But Surrey had, of course, his own independent access to the Italians and the Romans, and his technical standards were, in their own way, higher than any that Wyatt could have taught him. In some respects he hardly competes with Wyatt. He is much less affected by the native lyrical tradition: perhaps less related to music at all. The pieces in which he is closest to Wyatt ('Although I had a check', 'O lothsome place', or 'Though I regarded not') are neither his best nor his most characteristic. He does not care for refrains, and is happiest as a lyric poet in octosyllabic stanzas. He loves what was newest (and worst) in Wyatt, the poulter's measure. He is less medieval; with him the Drab Age is fully established.

His Petrarchan pieces are by no means his best; yet even in them it is easy to see why the Elizabethans preferred him to Wyatt. He was more accomplished, more useful. For the sonnet he often adopted that modified form less greedy of rhymes, which Shakespeare perfected, and availed himself of its greater ease to make sonnets which, if never very moving, are smooth and elegant and work up to a tolerable climax. Sometimes he produced equally good results with a more exacting rhyme scheme; as in 'The Soote Season' and his sonnet on sleep. His lyrics nearly all have the completeness, the shape, which Wyatt sometimes lacked. But the truth is that his love poetry is usually best when it is least about love. He takes every opportunity of bringing in external nature, or narrative, as if to take a holiday from the erotic treadmill. Oddly enough, the only two poems in which we are really moved by the theme of love are both put into the mouth of a woman; and of these women one certainly is, and the other may be, a wife in love with her husband. The better of the two is the lyric 'O happie dames' (freely adapted from an Italian original) which contains the best stanza he ever wrote. The other, in poulter's ('Good Ladies'), nearly triumphs over that jigging metre.

But if Surrey as a love poet is for the most part 'correctly cold and regularly low', he can express real feeling on other subjects: especially on friendship. His elegy on Wyatt has already been

mentioned: it is a little clumsy and a little too like a catalogue,
yet a credible picture emerges from it. More moving is the epitaph on his follower and comrade in arms, Thomas Clere. Best
of all is the poem on his imprisonment at Windsor. It has its
flaws (the tiger in l. 11 comes in very oddly) but it has caught
the very spirit of that pleasure which flows over like-minded
young men when they are all together and making their first
friendships. We shall meet so many satires on the Court in the
sixteenth century that it is important to learn from Surrey the
other side—

> The secret thoughtes imparted with such trust,
> The wanton talke, the dyuers chaunge of playe,
> The frendshipp sworne, eche promyse kept so iust
> Wherewith we past the winter nightes away—

for though they were great lords, and skilled knights, huntsmen,
and lovers, these courtiers were very young and very crowded,
sleeping two in a room and talking late like schoolfellows.

The *Satire* against the citizens of London wins us by its sheer
Falstaffian audacity. Surrey is in the Fleet for breaking windows.
Breaking windows?—he admits the charge, but claims that he
had the highest motives. He was acting as a prophet, almost as
'the scourge of God', awaking the conscience of that very
wicked city. But the idea, which might have made an amusing
epigram, hardly suffices for so long a poem. His religious works
—a paraphrase of Ecclesiastes i–v, and another of certain psalms
—are, of course, not good. Hebrew poetry, and Pindar, have
led better poets than Surrey to disaster, and he had certainly
not solved the problem raised by oriental imagery when he
wrote—

> Butter falles not so softe as doth hys pacyence long.

One line ('In booste of outwarde works he taketh no delight')
suggests an unexpected sympathy with Lutheran theology. But
the real interest of the paraphrases is metrical: not chiefly
because in Psalm lv Surrey attempts the unrhymed alexandrine
(nothing was to come of that till the *Testament of Beauty*) but
because he is now trying to reform the poulter's measure.

The vices of that metre are two. The medial break in the
alexandrine, though it may do well enough in French, quickly
becomes intolerable in a language with such a tyrannous stress-
accent as ours: the line struts. The fourteener has a much

pleasanter movement, but a totally different one; the line
dances a jig. Hence in a couplet made of two such yoke-fellows
we seem to be labouring up a steep hill in bottom gear for the
first line, and then running down the other side of the hill, out
of control, for the second. In his *Paraphrases* (chiefly in the
Ecclesiastes) Surrey is, I think, attempting to remedy this by
restraining the run-away tendency of the fourteener. He does
this sometimes by putting in another pause as strong as that at
the eighth syllable, and thus cutting his line in three—

> The World is false, man he is fraile, and all his pleasures payne

sometimes by inversions of stress in the neighbourhood of the
pause—

> Then aged Kings, wedded to will, that worke without advice—

sometimes by trisyllabic feet—

> And carrey the roodde that skorgeth them that glorey in their
>   gold.

With the alexandrine he takes fewer liberties, but those which
he allows himself yield impressive lines, as

> I, Salamon, Dauids sonne, King of Jerusalem,

or

> We that live on the earth draw towards our decay.

Even if the process had been carried further it would hardly
have made poulter's a good metre, but it might have made
more of the fourteener than Chapman ever did, and shows the
continually growing and exploring artistry of Surrey.

His greatest exploration was that which led him to translate
two books of the *Aeneid* in what the printer of the first edition
called, on his title-page, 'a strange metre', and what we call
blank verse. In this metre he had been anticipated by the Italians,
and it is reasonable to suppose that he derived the idea from
them: the suggestion that he found blank verse in the *Tale of
Melibeus* does not seem to me worth considering. Trissino and
others had already used the metre and Ippolito de Medici had
used it for translating Virgil. Surrey's version exists in the
Hargreave MS., in the print by John Day, and in Tottel:
variants are numerous and detailed criticism is inhibited by
our uncertainty as to which text, if any, represents Surrey's
final intentions. Even if that were known, critical judgement

would still be difficult: the original is so good that it will triumph over great defects of translation and to calculate what percentage of our pleasure is due to Surrey is a matter of great nicety. If, amid these perplexities, I am to hazard a verdict, it would be this; that Surrey has made a poor translation but good verses—for a pioneer, astonishingly good. A certain stiffness which we feel in his lines is not due to excessive end-stopping. It is rather a syntactical than a metrical stiffness. In his effort to keep close to the Latin Surrey does not leave himself room for flowing sentences. He thus becomes lapidary and laconic. This quality is not fatal to poetry but it is excessively anti-Virgilian. Virgil, like every great poet, is no doubt economic in fact ('no word he wrote in vain') but the impression he produces is one of lavishness—as of a rich wine swelled above the brim of the glass. He is full of echoes and vistas and partial repetitions. How different Surrey is, an example will show:

> Chorebus then encouraged by this chaunce
> Reioising sayd: Hold forth the way of health,
> My feres, that hap and manhod hath us taught:
> Chaunge we our shields: the grekes arms do we on.
> Craft or manhod with foes what reckes it which?

That *manhod* in the third line is probably a misunderstanding of the Latin does not matter much. What matters is that we have asyndeton where Virgil has *atque* once and enclitic -*que* thrice, that *my feres*, as Surrey tucks the words in, has none of the enthusiasm of *o socii*, that the construction of *reioising sayd* (later so dear to the Miltonists) strikes a foreign and 'classical' note which nothing in the original would have struck for Roman readers, and that the hortatory inversions of the fourth line prolong the same effect. The generosity of the wine has been lost in the decanting. Surrey's version as a whole is a little too severe, too cold. It is Virgil in corsets. If this effect is wholly unintended, it would be harsh to dwell on it: for we should stand by the first English blank verse as reverently as we stand by the springs of the Thames. But it may not be unintended: it may reflect the humanist or 'classical' misunderstanding of the ancients. In no case can Surrey be regarded as a rival to Douglas: he is less medieval and (almost in the same proportion) less Virgilian.

Nearly all that is good, and some things that are bad, in the Drab Age, can be found in Surrey's poetry. He can, in poulter's, give us specimens of its lumbering clownishness—

Unhappy hand, it had been happy time for me
If when to write thou learned first uniointed hadst thou be.

But he also contributed to our poetry a certain smooth and
controlled dignity or propriety: and if the word 'politeness' rises
to our lips we need not reject it, for the Drab Age has certain
real affinities with that of the Augustans. He does not warble
woodnotes nor thunder in high astounding terms nor wanton
in luscious imagery: when he reminds us of the Elizabethans at
all, he reminds us of 'well languaged Daniel' or sober *Nosce
Teipsum*. He can make trifles pleasing by their neat structure
and by the ease and consistency of his language. Once or twice
he goes higher than this. Metrically, he is one of the great
road-makers. If we adopted the ludicrous principle of judging
poets not by their own work but by their utility to their successors, he would have to rank not only above Wyatt but above
Chaucer and Milton; perhaps above Shakespeare too. By any
sane standard, however, he is merely a man who served his
generation well and has left one or two poems of permanent,
though moderate, value.

It is natural to compare Surrey's blank verse with the two
pieces which Nicholas Grimald (1519–62) wrote in the same
metre and which Tottel printed in his *Miscellany*. It is not
certain that they owe anything to Surrey. Both are translations,
the one from the twelfth-century *Alexandreis* by Philippus
Gualterus and the other from Beza's *Mors Ciceronis*, and both
record heroic deaths. Grimald can be very clumsy. He omits
articles in a fashion which English ears cannot tolerate and uses
uncouth inversions, as in 'Wherefore the hands also doth hee of
smyte'. Yet in a sense he carries out his undertaking more successfully than Surrey. The *fee-fo-fi-fum* manner of the *Alexandreis* was much less worth reproducing than Virgil, but it was
really within Grimald's reach as Virgil was not within Surrey's.
Witness the opening lines:

Now clattering arms, now ragyng broyls of warr
Gan passe the noyes of taratantars clang:
Shrowded with shafts, the heuen; with clowd of darts
Covered, the ayre—(Tottel, 265.)

There is life, of a sort, in this, and the pauses are not badly
managed. The last line of the poem ('From derk obliuion of
deuouryng death') is worthy of Marlowe.

With Grimald we have already reached Tottel's *Miscellany*. Richard Tottel was printer and bookseller and his *Miscellany*, which he called *Songes and Sonettes*, first appeared in 1557 to be republished with additions and deletions in the same year and frequently after that till 1587. It was a goldmine to its publishers. With the additions it contains 310 poems: first come those of Surrey, Wyatt, and Grimald, and then follow the 'Uncertain Auctors'. Some of these have been identified: but the appearance of Chaucer among them warns us that we have no certain knowledge of the period covered by the collection. Among the known authors Lord Vaux died in 1556, Sir John Cheke and W. Gray in 1557, Sir Anthony St. Leger in 1559, Grimald about 1562. Combining this with Puttenham's statement that the 'new makers' came up in the latter years of Henry VIII, we ordinarily conclude that Tottel represents a movement which began about 1530 and was still going on when he went to press in 1557. But we must remember that this is only probable. Earlier work may be included, and what we take to be minor tendencies within the Drab Age may really be relics from a previous period. Only philological evidence could give us complete certainty, and unfortunately Tottel's text, wherever it can be tested by manuscripts, proves so licentious that it can give the philologist no sure foothold. But though our common assumption is only probable, the probability is strong: almost nothing in Tottel looks as if it belonged to the fifteenth, or even the early sixteenth century. I take it to be essentially a Drab Age anthology.

'Essentially'—for there are pieces in it which look forward, and pieces which, without looking forward, are anomalous. 'Phylida was a fayer maid' (181, p. 138),[1] with its pastoralism and its flowers and beasts, looks forward: so does the eloquent opening of No. 233 (p. 189),

> Though in the waxe a perfect picture made
> Dothe shew as fayre as in the marble stone,

and you may add, though from that most unpromising strain 'Grimald out of Beza',

> Gorgeous attire, by art made trym and clene,
> Cheyn, bracelet, perl, or gem of Indian river (146, p. 107).

---

[1] In these references the number is that which the piece bears in H. E. Rollins's Harvard edition (1928–9); the page, that on which it occurs in Arber's reprint (1897).

Or again, Grimald translating Pseudo-Ausonius, may momentarily anticipate the tone of Sylvester:

> So greeted floods: that, where ther rode before
> A ship, a car may go safe on the shore (157, p. 112).

But these are not typical. The other class of anomalous poems is, in a way, more interesting: they show not where poetry was going but where it might have gone. The grand function of the Drab Age poets was to build a firm metrical highway out of the late medieval swamp; but in Tottel we can discover traces of one or two uncompleted highways, systems of metre that were never worked out. That the authors were not simply losing their way (as some still suspect Wyatt of doing) but genuinely working on an alternative route is shown by the fact that Lord Vaux, who can elsewhere be as iambic as Tate and Brady, is one of them. His No. 217 (p. 177), 'O temerous tauntres', and someone's No. 220 (p. 179), 'Cruel and vnkind', both regularize the floundering line of Hawes and Barclay not into decasyllables but into five 'lifts' and 'dips' (or, if you prefer, five anapaests or dactyls) and produce a very clear rhythm:

> Cruell and vnkind whom mercy cannot moue,
> Harbour of vnhappe where rigours rage doth raigne,
> The ground of my griefe where pitie cannot proue,
> Too tickle to trust, of all vntruth the traine.

Elsewhere, in an iambic poem ('Sith that the way'), alliteration is so persistently used that it is no longer a decoration but structural, and we almost return to the technique of *Pearl*:

> And take no skorne to scape from skill,
> To spend my spirits to spare my speche,
> To win for welth the want of will;
> And thus for rest to rage I reche (192, p. 156).

Such experiments are, however, rare. Much commoner, and more important, is what may be called the neo-medieval manner. Several poems, and some of them very good, apply the language and metre of Surrey to themes and to an outlook indistinguishable from those of the fourteenth century. Thus Lord Vaux's 'Assault of Cupid' (211, p. 172) gives us in Drab Age stanzas an erotic *psychomachia* which is perfectly medieval. 'The Sun when he' (278, p. 230), which some have attributed to Surrey, is simply Gower brought up to date. Without any servile imitation the poet has caught exactly the equable flow, the tenderness, and wistfulness of the *Confessio Amantis*, but all in the prosody of his own time. But the best and most interesting poem in this class is 'Sythe singing gladdeth oft' (185, p. 144), which illustrates once more how misleading some of our traditional categories may be. It is based on Petrarch's canzone *Nel dolce tempo* (*Rime. In Vita*, xxiii), but a reading of the poem at once dispels the idea that it must therefore be new or of 'the Renaissance'. The canzone is Petrarch at his most medieval. The English poet has omitted the characteristically Petrarchan transformations of the lover into a fountain, a stag, and a laurel. He sees his original through the eyes of Chaucer and produces what is almost exactly an abridged version of the mourner's narrative in the *Boke of the Duchesse*. The result is a very gem of this transitional art, the disarming tenderness of the Middle Ages in the sober quatrains of the Drab Age: so good, and so little known, that I feel justified in quoting three stanzas:

> I lingred forth tyll I was brought
> With pining in so piteous case,
> That all that saw me sayd, me thought,
> Lo, death is painted in his face . . .

> And closed up are those faire eyes
> That gave me first the signe of grace:
> My faire swete foes, myne enemies,
> And earth dothe hide her pleasant face . . .

> And ending thys my wofull song,
> Now that it ended is and past,
> I wold my life were but as long
> And that this word might be my last.

But the bulk of the collection does not thus look back, and (I think) looks forward only in so far as its metrical regularity will presently make possible the freedoms of the Golden Age. It is the great treasure house of Drab style, both good and bad. At its worst the Drab can be very loutish, as in Grimald's

> From yeres tuise ten if you in count wil but one yere abate,
> The very age then shall you finde of Lord Mautrauers fate (163,
>   p. 118).

or in

> I would not have it thought hereby
> The dolphin swimme I meane to teach (170, p. 129).

From these abysses it sometimes attempts to rise by means of the
Ercles vein, as in 'The restlesse rage' (179, p. 137) which is all
about deep, devouring hell and 'Tantale' and 'Promethus,' or
in No. 246 (p. 201), possibly by Churchyard, which begins a
compliment to a lady with the line 'I heard when Fame with
thundrying voice did sommon to appere'. At other times there
is an attempt to escape from dullness by excessive rhetoric, as in
the intolerable No. 174 (p. 132), 'The lenger lyfe', an example
of Puttenham's 'marching figure'. Most often, however, the
poets do not seem to feel the need of any enrichments. They
sacrifice to the Muses with great parsimony and think they have
done enough. The lines, the sentences, and even the words are
short and this often produces an unpleasantly *staccato* effect,
aggravated by a fondness, which the Drab Age bequeathed to
its successor, for filling up their poems with short 'gnomes' or
pithy maxims. And when the Drab style becomes good it does
not do so by departing from its plainness, its sententiousness, or
its brevity. It is good when these very qualities somehow attain
dignity and force. In 'The plage is great' two lines,

> The cause of things I will not blame
> Lest I offend the prince of peas (176, p. 134),

are very clearly in the same manner as the absurd lines about
teaching the dolphin. They are plain and monosyllabic, closed
up in themselves. The difference is that they have something to
say, have no clumsy inversion, have a half alliteration, and two
Kenningar. Thus again, that air of finality, which elsewhere
produces the *staccato*, gives most of its charm to the following
stanza from 'The smoky sighes':

> The frutes were faire the which did grow,
>   Within my garden planted,
> The leaves were grene of every bough,
>   And moysture nothing wanted,
> Yet or the blossoms gan to fall,
> The caterpillar wasted all (214, p. 175).

It might almost come from Cowper or from one of the great
eighteenth-century hymn writers: and the resemblance is not
accidental. Nothing is gained by treating Drab Age poetry as if
it were Golden Age poetry in embryo; that, indeed, is the way to
miss its real merits. At its best it has a severity, a neatness, a

precision, which bring it much closer to the work of the
Augustans than to Sidney, Spenser, and Shakespeare.

Some pieces in Tottel have just been classified as 'neo-
medieval', but the most fully developed specimen of the class
comes elsewhere. It is the anonymous *Court of Love* which
Stow printed in his *Chaucer* of 1561. The arguments by which
Skeat demolished the attribution to Chaucer and moved the
date of the poem forward into the sixteenth century need not be
repeated here. The unknown poet was trying to do to Chaucer
what the neo-Latin poets of that age did to the classics; to make
a *pastiche* so good that it could succeed as a forgery. And though
he had not philology enough to deceive modern scholars he was
astonishingly clever. Considered as an original poem, his work
towers above most Drab Age verse by its sheer accomplishment.
Except here and there in Wyatt this chapter has not yet led us
to mention anything so light, so graceful, and so sophisticated as
the *Court of Love*. The matter is in places wanton, even scabrous,
but in the allegory all grossness disappears, and there is music,
humour, and even at times a lyrical intensity.

After Tottel the greatest composite monument of the Drab
Age is the *Mirror for Magistrates*. In a way, just because it is so
much worse, it reveals the movement of taste more clearly than
Tottel—as a derelict shows the set of the tide more clearly than
a ship under sail. Its earliest *strata* are late medieval, and its
latest pieces were written when the Golden Age had begun. It
thus overlaps the Drab Age at both ends and in a sense records
its whole history.

The conception of the book was derived, of course, from
Boccaccio's *De Casibus* and in its earliest form (the suppressed
edition of about 1555) the *Mirror* appeared along with Lydgate's
Fall of Princes and as an addition to them. The new 'tragedies',
according to the title-page which is almost all we have of this
print, were 'diligently collected out of the Chronicles'. The
advertisement is significant. The printer and the editor (William
Baldwin) are appealing to an historical, not to a purely literary,
taste. This attitude continued in the historical verse of Drayton
and Daniel: it is to be judged as applied poetry. This fusion of
poetry and history descends from the epic, the common parent
of both those arts, and had long been practised in the metrical
chronicle. But Baldwin and his collaborators were departing
from pure metrical chronicle under the disastrous, late medieval

influence of 'tragedy' (as Chaucer's Monk understood it) just as Drayton and Daniel were to depart from it under the influence of Lucan and Ovid. Both changes were for the worse: the monotony of 'tragedy' and the laborious dignity of the pseudo-epic are a poor exchange for the springy variety of the unambitious chronicle.

The oldest work in the *Mirror* is found not in the first extant edition of 1559 but in that of 1587. In that, there occur two pieces, on Flodden and on James IV, which, as the prose link tells us, were composed 'even shortly after the death of the sayd King'. Internal evidence supports this statement. Both are in the style and metre of the first decade of the century, and both beneath contempt. One line ('My rewarde is no more but the showle and the spade') lives in the memory. Of the same vintage is No. XIX (*Edward IV*) in the 1559 volume, in a twelve-line stanza with a Latin refrain. It is better, in so far as the lines approximate more consistently to a rough four beats.

In the same volume we have two tragedies (*Tresilian* and *Thomas of Woodstock, Duke of Gloster*) by George Ferrers, a lawyer and courtier who had the knack of surviving many unfortunate patrons. To the 1563 volume he contributed *Edmund of Somerset*: to the 1578, *Eleanor Cobham* and *Duke Humfrey of Gloster*, but it is probable from bibliographical evidence that the *Duke Humfrey* and the *Somerset* were written, or bespoke, for the 1559 edition, and *Eleanor Cobham* written before 1563. Ferrers was old enough to publish a translation of Magna Carta in 1534 and we shall probably not be far wrong if we date none of his works later than the fifties.

Ferrers is no poet but he is of curious interest as a metrist. None of his five pieces is in regular decasyllabic verse. *Eleanor Cobham* comes nearest to it, but strays into the irregular nursery-rhyme movement of *Beryn*. *Duke Humfrey* begins in pure decasyllables but by line 15 has dropped into

> In their most weal to beware of vnhap,

and later, as if to emphasize the skipping measure with internal rhyme,

> Not heeding, lesse dreedinge al unaware (34).

In these two poems, since there is some attempt at decasyllabics, the irregular lines can, if we please, be regarded as mere blunders; but his remaining tragedies are in a different category. In *Tresilian* Ferrers keeps throughout within the norm of *Beryn*; and here again we meet internal rhyme:

> Greedy and euer nedy, prollyng for theyr praye (61).

This is not the work of a man trying unsuccessfully to write decasyllables but of a man deliberately writing a different metre. In *Thomas of Woodstock* he is again following a path of his own, but a different one: the four beat line (precursor of some eclogues in the *Shepherd's Calendar*) predominates:

> And the soldiers of Brest were by me made bolde
> To claym entertainment, the towne being solde (146)

or with internal rhyme

> With swurdes and no wurdes we tryed our appeale (123).

Close to this, from *Edmund of Somerset*, though there decasyllabics are creeping in, is the couplet

> The more ye lop trees the greater they growe,
> The more ye stop streames the higher they flowe (27).

Thus in Ferrers, as sometimes in Tottel, we find a hint of things that might have happened; his work is the beginning of one more unfinished causeway across the swamp.

If Churchyard spoke the truth when he said that his *Shore's Wife* (No. XXV in the 1563 volume) was written 'in King Edwardes daies' we must place it in an early stratum of the *Mirror*. Here, in sharp contrast to the work of Ferrers, we see the triumph (at first a desolating triumph) of the new Drab poetry. The lines are of wooden regularity and the story is drowned under declamation and proverbs. Yet Shakespeare used a similar narrative technique in his *Lucrece* and Marlowe may have remembered from Churchyard the line 'And bent the wand that might have growen full streight' (140).

Other named poets in the 1559 volume are Thomas Phaer, the translator of Virgil, here notable for being wooden without being regular; Thomas Challoner, a diligent translator whose *Richard II* scans and is dull: and William Baldwin, the editor. Three tragedies are certainly by him (VIII, *Richard Earl of Cambridge*, XIII, *Richard of York*, XVIII, *Duke of Clarence*). Most of the remaining twelve, though not No. XVII (*Henry VI*), may be his. All are regular, or nearly regular, in metre and all set the execrable example followed by Daniel and Drayton of oscil-

lating between passages where political and genealogical fact is
forced into verse without the slightest poetical colouring and
others of gnomic digression. In No. IX (*Montague Earl of
Salisbury*) there are two good satiric lines:

> Duke Thomas' death was Iustice two yeres long.
> And euer sence, sore tiranny and wrong (34).

But in general the work is disastrous: just not bad enough to be
harmless to public taste. One other piece in this volume which
deserves mention is No. XVII, *Henry VI*. This is a very up-to-
date metrical experiment whose stanza, rhyming *abab*, consists
of three alexandrines followed by one fourteener. The design
is indeed utterly tasteless: but it proves that the new regularity
has reached the stage at which you can begin to play tricks with
it.

In 1563 Thomas Marsh printed the *Second Part of the Mirror
for Magistrates*, but there is evidence that most of its eight new
tragedies were written in the reign of Queen Mary. Two of them,
the work of Ferrers and Churchyard, have already been dealt
with. No. XXIV, *Richard Duke of Gloster* by Francis Seager, and
No. XXVII, *The Blacksmith* by H. Cavell, are in the old,
shambling metre: but this is now so out of fashion that it has to
be defended in the prose links on grounds of dramatic decorum.
What matters very much more is that in this volume the
Mirror for the first time offers us two poems which deserve
attention on their own merits. The first is *Hastings* (No. XXI)
by John Dolman, a fellow of the Inner Temple who translated
Cicero's *Tusculans* in 1561. It is not a satisfactory poem: it is
obscure and tormented and in actual achievement the dull work
of Baldwin might, without absurdity, be placed above it. It is
inferior to Baldwin's poetry as a baby at six months is inferior
to a dog at the same age: but then the baby is full of possibilities
that the puppy lacks. In the same way Dolman is full of—is
partly disabled by—an inner fermentation of poetry with which
Baldwin never was embarrassed. He understands better than
any of his collaborators, better even than Sackville, what a
poem ought to be. The other ghosts are mere mouth-pieces of
moral and political doctrine: but Dolman really tries by changes
of mood and human inconsistencies to dramatize his Hastings.
He attempts the conceit, and tough, sinewy conceits too, not
mere flowers, as in 'Yet circlewise into themselves do run' (60),

or, of a beast inspired to carry God's warning, 'Who is deaf
bearer of His speaking dumb' (464). His description of Richard
enraged (555–560) is something better than the usual Drab Age
fustian, and even when he is gnomic there is music and passion
in his saw:

> God for adultery slay'th
> Tho' ye it thynk too sweet a synne for death (616),

or again,

> In Lethe's floud long since in Stigian vale
> Selfe-love I dreynt (10).

Above all, here at last the sweet richness which was soon to
transform English poetry begins to appear:

> Shonning those synnes that shake the golden leaves
> Perforce from boughes ere Nature bare the greaves (37).

and

> That twynckkling sterres fling downe the fixed fate (501).

The poem is confused (the prose link acknowledges it 'very
darke and hard to be understood'), crowded, and uncomfort-
able. But it anticipates, in however dim a form, nearly every one
of the excellences which were soon to be knocking at the door—
the Golden tongue of Spenser, the turgid grandeur of Chapman,
the twisted strength of Donne.

Thomas Sackville, in this volume, has come far nearer than
Dolman to achievement, but his promise is less various. His
Buckingham (No. XXII) is quite unremarkable and, as readers
of *Gorboduc* would expect, shows none of Dolman's dramatic
capacity. He tears passions to tatters and endeavours to compensate for lack of real sympathy by mechanic exaggerations.
His fame must rest on the *Induction*. The idea of writing an induction at all and of thus giving some artistic unity to the
Mirror is itself praiseworthy: and the vision poetry of which it
consists is well suited to a writer who is more at home among
moods and atmospheres than among passions. There are too
many *exempla* for a modern taste, but where these do not clog
Sackville's flow the images follow one another with a satisfactory stateliness of gloom. Some of the allegorical personages
are described with a woodcut energy not below Spenser's: and,
in the famous lines on sleep we hear, in momentary perfection,
the note of the coming 'Golden' age.

In 1574 the persistent Thomas Marshe published the *First Part of the Mirrour*, so called because it deals with earlier periods than those touched in the previous collections. Its sixteen tragedies are all by John Higgins, a diligent lexicographer and book-maker born about 1545. In 1575 Higgins added one more, and in 1587 all of his work (some of it re-written) was included in a new edition along with that of the original team. He made about forty tragedies in all. His name cannot have sounded in sixteenth-century ears as it does in ours, for he considers it suitable to verse and lets a ghost say

I pray thee *Higgins* take in hand thy pen (*Bladud*, 1, 1587).

Wordsworth similarly began a sonnet with the word *Jones*. The matter is worth more than a smile: the downward trend in the overtones of common surnames must have a cause and the cause would be worth finding. Higgins is a gnomic and pedestrian poet of no merit; his importance is that he illustrates the riot of metrical experiment which provides the background to Spenser's early work. We are here miles away from the confusions of the late Middle Ages. Higgins understands many different types of line and is experimenting with new combinations. In *Albanact* the story is in rhyme royal but the oracles in fourteeners. In *Cordila* we have the rhyme scheme of rhyme royal but the first four lines are alexandrines and the remaining three are decasyllables. In *Nennius* the story is again in rhyme royal, Caesar's letter in decasyllabic quatrains and Casibellane's in alexandrine couplets. *Porrex* in its 1574 form is in eights and sixes. In 1587 he was still experimenting (the re-written *Bladud* is an extraordinary gallimaufry) but by 1587 he has ceased to have even historical significance, is only an owl that ought to have gone to bed or a ghost that has stayed for breakfast. In 1574 he was still a precursor. His experiments are quite tasteless, his combinations arbitrary, but as far as knowledge goes he has mapped the whole metrical world which the 'Golden Age' was to inhabit. He thus illustrates those conditions without which that 'Golden Age' could not have come into existence, though he is quite powerless to anticipate it. He is a hen that mothers ducklings but will never learn to swim.

With Higgins the history of the *Mirror* is almost at an end. Of Thomas Blenerhasset, whose *Second Part of the Mirror* (1578) was an independent and rival venture, little need be said except that in his *Cadwallader* you will find some alexandrine blank verse in a very tedious vein of *fee-fo-fi-fum*.

No one lays down the *Mirror* without a sense of relief. An immense amount of serious thought and honest work went to its composition and it remains, with Tottel, the chief poetical monument of the Drab Age. Like Tottel it did useful work in re-establishing metrical regularity, but in other respects its influence on succeeding poets was mainly bad. It encouraged that taste for heavily doctrinal history in verse which is partly responsible for the *Mortimeriados* and *Polyolbion*.

To Tottel and the *Mirror* we must add the third great composite work of the Drab Age, the rhyming psalter commonly known as 'Sternhold and Hopkins'. The French metrical version had been begun by Marot in 1533 and finished by Beza in 1562. Thomas Sternhold, a courtier of Henry VIII's, working independently, had begun in the forties. His work was continued by the parson John Hopkins, and later by the Protestant exiles at Geneva. The *Whole Book* of 1562 includes work by William Whittingham, W. Kethe, Thomas Norton, T. Becon, Robert Wisdom, and John Craig. Some attribute to Kethe the 'old hundredth' (All people that on earth do dwell) but without conclusive evidence. Whittingham is perhaps the best of the team and offers considerable metrical variety. He is happiest in heroic couplets:

> I have no need to take of thee at all
> Goats of thy fold or calfe out of thy stall—
> I know for mine all Birds that are on mountaines;
> All beasts are mine that haunt the fields and fountaines (L).

Norton ventures on rhymeless octosyllabics for No. CXXXVI. Kethe, for No. CIV, uses what we must call anapaests till some better word wins general acceptance;

> By these pleasaunt Springs and Fountaines full faire
> The fowles of the aire abide shall and dwell,
> Who moued by nature to hop here and there,
> Among the greene branches their songs shall excell.

But the staple of the book is poulter's and fourteeners (or 'eights and sixes'). Its poetical level has been a butt for critics almost ever since it appeared; the common people accepted it as an inspired book. Something like poetry of a rude, ballad kind can here and there be found in it. Thus the sun is likened to

a valiant champion
Who for to get a prize
With ioy doth hast to take in hand
Some noble enterprize (XIX)

or again

The voice of God doth rent and breake
The cedar trees so long,
The cedar trees of Libanus
Which are both high and strong (XXIX)

or even

Lord, make the·King unto the iust
Like raine to fields new moune,
And like to drops that lay the dust
And fresh the land new soune (LXXII).

But these are exceptional. The book did no harm to taste: neither its faults nor its few merits were of a kind to appeal to cultivated writers. Those who used it in church were not looking for poetry and such poetry as they got crept into their mind unconsciously mixed with the devotion and the music. Hence we do these artless verses a kind of outrage in wrenching them from their natural context and dragging them before the bar of criticism. They are to be enjoyed, if at all, as we enjoy the epitaphs in a village churchyard.

Much of the most characteristic work of the Drab Age is to be found in its copious translations from the Latin, which are so homogeneous that only a super-human critic could attribute them to their several authors on internal evidence. But almost anyone could attribute them to their period. Their metres (fourteeners, poulter's, and, more rarely, blank verse) mark them off from medieval work; their clumsiness and their diction, from the Golden Age. That diction may now give pleasure, but a pleasure wholly alien from most of their originals. It now pleases by sounding rustic, quaint, and even 'low'. The difficulty is to find whether it was low then. No one can read Drab and even Golden verse for long without coming to the conclusion that the overtones of, say, the noun *gripe* and the verb *fry* have deteriorated since the sixteenth century; otherwise even moderately good poets would not have used them where they did. But once the question has been raised we become sceptical about our whole reaction to the diction of the Drab Age

translators. They are full of words like *clummes*, *grunt* (of a woman
in travail), *patch* (as a term of abuse), *snudge*, *sluttish*, *trull*, *glumme*,
and *wagge* (both as noun and verb). Were these bad when they
were written or were they as innocent of the modern over-tones
as Anglo-Saxon *stincan*? We can only guess, guided by the following considerations: (1) most of them were soon abandoned by
good poets in elevated contexts, and Puttenham condemns *trudge*
and *tugge*; (2) there is some evidence that the Drab Age was in
fact grossly insensitive to the quality of the Latin poetry it was
translating. Thomas Blundeville in 1566 praises Golding for
translating Ovid's *Metamorphoses* in a 'thondrying' style—
which is as if we praised a translation of the *Rape of the Lock* for
sounding like Aeschylus. My tentative conclusion is that the
diction of the Drab translators, as a whole, was already a little
mean and clownish when they used it, and became much more
so as usage changed: but this conclusion is much more doubtful
about any one given word than about the cumulative effect. At
the very least we are probably safe in inferring from it that none
of them was being strongly affected by a humanistic feeling for
dignity. To that extent they belong with Douglas, not with
Surrey or Dryden. And with all their faults they are honest
translators who try hard to get the sense of the original, though
in places either their Latinity or, more probably, their texts
were very odd.

The earliest of these translators, Thomas Phaer (1510?–1560)
seems to me very much the best. His *Seven first books of the
Eneidos* (1558) can be very easily misrepresented in whichever
direction you please either by quoting bad lines like

> But we your stock whom to the starres of heauen admit you
> please (i. 250)

or good ones like

> The grenewood like a garland growes and hides them al with
> shade (i. 164).

But the only fair test is prolonged reading. His faults, even with
the linguistic allowances suggested in the preceding paragraph,
are obvious. He has strained inversions, and he can be flat. He
can badly misrepresent the original as in i. 170 or again in iii.
325 (*Nec victoris heri tetigit captiva cubile*) where 'Nor neuer she to
masters bed was captiue *fixed fast*', besides suggesting a ludicrous domestic arrangement, does very little justice to the

Most of us, I suspect, would advise a mediocre poet, if he must translate, to avoid the greater originals and choose the less, as if these would be easier. But this is probably a mistake. The great poets have so much wealth that even if you lose two-thirds of it on the voyage home you can still be rich on the remainder: slighter art, when it loses the perfection of its original form, loses all power of pleasing. Thus not only Douglas's Virgil, but Surrey's and Phaer's Virgil are still worth reading, but the Drab translators of Ovid are not. Ovid without his neatness, his pert dexterity, is nothing, except (as we shall see) in the *Metamorphoses*.

In 1560 there appeared anonymously *The Fable of Ovid treating of Narcissus*. It consists of a translation in poulter's measure, a long *Moralization* in rhyme royal, and two stanzas *From the Printer to the Booke* which use the floundering Late Medieval line. In the *Moralization* the author's desire to show that Ovid 'no follye mente' is no more specifically puritan than it is medieval. He reveals some sensibility to one important aspect of Ovid's art by pointing out that

> Hys tales do ioyne in suche a goodly wyse
> That one doth hange upon anothers ende.

The poetical quality both of his translation and of his original verse is beneath criticism, but the unmetrical lines are rare enough to be attributed to the printers' errors.

In 1565 Thomas Peend brought out his *Pleasaunt Fable of Hermaphroditus and Salmacis*. In it the humanistic fashion of strict translation has not yet fully emerged from the medieval fashion of helping yourself to Ovid as you pleased. Peend is retelling the story in his own way, with references to Dame Nature and her mould and plenty of medieval stopgaps ('as ancient stories tell', 'if poets truly wryte') and only at times keeps close enough to Ovid to be called a translator. He uses poulter's but every now and then horribly slips in an octosyllabic couplet (printed as a single long line). Like Chaucer, he is inconsistent in his scansion of classical names, accenting Hermaphrodite sometimes on the second and fourth but sometimes on the first and third. He too adds a moral, and he too is very, very bad.

In the same year Arthur Golding (1536–1605?) produced the first four books of the *Metamorphoses*; the whole fifteen followed in 1567. This industrious man also translated Aretine's *History*,

shrinking *tetigit*. These faults he shares with all the D
lators; but in the others they become less endurable t
we read, whereas in Phaer the general effect is so good
come to overlook them. The explanation is that he is a
of his metre. He uses hardly any enjambment (the fou
will not stand it) and relies for variety on a free use of elisi
other variations within the line. In quotation such an elis
'To come to Italia where we trust to fynd our resting end
205) may seem harsh, but it is not so when we meet it i
context; nor is the disregard of the medial break in '
Mighty Gias and Cloanthus mourned he most of all' (i. 2
To an ear numbed with the monotony of Turberville or rack
with Golding's cacophonies Phaer offers refreshment. T
phrasing too is often (not always) good: 'of precious Ladi
seven and seven about me do I keepe' (i. 71), 'Robes and painted
pomp of Troy' (i. 119), 'the gladsome giftes of God' (i. 636),
or, for *umbraeque silentes*, 'soules of silence dumme' in vi. 264.
Sometimes for two or three lines together he keeps a level
almost worthy of Virgil;

> And now the mornyng read doth ryse and starres expulsed be
> When, farre aloof with mountaines dymme and low to looke,
>   we see
> Italia land. 'Italia' first of all Achates cryed,
> 'Italia' than with gretyng loude my mates for ioy replied
>   (iii. 521).

At some of the great lines (not at *lacrimae rerum*) he has come as
near to success as anyone: as in

> Alas to thinke how sore berayed, how from that Hector sore
> He chaunged was (ii. 274).

or

> Why should we hennes remove? Who letts us here our wall
>   to bylde (iii. 631)

or

> And stretching held their hands desiring moch the furth
>   shore (vi. 314).

Phaer naturalizes and even medievalizes Virgil, mak
Nereids into mermaids and *domos Ditis vacuas* into 'Lym
Kingdoms wast', but he is little the worse for that. On the wh
any man who cares for epic and cannot master either Vir
Latin or Douglas's Scots will be tolerably safe with Phaer

Calvin's sermons, Trogus, Caesar, and what not? His version of
Ovid providentially forestalled one which Peend, by his own confession, had intended: providentially, because Golding is a little
better. At the same time the indulgence which more than one
writer has extended to his ugly fourteeners demands some explanation. The truth is, I think, that he is saved by his original.
The Ovidian manner, the flippant and sophisticated brilliance,
was beyond his reach as it was beyond the reach of all the Drab
poets. But in the *Metamorphoses* this manner surprisingly co-
exists with an unspoiled and hearty relish in sheer story-telling;
it is puff-pastry (the finest ever cooked) but puff-pastry enclosing
a homely and nourishing food. This element in his original, and
this alone, Golding cannot destroy. He can therefore be read
with a simple pleasure which is very unlike the total pleasure
given by Ovid, though it made part of that total. Thus *Materiam
superabat opus* (ii. 5) is very much weakened in

> But yet the cunning workmanship of thinges therein farre past
> The stuffe whereof the doores were made.

But we are still getting on with the story of Phaethon and Golding cannot kill it. The great defect of his version is that he uses
enjambment not for musical delight but (as he also uses strained
inversion) for mere convenience, and to a degree which the fourteener will not endure. He uses it like this:

> My God Apollos temple, I will set you open and
> Disclose the wondrous heauens themselues (xv. 144).

If I quoted from his introduction 'there is alreadie shewd sufficient to detect that Poets tooke the grounde of all their deepest
fables out of Scripture' who (if not warned by the present context) would suspect that the introduction was in verse? He
expands freely. *Lucum* (iii. 35) becomes 'a thicke and queachie
plot' because he wants a rhyme to 'sticke'. *Notitiam primosque
gradus vicinia fecit: Tempore crevit amor* (iv. 59) is dragged out into
the shuffling rigmarole of

> This neighbrod bred acquaintance first, this neighbrod first did
> stirre
> The secret sparkes, this neighbrod first an entrance in did
> showe
> For love to come to that to which it afterward did growe.

It ought to be unendurable, and it almost is—but not quite. The stories keep us going, and some not very Ovidian traits in Golding's language—his 'thondryng' style, which makes *sanguinea lingua* a 'blo and blasting tung' or *immensos saltu sinuatur in arcus* 'and bending into bunchy bowghts his bodie forth he hales' (iii. 42) have an Englishness and pungency which wins from us a smile (partly) of pleasure. If a man had read Golding in boyhood, and knew the stories first or only through him, he would probably have an affection for Golding which maturer taste would never quite reject. But if we are to be pleased we must read him, like Sternhold and Hopkins, with indulgence. Prospero's speech in the *Tempest* and Medea's in Golding have five or six words in common, but there the resemblance ends.

His versified preface, though it shows Golding at his worst as a poet, is of interest. Like the anonymous translator of 1560, and like the medievals who had 'moralized' even the *Romance of the Rose*, he believes that Ovid is profitable and philosophical. He bases his belief not only on the supposed morals of the individual stories but on the theme of the whole work—'this same dark Philosophie of turned shapes'. By this Ovid teaches us that nothing 'doth in stedfast state remayne' but also that 'nothing perisheth', and the Pythagorean doctrine of Metempsychosis in Book XV is true, if not of the rational, yet of the sensitive and vegetable souls. Ovid is thus found to contain most of the 'philosophy' which reappears in Spenser's Garden of Adonis and cantos of Mutabilitie. He also in many places agrees with scripture. I think we shall misunderstand the age if we take this to be the special pleading of the 'Humanist' in Golding against the 'Puritan'. He is not merely finding excuses. This is how our ancestors really approached Ovid. The all-embracing syncretism of their thought and a readiness (inherited from the Middle Ages) to expect multiple senses and heterogeneous pleasures from a single text made it natural for them to do so.

The year 1567 which saw the completion of Golding's *Metamorphoses* saw also Turberville's *Heroical Epistles*, a version of the *Heroides*: ten in poulter's, six in blank, and five in fourteeners. The blank verse is not perhaps intrinsically better than the fourteeners (anything is better than poulter's) but it refreshes our jaded ears. Turberville is a better poet than Golding, but not a good one. He has one beautiful line, 'Demophon to the windes ingagde his promise with his sayle' (ii. 25), but the elegant rhetoric of the original usually evades him and when that is lost the *Heroides* has nothing to offer us. The 'low' diction of the Drab Age (if it was low) is more marked in him than in any of the other translators. He accents classical proper names very erratically, and once preserves in English the vocative inflection 'O Macareu' (as Kingsley wrote 'Andromeden and Persea' in his *Andromeda*, 423). Few books less repay perusal.

Thomas Underdowne has deserved well of us all by translating Heliodorus: his *Ovid his invective against Ibis* (1569) in ordinary Drab fourteeners, with notes (as we should now call them) on mythology and archaeology, adds nothing to his fame. Thomas Churchyard's *Three first Books of Ovid de Tristibus* (1572), also in fourteeners, is one of the better specimens of its kind. He stops his couplets with almost Popian regularity, surrenders himself to the swing of the metre, and is not unmusical. But the original has few qualities that can survive in Drab style and homely verse.

Other translators were meanwhile attempting an even harder original. The plays which go under the name of Seneca (though it is hard to believe that he wrote *Hercules Furens*, 858–67) are by no means contemptible. They excel, as Mr. Eliot says, in 'the verbal *coup de théâtre*' and if the poet were not so incessantly on his top note would even have a kind of greatness. But he was doubly unsuitable for our Drab translators. In him the prehistoric tales of anguish were re-clothed in despairing epigram and enormous rhetoric, not quite wantonly but because they really, if 'obliquely', represent such an outlook on life as the expiring Roman nobility must have had under the successive imperial Terrors. The real world was for them not very unlike the world of Senecan tragedy: Agrippina's *Occidat dum imperet* or Arria's *Paete, non dolet* might have come in the plays. Art raised on so volcanic a soil could only be a monstrous exotic when transplanted to England. And secondly, the Drab poets were of all men least able to reproduce the epigrammatic. They muff it every time. Thus in *Medea*, 166 (out of which Corneille made his famous *Dans un si grand revers que vous resta-t-il? —Moi*), Studley gives us:

Medea yet is lefte (to much) and here thou mayst-espye
The seas to succour us in flyght and lands aloofe that lye.

For *magna momento obrui Vincendo didici* (*Troades*, 263) Jasper Heywood has:

In beating downe that warre hath wonne by proofe I have
ben taught
What pompe and pride in twinke of eye may falle and come to
naught.

In Studley's *Agamemnon* (287) *Pretio parata vincitur pretio fides*
becomes

The trust that hyred is and bought by brybes and moneies fre
Thy counsell to bewray agayne with brybes entyste wil be.

Even the fact that he was misled by a false attribution in his text
can hardly excuse the same Studley for translating *Fortem facit
vicina libertas senem* ('Freedom, now near, makes bold the white-
haired slave', *Hippolytus*, 139),

The neighbors weale great comfort brings unto the horie head.

Thus the translators go on. All the sharp detonations of the
original (without which it is nothing) disappear in the yokel garrulity of their style. One begins to suspect that they hardly perceived or did not value the epigrams, and were interested only in
the fustian which gave them an excuse for such phrases as 'Whose
growyng gutts the gnawing grypes and fylthie foules doe fyll', or
'Thwack not about with thunder thumpes'. And very small
excuses satisfied them. In Newton's *Phoenissae* (or *Thebais*, 5)
permitte labi is swollen into 'Let mee I pray thee headlong slyde in
breaknecke tumbling plight', and the original *Oedipus* has nothing at all to correspond to Neville's 'And filthy feendes spout
out their flames out of their darksome caues'.

This unhappy enterprise was begun by the Jesuit Jasper Heywood (1535–97), son of old Heywood the epigrammatist. His
Troas (which we call *Troades*) appeared in 1559, his *Thyestes* in
1560, and his *Hercules Furens* in 1561. In this short period he
moved from a medieval to a humanistic conception of his task.
In the *Troas* he treats his original with great freedom, adding a
new character, and substituting a chorus of his own for one
which, he thinks, 'should have no grace in the englishe tonge'.
The rhyme royal stanzas which he inserts at one point are
not dramatic, but addressed to the reader: 'good ladies have
your teares in reddines'. It is the Chaucerian technique: *Auctour*
should be written in the margin. *Thyestes* is preceded by a
dream (purely medieval but for its fourteeners) in which Heywood meets Seneca's ghost. The *Hercules Furens* is quite a dif-

ferent matter, translated 'verse for verse' and 'word for word'
and accompanied with the Latin in an eclectic text of his own
manufacture. In all three alike he uses fourteeners for the iambic
parts, and octosyllabic or decasyllabic metres for the lyrics. The
general superiority of these, and especially of his original chorus
(*Troas*, 814 et seq.) suggests that he had poetry in him but ship-
wrecked on an ill-chosen metre and an ill-chosen original. He is
interested in the 'augmentation' of the vernacular, rendering
rogae as 'roges' and *stadia* as 'stadies'.

Alexander Neville (1544–1614) produced his *Oedipus* in 1563.
In the collected *Ten Tragedies* of 1581 he made a great point of
his precocity, but since the 1581 text is in fact almost a new version (of which he says nothing) there was some *suggestio falsi* in
this. Neville follows Peend's strange practice of slipping in a six-
teen-syllable line (or octosyllabic couplet) every now and then
among his fourteeners. Once, his excuse is that he is translating
trochaic septenarii, but he forgets about this and reverts to fourteeners after two lines that remind us irresistibly of a Gilbert and
Sullivan 'patter song':

> God graunte I may it safely tel, the hearyng was to terrible,
> My senses al amased are, it is a thing so horrible (*Oedipus*, 223).

Unlike Heywood he often used fourteeners even for the choruses.
He is very, very bad.

He was succeeded by Thomas Nuce (ob. 1617) who translated
the *Octavia*. To this work, simply because it is in decasyllabics,
the reader turns in hopes of relief, but they are soon dashed. It is
like this:

> Though much I beare that boyling brest do beate
> And tolerably take divorcements threate,
> Deathes only deadlie darte, I see, &c. (*Octavia*, 100 et seq.).

After Nuce came John Studley (who took his B.A. in 1567) with
the *Agamemnon* (1566), *Medea* (1566), *Hercules Oetaeus*, and *Hippolytus*. Like Heywood in the *Troas* he treats his original freely
and inserts a chorus of his own in the *Medea*: it is very medieval
and throws the emphasis, as Chaucer would have done, on
Jason's inconstancy in love. Here, for a moment, as if he had
thrown off an incubus, he achieves a shadow of poetry:

> Who lysteth to the flateryng Maremaides note
> Must needes commit his tyred eyes to sleepe,

but against this must be set the fact that he pursues us even in tragedy with the poulter's measure (*Hercules Oetaeus*, 172 et seq.) and that he scored the record failure of them all in rendering a Senecal Gnome:

> *Curae leves loquuntur, ingentes stupent.*
> Light cares have wordes at will, but great do make us sore agast (607).

He also uses more often than his fellows that diction which, whether 'low' in his own day or not, cannot now be read without a smile—'frostyface', 'topsy turvy', and (for *Tacitae Stygis* in *Hippolytus* 625) 'Stygian puddle glum'.

In 1581 Thomas Newton (b. 1542) shovelled all the existing versions together, added his own of the fragmentary *Phoenissae*, and published the whole as *The Ten Tragedies*. Out of this bog of verbiage Mr. Eliot has picked, with exquisite taste, the only lines (*Hercules Furens*, 1131 et seq.) which deserve praise: and even those no man could construe unless he had seen the Latin first. In my sad progress I have sometimes thought that I could find others to set beside them: but it was only the same sort of illusion which might make a man, by long residence in Lincolnshire, come to take a mound for a mountain. As soon as we return to good literature, or even to ordinary conversation, the imagined beauties fade. 'English Seneca' is execrable: the metre a torment to the ear, the language at once artless and unnatural. Its influence on English drama is reserved for an abler pen. But I suspect the chief value of that story will be to increase our admiration for the native genius that could so soon and (on the whole) so completely recover from it.

Thomas Drant (ob. 1578) who published a version of Horace's *Satires* in 1566, followed by the *Ars Poetica* and *Epistles* in 1567, makes far better reading than the Senecans, not because he is very much better either as a poet or a translator but because Horace suffers less than the tragedies from such style and metre as the Drab Age could afford. Drant's homely and pungent manner gives us a quality which, if different from the Horatian urbanity, is at least not simply antagonistic to it. With what eyes he saw Horace may be inferred from the fact that he called him 'a muche zealous controller of sinne' and combined his *Satires* in one volume with the *Wailings of Hieremie*, comparing his two authors with the laughing Democritus and the weeping Hera-

clitus and entitling the whole *A Medicinable Moral*. Though he
claims to have 'waied' his version of Jeremiah 'with the Chaldie
Targum' he is not always master of Horace's Latin: as when *dum
ingenuus* (i. vi. 8) becomes 'so that our oune demeanour be not
yll'. In general there is no knowing what trains of English
imagery any phrase of the original may start in his lively mind,
and they are often delightful. Thus in i. i. 37 Horace's colourless
Non usquam prorepit et illis utitur ante Quaesitis sapiens blossoms into

> Then ladye Pismyer stirrs no where, shes claspde in closset
> deepe,
> She keepes her Chrystenmasse in cave and ther they make bon
> cheare.

A man can only say, 'Bless thee, Horace, thou art translated'.
More legitimately, but with equal pleasure, we find *loquaces*
(i. ix. 33) rendered 'iangling iacks' and *furcifer* (ii. vii. 22) 'thou
stretche-hempe'. Some of his more violent departures from the
original are made for decency in obedience to the maxim quoted
from St. Jerome on his title-page, *quod malum est muta*; but these
too may lead us into pleasant by-paths. Like Peend and Neville
he allows himself amid his fourteeners an occasional line of
eight beats. His own Latin verses, oddly called *Epigrammata* and
appended to the *Medicinable Moral*, are very curious. Such a
line as *O Mors, Mors, quid ages? quove feres pedem?* is indeed in a
metre that Geoffrey de Vinsauf never knew: that it marks in any
other respect an advance from *O Veneris lachrymosa dies* is not clear.

This list of Drab translations from the Classics (which does
not claim to be exhaustive) may close with the first attempt at an
English Homer, by A. H. (Arthur Hall, 1563–1604). Though not
published till 1581, this work had been started 'about eighteen
or nineteen years' earlier and had been encouraged by Jasper
Heywood. It consists of *Iliad*, i–x done into fourteeners, not from
the Greek but from the version of Hugues Salel in French decasyllabics which was finished in 1545; hence the jibe about 'the
French Midwife' in Chapman. In reality very few of Hall's
faults are due to Salel. His version is extremely bad and worth
mentioning only because a comparison between it and Salel and
Chapman brings out so prettily (thus summing up the whole
lesson of the last few pages) the character which sets the Drab
translators apart from all others. A single quotation will do it.
Homer said,

Αὐτίκα δ'ἀργεννῆσι καλυψαμένη ὀθόνῃσιν
ὡρμᾶτ' ἐκ θαλάμοιο τέρεν κατὰ δάκρυ χέουσα (iii. 141).

Salel renders it

> Si se leva debout et se vestit
> De beaux habits puis quant et quant sortit
> Hors son logis, iectant la larme tendre
> Que l'on voyait par ses joues descendre.

Hall, thus

> She riseth vp and deckes herself with gorgeous attyer
> And out she goes distilling teares as they wel saw stoode by her.

And finally Chapman

>   she hied,
> Shadowed her graces with white veils, and (though she took a
>   pride
> To set her thoughtes at gaze and see in her cleare beauties flood
> What choice of glorie swum to her yet tender womanhood)
> Seasonde with teares her ioyes to see more ioyes the more offence
> And that perfectioun coulde not flowe from earthlie excellence.

The style of the French, a little cold yet beautifully limpid, is above all a narrative style. French poetry has not yet lost the power that had made the romances and the *chansons de gestes*: something of Homer comes through. Chapman's lines, filled with rich beauties foreign and even opposite to those of the original, illustrate the deeply unclassical richness of the 'Golden' manner in its later and almost overripe development. Homer has completely vanished but we are given something else instead. Hall cannot preserve Homer (nor even Salel) and cannot compensate for the loss: between the other quotations his couplet shows like a splash of mud on our page.

We must now turn to the original poets of the Drab Age. These are more numerous than we easily remember and not all of them deserve critical mention in a work on this scale. Thus the religious poems of William Hunnis (ob. 1597)—the *Seven Sobs*, the *Handful of Honeysuckles*, the *Poor Widow's Mite*, and the *Comfortable Dialogues*, all in 1583—belong to the history of piety rather than that of poetry; Hugh Rhodes's *Book of Nurture* (1545?), to the history of manners.

Barnaby Googe (1540?–1594) was a diligent translator from the neo-Latin and an anti-papistical propagandist. He began

his career with a translation of the first six books of Palingenius'
Zodiacus Vitae which he completed in 1565. The original, a
diffuse and tedious satirical-moral diatribe in hexameters, lost
little in Googe's fourteeners. Perhaps it gained; *Vincit amor
Musae, vincit deus* is ordinary schoolroom nullity, whereas 'The
love of Muse and Hie Jehoue doth both within me dwell' is at
least a curiosity. In 1570 followed the *Popish Kingdom* from the
Latin of Thomas Naogeorgus (or Kirchmeyer), and Googe
may be the 'B. G.' responsible in 1579 for a *New Year's Gift*,
a scurrilous scissors-and-paste compilation against the Papists.
The *Four Books of Husbandry* in prose translated (with additions)
from Heresbachius in 1577 make slightly better reading. His
claim to be an original poet rests on the *Eclogues, Epitaphs and
Sonnets* of 1563. The eclogues (in fourteeners) conform to
humanistic ideas of 'imitation' by introducing pederasty and a
suicide for love, and to Christian morals by bringing back the
suicide's ghost to tell us he is damned; *omne tulit punctum*. The
story of Faustus in the fifth eclogue resembles one of the plots
in *Twelfth Night*. The so-called sonnets are grave compliments
in decasyllabic quatrains. The decasyllables are cut up into two
lines each, an arrangement which, if it derives from the author,
may throw some light on his conception of that metre. *Cupido
Conquered* is a purely medieval poem, an allegory complete
with spring morning, complaint, well of Narcissus, and a
psychomachy. Two of the epitaphs show clearly, what the
eclogues sometimes suggest, how close to the surface the ballad
spirit and broadsheet style lie beneath Googe's veneer of Tot-
telianism. He is at his poor best when he forgets to be a courtly
maker and thumps out

> Ten Scottes to one (a dredeful thyng
> A dolfull fyghtyng daye).

Arthur Broke (ob. 1563) owes his shadowy immortality to
the fact that Shakespeare used for a play his *Tragical History of
Romeus and Juliet* (1562). It is derived from Bandello through
Belleforest and Broke adds something of his own. He did not
add much poetry. His *History*, in poulter's, is extremely long and
his style can descend to

> How happie had he been had he not ben forsworne,
> But twice as happie had he ben had he ben never borne.

George Turberville (1540–95?) is a little better than Googe
and Brooke. He has already met us as a translator of Ovid. He
also followed Barclay by translating both Mantuan (before
1567) and Mancinus (*A Plain Path to Perfect Virtue*, 1568). Turberville's Mantuan set beside Barclay's fourth and fifth eclogues
thus give us an instructive contrast between the Late Medieval
and the Drab technique when both working under the same
humanistic impulse. Barclay takes you bumping over a ploughed
field; Turberville keeps you ruthlessly on the march along the
hard shadeless road of poulter's and fourteeners. It is merely
a matter of temperament which you find worse. His *Epitaphs,
Epigrams, Songs and Sonnets* seem to have been published before
1567. Many of them are imitated from classical trifles which
demand, more than any other kind of poetry, the lightness that
Turberville lacked. His play is elephantine. He is less unhappy
when he attempts the Tottelian lyric. Wyatt is his chief model
and he sometimes varies Wyatt's stanza-forms with new complexities. He often spoils what he borrows but one or two of his
pieces can give a faint pleasure: 'The green that you did wish
me wear', 'Shall Reason rule', or 'The Phoenix shall have
many nests'. The stanza used in 'Of Tantalus plight' seems to
me tasteless but might be redeemed by the music. 'Of Lady
Venus' is an interesting, though unsuccessful experiment in
alexandrines written with no medial break. The verse epistles
written from Russia in 1568 (and printed in Hakluyt) are
wretched stuff.

But this is not the whole story about Turberville. There are
indications that far from being a man raised to the little stature
he has by Petrarch and humanism and the Tottelians, he is
a man who might have done better if he had heard of none of
them. His two prose treatises of *Faulconry* and *Hunting* (1575) are
of course compilations 'collected out of the best approved
authors': but Turberville on kennels is much better reading
than the Ovidian and Tottelian Turberville, and the poems
put into the mouths of the beasts are not without interest: one
regrets that the Badgerd (of whom there is a most fearsome cut)
had apparently no turn for verse. Even more interesting from
this point of view are his *Tragical Tales*. Seven of these are from
Boccaccio; the other three, as modern research has shown, have
a more complicated descent. Now those which are not damned
(as four are) by poulter's measure do not quite fail: you can

still read them for the story. And the odd thing is that their most obvious fault is very closely connected with their sole merit. Their fault is their ready acquiescence in the stopgaps of the debased ballad style— 'As here my penne will show', 'As I before have penned', or even 'He was content to hold his tong and so he went to bed'. Yet at the same time Turberville is best when he is content to keep closest to this humble kind of art. The beer is indeed very small, but even the smallest beer is better than grocer's port. Hence the sixth tale ('Gerbin and the King's daughter of Tunis'), which has a purely medieval content and admits ballad irregularities of metre, is easily his best work; at one moment, just before the sea fight, it strikes the note of the great ballads:

> Good faith, quoth he, I neede no glove
> My Faulcon is not here.

Turberville like Googe, thus suggests that if the poetry of the Drab Age was usually bad, that might be because new models induced minor talents to turn away from the thin, but real, trickle of poetry that still survived among the people, and might have saved them. This is the most interesting thing about Turberville. For the rest, he has several peculiarities of language. He carries the 'low' vocabulary further than any of his contemporaries. He omits auxiliary *have*, writing *might tolde* and *might been*, which can be paralleled, and repeatedly puts *mother law* for *mother in law*, which (I think) cannot.

Thomas Howell, who published *The Arbor of Amity* (1568), the *New Sonnets and pretty Pamphlets*, and *Howell his Devises* (1581), does all the things we have learned to expect from a Drab poet —neat, but tepid, lyrics in the Tottelian vein, thumping four-teeners ('Most greedie gripes and plunging paines do pierce his ruthfull harte'), poems in 'the Marching Figure', and poulter's. He is full of gnomic morality and much indebted to Petrarch and Chaucer. He attempts 'anapaests', not very melodiously, and acrostics. But he has also something of his own. 'Jack to Jone', in dialect, faintly reminds us of the Scotch essays in poetical rusticity. 'Sing all of greene laurell', in a complex stanza, has some merit. 'A Dreame' uses, not quite consistently, the stanza of Sir Richard Maitland's poem on the Fall. The complaint of a betrayed woman *To her Lover* contains the only lines still quoted from Howell,

> I doubt the Dryades
> Amidst the forest chase
> And thinking on the seas
> I dread the Marmayds grace.

The rest is not so good. The following, though defenceless against a stern critic, has its charm:

> Tell her I will come
> Knowing not how soone,
>   Speede well.
> Love may no let have,
> This is all I crave,
>   Farewell.

If Googe and Turberville misapplied their small talents, Thomas Tusser (1529?–80) knew exactly what to do with his. The *Hundred Good Points of Husbandry* (1557), 'maried' in the 1570 edition to a *Hundred Good Points of Huswifery*, was revised and augmented into the *Five Hundred Points* of 1573, and ran through many editions. Here is one of those works before which the literary critic hesitates, doubtful whether his commission extends so far. Though Tusser had been at Eton (he records Udall's detestable cruelty) and at Trinity, he writes no Georgics and seems to claim no literary honours:

> What lookest thou herein to haue?
> Fine verses thy fancie to please?
> Of many my betters that craue,
> Look nothing but rudenes in these.

It is doubtful whether his work is to be treated as literature. If we complain that his 'anapaests', though at first a relief from the eternal fourteener, prove in the end only a variety of torment, may it not be replied that we are absurdly judging as poetry what were only meant to be mnemonic jingles? Yet we cannot so leave them. The truth is that, after Wyatt, Tusser is the most readable of all the Drab versifiers. The pleasure, no doubt, results partly from our nostalgia for the land and for an age which, if not much softer than our own, was hard in different places. Tusser can be stern and suspicious: 'shew servaunt his labour and shew him no more', 'Maids, vp I beseeche yee, least Mistress doe breach yee', 'Make hir crie creake and teach hir to stirre'. But one can set against this his precepts of alms-giving, his demands that from May to August

'Patch' must be allowed 'an hower or two' for midday sleep or that nothing be 'grutched' to sick labourers, above all the vanished community of country life:

> In haruest time haruest folke, seruants and all
> Should make all togither good cheere in the hall
> And fill out the black boule of bleith to their song,
> And let them be merie all haruest time long.

So also at Christmas, since our plenty 'was sent us (no doubt on) good houses to keepe'. And all the year round the best workers are those who 'sing in their laboure as briddes in the wood : therefore 'disdaine not the honest though merie they seeme'. To the beasts, too, he displays a farmer's characteristic blend of callousness and tenderness. All this, no doubt, gains by distance. So does his unquestioning piety, a piety not specific-ally Christian but inherent in the life of the farmer from times before all record: Virgil, with a few explanations, could have understood it. There is, as Tusser says, 'no doubt' about any-one's duty at any moment, and duties cannot be altered by the character of particular people:

> Though Vicar be bad or the Parson as euill
> Go not for thy tithing thyself to the deuill.

Closely connected with this is a piety towards the very earth which finds expression in a kind of anthropomorphism or 'pathetic fallacy' unaffected by literary models and indeed current down to our own day. Excessive carting 'brings out of hart' both the land and the horse. North winds are as ill to the hops 'as a fraie in a feast' but south wind is 'ioy' to them like 'a welcomed gest'. A bad farmer 'defraudeth the land': you must give nature her way, 'let seede have her longing, let soile have her lust'. That, indeed, is almost a description of what has happened in Tusser's homely verses. They are scarcely art: they let Nature have her way and she almost saves the book as literature. You cannot read long without feeling earth between your fingers. He thus comes far closer to one real classic (Hesiod) than his courtly rivals ever came to the real Ovid or the real Petrarch. In a sense, to be sure, Tusser is of no importance: the course of English poetry would be the same if he had never written. The chief critical truth we learn from him is that very minor talents should stick to 'applied' poetry and avoid the 'pure'. The eighteenth century was quite right in recommend-

ing to them such subjects as the Mediterranean and the
Barometer.

As far as chronology is concerned, Thomas Churchyard
(1520?–1604) might be placed almost anywhere in this book.
He had known Surrey and he lived to celebrate James I's entry
into London. His long and chequered career as hack poet,
would-be courtier, and soldier would make a good subject
for an historical novel: the impression it left on poor Churchyard
himself was summed up in the lines

> If fiue and forty sons I had
> Not one to court nor wars should goe.
>
> (*A Pleasant Discourse*, 1596.)

But by his literary character he belongs to this chapter. In
his earliest work we can, indeed, detect a pre-Drab, a late
medieval stratum. In the *Mirror of Man*, which he declared to be
'almost fifty yeares old' in 1594, his metre is close to that of
Robert Crowley: each line is divided into two half-lines which
are usually dimeters in rising rhythm, but which sometimes fail
to reach that norm and thus surrender the whole line to the
floundering metre of Barclay. And at the other end of his career
we find sporadically, faint and belated, a tinge of 'Gold', as in
A Musicall Consort.

> Among the Dames of faire Dianas traine
> Where beautie shines like silver drops of raine
> In sunnie day.

But the most part of his work is purest Drab and explores all
varieties of Drab poetics except the genuine lyrical impulse
that descends from Wyatt. His best work was done in the neo-
Chaucerian manner. In the 'Spider and the Gowt' and 'Church-
yards Dream' (both found in his *Chips*) he attempts, not quite con-
temptibly, the humorous garrulity of Chaucer's octosyllabics.
Much more often he was driven to the sort of poetry that paid:
pageant-verses for royal progresses, epitaphs, 'tragedies',
metrical journalism about the wars, an advertisement for a
new paper mill, what not? He was, as he says, 'apt to take any
theam'. In the *Worthiness of Wales* (1587) he even translates the
law-Latin of an Earl's patent into fourteeners. His pageant
verse and his heavily gnomic style often bring him very close to
the Emblematists: in *A Pleasant Discourse* (1596) the stanzas
which successively compare the court to a cage, a crossbow,

a maze, &c., seem incomplete without the allegorical plates. He has no standards. Here and there we meet a poem less bad than the rest ('Of my Lord Chief Baron', for example, or 'Mistress Mabel Broune') and here and there a pleasing line ('In peascod time when hound to horne gives eare til Buck be kilde'): but they are probably accidental. In metre, he drums away regularly enough and invents some rhyme schemes (bad ones) of his own. The poor man knew already by 1580 that 'yong witts hath ronne old Churchyard out of breathe'. It is of some interest that in the Epistle Dedicatory to his *Light Bundle* (or *Charge*, 1580) he seems to feel that the new, Golden poetry differed from his own kind by superior gravity, complaining that the world now grows weary of 'frevolous verses', yet re-affirming his own belief that 'the nature of Rime is to reuiue the spirites or moue a smile'. This, with his 'crank' spelling and the interest of his biography, is now, I fear, his chief claim on our attention.

Churchyard, then, continued to write Drab all through the age of Gold. Nicholas Breton (1551?–c. 1623), on the other hand, after starting as a Drab poet, had strength to follow the lead that his betters gave him and become a minor Golden poet. He cannot be called a transitional poet for he contributed nothing to the change; he is merely a convertite. His *Flourish upon Fancy* (1577) and *Toys of an Idle Head* (1582) show that in his Drab and unconverted days he was not one of the worst of his kind. His 'Service is no heritage' is a passable song and there is even a faint anticipation of Donne's conversational openings in:

> If any man do liue of ioyes berefte,
> By heauens I sweare, I thinke that man am I.

His seventeenth-century works are dealt with in another volume.

One poet remains who will perhaps claim more attention from the historian of drama than can be given him in this volume. George Whetstone (ob. 1587) in the *Rock of Regard* (1576) offers us a very mixed bill of fare. The metre of 'Medea's Complaint', where each stanza consists of a poulter's couplet followed by two octosyllabic lines, illustrates the freedom to experiment which the Drab Age had achieved and also the lack of taste which renders their experiments so fruitless. The burlesque mythological poem on the wedding of Venus, in which Vulcan becomes 'a Croydon Chuffe', can still almost extort a smile. What he liked best was narrative. His *Rock* includes one prose *novella*. In verse (fourteeners) we have the story of Lady Barbara, whose virtue, like Imogen's was subjected to a wager by her husband and who clapped the unsuccessful Iachimo in prison and set him to spin. Spenser's Radigund may owe something to this episode. In 'The Disordered Life of Bianca Maria' and 'Cressid's Complaint' Whetstone prefers the technique of the *Mirror for Magistrates* and puts the 'tragedies' (both in rhyme royal) into the mouths of their protagonists. Indeed he was so wedded to this device (tasteless when not inspired by the imagination of a Browning) that when, in 1577, he brought out a 'Remembraunce' of his friend George Gascoigne, he made it also into a sort of 'tragedie' and put it into Gascoigne's mouth. He is a very lugubrious and sententious poet; the title of one of his pieces (*Fiftie apples of admonicion late growing on the tree of good government*) is significant.

Mere literary criticism is not wholly competent to deal with the three miscellanies which will conclude this account of Drab Age verse. All of them were intended to provide singing matter; the purchaser paid his money for an aid to social success not for a pleasure to be enjoyed in his study. The earliest of these is *A Handful of Pleasant Delights* by Clement Robinson 'and divers others'—at least, if we follow its latest editor in identifying it with *Very pleasant sonettes* entered in the Stationers' Register in 1566. But what matters more than its date is that character which sets it apart from its two rivals. The *Handful* is clearly intended for citizens, not courtiers: it knows nothing of a Renaissance, or of the Italians, cares for no 'tragedies' and relies on broadsheet material. Some of its pieces hardly exist without the music: even 'Greensleeves', if we could forget the tune, would die in print. But in general the effect of turning from most Drab poetry to the *Handful* is like that of passing from a gimcrack parlour into sweet open air:

> Tantara, tara, tantara, this trumpet glads our hearts.

The 'Nosegaie' had perhaps a place in Shakespeare's memory. In 'Diana and Acteon' we read:

> The leaves were gay and greene
> And pleasant to be seene,
> They went the trees betweene
> In cool array.

Surely these lines, or even the two last words of them, outweigh in value 90 per cent. of the verse that has been considered in this chapter? But with the *Paradise of dainty devices* (1576) 'written for the most part by M. Edwards, sometimes of her Maiesties Chappel', we are back at court, back among poulter's and 'sentences' and verse knick-knacks in which the first two feet of every line read downwards as well as across. Edwards, who had died ten years before the *Paradise* was printed, might be excused for being old fashioned, but there is no sign that taste had outgrown his sort of poetry. On the contrary, the popularity of his collection (reprinted in 1578, 1580, 1585, 1596, 1600, 1606) is shocking. We must again remind ourselves that its contents were 'aptly made to be set to any song in fiue partes' besides being, in general, very staid and edifying. Here was 'honest' recreation; doubtless a suitable present for a gentlewoman or for young master. The very knick-knacks were admired. They gave the Elizabethans the same sort of pleasure which the Victorians drew from a summer-house curiously lined with shells or a model of the Leaning Tower made out of coal. Not all the authors have been identified. Edwards himself once raises hopes (in the poem that begins 'In goyng to my naked bed') but the flicker of narrative is soon over and the gnomic deluge descends. William Hunnis is a little better here than in his independently published devotional verses. Francis Kindlemarsh is better than either of these. His poems on Christmas and Whitsunday show 'promise'. Edward de Vere, Earl of Oxford, shows, here and there, a faint talent, but is for the most part undistinguished and verbose. Lord Vaux in 'Of a Contented Mynde' transforms what would easily have been a dull moral poem by his opening—'When all is doen and said'—which produces the illusion of real speech in a real situation. But the *Paradise* is a poor book, and its texts often look to me unsound. It was followed two years later by *A Gorgeous Gallery of Gallant Inventions*. Thomas Proctor was the editor: Owen Roydon, Churchyard, Howell, Jasper Heywood, and others contributed. It was much less successful than the *Paradise*, perhaps because it came later, certainly not because it is worse. How inferior it is to the *Handful* may be seen by comparing its 'Pyramus and Thisbie' (in fourteeners) with the *Handful*'s ballad on the same story. But it contains better work than the *Paradise*, besides printing in a better text the best piece which the

Paradise offered ('I woulde I were Acteon whom Diana did disgrace'). The finest poem in the book, in a strangely, yet pleasingly, inconsequent metre, is the song 'Ay mee, Ay mee, I sigh to see the Sythe a field'. But there is also much inferior work. The tradition of 'tragedie' is still strong and Helen speaks from the abyss to tell us 'the rewarde of Whoredome'.

Though the mind sickens at the task of dragging all these poetasters back to the cruel light, our labour will not have been wasted if we are now cured of some false notions about the Drab Age. It is not a period during which the genial spring of a 'Renaissance' gradually ripens poetry towards its 'Golden' summer. In this age there was no such advance; save in metrical smoothness, there was a decline. The earliest Drab poetry, that of Wyatt, was the best: so incomparably the best that his inclusion in the Drab Age at all might be questioned if we forgot that the plain diction which can be so admirable in him is, in a sense, the other side of the fatal flatness which damns his successors and that he, soon heavily reinforced by Surrey, inaugurated the vogue of the poulter's measure. Nor is there any indication that humanism or the Italians had a tendency to arrest the decline. Except on Surrey it is doubtful whether they were good influences. Wyatt himself is not best when he is most Italianate: left wholly to Petrarch and stripped of what he owed to the English song, he would perhaps hardly be a poet at all. As for the rest, the Drab poetry which can still be read with some approach to pleasure is that which owes most to the Middle Ages or to the popular tradition. Even the metrical regularity which, if not delightful in itself, is yet the most useful legacy which the Drab Age bequeathed to later poets, was almost certainly not learned from the humanists. In a later chapter the controversy about classical metres will show—what some of us have learned from our own experience as teachers—that 'doing Latin verse' at school is a hindrance rather than a help to the understanding of English prosody. If our knowledge of literature ended with these poets there would be nothing to suggest that English poetry was soon, or ever, going to rise again. We should suppose that we had been watching by its death-bed: and all the evidence would be consistent with the belief that the 'Renaissance' was helping to kill it. It has, of course, been suggested that Henry VIII (that hard-worked whipping boy) was responsible for the Drab Age by cutting off the heads of scholars or poets. But who (save Surrey) were the promising poets that he killed? It is not clear that our poetry would be much the poorer if he had beheaded nearly every writer mentioned in this chapter.

George Gascoigne (1539?–77) I have set apart because he does not belong completely to the Drab Age. In him at last we find what we have vainly sought among his contemporaries, a transitional poet—one in whom we see the Golden quality coming to birth. He has set posterity a number of small but intricate problems which cannot be adequately discussed here. It is disputed whether he wrote all, or only some, of the poems in *A Hundred Sundry Flowers* (1573). It is disputed whether his prose narrative, *The Adventures of Master F. J.*, is really translated, as he himself said, from the Italian of an unknown 'Bartello' or is, as contemporaries believed, a libellous *roman à clef*. (It is always difficult to convince unimaginative readers that anything is invented.) If the *Adventures* are original fiction they rise to some importance as our earliest novel or (longish) short story. They tell an adulterous love story in easy and elegant prose with sufficient psychology and good dialogue; but the inset poems and letters have, for Gascoigne, more importance, and the narrative less, than modern taste demands. A very different kind of prose story appears in the *Tale of Hemetes the Hermit*, 'pronounced' before the queen at Woodstock in 1575. This, in little space, shows the 'heroic romance' just branching off from the medieval, chivalric stem. It is rhetorically written, winds up with a compliment, and was probably, for its purpose, a pretty enough trifle. In his more serious vein (for he was intermittently a moralist) he made a version of the *De Contemptu Mundi* which he called *The Drum of Doom's Day*, and in the same year (1576) a temperance tract, the *Delicate Diet for dainty-mouthed Drunkards*. It is slightly rhetorical and not without vigour. His finest prose work, *The Supposes*, falls to the historian of drama, and so perhaps should the *Glass of Government* (1575): but though it is divided into Acts and Scenes, the speeches (highly edifying) are so long and many scenes so undramatic that it reads more like an Erasmian 'colloquy' than a play. The *Spoil of Antwerp* (1576), almost certainly by Gascoigne, is a good, straightforward piece of reporting. His poetry displays the same versatility as his prose.

The *Steel Glass*, because it is in blank verse and can, in a sense, be called our first satire, has had more attention than it deserves. It is medieval in everything but metre; an allegorical account of the birth of Satire followed by the traditional flyting of all 'estates'. *Dan Bartholmew of Bath* teases us with the expectation of a story, and its flowing stanzas could well have carried one; but Gascoigne has no story to tell, fills up with indifferent lyrics, and leaves us in doubt where we are meant to laugh. Much better is the *Fruits of War*, which begins with mere diatribe but blossoms unexpectedly into a narrative of the poet's own military experience in Flanders. It is the sort of thing that would now be done in prose and is very like many memoirs written by officers—quite free from fire-eating rhetoric, and characteristically full of respect for enemies, hatred for allies, and distrust of the General Staff. But it is on his shorter pieces that Gascoigne's fame as a poet depends. He writes poulter's, fourteeners, songs, sonnets, decasyllabic stanzas, and couplets. What sets him at times above the Drab poets and brings him to the verge of the Golden quality is his grace and melody. He is only a minor poet. He has neither enough invention for narrative nor enough passion for lyric. If he had followed, instead of anticipating (however faintly) the Golden poets, he would be nothing. As things are, he is like the first streak of dawn. Two of his songs, the 'Lullaby' and 'In Praise of Philip Sparrow', cling pleasantly to the memory. He often reminds us of the weaker parts of Spenser; and once, if I am not deceived, of Shakespeare himself:

> When I recorde within my musing mynde
> The noble names of wightes bewitcht in loue,
> Such solace for my self therein I fynde
> As nothing may my fixed fancie moue . . .

We have left the hard high-road at last; we are already 'gliding meteorous', though only an inch from the ground.

His unpretentious *Certain Notes of Instruction* on English verse are of great importance because they tell us what he really wanted and what difficulties he found (he recommends lists of rhyme-words). 'The rule of Inuention . . . of all other rules is most to be marked' . . . 'if I should vndertake to wryte in prayse of a gentle-woman, I would neither prayse her christal eye nor her cherrie lippe &c., For these things are *trita et obuia*. But I would either

finde some supernaturall cause wherby my penne might walke
in the superlatiue degree, or els I would vndertake to aunswere
for any imperfection that shee hath.' The 'Invention' here is the
'conceit', or the 'idea', the thing that makes the poem different
from what any man might say without being a poet. It secures
in poetic thought that departure from the literal and ordinary
(the κύριον and the ἰδιωτικόν) which Aristotle demands in
poetic language. When Donne thought of his flea or his will,
ideas which organize the poems named after them, he had
made an 'invention'. In many Shakespearian sonnets only the
last couplet directly bears on the theme of love; the preceding
twelve lines, which place this theme in a new light, are the
'invention'. The knick-knacks in the *Paradyse* are an earlier, and
much lower, kind of 'invention'. In other words, Drab poetry,
Golden poetry, and metaphysical poetry alike are dominated
by an impulse which is the direct opposite of Wordsworthianism,
naturalism, or expressionism. The poets are never concerned
solely to communicate an experience; they are also concerned
—usually more concerned—to fabricate a novel, attractive,
intricate object, a dainty device. They would hardly have
understood how a modern can use words like 'pretty' and 'clever'
in dispraise of a poem. There are, no doubt, other passages in
the *Notes of Instruction* worth remembering. But this passage on
invention is the most important and should be constantly
borne in mind as a prophylactic against that continual slight
misinterpretation of the Elizabethans to which our own
austerer tastes incessantly tempt us.

III

DRAB AND TRANSITIONAL PROSE

WITH few exceptions the prose which we were considering two chapters ago was 'applied' prose, such as never owed too much and often owed too little to conscious artistry. Of such plain writing some awaits us in the present chapter, but we shall also have to deal with picked prose and even with adorned prose—*Kunstprosa* as the Germans call it. In order to be fair to the latter we must put considerable constraint upon ourselves. Nothing in literature is so 'desperately mortal' as a stylish prose. On the other hand, the prose of men who are intent upon their matter and write only to be understood tends, not quite fairly, to gain from the passage of time. Its content, even when mediocre in itself, acquires historical interest; its most commonplace terms of expression grow pleasantly archaic; proverbs and idioms which were part of the common speech seem to the inexperienced reader to be proofs of individual genius; even characteristic faults are at worst refreshingly unlike the faults of our own prose. To all these general causes of misjudgement there must be added in our age a strong bias in favour of strictly functional beauty and a quite unusual distrust of rhetoric. Decoration, externally laid on and inorganic, is now hardly tolerated except in the human face. We must therefore throughout this chapter endeavour, not indeed to exchange our own prejudices for those of the sixteenth century, but to bring ourselves a little nearer to the ideal middle point. We must practice some deliberate indulgence to the adorned prose, and be strictly critical when we read the plain. For not all plain prose is good. Such efforts as ink-horn terms or euphuism may have been misdirected, even barbarous, but those who made them were not wrong in their belief that our prose needed to be heightened and coloured and 'strongly trussed up'. We forget too easily the faults of the plain Drab. Here, from Harpsfield's *Life of More*, is a specimen of the sort of thing the more ambitious stylists were trying to escape from:

The see of Rome being at that time voyde, the Cardinall, being a man very ambitious and desirous to aspire to that dignitie, wherein he had good hope and likelyhood, perceauing himselfe frustrate and eluded of this his aspiring expectation by the meanes of the Emperour Charles commending Cardinall Adrian, sometime his schoolemaster, to the Cardinalls of Rome, for his great learning, vertue and worthines, who therevpon was elected Pope (and comming from Spaine, whereof he had vnder the saide Charles the chiefe gouernment, before his entrie into the Citie of Rome putting off his hose and shoes and, as I haue hearde it credibly reported, bare foote and bare legged passed through the streetes towardes his pallace, with such humblenes as all the people had him in great reuerence) the Cardinall (I saie) waxed so wood therewith that he studied to . . ., &c.

This effect, as of a man speaking with his mouth half full of gravel, had been tolerated long enough.

Sir Thomas Elyot[1] (1490?–1546) though not a self-made man, for he came of a good family, boasts that he is a self-taught one who, from his twelfth year, had no instructor but himself *tam in scientiis liberalibus quam in utraque philosophia*, though he also tells us that before he was twenty a 'renoumed' physician had taken him through Galen. His earliest publication was the *Book of the Governor* (1531). This was followed in 1532 by *Pasquil the Plain* and in 1533 by *The Knowledge that maketh a Wise Man*. The former, possibly derived from an Italian source, is a dialogue in the early Platonic manner between Pasquil, the personification of free speech, and a flatterer called Gnato. Gnato represents Protestantism and is painted as an ignorant hypocrite, one of those who 'will be in the bowells of diuinitie before they know what belongeth to good humanitie'. He carries in his bosom a copy of the New Testament, but cheek by jowl with it (and 'Lorde! what discorde is bitweyne these two bokes!') Chaucer's *Troilus*. We have heard from the other side so much about idle monkes and wanton chanouns as the authors of chivalrous romance that the jibe is unexpected. The truth is that in 'advanced' circles at that time any party might accuse any other of medieval proclivities; the romances were out of fashion. In 1534 came *The Castle of Health*, a novelty in so far as it is a medical treatise written by a layman and in the vernacular. Elyot was attacked for writing it both by the doctors who

[1] b. c. 1490. Clerk of Assize on Western Circuit, 1511. In Commission of the Peace for Oxfordshire, 1522. Sheriff of Oxon. and Berks., 1527. Friend of Cromwell's by 1528. Knighted, 1530. Ambassador to the Imperial Court, 1531 and 1535. Tells Cromwell 'the amity between me and Sir Thomas More was *usque ad aras*', 1536. M.P. for Cambridgeshire, 1542. Ob. 1546.

resented the intrusion of an amateur and also by men of his own class who held that such work 'beseemeth not a knight, he mought haue been much better occupied'. This criticism provoked from him in the second edition a vigorous defence both of the vernacular and of the 'histories' or anecdotes with which he had plentifully besprinkled his discourse: 'they may more surely cure mens affections then diuers physitions do cure maladies'. In 1538 he brought out his *Latin–English Dictionary*, dedicated to the king whom he obediently salutes as 'supreme head of the Church under Christ' and praises for his 'evangelical faith'. In 1539 came a *Banquet of Sapience* and in 1540 an *Image of Governance*. There is evidence that he also began in Latin a book *De Rebus Memorabilibus Angliae*.

Elyot's *Dictionary* is probably the most useful thing he did, but as an English author he is chiefly remembered for the *Book of the Governor*. By a Governor he means one who rules under a king, a member of the governing classes. His book is thus a sort of blue-print for the education of the aristocracy and falls into place beside those numerous works in which humanists and others at that time endeavoured, not quite ineffectively, to alter their masters. A new type was in fact produced, even if it was not very like what the humanists wanted. Castiglione's *Il Cortegiano*, Machiavelli's *Prince*, Vives' *De Christiana Femina*, Erasmus' *Institutio Regis Christiani*, and the *De Regno et Regis Institutione* of Patricius (Francesco Patrizi) all reveal the impulse; so in its own way does the *Faerie Queene*. Patricius and Erasmus were the two that influenced Elyot most. But he is less philosophical and universal than they, more rooted in the realities of a particular time and place. Erasmus begs rulers to remember how unreasonable it is (*quam sit absurdum*) for them to be elevated above the people in splendour if they are not proportionately elevated in virtue. Elyot substitutes for *quam absurdum* 'what reproche', changing a sage's into a gentleman's censure (II. i). He borrows from Patricius the point that *res publica* means not 'common' but 'public' weal. But in Patricius this had been not much more than a philological note; in Elyot (I. i) it is the starting-point for a refutation of egalitarianism and a glowing eulogy of degree which anticipates, as so many authors have done, the speech of Shakespeare's Ulysses.

Of education in its nursery stage Elyot has nothing of value to say. Like all his kind he issues rigid instructions which would be scattered to the winds by ten minutes' experience of any real child or any real nurse (he died without issue). In the later chapters of his First Book he is really laying the foundations of the system which, in a narrower but not unrecognizable form, became the 'classical education' of our public schools. He has to fight on two fronts. On the one hand he has to rebut the lingering medieval idea (Castiglione says it died hardest in France) 'that to a great gentleman it is a notable reproche to be well lerned and to be called a great clerke' (I. xii). It was on this front that the humanists triumphed most completely. The tradition of gentlemanly philistinism slowly but surely decayed and was not reinstated till compulsory games altered the whole character of school life. There was thus a long lucid interval between Squire Western and Bertie Wooster; it is arguable that during that interval England was at her greatest. On the other hand, Elyot has to fight against the current practice of his own day whereby boys having once learned 'to speake Latine elegantly' and 'to make verses without mater or sentence' (I. xiii) are snatched away to the illiberal but lucrative study of the law, when they ought to be 'forming their minds' on the great poets, orators, and philosophers. For these Elyot expresses, and in some sense no doubt sincerely feels, a boundless enthusiasm—'I feare me to be to longe from noble Homere'. Yet his own praise of Homer does not suggest anything that would now be regarded as discriminating enjoyment. On Virgil he is more convincing (I. x).

Perhaps the most interesting thing in Elyot's advice is his plea for what we should now call aesthetic education. He laments a decay of the arts in England, by which it has come about that 'if we wyll haue any thinge well paynted, kerued, or embrawdred' we must 'resorte unto straungers' (I. xiv). A young nobleman who shows any talent for drawing should be given lessons in it; not only for its possible military uses, but for a deeper reason. The man who can draw will 'alway couaite congruent mater . . . and whan he happeneth to rede or here any fable or historie, forthwith he apprehendeth it more desirously and retaineth it better than any other' (I. viii).

The *Book of the Governor* is thus by no means contemptible for its content; at the same time there is nothing in it which suggests a mind of the first order. Elyot is a well informed man, not a scholar; a sensible man (for the most part), not a deep thinker. As a stylist he has perhaps higher claims. His verse, which appears frequently in short translated extracts from the ancients, is Late Medieval and worthless. Within his prose we must make distinctions. The florid *Proheme*, to Henry VIII, is not characteristic. Nor is II. xii, where his Burtonian love of 'histories' overflows all bounds and produces in the story of Titus and Gisippus (from Boccaccio) what is really a full dress *novella*. Here he is a little aureate ('Am I of that vertue that I may resiste agayne celestiall influence preordinate by prouidence diuine?'). But that is not the true Elyot. The love of long words is indeed a constant trait. In this respect Elyot is at the opposite pole from the purist Cheke. He is a convinced and conscious neologist, and is prepared to defend his practice 'for the necessary augmentation of our language' (I. xxii). No one will now seriously deny the necessity; and fortune so sways the destiny of words that it would be harsh to blame Elyot if his *mansuetude*, *pristinate*, and *levigate* have not succeeded. It is not these, whether we praise or blame them, that should determine his place as a writer. The important thing is that Elyot is aware of prose as an art. His sentences do not simply happen, they are built. He keeps a firm hold of his construction, he is nearly always lucid, and his rhythm is generally sound. In a word, his prose is, for good as well as for ill, more literary than More's. Hence some loss of race and intimacy (humour he probably had little to express) and hence also a freedom from confusion and monotony. The difference is still a very fine one, not easily to be discovered by comparing a sentence or two of his with a sentence or two of More's. After a day's reading it becomes noticeable. If it were possible for authors to be always either as lively as More or as lyrical as Tyndale at their best, the appearance of such prose as Elyot's would be a disaster. As things are, the gain almost equals the loss. I am not suggesting that Elyot, or a thousand such as Elyot, matter to the mind and heart of man as More matters; but the ear of man must sometimes prefer him.

The same impulse towards a more formal prose appears in the historian Edward Hall (1499?-1547) and has in him been compendiously damned by Ascham as 'indenture Englishe' and 'strange and inkhorne tearmes'. 'Indenture English' refers no doubt to coupled synonyms such as Hall's 'gredy and auaricious', 'an innocent with a nocent, a man vngilty with a gilty', 'poore and needy'; 'inkhorne tearmes', to such real or supposed neologisms as *abbreviated, parasite, culpe,* or *sepulted*—not all of which the language would now willingly spare. Hall is deliberately trying to write better than he talked. He is fond of the allegorical figure; 'that venemous worme, that dreadfull dragon, called disdain of superioritie' or 'the slowe worme and deadely Dormouse called Idlenes'. He is much indebted for style, as for matter, to Polydore Vergil. In his character sketches Latin models make their presence very noticeable, as when he writes of Henry V, 'No Emperoure in magnanimitie euer him excelled. No potentate was more piteous nor lorde more bounteous. No prince had lesse of his subiectes and neuer king conquered more.' He seldom lets slip any occasion for a (fictitious) set speech: Thucydides, who alone could really bend that bow, has much to answer for. He is fond of what medieval rhetoricians called *Occupatio*; 'What should I reherse?'—'What should I write?' Sometimes we seem in Hall to hear the premonitory drops of what later became the shower of euphuism:

What so euer man intendeth, God sodainly reuerseth, what princes wil, God wil not, what we thinke stable God sodainly maketh mutable. . . .

But here, as always whether in prose or verse, a narrative style is not to be judged by snippets. You must read for at least half a day and read with your mind on the story. If Hall is given a fair chance he will be found, at worst, very tolerable. Ascham exaggerates: it is indeed significant that the purists could never make their case without exaggeration or without inventing men of straw to attack, such as Wilson's 'Lincolneshire man' in his *Art of Rhetoric*. I do not think that many who, without reading Hall, read Holinshed where he follows him almost *verbatim*, make any complaint of the style; change the dog's name and no one will hang him. Hall's narrative—proems and conclusions are no fair test—is nearly always readable, and sometimes splendid. Even where the art is most apparent, the effect may be good, as in this of Shrewsbury:

The prince Henry that daie holpe muche his father, for although he wer sore wounded in the face with an arow, yet he neuer ceased ether to fight where the battail was moste strongest, or to courage his men where their hertes were moste danted.

This has, in Johnson's words, 'the formality of a settled style in which the first half of the sentence betrays the other'. But the demands of the rhythm are properly met by the matter. We should have had no Johnson, no Gibbon, and perhaps no Thomas Browne if the road on which Hall was setting out had been effectively closed by the doubtful canon of 'writing as you talk'. To some tastes, including my own, this new kind of history will always seem a poor thing compared with the best of the old—with Snorri or Froissart. But for most Englishmen in Hall's time there was no such alternative. That clear, effortless narrative was not within their reach. If Hall had not been artificial he would probably have sunk to the level of his editor and (in 1562) successor, Richard Grafton:

He banished out of his Court nicenesse and wantonnesse, and committed Reynulph Bishop of Duresme, a man hated of all men for oppression, bribery and diuerse other notable crymes, and a chiefe Counsaylour and perswader also of the King his brother in all his lewde and vngodly attemptes to the tower of London, the which before you haue heard was so great with his brother William (*Chronicle at Large, Henry,* 1).

The sentence may not be by Grafton (very little of his *Chronicle at Large* is) but it will illustrate the point equally well whoever wrote it.

So much for Hall's place in the history of style; but his book, *The Union of the Two Noble and Illustre Families of Lancaster and York* (1548) has other claims on our attention. Except for the reign of Henry VIII (where the historians value him) Hall does not claim to be an original authority; indeed he expressly tells us that his work was 'compiled and gathered (not made) out of diuerse writers'. Still less can he be praised for impartiality. In religion he is frankly on the Protestant side, in politics he is the spokesman of the official Tudor point of view. Yet he has a twofold literary importance. His work, after More's *Richard III,* is the first English attempt at history in the grand manner. In a previous chapter we saw historiography budding off from the Chronicles of London. Hall, inspired by More and Polydore Vergil, whose *Historia Anglica* (1534) did for us (and much better) what Boece had done for the art of history in Scotland, severs that old connexion. The very title of his book is significant. He is not an annalist, bound to record whatever happened, but a man selecting a subject and writing with a standard of relevance in view; he can omit things which are 'no parte of my processe'—though it must be confessed that he does not always do so. And secondly, he is the great transmitter of the English legend as it was fashioned by Vergil and as it lived in the minds of the Elizabethans. His good Duke Humphrey, his Margaret, his Suffolk, together with More's Richard, are substantially those of Shakespeare. His love of pageantry offends some moderns, but the taste for it must be acquired if we are to understand the sixteenth century. The splendours which he describes did not seem to him mere externals. A fine armour is almost part of the personality of the knight who wears it; and there was doubtless to him an almost spiritual significance in the appearance of Richard III's guard at his coronation, 'euil appareled and worse harneissed in rusty harneys neither defensable nor skoured to the sale, to the great disdain of all the lookers on'. On the whole it is difficult (though not impossible) to understand why Hall receives from most critics so much less attention than either Elyot or Ascham.

As regards Elyot and Ascham in common, the explanation presumably lies in that exaggerated reverence for humanism which has long infected our critical tradition. But as regards Roger Ascham (1515–68),[1] considered by himself, there is another and better reason. There is nothing about Hall that excites love: we praise the writer, but feel that the man may have been little better than a government tool. Ascham, on the other hand, is everyone's friend. He is irresistible. In his own day nearly everyone seems to have liked him. Despite his avowed Protestantism, Mary made him her Latin Secretary and he found it possible all through her reign to abide by his religion with (let us hope) no disgraceful degree of prudence. His very weaknesses—'too much given to dicing and cock-fighting', says Camden—were of a genial sort, and it is plain that he was a good schoolmaster, a good husband, and a good friend. His delightful, and delighted, temperament has flowed into his writing.

[1] b. 1515. Serves in house of Sir Anthony Wingfield. Enters St. John's, Cambridge, 1530. Gets to know Sir John Cheke. B.A., and Fellowship, 1534. Reader in Greek, c. 1538. Serious illness, 1539–40. Sides with Cheke in support of an Anglicized pronunciation of Greek. Pension from Henry VIII, 1545. Public Orator, 1546. Writes against the Mass, c. 1547. Tutor to Princess Elizabeth, 1548–9. Visits Lady Jane Grey, 1550. Becomes Secretary to Sir Richard Moryson, Ambassador to the Emperor, 1550; visits Louvain, Maine, Worms, Venice, &c. Latin Secretary to Queen Mary, 1553. Marries Margaret Howe, 1554. Prebendary of Wetwang, 1559. Ob. 1568.

His *Toxophilus* (1545) is one of the most genial and winning books that had yet appeared in English. The modern reader who feels the subject of archery to be a little remote has only to realize that it was to Ascham what cricket has been to many of his successors and all will be well. The tone is unmistakable. Archery is England's safety and glory (for it is a vile French lie that the Scotch shoot better than we); these new fangled guns are unreliable and at the mercy of the weather; nothing keeps a man so fit as shooting at the butts; archery gets boys out into the open air, and away from those nasty cards. Archery, that is, with your true English long-bow. Cross-bows are a poor affair. You find no mention of them 'in any good Authour'. Shooting is far better sport than bowls or music—especially the sort of music that is increasingly popular nowadays with its 'nice, fine, minikin fingering', only fit for use 'in the courte among ladies': if they used pricksong and plainsong, it would be another matter. Thus the book is, if you will, a farrago of prejudices: but then that is its charm. Ascham is everywhere writing of what he knows and loves, and is full of reality. The attack on gaming (which he was in one sense only too well qualified to deliver) introduces some lively painting of low life. The reminiscences of Erasmus, Cheke, and Elyot are pleasant: still more so, Ascham's memory of his own childhood when kind Sir Humfrey Wingfield would come down from London with a bow and shafts and set all the boys to shooting. What is best of all is the passage about air and snow: I hardly know where such loving observation can be found again till we come to the Journals of Dorothy Wordsworth. The only real weakness of *Toxophilus* is that the dialogue (for it is cast in that form) does not come to much life, though in the digression on Excellence and Possibility the Platonic manner is closely imitated.

The Schoolmaster, posthumously published in 1570, occupied the last years of Ascham's life. Its starting-point was a conversation in 1563 about some Eton boys who had run away 'for feare of beating'. This provoked from Ascham, to his lasting glory, a protest (I think the first in English) against cruelty in teaching. As a treatise on education his book is in a very different class from the works of Erasmus and Elyot. There are no grandiose projects. Instead, we have the technical advice of a practising teacher who knows what pupils, whether 'hard' or 'quick' wits, can really do. On this side Ascham's precepts are to be judged only by those who have had some experience of his trade; the literary historian can have no opinion on the mischief of 'making Latines' or the virtues of the 'two paper bokes'. The author's love both of boys and of learning is, however, plain for all to see. What is less attractive is his general conception of literature. Ascham is a rigid humanist, a professed follower of his contemporary Sturmius, a Ciceronian, and a whole-hearted adherent to the doctrine of Imitation. This does not mean Aristotle's imitation of Nature, but that imitation of authors by authors which the dependence of Roman literature upon Greek had elevated into a principle. By Ascham's time it has become imitation of imitation. We are to learn how to copy Tully by studying his methods of copying Demosthenes and then copying them. Ascham's belief in the nutritive value of this feast of husks is astonishing; he quotes with approval Cheke's optimistic statement, 'he that will dwell in these few bookes onelie, first in Gods holie Bible, and than ioyne with it *Tullie* in *Latin, Plato, Aristotle, Xenophon, Isocrates* and *Demosthenes* in *Greke*, must nedes proue an excellent man'. Contrariwise, he is confident that 'who so euer be founde fonde in iudgement of matter, be commonlie found as rude in vttering their mynde'. Such are 'Stoickes, Anabaptistes, and Friers, with Epicures, Libertines and Monkes'. Style (and that very narrowly conceived) is coming to be the whole of learning. 'Musicke, Arithmetick, and Geometrie', if not kept firmly in their place, 'sharpen mens wittes ouer moch' and 'change mens maners ouer sore.' And in *Toxophilus* Ascham had already told us that eloquence is 'a thinge moste necessary of all other for a captayne'.

It is no kindness to Ascham to give him a place among English critics. His attack on medieval romance is a humanist commonplace. His reference in *Toxophilus* to Chaucer as 'our Englyshe Homer' will do well enough as a conventional bow to a venerable figure: if taken more seriously it would indicate a most imperceptive reading of both poets. His general theory of poetry, in the same book, is the common and disastrous one that poets 'vnder the couering of a fable do hyde and wrappe in goodlie preceptes of philosophie'. His attack on rhyme was important only in so far as it was mischievous. He makes no attempt to analyse; the only approach to an argument is, characteristically, the statement that rhyme is derived from the

K

'Gothes and Hunnes'. The best we can say for Ascham as a critic is that if he has no virtues, at least his faults are not original but those of his school. And all the time, even in his driest or most perverse pages, we feel the presence of a humanity which his humanism could never quite defeat.

Ascham's English style is praised in Gabriel Harvey's *Ciceronianus* (1577) as *eleganti, perpolitoque sermone praeditus*, as *limatus* and *nitidus*. A modern reader who worked back to Ascham from Sidney or Hooker would not perhaps immediately notice this polish, this labour of the file. Ascham would strike him as a plain writer. In reality he is as conscious as Elyot or Hall and belongs with them to the refining party; but he is on the other wing of that party, a purist like his friend Cheke. He rebukes the neologists for 'using straunge words as latin, french and Italian' till they 'make all thinges darke and harde'. He would rather write 'faule of the leafe' than 'Autumn'. But to avoid ink-horn terms meant, not to write as you spoke, but to depend on other devices. Notice the (perhaps excessive) balance of the following:

Howe honest a pastyme for the mynde, how holsome an exercise for the bodye, not vile for great men to vse, not costlye for poore men to susteyne, not lurking in holes and corners for ill men at their pleasure to misuse it, but abiding in the open sight and face of the worlde for good men, if it fault, by theyr wisdome to correct it.

We also find alliteration; 'but seeing with wishing we can not haue one nowe worthie' or 'muche musike marreth mennes maners, sayth Galen'. Sometimes we find alliteration and antithesis together—'being not so paynfull for the labour as pleasaunt for the pastyme'. These tricks, if used more continuously and seasoned with enough similes would amount to what we have been taught to call euphuism. Euphuism is, in fact, an extreme development of the purist type of refinement. In Ascham that extreme is still a fair distance away. The symmetry does not usually force itself upon our attention and is often perceived only by its happy result—the ease with which the sentences take their place in our mind. Ascham at his best is too full of things to be the slave of his own stylishness. He had eyes as well as ears—eyes not only for the snow but for the unlucky archer 'crying after the shafte', for the optical illusions produced by broken ground, for a cook in the kitchen chopping herbs 'with such a measure . . . as would delyte a manne both to

se hym and heare hym'. Ascham the humanist is narrow enough;
once get him out of the schoolroom and he pleases us all because
he is pleased with everything.

Ascham's fellow collegian John Cheke (1514–57), though his
senior and indeed his tutor, appeared later as a writer in the
vernacular. In that capacity he is not of much importance.
Cheke was primarily a don, the first Regius Professor of Greek
at Cambridge, the tutor of William Cecil, of Edward VI, and
occasionally of Elizabeth, the man who helped to make St.
John's a centre of early Protestantism and early humanism.
He was also, less happily, an early specimen of the fashionable
and political don. His reforming zeal was by no means confined to religion. He wanted men to approach not only theology
but all subjects 'without being at all prepossessed', says Strype,
by the 'commonly received notions'. He was a believer in the
'clean sweep', a sharp, scrutinizing man of the type common at
Cambridge in the sixteenth century and happily not extinct in
the twentieth. One of his innovations, the 'new' pronunciation
of Greek, was almost certainly in the right direction. His life
was a medieval 'tragedie' of rise and fall. At one time he was
influential with Anne Boleyn, later with Edward VI, enriched
with monastic lands, knighted, made Provost of King's. Then
came Mary's reign, exile, poverty, a treacherous safe conduct
to Brussels, capture, the Tower, the threat of Smithfield. His
courage failed, he recanted, and died a miserable man.

It was not out of character that such a man should be a keen
astrologer. He was also, to speak freely, something of a crank.
He had a bee in his bonnet about 'pure and unmixed' English
and another about spelling reform. His translation of St.
Matthew is a monument of both. From this curious work it
appears that Cheke, like so many purists, had not given much
serious thought to the language he wished to purify. If 'lunatic'
is to become *moond*, and 'apostle' *frosent*, and a 'proselyte' a
freshman, and to be 'crucified', to be *crossed*, it is not easy to see
why he retains such words as *conforted*, *persequuted*, and *vnsaverie*.
But perhaps his motives were not purely philological. Romance
words, or at least such romance words as the accidents of habit
and prejudice made noticeable to him, smelled of aureation
and therefore of the Middle Ages—away with them! There
might also be a wish to recede as far as possible from Gardiner
and his 1542 list of words that must not be translated; for

Gardiner was not only a Papist but a Chancellor of Cambridge who had used his authority to suppress the new pronunciation of Greek. But the matter is of little consequence; Cheke as a translator of scripture is only a curiosity. His *Hurt of Sedition* (1549) is a government pamphlet addressed to the rebels; the 'other learned and useful tracts' with which tradition credited him are not now easily to be identified. The *Hurt of Sedition*, though better than anything of the same sort would be likely to be in our own days, is not very memorable. It bears no trace of his purist fancies. There is a plentiful, yet not obtrusive, employment of antithesis and he likes to accumulate clauses of the same type—'disobedience is thought stoutnesse and sullennesse is counted manhood and stomaking is courage and prating is iudged wisedome and the elvishest is most meete to rule'. In general the style is much less visibly artful than that of Elyot, Hall, or Ascham; it is nearer to More's. It even has something of the old pungency: 'ye haue encamped your selfe in fielde and there lyke a byle in a body, nay lyke a sinke in a towne, haue gathered togither all the nastie vagabondes and ydle loyterers.' But whatever Cheke does well others do better, and the fads which may have impressed the combination-room make a thin sound across the centuries; *vocem exiguam, inceptus clamor frustratur hiantem.*

The *Dialogue* of Thomas Starkey (1499?–1538), composed about 1534, uses a style less artificial than Elyot's or Hall's but generally avoids the contusion of the old go-as-you-please manner. He does not seem to attempt eloquence but becomes eloquent unawares in the passage beginning 'Let vs, as hyt were, out of a hyar place' (1. i). As a writer of dialogue he does not rank very high. His speakers are feigned to be Thomas Lupset and Cardinal Pole (men well worth a digression each if the scale of my book allowed it) but they might almost as well be nameless and there is little pretence of dramatic life. The content of the work is extremely interesting. After a 'vnyuersal and scolastycal consideratyon' on the active and contemplative lives and on Natural and Civil Law (this part is really very well done) he unfolds his plans for England. They include an elective, and strictly limited monarchy, the imposition of Roman Law, the suppression of 'curyouse deuysarys of new songs', the closing of public houses, and a tax on bachelors. In religion, though Starkey has no sympathy with

Protestant theology, he approves many Protestant practices—
a married clergy, services in English, and resistance to papal
dispensations. A most interesting trait is his passionate love of
urban life. The old Stoic idea that man lived best in 'the wyld
forest' is produced only to be contradicted. Gentlemen like
living in the country but 'thys ys a great rudenes and a
barbarous custome'; they must be compelled 'to retyre to cytes
and townys and to byld them housys in the same'. Gentlemen
have so often been urged to do exactly the opposite that we read
this passage with bewilderment: the explanation is perhaps to be
found in Starkey's humanism. Town may have seemed to him
more 'classical' than country, more redolent of Terence; he has
much to say of the 'ornamentys' of cities and possibly dreamed of
a little Athens in every county. Starkey is no Solomon and thinks
that the disorders usually attendant upon elective monarchy
could be avoided by confining the election to 'the auncyent
famylys'. In one passage (1. ii) he anticipates Milton's refusal
to praise a fugitive and cloistered virtue and maintains that the
man who lives well 'in daungerous prosperyte' deserves more
praise than he who 'for feare of the same daungerys runnyth
in to a relygyouse house'.

All the writers I have yet mentioned are in some degree
artists; a much homelier and less ambitious prose is offered
by the Protestant Brinkelow, and the Papists Roper and
Harpsfield.

Of Henry Brinkelow we know almost nothing except that he
died in 1546, that he had been 'somtyme a grey fryre', and that
he was in Bale's opinion a pious man *fide magis quam eruditione
clarus*. Of the three books which Bale attributes to him two can
be certainly identified with the *Lamentation of a Christian against
the City of London* (1542?) and the *Complaint of Roderick Mors*
(1548?). The *Lamentation* is mainly moral and theological, the
Complaint economic and political as well. It records the disappointment of an ardent Lutheran who had approved (and
still approves) the dissolution of the monasteries on doctrinal
grounds, but is shocked by its actual results. The new owners
are even worse landlords and worse patrons than the abbeys;
and 'this is a fayre amendment . . . it is amendid euen as the
deuel amended his damys legg'. The great merit of this piece is
that Brinkelow goes beyond the common medieval appeal for
perfect moral virtue in all 'estates' and shows us economic

necessities. Rising rents must produce a rise in prices, and a rise in the price of wool must lose us our foreign markets, 'make what actes ye can deuyse to the contrary'. All this is done in a prose which has not perhaps been sufficiently praised. It goes about as far towards excellence as a merely natural style can go when the author is neither a humorist nor a poet, and is far less confused and monotonous than such styles usually are. It has even its own untaught eloquence:

> Death, death, euyn for tryfyls, so that thei folow the High Prystys in crucifyeing Christ, saying *nos habemus legem* and *secundum legem nostram debet mori*, we haue a lawe and by our lawe he ought to dye. This *mori, mori*, dye, dye, went neuer owt of the pristes mowthes syns that tyme, and now thei haue poysonyd the temporal rulars with the same.

Brinkelow's style, intelligence, and honest passion deserve more attention than they usually receive.

Harpsfield and Roper both availed themselves of the brief freedom which their religion enjoyed under Mary to produce Lives of Sir Thomas More. Both works are of great interest but not of equal literary merit. Nicholas Harpsfield (1519–75) was the Marian Archdeacon of Canterbury and is of some importance as a neo-Latin controversialist and historian. His *Life and Death of Sir Thomas More* was composed while the folio of More's *Works* was going through the press; presumably in 1556. It is far more ambitious than Roper's, and its historical merits have been praised by students on both sides, but it is hardly a satisfactory book. All its best passages are taken, often word for word, from Roper whose manuscript, perhaps in an unfinished state, had been placed at Harpsfield's disposal. His own writing can ill bear the comparison. Most authors in this period can be classified either as 'plain' or as 'literary', and there is something to dislike in each class; Harpsfield unhappily shares the faults of both. His intermittent decorations do not please. We weary of triplets like 'impaired, blemished, or defaced', 'quicken, refresh, and exhilerate'. All good men love Margaret Roper; but no man will love her more for hearing her compared, all in one breath, to Sappho, Aspasia, Damo, Cornelia, Fabiola, Marcella, Paula, and Eustochium. Yet at other times Harpsfield is only too natural; he will set off without forethought on too long a sentence and sink over boots and breech in a quagmire of clauses. Neither fault, however, is incessant, and specimens of good (or goodish) plain prose can be found. Yet when all is said, his book lives by the beauty and greatness of its matter and not by Harpsfield's skill.

William Roper (1496–1578) in small compass produced a masterpiece. In narrative his prose may sometimes be a little heavy, but his dialogue is excellent. He shares with Boswell the power of giving to reported conversation that appearance of reality which we demand of conversations in fiction. The gift is extremely rare; neither Spence nor Eckermann had it in a comparable degree, and in Plato we suspect a larger element of fiction. And it has every right to be regarded as a literary gift. Roper also shares Boswell's humility; he will cast himself for the fool's part if the anecdote demands it. All the best stories about More come from him. One merit which he and Harpsfield have in common deserves to be pondered: both write almost pure panegyric without awaking either disgust or incredulity. One would have to mount into very high regions indeed to find a parallel.

A third Marian biography, also on the Roman side, is Cavendish's *Life and Death of Thomas Wolsey*. George Cavendish (*c*. 1500–61?) had been one of the cardinal's gentlemen ushers; internal evidence shows that he wrote between July 1554 and February 1557. His *Life* is a work of singular beauty, not so much for its style (which is perhaps a little better than Harpsfield's) as for its unity of effect. In any later period such a life would tend to have the purpose either of blackening or defending its hero. That is not Cavendish's aim. He extenuates little or nothing and sets down naught in malice. He notes his master's faults—'pride and arrogance' and 'more respect to the worldly honour of his person than he had to his spiritual profession'. Yet it is not his chief concern to show, in the Greek fashion, how *hybris* provokes *nemesis*. That comes in; but in the main the life of Wolsey is to Cavendish one of the 'falls of princes', an illustration of Fortune's turning wheel. The moral is, 'let all men to whom Fortune extendeth her grace not trust too much to her fickle favour', and his book conforms perfectly to the medieval pattern of 'tragedie'. That pattern justifies (what Cavendish would probably have loved to write even without justification) the piled-up descriptions of magnificence with which the story is filled; Wolsey's gentlemen 'in coats of crimson veluet of the most purest colour that might be inuented', himself in 'fine

scarlet or else crimson satin, taffety, damask or caffa', his table
served with confections in which birds, beasts, dancers or battles
were 'most liuely made and counterfeited', his train a quarter
of a mile long, his very mule 'trapped with a foot-cloth and
traps of crimson veluet upon veluet purled with gold'. It goes on
perhaps too long. It betrays something of the nostalgic loquacity
we may meet today in an old domestic who remembers the age
of great houses. But on the whole it is proper to Cavendish's
theme. All builds up to the hour when Fortune with Venus (in
the person of Anne Boleyn) as her instrument 'thought she
would deuyse a mean to abate his high port'. The end ('If I
had serued God as diligentlie as I haue done the King', &c.)
is familiar. The behaviour attributed to Wolsey in disgrace is
strikingly unlike that of an Elizabethan hero or an Elizabethan
villain. He is more like a whipped dog; such is the medieval
acquiescence in Fortune's decree. This is perhaps the last work
written in English which belongs completely to the Middle
Ages. The prefatory verses are, appropriately, in the style and
metre of Hawes.

The Life of Fisher found in MS. Harleian 6382, though
clearly composed after Mary's death, belongs to the school of
Harpsfield and Roper. Since the author feels it necessary to say
that London is 'the head cittie of England' he presumably had
foreign readers in view and intended his book to be turned into
Latin. Save for a few clusters of rhetorical questions, his prose is
very artless and there are some long, dishevelled sentences. If
in a few passages—on Queen Katharine before the Legate's
court and on the sufferings and death of Fisher—his work is as
moving as anything in the whole range of English historical
writing, this is chiefly due to his matter. Chiefly, not wholly:
for while he has none of the literary talent which could set off
a dull theme, he is at least free from all those literary vices which
really offend a reader. He has the old infirmities, but no
vulgarity, no fashionable grimaces.

Protestantism under Mary found an interesting expression
in the *Short Treatise of Politic Power* by John Poynet or Ponet,
the exiled Bishop of Winchester, posthumously and anonymously printed in 1556. It is a well-pressed attack on the
(momentarily papistical) Tudor Monarchy in the light of the
medieval conception of Natural Law. Its style displays very
varied powers in short space. In the flyting of Bonner we have

the slapstick manner dear to More and later to be revived by Nashe: ('Some of you chaplaines get my lorde a cup of sacke to comforte his spirites. My lorde and I agree almost like belles, we iare somwhat but not muche, his lordship meaneth that men ought to be alwaies but not at all tymes honest, but I saie they must be honest alwaies and at all tymes.') In sharp contrast to this we find almost Johnsonian weight and precision in the statement that those who admit absolute sovereignty 'purchase to themselves a perpetuall vncertaintie both of life and goodes'. Elsewhere, on Hooker's own theme, he can at times be as lofty as Hooker himself;

The Ethnikes (albeit they had not the right and perfite true knowlage of God) were endued with the knowlage of the lawe of nature. For it is no priuate lawe to a fewe or certain people but common to all; not written in bokes but graffed in the heartes of men; not made by man but ordained of God; which we haue not learned, receaued, or redde but haue taken, sucked, and drawne it out of nature; wherevnto we are not taught but made.

If he had fully known how good the last clause is, he might have spared some of the others; but clearly we are dealing with a strong writer.

In contrast to Poynet we may place Sir Thomas Smith (1513–77), the humanist, the learned civilian, and the man of affairs. His *De Republica Anglorum*, partly written in the sixties, was not published till 1583. Smith's political thought is singularly free from moral and theological elements and he is not interested in Natural Law. The 'lawe already put' in any commonwealth seems to be almost the final standard by which conduct is to be judged; hence 'if it be ciuilly vnderstood' Thrasymachus' definition of justice as the interest of the stronger 'is not so far oute of the waie as Plato would make it' (I. ii). Ultimate questions, as whether rebellion is ever justifiable (I. v) or whether every monarch have παμβασιλείαν 'if he would vse the same' (I. viii) are mentioned only to be waived. His beliefs about the origin of the State are largely derived from Aristotle. His main purpose, however, is not to speculate but to describe, and he thus becomes an author of value to constitutional historians. For the literary student he is of only moderate interest. His sentences, wholly unadorned, are usually long and have a dry lucidity.

A far feebler, and anonymous, work of the same period is

The Institution of a Gentleman (1555). It is of some interest to social historians and has been mentioned from that point of view in a previous chapter. The distinction between 'gentle gentle', 'gentle ungentle', and 'ungentle gentle' is well expounded and the style has no serious fault. But the author has no light to throw on the theory of aristocracy, defining his 'gentleman' in purely ethical terms and thus failing to define the very thing he is concerned with: for the word *gentleman* never meant simply 'a good man'. At the same time he is not ethical enough and among the virtues which he attributes to gentlemen we find not one word about their duties as landlords.

With Thomas Wilson (1525?–81) we return to humanist circles. Wilson is the friend of Cheke and Ascham and the translator of *Three Orations* (1570) from Demosthenes, besides being a civilian and a public servant who had both suffered torture in Rome from the Inquisition and inflicted it on Norfolk's followers in the Tower. He has left us in English three treatises. *The Rule of Reason* (1551) is an introduction to logic commissioned by the printer Whitchurch. Its dedicatory epistle to Edward VI reflects the optimism of a man who found his own age congenial for its 'forwardnesse' whereby 'the very multitude are prompte and ripe in al sciences'. The book is of course a mere work of popularization and aims at no originality. A modern reader, heir to many improvements in the art of making textbooks, will find it dark and crabbed. *The Art of Rhetoric*, first issued in 1553, but revised and enlarged in 1560 and then frequently reprinted, has won more celebrity: not so much, perhaps, by its intrinsic merits as because it happens to tell us things that we are now glad to know. Wilson's conception of fine writing shows the drift towards euphuism, and that in two respects. He recommends the use of similes from supposed natural history; 'brute beastes minister greate occasion of right good matter'—'in young Storkes we may take an example of loue towards their damme'—'in young Vipers there is a contrary example'. He also praises like ending (as 'in deede miserably, in fashion cruelly, in cause deuilishly') and like falling ('by great travaile is gotten much auaile') and notes the logical and phonetic conditions under which these two kinds of 'exornation' are 'most delitefull'. All are fulfilled in such a sentence as 'a meeter man to driue the cart then to serue the court'. It will be noticed that Wilson is silent about Spanish or Italian

models for this way of writing: its extreme representative is for
him St. Augustine. Elsewhere, when he tells us that 'the fine
courtier' in his day 'will talke nothing but *Chaucer*' he introduces
us to another side of the Drab Age—the 'neo-Medievalism'
which we found in some Tottelians. On vocabulary he is a
moderate purist, attacking what he calls 'ynkehorne termes' but
admitting such Latin and Greek loan-words as usage will
sanction. These *obiter dicta*, together with a tolerable vein of
anecdote, have saved his book from oblivion. To judge its
essential merits as a handbook is not easy for us who do not
know the art Wilson is teaching; I suspect, rather than believe,
that it is not very good. His definitions are not always easy to
understand, and if we are seeking 'an especiall and soueraine
preseruatiue against the infection of cankard obliuion' it helps
little to be told to 'cherish the memorie from time to time'. But
Wilson's literary fame ought not to rest upon his *Rhetoric*; the
Discourse upon Usury, finished in 1569 but not published till 1572,
handles with more intelligence and more imagination a theme
of more permanent interest. It is a dialogue in which a Merchant (Gromel Gayner) a Common Lawyer, a Civilian, and a
Preacher (Ockerfoe) are the speakers. Its great merit is that,
unlike most literary dialogues, it gives fair play to both sides.
The defence of usury is divided between the Merchant and the
Common Lawyer. This enables Wilson to put into the character
of the Merchant (who combines the avarice of Scrooge with the
cheery brutality of Squeers) all his real hatred of usury while
allowing the Common Lawyer to advance whatever can be
reasonably, and therefore formidably, said in its defence. Full
dramatic life was not of course aimed at, but his speakers are
not mere names, or not till the last page when no one believes
for a moment in Gromel Gayner's conversion. In his earlier
speeches he was a man; 'I see here is some sporte towardes; there
will be snappyng and snarring'—'I will heare further before I
geeue vp because it may bee there is some shifte to saue a mans
conscience with all'—'I will neither saye buffe nor baffe, for as
you may perceyue I haue often greeted your good talk with a
nodde'. Wilson's own views are expressed, often with great
lucidity and energy, through the mouths of the Preacher and the
Civilian. Some understanding of these views is the best preparation for seeing the *Merchant of Venice*. 'What is more against
nature then that money should beget or bring forth money,

which was ordeined to be a pledge betwixt man and man . . .
and not to increase itselfe as a woman doth that bringeth foorthe
a childe, cleane contrarye to the firste institution of money':
and again 'Nature cannot afoord yt that *once one of dead things*
should become twice one'. I have ventured to italicize five
words here because they reveal the whole point of the scene
where Shylock attempts to justify his trade by Jacob's genetic
stratagem with the flocks. The difference between cattle, which
breed by nature, and *dead things* is the crux of the whole matter
and Shylock blandly displays his incurable blindness. Throughout the *Discourse* there is real learning, real thought, and some
passion. The style is occasionally adorned with verbal tricks
('These be marmaides not merchants') or with alliteration ('As
deafe as a doore nayle, as blynde as a bittle') but is in general
plain though by no means artless.

The possibilities of the dialogue were explored further by
William Bullein (ob. 1576). Most of his works were purely
medical and so belong to the history of science rather than to
that of literature, and when in these the dialogue form is used it
provides only the thinnest gilding for the pill. In the *New book
Entitled the Government of Health*, which was finished in 1558, one
of the characters promises well enough when he begins by
attempting to dismiss his importunate adviser with the words
'What good sir I require not your counsell, I pray you be your
owne caruer', but by the end he has become a dutiful 'feed' (in
the theatrical sense) asking such questions as 'What be cloues,
Galangell, and pepper?' Once, however, Bullein attempted
to combine pleasure with profit in a full-blown Erasmian 'Colloquy', the *Dialogue . . . against the fever Pestilence* (1564). This is a
tantalizing book. In Bullein's hands the form bids fair to rival
the novel and the drama as a mirror of life. He is free of several
different social circles, describes the country as well as the town,
and keeps in action five major characters who, if far from
Shakespearian, are not far from Jonsonian. *Volpone*, indeed, may
be indebted to the *Dialogue*. Yet Bullein never seems to understand what excellences were within his reach. One reason is
that he was trying to do too many things at once. He wanted to
write prescriptions against the Plague, satire against usurers,
satire against lawyers, a Protestant tract, a catalogue of Emblems, and a Dance of Death. These designs were not harmonized. The terrible scene at the death-bed of Avarus (half

farce and whole tragedy) is spoiled because the Doctor, from being a real and sinister character, presently becomes a mere lecturer on physic. Theologus at the bedside of Civis (which had promised to be most moving) fails both as a character and a comforter because a systematic compendium of Protestant theology is forced into his mouth. Civis's man, the hitherto delightful Roger, is made to deliver a diatribe on usury which is quite out of character. Yet what comes through between these incidences of doctrinal *corvée* is good enough to make us demand more. Civis himself, the kind husband of a close-fisted wife, is nearly always natural and we are made to love him. The wife is not much inferior to some of More's sketches. Mendax, recounting his voyage to Terra Florida, is an amusing member of the Munchausen family. The change from London to the country is sensitively imagined, Roger's fable delightfully told. The last scene in which Civis finds that his flight from London has been in vain and meets Mors in person, though it conforms to a familiar pattern, is so managed that we feel surprise and horror. Death's speech has real eloquence, and some of the references to rural sights and sounds have the freshness of Izaak Walton. But neither of these two passages is typical of Bullein's manner, which is studiously simple. His scenes of low life are less racy and his decorations rarer than we might expect: not, I think, through any defect of power but because Terence and Erasmus are his models. He aims, not unsuccessfully, at something as easy as real conversation but a shade more elegant. His prose is, like Gascoigne's, a civilized prose. This, together with his invention and his knowledge of human nature, puts him above many writers of the period whose names are better known. Hence, ungratefully, we read him with an irritation which Ascham or Harpsfield do not arouse; he might so easily have been better. It is like seeing a man throw away a good hand at cards.

I have placed Bullein immediately after Wilson because Wilson in my opinion should be remembered as a writer of colloquy rather than as a teacher of rhetoric. In the latter capacity he had, however, predecessors and successors of whom some ought perhaps to be mentioned.

Richard Sherry, a schoolmaster, finished his *Treatise of Schemes and Tropes* in 1550, and though the *Rhetoric* of Leonard Cox had appeared in 1524 regards himself as a pioneer, his title 'straunge vnto our Englyche eares' and likely to be scorned as 'newe fangle'. In his preface he observes that the *De Oratore* is not of much practical use because Cicero 'wyth his incomperable eloquence hath so hid the preceptes'; an admission which, one would have thought, might have given a teacher of rhetoric some uneasiness. The earlier and more general parts of Sherry's book are badly done. We understand what he means by the 'great', 'small', and 'meane' kinds only because we have seen them exemplified and better explained elsewhere: if we relied on Sherry himself we should be completely mystified. Later, when he tabulates and defines the schemes and figures, he becomes tolerably clear. He has also the good sense to warn us that we should always speak 'wyth as playne wordes as may be' and notes in the margin 'A figure not to be vsed but for a cause.' His own prose style is mediocre, but his *Treatise*, as a practical handbook, is, I believe, better than Wilson's *Art*.

Richard Rainold in his *Foundation of Rhetoric* (1563) hardly attempts to rival Wilson (whom he mentions with respect) for it consists almost entirely of specimen orations. These were intended to teach more than rhetoric, being devoted to 'soche questions as are right necessarie to be knowen', and ballasted with 'vertuous precepts' and 'famous Histories'. Their construction will teach us 'copiously to dilate any matter'. This promise is well kept. Thus, if you begin with Aesop's fable of the wolves who persuaded the shepherds to kill their dogs, you can first tell the fable at length, and then expound the moral at length, and then digress into the natural history of wolves (and sheep), and then re-tell the fable at greater length including a speech by the Chief Wolf . . . and so forth. Yet even this foolish book can teach us something. Much light is thrown on Elizabethan methods of composition by Rainold's passage on the figure *Chria*. A Chria is 'a rehearsall in fewe wordes of any one fact or of the saying of any man vpon the whiche an occasion can be made'. Hence those countless sentences which begin 'Diogenes seeing a boie wanton' or the like; hence too the immense value to our ancestors of books like Laertius and Plutarch. For Chria is a hungry figure.

Henry Peacham's *Garden of Eloquence* which appeared in 1577 is probably the best of the books on rhetoric. It is a systematic (not alphabetical) lexicon of the rhetorician's terms, with clear definitions and examples. I think one could really learn the art from this book, as one could not from Wilson's or Rainold's. As we read his pages we perceive how the rhetorical standpoint, once adopted, accounts (in one sense) for everything that can be said or written and thus (in another sense) excludes nearly everything. Those accidents which we call Spoonerisms are for Peacham the scheme *Hypallage*; poetical forms of words (such as Dian for Diana) are schemes orthographical. The trope *Metonimia*, which puts 'the inuentor for the thing inuented' is exemplified by 'Neptune for the sea' and 'In Christ, for in the fayth of Christ'. It is doubtful if most pagans would be satisfied with the first, or most Christians with the second, example.

More interesting than the rhetoricians is Thomas Harman, of whose life we know little. His *Caveat or Warning for Common Cursetours* (1567) reveals him as a hard, inquisitive man with one literary gift and no literary standards. Where he is trying to be literary, as in his dedication, he relies on Berners's trick of synonyms ('relief, succour, comforte, and sustentacion') or hunts the letter ('peuishe, peltinge and prickinge parasites'). In the body of his work these decorations rarely appear. His book belongs to that literature of roguery which has crossed our path once or twice before and which had been enriched (probably before 1566) by the *Manifest Detection of Dice Play*, attributed by an early scholiast to one Gilbert Walker. This is a work of considerable literary merit. The author's intentions were perhaps wholly serious but as he paints his cheats and sets them talking in a lifelike manner an effect of comedy is produced. In 1560 came the *Fraternity of Vacabonds*, a short dictionary of cant, printed and perhaps written by one Awdeley. Harman goes far beyond his predecessors. His first page is not promising but almost at once the stories begin and on them the whole literary value of his book depends. They grow better and better as he proceeds. At first we are not quite sure whether he sees how funny they are; there is considerable *naïveté* in the account (xi, xii) of his own amateur detective work, regrettably carried out by the private and unauthorized torture of a suspect. But our doubts are allayed by the great story in chapter xix. Here, it is important to notice, some of the best scenes could not have been witnessed either by Harman or by his informant. This ruins Harman's claim to be a serious sociologist. Those scenes must be invention. But if they are Harman's invention, his place in the history of fiction, though very small, is secure. His dialogue, too, can be exquisitely natural—'Now by my trouth I knowe not, quoth she, you bring me out of my tale so, you do'. Yet when he writes in his own person you might often take him for little better than a dunce. It would seem impossible for a man to lose his construction in sentences so short and unpretentious as Harman's, yet Harman contrives to do it. But he used his single talent well: he has set before us rogues who talk so that they could mix undetected among the rogues of Shakespeare. For the misery behind the roguery he shows no more pity than a stone; though he claims (as such men always do) to have reached his present state of mind after having often given and been often deceived.

Edmund Tilney's *Brief and pleasant Discourse of Duties in Marriage* (1568) is in its way a more ambitious specimen of the Dialogue than Wilson's or Bullein's. The model was perhaps Castiglione. We set off in the florid manner of the *Complaynt of Scotland* ('What time Flora had clothed the earth', &c.) and are conducted with much circumstance to the house of a certain Lady Julian. A rich background of palaces and gardens is painted and we find Vives and Erasmus among the company. Neither of them, however, has much to say and Tilney's actual teaching about marriage is too short and homely to justify its elaborate setting. The ladies' speeches are the liveliest. The book is interesting as an unsuccessful attempt to create that world of courtesy which we find in Sidney's romance or in Lyly's or Shakespeare's comedies.

Among historians and antiquaries (whom I shall treat together) John Bale (1495–1563) comes first in time. His doggerel tragedy *King John* will be dealt with in another volume. His value as an antiquary is best seen in the *Illustrium Majoris Britanniae Scriptorum Summarium* (1548) and the later *Catalogus* (1557) and also in his surviving notes on the same subject. Here Bale is sincerely concerned with fact, and is free both from literary adornment and scurrility, which elsewhere, for Bale, are much the same thing. In his published vernacular works he is the most vitriolic of the Protestant controversialists, and enriches the vocabulary of abuse with the words *prostybulous* and *bluddering*. His *Acts of English Votaries* (1546), provoked by some extreme disparagements of matrimony on the Roman side, attempts to show that those who embrace the celibate life are nearly always 'whoremongers' or 'most fylthie Gomorreans'.

The charge is not confined to popish celibates; the Vestal Virgins, and even the Druids, were no better than they should be. The book, however, is not so prurient as this kind of propaganda has often been, and at times, as in his discussion on Ursula and the eleven thousand virgins, his concern is, in part, genuinely historical. Much better are the *Brief Chronicle concerning Sir John Oldcastle* (1544) or the *First Examination* (1546) and *Latter Examination* (1547) of Anne Askew. The parallel between Oldcastle and Becket shows Bale's polemical abilities at their best, but in the Askew pamphlets his prose, though readable, cannot stand up to the simple words of the martyr herself:

Then they did put me on the rack because I confessed no ladies or gentlewomen to be of my opinion: and because I lay still and did not cry, my lord chancellor and Master Rich took pains to rack me in their own hands.

Perhaps the most interesting thing we can discover in Bale, as in Leland's *Assertio inclytissimi Arturii* (1544), is the emergence of a theory by which Arthur was regarded almost as a Protestant and thus rescued for Spenser and Milton from the disfavour in which Protestant humanism had plunged him. 'The Romysh Byshop sought all meanes possyble to vphold the Englysh Saxons in a Kyngedome falselye gotten, the Britaynes hatynge hym for yt.' The Augustinian church was 'rather polytyke' than 'Christian' and this, as Leland argues, explains Bede's silence about Arthur. As for Polydore Vergil's scepticism, 'no men are learned with him but Italians' says Bale in his *Oldcastle*.

If we deny that John Leland himself (1506?–52) is an author in the literary historian's sense of the word, we intend no quarrel with those who will maintain that he is something quite as good. He first (and last) held the office of King's Antiquary, and great things were expected of him, but the *magnum opus* on our histories and antiquities for which he undertook all his journeys was never written. His voluminous manuscript notes, which supplied much to Bale, Stow, Harrison, and Holinshed, survive in the famous *Itinerary* (English) and *Collectanea* (Latin). The jottings of the *Itinerary*, never intended for the public, are not without their charm. 'Soone after I enterid, withyn the space of a Myle or lesse, ynto the very thik of the woddy Forest of Shirwood where ys great game of Deer'—it is almost as good as a sentence of Malory. But it is most unlikely that if he had written the book he intended, it would have had any such beauties. His short English address to Henry VIII—*The Laborious Journey and Search ... given ... as a New Year's Gift* (1549) — is florid and heavy in accordance with the demands of an age when 'a florishing style' was 'yn such estimation that except truethe be delicately clothid yn purpure her written Verites can scant finde a Reader'; and in the *Assertio* he puts a Livian oration into Arthur's mouth. As an antiquary he has been generally praised by his successors, and though he seems to have defaced at York Minster in 1534 an inscription displeasing to Government, there is no doubt that he was in general a zealous rescuer of materials which the Dissolution had endangered. Some, he tells us, were already finding their way out of the country. Though a vocal Protestant when the time came, he had enjoyed Clement VII's dispensation to hold four benefices, and has none of Bale's scurrility. Sometimes in his work, as in Bale's, we can see northern and western scholarship becoming restive under the long dominance of the Italians. His Latin poetry has been praised, but I cannot think that a man who would use such a metre as the hendecasyllable for a poem seven hundred lines long was really very sensitive.

Thomas Cooper (1517?–94) whose theological work I reserve for a later chapter, continued to the reign of Edward VI the world chronicle which Thomas Lanquet had left unfinished at his death in 1545, and published this composite work in the *Epitome of Chronicles* in 1549. Both authors are mere annalists and added nothing either to the science or the art of history. Their book was re-issued with a continuation by the poetaster Robert Crowley in 1559. Richard Grafton, whose *Abridgement* (1563) was followed by the *Chronicle at Large* in 1569, has already received such mention as he needs. He had the audacity to enter into historical controversy (*impar congressus*) with the great John Stow (1525–1605). This 'merry old man', footing it over England in search of antiquities because he could never learn to ride, sometimes suspected by Government of being insufficiently Protestant, now begging with a basin in the street, now spending £200 a year on his library, holds a very high place in the history of learning. Even those who, like Camden, distrusted his judgement, allowed his industry. His *Chaucer* (1561) was his first but by no means his best work: he helped to swell the Chaucerian apocrypha. His *Summary of English Chronicles* (1565) looks at first like a retrogression from Hall; we are back at the annalistic form and the London tradition with its lists of bailiffs and mayors. But the important thing is that Stow is not a mere compiler but (as we call it) a 'researcher'. He uses the literary sources but he adds 'paynfull searche' into records, and 'diligent experience'. He collected not only books but charters and legal documents. He bought up the collections of others, and his own assisted both Speght and Parker. In 1580 came the *Chronicle of England from Brute vnto this present year*, re-issued in 1592 as the *Annals*. The *Survey of London* (1598) was re-issued in 1603 and afterwards enlarged by other hands. Its modern editor finds this work 'instinct with' a 'life' which the *Annals* lack. It is a treasure-house of old customs, old splendours, old gaieties and hospitalities, already vanished or vanishing when the author wrote. Stow had no stylistic ambitions; his works were, as he said, 'written homely'. His prose varies between mere note-making (see the account of printing under year 1458 in the *Summary*) and tolerably vivid narrative. In general it is just such an unobtrusive medium as keeps our attention on the facts, and therefore good for its purpose; *recte olet ubi nihil olet*.

The good fame of John Foxe (1517–87) has had many vicissitudes. In his own time he was, naturally, attacked from the Roman side by John Harding in 1565 and by Harpsfield under the pseudonym of Alan Cope in his *Sex Dialogi* (1566). Among Protestants he soon acquired and long retained almost scriptural authority, but in 1837 the work of S. R. Maitland ushered in a violent reaction. Maitland had many successors and the nineteenth-century tradition represents Foxe as an unscrupulous propagandist who records what he knows to be false, suppresses what he knows to be true, and claims to have seen documents he has not seen. In 1940, however, Mr. J. F. Mozley re-opened the whole question and defended Foxe's integrity, as it seems to me, with complete success. From his examination Foxe emerges, not indeed as a great historian, but as an honest man. For early Church history he relies on the obvious authorities and is of very mediocre value. For the Marian persecution his sources are usually the narratives of eyewitnesses. Such narratives, whispered in secret during a Terror and emulously proclaimed as soon as the Terror is over, are liable to distortion. Men who have seen their friends die in torture are not always inspired by that coolly scientific spirit which the academic researcher so properly demands. But there seems no evidence that Foxe ever accepted what he did not himself believe or ever refused to correct what he had written in the light of fresh evidence. The most horrible of all his stories, the Guernsey martyrdoms, was never refuted, though violently assailed; in some ways the defence may be thought scarcely less damaging than the charge. And in one respect—in his hatred of cruelty—Foxe was impartial to a degree hardly paralleled in that age. His earliest original work, the *De Non Plectendis Morte Adulteris* (1548) is a plea for mercy; he confesses that he could never pass a slaughter-house without discomposure; and when his own party was on top he interceded (vainly, of course) to save Anabaptists from the stake in 1575 and Jesuits from the gallows in 1581.

Foxe's enormous influence is curiously out of proportion to his actual status as an English man of letters. Latin was the medium he preferred. The first form taken by his Martyrology was the *Commentarii* published at Strassburg in 1554, which dealt mainly with the Lollards. This was enlarged to include the Marian persecution and published as *Rerum in Ecclesia Gestarum. . . Commentarii* at Basel in 1559. The *Acts and Monuments* of 1563 contains a translation (not by Foxe) of the *Rerum* and adds masses of new material which had poured in on him since his return to England. The narratives of others are sometimes reproduced *verbatim*, sometimes abridged, sometimes conflated. The *Ecclesiastical History* (1570) extends the story back to Apostolic times and abridges (not always judiciously) the later periods. It will be seen, therefore, that it is only in the earlier portions of the 1570 text that we have long stretches of pure Foxian English composition as distinct from Foxe translated by others or Foxe working with scissors and paste. This section is in every way the least valuable part of his work and his English style has no high merits. The sentences have not energy to support their great length. In the Marian parts, as in Malory, we find plenty of good reading without being able to trace our pleasure confidently to any single author's skill. But the composite result is by no means to be neglected. Many excellent scenes recur to the mind: Jullins Palmer talking to his mother, Mrs. Wardall's lodger coming to the window to explain that she is a stranger in these parts and is afraid of spirits walking by night, Mr. Lewes making a sumner eat his citation. Better than all is the moment at which Elizabeth Folkes, stripping for the fire and prevented by the police from giving her petticoat to her mother, flings it away with the words,

'Farewell all the world! Farewell Faith, farewell Hope, welcome Love!'

If Foxe is primarily, Matthew Parker (1504–75) is almost exclusively, a neo-Latin author. His great work *De Antiquitate Britannicae Ecclesiae* (1572) hardly concerns us, but he deserves grateful memory from all English scholars as one of the pioneers in the study of Anglo-Saxon.

Holinshed's *Chronicles* (1577 and 1587) are all that survives of a far more ambitious scheme, a 'universall cosmographie' with 'histories of euery knowne nation', projected many years earlier by Reyne (or Reginald) Wolfe, printer to Queen Elizabeth. At Wolfe's death in 1573 his successors reduced the design to a history and geography of the British Isles. The work was carried out by Raphael Holinshed, Richard Stanyhurst, John Hooker (*alias* Vowell), Francis Thynne, and William Harrison. It defies the ordinary methods of literary criticism for a reason which an example will make clear. 'Holinshed' describing the preliminaries to the battle of Crecy writes:

When euerie man was gotten into order of battell, the king leapt vpon a white hobbie and rode from ranke to ranke to view them, the one Marshall on his right hand and the other on his left, desiring euerie man that daie to haue regard to his right and honour.

Turn back to Grafton at the same place and you will read:

When all these battayles were set in an order, then the king lept on a Hobby with a whyte rodde in his hande, one of his Marshalles on the one hande, and another on the other hande, and he road from ranke to ranke, desyring euery man to take heede that day to his right and honour.

Turn back again to Berners's *Froissart* and you find:

Then the king lept on a hobby with a whyte rodde in his hande, one of his Marshalls on the one hande, and the other on the other hande; he rode from ranke to ranke desyringe euerie man to take heede that daie to his right and honour.

Clearly there is nothing that can be called original composition except in Froissart: yet at the same time Grafton and Holinshed are not exactly transcribing. We are in a world where our modern notions of authorship do not apply. I do not promise that 'Holinshed' everywhere follows its predecessors quite so closely as this, though I could quote places where it is as close to Hall. The point is that no one can pronounce any sentence to be pure

Holinshed until he has looked at the corresponding place in every previous chronicler. That is work for an editor; the literary historian must be content to warn the student that at this period a new chronicle is not necessarily what we should call a new book. The 'English story' is a sort of national stock-pot permanently simmering to which each new cook adds flavouring at his discretion.

There is, however, one part of 'Holinshed' which can be treated as the original work of a single author. The parson William Harrison (1534–93) had already been engaged on a *Chronology* when he was invited to supply the 'cosmographicall' part of the new venture and thus came to write his celebrated *Description of Britain*. In some respects he was not very well qualified for the work. His account of Scotland is merely an Anglicization of Bellenden's Scots version of Boece. Even in England he was not a great traveller and researcher like Leland or Stow. He relies on many sources—Leland himself, Smith, Bale, Harman, Humphrey Lloyd, Dr. Caius *On English Dogs*, and that inaccurate but never uninteresting authority, 'old men yet dwelling in the village where I remain'. But he was clearly a great questioner and listener and produced a book which has much historical value.

For the general reader his value is higher still. He is the most Herodotean of our writers; a cheerful gossip. Some of his digressions—and he often has to pull himself up with a 'But whither am I digressed?'—are perhaps scarcely to modern taste; we may doubt whether in an account of Elizabethan shipping 'It shall not be amisse to begin at the nauie of Xerxes' (II. xvii), or whether English meals need to be compared to those of the Romans, Greeks, Persians, 'Canariens', Indians, Caspians, and Tyrhenians (II. vi). But then most moderns will be delighted with his passage on brewing (his wife's recipe included) for which he seems to apologize; 'beare with me, gentle reader (I beseech thee) that lead thee from the description of the plentiful diet of our countrie. . . into a mustie malthouse: but such is now thy hap, wherefore I praie thee be contented' (ibid.). The confiding tone is characteristic. Whatever else Harrison gives us, he always gives us himself; his devout love for both universities, his dislike of Italian travels, his scarce acquaintance 'with any siluer at all, much lesse then (God it wot) with any store of gold', his honest pride in his garden, his distrust of the potato. On the strength of one sentence ('When our houses were builded of willow, then had we oken men', II. xxii) he has sometimes been set down as a *laudator temporis acti*. This is unjust. Of the changes that had occurred within living memory, Harrison thinks, as in most periods a man of sense must think, that some were for the worse and some for the better. He believes that our 'husbandmen and artificers' were 'neuer so excellent in their trades as at this present' (II. v), thanks God that the number of meals has been reduced to two a day (II. vi), and mentions the improved table furniture in nearly all classes of society not 'in reproche of anie man, God is my iudge, but to shew that I do reioyse rather to see how God has blessed vs' (II. xii). He is delighted at recent progress in horticulture and thinks that our modern gardens probably surpass those of the Hesperides (II. xx). Though he is no friend to excessive troops of serving men he can enjoy their liveries, 'to see them muster at court, which, being filled with them, dooth yield the contemplation of a notable varietie vnto the beholder, much like to the shew of the pecocks taile in the full beautie' (II. xv). If, on the debit side, he laments deforestation, rising rents and prices, oppression of small holders, increasing poverty and rings in markets, no doubt he had good reason.

For our purpose Harrison's style is no less important than his matter; in reading him we find that we have quite clearly emerged from the Drab Age. This impression is all the stronger and more reliable because he is not one, like Hall or Ascham, who is consciously labouring to improve our prose. 'I neuer made any choise of stile or words', he says in his preface, and refers to his work as a thing 'scambled up', a 'foule frizeled Treatise'. And this is true. He is an inartificial writer like More, Roper, or Brinkelow. Yet he is very different from them. A new familiar style has arisen; a brisk, cheerful, voluble style. Roper and Harrison both suggest talk, but where Roper suggests a man talking slowly, Harrison suggests a man talking quickly. More's drollery requires the grave tone and even the drudging pace of his sentences: it is irresistibly comic because the funniest things are said with a straight face. Harrison's jokes are high spirited and effervescent. In the Drab Period nearly all prose writers sound middle-aged; in Harrison we recover that spirit of youthfulness which is often characteristic of the 'Golden' period. A hostile critic could say of Harrison, as no one could possibly say of Harpsfield or Cheke, that he prattles. It is less important that we should criticize than that we should perceive the change—whether we describe it by saying that the fog has lifted, or that the age of the martyrs has given place to that of the fantasticals, or that Mercury has succeeded Saturn. Not comparing the two orders, but considering Harrison as a specimen of the new, we must praise him. His sentences are long and sometimes (note that which introduces the quotation from Agrippa in II. xv) he loses his way, but when he does not they have great liveliness. In general he has the 'easie ambling pace' which he attributes to a good gelding, 'pleasant and delectable' to the rider's ear (III. i). Much that now pleases us flows, no doubt, less from his own talent than from the common language of the age. The very names which he mentions for strong beer are a sort of mental carouse—Huffcap, Go-by-the-Wall, Mad Dog, and Merry-go-down (II. xviii).

From historians I turn to translators of whom the earliest and most memorable is Thomas North (1535–1601?). His *Dial of Princes* renders Guevara's *Libro Aureo* from an intermediate French version. It appeared in 1557 and again in 1563 with a so-called 'fourth booke', really a translation of Guevara's *Aviso de Privados*. The abandoned theory which traced euphuism to North's Guevara has perhaps given this book a place in literary history which it hardly deserves. Sentences that anticipate Lyly can be found in it, but not more often than in Hall and less often than in Ascham. Lyly's real debt to Guevara is for matter not for style. The *Lives of the Noble Grecians and Romans* (1579) is very much more important. It is not a scholarly production. North works from the French of Amyot (1559) which he sometimes misunderstands, and Amyot had sometimes misunderstood the Greek. Plutarch himself was not a scientific nor (in our sense) a philosophical historian. The process of history is not his concern and he has little sense of period; mythical heroes and well-known statesmen are treated in much the same way. Heroic gossip is his line—the striking reversal of fortune, the curious anecdote, the apophthegm, the examples of vices and virtues. For this very reason he suited the Elizabethans far better than Thucydides; his love of pageantry and his monotheistic piety, added to the attraction. He furnished their picture of antiquity with traits at least as important as those provided by the ancient poets. The *Renascentia* did not people our imagination exclusively, nor chiefly, with gods and goddesses, or shepherds and nymphs.

From Plutarch (and Laertius) comes that almost oppressive crowd of generals, sages, courtesans, politicians, soothsayers, and noble dames who haunt the *Essais* and the *Anatomy*. It was a picture without historical perspective, in which the 'ancients' were all of a piece. It was not even a 'costume' picture; by the time we reach North's English, *flamens* are 'bishops' and chariots are 'carts'. This helped the examples and the maxims, whether magnanimous or Machiavellian, to strike home. It is thus, not as a model of form but as a storehouse of matter, that ancient literature produced its deepest effect.

Of North as an English writer Charles Whibley said, 'He held a central place in the history of our speech' and 'he played upon English prose as upon an organ whose every stop he controlled with an easy confidence'. This seems to me excessive: I know no writer of whom it could be said with strict truth. But North's prose is lively, idiomatic, and masculine in rhythm. Some passages perhaps seem more eloquent than they are because we cannot read them without remembering what Shakespeare made of them by small but momentous changes. But the word *small* is important; what Shakespeare had to work on was already good.

As Plutarch's *Lives* built the heroic ideal of the Elizabethan age, Castiglione's *Libro del Cortegiano* (1528), translated by Sir Thomas Hoby in 1561, built their courtly ideal. This is another of those books which mark and, I hope, justify my distinction between a Drab and a 'Golden' Age. Anyone who compares the *Courtier* with Elyot's *Governor* or Erasmus's *Institutio* will see what I mean. The courtly ideal has its own severities and Castiglione can even speak of the 'horrible face of true vertue', much as Horace speaks of the *atrocem animum Catonis*. Yet this 'Vertue' remains a mistress, not a schoolmistress, to gentle hearts; and what is a mistress without *Daungier*? Its ardour and delight in the pursuit of ideal conduct make the *Courtier* an attractive book. Here, as in Harrison's *Description*, but on a far higher level, we see the air and fire of youth chasing away the staidness of the Drab Age. Even old men, as Castiglione explains, can still be lovers in their proper mode. And he has a right to sound youthful for his book really marks a rejuvenation or re-birth, though a different one from the *renascentia* in its proper sense. He is retrieving, with modifications, the medieval ideal; the knight and lover who might, to our endless loss, have been simply rejected in favour of the half Plutarchan, half Machiavellian, Great

Man, is recalled and refashioned and set forward on a new career, with the characters of poet, patron, and philosopher now added to him. For Castiglione's art of courtly life is not a mere *moyen de parvenir*. The courtier is not judged by his success in winning the prince's favour; the prince is judged by his worthiness to have such a courtier. And though all is serious, all is graceful, spontaneous, unconstrained. In his picture of a court he creates (at least for literature) what he preaches. The stage is set for Pamela, Florimel, and Viola. Hoby's translation does little justice to the golden manner of the original, but the golden content gets through. He prints Cheke's foolish letter about 'pure, unmixt' English, but I do not think it influenced his practice.

Of the theologians who might be mentioned in this chapter I reserve Thomas Cartwright for later treatment. John Jewel (1522–71) is of great importance for his *Apologia Ecclesiae Anglicanae* (1562) but not for his vernacular writings. These include sermons, a commentary on Thessalonians, and a jungle of controversies to which he rashly committed himself by his so-called Challenge Sermon in 1559. This is close fighting and seldom without interest, but stands at about the same distance from literature proper as the debates in Hansard. One passage is worth noting. 'Ye teach the people', says Jewel to his Roman adversary, 'thus to pray vnto the Blessed Virgin, *Monstra te esse matrem*, command thy son, vse thy motherly authority ouer him, let him know thee to be his mother. This you say is no blasphemy but a spiritual dallying. Now verily, M. Harding, this must needs be a blessed kind of diuinity that can turne prayer into dalliance.' Here I suppose Jewel and Thomas Harding to be equally sincere and equally shocked. They are divided by a difference of devotional temper which sharpened, and had perhaps long preceded, the strictly doctrinal differences. One of Jewel's very minor works in Latin, the early *Oratio contra Rhetoricam* would be of great literary interest if we could be sure that it was seriously intended. We should have to salute a man who stood almost alone in maintaining that rhetorical study is a total waste of time, that rhetoricians are neither better understood nor more believed than natural speakers, and that an art which bad causes need far more than good ones is the ruin of states. The *Oratio* has been so taken by an eminent scholar, but I cannot agree with him. What first awakes suspicion is the absence of all arguments drawn from religion. Its whole atmosphere is that of literary paganism. And towards the end we find a passage which, from such a man at such a date, must surely be ironical. It might be translated thus:

Our owne country men not many yeares sithence whan they had no shadowe, I saie not of eloquence but of verie Latine and clene language, whan Cicero lay despised and scorned in kennels and darke corners and Scotus blocked vp the gate and entrie of all the scholes, how well learned neuerthelater, of how sharpe iudgment in philosophie, how graue in diuinity they were esteemde? Oh blessed vniversitie! Oh the goode worlde! For than naught might be done against oure sentence, than might we make peace and warre and stirre vp tumultes and sette prynces by the eares.

What can this be but an insinuation that none could seriously attack (as Jewel has been ostensibly attacking) the new Ciceronianism, unless he were a Papist and a scholastic? The whole *Oratio* is a laboured academic joke of the kind not then uncommon. Jewel was no more seriously condemning rhetoric than Erasmus was seriously praising folly.

Anne Lady Bacon who translated his *Apologia* in 1564 deserves more praise than I have space to give her. Latin prose has a flavour very hard to disguise in translation, but nearly every sentence in Lady Bacon's work sounds like an original. Again and again she finds the phrase which, once she has found it, we feel to be inevitable. *Sacrificuli* become 'massing priests', *ineptum* 'a verie toy', *quidam ex asseclis et parasitis* 'one of his soothing pages and clawebackes', *lege sodes* 'in goode fellowshipe I pray thee reade', *operae pretium est videre* 'it is a world to see', and *magnum silentium* 'all mum, not a worde'. If quality without bulk were enough, Lady Bacon might be put forward as the best of all sixteenth-century translators.

The literature of exploration and travel, soon to be so copious, was stimulated during this period both by recent adventure and by the example of such works as Fernandez de Oviedo's *Summario* (1526), Ramusio's *Navigationi* (1550), and Lopez de Gómara's *Istoria de las Indias* (1552). The slaver John Hawkins in his *True Declaration* (1569) tells a plain tale of shipping blacks from Africa and selling them, sometimes with the help of a little gunnery, in Spanish America; deploring incidentally the low standards of international morality among 'negrose' and Spaniards. His prose is free from affectation but shows no remarkable strength or race. Sir Humphrey Gilbert's *Discourse* (1576) has for modern readers an accidental charm which is hard to resist. In it we recapture the moment, so rich in suggestion, at which ancient tradition or myth and recent exploration seemed on the point of joining hands; when 'Plato *in Timaeo*', Philo, Cartier, and Cabot could all equally be called as witnesses. Considered more objectively, it is a workmanlike essay, well arranged, well informed, and free from rhetoric. Richard Eden (1521?–1576) was a diligent translator of geographical works, censured by the purists for words 'smellyng to much of the Latine', such as *ponderous, portentous, despicable*, and *destructive*. He tells us something of contemporary taste by his modest admission, 'I haue not for euery worde asked counsayle of eloquent Eliot or Sir Thomas More'; and in his pages Shakespeare found the name *Setebos*. His collected works were edited and 'augmented' as the *History of Travel* in 1577 by one Richard Willes who is probably Spenser's 'pleasant Willy' in the *Tears of the Muses*, the neo-Latin poet Ricardus Willeius. This same Willes is the author of three pieces which can be read in Hakluyt and which betray stylistic ambitions. His most interesting production is, however, his preface to the *History of Travel*, for here, to the best of my knowledge, we first meet that type of advertisement, since so common, which may be called chronological intimidation. Willes would have us buy his book because geography is the science of the future, because we are entering upon the geographical age. 'There was a time whan the arte of grammar was so muche esteemed. . . . Than was it honourable to be a Poet . . . that tyme is paste. There was a tyme whan Logike and Astrology so weeried the heades of young schollers . . . that tyme is past. Not long since happy was he that had any skil in the Greke language.' But we have changed all that, and now 'all Christians, Iewes, Turkes, Morres, Infidels and Barbares be this day in loue with Geographie'.

But these works are of minor interest. What the lover of voyages really wants first appears in George Beste's *True Discourse* (1578), a subordinate officer's first-hand account of Frobisher's three attempts to find the North-West Passage and (what interested Elizabeth more) a gold-mine in Meta Incognita. Here, as Beste promises us, we can learn both 'how dangerous it is to attempt new Discoueries' and also 'how pleasant and profitable'. The scientific preface—a close argument to prove that all zones are habitable—is, no doubt, superseded in manner as well as in matter; this is one of the kinds of literature which we do better than the Elizabethans. But the narrative is of a very high order. Everything is as it should be. The motive attributed to Frobisher is heroical, 'to accomplish or bring true certificate of the truth, or els never to returne againe, knowing this to be the only thing of the world that was left yet vndone whereby a notable minde might be made famous and fortunate'. The author's generous admiration for his leader heightens his whole work. He has that unemphatic and commonsensible piety which could now hardly be expressed without self-consciousness, telling how they escaped imminent danger in the ice 'God being our best Steresman and by the industry of Charles Jackman and Andrew Dyer'. Many a frightful landscape is brought vividly, and effortlessly, before us in a few words. The praise and blame which he allots to his comrades carry conviction. A malicious reader might whisper that Beste's own speech and conduct are by no means hidden under a bushel; but then, as Johnson says of Dryden, 'while he forces himself upon our esteem, we cannot refuse him to stand high in his own'. His book is so delightful that on a first reading we are tempted to exclaim that the thing could not be better done. But we must keep our heads. This kind of Elizabethan prose, though full of sap, is yet not quite a perfect medium. Beste is a master of the phrase; not so completely a master of the sentence. The multiplication of subordinate clauses sometimes blurs the effect. Defoe could write, on the whole, a little better. But though we must keep our heads we must also be grateful for meeting (at last) an author who can tempt us to lose them.

The *novella*, from which matter had often been borrowed before, enters English literature as a form with the work of Painter, Fenton, and Pettie. Of this form the modern critic is apt to make demands which it never attempted to satisfy: he is half angry with the authors for not developing it in the direction of the modern novel. But except in so far as it marks the appearance of story-telling naked and unashamed, story-telling without roots in legend or supposed history, the *novella* seems to have little connexion with later developments of fiction. It is an elaboration of the oral anecdote. Interest is concentrated on what happened: character, sentiment, manners, and atmosphere exist only for the sake of the event. In English its historical function was not to produce higher forms of fiction but to serve as a dung or compost for the popular drama. Its anecdotal character perhaps explains its tendency to become either licentious or bloodcurdling.

Certainly it had been under heavy moral criticism almost from its birth; there is nothing new, and nothing specifically Protestant, in Ascham's attack on the first English specimens of the *genre*.

The pure Italian *novella* came to the hands of Painter and Fenton already modified by a French intermediary, the *Histoires Tragiques* (1559–82) of Boaistuau and Belleforest. Belleforest had felt that the form invited further developments, but the developments he chose were not those which will appeal to a modern. He was a rhetorician and a moralist and he expanded dialogue and soliloquy, besides interpolating direct diatribe, in the interests of eloquence and edification. Not surprisingly, he is credited by one of his few modern readers with 'a positive genius for destroying the narrative movement of a story'. But his methods were congenial to sixteenth-century English taste.

William Painter (1540?–94), a civil servant and apparently a swindler, published his *Palace of Pleasure* in 1566, and a second volume of it in 1567. One of its stories ('The Horrible and cruel murder of Sultan Solyman') had appeared separately, about 1558. Other, not very memorable, translations are to his credit. In the *Palace* we find tales from Cinthio, Plutarch, Margaret of Navarre, and Boccaccio, but more from Bandello through Belleforest. Bandello's own text Painter rather despised for the 'barren soile' of his 'vain': it has, indeed, been accused by the Italian critics of *Lumbardismi e gallicismi*. Painter takes some pains to defend his stories as morally profitable, but also recommends them on the ground that they will 'recreate and refreshe weried mindes, deiatigated either with painefull travaile or with continuall care'. Literary fare 'for tired business men' is as old, then, as that; perhaps not much older. Except in his dedicatory epistle where he is a little inclined to ink-horn terms, Painter writes a tolerably plain prose. He includes as 'novelles' some things which are only *bons mots*, and these could hardly be less effectively told. His longer pieces, if you do not happen to know the story already, can be read with moderate pleasure.

All that we know about Geoffrey Fenton (1539?–1608) as a man excites disgust, but he has more claims than Painter to rank as a semi-original author. He published *Golden Epistles* 'gathered' out of Guevara and 'other Authours Latine, French and Italian' in 1575, besides translating Etienne Pasquier's *Monophile* (1572) and Guicciardini's *History* (1579). But his name is chiefly remembered for the *Tragical Discourses* of 1567. In them Fenton does to

Belleforest what Belleforest had already done to Bandello; loads, or stuffs, every rift with rhetorical, proverbial, and moral ore. We must repeatedly remind ourselves that harsh morality was as modish then as flippant immorality in the twenties of our own century; it may be questioned whether the Elizabethan mode was not the more odious of the two. The glib severity of a Fenton or a Lyly has something shocking in it. In a style so rhetorical as Fenton's nearly every device occurs sooner or later, and it is therefore possible to pick out Euphuisms in the *Tragical Discourses*. But in general his prose is not, I think, so euphuistic as Ascham's. It is in the next author on our list that we find something more like the real thing.

George Pettie (1548–89), if we are to believe the prefatory matter to the *Petite Palace of Pettie his Pleasures*, (1576) was responsible neither for the publication nor for the title of that book. A certain R. B. ushers it in with an address to the 'Gentle Readers whom by my will I woulde haue only Gentlewomen' and explains that he has pirated a manuscript lent him by the author. His disarming defence is that 'he cares not to displease twentie men to please one woman'. Then follows the letter which Pettie is supposed to have written to R. B. when he lent him the manuscript. He reminds R. B. that all these stories were told *ex tempore* 'in sundrie companies' and suggests that if the written version seems better than the oral this is probably because the author's 'lisping lips' did not do his composition justice. He also hints that some of them are *romans à clef*. One would like to believe that the lisp is historical, but it is not necessary to regard the whole affair as anything more than an advertisement. With one exception (*Alexius*) Pettie's twelve stories are all drawn from classical sources; chiefly from Ovid and Livy. To complain that they have hardly any narrative vitality is to complain that Pettie has not done what he never intended to do. His art is at the opposite pole from that of the Italian *novella*. The story interests him solely as a trellis over which to train the flowers of rhetorical soliloquy and tirade: Johnson's warning to those who read Richardson 'for the story' comes to mind. And in Pettie's rhetoric we find euphuism at last fully developed and more or less continuous. 'Faithfully without doubting, truely without doublyng, willingly without constraint, ioyfully without complaint', he writes in his first tale; or again 'As a stroke or blowe the higher it is lifted the hevier it lightes, so Gods vengeance the

longer it is defered, the more it is to be feared'; or in V, 'It is her
bountie not her beutie that bindeth mee, it is her curtesie not her
comlinesse that I care for'. Pettie is also a great imitator of the
recent English poets and sometimes preserves their metre in his
own prose. Thus 'for like as streames the more ye stop them the
higher they flow, and trees the more yee lop them the greater
they growe' reproduces almost *verbatim* a couplet we have already
met in the *Mirror for Magistrates*. He is a great retailer of proverbs. His translation (through the French of Chappuys) of
Stefano Guazzo's courtesy book *La Civile Conversatione* (1574) was
published in 1586 and contains a spirited rebuke 'to such curious
fellowes who, if one chaunce to derive any woord from the
Latine, they foorthwith make a jest at it and terme it an Inke-
horne terme'. But it is as the euphuist in embryo that Pettie
holds his place in literary history.

We now come to Lyly (*c.* 1553–1606)[1] himself, an author once
unjustly celebrated for a style which he did not invent, and now
inadequately praised for his real, and very remarkable, achievement. If Lyly had never written *Euphues* I should have placed him
in the next chapter among the 'Golden' writers: that fatal success
ties him down to the 'transitional' category.

The wild goose chase for a particular 'source' of euphuism,
which began roughly with the publication of Landmann's
Euphuismus in 1881, is now, I take it, pretty well at an end. No
literary development, perhaps, can be fully explained but few
are less mysterious than this. In the present chapter we have seen
its gradual emergence as a structural decoration alternative to
the ink-horn decoration of vocabulary and therefore dear to
purists. Its elements—antithesis, alliteration, balance, rhyme,
and assonance—were not new. They can be found even in
More and in the Latin of the *Imitation*. So far as the elements
are concerned we are indeed embarrassed with too many
ancestors rather than too few: those who inquire most learnedly
find themselves driven back and back till they reach Gorgias.

---

[1] b. 1553 or 1554. A Kentish man. Commoner, Magdalen, Oxford, perhaps with
the assistance of Burleigh, 1569(?). B.A., 1573. Unsuccessful attempt through
Burleigh to get royal nomination to a fellowship, 1574. M.A., 1575. In London at
the Savoy, 1578. Patronized by Earl of Oxford, 1580. Loses Oxford's favour, 1582.
Post in the Revels: also Vice Master (?) of St. Paul's, 1585. M.P., 1588–9. Possibly
a reader of books for licensing to the Bishop of London. Involved in Marprelate
Controversy on the bishops' side, 1589. Petition to the queen, 1595. Second
petition, 1598. Ob., 1606.

What is added in full blown euphuism is a wealth of pseudo-scientific simile—'new stones, new Fowles, new Serpents'. Of course that sort of simile neither began nor ended with the euphuists. Chaucer's reference to hyena's gall in his *Response de Fortune* would have delighted Lyly: the ostrich still hides her head in the sand for the convenience of political orators. What constitutes euphuism is neither the structural devices nor the 'unnatural history' but the unremitting use of both. The excess is the novelty: the euphuism of any composition is a matter of degree. We are all greatly indebted to a modern scholar for drawing our attention to the Latin orations of Joannes Rainoldus, delivered in the seventies and published as *Orationes Duodecim* in 1614 and 1619. Reynolds, a scholar of Corpus and tutor of Hooker, was a distinguished man in his day and the orations he delivered as Greek reader at Merton may have been the final and crucial influence upon Lyly, Lodge, Gosson, and others. Read in quotation, he may well appear as the original euphuist. It seems hard to demand more than a sentence like *ut videmus herbam Anthemidem quo magis deprimitur eo latius diffundi*. But if we sit down to Rainoldus for a whole morning we shall be disappointed. The euphuisms are there but they are not continuous; we wade through many a page of (moderate) Ciceronianism to reach them. The credit—or discredit—of having first kept the thing up for whole pages or decades of pages at a stretch must still, I believe, be given to Lyly. I speak, of course, of 'euphuism' as we now understand it; in Lyly's own time the word referred exclusively to the learned similes.

Euphues itself is related to Lyly's literary career rather as the Preface of the *Lyrical Ballads* is related to Wordsworth's; each marking a temporary aberration, a diversion of the author from his true path, which by its unfortunate celebrity confuses our impression of his genius. John Lyly belongs to a familiar type. He is a wit, a man of letters to his finger tips. He comes of erudite stock. His grandfather is Lyly of the Eton Grammar; his aunt marries two schoolmasters of St. Paul's in succession and her children have names like Polydore and Scholastica. At Magdalen (Oxford) he is 'a dapper and deft companion' much averse to 'crabbed studies', behindhand with his battels and (need we add?) very critical of the dons. In our own age he would have been a leading light of the O.U.D.S. and when he went down would have become a producer. And that, in a sense, was what he actually became. He gets some post in the Revels and also at St. Paul's choir school; officially to teach the children Latin (judging by his own verses, he did it very badly), but unofficially to be dramatist, trainer, and producer to what is, in effect, a theatrical company. To that world of 'revels', of pretty, pert, highly trained boys who sing elegant poems to delicious music and enact stories that are 'ten leagues beyond man's life', in dialogue of exquisite and artificial polish, Lyly belongs. There he does (though with much financial discontent) the work that he was born to do. Unfortunately, however, once in his life, Lyly, then resident at the Savoy, anxious about his career, and much concerned to please his patron, the precisian Burleigh, in an evil hour (evil for his lasting fame) had decided to turn moralist. He would write a palinode against excess of wit and other youthful follies. He would line up with Ascham and others against the dangers of Italian travel. Of course such a design was a less violent departure for him than it would be for the same type of intellectual in many other periods. Moral severity was modish as well as prudent. The palinode against wit could be very witty. One did not need to step out of 'the Movement' in order to be a *censor morum*. No moral theology, no experience of life, no knowledge of the human heart were required. The plan had, from his point of view, everything to recommend it, and was carried out in *Euphues. The Anatomy of Wit* (1578).

I cannot agree with critics who hold that *Euphues* marks any advance in the art of fiction. For Lyly, as for Pettie, the story is a trellis. The difference is that Pettie's trellis was an inoffensive thing which you could forget once the roses were in bloom, while Lyly's is a monstrosity. Euphues betrays his sworn friend in love, is himself betrayed, undergoes a sudden conversion to philosophy, is reconciled (apparently without apology) to the injured friend, and for the rest of the book lectures the friend and the human race on morals in a style which would be rather too lofty for Cato to use to Heliogabalus. It is like seeing the *School for Scandal* re-written with Joseph Surface as the hero. It is no kindness to Lyly to treat him as a serious novelist; the more seriously we take its action and characters the more odious his book will appear. Whether Lyly's moralizing was sincere or no, we need not inquire: it is, in either case, intolerable. The book can now only be read, as it was chiefly read by Lyly's contemporaries, for the style. It is worst where it is least euphuistic. In the dialogue between Euphues and Atheos euphuism is almost wholly abandoned, and it is here that the confident fatuity of Lyly's thought becomes most exasperating.

Fortunately Lyly's didactic fit did not last long. The recovery is already beginning in *Euphues and his England* (1580). Here Euphues himself remains as detestable as he was before (the unfortunate Philautus is lectured even while sea sick) but there are three changes. In the first book Lyly addressed himself only to gentlemen; he now solicits the attention of ladies. In the first book we had a *remedium amoris* based on a condemnation of all women and therefore unrelated to any possible life in the real world: in the second, honest loves are distinguished from dishonest and the virtuous, though loving, Iffida has a little (a very little) vitality. Finally the narrative element is increased in quantity and improved in quality. In the *Anatomy* the story had played a very small part, and the book had to be filled out with a dialogue on atheism, a tractate on education (mainly from Plutarch), and numerous letters. In the *England* there are still plenty of instructive letters, but rather more happens and there are inset stories within the main story. The change must not be exaggerated. Lyly is still more interested in rhetoric than in character or situation; far further from the true novel than *Amadis* or *Huon* or Chaucer's *Troilus* had been. In the history of fiction his book is not an advance from medieval art but a retrogression. It is, however, an advance from its predecessor. And in becoming less severely didactic Lyly has become, in every sense that matters, more moral. Values that a man might really acknowledge hang about *Euphues and his England*.

The chief pleasure now to be had from both books is our participation in the author's obvious enjoyment of his own rhetoric. We despise his sermons; but seeing him so young and brisk, so delightedly preoccupied with the set of his bonnet, the folds of his cloak, and the conduct of his little sword, we feel our hearts softened. But neither Lyly nor euphuism can be fairly judged from the two *Euphues* books. No style can be good in the mouth of a man who has nothing, or nonsense, to say. It is in the plays that euphuism shows its real value.

The difference may be illustrated by two quotations. Endimion soliloquizing in act II, scene i, says

I am none of those Wolues, that barke most when thou shinest brightest; but that fish (thy fish *Cynthia* in the floode Arares) which at thy waxing is as white as the driuen snowe, and at thy wayning, as blacke as deepest darknes.

Philautus, at the moment of discovering Euphues' treachery, says

I see now that as the fish *Scolopidus* in the floud Araris at the waxinge of the Moone is as white as the driuen snowe, and at the wayning as blacke as the burnt coale, so Euphues, which at the first encreasing of our familyaritie, was very zealous, is nowe at the last cast become most faythlesse.

There are minor differences, no doubt. *Deepest darknes* is more evocative than *burnt coale*. The laboured exposition of the analogy in Philautus' speech leads to a flat anticlimax—*very zealous . . . most faythlesse.* But the fundamental difference is that Philautus (in angry conversation) is merely talking about the moon, Endimion (in solitary passion) is adoring her; that the relation between this moon-struck fish and the behaviour of Euphues is purely intellectual, while Endimion can identify himself with the fish and his voice breaks at the identification in the parenthesis *thy fish Cynthia*. Hence Philautus' simile is frigid; in Endimion's the crazy exaltation is really suitable to the tale of a man who loved the moon. In Lyly's novels the euphuistic style is plastered over scenes and emotions (not themselves very interesting) which neither demand nor permit it; in his plays he creates a world where euphuism would be the natural language. And of course the antithesis—what M. Feuillerat calls *le tic-tac métronomique* of Lyly's style—is far better in dialogue than it could ever be in narrative. Not infrequently it achieves grandeur: as in 'He cannot subdue that which is diuine—Thebes was not— Vertue is' (*Campaspe*, 1. i) or 'Shee shall haue an ende—so shall the world' (*Endimion*, 1. i). Let us note in passing that it is here, not in the wretched work of Studley and his colleagues, that the Senecan 'verbal *coup de théâtre*' is really Englished.

The history of drama is not my concern, so I will say nothing of Lyly's plays as 'theatre' beyond recording that when I saw *Endimion* the courtly scenes (not the weak foolery of Sir Thopas) held me delighted for five acts. But these plays have a literary importance which cannot be passed over in silence without crippling the whole story that this book sets out to tell. Lyly as a dramatist is the first writer since the great medievals whose taste we can trust: the first who can maintain a work of any length

qualis ab incepto processerit. Having conceived the imaginary world
in which most of his plays are set—whether antique-heroical as
in *Campaspe* or pastoral-Ovidian as in most of the others—he
brings everything into keeping. He is consistently and exquisitely
artificial. If we miss in him that full-bloodedness which delights a
modern in so many Elizabethans, we must remember that it was
a quality of which our literature had then too much rather than
too little. Belly laughter or graphic abuse could then be supplied
by almost everyone; the fault was that they often intruded where
they were ruinous. The lightness of Lyly's touch, the delicacy,
the blessed unreality were real advances in civilization. His
nymphs and shepherdesses are among the first ladies we have
met since the Middle Ages. They have all the character they
need; to demand more is like asking to have a portrait head by
Reynolds clapped on to a goddess out of Tintoretto. His only
serious fault is the weakness of the low comedy scenes between
the pages. In *Love's Metamorphosis* he omitted the clowns and com-
pensated for their absence by making the heroines a little lighter
and more playful. The result is something sweeter and fresher,
but hardly less piquant, than Millamant. It is on these bubble-
like comedies, not on *Euphues* nor on his anti-Martinist pamphlet
Pappe with a Hatchet, that Lyly's fame must rest. And they are
good, not despite, but by means of, his style. It is the perfect
instrument for his purpose, and he can make it pert, grave,
tragic, or rapturously exalted. If, as most scholars think, he did
not write the admirable songs which appeared in the 1632
collection of *Six Court Comedies*, he certainly wrote plays exactly
fitted to contain those songs. For in the larger and older sense of
the word his genius was essentially poetical and his work 'poesie'.
Here is the 'Golden' literature at last.

BOOK III
'Golden'

———

I
SIDNEY AND SPENSER

Aᴛ the outset of this chapter I once more beg the reader to remember that the adjective *Golden* is not here used in a eulogistic sense. By 'Golden poetry' I do not mean simply good poetry (that is another question) but poetry in its innocent —as the theologians would say, its 'once-born'—condition. Marlowe's 'Come liue with me' is Golden, Donne's answer to it is not. The rhythm in 'beauty making beautiful old rhyme' is Golden, that in 'Burnt after them to the bottomless pit' is not. Phoebus dancing forth from the oriental gate is a Golden image; snow coming down to periwig the baldpate woods is far otherwise. A clear recognition of the difference should be common to those whose preferences are quite opposed.

Though individual critics will be noticed as we proceed, it will be well to start with a glance at the general outlook on poetry which lies behind the whole Golden achievement. This outlook was expressed in a more or less common defence and theory of poetry; criticism on particular poems was less plentiful and much less important.

The defence of poetry will not be rightly understood unless we keep two facts carefully in mind. In the first place, it is a defence not of poetry as against prose but of fiction as against fact. The word *poetry* often covered all imaginative writing whether in prose or verse, and even those critics who did not so extend it thought of poetry primarily as invention. What is in question is not man's right to sing but his right to feign, to 'make things up'. In the second place, the attack which necessitates this defence is not, save locally and accidentally, a puritan attack. In England, no doubt, most of the attackers were Protestants. But so were most of the defenders. The controversy had begun far from England and long before the Reformation. Boccaccio's

De Genealogia Deorum (XIV and XV) is as much a defence as Sidney's *Apology*. So is Plutarch's *De Audiendis Poetis*. Our sixteenth-century critics are really contributing to, or concluding, an age-old debate; and that debate, properly viewed, is simply the difficult process by which Europe became conscious of fiction as an activity distinct from history on the one hand and from lying on the other.

It was, of course, Plato who opened this debate, and he made two very different contributions to it. On the one hand, in the *Ion* and the *Phaedrus*, he stated in an extreme form the doctrine of inspiration. He denied that poetry was an art. It was produced in a divine alienation of mind by men who did not know what they were doing. The non-human beings who were its real creators showed this by sometimes choosing as their mouthpiece the worst of men or even the worst of poets. On the other hand, in the *Republic* he condemned poetry along with all the other 'mimetic' or representational arts. This condemnation was two-sided. In part it is directed (and so indeed is his theory of inspiration) against the old error, still dangerous when Plutarch wrote, of mistaking art for science and treating Homer as an encyclopedia. To that extent it was a real advance. In part it was metaphysical. Nature, the phenomenal world, is in Plato's dualism a copy of the real and supersensuous world. Dialectic leads us up from unreal Nature to her real original. But the arts which imitate Nature lead us down, further away from reality, to 'the copy of a copy'.

Two different answers were given to Plato, which may roughly be called the Aristotelian and the neo-Platonic. Aristotle gave his almost at once. Poetry, he maintained, does not copy the particulars of Nature; it disengages and represents her general characteristics. The poetic myth shows us what would necessarily or probably or possibly happen in all situations of a certain kind. If you like, it reveals the universal and is thus more scientific (φιλοσοφώτερον) than history. The neo-Platonic answer, far later and more gradually, arose from prolonged reflection on sacred iconography; even, it would appear, from reflection on a single sacred image. In the first century A.D. we find Dio Chrysostom putting into the mouth of Pheidias the words, 'What is hardest in making such a work as my Olympian Zeus is that the same image has to be preserved unchanged in the mind of the artist until he has finished the statue, which may be a matter of years'. The model, apparently, is not a natural object, but an image in the artist's mind, invented, says Dio, because 'wisdom and reason cannot be directly portrayed. Therefore, knowing the object in which they do occur, we have recourse to it and attach a human shape to wisdom and reason, showing forth the invisible by the visible' (*Orat*. XII, *De Dei Cognitione*). This could, by a little manipulation, be reconciled with Aristotle, but is already pointing in a different direction. A century later Philostratus has gone farther. Again citing the works of Pheidias, and this time adding those of Praxiteles, he says that they were never produced by imitating nature. 'Imagination made them, and she is a better artist than imitation; for where the one carves only what she has seen, the other carves what she has not seen' (*De Vita Apollonii*, VI. xix). In the third century Plotinus completes the theory. 'If anyone disparages the arts on the ground that they imitate Nature', he writes, 'we must remind him that natural objects are themselves only imitations, and that the arts do not simply imitate what they see but re-ascend to those principles (λόγους) from which Nature herself is derived. . . . Pheidias used no visible model for his Zeus' (*Ennead*, v. viii). Art and Nature thus become rival copies of the same supersensuous original, and there is no reason why Art should not sometimes be the better of the two. Such a theory leaves the artist free to exceed the limits of Nature. Of these two conceptions it is the neo-Platonic, not the Aristotelian, which is really demanded by most Golden poetry; by the *Furioso*, the *Liberata*, the *Arcadia*, the *Faerie Queene*, and by many elements in Shakespearian 'comedy'. It is also directly asserted by some of the critics. 'The poet,' says Scaliger (*Poet.* I. i), 'maketh a new Nature and so maketh himself as it were a new God.' It will be remembered how closely Sidney follows him. The poet, unlike the historian, is not 'captiued to the trueth of a foolish world' but can 'deliuer a golden'. Bacon defines poetry as 'feigned history', and the purpose of the feigning is to give us 'some shadow of satisfaction' in those points where 'the nature of things doth deny it'. To most moderns this will necessarily appear a kind of 'escapism'. It did not seem so to Scaliger, Sidney, or Bacon, because they inherited, in a Christianized form, the Platonic dualism. Nature was not the whole. Above earth was heaven: behind the phenomenal, the metaphysical. To that higher region the human soul belonged. The natural world, as Bacon said, was 'in proportion inferior to the soul'. Such a conception excluded that kind and degree of reverence for natural fact which romanticism and science have combined to instil into us. The man who, in his 'feigned history', improved on Nature and painted what might be or ought to be, did not feel that he was retreating from reality into a merely subjective refuge; he was reascending from a world which he had a right to call 'foolish' and asserting his divine origin.

Such unambiguous statements of the neo-platonic creed are not, however, very common. The men of that age were such inveterate syncretists, so much more anxious to reconcile authorities than to draw out their differences, that the Aristotelian and neo-Platonic views are not clearly opposed and compared, but are rather contaminated by each other and by many more influences as well. Aristotle himself was sometimes misinterpreted in a sense which brought him very close to Plotinus. Thus Fracastorius (1483–1553) in his *Naugerius* explains that while other writers give us the naked fact (*rem*), the poet gives us the form (*ideam*) clothed in all its beauties (*pulchritudinibus vestitam*) 'which Aristotle calleth the vniuersal'. These 'beauties' however are not very relevant to Aristotle's immanent universal—the general character in situations of a given kind, the 'sort of thing that might happen'; they have come in because Fracastorius is really thinking of a Platonic and transcendent form, a reality prior to, and exalted above, Nature. And Aristotle himself had unwittingly invited such a confusion when he allowed, in contexts which had nothing to do with poetry, that Nature often tends to or aims at ($\beta o \acute{v} \lambda \epsilon \tau a \iota$ $\pi o \iota \epsilon \hat{\imath} v$) a greater perfection than the indeterminacy of matter allows her to achieve (*De. Gen. Anim.* 778ª; *Polit.* 1255ᵇ); words which Sidney remembered when he wrote in the *Arcadia* (1590, II. xi) of forms such as 'Nature, often erring, yet shewes she would faine make'. Aristotle was also contaminated by that late and vulgarized version of his own poetics which appears in Horace's *Ars Poetica*. Here the doctrine of the universal has shrunk into a doctrine of fixed theatrical types, arbitrary rules abound, and the seed of neo-classicism is sown. Side by side with this, the medieval doctrine of allegorical interpretation throve with unabated vigour, and with it the old error refuted by Plato and Plutarch which treated poems as encyclopedias. Added to all this, and forming the most characteristic common

mark of the whole school, was the Platonic theory of inspiration.
On this Politian (in the *Nutricia*), Ficino (*De Furore Poetico*),
Scaliger, Tasso, Spenser, and Milton are agreed, and Horace's
rationalism is ignored.

It is important to realize that these claims to inspiration are
not, like similar claims in the Romantics, rhetorically or hyper-
bolically made. They are serious and literal. Tasso and Milton
invoke the Holy Ghost; but inspiration could also be traced to
a lower, though still superhuman, source. When Scaliger (*Poet.*
III. xxv) attributes compositions to his *Genius* he does not mean
by that word some condition of his own mind. He means an
objective, created, personal being, distinct from himself, known
to him, indeed, only by its effects, but to some favoured people
actually audible or visible. This pneumatology may lie behind
Shakespeare's line about the rival poet and his 'spirit by spirits
taught to write'.

The Golden poetics, it will be seen, are by no means free
from confusion. But it is, in my opinion, the claim to inspiration
and to limitless freedom of invention, and not the occasional
Horatianisms about following Nature, that really provide the
key. Most of the Golden poetry was not primarily intended
either to reflect the actual world or to express the personality
of the poet. Shakespeare himself might well have agreed with
Professor Stoll that his great heroines are not such women as
we may ever hope to meet. The poets of that age were full of
reverence—for God, for kings, for fathers, for authority—but
not of our reverence for the actual.[1] Fortune (which in some
contexts we call 'history') was a blind hussy, a strumpet. To
adorn external Nature with conceits and mythical personifica-
tions was as legitimate as to tie a ribbon round the neck of one's
own kitten or cut one's own yew-tree into the shape of a pea-
cock; for we are of a higher birth than nature and her masters
by divine right. In his graver *enthousiasmos* the poet calls down
fire from his native heaven to make this 'foolish' though lovely
world 'more lovelie'. His aim is indeed ethical as well as
aesthetic, *docere et delectare*, *docere delectando*, *jucunda doctrina*. But
this is part of the loveliness, for virtue is lovely, not merely
obligatory; a celestial mistress, not a categorical imperative.

---

[1] The bee on the title-page of Thomas Cutwood's *Caltha Poetarum* (1599) has
only four legs; some horses in the plates to Harington's Ariosto have human
eyebrows.

The change which English poetry underwent at the hands of the Golden poets was twofold: a great change in power (a change from worse to better) and a slighter change in character. 'Drab' does not mean 'bad', but most Drab poetry had been bad in fact. The Golden poets rejected some of its metres almost entirely, set a new standard of melody for those they retained, and purged its vocabulary. The change in character was, as I have said, slighter. The chief merit of good Drab—plain statement which carries the illusion of the speaking voice—was not lost, but it becomes very subordinate. The main effort is directed towards richness, to a poetry which no one could mistake for speech; and this is increasingly so as the Golden Age proceeds. With the Golden manner there goes, usually, a Golden matter; ideally ardent lovers or ideally heroic wars in an ideally flowery and fruitful landscape are the staple. Verse is praised for being 'sugared' or 'with Nectar sprinkeled'. These two changes, taken together, make up what might in the cant sense be called a 'revolution'. It is, however, important to realize that the Golden poets were not revolutionary in the same sense as Donne, or the pioneers of *Vers libre*. They wrote the same kinds, if not the same kind, of poetry as their predecessors. The Golden sonneteers had Wyatt, Surrey, and other Tottelians behind them. Spenser and Marlowe translated from the Latin as Surrey, Turberville, and Drant had done. The neo-medieval work of Spenser follows the *Court of Love*, certain pieces in Tottel, Googe's 'Cupido Conquered' and 'Church-yard's Dream'. Erotic epyllia such as *Hero and Leander* or *Venus and Adonis* had prototypes in Peend or the *Fable of Narcissus*. Barclay and Googe preceded Spenser in Eclogues. The historical impulse seen in the *Mirror* continues in Drayton's epics and *Heroical Epistles*. This possibly helps to explain the arrival of the Golden Age. We do not know why men of genius are born at one period rather than another. But granted the genius, it may find more or less favourable conditions. And surely no genius is so fortunate as he who has the power and wish to do well what his predecessors have been doing badly. He need neither oppose an existing taste nor create a new one: he has only to satisfy a desire which is already aroused. None of his powers are dissipated or embittered by the struggle to make his aims understood: he can get to work at once. This advantage the Golden poets enjoyed. Perhaps it is under such conditions that the perfect work comes, ripe and not over-ripe: a Jane Austen following on a Fanny Burney, a Racine on a Corneille, an Ariosto on a Boiardo.

Though Spenser was two years older than Sidney,[1] Sidney's work was done before Spenser had published anything of comparable value. To settle the exact precedence between them would be difficult; if I here treat Sidney first, the reason is, I confess, pedagogic. To reverse the order would mean beginning with the *Shepherd's Calendar* and thus helping to maintain the importance—in my opinion, mistaken—which critical tradition has come to give it. Spenser's effective contribution to our Golden literature begins with the first fragment of the *Faerie Queene* in 1590; the revised *Arcadia*, a work equally Golden and perhaps even more influential upon the Elizabethan and Jacobean mind, belongs to the early eighties.

Even at this distance Sidney is dazzling. He is that rare thing, the aristocrat in whom the aristocratic ideal is really embodied. Leicester's nephew, Pembroke's brother-in-law, an eligible *parti* for a princess, painted by Veronese, poet and patron of poets, statesman, knight, captain—fate has dealt such hands before, but they have very seldom been so well played. Little of the Spenser whom we love is to be found in the letters to Harvey or the *View of the State of Ireland*; but the Sidney revealed in his life and letters is just what the author of the *Arcadia* ought to have been. He is a young man ambitious of learning, anxious to read Aristotle in the Greek, though French will do for Plutarch, sufficiently of his age to like the *Imprese*

[1] b. Nov. 1554. Entered at Shrewsbury (with Greville), 1564. Entered at Christ Church, Oxford, 1568. Proposed match with Anne Cecil, 1569. Leaves England, with L. Bryskett, in train of Earl of Leicester; at Paris is made Gent. of Bedchamber to Charles IV; meets Ramus at Frankfort, 1572. At Padua; painted by Veronese; meets Edw. Wotton; studies horsemanship under Pugliano; meets Sturmius and Languet, 1573–4. With his father (now Lord Deputy) in Ireland; proposed match with Essex's daughter Penelope Devereux, 1575. Writes elegy on Essex, *Shepherd of Shepherds?* 1576. *Arcadia* begun? Sent ambassador to Emperor Rudolph; meets Don John at Louvain, P. John Casimir, the emperor and Edm. Campion at Prague, William of Orange at Geertruidenberg; proposed match with Orange's sister, 1577. Produces *Lady of May*, 1578. Quarrels with Oxford; discusses classical metres with Dyer and Spenser, 1579. Writes Memorial on Queen's Marriage and, perhaps, *Defence*, 1580. Finishes cancelled version of *Arcadia*; Pen. Devereux m. Lord Rich; Sidney becomes M.P. is offered the Forfeitures (*v.* Letter LII), 1581. Knighted; m. Frances Walsingham; meets Bruno, 1583. Works under Warwick in Ordnance, 1584. Becomes Joint Master of Ordnance; narrowly prevented from joining Drake's West Indian expedition; is made Governor of Flushing, 1585. On service in Netherlands; dies of wounds at Arnhem, 1586.

of Ruscelli and to quote Buchanan, yet independent enough of its worst folly to call Ciceronianism 'the cheife abuse of Oxford'. He is a serious-minded young man, zealous for the whole European *respublica Christiana* (of which he thinks Rome a *putridum membrum*) and fervent as Ascham against the corruptions of Italy. He is a keen student of affairs, policies, constitutions, but also of 'the true points of Honour', best learned from the French and Spaniards 'wherein if they seeme ouer curious, it is an easie matter to cutt of, when a man sees the bottome'. He complains (perhaps yielding somewhat to the fashion) of melancholy, but there is little of it to be found in his letters; least of all when he is once launched on his utterly hopeless command in the Netherlands. It is then, as one critic rightly says, that his words breathe a certain exaltation. If the Queen were the fountain, he would see nothing ahead but despair. But she is only a means. Even if she cried off altogether 'other springes would ryse to help this action'; for we are engaged against 'the great abusers of the world'. Before he sailed he had 'cast his count' not of danger only, but of 'want and disgrace'. In those last few months the man rises above the author. His care for 'the miserable souldier', and the famous sacrifice of the cup of water at Zutphen, are traits we might not have anticipated from the *Arcadia*.

Apart from the *Lady of May* (1578), a trifle now chiefly remembered for the possible connexion between its Rombus and Shakespeare's Holofernes, Sidney's poetical output consists of the Arcadian pieces and the *Astrophel and Stella*, with some poems added to it in the folio of 1598.

It is not on the Arcadian group that Sidney's lasting fame depends, but they establish his position as the pioneer of Golden poetry. This is best seen by comparing him with one of his predecessors. Here are three lines of Sackville:

> O Sorrow, alas, sith Sorrow is thy name,
> And that to thee this drere doth well pertaine,
> In vayne it were to seeke to cease the same . . .

And here three of Sidney's:

> You Gote-heard Gods that love the grassie mountaines,
> You Nimphes that haunt the springs in pleasant vallies,
> You Satyrs joyde with free and quiet forrests . . .

Everyone feels the clogged, laborious movement of the first, the sense of liberation and ease in the second. And some of the causes are obvious; the hissing alliterations in Sackville, and the lack of vocalic melody; against this, in Sidney, the admirable variety of vowels (*Nimphes* and *springs* being the only exception) and the sub-alliterations of G–GR, FR–F. But there is a difference even more important than this. In the Sackville the words which make any appeal to the emotions or imagination are almost lost in dull connectives. Thus in the second line the noun *drere* is the only live word. In Sidney every single word, except the inevitable *that*'s and *the*'s and *with*, does something for us; there are gods, nymphs, and satyrs who love and haunt and enjoy, grass on the mountains, water and pleasure in the valleys, and, best of all, liberty and silence in the woods. There are no non-conductors. Sidney knows, what few Drab poets ever learned, that verse must carry the smallest possible cargo of words which exist solely for the sake of other words.

If this example seems unduly favourable to the Gold and unduly hard on the Drab, I will take another where the Drab may, without absurdity, be preferred. Petrarch writes:

> Rotta è l'alta colonna e 'l verde lauro
> Che facean ombra al mio stanco pensero;
> Perduto ho quel che ritrovar non spero
> Dal boreo a l'austro o dal mar indo al mauro . . .

Wyatt adapts it thus:

> The pillar perish'd is whereto I leante
> The strongest stay of mine vnquiet minde;
> The like of it no man agayne can finde,
> From east to weste stil seekynge though he wente.

And here is the opening of a dirge for a dead Arcadian king:

> Farewell O Sunn, *Arcadias* clearest light;
> Farewell O pearl, the poore mans plenteous treasure:
> Farewell O golden staffe, the weake mans might:
> Farewell O Joy, the joyfulls onely pleasure.
> Wisdom farewell, the skillesse mans direction:
> Farewell with thee, farewell all our affection.

The Drab specimen here seems to me sound, masculine writing in Wyatt's graver manner, and the vapidity of the fourth line in the Golden specimen will be obvious to everyone. What here concerns us is to notice how Wyatt (perhaps not for purely aesthetic reasons) has, so to speak, turned down the lights of the Petrarch. The picturable *rotta* has become the highly general *perished*: the green laurel has gone; the first person of *perduto ho* has become the gnomic 'no man'; and the last line substitutes east and west for two winds and two seas. In Sidney we see a sun eclipsed, a pearl lost, a wand of gold destroyed, poor men enriched, weak men strengthened, ignorant men guided. Notice, too, how the Farewell phrase runs to four syllables in the first two lines, then to six in the third, then back to four in the fourth, is reversed in the fifth, and doubled in the last, giving the illusion of chant-like monotony without monotony itself. The bad fourth line reveals the temper of Golden poetry as clearly as the others; where it lacks riches it will still pretend to have them.

In his Arcadian poems Sidney offers a much wider range of metrical experiment than Spenser. He has a more delicate ear and is more learned in the art. The poems which stand out will usually be found to do so by some novelty or other excellence in their music. Such are 'The ladd Philisides', which may have suggested the stanza of Milton's *Hymn* on the Nativity, 'Get hence foul grief', which pleases by its metre alone, and the stately 'Why dost thou haste?' Even the pieces in classical metres, which Sidney understands far better than either Harvey or Spenser, are not all failures. The Asclepiads ('O sweet woods') have real charm.

Since *Astrophel and Stella* is the first full-blown sonnet-sequence we have met, something must be said about that misunderstood Form. The difference between the *Vita Nuova* and Petrarch's *Rime* is that Petrarch has abandoned the prose links; and it was they that carried the narrative. The first thing to grasp about the sonnet sequence is that it is not a way of telling a story. It is a form which exists for the sake of prolonged lyrical meditation, chiefly on love but relieved from time to time by excursions into public affairs, literary criticism, compliment, or what you will. External events—a quarrel, a parting, an illness, a stolen kiss—are every now and then mentioned to provide themes for the meditation. Thus you get an island, or (if the event gives matter for more than one piece) an archipelago, of narrative in the lyrical sea. It is not there in order to interest you in the history of a love affair, after the manner of the novelist. To concentrate on these islands, and to regard the intervening pieces as mere links between them, is as if you valued a Mozartian opera chiefly for the plot. You are already turning away from the work of art which has been offered you. To go further and seek for the 'real' (that is, the biographical) story is to turn your back on it altogether. To go further still and to start rearranging the pieces in the hope of mending the story or squaring it with other biographical data is, in my opinion, to commit yourself to unresisted illusion. If you arrange things to make a story, then of course a story will result from your re-arrangement; have we not all done it as a parlour game with pictures torn at random from the daily papers?

Facts may, of course, lie behind (and any distance behind) a work of art. But the sonnet sequence does not exist to tell a real, or even a feigned, story. And we must not listen at all to critics who present us with the preposterous alternative of 'sincerity' (by which they mean autobiography) and 'literary exercise'. The only poet (unless I am mistaken) who has edited Sidney, Mr. Drinkwater, makes short work of that dichotomy. 'Look in thy heart and write' is good counsel for poets; but when a poet looks in his heart he finds many things there besides the actual. That is why, and how, he is a poet.

The narrative, still more the biographical, reading of a sonnet sequence may obscure its real qualities. Where the poet (thinking symphonically, not historically) has put in a few lighter or more reflective sonnets for relief or variety, the reader who wants a 'human document' will thrust them aside as frigid and miss any structural fitness they may really have. Something like this has happened with Sidney. Scholars draw a distinction between the first thirty-two sonnets and the rest. At XXXIII the 'real' (that is, the historical) passion is supposed to begin. The change, we are told, coincides with the marriage of Penelope Devereux to Lord Rich; and XXIV, which does not fit the theory, must have been put in (as God, in some anti-Darwinian theologies, put in the fossils) to deceive us. My concern is not with the truth or falsehood of the theory, but with its inutility. Grant it true, and what have we gained? Nothing, apparently, but an obstacle to our appreciation of the first thirty-two son-nets. These seem dull only because they do not fit into the story. Read without the perverse demand for story, they will not be found to differ much from the others either in subject or merit. They introduce most of the themes on which the sequence is built. We have in them sonnets about sonnet-writing (why not?

Milton writes about the epic in his epic, Pindar about odes in his odes) as we shall have again in XXXIV, L, LVI, and XC. We have glances at the outer world of moralists, *losengiers*, and impertinents; we shall meet them again in XXXV and XLVIII. The 'Platonic' solution which occupies us from LXIX to LXXI has already been hinted in XI. The direct or conceited celebration of the lady's beauty occurs as often after the thirty-third sonnet as before it. That none of the most passionate sonnets come before XXXIII is true. I know no reason why they should. The earlier pieces deal with the conflict between Love and Virtue (or 'Reason'). Structurally it is very proper that this theme should come at the beginning. Such a conflict may not interest all modern readers so much as the pictures of passion triumphant, but it interested Sidney. Pyrocles and Musidorus talk about it at great length in the *Arcadia*. It is significant that the poet makes no attempt to explain what particular circumstances threw Love and Virtue into opposition. He takes the opposition for granted. Everyone knew that Passion and Reason, or Will and Wit, were antagonists. It was assumed that they would be at loggerheads, as we assume that a dog will go for a cat. Similarly, when he deals with a lovers' quarrel (Song 10 to Sonnet XCV) he does not say what the quarrel was about. Everyone knows that lovers have quarrels. He is writing not a love story but an anatomy of love.

There is so much careless writing in *Astrophel and Stella* that malicious quotation could easily make it appear a failure. Sidney can hiss like a serpent ('Sweet swelling lips well maist thou swell'), gobble like a turkey ('Moddels such be wood globes'), and quack like a duck ('But God wot, wot not what they mean'). But *non ego paucis*. With all its faults this work towers above everything that had been done in poetry, south of the Tweed, since Chaucer died. The fourth song alone, with its hurried and (as it were) whispered metre, its inimitable refrain, its perfect selection of images, is enough to raise Sidney above all his contemporaries. Here at last a situation is not merely written about: it is created, presented, so as to compel our imaginations. Or consider Sonnet LXXI. In almost any other poet the first thirteen lines would have the air of being a mere 'build up' for the sake of the last. But Sidney's sonnet might have ended quite differently and still been equally, though diversely, admirable. Nearly all the trochaic songs hint at the incantatory music of the *Phoenix and the Turtle*. They do not quite achieve it. Lines rhythmically dead, such as 'But when their tongues could not speake' always break in and mar the spell. But to have gone so far is immense praise.

Considered historically, then, and in relation to his predecessors, Sidney is one of our most important poets. Nothing which that century had yet produced could have led us to predict the music, passion, and eloquence of *Astrophel and Stella*. It is not all in the 'sugared' manner. Sidney can come down to earth when he chooses—'He cannot love: no, no; let him alone', or even 'Is it not ill that such a beast wants hornes?' And these passages may please the modern reader as much as any. The historian, who comes to it almost numbed with Drab, is more likely to notice what is unprecedented, the conceits that 'with wings of love in aire of wonder flie', the 'golden sea whose waves in curles are broken' or the

> shafts of light
> Closed with their quivers in Sleeps armorie.

Notice again how few of these words exist only for the sake of other words; notice the variety of the vowels; notice the hint, the finer spirit, of alliteration. Then consider how far it overgoes the common (though excellent) equation of eye-glances with arrows, and yet preserves it. There had been nothing like this in English before. There had hardly been anything like it in Latin; you must go back to Greeks, whom Sidney almost certainly did not know, to find a parallel.

Poetry still has its militant, though tiny, audience: but the taste for romance seems in our age to be dead, and the very corpse mutilated and mocked. Yet if we are ever to enter into the life of our ancestors we must try to appreciate the *Arcadia* as well as the *Astrophel and Stella*. For those (I am not one of them) who find it unattractive the first step must be to replace it in its setting. It was not, when Sidney wrote it, a *bizarre*, irrelevant book. Its style may not be what they now call 'functional'; no more were the architecture, clothes, furniture, and etiquette of the period that begot it. As we read it we must have in mind the ruffs, the feathers, the tapestries, the rich carvings, the mannered gardens, the elaborate courtesies. Even its sentiment was at no such distance from life as we suppose. How near it came to Sidney's own life we know; when he threw away his cuisses at Zutphen, by which he got his death wound, he was obeying a heroic punctilio worthy of Argalus or Amadis. But love could be as romantic as war. 'He told him of a gentleman who not long before found all the people bewailing the death of a gentlewoman that had lived there, and grew so in love with the description that he grew desperately melancholy and would goe to a mount where the print of her foote was cutt and lie there pining and kissing of it all the day long, till at length death concluded his languishment.' You would think that was from a heroic romance: actually, it comes from Lucy Hutchinson's memoir of her husband, and his own passion, a few pages later, is almost of the same kind. Many readers may ask whether the reality is not as foolish and tasteless as the fiction. It is a good question; and sympathetic reading of the *Arcadia* will enrich our data for answering it. To judge between one *ethos* and another, it is necessary to have got inside both, and if literary history does not help us to do so it is a great waste of labour.

Some time between 1577 and 1580 Sidney wrote for his sister a prose romance; an 'idle worke', partly written in her presence and partly sent to her sheet by sheet. In 1581 or 1582, as we know from a letter of Greville's, he began to re-write it in a more serious spirit and on a much larger scale, but left off in the middle of a sentence in Book III. This fragment was published by Ponsonby after Sidney's death in the quarto of 1590. Such a truncated text must have tormented all gentle hearts, and in 1593 the best that could now be contrived was given them in Ponsonby's folio: this reprints the fragment which had appeared in the quarto and adds Books III to V 'out of the Authors owne writings and conceits'. This composite text is the *Arcadia* which our ancestors knew. But the original 'idle worke' had not perished, and in the present century several manuscripts of it have been discovered. It was then found that this 'old *Arcadia*' differed in some respects not only from the revised fragment (as we knew it would) but also from those later parts of the Ponsonby folio which had been 'supplied' from Sidney's 'owne writings and conceits'. It thus comes about that, instead of the work which Sidney intended to leave us, we have three things: (1) The 'old' or cancelled *Arcadia* in its entirety, (2) the fragment of revised *Arcadia*, (3) the last three Books (III–V) of the cancelled *Arcadia* modified for inclusion in the folio.

The difference between the first and second is structural. The cancelled *Arcadia* had told a fairly simple tale; in the revised fragment Sidney complicated it by a labyrinth of interwoven stories in conformity with the epic practice of his time. He turned, in fact, from something like the technique of the modern novel to the technique of Spenser, Ariosto, Malory, the French prose romances, and Ovid's *Metamorphoses*. It was therefore to be expected that many modern critics, bred on the novel, should prefer the cancelled *Arcadia* to the revised; but to say that it was better, that Sidney in his revision was spoiling his work, would be rather ingenuous. Our own taste in fiction has not yet lasted as long as the taste for the interwoven sort lasted. When we find ourselves rejecting a method in which so many spirited and polished generations took pleasure, it requires great boldness—or impudence—to assume that we are in the right.

The differences between the cancelled *Arcadia* and the later parts of the folio are small but important: the two that matter most are these. In the cancelled *Arcadia*, at the end of Book III, Philoclea (under very extenuating circumstances) surrenders her virginity to Pyrocles without marriage; and earlier in the same book (under circumstances of most aggravated treachery) Musidorus is restrained from the rape of Pamela only by a timely interruption. In the corresponding parts of the folio the honour of Philoclea and the good faith of Musidorus are both preserved. This does not imply any change of morality, for the acts which are omitted in the folio had been condemned in the cancelled version. The artistic value of the change is very difficult to judge. For those of us who have been early steeped in the traditional version, the difficulty is not one of morals but of credibility. We cannot suspend our disbelief in a Musidorus who commits indecent assaults: it is as if, in some re-discovered first draft of *Emma*, we were asked to accept a Mr. Woodhouse who fought a duel with Frank Churchill. Philoclea's lapse is in comparison a trifle; and in the folio text, where so much of the scene is retained and the main purpose of the scene omitted, the result is certainly inferior.

It is tempting to assume that Lady Pembroke made these changes with no authority, in obedience to what some call her 'prudery'. But this is by no means certain. Ponsonby said that the later books were derived not from Sidney's writings only, but from his 'writings and conceits'. This may, no doubt, be merely a redundant expression; but it is equally possible that Ponsonby means what he says, and that Lady Pembroke retouched the 'writings' or manuscripts in the light of the 'conceits'—that is, of alterations which, to her knowledge, Sidney had intended to make. In revising his romance, he was turning it from a 'toyfull booke' into a prose epic which would have no need to shun 'severer eyes'. This might well have involved heroines more chaste and heroes more heroical than he had previously intended, and it would be natural enough that he should discuss these changes with his sister. It was, after all, her book.

But these questions, however interesting to the student of Sidney, do not much concern the literary historian. To him 'the *Arcadia*' must mean the composite text of 1593: it, and it alone, is the book which lived; Shakespeare's book, Charles I's book, Milton's book, Lamb's book, our own book long before we heard of textual criticism. If the recovery of the cancelled version is to prevent our looking steadily at the text which really affected the English mind, it will have been a disaster.

The two great influences on Sidney's romance are the *Arcadia* (1501) of Sannazaro and the *Ethiopian History* (fourth century A.D.) of Heliodorus. There are of course others; Malory possibly, *Amadis* probably, and Montemayor's *Diana*. But Montemayor is himself largely a disciple of Sannazaro: it is from Sannazaro and Heliodorus that the two kinds of fiction which Sidney is fusing really descend.

Sannazaro's work belongs formally to an extinct species, the Varronian *Satura Menippea* in alternating proses and metres, as used by Boethius and Alanus. Since it was originally entitled *Ecloghe* we may perhaps conclude that for Sannazaro the poems were the important thing and the intervening proses were intended merely as links. If so, his actual achievement is different from, and better than, his design. The thread of narrative in the proses, though enriched with epic material (the funeral games in XI) and romantic (the subterranean journey in XII or the Wood of Dreadful Beauty in X) is indeed very slight. But it has a momentous effect. It creates for the singing shepherds a landscape, a social structure, a whole world; a new image, only hinted by previous pastoralists, has come into existence—the image of Arcadia itself. That is why Sannazaro's work, though in one sense highly derivative—it is claimed that almost every phrase has a classical origin—is, in another, so new and so important. If Pope was able to take it for granted that 'Pastoral is an image of what they call the Golden Age', this was largely the result of Sannazaro's *Arcadia*. It was Sannazaro, more than any one else, who turned pastoral away from the harshness of Mantuan (or our own Barclay), made of it something to be pictured not in grotesque woodcuts but in the art of Poussin, and so created one of the great dreams of humanity. To that extent he is a founder.

Heliodorus, translated by Thomas Underdowne in 1569, not from the Greek but from an intermediate Latin version, had in Sidney's time an importance which the successive narrowings of our classical tradition have since obscured. In order to see that importance we must once more remind ourselves that the word 'poesie' could cover prose fiction. We must remember the taste for interlocked and endlessly varied narrative to which the medieval romances and Italian epics equally bear witness. These facts, taken together, explain why Scaliger cites the *Aithiopica* as a model of epic construction; why Sidney and Tasso both mention it among heroic poems, and Racine (it is said) thought of turning it into a tragedy. And though it is not literature of the greatest sort, it partly deserved Scaliger's praise. The plot is cleverly devised so as to combine a breathless variety of adventure with an ultimate unity of action. This supplied the *delectare*; the *docere* was provided by the constancy, lawfulness, and (almost medieval) courtesy of the love between Theagenes and Chariclea. It was widely read. Shakespeare makes Orsino remember its 'Egyptian thief'. Fletcher in his *Shepherdess* borrows from it the taper that will not burn the chaste. Details about the 'church' and priesthood of Isis reappear in Spenser's story of Britomart. Its elaborate descriptions of dress may have encouraged an existing Elizabethan taste for such things.

From Sannazaro Sidney took over the Menippean form (though he made his proses so long that we hardly notice it) and the idea of Arcadia itself. From Heliodorus he took over the conception of the prose epic, filling his story with shipwreck, disguise, battle, and intrigue. For the battles he drew upon Homer (but no doubt, Homer strained through Virgil). The first thing we need to know about the *Arcadia* is that it is a heroic poesy; not Arcadian idyll, not even Arcadian romance, but Arcadian epic.

To call it a pastoral romance is misleading. The title seems to promise that, and the first few pages keep the promise. But almost at once Sidney leads us away from 'the shepherdish complaynts of Strephon' to a shipwreck, to the house of a country gentleman, to affairs of state, and to the royal family. The shepherds sink to the rank of minor characters, their eclogues to a recurrent interlude. It is true that Basilius and his court for the sake of the plot are in rustic retirement. But they are not figures in an idyll; their complicated domestic life contains both tragic and comic elements. The loves of the major characters are not 'shepherdish'. Those of the heroes are heroical, that of Basilius, senile and ridiculous, that of Gynecia, a sinister obsession like the love of Phèdre, and felt as such by its victim. But as the *Arcadia* is not mainly pastoral, so neither is it wholly amatory. Already in the first two books we are struck by the high proportion of chivalrous adventure to amorous complaint. When we reach the third the epic quality increases. There is less interweaving of separate stories in the medieval manner. There is an increasingly tragic atmosphere. The battles, though no less chivalrous, are more filled with Homeric echoes. The main story, now marching steadily forward, holds us for its own sake.

But even when we have added the heroic to the amatory and realized that the pastoral is quite subordinate, we have still left out one of the elements that go to make the *Arcadia*. Sidney is not merely a lover and a knight; he is also a moralist, a scholar, and a man of affairs. He aspires to teach not only virtue but prudence. He often exchanges his poetical prose for that style which the ancients called *politike*; and he dearly loves a debate or a set speech. No one has really tasted the *Arcadia* who does not remember the epistle of Philanax in Book I, Zelmane's speech to the rebels in Book II, the discussions on beauty and on the existence of God in Book III, or that on suicide in Book IV— not to mention the maxims of law, government, morals, or psychology, which are scattered on nearly every page. It is significant that the whole story moves neither to a martial nor an amorous, but to a forensic, climax; the great trial scene almost fills the fifth book. We are expected to enjoy the rhetoric of the chief speakers and (what is really part of their rhetoric) their carefully chosen dress. We are expected to revere the inflexible gravity of Euarchus. It was only the conventional modesty of a 'gentle' author that led Sidney to describe even his cancelled version as a 'toyfull booke'; and to the real *Arcadia* such words have no application at all. Beyond all doubt he was intending to express *totius vitae imaginem*. If he offers sweets in plenty for the young and amorous reader, he also provides solid nourishment for maturer stomachs.

This many-sided appeal can easily be misrepresented by a one-sided choice of quotations. We can paint Arcadia all 'humble vallies comforted with refreshing of siluer riuers', all trees that 'maintaine their flourishing olde age with the onely happinesse of their seat, being clothed with a continual spring because no beautie here should euer fade'. We can people it with lovers who 'stoppe their eares lest they grow mad with musicke' and who, on seeing their mistress in an orchard, exclaim 'the apples, me thought, fell downe from the trees to do homage to the apples of her breast'. We can mention the war horse 'milk white but that vpon his shoulder and withers he was fretned with red staines as when a few strawberies are scattered into a dish of creame', his mane and tail 'died in carnation' and his harness 'artificially made' like vine branches. Such is the *Arcadia* we know from popular tradition before we open the book. And all this is really there. But it is not there alone. Against these passages we can quote almost as many of a sterner and graver kind. 'Judgement', says Euarchus (as if he had been reading Burke), 'must vndoubtedly bee done, not by a free discourse of reason and skill of philosophy, but must be tied to the lawes of *Greece* and municipall statutes of this kingdome' (1593, v). 'Hope', says Pamela, 'is the fawning traitour of the minde, while vnder the colour of friendship, it robbes it of his chiefe force of resolution' (iii. xxxvii). Noble youths 'looke through loue vpon the maiesty of vertue' (iii. xvii) and 'the journey of high honour . . . lies not in plaine wayes' (ii. xxiii). If Charles I used Pamela's prayer in prison, he was not ill advised: even the less known prayer of Musidorus, if somewhat unregenerate in its object, is noble in style and rhythm (1593, iv). The fantastic equipage of the knights does not mean that Sidney ignores the reality of battle. He draws both sides of that picture and himself points the contrast:

For at the first, though it were terrible, yet Terror was deckt so brauelie with rich furniture, guilte swords, shining armours, pleasant pensils, that the eye with delight had scarce leasure to be afraide; But now all vniuersally defiled with dust, blood, broken armours, mangled bodies, tooke away the maske, and sette foorth Horror in his owne horrible manner (III. viii).[1]

Quotation to illustrate this less Arcadian side of Sidney could be endless, but I must content myself with one more specimen, the magnificent *viximus* of Musidorus and Pyrocles in their condemned cell:

We haue liued, and liued to be good to our selues and others: our soules, which are put into the sturring earth of our bodyes, haue atchieued the causes of their hither coming: They haue knowne, and honoured with knowledge, the cause of their creation, and to many men (for in this time, place and fortune, it is lawfull for vs to speake gloriously) it hath bene behouefull that we should liue (1593, v).

The elaboration of the style, always, of course, most notice-able to those who have no taste for the matter, seems to me to lessen as the book goes on. But even at its most elaborate it does not exclude reality, though it is usually a heightened reality. Most of the characters are, no doubt, types and much that happens is improbable; but Sidney contrives to let us know very well the sort of people he is talking about. His artificiality is not of the kind which needs to be carefully pro-tected; whenever he pleases he can drop into simplicity and no shock is felt; as in the sentence 'At that Philoclea smiled with a little nod' (II. xx). He can afford to let us hear Zelmane stutter-ing or Kalander lecturing the young men on early hours. He can show us Zoilus 'turning up his mustachoes and marching as if he would begin a paven', or old Basilius 'stroking vp' his stockings and nodding his head 'as though they mistook him much that thought he was not his wiues maister' (1593, III). The comic relief supplied by Dametas and his family is by no means contemptible; at the end of the old fourth, in the story of the buried treasure and the ash-tree, it is really good. Sidney does not, like Shakespeare, love his clowns, but he has made me laugh.

Of the characters, Basilius is a stock comic type and the two heroes, though adequate in their context, do not live on in the mind. It is in his women that Sidney shows himself a true maker. Gynecia I have already compared to Phèdre, not, of course, because there is any equality of art between Sidney and

---

[1] This passage may owe something to Boiardo, *Orl. Innam.* II. xxiii. 22, 23.

Racine, but because both are studies of the same thing, and against the same background of Augustinian theology. Each pictures the tormented human will, impotent against the depravity of fallen human nature. The horror of Gynecia's state is that, while the will is instantly enslaved, the judgement of good and evil remains clear. Her very virtues, being merely natural, and therefore only *splendida vitia*, give her no help against the 'hideous thing', nay rather aggravate her fall: in Sidney's terrible words she had been 'guiltie of a long exercised virtue which made this vice the fuller of deformitie'. In defiance of the supposed paganism of Arcadia he allows her to make the theology explicit when she says, 'strange mixture of humaine mindes! Only so much good left as to make vs languish in our owne euills' (1593, III).

Pamela and Philoclea, on the other hand, are true natives of Arcadia. They can be praised without reservation. English literature had seen no women to compare with them since Chaucer's Crisseid; and, apart from Shakespeare, was to wait centuries for their equals. They are, of course, idealized; but then they are lifelike as well. It is easy to produce lifeless idealisms; it is perhaps easier than we suppose to paint people (think of Trollope's Johnny Eames) as real, and also as dull, as some people we meet. But to idealize discreetly, to go beyond Nature yet on Nature's lines, to paint dreams which have not come through the ivory gate, to embody what reality hints, forms such as 'Nature, often erring, yet shewes she would faine make'—this is a very rare achievement. And Sidney has almost done it. I do not think that the majesty of Pamela is ever strained or the simplicity of Philoclea ever insipid. The contrast between the two cynosures, worked out in every detail, down to the difference of their toilets in prison (III. v, x), helps to save them from abstraction. Here are great ladies; the first fruits of returning civilization and an earnest that this civilization will rise high and last long.

Yet characterization is not Sidney's main interest. The heart of the *Arcadia*, the thing for which it exists, which wrung from Milton even in his anger an admission of its 'wit and worth', is its nobility of sentiment. We can almost say of Sidney as Johnson said of Richardson, 'You must read him for the sentiment.' Sidney assumes in his readers an agreed response to certain ideals of virtue, honour, friendship, and magnanimity.

His conception of love is a Platonic elaboration of medieval *Frauendienst*—the theory, later expressed by Patmore, that erotic love can be a sensuous appetite of intelligible good. Hence he can speak of noble women as having 'throwne reason vpon our desires and, as it were, giuen eyes to Cupid' (I. i). We are meant to feel as an unpurchasable grace that single kiss which Pamela vouchsafes to her lover, 'either loue so commanding her, which doubted how long they should enioy one another; or of a liuely spark of noblenes, to descende in most favour to one when he is lowest in affliction'. And the second alternative is to be taken seriously. A lover is not to be suspected of self-deception when he says

> the roote of my desire
> Was vertue cladde in constant loues attire (1593, III).

At the same time, there is no notion that love has a right to override all claims. Infinite, so to speak, in one direction, it is, in another, rigidly bounded by different parts of the pattern of honour. It leaves the laws of friendship sacred. 'Life of my desires,' says Musidorus to Philoclea, 'what is mine euen to my soule is yours; but the secret of my friend is not mine.' And the friendship of which we here speak is 'a child and not the father of Vertue'. Everything proposed for our admiration in the *Arcadia* is on that level, everything is good and fair and beyond the common reach. It was not written for a democracy. And though this exaltation may strain a modern reader it is never itself strained, never rings false like the later heroic drama. We can hardly doubt that it was among the lofty romances which Milton acknowledged as his textbooks of love and chastity, replete with those beauties whereof 'not to be sensible argues a gross and swainish disposition'.

In that way the *Arcadia* is a kind of touchstone. What a man thinks of it, far more than what he thinks of Shakespeare or Spenser or Donne, tests the depth of his sympathy with the sixteenth century. For it is, as Carrara says of the earlier Italian *Arcadia*, a work of distillation. It gathers up what a whole generation wanted to say. The very gallimaufry that it is— medieval, Protestant, pastoral, Stoical, Platonic—made it the more characteristic and, as long as that society lasted, more satisfactory.

The style is not one that naturally appeals to most modern ears. Its essence is fullness, its danger, overfullness. Every rift is loaded with ore; this 'ore' mostly consisting of descriptive detail, simile, metaphor, or conceit. The sentences are usually long: whether too long, may be disputed. A sentence is too long either when length makes it obscure or unpronounceable, or else when the matter is too little to fill it. Sidney seldom offends against the first canon; about the second it is not so easy to decide. Much that seems otiose if we consider only the necessities of plot and character, may yet be necessary to the atmosphere. The looks and clothes and retinues of the characters, and the scenes in which they appear, are really essential to the Arcadian quality. The world which Sidney is imagining could not, perhaps, be described without conceits. Even the real world, as he saw it, was allegorical, emblematic: Arcadia, of course, more so. I believe we should seldom blame Sidney for saying too much if we were in full sympathy with his mode of appreciating external nature. When the princesses are drying after their bathe, 'the water (with some drops) seemed to weepe that it should parte from such bodies' (II. xi). We are apt to regard such conceits as a frigid substitute for real observation and enjoyment. More probably they are fantasies wrought upon an observation and enjoyment which were real but very different from ours. I remarked before that the Elizabethans had neither the romantic, nor the scientific, reverence for nature. Her beauties were, for them, not degraded but raised by being forced into real service to, or fanciful connexion with, the needs and moods of humanity. Their outlook was anthropocentric to a degree now hardly imaginable. This comes out well in a place where Sidney is not writing fantastically at all. He tells us that the shepherds' arena was surrounded by 'such a sort of trees as eyther excellency of fruit, statelines of growth, continuall greennes, or poeticall fancies haue made at any time famous' (I. xix). Every one of these qualifications is illuminating. Sidney likes things to be useful, healthy, and perfect in their own kinds. To that extent he is at one with Jane Austen's Edward Ferrars; 'I do not like crooked, twisted, blasted trees. I admire them much more if they are tall, straight and flourishing. . . . I am not fond of nettles or thistles or heath blossoms.' But, unlike Ferrars, he is a poet, a mythologist, and a scholar. He wants 'poeticall fancies' and 'fame' as well as fruit and shade. He values, in fact, those parts of nature which, for whatever reason, have already made good their claim on man's attention. His

'Nature' is a nature thoroughly humanized, thoroughly sub-
jugated to man's pleasure, and now, after so many centuries
of planting, pruning, mowing, myth-making, after so many
physic gardens, emblems, languages of flowers, and topiary,
almost an extension of ourselves. He would not understand our
objection to the conceits. The Romantic poet wishes to be
absorbed into Nature, the Elizabethan, to absorb her.

The case against the *Arcadia* does not rest upon its style.
Doubtless it is no perfect style, but it has its own appropriateness and admits more vigour and variety than is popularly
supposed. Probably no man, qualified in other respects to enjoy
the book, was ever really deterred by its style. Those who dislike
Sidney's manner also dislike his matter. A simple style could
not carry that matter at all. In that sense his decorations can be
called 'functional', if not in each particular sentence, yet in
their total effect. Jonson placed him beside Hooker as a master,
not only of invention and judgement, but of language.

A more serious criticism against him might be that the
elements he has taken from Sannazaro do not really lie down
at ease with those he has taken from Heliodorus. Sannazaro's
Arcadia was a golden world; Heliodorus offers us a world of
battle, murder, and sudden death. When Sidney has blended
the two, some may ask how Arcadia can admit such disorders,
or what was the use of taking us to Arcadia at all if this is what
we find there. But I think such criticism would reveal a misunderstanding. Sidney by no means commits himself to the
claim that his Arcadia represents the state of innocence in any
strictly Christian or Stoical sense. Its woods are greener, its
rivers purer, its sky brighter than ours. But its inhabitants are
'ideal' only in the sense that they are either more beautiful or
more ugly, more stately or more ridiculous, more vicious or
more virtuous, than those whom we meet every day. The world
he paints is, in fact, simplified and heightened; because it is the
poet's business to feign 'notable images' of virtues and vices.
But we must not exaggerate the extent to which he intends his
heroes and heroines for images of virtue. Their faults are conceived, no doubt, as the faults of noble natures: yet still as
faults. Musidorus exhorts Pyrocles against the 'base affection'
of love (1590, 1. ix) as a thing which will 'divert his thoughts
from the way of goodnesse' (ibid. xii); when conquered himself,
he apostrophizes love as a 'celestial or infernal spirit' (ibid.

xviii). Not that Sidney thinks thus of love *simpliciter*; but he sees
in these loves an element of 'ill governed passion' and they lead
to actions which he does not approve. In that respect the expur-
gation of Philoclea's weakness and Musidorus' attempted rape
alter the nature of the story only in degree. Imperfection, not
condoned because it is lovely imperfection, remains and is
rebuked by Euarchus: 'Loue may have no such priviledge.
That sweete and heavenly vniting of mindes, which properly is
called loue, hath no other knot but vertue, and therefore if it
be a right loue, it can never slide into any action which is not
vertuous.' The 'uniting of mindes' does not here, of course,
exclude the uniting of bodies in marriage; what is condemned
is disguise, trickery, hypocrisy, and abduction—and probably
marriage without parents' consent. These things bring his
heroes within an ace of death under the sentence of a just judge.

Theoretically we are all pagans in Arcadia, and there is
nothing necessarily foreign to paganism in the judgement of
Euarchus. Nevertheless, Christian theology is always breaking
in. Thus a single phrase like 'Since neither we made ourselves
nor bought ourselves' (1593, IV) casually and perhaps unconsciously lets in the whole doctrine of the Redemption. Pamela's
prayer is Christian in all but name. This superficial discrepancy
does no more harm here than in *Comus* or in the *Winter's Tale*,
where Leontes consults the Delphic oracle but Polixenes knows
all about original sin, 'the imposition hereditary ours'. The
convention was well understood, and very useful. In such works
the gods are God *incognito* and everyone is in the secret. Paganism
is the religion of poetry through which the author can express,
at any moment, just so much or so little of his real religion as
his art requires.

The *Arcadia*, as I have said, is a work of sentiment. It expresses
an ideal. Whatever we think of that ideal, we must not mistake
it for a mere emotional indulgence. The balance and tension
within it of many diverse ardours—erotic, heroic, political,
ethical, religious—save it from that charge. In Dryden's heroic
plays all is subordinate to love, in Mackenzie, all to 'feeling', in
Kipling, all to discipline. Sidney is not like that. His ideal is not
a reverie but a structure. A sane man could—I think sane men
did—attempt to live by it. His constancy to so builded an ideal
gives to him, as to the young Milton, the quality of joyful seriousness. And that, to some tastes, compensates for many faults.

The *Defence of Poesie* or *Apology for Poetry*, as the two quartos of 1595 respectively name it, is, I suppose, universally accepted as the best critical essay in English before Dryden; and it is not obvious that Dryden wrote anything so good. In his comments on individual writers he is no doubt happier than Sidney, but in the theory of poetry he is much less consistent and complete. He lives from hand to mouth. Sidney's theory, for good or ill, springs organically from his whole attitude to life. If we want to refute it we must grub up the roots.

Because that attitude was widely shared Sidney can make much use of his predecessors. His central doctrine, that the poet is a second Creator producing a second Nature, is taken from Scaliger. The historical doctrine that poetry is the eldest of the arts probably comes from Minturno. Aristotle is misunderstood and pressed into the service of a Poetics different from his own. His 'universal' becomes 'what is fit to be said or done' and the unities of place and time are foisted upon him. Sometimes a commonplace in Sidney has a longer and more complicated history than this; the idea that poetry is a 'speaking picture' is to be found in Vives, Horace, and (perhaps this is the fountain head) Simonides. Behind Scaliger, as we have seen, lies Plotinus. Rummaging thus in the genealogy of ideas we may get the impression that the copious works of our ancestors were all spun out of a very small stock of thought, but posterity, rummaging in our works, may find the same. It is when a commonplace ceases to be common that it is first recognized as such.

Sidney's own taste is that of a chivalrous, heroic, and romantic person, slightly modified at certain points by humanistic rule of thumb. Thus, on the one hand, he welcomes, from Minturno, the idea, unknown to Aristotle, that tragedy should move admiration. He thinks 'high flying libertie of conceit' proper to a poet. Epic is the 'best and most accomplished' (that is, the most perfect) of the kinds. He thinks peace may be hostile to poetry, for it is the companion of camps. A soldier will never reject Ariosto or 'honest king Arthur'—where 'honest' is probably a conscious contradiction of Ascham. Chaucer, unexpectedly but delightfully, is praised not for the *Tales* but for *Troilus*. Even compositions which Sidney the humanist feels bound to disparage, such as *Amadis* and the ballad of *Chevy Chase*, are obviously dear to him. On the other hand, *Gorboduc* is praised for its Senecal style and damned (along with all our rising school of drama) for its disobedience to the unities. The 'olde rusticke language' of Spenser's *Calendar* is disapproved not on any analysis of its effect but solely on the ground that it does not follow precedent—'neither *Theocritus* in Greeke, *Virgill* in Latine, nor *Sannazaro* in Italian' had used it. In what sense this is true of Theocritus he does not explain. Sidney's discussion of comedy is unsatisfactory and perhaps inconsistent. On the general state of English poetry in his own time he does better. The frigidity of most love poetry (it lacks *Energia*), the excessive alliteration, the 'surfet' of similes from 'beasts, fowles, and fishes' were real faults. On versification he seems to understand his own meaning better than most Elizabethan writers. *Accent* here means, as it does not always, stress accent, and he has some notion of its importance for our prosody. On More's *Utopia* he makes a good distinction between the 'Way' or method and the commonwealth presented, reserving his praise for the former.

When we have eliminated the Exordium (with *Chria*) and the jocular peroration, the logical structure of the *Defence* becomes plain with one exception. The exact relation between Sidney's first account of the poet as maker or ποιητής and the 'more ordinarie opening of him' as an imitator is not at once apparent. In reality the 'more ordinarie opening' is concessive and strategical. If the first account has seemed to some readers too ambitious and metaphysical, here for their comfort is something 'which no man will denie'. But when once we have been thus lured into agreement we shall find that it all comes to the same thing in the end and we are committed to Sidney's full doctrine. For of poets, thus 'more ordinarily opened' there are three kinds, the devotional, the philosophical, and the fictional, and it is the third who are 'indeed right Poets' and with whom the rest of the *Defence* is to be concerned. And these imitate in such a curious sense (it is not explained) that they 'to imitate, borrow nothing of what is, hath bin, or shall be, but range onely reined with learned discretion into the divine consideration of what may be and should be'. And so we return to the real Sidneian position.

The basis of that position is the *de jure* superiority of Man in the natural universe. He is set 'beyond and over' it. Nothing shows both that superiority and its loss (*de facto*) by the Fall so clearly as poetry. For in it we produce what surpasses Nature;

our 'erected wit' still enabling us to conceive perfection though our 'infected wil' hinders us from achieving it in action. Because the infection lies in our will, not in our wit, the pretensions of the moral philosopher are spurious. The 'inward light' has already shown us the goodness he professes to teach. What keeps us back is not defect of reason, but our 'combersome servant passion'—to whom the philosopher has nothing to say. He heals that in us which is not sick and abandons that which is. Passion needs to be enticed to virtue, and poetry provides the enticement by her 'notable images of vertues, vices, or what els'. This is her share in the common function of all learnings, which is 'to lift up the minde . . . to the enjoying of his owne diuine essence'. To that end she is set free from Nature, not 'captived' like history to 'the trueth of a foolish world' but licensed to create 'things either better than nature bringeth foorth, or quite anew, formes such as never were'. Or, if she is in some way dependent on Nature, she acts and plays not what Nature in fact produces, but what Nature 'will have set forth' (doubtless Aristotle's βούλεται ποιεῖν). Sidney is aware that this conception may seem megalomaniac—'too saucy' are his own words. But it is seriously held. Sidney has faced the objection that poetry does not 'make' anything in the sense in which Nature makes, because the products of poetry are not real. ('The workes of the one be essenciall, the other in imitation or fiction.') To this there are two answers. What matters about anything is not its reality in the sense demanded but its *idea*. What would it add to the idea of Pickwick if parish registers and death certificates told us that such a man had veritably lived and died? And secondly, in so far as poetry makes its readers enamoured of virtue and thus modifies their behaviour, poetry does produce results in the historical world. In that sense, Xenophon by feigning one Cyrus may have helped to make 'many Cyrusses' who are not feigned.

In this abstract the danger is lest Sidney's theory should seem too bleakly didactic. And there is one point at which it threatens to become so in reality. When he defends the poet from the charge of lying by the example of the lawyer who puts a case under the names of 'John of the Stile and John of the Nokes' or the chess player who calls a piece of wood a bishop, and continues 'the *Poet* nameth *Cyrus* and *Aeneas* no other way then to shewe what men of their fames, fortunes, and estates, should

M

doo', we become uneasy. The respectable theory that poetry is 'delightfull teaching' is here ready to slip into the manifestly absurd theory that the scenes and persons of the poem are mere examples, in themselves as arbitrary and sapless as the symbols of algebra. But any such development is precluded by the whole nature of Sidney's thought. If poetry does not ravish, it is for him nothing. The 'Golden world' which it presents must be set forth 'in so rich Tapistry' as Nature never knew, must lure us into itself. The images of virtue are no mere *moralitas*, no powder hidden under jam. They are the final sweetness of that sweet world, 'the form of goodness, which seen we cannot but love'. The assumption (to put it in our language) that the ethical is the aesthetic *par excellence* is so basic to Sidney that he never argues it. He thought we would know.

Many causes make it unlikely that most of my readers will accept Sidney's theory of poetry. One element in it has indeed been too cavalierly dismissed. His belief that poetry (by which he means fiction) can help men to be good now raises a smile; yet in a world where no discussion of juvenile delinquency is complete without a reference to the dangers of the film, this is surely very strange. Why should fiction be potent to corrupt and powerless to edify? But to accept Sidney in his entirety a man would have to share his theology, his ethics, and his delight in heroic narrative. If he did share them, he would not find Sidney's theory easy to reject. That is where its greatness lies. It was not manufactured and the facts, as Sidney saw them, did not have to be falsified to fit it. Apart from the few humanistic pedantries which I have noted, it is the form into which the actual taste and ethics and religion and poetic practice of his age and class (some courtiers have 'a more sound stile' than scholars) naturally fell when reflected on and harmonized. This does not by any means imply that he ever follows mere fashion; he explicitly dissents from the popular Platonic doctrine of Inspiration. He is not a man following a 'Movement'. He is the man in whom the 'Golden' poetics, as by right, become most fully articulate.

There is great variety in Sidney's prose style, ranging from the richly decorated parts of the *Arcadia* to that of the Letter to Molyneux ('I assure you before God that if ever I know you do so muche as reede any lettre I wryte to my Father, without his commandement, or my consente, I will thruste my Dagger into you. And truste to it, for I speake it in earnest'). The style of the *Defence* lies about in the middle; rich, but not over-rich, in images, pressing on at a good pace, and full (like all his work) of gusto.

We know Edmund Spenser[1] (1552–99) as a man less well than we know Sidney; and probably, as a man, he was less worth knowing. He developed more slowly. Sidney's work rises out of the contemporary Drab almost as a rocket rises: Spenser climbed out slowly and painfully, like Christian from the slough. His work has, nevertheless, excited a wider and more enduring interest. It has perhaps more commerce than Sidney's with our subconscious and semi-conscious minds; probes deeper. That may be his compensation for being a more ordinary man, less clever, less easily articulate. Here, as often, defects and virtues are closely connected. His not infrequent dullness and flatness may owe something to that same simplicity and quietness of mind which give his great passages their peculiar depth and, as it were, rectitude. We feel that they could not have been otherwise, that nothing has been merely 'made up'.

Before dealing with his poetry I shall touch briefly on some people and things which may be supposed to have influenced him.

Of his old headmaster, Richard Mulcaster (1530?–1611) we know a good deal, and though his *Positions* did not appear till 1581 nor his *First Part of the Elementary* till 1582 they were probably based on ideas and experience which he already had when Spenser worked under him, and it will be convenient to deal with them here. He is on many accounts a memorable man. First,

[1] b. 1552. Ed. at Merchant Taylors' School. Sizar at Pembroke Hall, Cambridge; appears in *Theatre of Voluptuous Worldlings*, 1569. Proceeds M.A., 1576. Secretary to Bishop Young of Rochester, 1578. At Leicester House; 'in some use of familiarity' with Sidney and Dyer, 1579. *Calendar*, 1579–80. At work on *Dreames, Pelican, Stemmata, Epithal., Thamesis, Mother Hubbard*; Dedication to *Gnat*; becomes secretary to Lord Grey of Wilton; arrives in Dublin (Aug.), 1580; Clerk of Faculties in Irish Court of Chancery; lease of manor and abbey of Enniscorthy; house in Dublin, 1581. Lord Grey recalled; Bryskett's *Discourse*; gets New Abbey, Kildare, 1583. Commissioner for Musters, Co. Kildare, 1583. Sonnet to Harvey; gets Kilcolman, 1586. Deputy Clerk to Council of Munster *vice* Bryskett, 1584–8. Visited by Raleigh; litigation with Lord Roche; re-visits England, 1589. *Faerie Queene*, Fragment A; *Muiopotmos*, 1590. *Daphnaida*, 1591. Harvey publishes *Foure Letters*, 1592. Sued by Lord Roche, 1593. m. Elizabeth Boyle; sued by Lord Roche, 1594. *Amoretti*, &c.; re-visits England, 1595. *Prothalamium; Faerie Queene*, Fragment B; *Hymnes*; King James's protest against character of Duessa, 1596. Returns to Ireland, 1597. Recommended as High Sheriff of Cork; his house sacked by Tyrone's men; returns to England, 1598. Ob. 1599.

for his style. I should not blame a student who at sight attributed the following to the *Laws of Ecclesiastical Polity*:

For we do confesse that this multiplicitie and manifold vse in the force and seruice of our letters, wold haue som distinction, whereby to be known, if generall acquaintance with our own writing be not sufficient enough to perceiue that in vse which we put down by vse; but withall we defend and maintain the multiplicitie it self, as a thing much vsed in the best tungs, and therefore not vnlawfull, tho' there were no distinction (*Elementary*, XIV).

It is not only Hooker's manner; the very quality of Hooker's mind is there, the sequaciousness, the gentle, quiet persistence. At his best Mulcaster is Hooker's precursor in English prose. But of course he is not always at his best. He is more euphuistic than Hooker and fond of alliteration; one of his reasons for loving English was that he thought it a tongue which 'doth admit such dalliance with the letter as I knowe not anie' (ibid. *Peroration*). Unlike Hooker he is often obscure, and is apt to plunge into refinements before he has made the main issue perfectly clear. He is impenitently aware that his style is not easy. He did not mean it to be; he wanted it 'to print depe euen bycause it semes dark, and contains a matter, which must be thrise lookt on, ear it be once gotten' (ibid.). We are to 'read at leasur and not all at once' (ibid.). It is a high tone from a man who is writing a glorified spelling book; for that, after all, is Mulcaster's achievement. The *Positions*—by 'positions' he means postulates or preliminary maxims—introduces the 'first part' of the *Elementary*, and the four other parts which he failed to write would still not have brought the pupil to his Latin grammar. If we quail at the prospect, then we are shallow creatures in Mulcaster's eyes, smatterers who only 'bid a book goodmorrow'; he does not write for us. *Nil in studiis parvum est*—'leave time to dogs and apes'. There is a kind of heroical absurdity in all this. Indeed it is impossible to read Mulcaster long without smiling. Sometimes he meant us to smile. He recalls innumerable scenes in headmasters' studies when he writes of the father who will 'very carefully commend his silly poore boy at his first entry, to his maisters charge, not omitting euen how much his mother makes of him, if she come not her selfe and do her owne commendation' (*Positions*, IV). But he is quite serious when he recommends holding the breath as a beneficial physical exercise 'though all men can tell what a singular benefit breathing is' (ibid. XV) or writes 'Consider but the vse of our legges, how necessarie they be' (ibid. XX). Yet as we read on we become aware that we are dealing with a learned, an original, and almost a great mind. In Mulcaster humanism has grown ripe and is beginning to correct its first harshness and narrowness. He accepts the doctrine of a classical age in every tongue (*Elementary*, XII), but he is also aware of tongues as living and growing organisms each governed (as we should say) by its 'genius', in his language by its 'prerogatiue', which is its 'secret misterie, or rather quikning spirit'. For 'there is som soulish substance in euerie spoken tung'. Hence after a language has been 'fined' into its classical period it will again decay 'and a new period groweth, different from the old, tho' excellent in the altered kinde, and yet it selfe to depart and make room for another, when the circular turn shall have ripened alteration' (ibid. XXIII). These words lay the foundations for a genuinely historical and sensitive philology and sweep away (perhaps more effectively than Mulcaster knew) a great deal of ignorant dogmatism. On loan words (ibid. XXII) he goes at once to the root of the matter, and his refutation of phonetic spelling (XII) is far in advance of much that is talked and printed in modern England. Though deeply in love with learning he is well aware of the cruelty involved in breeding to it more men than the learned professions can support, and faces the problem honestly (*Positions*, XXXVI, XXXVII, *et passim*). He is a great defender of women and advocates their education; not because he would be progressive, but, on the contrary, because it is already 'the manner and custome of my countrey' (ibid. XXXVIII). The reason is characteristic. Mulcaster again and again expresses his reverence for custom. He deliberately writes so that he need 'feare no note of noueltie': he is 'nothing giuen to the vnpossible'. That is why he abandons the Burtonian or Shandean habit of supporting everything with classical or continental authorities. For in reality the 'circunstance of the countrie' usually makes such transplanted maxims irrelevant and 'the likeness of vnlike things' is deceptive (ibid. III). Here again we are reminded of the caution of Hooker, or of Burke: Mulcaster is no doctrinaire with a blue print. 'Ripeness' is one of his favourite words. He reverences the spirit of actual institutions as he reverences the spirit of a language. In that way, though he sometimes happens to agree with the moderns, he is a true Elizabethan. He values learning as 'the instrument of quietnesse'. Students must have 'mindes giuen to peace'. Rest, private and public, is the true end of all activities. (*Elementary*, *Epistle*, and *Peroration*.)

Though I believe that we of the teaching professions often exaggerate the influence of teachers, it is irresistible to glance through Mulcaster for thoughts that possibly influenced, or were at least congenial to, the mind of Spenser. Thus we may notice that for Mulcaster Ate is one of the great enemies (*Elementary*, I), that the body is likened to a house in which the brain occupies the 'principall chamber' (ibid. VII), and that the defence against phonetic spelling takes the form of an allegorical history of Old King Sound (ibid. XII). Mulcaster professes himself a reader of Ariosto (*Positions*, XXXVIII). The passage quoted above about the 'circular turn' which brings in excellence in an altered kind may, to some readers, suggest lines in Nature's answer to Mutabilitie; and it is certainly hard to keep the *Faerie Queene* out of mind when we read in the *Peroration* to the *Elementary* 'euerie priuat man traueleth in this world to win rest after toil, to haue ease after labor'. But none of these goes beyond easy possibilities of coincidence. We are on safer ground if we attend more to Mulcaster's general attitudes—his reverence for usage and order, his reverence for women, his delight in the vernacular, his longing for 'honest contentment and rest . . . the priuat man's hauen'—and admit that he may have passed on some of them to his pupil. About the possible significance of Mulcaster's love for archery something will be said presently.

The picture would not be complete without some notice of Mulcaster's cruelty. He was, as Fuller tells us, *plagosus Orbilius*, inexorable as Atropos; 'the prayers of cockering mothers . . . rather increasing than mitigating his severity'. (He had observed in the *Positions* that 'parentes and freindes will be medlars sometime'.) In this, as in all else, he followed the custom. But whatever else he may have been, he was certainly a character; and that, at least in memory, heals many wounds. It is better (in retrospect) to have been flogged by Keate than smacked by Perrin.

Spenser was in his second year at Pembroke Hall when Gabriel Harvey became a fellow, and a close friendship arose between them. Of Harvey our materials offer us three pictures.

First, we have Spenser's sonnet, 'Harvey, the happie above happiest men'. It is a clear and striking portrait of the tranquil spectator in the world's show, the man detached 'as if he were God's spy'. Secondly, we have Harvey as he is revealed in contemporary records or in his own books and letters. This is Nashe's Harvey, 'Gorboduc Huddleduddle'; a misfit, arrogant, unclubbable, unpopular, tactless, vindictive, laboriously jocose, a man who feels himself above his profession. 'I neuer found ani fault with them for duelling in there own stale questions', he writes; or again, 'You suppose vs students happye . . . Look them in the face . . . they are the dryest, leanist, ill-favoriddist, abiectist, base-minddist carrions.' Thirdly (which is rather unfair) we have the secret Harvey, Harvey in solitude, pouring out his thoughts in commonplace book and marginalia. This Harvey sees the world as his oyster and has not the slightest doubt of his ability to open it. He hardly mentions religion; he cares nothing for learning; he abhors the life of a scholar. 'The foole hideth his Talent. Λαθε βιωσας is a beggarly maxim' (*ignavum praeceptum*). Only an ass wastes time on studies that lack 'sum prospect to actual commodity and praeferment'. A man must be ruthless, practical, realistic. 'We live in Smith's commonwealth not More's Utopia.' 'From tablets to meditation, from meditation to action' is the rule. Fortunately, if one is a great man, one of the *megalandri*, it is astonishingly easy to arrive. Examples of those who have risen with meteoric speed from obscurity to power are always before his mind: especially Joan of Arc. Fencing, riding, and shooting can each be learned in a week: any art or science in the same time. Every profession or faculty is 'but a feate and a slight'. 'Gallant audacity is neuer out of countenance.' One must become 'a right fellow to practise in the world, one that knowith fasshions . . . Machiaevel and Aretine knew fasshions'. Machiavel is a 'principal author'. In every emergency you must ask yourself 'What would Speculator or Machiavel aduise?' All this can be reconciled with the Harvey of the records. Putting the two together, we get the tragicomedy of the man; in dreams a Machiavellian, a 'politique' who admires Wolsey and Cromwell; in reality, worsted by every college intrigue. Nothing indeed was less practical than the desperate practicality of his maxims. He was one of those men who are always (in fantasy) surrendering their virtue to glittering temptations which neither their talents nor their circum-

stances will ever present to them. There remains, on the other
side, Spenser's sonnet. We could, of course, suppose that Spenser
(following a precedent then well established in encomiastic
verse) hid advice as flattery and recommended virtues by feigning that they already existed. We could, on the other hand,
suppose that Spenser was deceived. The Harvey of the sonnet
may have been the *persona* which Harvey presented to his few
friends. It would be quite in character that he should laugh
away among them the slights and rebuffs at which he writhed
when he was alone. But after we have explained the sonnet we
still have to explain the friendship that begot it. One would not
willingly believe that the man whom Spenser loved was simply
Nashe's Huddleduddle. It is not certain that the marginalia
reveal the deepest truth. They may give us only Harvey's imagination of Harvey, and the real man might be better than that.
I am inclined to think that in a tête-à-tête, his watchful inferiority complex lulled asleep, this uncouth creature may have
revealed qualities of loyalty and affection. He seems to have
been a good brother. And whatever else he may have been, the
marginalia (unlike the letters) show that, off his guard, he was
not a bore.

Despite their friendship his influence on Spenser was, I believe, superficial. Poets are not so like putty as is sometimes implied. There were differences of outlook between them about
which Spenser was quite immovable. A modern critic has expressed it by saying that Harvey objected to Spenser's 'backward looking views'. That seems to me about right. Spenser
looked by preference to the past. There is no evidence that he
resented it when Harvey jeered at his 'elvish queene'; but also
no evidence that he paid the slightest attention. He would
probably have resented it more if he had been less sure that he
was making the right choice. He liked looking at the past, the
legendary past, and continued to look; and out of it he made
not, as we idly say, a dream—for the dreamer takes all he sees to
be reality—but a vast, invented structure which other men
could walk all round and in and out of for four centuries. Harvey was quite a different sort of man. He was almost, like a
modern, concerned with period, with being contemporary,
anxious to follow the change of times. He proclaims in 1595
that 'the date of idle vanityes is expired' and a new age of
Spartan austerity about to begin. Much earlier he had an-

nounced that the great period of 'the tunges and eloquence' was coming to an end, and philosophy in 'diuers morall [and] naturall matters' would soon have all the credit. He is thus to be classed with Willes as a very early instance of that historical attitude towards the present which has since become so common. I have often wondered that modern critics do not on that account make more of him. Perhaps it is still to come.

Of Harvey's views about English metre I will speak presently. As a critic in general (and there are many short critical *dicta* in his works) he is neither good nor notably bad; certainly not worse than most of his contemporaries. Praise of the ancients tells us nothing, for all then praised them. He admires Chaucer, Lydgate, and Henryson for 'notable descriptions and not anie so artificiall in Latine or Greeke', but significantly admires still more their 'Astronomie, philosophie and other parts of profound or cunning art'. Of the moderns he praises Guevara, Tasso, Sidney, Watson, Daniel, Heywood, and of course Spenser, having apparently come in the end to admire 'the pure sanguine' of the *Faerie Queene*: but he also praises the translations of Drant, Golding, Stanyhurst, and the Senecans. His favourite poet, the one to whose praises he returns most often, is *Bartasius*, du Bartas. His polemical writings (we can hardly call them controversial) are not quite without merit. He was drawn into them almost by accident. In his *Three Proper and witty Letters* (1580) Harvey wrote some English hexameters on *Tuscanism* which reflected on, or were held to reflect on, the Earl of Oxford. Lyly, on Oxford's side, replied with some flyting of Harvey in his anti-Marprelate *Pappe with an Hatchet*. Harvey thus became involved with Lyly, Greene, and Nashe and the results were the *Four Letters* (1592), *A New Letter* (1593), two pamphlets both entitled *Pierce's Supererogation* and both dated 1593, and the *Trimming of Thomas Nashe* (1597). Although he was lashing the anti-Martinists Harvey was by no means a Martinist. In the *Supererogation* he strongly deprecates any attempt to thrust the Genevan theocracy upon England, though his grounds are not those which would please either a modern Christian or a modern atheist. Harvey's view is that England is a monarchy with aristocratic elements and that in such a state you must not 'build a reformation . . . vpon a popular foundation or a mechanicall plott'. Calvin had been dealing with a town of 'meane marchantes and meaner artificers'. 'M. Cartwright or

M. Traverse' are welcome to try their hands 'on any like popular towne . . . where Democraty ruleth the rost'; it will not do here. But for the most part Harvey's only concern is to retaliate personal offences. He is completely overmatched by Nashe in comic abuse and what is fun to the adversary is death to him. Yet that future rehabilitator of Harvey whom I antici-pate will not find his work absolutely hopeless. It is true that the 'hard sanctimoniousness' (I quote Grosart) with which Harvey gloats and jeers over Greene for dying in poverty and over Marlowe, as far as we can make out, for dying at all— Harvey thought it was the plague that had killed him—were revolting to nineteenth-century taste, as they are to mine. But standards change and a day may come when such worm's work will no longer militate against Harvey's fame. What is more certainly damaging is that Harvey gives us at his best only what we can get better elsewhere. Many Elizabethans were good at flyting and he is not in the first rank. Much weight will have to be placed by his defender on those passages where he seems aware, as his contemporaries so seldom seem, of the greatness of his own age, talking with spirit of the Armada, the western voyages, and Lepanto 'the glory of Christendom'. This is in the *Supererogation*.

With Gabriel Harvey we naturally associate the glossator of the *Shepherd's Calendar*, E. K. It matters little whether his name was Kirke or not, but it would matter a good deal if we supposed him to be Spenser himself. Good scholars have thought so, but I cannot understand why. E. K. dislikes alliteration which Spenser loves, and despises Marot whom Spenser translates. Above all, he twice goes out of his way (in the Glosses on *April* and *June*) to express his humanistic and Protestant detestation of that medieval or 'Gothic' mythology which was Spenser's life-long delight. It is for him 'unlawfull leasing', feigned by 'bald Friers', and he would 'roote that rancke opinion of Elfes oute of mens hearts'. It is a little surprising that he does not add a more literary objection on the ground of *decorum* to Spenser's mixing fairies and nymphs in the same line. Perhaps he had not the wit: or perhaps Spenser silenced him by pointing to Ronsard's 'Afin de voir au soir les Nymphes et les Fées'. However that may be, it seems to me certain that E. K., far from being Spenser, is a very good specimen of the friendly, yet in the long run wholly uncongenial, *coterie* who patronized Spenser in his nonage but from whose principles he departed as widely and easily as the duckling from the hen that mothered it. The rift already existed when the *Calendar* appeared. If Spenser had fully shared their tastes he would not have written the lines about fairies. Indeed that text and that gloss make very clear the curious *modus vivendi* between him and his set. He will let them gloss his lines but will not delete them: they will let him print the lines but not without protest. It speaks well for all concerned that there is no trace of a quarrel: but the balance of power could not last long. E. K. and Harvey and the rest (there must have been others: there always are in such a covin) would have killed Spenser poetically if he had let them. For the rest, E. K. is a very ridiculous person. His learning is shaky and his positive contribution to our understanding of the text is pretty fairly represented by glosses like '*Neighbour towne*, the next towne: expressing the Latine Vicina'.

A full account of Spenser's reading would perhaps illuminate his work more than an account of his friendships. But it is not very easy to be sure what he had read. He was not an exact scholar, and his mind was so concoctive and esemplastic that the fruits of his reading met and mingled and transformed one another till they became unrecognizable—as happens on the 'road to Xanadu'. If Phaedrus and Phaedo and Xenophon and Cicero are all confused in a single passage (*F.Q.* IV, Prol. iii), as one scholar maintains, we cannot thence conclude with certainty that he had never read Plato. Lodowick Bryskett who introduces Spenser as a speaker in his *Discourse of Civil Life* pronounces him 'perfect in the Greek tongue' and 'very well read in Philosophie both morall and naturall'. But a man is not on his oath in an Erasmian colloquy and we do not know Bryskett's qualifications as a judge of scholarship. For the natural philosophy we can check his evidence by Harvey's statement that Spenser admitted with shame his lack of skill in 'the Canons, Tables, and instruments' of astronomy; while at the same time he delighted in Du Bartas (Week I, Day iv) as 'the proper profession of Urania'. This, I suppose to be characteristic; that Day, with its riot of quaint anthropomorphism, was a sort of astronomy that suited Spenser much better than the tables and instruments. Aristotle's *Ethics* I think he had read—or as the schoolboys say 'done'—probably with much help from a Latin version, but it was clearly not one of the books he had lived with. The Bible and the commoner classics we may take for granted; and with them masses of neo-Latin—Pico, Ficino, Palingenius, Erasmus, Natalis Comes, Bodinus, Sannazarus, Buchanan. It is in that direction that his reading most often goes beyond ours. Marot and the Pléiade he knew well. The great, lifelong influences upon him were the Bible, Ovid, Boiardo, and Ariosto. From the two last he derived almost exclusively his conception both of romantic matter and romantic method, though he seems also to have looked at *Arthur of Little Britain* and some metrical romances. Chaucer and pseudo-Chaucer were less important to him than he himself liked to believe. Of Malory he made extraordinarily little use; I shall suggest a reason for this below.

It is of some importance to remember that Spenser's imagination was moulded by many extinct arts. A more or less agreed mythology and allegory poured in upon him from masque, pageant, tapestry, emblem, carvings, tournaments, woodcuts (and their manuscript predecessors). This provided the forms with which he found it natural to work. Some of his figures were instantly recognizable by his first readers; as if a modern poet used Father Christmas, John Bull, Johnny Walker, and Father Time. But Father Time (his name was once Saturn) is the only form common to Spenser's age and ours.

Finally we must remember the long years in Ireland, though we can only guess how they affected him. Between him and the Irish (though he rather liked some of their poetry in translation) no relations save those of the *lex talionis* were possible; but we note with some surprise that he was charmed by the country-side. He would have been more typical of his age if he had regarded it as a howling wilderness only endurable in the hope of release and promotion. Instead, we read of its rivers 'no lesse famous than the rest', spacious Shenan and 'fishy fruitfull Ban' and Mulla superlative for trout, of the shady grove under Slew-boome, of Arlo hill dear to the Olympians with its oaks and marble and flowery dales. What sort of reactions lurk behind all this we do not know, but what Ireland can do to some minds we learn from Bernard Shaw: 'Such colours in the sky . . . such lure in the distances . . . such sadness in the evenings. Oh, the dream-ing! the torturing, heartscalding, never satisfying dreaming!' It would be very rash to assume that Spenser felt that, but it is not quite impossible. The endless quest on which, with no authority, he sent his Arthur, would fit in well with such an experience. Not, of course, that he would, like Shaw, have regarded it as a horrible form of spiritual dram-drinking. That is the language of a progressive and one who worships the *élan vital*. To a Christian Platonist these formless longings would logically appear as among the sanest and most fruitful experiences we have; for their object really exists and really draws us to itself. This is, however, the merest conjecture. We are on rather more certain ground in thinking that Spenser was increasingly reconciled, though never perfectly, to the rusticity, the homeliness, and the freedom of life in a wild country. The passages in which he forswears court and courtly shows and praises the hermit's or the shepherd's life do not sound to me like affectation or the cry of sour grapes. I think they represent a real, though only recurrent, mood; and that mood perhaps, while it lasted, the deepest. His exile may have been a gain to English poetry. But it is high time to turn from these supposals to the works he actually wrote.

Let us notice at the outset that Spenser's publications, taken in their chronological order, do not represent his actual career as a poet. The *Shepherd's Calendar* indeed may have appeared exactly when and as he would have wished. Vida and others had laid it down that a young poet should begin with Pastoral. Yet this début according to the rules may have owed more to the orthodox humanism of friends than to Spenser's own initiative. From the editorial matter in the *Calendar* we learn that Spenser had already written *Dreames*, *Legendes*, *Pageaunts*, 'sonetts', and a *Court of Cupide*. We learn also that he was reluctant to publish them; while at the same time nine words from one of them, 'that feeles the deep delight that is in death' (quoted in the gloss on *October*) are better, and more characteristically Spenserian, poetry than anything in the *Calendar* itself. It will also be noticed that the single line which E. K. quotes from the *Pageants* ('An hundred graces on her eyelids satte') is very close to *Faerie Queene*, II. iii. 25, and that in II. i. 33 the knights refer to their own quests as 'pageants'. And it is obvious that matter suitable to the titles of the lost works might well be equally suitable for later inclusion in the *Faerie Queene*. It is therefore quite possible that in 1579 Spenser had already written work better than the *Calendar* and more like the *Faerie Queene*, some of which the *Faerie Queene* absorbed. If so, the *Calendar* itself was in some sort the interruption of a life's work already begun. But however that may be, it is certain that Spenser very soon after 1579 embarked on his gigantic project. This project, I believe, satisfied him completely as a poet; but as a man he was faced with the problem of keeping his name before his patrons and the public while he worked at the epic. His solution was to seize the chance of a holiday from Ireland in 1590 and bring out a specimen of 'work in progress'—Books I to III. There is no reason to believe that he had any aesthetic grounds for choosing to publish just those Books in just that state of finish in that particular year. On the contrary, in order to give the fragment some appearance of completeness, he had to patch up a provisional happy ending for the story of Amoret. The fragment was a success and of course his publisher urged him to follow it up. Hence a volume of *Complaints* (1591) was put together from such manuscripts, mostly old ones, as he could offer. Then came a *pièce d'occasion*, the regrettable *Daphnaïda*. In 1595 he was once more on leave in England. This time he had fresh work to publish (*Amoretti* and *Epithalamium*) but he also refurbished the earlier *Colin Clout's Come Home Again* and brought out an extremely belated elegy on the death of Sidney. In 1596 came the second fragment of *Faerie Queene* and two Platonic poems, written in 'the greener times of his youth', were furnished with a 'retractation' as the *Four Hymns*. It will be seen that very few of Spenser's works indicate the interests, or the powers, which were his at the moment of publication. It will also be seen how profoundly right the common reader has shown himself in regarding Spenser almost exclusively as the poet of the *Faerie Queene*. Almost everything else he did was something of a digression. All his life he was in the position of a painter who, while engaged on some great work, frequently has visitors in the studio. They have to be entertained (it is his only chance as a man, if not as an artist) with anything he can lay his hands on. Old canvases that he himself cares nothing about will be brought forward. Worse still, they must be shown the great work itself in various stages of incompleteness. This helps to explain the extraordinary disparity in value between the *Faerie Queene* and nearly all the minor poems. Virgil without the *Aeneid*, Milton without *Paradise Lost*, Goethe without *Faust*, would still rank as great poets. But if Spenser were shorn of the *Faerie Queene*, though the *Epithalamium* (perhaps truncated) would appear in anthologies, the rest of his work would be known only to professional scholars. Even as things are, it is perhaps read by hardly anyone else.

The earliest poetry of Spenser's that we have was printed anonymously. In 1569 appeared the English translation of a tract by the Dutch Protestant refugee Van der Noodt. Its cumbersome title is usually abbreviated as the *Theatre of Voluptuous Worldlings*. Most of it is in prose but what concerns us is the verse. This amounts to twenty-one pieces, with woodcuts, which fall into three classes. In the first are six pieces translated from Marot's version of Petrarch's *Rime*; perhaps by one who glanced at the original Italian as well as the French. In the second are eleven translations from du Bellay's *Songe ou Vision*. In the third are four pieces based on the Apocalypse. The first or Petrarchan group are rhymed, the remaining fifteen in blank verse. Now in the *Complaints* of 1591 Spenser printed *The Visions of Petrarch: formerly translated*. They are seven sonnets of which six are almost identical with the first group of poems in the *Theatre*, except that in four instances twelve-line pieces in the *Theatre* are extended to make them full sonnets. It is therefore clear that Spenser is the author of the first six in the *Theatre*. In the *Complaints* he also printed fifteen sonnets which he entitled *The Visions of Bellay*. There is here no mention of former translation and the eleven of these sonnets which correspond to the second group in the *Theatre* have many variants from the text of that group. These variants, however, are no greater than would necessarily be involved in cobbling blank verse into the rhyme-scheme of the sonnet. It is therefore overwhelmingly probable that Spenser wrote the second group of poems in the *Theatre*. The four Apocalyptic pieces in the third group were never reprinted in any of Spenser's publications. A man who wished to maintain that he was not their author would therefore have no external evidence against him; but he would be introducing an unknown poet into the *Theatre* without necessity and thus breaking Occam's rule against 'multiplication of entities'.

These early translations are not of much poetical value. Such interest as they have for us is twofold. First, their re-appearance in the *Complaints* illustrates what was said above about Spenser's methods of publication. Secondly, they contain several departures from regular metre; such as

Cruell death vanquishing so noble beautie.

Vnto the gentle sounding of the waters fall.

To beare the frame, four great Lions of golde.

In the *Complaints* the second of these has been altered from an alexandrine into a five-beat line,

> To the soft sounding of the waters fall,

but the others remain. Their preservation may be taken, I suppose, as evidence that in the *Theatre* they were not bungles but deliberate experiments; and a critic who disagrees with my view about Wyatt's irregularities might find help in this.

The plentiful literature which scholars have written about the *Shepherd's Calendar* (1579) is concerned much more with the problems it gives rise to than with its poetical merits. This is inevitable. From the first it invited such treatment. E. K.'s learned (or what he thought learned) deck-hamper is so disproportionate to the small cargo of poetry that if the book were not known to be Spenser's it would now be mentioned chiefly to be mocked. Some find the confidence with which E. K. announces the new poet impressive. But it is impressive only in the light of Spenser's later works. In itself it is not remarkable; to hear young men proclaiming that their circle or someone whom their circle has 'taken up' is the only hope for poetry is no more wonder than to see a goose go barefoot. This time they were not so far wrong; but the more we study E. K., the more we shall be convinced that he was only lucky, not judicious. I cannot help thinking that any other poet who was a Cambridge man, and who would write in a humanistic form and let E. K. write Notes, would have received equal commendation from E. K. He hails Harvey as a 'most excellent poete'.

Two ways in pastoral lay open before Spenser. One, which we may venture to call the true way since it led to the *Muses' Elizium* and *Lycidas*, was that of delicate Arcadian idealization; the way of Sannazaro and Guarini. The other was that of Barclay: rough, superficially realistic, full of hard words, satiric, and much indebted to Mantuan. His simple plan was to follow the first method in *January, April, June, October, November, December*, and the second in *February, March, May, July, and September*. *August* partakes of both. In three 'aeglogues' of the second type (*February, May*, and *September*) we find metre which is by later standards anomalous. *August*, the composite aeglogue, begins with nine regular decasyllables and then changes into the rougher verse. *April* is the strangest. We begin with thirty-six decasyllabics and then have a Ronsardian ode.

Long and short lines are mixed in a regular pattern and the
first two stanzas have a regular iambic movement. In the later
stanzas the short lines become irregular (cf. 62, 67, 74, 76, 79,
83, 85, 88, &c., with their earlier counterparts 38, 40, 43, 44, 47,
49, 52, 53, 56). Some even of the longer lines cease to be plain
decasyllables—as 60, 84. Line 87, 'Such follie great sorrow to
Niobe did breede', is pure Barclay or Hawes, and the penulti-
mate stanza ends with a rough trimeter 'shall match with the
fayre flowre Délice' (for *delice* here must be pronounced to
rhyme with *lillies*).

I could wish that critics had devoted less time to praising this
ode and more to explaining its structure; but elsewhere I do not
think Spenser's rougher metres raise any great problem. Looking through the English poetry of his own century, Spenser
found two kinds of verse; the syllabic verse of Surrey, Sackville,
Gascoigne, and others, but also the roughly rhythmical (or even
wholly unrhythmical) verse of Tottel Nos. 217 and 220, of
Seager's and Ferrers's pieces and *Flodden* and *James I* in the
Mirror, not to mention Barclay, Hawes, Skelton's rhyme royal,
and the pseudo-Chaucerian *Pilgrim's Tale*. This kind had been
attributed to Chaucer by Gascoigne in his *Notes of Instruction*,
and is used, if not as Harvey said in 'the most part' of Sidney, at
least in the song 'Who hath euer felt the change of love'. I do
not think any contemporary reader would have been puzzled
by the metre of *February*; it was part of the English inheritance.
I think it seemed rude and archaic in 1579; that, no doubt, was
why Spenser thought it suitable to pastoral, and especially to
pastorals in his rougher style. Sometimes, for a few lines, it does
perhaps really achieve the pungent, homely effect that he intended. More often it is detestable, and to compare it with the
delicacies of *Christabel* is an injury to Coleridge. But Harvey
would have liked it and encouraged it.

Other problems are raised by the fact that the *Calendar* is a
roman à clef. Hobbinol, we know, is Harvey. (Note in *January*
the suggestion of pederasty advanced to show that we are classical, and withdrawn in the gloss to show that we are Christians.)
Algrin is pretty certainly Grindal. Thomalin, Rosalind, and the
rest continue to afford the pleasures of the chase to many re-
searchers. The possible or probable chronology of the aeglogues
has been discussed as a key to details in Spenser's biography:
perhaps certainty cannot be reached.

The theological position of Spenser in the *Calendar* is not easily determined, and since it may have changed during the period of composition we are hampered by not knowing the order of the poems. Cambridge in his day was certainly a centre of puritanism; but Harvey, as we have seen, explicitly rejected the puritan position. *May* and *September* ostensibly attack the Roman and defend the Protestant clergy and E. K.'s gloss on *May* (118) tells us that what is said against Roman prelates is not meant 'to deny fatherly rule and godly gouernance (as some malitiously of late haue done)'. This is clearly intended to dissociate Spenser's position from the puritan attack on Anglican episcopacy. But then it may well be that this was part of Spenser's and E. K.'s strategy—to write what all friends would recognize as 'Marprelate' work, but in such a way that it could always, at need, be defended to government as merely anti-papistical. In *September*, Diggon Davie appears to one excellent editor as 'a central Anglican parson defending his kind' and even cursing those puritans who attack it as Piers had done in *May*, 73–102. But was Spenser's purpose in putting that curse into Diggon's mouth ironical? In *July* we seem to be on firmer ground. Algrin is almost certainly Grindal and is certainly approved by the poet, and Grindal (London 1565, York 1570, Canterbury 1576) had suffered at Elizabeth's hands for his failure to suppress puritan 'prophesyings'. Yet one scholar has questioned Grindal's puritan sympathies. Much depends on our interpretation of *February*. The moral of that fable is that the Briar who wants the Oak cut down will find, when his wish is granted, that he cannot get on without it. Yet at the same time the Briar's dislike of the Oak is almost (certainly not quite) condoned by the fact that the Oak has been associated with popery (207–12). The most natural explanation seems to be that the Briar is Protestantism and the Oak episcopacy; if this is accepted, then Spenser, at least when he wrote *February*, held the official Anglican position. His tenderness for the Oak, as for all medieval survivals, combined with his frank admission that it had been contaminated with 'foolerie', and his dislike for the cocksure and upstart character of the Briar, would fit in well with all that we know of his outlook.

Some scholars find in Spenser an 'extreme antipathy to marriage among the clergy'. It is not impossible that he felt so: Elizabeth did, and in the *Faerie Queene* Spenser praises both vocations, marriage and celibacy, with equal ardour. But the relevant passages—*May* 81–102, *September* 112–15, and *Mother Hubberd's Tale* 475–8—do not prove it. The two first apply to the clergy the perennial complaint *ces pères de famille sont capables de tout*. But when we complain thus of any profession we do not necessarily mean that it ought to be filled only by celibates, though of course we are incidentally providing ammunition for those who do. In *Mother Hubberd* the idle and ignorant parson congratulates himself on being free to marry. But he also congratulates himself on having no 'penie Masses', Complines, Dirges, Trentals, and Confessions. We are not obliged to infer that Spenser desires the revival of celibacy any more than that he desires the revival of all these; which is highly improbable.

Of the *Shepherd's Calendar* as poetry we must frankly confess that it commits the one sin for which, in literature, no merits can compensate; it is rather dull. It would be interesting to know whether a hundred people (or ten) not officially connected with English studies have read it in the last fifty years. I have never in my life met anyone who spoke of it in the tones that betray real enjoyment. Nothing at all is gained by talking as if it were comparable in value to the best, or even the second best, of Sidney's poetry. The fables in *February* and *May* are told not badly: that is as far as praise of them can extend. The roundelay in *August* goes with a swing, but much real popular poetry, even in that century, had been better. The real merit of the *Calendar* lies in achieving more often and keeping up for longer stretches the easy, liquid movement which Gascoigne sometimes just reached. Lines like

> The blossome which my braunch of youth did beare,
> With breathed sighes is blowne away and blasted,

or

> Whence is it, that the flowret of the field doth fade
> And lyeth buryed long in Winters bale?

are not much in themselves. But they are the medium in which much can be done. In *December* there are beautiful metrical audacities, not to be confused with the joltings of his *February*,

> Áll was blówne awáy of the wávering wýnd

or

> Gáther yé togéther my líttle flócke

But Spenser was soon to write and had perhaps already written poetry which deprives the *Calendar* of all importance. We know from E. K. that he was slow to publish, and I think the friends he then had would encourage him to publish his worst work. Pastorals were so very classical, and gave a pretext for satire, and Rosalind and Hobbinol and the whole circle could be brought in. It was the next best thing to publishing a poem themselves.

In 1580 appeared *Three Proper and witty familiar letters*, followed in the same year by *Two other very commendable letters*. The *Three Proper* contain one letter from Spenser to Harvey and two from Harvey to Spenser; the *Two other*, one from each. The letters in the second publication were written before those in the first. Harvey afterwards talked as if they had been published without his consent. As specimens of the epistolary art all five letters are dull, laboured things and we read them only because they show Spenser exploring what was for him a dead-end in English prosody. For at that time the attempt to use classical metres in English could hardly lead to good. Most of those who discussed the project lacked certain necessary knowledge. They did not clearly understand what quantity and accent are; that the first of *merry* is short and the first of *Mary* is long, though both are accented. They did not clearly understand that prosody is based on phonetic fact, not arbitrary rule, and that spelling has nothing to do with it; that the two (graphic) R's in *merry* are irrelevant, or that Latin *bellum* has the first long not because the Romans wrote, but because they pronounced, a double consonant. This is revealed by Spenser's and Harvey's controversy about the scansion of *carpenter*. Spenser assumes that the 'middle sillable' is 'shorte in speache' but will have to 'be read long in Verse'. Harvey replies that since it is short in speech it must be short in verse too. By 'short' both really mean 'unaccented', and are puzzled because unaccented syllables (very naturally) do not conform to the supposed Latin 'rules' about 'length by position'. (There are, of course, no such rules: it is a fact, not a rule, that *cumber* takes longer to say than *cutter*.) Spenser, if I understand him, would solve it by having a distorted pronunciation for verse, while Harvey will boldly substitute accent for quantity throughout. Thus Harvey is, if you like, wiser than Spenser, for Spenser is embarking nowhither and Harvey is sailing to a possible, though in my judgement very

undesirable, destination: the accentual hexameters of Long-
fellow.

Ascham had begun the mischief. Drant—'gorbellied' Drant
the translator of Horace—had evolved rules of prosody. Harvey,
independently of Drant, had experimented himself and urged
Spenser to do likewise. At that time Spenser had ignored Harvey's advice, as he so often did. Later, when he found himself at
Leicester House and 'in some vse of familiarity' with Sidney and
the shadowy 'Master Dyer', who were already at work on a
modified version of Drant's system, he was 'drawen' into their
'faction'. His allegiance did not continue long and none of his
surviving experiments were successful. Sidney did better. In
1582 came Richard Stanyhurst's *First Fovr Books of Virgil his
Aeneis* in hexameters, a monstrosity which Harvey admired but
Nashe and Joseph Hall and Thomas Warton trounced as it
deserves. It has no place in the history even of the English hexa-
meter, for it is barely English. Richard Barnefield in *Hellen's
Rape* used the same metre much better for a comic purpose;
which is perhaps its proper English use. Campion, who is an
exception to all rules, the seraphic doctor of English prosody,
will be dealt with in his proper place.

The most important work of Spenser's youth lies outside the
Calendar. We know that the *Faerie Queene* had been begun, and
a specimen of it sent to Harvey, early in 1580. If we could
identify the earliest passages in it—which of course need not be
those that come first in the text—they would be the proper
starting-point for a study of Spenser's effective career as a poet.
There are also some minor poems which may be as early as the
Calendar, or very little later. *Virgil's Gnat* is dated 1580 by a good
critic. *Mother Hubberd's Tale*, if the most popular interpretation
of it is correct, cannot in its original form be much later than
1579. Both these are more interesting and accomplished than
the *Calendar*.

The *Gnat* is a version of the Virgilian *Culex* in *ottava rima*. It
has its faults, but to compare it with the verse-translations which
we painfully studied in an earlier chapter is to realize that here
at any rate the ascent from the Drab to the Golden is not like a
slope but like a cliff. It keeps on the whole very close to its
corrupt and difficult original but there is very little constraint,
and there are lines of what must at that time have been a startling beauty:

And paint with pallid greene her buds of gold

or

The Sunnes sad daughters waylde the rash decay
Of Phaeton

or the whole stanza which begins 'The verie nature of the place'. The ugly anacoluthon at line 170 is Virgil's fault, not Spenser's. But it is Spenser who unfortunately gives the gnat's ghost a 'grieslie countenance and visage grim', unsuitable I think to the tone of the poem. The prefatory sonnet to Leicester hints, in words not meant to be understood by an outsider, that Spenser had some special intention either in translating the *Culex* at all or in dedicating it at some particular juncture to that patron. Everything in his version is, however, fully accounted for by the original, and allegorical interpretations are now purely speculative.

In *Mother Hubberd's Tale* Spenser assumes his true role as a neo-medieval poet. He ignores Roman satire and goes back to the Renard tradition. Critics usually connect his Ape with the French agent Simier ('My Ape' as Elizabeth called him) who visited England in 1579 in the hope of making a match between the queen and his master the Duc d'Alençon. Apart from the phonetic relation of Simier and *simius* the resemblance is not really very strong: that between the Fox and Burghley is in some passages stronger. The allusion, on any view, concerns only the last episode in Spenser's poem, which is probably a mass of allusions but not a detailed and unified allegory like Dryden's *Absalom*. Thus the Lion is certainly the queen in line 629 but probably not the queen when rated for sloth in line 1327; and the picture of tyranny supported by foreign mercenaries (1118–24), though it may glance at the probable results of a marriage with Alençon, may also be merely general political wisdom from classical sources such as *Republic*, 567[d]. Spenser, looking round on a great variety of evils (sturdy vagabonds disguised as old soldiers, idle parsons, dishonest and venal patrons, frivolity and unmanliness at court, and the insolence of upstarts in office) invents as their cause the ubiquitous activities of an Ape and a Fox. His poem is thus a satire on nearly all 'estates'. It escapes the dullness to which such things are liable, partly by its thread of narrative which is often very lively (note, especially the Ape's approach to the sleeping Lion, 1005–14), and partly because Spenser, unlike some satirists, can paint his positive ideal in contrast to the abuses. Nowhere else do we find him at the same time so far away from the *Faerie Queene* and so good. But the distance must not be exaggerated. If the *tempo* of the *Tale* is brisk, that of the *Faerie Queene* is not nearly so languid as skimming readers suppose; and

To plough, to plant, to reap, to rake, to sowe (263)

is close to the tone of Terpin's

To spin, to card, to sew, to wash, to wring. (*F.Q.* v. iv. 31.)

The Ape has much in common with Braggadocchio. I have often wondered in re-reading this poem why, with all its brilliance, it does not wholly please, and am inclined to think it leaves the ear unsatisfied. The couplets are very often end-stopped but they lack the balance and resonance which the Augustans (I think, rightly) have taught us to expect in that form. There are too many rhymes on unaccented syllables. The effect is a little flaccid. No doubt Spenser would point out to me his warning 'Base is the style, and matter meane withall'; but what is intentional is not therefore necessarily good.

Muiopotmos, from its metre and subject, looks as if it might have been written soon after the *Gnat*. If we were sure of its allegorical meaning we might be able to date it accurately: but we are not sure that it has an allegorical meaning at all. Some think it concerns an abortive duel between Essex and Raleigh in 1588 or between Sidney and Oxford in 1579. The parallel between a successful assassination (which is what happens in the poem) and an unfought duel escapes me. Spenser's poem is 440 lines long. Forty of these are a description of a garden; eighty are an adaptation of Ovid (*Met.* vi. 70–145); forty an account of the butterfly's armour; eight an apology to Cupid for preferring its wings to his; twenty-four describe a cobweb. The topical allegory must presumably come in the remaining two hundred and fifty-two. We can never prove that it does not, but the whole poem, as a playful exhibition of artifice in the Alexandrian manner, seems to require no such explanation. It is full of sunshine and flowers and short enough for its levity not to weary the reader. From it and from the *Gnat* we can see that Spenser did not reject *ottava rima* for his epic because he found it difficult. Its speed and lightness become him very well, but they were excellences he deliberately rejected from the *Faerie Queene*.

I believe it is impossible to date the *Tears of the Muses*. Some

put it later than 1588 because Clio says 'I nothing noble have to
sing' and they think she ought not to have said this after the
defeat of the Armada; but later on Melpomene complains that
'mourning matter she has none'. Euterpe says that 'now no
pastorall is to bee hard', which hardly fits any of the possible
dates. The 'light foote Faeries' of line 31 might seem to 'link' it
(as critics say) with the *Calendar* which has 'lightfote Nymphes'
(*June*, 26), and 'Ye gentle Spirits breathing from aboue' (361)
with 'Most gentle spirite breathed from aboue' in the *Ruins of
Time* (281), and the collocation 'carefull comfortlesse' (349)
with *Faerie Queene*, I. vi. 6. But it is not obvious that when poets
repeat themselves they must be repeating their recent works:
they are surely at least as likely to repeat lines written so long
ago that they do not recognize the repetition. Again, we
might place it early because in it so much of the Drab Age
manner survives; its impotent violence and ill-timed realism.
The lamentation of Spenser's Muses consists of 'yelling shricks',
'shrikes and groanes', and 'lowd shrieks', till we think we are at
a cats' concert. They cry till their eyes are 'swollen'. Ineffective
epithets abound: 'dismall heavinesse', 'dreadful uglinesse',
'loathly idleness', 'lamentable wounds'. Urania tells us at some
length that we know by means of knowledge. Unfortunately,
however, these are faults that Spenser never quite outgrew; we
call him a Golden poet because there is so much gold, not because
there is so little Drab, in his work. The complaints which the
Muses make of contemporary bad taste and indifference to
poetry are far too general to date the poem; authors in nearly
all ages say that kind of thing. I should like to believe that the
Tears is early, for it is a helpless, laboured thing.

The rest of the 1591 volume of *Complaints* was filled out with
the *Ruins of Rome*, a poor translation from Du Bellay's *Antiquités*, the *Visions* of 'Bellay' and Petrarch, cobbled up from the
Theatre, the *Visions of the World's Vanity*, and the *Ruins of Time*.
The *World's Vanity* consists of twelve sonnets all illustrating one
theme (that great things can be destroyed or helped by small)
with emblematic instances. There are interesting peculiarities of
metre, and the ninth and twelfth have some merit.

The remaining piece in the *Complaints* is the only one which
we know to have been recent work when that volume appeared
in 1591. This is the *Ruins of Time* which refers to the deaths of
Sidney (1586), Leicester (1588), and Walsingham (1590). When

Spenser visited England in 1590 he found himself criticized for not having lamented these deaths. That is the external occasion of the poem. There may well have been internal pressure; an exile back on leave feels mutability with a fiercer shock than home dwellers for whom change proceeds gradually. The England to which Spenser returned was not the England for which he had been homesick. He had also been reading in Camden or others about the vanished splendours of the Roman city of Verulam. Following the precedent of du Bellay's *Antiquités de Rome*, and unconsciously reviving a favourite theme of Anglo-Saxon poetry (*Hryðge ða ederas, woriaþ þa winsalo, waldend licgaþ*), he made Verulam the ostensible theme of his poem. The ruined city personified appears to the poet and laments her fate, passing gradually into elegies on the lately dead. This is one of the weightiest, the most chastened, and the most sonorous of Spenser's minor poems. It is almost entirely free from rhetorical violence and sometimes approaches a harder and more austere and genuinely classical manner than was usual with him; as in the lines

> For not to have been dipt in Lethe lake
> Could save the sonne of Thetis from to die (428).

It thus occupies among his works somewhat the same place as *Laodamia* among Wordsworth's. The nine stanzas on Sidney are the best elegiac poetry he ever wrote. The choice and preservation of tone (in Dr. I. A. Richards's sense of that word) was not Spenser's strong point, but here both are excellent. I think the *Ruins* would have been better without its *coda* of six emblematic visions, but even these are much better than most things of their sort. One of them glances at an episode for the *Faerie Queene* which was either never written or not included in the surviving fragments.

It is a pity that Spenser was not whisked away from court and England, and back to Ireland and the *Faerie Queene* immediately after finishing the *Ruins of Time*. Unfortunately he remained to write *Daphnaïda*, an elegy on the wife of Arthur Gorges. Here, as in *Mother Hubberd*, he chose the neo-medieval manner. He resolved to bring up to date the *Boke of the Duchesse*. Nothing could show more clearly how imperceptively he read the Chaucer[1] whom he so revered. I do not think the fault is

---

[1] It must always be remembered that all his 'Chaucer' was corrupt and much of it spurious.

personal to Spenser. *Daphnaïda* really brings to light an aspect of
what I have called the New Ignorance, for its immense inferiority to the *Duchesse* (itself by no means one of Chaucer's best
works) is not an inferiority of technique, but of what we should
now call civilization; what the medieval poets themselves would
have called *freedom*, *gentilesse*, and *mesure*. It is instructive to compare Chaucer's man in black with Spenser's. Chaucer's man is
found dressed in black, sitting against a tree, composing verses,
and looking wonderfully sad. He apologizes for not having replied to Chaucer's first question ('Be not wrooth, I herde thee
not') and accepts Chaucer's apology. Spenser's man has to be a
pilgrim with 'carelesse locks, vncombed and vnshorne' and
'beard all ouer growne', glancing aside 'as in disdainefull wise'
and 'half wrothfully' bidding Spenser 'Cease foolish man'. There
is an equally disastrous contrast between Spenser and another
poet whom he approaches in *Daphnaïda*. Bembo in his *Rime*
says that the death of the beloved has left the day without sun,
the night without stars, the birds without song. Spenser's Alcyon
instead of saying that the world has altered, commands it to
do so:

> Let birds be silent on the naked spray,
> And shady woods resound with dreadful yells—

thus turning a legitimately hyperbolical expression of what
passion really can do to our minds into a shrill witch's or
maniac's curse. Thus throughout the poem we have 'endless
labour to be wrong'. Chaucer's is like a piece of wood-carving,
not of the finest workmanship but showing (when you examine
it) the traces of a sound tradition and of an honest workman
who blundered at times but was a man of sense and feeling;
Spenser's is a great, flamboyant, garish thing of stucco disguised as marble. There are, to be sure, good lines and good
images, but it is radically vulgar. I think it reasonable to lay the
blame chiefly on the age, because Spenser (like Sidney and
Shakespeare) spent most of his literary career in successfully
resisting and curing the new vulgarity. But on this occasion it
conquered him.

By December 1591 we find Spenser restored to poetical health,
to his own house at Kilcolman, and probably to the *Faerie
Queene*, and dedicating to Raleigh a poem which narrates the
inception, progress, and results of his recent English holiday:
Colin Clout's Come Home Againe. Under a thin disguise of pastoral

this is the most familiar and autobiographical of Spenser's poems. Its mood is ambivalent. On the one hand, England is a paradise governed by a goddess, and the court a constellation of excellent poets and bright nymphs: on the other, that same court is a den of false loves, backbiting and intrigue, no place 'for any gentle wit', from which Colin 'rather chose back to his sheep to tourne'. This is very natural. Thus many an exile feels when he comes back (he had almost said 'comes *home*') to his post after the longed for, the exciting, and yet ultimately disappointing holiday in England. Doubly disappointing, because he has failed to get the job in England that he hoped for, and also wonders whether there are not, after all, many consolations for living abroad. I think that with Spenser these consolations were now more valuable than he fully realized, for though the poem contains bitter lines the prevailing air is one of cheerfulness. This pleasant work, like *Mother Hubberd*, fails to satisfy the ear. The truth is that Spenser's ample Muse was unwise ever to appear in public without the *corsage* of stanzaic form; continuous alternate rhyme was not enough. The catalogue of recent or contemporary poets and wits is naturally of great interest to scholars. William Alabaster (a neo-Latin poet) and Daniel are mentioned by name. Alcyon (Arthur Gorges), Palemon (Churchyard), Thestylis (Ludovic Bryskett), and Urania (Lady Pembroke) can be identified. After others the hunt is still up. When we learn that Aetion has been variously taken for Marlowe, Drayton, and Thomas Edwards, or Harpalus for Churchyard, Googe, Puttenham, Sackville, and Turberville, we may perhaps conclude that the quarry is in no imminent danger.

Colin Clout's Come Home Againe was partly re-written and published in 1595 along with elegies by various hands on the death of Sidney. Spenser's own contribution to this collection is *Astrophel*, a poem difficult to date. *A priori* we should expect it to have been written soon after Sidney's death in 1586; especially since Ludovic Bryskett's contribution, *The Mourning Muse of Thestylis*, appears in the Stationers' Register in 1587. But then in the Dedicatory Epistle to the *Ruins of Time* (1590) Spenser confessed that at that date he had still failed to elegize Sidney. It is not impossible that he had already written *Astrophel* and rightly judged it unworthy of the occasion. Nine years later, anxious once more to fill up a volume for the press, he might have glanced at the old manuscript and suffered one of those recrudescences of partiality which are among the dangers of a literary life. In such a mood, with an eager publisher at his elbow, he might come to think that it would just do after all. If so, he was mistaken, but not dreadfully mistaken. *Astrophel* has none of the elaborate ugliness of *Daphnaïda*. It is merely insipid. The eighth stanza has some merit.

In June 1594 Spenser was married, not for the first time. In November of the same year the volume entitled *Amoretti and Epithalamium. Written not long since* was entered in the Stationers' Register. I think we were meant to believe that all the *Amoretti* were addressed to Elizabeth Boyle, the bride of the *Epithalamium*, and present a poetic picture of his recent courtship, and there is really no reason why we should not; though, of course, the merit of the sonnet sequence does not depend on any narrative qualities, much less on their historical value. Spenser was not one of the great sonneteers. Yet his *Amoretti* do not quite fall into the class of works which are negligible because all they can do for us is done better elsewhere. I can imagine (though I have not yet experienced) a day, an hour, and a mood in which they would be the one book we desired. More brilliant and certainly more passionate love poetry is easy to find; but nowhere else exactly this devout, quiet, harmonious pattern. The effect (perhaps incompatible with some other and more exciting beauties) is close to Petrarch's own but without the melancholy. Spenser refers of course to the pains of love; but I cannot help thinking that his love, if not the best kind to read about, was a happy kind to live in. This is confirmed (as the *Amoretti* themselves are eclipsed) by their glorious lyrical sequel.

The *Epithalamium* is our only evidence that Spenser, had he chosen, might have been among the very greatest lyrical poets: lyrical, of course, after the manner of Pindar, not that of Herrick or Burns. The song, as practised by Wyatt, was a form which he either never attempted or attempted so unsuccessfully that he destroyed the result; his talents did not lie in that direction. But for the Greater Ode he had powers unequalled in English.[1] The *Epithalamium*, despite its Italian and Latin affinities, is the most Pindaric thing we have. It has one, or perhaps two, faults; the refrain loses some of its beauty when, at line 333, it has to pass into the negative, and the choir of frogs that make us 'wish theyr choking' is either too comic or else not comic enough. All

[1] Except, perhaps, by Hopkins and Charles Williams.

the rest is, I think, perfection, and here, if nowhere else, the Drab has been completely purged away. The resemblance to Pindar lies in the festal sublimity (a thing much rarer than tragic sublimity) and in the triumphant fusion of many different elements. The Bacchanalian or fescennine jollity of the fourteenth strophe, the hushed sensuousness of the seventeenth, the grotesque night fears of the nineteenth, the realism of 'Those trouts and pikes all others doo excell', and the transformation whereby a small Protestant church becomes a Salomonic or even a pagan temple and at the same time a great cathedral of the old religion with high altar, roaring organs, and crowds of hovering angels, are very different and drawn from different traditions. What organizes them all is the steady progression of the bridal day. Catullus began with evening: thus losing all the alacrity of Spenser's earlier strophes with their 'Awake', 'Bid her awake', 'Hymen is awake', 'The wished day is come at last'. Joy does not begin to pass into 'merriment' (with a medieval chorus of birds) till strophe five. The suggestion of heat (it is high summer) is delayed till seven. At the same time the emotional development is artfully varied and interrupted as in a good symphony. The lustiness which breaks out fully in fourteen had been just hinted by the 'strong confused noyse' in eight and then hushed by the processional movement of the five that follow. The moonlight in twenty-one comes as unexpectedly as a new turn in a novel or a play. The intense desire for posterity (who will people not only earth but heaven) and the astrological connexion of this with the 'thousand torches flaming bright' above the house-tops add not only a public but almost a cosmic solemnity to the poem; which remains, none the less, a thoroughly personal love poem—'Let this day let this one day be myne'—with a remembrance of 'sorrowes past'.

In the *Prothalamium* (1596) his success was not so complete. The central structural idea, that of the swans' gliding progress down the river, is a happy one, and the refrain is more emotionally relevant than the refrain of the *Epithalamium*. But I cannot feel that perfect unity has been achieved. The references to Spenser's own discontents, to the history of the Temple, and to the achievements of Essex, interesting as they are in themselves, do not seem to have been made to contribute much to the total effect. And there is perhaps a little awkwardness at the end of the sixth strophe.

In 1596 came *Four Hymns*. This presents so many problems

that, unless our discussion is to be out of all proportion to the
literary value of the text, I must beg leave to state my views with
a somewhat dogmatic brevity. In the dedication Spenser tells us
that the two first 'Hymns' were composed in 'the greener times
of his youth'. I do not doubt that this is honest, but it is vague,
and I do not believe that we can fix their date by internal
evidence. Spenser's style does not, like Shakespeare's or Milton's,
develop through well-marked periods; he wrote sometimes
better and sometimes worse but his virtues and vices were much
the same throughout, save when he essayed a different *genre* as
in *Mother Hubberd*. Secondly I believe that the *Four Hymns*
defy all attempts (I have made many) to read them as an exposition of the 'Ladder' in the *Symposium*. The first two do not
provide steps or rungs by which to climb to the position adopted
in the third and fourth. The latter are simply, as Spenser says,
a 'retractation' on the lines of 'I lothe that I did loue' (Tottel,
212) or the end of *Troilus*. The mood which found it necessary
to retract loves so very chaste and honest as those celebrated in
the first two hymns is surprising. It is not Christian, for all
Christians allow marriage; nor Protestant, for Protestants
exalted marriage and distrusted celibacy; nor Florentine-
Platonic, for Ficino said of the two loves, natural and mystical,
uterque honestus et probandus (*In Platonis Convivium*, II. vii); and
it is wholly inconsistent with the tenor of the *Faerie Queene*.
Some scholars have thought that even if there is no ladder
in the *Hymns* as a whole, some rungs can be discovered in
the first two. I cannot agree. The *Hymn of Love* is in general
very much more medieval than Platonic. The invocation to
the God of Love and the Muses (1–35), the cruelties of Cupid
(120–61), the effects of love in producing nobility and knightly
deeds (176–237), the pains of jealousy (252–72), the passage
from Love's Purgatory to Love's Heaven (273–93), and the
concluding collect (294–307), are exactly in the manner of
Frauendienst and its religion of love. But for the language, they
could all have been written two hundred years earlier. They are
well done, though not in Spenser's greatest manner, and by
them the poem stands or falls. The birth of Love and his cosmic
operations (43–91) owe much to the *Symposium*, though the
dreadful blunder which gives Love three parents (52, 53) was
not Plato's fault. Nor will Ficino's two Veneres help us here, for
in his commentary (VI. vii) there is no question of the second

Venus at this point, and *Penia* (Spenser's Penurie) is simply the first Venus herself, the receptive intelligence of the angelic mind, before *Porus* (Spenser's Plentie), the ray of Deity, illuminates it. At lines 99–112 we get what looks for a moment like a possible rung. But Spenser's distinction does not seem to be between those who desire carnal fruition and those who desire union of souls (Plato's fourth rung), but between those who merely wish to 'quench the flame' and those who desire progeny 'for eternitie' (cf. *Epithalamium*, 420 et seq.). Lines 190–7 are, I admit, obscure, but I see no evidence that their obscurity conceals a rung. The *Hymn of Beauty* contains much more Platonic or neo-Platonic matter. The Form of Beauty, the supercelestial Venus, the model from which the Creator drew the visible universe (29–63) is the παράδειγμα of *Timaeus*, 28 c et seq. Her relation to Ficino's complexities is not so easily determined. His First Venus is the Angelic Mind considered in its contemplation of Divine Beauty. His Second is the generative power in the *Anima Mundi* (a being inferior to the angels). Since this Second Venus endeavours to procreate material things in the image of the Divine Beauty (Ficino, op. cit. II. vii), Spenser's Venus ought really to be the Divine Beauty itself. Perhaps he was not following Ficino closely at this point. By lines 99–112 he is I think much less concerned with any of these metaphysical Veneres than with the astrological Venus in the third sphere; and his interpretation of *Phaedrus*, 252 and 253 (in lines 197–203) is also astrological. Plato's doctrine that the beloved finds his own beauty mirrored in the lover is used at 176. Spenser, envisaging of course a heterosexual love, wants this to be reciprocal, and that, I believe, was the real meaning of lines 190–6 in the previous hymn. In the lady the lover sees his potential and more beautiful self. But Spenser sadly bungles the idea by likening the two lovers to two mirrors which face one another. Surely the results would be very uninteresting. Lines 211–31 tell us that the lover, in his imagination, fashions the beloved fairer than she really is. If this led him to pass on from her to all beautiful bodies and thence to the beauty of laws and sciences we should at last have our feet on the Platonic ladder. But it does nothing of the sort. Spenser immediately returns to courtly love and winds up with a medieval prayer to Venus (now Love pure and simple with no Plato or Ficino about her) and to his 'Soueraine' Lady.

It is we, after all, not Spenser, who have called these poems Platonic. They are substantially meditations on chivalrous, monogamous, English love, enriched with colourings from Plato, Ficino, Lucretius, and the medieval poets. If we speak of the Platonic colourings at all we have to do so at some length because they are difficult: not because they are of immense importance.

In the *Heavenly Love* we bid farewell to Platonism almost completely. Most of this poem is a straight account of the Creation, Fall, and Redemption, such as any child in a Christian family learns before he is twelve. The earlier stanzas can be pressed into something Platonic (and heretical) if great skill and force are applied to them. The gravamen of the charge is that Spenser describes God as 'begetting' the angels. I think Spenser would have been astonished if anyone had supposed that he was confusing the creation of the angels with the eternal generation of the Son ('ere flitting Time could wag his eyas wings'). I think it would have seemed to him obvious that the word *beget* (like the word *Father*) could be used in this lower sense, especially when rhyme encouraged it. He could always defend himself by Luke iii. 38. One critic thinks it 'important' and neo-Platonic that Spenser describes the Son as creating Man (127–8): but Spenser, long before he heard of Ficino, had learned from the Fourth Gospel and the Nicene Creed that the Son created everything. The truth is that the *Hymn of Heavenly Love* is a very simple, pious poem; eloquent and (to Spenser's co-religionists) edifying, but not, on its poetic or philosophical merits, to be very strongly pressed on other readers.

The *Hymn of Heavenly Beauty* is a little harder. We begin, in correct Pauline fashion, by contemplating the beauty of the visible universe. Having ascended through the spheres we pass, as Dante does in *Paradiso* XXX and Plato dreams of doing in *Phaedrus*, 247 c, beyond the Primum Mobile into the 'supercelestial place'. It also has its hierarchical divisions: lowest the abode of blessed souls, then the region of Forms, and above that the angelic orders. From then, on to line 182, we have a simple and orthodox meditation on the Divine majesty. But this gives way to the figure of Sapience. No doubt Spenser chose this feminine image to provide a parallel to the Venus of the second hymn. Her chief origin is in the Book of Wisdom, but Spenser is also remembering *Phaedrus*, 250 c–d. We have seen all the forms—Justice, Beauty, Wisdom, and the rest—when we too, before our birth, were in the supercelestial place. In the present life it is the reminders of Beauty that especially inflame us. And Plato explains why. Not because Beauty in herself is more desirable than the others, but because the reminders of Beauty are visual, and sight is the clearest of our faculties. If the reminders of Wisdom could come home to our senses in the same way—why, then δεινοὺς ἂν παρεῖχεν ἔρωτας, terrible would be the fire of longing in which we should burn. Hence Spenser's words (239–45) about the direct vision of Sapience to be enjoyed hereafter. Sapience in the fourth hymn thus, in a sense, recovers from that unfair disadvantage (invisibility) which led us to exalt Beauty in the second. The vision of the Divine Wisdom (Hagia Sophia) is not purely a bookish conception. She has had her place in Christian devotions: Soloviev claimed to have met her face to face even in this life. She is, of course, a being higher than Ficino's First Venus: for even the First Venus is an aspect of created (angelic) mind, whereas Sapience is a Divine attribute personified or even the Second Person of the Trinity, from a particular point of view. I cannot find anything either confused or heretical in this poem. The Angelology is that of Dante and ultimately of Dionysius. The Christian saints in bliss and the Platonic Forms are conceptions which, though they do not imply, do not contradict, one another; and if both exist, where should they be except in the supercelestial place?—which is as much as to say, in no *Place* at all.

The length of this discussion must not be taken to mean that I reckon the *Four Hymns* among Spenser's best works. Their riot of syncretism, for reasons which I shall explain later, is not to be counted as a fault. Their confusions produce only local discomfort. Nor in their simpler passages—the medieval praise of love or the Christian gratitude for Redemption—do they lack honest and wholesome poetry. The trouble is that honest and wholesome poetry is utterly inadequate for the themes that Spenser is attempting. You cannot carry a reader beyond the flaming bounds of space and time simply by sincerity and conscientious workmanship. Poetry that deals with such towering conceptions as these must be either a continuous blaze of dazzling splendour or else fail completely. Great subjects do not make great poems; usually, indeed, the reverse.

With the *Four Hymns* our account of Spenser's minor poems

N

may end, but two pieces of prose must be mentioned before we turn to the *Faerie Queene.*

In 1592 Cuthbert Burbie published *A most excellent Dialogue . . . by Plato the Phylosopher . . . Translated . . . by Edw. Spenser.* It is a version, mainly through the Latin, of the *Axiochus,* and many scholars suppose it to be by the poet. The attribution to an Edward, not an Edmund, of that name is not fatal to their view; but it contains passages of verse translation which I do not believe that Edmund Spenser could have written at any stage of his career.

A View of the present state of Ireland was certainly written in 1596, though never printed till 1633. In it Spenser is speaking chiefly, but not exclusively, as a civil servant and a supporter of Lord Grey. His political theory (if that is not too grand a name for it) depends on a sharp antithesis beween Natural Law—'the streight rule of right' and 'Ius Polliticum'. The latter, though 'not of yt self Iust', becomes so 'by applycacion or rather necessitie . . . and this onelye respecte maketh all lawes iust'. From such principles it follows of course that 'all is the Conquerors, as *Tullie* to *Brutus* saith' and that 'a mischief' is better than an 'inconuenience'. The morality of his own plan for the reduction of Ireland has been shown to be not so indefensible as quotations might make it appear, but any stronger apologia would be a burden beyond my shoulders. *Let Dryghten deme.* As literature, the *View* does not rank very high. Spenser made little attempt to breathe dramatic life into the dialogue form. The prose, despite a few vivid phrases, is Drab. Even in describing things that he loves, Spenser has none of the liveliness of Harrison: the sentences are long and nerveless. Yet his essay will always have a certain interest not only for historians but for students of Spenser's poetry. His religious views are elusive, and he twice professes his laic ignorance; but they are certainly not those of a Protestant missionary nor of a bigot. He is sure that popery is not 'the pure springe of lyfe' but 'nothing doubtes' the salvation of many Papists. He loves Ireland strongly, in his own way, pronouncing Ulster 'a most bewtifull and sweete countrie as any is vnder heauen'. And he gives free rein to those antiquarian interests so characteristic of his age. The 'pleasure' of such studies is a recurrent theme and Eudoxus makes it clear that Spenser hoped to publish a substantial prose work on Irish antiquities.

Spenser did not live to complete the great poem which was his life's work. It would be salutary if instead of talking about the *Faerie Queene* we sometimes talked of Fragment A (I–III), Fragment B (IV–VI) and Fragment C (Mutabilitie). This would help to remind us that the inconsistencies we find in it are those of a partially written work. The letter to Raleigh prefixed to Fragment A gives us, no doubt, the design that was uppermost in Spenser's mind when he wrote that letter. It had not, in its entirety, been in his mind at all stages during the composition of that Fragment. It had been in some degree abandoned when he wrote Fragment C. There is nothing surprising about this. There is a stage in the invention of any long story at which the outsider would see nothing but chaos. Numerous alternatives, written, half-written, and unwritten (the latter possibly the most influential of all) ferment together. Passages which no longer fit the main scheme are retained because they seem too good to lose: they will be harmonized somehow later on if the author lives to complete his work. Even a final revision often leaves ragged edges; unnoticed by generations of readers but pointed out in the end by professional scholars. There is a psychological law which makes it harder for the author to detect them than for the scholar. To the scholar an event in fiction is as firm a *datum* as an event in real life: he did not choose and cannot change it. The author has chosen it and changed it and seen it in its molten condition passing from one shape to another. It has as many rivals for its place in his memory as it had for its place in the final text. This cause of error is of course aggravated if the story is labyrinthine, as Spenser's was. And it is aggravated still further if his professional duties permit him to work on his story only at rare intervals. Returning to work on an interrupted story is not like returning to work on a scholarly article. Facts, however long the scholar has left them untouched in his notebook, will still prove the same conclusions; he has only to start the engine running again. But the story is an organism: it goes on surreptitiously growing or decaying while your back is turned. If it decays, the resumption of work is like trying to coax back to life an almost extinguished fire, or to recapture the confidence of a shy animal which you had only partially tamed at your last visit. But if (as is far more probable) it grows, proliferates, 'wantons in its prime', then you will come back to find it

> Changed like a garden in the heat of spring
> After an eight-days' absence.

Fertile chaos has obliterated the paths. I do not know whether Spenser could have triumphed over all these difficulties if he had lived to revise his poem; but the actual imperfections are no more than we might expect. At the same time I think it quite impossible to reconstruct historically the phases in his invention of which particular inconsistencies are, so to speak, the fossils. The process is far too subtle and complicated for that.

Formally considered, the *Faerie Queene* is the fusion of two kinds, the medieval allegory and the more recent romantic epic of the Italians. Because it is allegory, and allegory neither strictly religious nor strictly erotic but universal, every part of the poet's experience can be brought in: because it is romantic epic, a certain unity is immediately imposed on all that enters it, for all is embodied in romantic adventures. 'Faerie land' itself provides the unity—a unity not of plot but of *milieu*. A *priori* the ways of Faerie Land might seem 'so exceeding spatious and wide' that such a unity amounted to nothing, but this is not found to be so. Few poems have a greater harmony of atmosphere. The multiplicity of the stories, far from impairing the unity, supports it; for just that multiplicity, that packed fullness of 'vehement adventures', is the quality of Faerie Land; as tragedy is the quality of Hardy's Wessex.

When I last wrote about the *Faerie Queene* some fifteen years ago, I do not think I sufficiently emphasized the originality and fruitfulness of this structural invention. Perhaps it can be best brought out by considering the problems it solves. Spenser, let us say, has experienced in himself and observed in others sensual temptation; frivolous gallantry; the imprisonment and frustration of long, serious, and self-condemned passions; happy love; and religious melancholy. You could, perhaps, get all this into a lengthy, biographical novel, but that form did not exist in his time. You could get it into half a dozen plays; but only if your talent were theatrical, and only if you were ready to see these states of the heart (which were Spenser's real concern) almost smothered by the Elizabethan demands for an exciting plot and comic relief. But in Faerie Land it is all quite simple. All the states become people or places in that country. You meet the first in the Bower of Acrasia, the second in Malecasta's castle, the third in the House of Busirane, the fourth on Mount Acidale, and the fifth in Orgoglio's dungeons and Despair's cave. And this is not scissors and paste work. Such bowers, such castles, such ogres are just what we require to meet in Faerie Land: they are as necessary for filling the country as the country is for accommodating them. Whatever incidental faults the poem may have, it has, so to speak, a healthy constitution: the matter and the form fit each other like hand and glove.

This primary structural idea is reinforced by two others, the first internal to each book, and the second striding across from book to book through the whole poem. Thus in each book Spenser decided that there should be what I have called an 'allegorical core' (or shrine, or inner stage) where the theme of that book would appear disentangled from the complex adventures and reveal its unity: the House of Holiness in I, the House of Alma in II, the Garden of Adonis in III, the Temple of Venus in IV, the Church of Isis in V, Mount Acidale in VI, and the whole appeal of Mutabilitie in the unfinished book. (Since the position of the core within the book is variable, no conclusion can be based on the numbering of those two cantos.) Next in dignity to the core in each book comes the main allegorical story of the book (Guyon's or Calidore's quest). Beyond that is a loose fringe of stories which may be fully allegorical (like Scudamore's visit to the cottage of Care) or merely typical (like Paridell's seduction of Hellenore) or not allegorical at all (like the story told by the Squire of Dames to Satyrane). Thus the appearance, so necessary to the poem's quality, of pathless wandering is largely a work of deliberate and successful illusion. Spenser, for reasons I have indicated, may not always know where he is going as regards the particular stories: as regards the symphony of moods, the careful arrangement of different degrees of allegory and different degrees of seriousness, he is always in command.

The second of the subordinate structural ideas is, of course, the quest of Arthur for Gloriana. In approaching Spenser's Arthur we must empty our minds of many associations. Very few places in Spenser's work show with certainty the influence of Malory, and most of them come late; in the Sixth Book of the *Faerie Queene* or the *State of Ireland*. His Merlin can be fully accounted for by Ariosto. If he had not used the form *Igrayne* (for Geoffrey's *Igerne*) in the *Letter to Raleigh* we might almost conclude that he had never met Malory's book till late in life. But the truth is that Malory's Arthur would not serve the Elizabethans' turn. He was too closely connected with the old reli-

gion and too little connected with later English history. The
Arthur whom Camden in 1586 pointed out as suitable matter
for a poet was a different figure. The same blood flowed in his
veins as in Elizabeth's. In opposing the Saxons he had very
nearly been opposing the Pope. At Henry VII's coronation the
Red Dragon of Cadwallader had been advanced, and Henry's
son was named Arthur (as Bacon says) 'in honour of the British
race of which himself was'. Arthur's conquests supported our
claims to Ireland. There may even have been in Spenser's mind
associations of a more homely and *bourgeois* sort. Mulcaster in
later life—and perhaps when Spenser sat under him—belonged
to an archers' club in London who called themselves the knights
not of King Arthur but of *Prince* (the *magnificent* Prince) Arthur.

Such an Arthur belonged to the antiquaries and to the patriots
far more than to Malory; but even from this new Arthur
Spenser turned away. He invented *enfances* for his hero which
had no precedent either in Tudor or in medieval tradition. His
Arthur was to be a lover endlessly seeking an unknown mistress
whom he had loved in a vision. For that theme he was presumably indebted to *Arthur of Little Britain*; whose hero, it
must be remembered, was not the British king at all. But it is in
Spenser that the myth of the visionary mistress effectively enters
modern literature. His prince is the precursor of Novalis's Hein-
rich, of Alastor, and of Keats's Endymion. Allegorically, we are
told, he is Magnificence; and it is clear that, in so far as this
means anything Aristotelian, it means Aristotle's Magnanimity.
He is seeking Gloriana who is glory, and glory is honour, and
honour is the goal of Aristotle's Magnanimous Man. The name
of his foster-father, Timon, underlines this. But then glory and
honour are difficult words. We found in Douglas's *Palace* that
the sight of true Honour was the vision of God. We know, if we
are Christians, that glory is what awaits the faithful in heaven.
We know, if we are Platonists—and a reading of Boethius
would make us Platonists enough for this—that every inferior
good attracts us only by being an image of the single real good.
The false Florimell attracts by being like the true, the true
Florimell by being like Beauty itself. Earthly glory would never
have moved us but by being a shadow or *idolon* of the Divine
Glory, in which we are called to participate. Gloriana is 'the
idole of her Makers great magnificence'. The First Fair is
desired in all that is desired. It is only, I think, in the light of

such conceptions that the quest of Spenser's Arthur can be understood. Arthur is an embodiment of what Professor Nygren calls 'Eros religion', the thirst of the soul for the Perfection beyond the created universe. Only this explains the terms in which Spenser describes his preliminary vision of Gloriana (I. ix). The laughter of all Nature, the grassy bed shared with the 'royall Mayd', the ravishing words ('no living man like wordes did ever heare') must, it seems to me, be taken for a picture not of nascent ambition and desire for fame but either of natural or celestial love; and they are certainly not simply a picture of the former. Only this explains the scene in which Arthur pursues Florimell (III. i, iv). Those who accuse him of inconstancy forget that he had seen the glory only in a vision by night. Hence, following Florimell,

> Oft did he wish that Lady faire mote bee
> His Faery Queene for whom he did complaine,
> Or that his Faery Queene were such as shee (III. iv. 54).

The best parallel to this is the repeated (and always disappointed) belief of the Trojans in *Aeneid*, III, that they have already found the *mansuram urbem*. It is in the very nature of the Platonic quest and the Eros religion that the soul cannot know her true aim till she has achieved it. The seeker must advance, with the possibility at each step of error, beyond the false Florimells to the true, and beyond the true Florimell to the Glory. Only such an interpretation will explain the deep seriousness and the explicitly religious language of Arthur's subsequent soliloquy (55-60).

We must not, of course, forget that Gloriana is also Queen Elizabeth. This was much less chilling and shocking to the sixteenth century than it is to us. Quite apart from any prudent desire to flatter his prince (in an age when flattery had a ceremonial element in it) or from any romantic loyalty which he may have felt and probably did feel as an individual, Spenser knew that even outside poetry all reigning sovereigns were *ex officio* vicegerents and images of God. No orthodox person doubted that in this sense Elizabeth was 'an idole' of the divine magnificence. It is also easy to misunderstand the sentence 'Gloriana is Elizabeth'. She *is* Elizabeth in a sense which does not prevent Belphoebe from also being Elizabeth nor Elizabeth from being also a remote, unborn descendant of Arthegall and

Britomart who are contemporaries of Gloriana. Modern readers, trained on a strict *roman-à-clef* like Dryden's *Absalom*, hardly know how to sit lightly enough to what is called the 'historical allegory' in Spenser. 'Historical parallels' or 'fugitive historical allusions' would be better names. The scene we have just been discussing is a good example. Arthur may at some moments and in some senses 'be' Leicester: but the poet is certainly not meaning to proclaim to the public that Elizabeth had shared her favourite's bed.[1] (For though Arthur met Gloriana in a vision, it was not quite a vision: there was 'pressed gras where she had lyen'.) In general it must be remembered that the identifications of Gloriana and Belphoebe are the only two in the whole poem that have Spenser's authority. That of Duessa was made so early that we may take it for certain. As for the rest, it is well to remember Spenser's own warning 'how doubtfully all allegories may be construed'. He can never have expected most of his historical meanings to be clear to more than a privileged minority of readers: it is reasonable to suppose that he seldom wrote a canto which depended on them for its main interest. No poet would embark his fame in such an unseaworthy vessel. Nor do I think that attempts in our own day to recover such meanings are at all likely to be fruitful. Great learning and skill have been spent on them. Every increase in our knowledge suggests a fresh allegory. If historical parallels were harder to come by they would convince more; but their multiplicity rather suggests to me how hard it is for a poet to feign an event which will not resemble some real event—or half a dozen real events.

In addition to the structural elements which I have already mentioned, Spenser at one time thought of stiffening his poem by dovetailing into it the Virtues out of Aristotle's *Ethics*. He was thinking that way when he wrote the Letter to Raleigh as a preface for Fragment A. Presumably he had not thought of Aristotle when he wrote Book I, and had ceased thinking of Aristotle when he decided to write a legend of Constancy. Aristotle's doctrine of the Mean is (rather dully) allegorized in II. ii. But the Aristotelian influence on Spenser is fitful and superficial. The *Ethics* was not at all his kind of book. His

---

[1] A friend points out that, after all, nothing but 'words' is said to have passed between Arthur and Gloriana. This makes the ice a little less thin: but nothing like thick enough for safe skating.

treatment of Justice suggests that he had forgotten, or never read, most of what Aristotle says about it.

Hitherto I have been speaking about the structural or (in that sense) 'poetic' ideas of the *Faerie Queene*, the inventions which make it the poem it is. Critics often, however, speak of a poet's 'ideas' in quite a different sense, meaning his opinions or (in extreme cases) his philosophy. These are not often so important in a work of art as its 'idea' or 'ideas' in the first sense; the first two books of *Gulliver* depend much more on the 'idea' of big and little men than on any great novelty or profundity in Swift's 'ideas' about politics and ethics. Spenser's thought, however, has been so variously estimated that we cannot pass it over without some discussion.

Some scholars believe that in parts of the *Faerie Queene* they can find Spenser systematically expounding the doctrines of a school. But if so, the school can hardly be defined as anything narrower than Platonized Protestantism. He certainly believes in Predestination. 'Why shouldst thou then despeire, that chosen art?' says Una to the Redcrosse Knight (1. ix. 53). But this will hardly make Spenser Calvinist as distinct from Lutheran, nor either as distinct from Augustinian, or simply Pauline. It is also true that the virtues we meet in the House of Holiness——Humility, Zeal, Reverence, Faith, Hope, Charity, Mercy, and Contemplation—can all be paralleled in Calvin's *Institutio*; but they are not arranged in the same order, and the things themselves would be likely to occur in any Christian teaching whatever. It is argued, again, that the quests on which the faerie knights are engaged, and especially the scene (1. x. 63) in which Contemplation commands St. George to turn back from the vision of the New Jerusalem and finish the 'royal maides bequeathed care', reflect the activism of Protestant (and, particularly, Calvinist) ethics and its rejection of the contemplative life. They may: but it is not certain. The quests of the knights are after all allegorical. A combat with Error or with the Old Dragon does not necessarily symbolize the active life. St. George's return from the mountain of Contemplation is quite as close to the return of Plato's 'guardians' (*Republic*, 519 d et seq.) as to anything in Protestant theology. And in any case, St. George in the poem must return because the story must go on. It is equally true that Spenser asserts total depravity ('If any strength we have, it is to ill', 1. x. 1) and 'loathes' this world 'this state of life so tickle' (*Mut.* viii. 1), and that this fits well enough with Calvinist theology. But hardly less well with Lutheran. Indeed expressions very similar can be found in nearly all Christian writers. And something not unlike them can be found even in Platonism. When scholars claim that there is a profound difference of temper between Platonism and these world-renouncing attitudes, I do not know what they mean. There is difference of course; but few pagan systems adapt themselves so nearly to total depravity and *contemptus mundi* as the Platonic. The emotional overtones of the words 'Renaissance Platonism' perhaps help us to forget that Plato's thought is at bottom other-worldly, pessimistic, and ascetic; far more ascetic than Protestant-ism. The natural universe is, for Plato, a world of shadows, of Helens false as Spenser's false Florimell (*Rep.* 586 A–C); the soul has come into it at all only because she lost her wings in a better place (*Phaedr.* 246 D–248 E); and the life of wisdom, while we are here, is a practice or exercise of death (*Phaed.* 80 D–81 A).

I am not arguing that Spenser was not a Calvinist. *A priori* it is very likely that he was. But his poetry is not so written as to enable us to pick out his own beliefs in distinct separation from kindred beliefs. When a modern writer is didactic he endeavours, like Shaw or M. Sartre, to throw his own 'ideas' into sharp relief, distinguishing them from the orthodoxy which he wants to attack. Spenser is not at all like that. Political circumstances lead him at times to stress his opposition to Roman Christianity; and if pressed, he would no doubt admit that where the pagan doctors differed from the Christian, the pagan doctors were wrong. But in general he is concerned with agreements, not differences. He is, like nearly all his contemporaries, a syncre-tist. He never dreamed of expounding something he could call 'his philosophy'. His business was to embody in moving images the common wisdom. It is this that may easily arouse distrust of him in a modern reader. We feel that the man who could weld together, or think that he had welded together, so many diverse elements, Protestant, chivalric, Platonic, Ovidian, Lucretian, and pastoral, must have been very vague and shallow in each. But here we need to remember the difference between his basic assumption and ours. It is scepticism, despair of ob-jective truth, which has trained us to regard diverse philosophies as historical phenomena, 'period pieces', not to be pitted against one another but each to be taken in its purest form and savoured on the historical palate. Thinking thus, we despise syncretism as we despise Victorian Gothic. Spenser could not feel thus, because he assumed from the outset that the truth about the universe was knowable and in fact known. If that were so, then of course you would expect agreements between the great teachers of all ages just as you expect agreements between the reports of different explorers. The agreements are the important thing, the useful and interesting thing. Differences, far from delighting us as precious manifestations of some unique temper or culture, are mere errors which can be neglected. Such intellectual optimism may be mistaken; but granted the mistake, a sincere and serious poet is bound to be, from our point of view, a syncretist. I believe that Sidney and Shakespeare are in this respect like Spenser, and to grasp this is one of the first duties of their critics. I do not think Shakespeare wrote a single line to express 'his' ideas. What some call his philosophy, he would have called common knowledge.

It is this that makes the thought of the *Faerie Queene*, as Professor Osgood says, 'somehow unmeasurable'. Spenser expected his readers to find in it not his philosophy but their own experience—everyone's experience—loosened from its particular contexts by the universalizing power of allegory. It is, no doubt, true that Spenser was far from being an exact thinker or a precise scholar in any department of human knowledge. Whatever he had tried to write would have had a certain vagueness about it. But most poetry is vague about something. In Milton the theology is clear, the images vague. In Racine the passions and the logic of events are clear, but the 'manners' vague and generalized. What is clear in Spenser is the image; Pyrochles beating the water while he cries 'I burne, I burne, I burne', or Disdain strutting, crane-like, on tiptoes, with legs that break but do not bleed, and as good as new, still glaring and still tiptoed, when he has been set up again. That is why it is at once so true and so misleading to call his poetry dream-like; its images have the violent clarity and precision which we often find in actual dreams, but not the dimness and evasiveness which the overtones of the word *dream-like* (based more on waking reverie than real dreaming) usually call up. These images are not founded on, but merely festooned with, philosophical conceptions. In IV. x we can find, if that is our interest, the following: (1) Love as friendship; (2) Venus distinct from Love (or Cupid) as mother

from son; (3) Love (Eros) as the brother of Hate (Eris) derived
ultimately from Empedocles (32); (4) the hermaphroditic
Venus whose obscure origins have been studied by Miss J. W.
Bennett (41); (5) Love naturalistically conceived in lines
adapted from Lucretius (44 et seq.). But Spenser did not set out
by collecting these concepts, still less by attempting a philosophical synthesis of them. His theme is courtship and his model
is medieval erotic allegory. How a gentle knight found the island
fortress of true love and overcame its defenders and won meek
Amoret—that is the substance. And that is all clear and vivid—
the bridge with its corbes and pendants, the door where the
porter Doubt peeps 'through a crevis small', the ubiquitous
sound of running water, the inner paradise, the Loves fluttering
round the statue, and the capture of the beloved. The philosophical matter merely adds a suggestion of depth, as if shadows
of old thought played about the temple: just as fugitive memories
of Donne or Dante or Patmore or Meredith might play about
our own minds during a real love affair. I do not mean that
Spenser thought of it quite in that way. He was too serious and
too syncretistic. Everything that the wise had said about Love
was worth attending to. He would not have said 'Let us shade in
here a little Platonism and there a little Epicureanism'. He
would have said 'Proclus *in Timaeum* doth report . . . Orpheus
hath it thus . . . read the like in that place of Ficinus'. But the
result is much the same. It produces that depth or thickness
which is one of the excellences of the *Faerie Queene*.

This is why work on Spenser's philosophical and iconographi-
cal background seems to me so much more rewarding than
work on his historical allegory. But though such studies are
enrichments they are not necessary for all readers. For those
who can surrender themselves simply to the story Spenser himself will provide guidance enough. The allegory that really
matters is usually unmistakable. Hazlitt can hardly have meant
what he said on that subject. Few poets are so radically allegorical as Spenser: it is significant that one of the few words he
has given to our language, Braggadocchio, though intended by
him as the name of a man, has become the name of a quality.
But it is not impossible that many who thought they were obeying Hazlitt have read the poetry aright. They receive the
allegory so easily that they forget they have done so, as a man
in health is unaware of breathing.

It has been the fate of the *Faerie Queene* to be attacked where it is strongest. The plan, the story, the invention are triumphant. If they have faults, they are such faults as never deterred any reader except those who dislike romance and would not be allured to read it by any perfections.

In his own day Spenser's narrative technique was highly individual; it has proved so widely serviceable in later fiction that we ignore this. The opening ('A gentle knight was pricking on the playne') seems to us the most ordinary thing in the world. We have seen a hundred novels begun in the same way; 'Dombey sat in the corner of the darkened room in the great armchair by the bedside', or 'It was early on a fine summer's day near the end of the eighteenth century when a young man of genteel appearance', &c. This method—the immediate presentation of a figure already in action—was not, however, the method of Spenser's predecessors and contemporaries. He had perhaps no perfect model of it except in Heliodorus; and Shakespeare, in his two narrative pieces, is almost his only follower within the sixteenth century. Homer is not quite so direct. Chaucer's *Troilus* does not show us Criseyde kneeling to Hector until line 105. The *Canterbury Tales* do not reach concrete particulars till line 20. Sackville's *Induction* begins with eleven stanzas of description and reflection. In the *Barons Wars* we wade through pages of political prolegomena to reach anything like a scene. *Hero and Leander* hardly becomes a story before line 156. Ariosto does not rise from synopsis to real presentation till his tenth stanza. And the promise of Spenser's opening line is kept in the canto that follows. Nineteenth-century critics, bred on *Marmion* and *The Bride of Abydos*, might think it leisurely; to an Elizabethan, reading it for the first time, the businesslike progression, the absence of what schoolboys call 'gas', must have appeared almost startling. Every line adds. We feel at once that the author has a tale to tell. The business-like progression creates faith. Hence, as Hazlitt (with my italics) says, 'In reading the Faery Queen, you *see* a little withered old man by a wood-side opening a wicket, a giant, and a dwarf', &c.

No critics seem to me farther astray than those who deny that Spenser is an essentially narrative poet. No one loves him who does not love his story; outside the proems to the books and cantos he scarcely writes a line that is not for the story's sake. His style is to be judged as the style of a story-teller. This is one

reason why, though eminently a poet of Golden matter, he does
not at all continuously exemplify the Golden manner. There is
unfortunately another reason: Spenser at times relapses into
the vices of the Drab Age.

We therefore have to distinguish three conditions of his style,
two good, and one bad. Here is a specimen of the bad:

> Tho when they had long time there taken rest,
> Sir Arthegall, who all this while was bound
> Upon an hard adventure yet in quest,
> Fit time for him thence to depart it found (IV. vi. 42).

It might come from the *Mirror for Magistrates*. Not one word in it
speaks to the senses or to the emotions. It is dry information, far
worse than prose because the language has been cruelly racked
to fit it into metre. That is Spenser in his Drab condition. Here
is Spenser in his Golden condition:

> By this the Northerne wagoner had set
> His sevenfold teme behind the stedfast starre
> That was in Ocean waves yet never wet
> But firme is fixed and sendeth light from farre
> To all that in the wide deep wandring are . . . (I. ii. 1).

That is plain gold; the unsubtle yet delicious flow, the frank
(yet here not excessive) alliteration, the frequent images, the
Homeric echoes. The last line here, like the last line of the
previous example, has an inversion. Yet the effect is quite
different. The one, with its clustered consonants and emotional
flatness, is felt as mere clumsiness; the other, coming in a line
full of melody and calling up great distances, adds a chant-like
solemnity. But thirdly, there is Spenser not Golden, not sugared
at all (in his manner) but thoroughly good, pressing his tale:

> And there beside of marble stone was built
> An Altare carv'd with cunning ymagery,
> On which trew Christians blood was often spilt . . . (I. viii. 36).

Or again:

> He durst not enter into th' open greene
> For dread of them unawares to be descryde,
> For breaking of their daunce if he were seene;
> But in the covert of the wood did byde,
> Beholding all. . . . (VI. x. 11).

It is as direct as good medieval verse: not to be lingered over,
carrying us equably forward. Much of the *Faerie Queene* is like

that; a 'poetry of statement'. The typical Spenserian line tells you what somebody did or wore or where he went. Thus Spenser both falls beneath the Golden norm by defect and is also free to go outside for his own good purposes. We class him among Golden poets for his matter—the whole story is a Golden invention—and because he can often command the Golden style. His lapses into the Drab cannot be palliated in the poem, however we may excuse them historically in the man. But his successful departures from the Golden manner are an added excellence. In an age when poetry was soon to be almost too poetical, he kept open the great thoroughfare of verse for long-distance travellers in workday clothes. Thus, while he touches hands with the pure Golden poets, he also touches hands with Chaucer, Byron, and Crabbe. Wordsworth acknowledged him as a model.

It will be noticed that speeches in the *Faerie Queene* are usually bad if they are meant to express personal passion, and good if they are essentially chants or meditations. The more nearly Spenser approaches to drama the less he succeeds. He does not know the rhetoric of the passions and substitutes that of the schools. This is because he is not the poet of passions but of moods. I use that word to mean those prolonged states of the 'inner weather' which may colour our world for a week or even a month. That is what Spenser does best. In reading him we are reminded not of falling in love but of being in love; not of the moment which brought despair but of the despair which followed it; not of our sudden surrenders to temptation but of our habitual vices; not of religious conversion but of the religious life. Despite the apparent remoteness of his scenes, he is, far more than the dramatists, the poet of ordinary life, of the thing that goes on. Few of us have been in Lear's situation or Hamlet's: the houses and bowers and gardens of the *Faerie Queene*, both good and evil, are always at hand.

From what has been said it follows that those who wish to attack Spenser will be wise to concentrate on his style. There alone he is seriously vulnerable. I have made no attempt to conceal or defend those places where, on any view, he must be admitted to write dully, shrilly, or clumsily. But we come to something more controversial when we consider that quality which, in his best passages no less than in his worst, will alienate many modern readers—the absence of pressure or tension. There are, indeed, metrical variations, more numerous than we always remember. But the general effect is tranquil; line by line, unremarkable. His voice never breaks, he does not pluck you by the elbow, unexpected collocations of ideas do not pour out red hot. There is no irony or ambiguity. Some now would deny the name of poetry to writing of which this must be admitted. Let us not dispute about the name. It is more important to realize that this style (when it is true to itself) is suitable for Spenser's purpose. He needs to create a certain quiet in our minds. The great images, the embodiments, as I have said, of moods or whole phases of experience, rise best if we are not flurried. A still, brooding attention, not a perpetual excitement, is what he demands. It is also probably true that the lack of tension in his verse reflects the lack of tension in his mind. His poetry does not express (though of course it often presents) discord and struggle: it expresses harmony. No poet, I think, was ever less like an Existentialist. He discovered early what things he valued, and there is no sign that his allegiance ever wavered. He was of course often, perhaps usually, disappointed. The actual court did not conform to his standard of courtesy: mutability, if philosophically accepted from the outset, might yet prove unexpectedly bitter to the taste. But disappointment is not necessarily conflict. It did not for Spenser discredit the things of which he was disappointed. It might breed melancholy or indignation, but not doubt. Why, after all, should it? Spenser inherited the Platonic and Christian dualism: heaven was set over against earth, being against becoming, eternity against time. He knew from the outset that the lower, half-unreal world must always fail to copy its archetype exactly. The worst that experience could do was to show that the degree of failure was greater than one had anticipated. If he had thought that the objects of his desire were merely 'ideals', private, subjective, constructions of his own mind, then the actual world might have thrown doubt on those ideals. But he thought no such thing. The Existentialist feels *Angst* because he thinks that man's nature (and therefore his relation to all things) has to be created or invented, without guidance, at each moment of decision. Spenser thought that man's nature was given, discoverable, and discovered; he did not feel *Angst*. He was often sad: but not, at bottom, worried. To many of my readers such a state of mind must appear a total illusion. If they cannot suspend their disbelief, they should leave Spenser alone; there are plenty of other authors to read. They must not, however, suppose that he was under an illusion about the historical world. That is not where he differs from them. He differs from them in thinking that it is not the whole story. His tranquillity is a robust tranquillity that 'tolerates the indignities of time', refusing (if we may put the matter in his terms) to be deceived by them, recognizing them as truths, indeed, but only the truths of 'a foolish world'. He would not have called himself 'the poet of our waking dreams': rather the poet of our waking.

What, then, should be our final judgement of Spenser? That question is, in one sense, unanswerable; in another, almost too easy to be worth asking. Among those who shared, or still share, the culture for which he wrote, and which he helped to create, there is no dispute about his greatness. He never, while that culture lasted, suffered any eclipse comparable to that which Donne suffered in the eighteenth century, or Pope in the nine-teenth. There are only minor fluctuations in his fame. Even for Rymer he is among the men 'whose intellectuals were of so great a making' that they may outlast 'founders of empires'. Even Dryden acknowledges that 'no man was ever born with so great a genius'. Pope imitated him as if he were an ancient. Within the older English tradition he is only less secure and central than Shakespeare and Milton. But of course this gives us no assurance that he will be mentioned a hundred years hence. His world has ended and his fame may end with it. To attempt an agreed estimate across the chasms that have now opened would be futile. There may—or may not—come a time when the culture for which Spenser wrote and the culture which is now replacing it can be compared, by men to whom English is a dead language, as coolly as we now compare two periods of ancient Egyptian history. At present it is not possible. We can only say that those who in any degree belong to the old culture still find in the ordered exuberance of the *Faerie Queene* an invigorating refreshment which no other book can supply. Doctor I. A. Richards's conception of a poem as a health-giving adjustment of impulses may not cover all poetry—I am not sure. But it certainly covers the *Faerie Queene*. Perhaps that is why, though it may fail to gain some readers, it seldom loses those it has once gained. I never meet a man who says that he *used to* like the *Faerie Queene*.

PROSE IN THE 'GOLDEN' PERIOD

IN the last quarter of the century we find a greatly increased
output of literature. There is on the whole a remarkable
improvement in quality; but even if this had not been so,
the mere quantity would be striking. Part of the explanation is
that literature is now finding its feet as a commercial art and
printers are eager for saleable copy. Many of the authors are
victims of that academic overproduction which Mulcaster depre-
cated, men who have been helped through the universities by
friends who could help them no further and who try to live (if
nothing better turns up) by the pen. The more fortunate of them
make plays for the new theatres; the others depend on the patron
and the bookseller. There are also, of course, many 'gentle',
pious, or learned authors who write from other motives.

Among the forms which commercial prose took at this time
fiction holds a very important place; so important that we may
wonder why this vein was so little exploited again before the
eighteenth century. But the truth is that Elizabethan fiction
points only rarely and uncertainly towards the novel properly so called. It appealed to rather different tastes and the
eighteenth-century novelists had to make a new start. The other
dominant form was the pamphlet; if indeed we can call it a
form. Often it contains matter that might well have been served
as fiction: presumably the taste for confessed fiction was then
(as it still is) rarer than the taste for sensational reading which
claims to be 'news'. The lowest sort of reader wants to be
assured (like Shakespeare's Mopsa) that what he reads is true.
Hence the pamphlet absorbed much that would now go into
the daily or Sunday papers; murders, apparitions, spy-stories,
executions, advertisement. Mr. H. Platt of Lincoln's Inn, in his
Discovery of certain English Wants (1595) finds himself 'forced even
by the bond of charity . . . and the tender loue and affection
which he owes his natiue countrey' to draw attention to the great
utility of 'colebals' and of an incredibly cheap and long-lived
candle that can be 'sodainly made'; interested readers may get
his address from the publisher. Controversy, if properly seasoned
with personal abuse, was a good line; a man who had bought

any one number of, say, the Harvey–Nashe flyting, would find it hard not to buy the next. Moralizing, preferably of an indignant, censorious kind, was highly popular. It need hardly be added that I attach no note of infamy to any text in calling it commercial. Many of the best books have been written for money.

I will deal first with the pamphlets, and where a pamphleteer has also written fiction, his work in that kind, if of sufficient importance, will be reserved for later treatment.

I

Stephen Gosson (1554–1624) and his *School of Abuse* (1579) are remembered because in that pamphlet he contributed to what is sometimes called the puritan attack on the theatre; a subject naturally interesting to historians of the drama. Taken in conjunction with his other works, it appears in a slightly different light. Gosson was no puritan; he came from Corpus, Oxford, the fountain head of pure Canterbury doctrine; in his sermon, *The Trumpet of War* (1598) he quotes Aquinas and Cajetan. At Corpus he imbibed, along with Anglicanism, the latest rhetoric, attending the lectures of Rainoldus who is the greatest single influence on his work. He was the son of a poor man and failed to get a fellowship; finding himself presently in London with empty pockets, he became a playwright. His plays appear to have been failures and have not survived. According to Meres, he also wrote pastorals; and however we rate Meres's authority, it is not unlikely that he did. Then, just as Lyly had done, he became a stern moralist, attacking in the *School of Abuse* not only drama but the arts in general, and working up his attack into a euphuistic oration well stuffed with classical anecdotes. I know nothing about his sincerity, and he may not have known much himself. There is some evidence to suggest that he was paid for writing the *School* by the Lord Mayor and Aldermen: but that is not inconsistent with a real change of his opinion. What Gosson has not changed is his general literary character. We must not contrast his plays as 'art' with his pamphlet as 'theology'. In the *School* he is still the artist, still indeed the commercial artist, catering for a well established taste in rhetoric. It advertises itself on the title-page as not only 'profitable for all that wyll follow vertue' but also 'pleasaunt for gentlemen that fauour learning'. The dedication to Sidney is significant. Gosson is just as modish and saleable in attacking plays as he had hoped to be in writing them. I doubt whether, at this stage, his quarrel with the players was very serious; later, when they had hit back, he warmed to his work, but in 1579 he may have valued his case against the stage mainly as a suitable peg for *chria* and simile. His next work, the *Ephemerides of Phialo* (in the same year) is equally moral and equally in the fashion. It derives from *Euphues*, and hangs many sententious discourses on a frail trellis of narrative. To it he added *A Short Apology* for the *School*. In 1582 he returned to the attack in *Plays Confuted*. By now (for all controversies gather momentum) he seems to be more in earnest. In 1595 he returned to poetry in the worthless book variously known as *A Glass to view the Pride of vainglorious women* and the *Quips for Upstart Gentlewomen*. Some critics have thought its coarseness inconsistent with the moral severity which Gosson elsewhere displays: but this is a misunderstanding. In those days it was the moralist who was expected to call a whore a whore; it was the 'vayne', 'wanton', or 'filthie' poet who called her Amaryllis and gave her goddesses for companions. Gosson's latest work, the sermon, is his best. The *School*, if taken seriously as argument, must be judged feeble in the extreme. Gosson mentions the 'right vse of auncient Poetrie' but gives us no criterion for distinguishing this from the later abuse. He admits that various ancient censures do not apply to the theatre of his own day but never answers an objection so apparently damaging to his main thesis. His pamphlet is hardly explicable except on the assumption that his main, almost his sole, purpose was rhetorical display. We take Gosson far too seriously if we try to give him a place in the history of English criticism.

The same is true of Thomas Lodge (1558?–1625) replying to Gosson, apparently in 1579. This reply exists in two copies only, both corrupt and both without title-page. Lodge, as we know, was refused a licence and the surviving texts are specimens of a privately printed and 'vnperfect coppye'. Its title, almost certainly, was *Honest Excuses*. It is, like Gosson's *School*, mainly a display of rhetoric, sometimes euphuistic, sometimes Biblical, and always heavily loaded with unreliable learning. Lodge's defence of poetry is substantially Boccaccio's. The authorship of this pamphlet has been questioned. But we know that Lodge answered Gosson and we know that his answer was suppressed: this book is an answer to Gosson and this book appears to have been suppressed. Nor can I see any internal evidence that it is not by Lodge. This is not demonstrative proof but it is as strong as the circumstances entitle us to look for.

To follow the details of the controversy which thus began is hardly, I think, the literary historian's business. As literary criticism it was not serious. It was of course serious enough in another way, which concerns historians of manners and of the theatre. Parents, employers, and magistrates (not all of them necessarily puritans in the proper sense) were very anxious to abolish the theatre; because it broke the Sabbath, because it drew young people away from their work and encouraged them to spend money, because it collected crowds (a thing both medically and morally suspect) and finally because, if you please, these players were becoming quite rich. All new ways of earning money at first excite indignation. The whole thing is very intelligible. But we must not build it up into an essential conflict between the claims of the moral and the aesthetic point of view. The defenders and the assailants shared the same moral premisses. I shall content myself with noticing one author, who is of permanent interest.

Philip Stubbes (c. 1555–1610+) began his literary career with broadside ballads, highly moral and poetically negligible. Success came to him in May 1583 with the *Anatomy of Abuses*, which reached a second edition in August of the same year and a fifth by 1595. It was followed, still in 1583, by a *Rosary of Christian Prayers* and the *Second Part of the Anatomy*, in 1585 by the *Intended Treason of Doctor Parrie*, in 1591 by the *Christal Glass*, in 1593 by *A Motive to Good Works*, and in 1610 by the *Perfect Pathway to Felicity*. He was probably not a commercial writer and in the preface to the *Anatomy* is nervously apologetic about his style. The 'palpable barbarisme' (*plus quam Vandalica*) which he confesses is apparent in his sad mangling of a line from Virgil, and what has since been christened 'elegant variation' never revealed itself more helplessly than in the sentence, 'as one doth ease the painfulness of the way, so doth the other alleuiate the yrksomnes of the iourney intended'. But when Stubbes warms to his work and forgets to be literary, his style is serviceable enough. Courage came to him with success and in later editions he removed most of the neologisms which abound in the 1583 *Anatomy*. In narrative he is not contemptible, but he breathed no life into the dialogue form (used in the *Anatomy*)

and failed to exploit his own promising idea of representing
England as a remote island called Ailgna. Indeed, later editions
removed the Erewhonian names.

The formula 'a Puritan attacking plays' does little justice to
Stubbes. He was no extreme puritan and the *Second Part of the
Anatomy* explicitly, though reluctantly, allows bishops' titles and
the surplice. Nor did the question of the theatre loom nearly so
large in his mind as in the minds of his modern readers. Stage-
plays are one item in his list of twenty-two profanations of the
Sabbath. He attacks usury, astrology, the growing exclusion of
the poor from the universities, the decay of alms-giving, and the
state of prisons as strongly as he attacks the theatre. Stubbes is
in fact a man much closer to Cobbett than to Gosson; a man
who feels, and hardly understands, a great change creeping over
society and attacks every manifestation of it. The *Motive to
Good Works*, full of things seen and well worth reprinting, has
indeed something in common with the *Rural Rides*. He is not so
wise a man nor so good a writer as Cobbett; but when you have
come to know him you may feel inclined to extend to his hatred
of plays the same sort of indulgence we extend to Cobbett's
hatred of tea. Of all the 'abuses' that he denounced, clearly the
one that excited Stubbes most was vanity and extravagance in
dress. He is very naïve on this topic. Sometimes vanity means no
more than novelty, as when he condemns the 'assy' use of hats
without hatbands; and he is delightfully credulous of assurances
from 'my Father and other wyse sages' that everyone had better
health before all the new-fangled clothes came in. This pre-
occupation with dress should be connected with his statement
that Pride is his 'chiefest argument'. That is not the only point
at which Stubbes, despite his Protestant theology, strikes a
medieval note. The whole lay-out of the *Anatomy*, with its inset
stories of dreadful judgements, would have commended itself
to Chaucer's Pardoner.

Though not a puritan of the first water, he is of course a
precisian. Like Gosson he begins by allowing that there is,
besides the abuse, a lawful use of plays, dances, and rich attire;
and like Gosson he makes no such distinction when he comes to
particulars. But then, unlike Gosson, he notices the inconsistency,
and removes the milder preface in his later edition. This leaves
his position one of great severity. But he is not the most repellent
kind of precisian; his angers are hot, not cold, and compassion

is a marked characteristic of his mind. It is of some historical interest that he has an almost nineteenth-century feeling for animals. Of bear-baiting he asks, 'What christian heart can take pleasure to see one poore beast to rent, teare and kill another'. Of hunting (save for necessary food) he says that our estrangement from the brutes is a result of the Fall 'which we are rather to sorrow for' than to exploit for pastime. This oddly sensitive side of Stubbes comes out stiffly, old-fashionedly, but beyond mistake in the *Christal Glass*, written to commemorate his young wife. The marriage, clearly, had been in reality what Dorothea Brooke vainly hoped her marriage with Casaubon would prove, and the bride '(let me speak it without offence), I think, the rarest in the world'. Less mawkish death-bed scenes than hers are not easily found in literature, for she lay 'red as the rose and most beautiful to beholde', and then, after her last conflict with Satan 'fell suddenly into a sweet, smiling laughter, saying . . . Now is he gone: do you not see him flie like a beaten cocke?' Stubbes did not at that moment care to note that her metaphor came from the cockpit.

George Whetstone (1544?–1587), a third son, an unsuccessful courtier, charged with dissipating what fortune he had on dice and *bona robas*, but himself charging others with having cheated him and thence plunging into ruinous litigation, was almost predestined to be a pamphleteer. The best of his adventuring lay outside literature, on active service in Holland (where he won some distinction as a soldier) or sailing with Gilbert for the North-West Passage in 1578: and the best of his literary adventuring lay outside the pamphlet. He tried everything— plays, poetry, and fiction; such is the 'sad variety' to which the commercial writer is often driven. In the pamphlet, grave moral warnings were his favourite line. The *Mirror for Magistrates of Cities* (1584, but re-issued as the *Enemy to Unthriftiness* in the following year) instructs magistrates by the example of Henry VII and Alexander Severus, whose oration fills most of the book. With the *Mirror* came also *A Touchstone for the Time*. Here, after a preliminary glance at the 'abuse' of the stage for 'scurylitie and vnchaste conveiance', Whetstone proceeds to an attack on dicing houses, ordinaries, 'the braue Shifter' (who 'hath inheritance in the Ile of Snatch' and 'adventureth to Cape Gripe'), the bawd, and the broker. It is not exactly bad, but other writers of the period have done the same kind of thing better.

The *English Mirror* (1586) is less interesting, a moral and political tract in two books, the first a warning against Envy, the second a defence of 'femenine gouernment', and a *caveat* against Jesuits.

Anthony Munday (1553–1633), exemplifies the life of commercial authorship at its lowest level and has more place in the history of police methods than in that of literature. He was a playwright except when attacks on the theatre became saleable, a spy, an *agent provocateur*, an evidence, the *commune refugium* (as one of his victims said) of tottering prosecutions, the dirty card that even government plays last. He hunted Jesuits and puritans with equal obedience: Jesuits paid best because, in addition to the profits of the chase, there was money in a good 'write-up' of the execution. His *English Roman Life* (1582) describes his journey to Rome and his residence there in the English College. It is readable. It would be even admirable if it were a picaresque novel, if its realism argued invention and its self-exposure were ironical. Being true (or at best being lies, not fiction), it is nothing. The style can sink very low: there is a sentence in chapter ii as helpless as those quoted before from Harpsfield and Grafton. The gap between this style and that of his *Zelauto* (which I reserve for treatment under the head of Fiction) shows how completely the rhetoric of such an author is laid on as an extra. Munday did not dream of being 'literary' when he had in hand work which would be bought for its matter. He wears his 'dicky' only when waiting at table.

Barnaby Rich (1540?–1617), though I must dismiss him briefly, is a more interesting writer than Munday. He was a soldier and anxious (what English soldier is not?) to arouse public feeling about the inadequacy of our army and the ill usage of our troops. To that side of his work belong the *Alarm to England* (1578), the *Pathway to Military Practice* (1587), and *A Soldier's Wish* (1604). In the first of these he argues the lawfulness of wars against radical pacifists, whom he calls by a livelier name, *peacemongers*, basing his case on scripture and on Cicero's maxim that it is 'as great iniustice not to defend an iniurie as to offer an iniurie'. Rich shows some of Burton's cheery garrulity in complaint. The *Pathway* is more technical. Rich comes nearest to Munday in his *True Report of a late practice by a Papist* (1582) which purports to give us the confession of a girl who was induced by 'a vile runnagate Papist' to set up as a prophetess.

His best attempts at fiction will be dealt with later, but we may here notice his *Farewell to Military Profession* (1581), now chiefly remembered because one of its eight inset *novelle*, *Apolonius and Silla* by Belleforest out of Bandello, was used in *Twelfth Night*. The stories, though not badly told, are more rhetorical than modern taste easily endures. His military grievances sometimes overflow into the narratives amusingly enough: 'this noble duke had no maner of skill in carpet trade' or 'now the Emperour beganne to repent hym of the slender accoumpt he had made of souldiours in the tyme of peace'.

Robert Greene[1] (1560?–1592) is in quite a different class from the Mundays and the Riches. His immense contemporary popularity, his early death, his miseries, and his somewhat heavily publicized but not therefore insincere repentance make him in some sort the hero and spokesman of all the commercial writers. As a poet he has permanent claims and as a 'novelist' (it is not quite the right word) he has at least historical importance: his pamphlets, in my opinion, contain little of his best work. Except for two translations (the *Debate Between Folly and Love* from the French, and *The Royal Exchange* from the Italian) and for the *Spanish Masquerado* (1589) which is mere victory-parade stuff, they fall into three classes. First in time— some would add, and in merit—come the 'conny catching' pamphlets. The first of these, *A Notable Discovery of Cousenage* (1591) comes as a welcome relief to a modern reader who reaches it by a chronological progress through Greene's works. Up till now he will have found in Greene mainly a rhetorical writer, the disciple and rival of Lyly; here at last is life and London and slang and humour. But this in itself does not prove that Greene is succeeding better than he had done in *Morando* or *Euphues his Censure*: only that he is now working in a genre which our age happens to prefer. In this genre his achievement is respectable but by no means brilliant. Harman's rogues had talked better. Lodge in *Wits Misery*, Greene himself in the *Quip*, Nashe almost everywhere, have more race and bustle. Greene blurs his point, without much comic effect in compensation, by making the Conny, in intention, as great a rogue as his Catchers. He makes

---

[1] b. Norwich *c.* 1560. Sizar St. John's, Cambridge, 1575. B.A.,1580. Transfers to Clare Hall. Studies medicine, M.A., 1583. By his own account visits Italy and Spain. Marries 1585 or 1586. Deserts his wife. Lives in London. Described by Nashe as careless of 'his credit' but not guilty of 'any notorious crime'. Dies in great poverty, 1592.

a trickster avow flatly 'As my religion is smal, so my deuotion is lesse—the two ends I aime at, are gaine and ease.' This is the language of an allegorical person introducing himself in a Morality. In the *Second part of Conny-catching* (1592) it is interesting to notice that Greene finds it necessary to defend (it would not have been necessary a few years later) that unadorned style which, for a modern, sets these pamphlets so clearly above his earlier work. He explains that he had abandoned his rhetoric in obedience to 'decorum' lest he 'should dishonour that high misterie of eloquence, and derogate from the dignitie of our English toonge, eyther to employ any figure or bestow one choyce English word vpon such disdained rakehels as those Conny-catchers'. The passage suggests that Greene felt himself not to be essaying a new kind of excellence but to be absolved from caring how he wrote, and the pamphlet itself confirms this. There are some long jog-trot sentences (notably near the end of the section on 'Vincents Law') which make us sigh for euphuism again. The latter part of the book is merely a collection of 'merry tales' and undistinguished. The *Disputation Between a He Conny-Catcher and a She Conny-catcher* (1592) is in part an advertisement for the previous pamphlets; the speakers, Nan and Lawrence, complain that their trade has suffered severely from that 'peevish scholler' R. G. The *Black Book's Messenger*, which appeared in the same year, is a collection of 'merry tales' about 'cross-biting' put in the form of an impenitent confession by one Ned Browne. He hardly comes to life.

The *Defence of Conny catching* (also in 1592) raises a problem. Grosart laughs at those who attributed it to Greene without noticing that it is an attack on him, but the question cannot be so easily dismissed. It purports to be written by Cuthbert Cunny-catcher who complains, like Nan and Lawrence, that his business has been ruined by R. G. In exasperation he has read Greene for himself and finds no mention of the greatest Catcher of all—the usurer. No book better calculated to increase the fame of Greene's recent pamphlets, and to sell some intended pamphlets, could be imagined. It is true that 'Cuthbert' accuses Greene of having written frivolous stuff which 'had better seemed T. D.' (probably Thomas Deloney). But this echoes what Greene (perhaps advertising a new line of goods for a new type of customer) had said himself in the epistle to his *Mourning Garment*. So far, the *Defence*, though ostensibly an attack is in reality a puff. The only passage which does not advertise Greene is the famous, 'Aske the Queens Players if you sold them not *Orlando Furioso* for twenty nobles, and when they were in the country sold the same play to the Lord Admirals men for as much more. Was not this plaine Conny catching?' One would suppose that only a real enemy could have written this; on the other hand, only one who was too big a fool to have written it at all would have been fool enough to write the rest of the *Defence* with the intention of harming Greene. Add to this that the *Disputation*—another oblique advertisement of the same type—was printed 'by A. I. for T. G.' and the *Defence* 'by A. I. for Thomas Gubbins', and we may perhaps conclude that the taunt about the *Orlando Furioso* is a slap-stick blow intended to be audible in the pit but innocuous to the actor who is struck, and that the *Defence* is either by a friend or, more probably, by Greene himself.

The second class of Greene's pamphlets is represented by a single work, the *Repentance* (1592). Its authenticity has of course been questioned but strenuously defended. From the purely literary point of view it is not very important. The modern reader will feel that the few lines written by Greene to his wife the night before he died (unless these also are spurious) are more moving than the *Repentance* itself. There, by painting himself totally black, Greene naturally fails to convince us. But he was not trying, like a modern author, to produce a 'portrait of the artist'. He was writing the kind of thing which the Elizabethans, accustomed to the 'last confessions' of bad men, well understood.

In the third class we have two pieces which come nearer to being 'pure' literature. The *Vision*, though said to be 'written at the instant of his death' and prefaced with an apology for previous 'lasciuious Pamphletting' ('Pouertie is the father of innumerable infirmities'), has none of the urgency of the *Repentance*, being in fact a fantasy with many medieval characteristics. Greene, fearing that his 'amorous trifles' will disgrace him after death, is comforted by Chaucer's ghost but scolded by Gower's. The two poets debate the question, Chaucer producing a list of twenty sound moral maxims from his client's works, and tell tales. Greene confesses, a little ungratefully, that he has followed Chaucer too much, and resolves for the future to devote himself to moral and natural philosophy: an illuminating comment on the claim that the *Vision* was composed at the 'instant' of death. Solomon then appears and explains that all sciences but theology are vain. The style of this piece, which is livelier than an abstract can suggest, is sometimes euphuistic. The *Quip for an Upstart Courtier: or, a quaint dispute between Velvet breeches and Cloth breeches* (1592) is the best of all Greene's pamphlets. The epistle, written in a style which is no longer euphuistic but has profited by the euphuistic discipline, is the finest specimen we have of Greene the rhetorician. The body of the work is medieval in conception. The allegorical garden, its sudden vanishing, the waste land, and the appearance of the velvet breeches ('I supposed it to be some monster nourished vppe in those desertes') are medievally vivid. The cloth breeches are 'seamed with a little couentry blewe, such as in *Diebus Illis* our grandfathers wore when neighbourhood and hospitality had banished pride out of England'. What follows is, of course, one of those laments for a vanished age of kindness and simplicity which men have made at all times, perhaps with as much reason as those who at most times have praised the new order. The difficulty of finding impartial arbitrators between the two pairs of breeches leads artfully to a lively satire on various professions. In this work Greene shows a balanced control of his powers which I do not find elsewhere. The story of the tailors 'eatinge their pease with their needels pointes, one by one' is worthy of Nashe.

A few pages ago I said that the playwrights had the same moral premisses as their 'puritan' critics. Greene illustrates this. He is not always moral at all, but when he is, his morality is of startling severity. He deplores his 'lasciuious pamphletting', his 'loue-trash'. Yet in our days a man who found his chastity endangered by the works of Greene would have to be, in Johnson's phrase, 'more combustible' than most.

Greene's career can roughly be divided into a rhetorical period and a period beginning in 1591, in which he attempts a more colloquial style. Lodge, as will be seen presently, though revealing a command of the colloquial style as early as 1584, does not venture to exploit it fully till 1596. Nashe, who was toying with a kind of semi-euphuism in 1589, achieves his own unmistakable manner in 1592. Thus, still very roughly, we may distinguish stylistically an earlier period when formal rhetoric dominated the pamphlet, and a later period in which the illusion of *ex tempore* speech is attempted. The dividing-line comes some-where about the year 1590. It is natural to connect it with the outburst of Martinist and Anti-Martinist publications which began in October 1588 and lasted into 1590.

By the autumn of 1588 the bishops, what between their control of the press and the powers of the detested High Commission established in 1582, had reduced their puritan critics to silence. At that moment, printed nobody knew where by Robert Waldegrave, appeared *Oh read over D. John Bridges* by 'Martin Marprelate gentleman'. The controversy to which 'Martin' was contributing will receive some attention later and from a different point of view. In that warfare Martinism was only a guerrilla episode and can the more easily be detached for our present purpose because, on the intellectual level, it was of no serious importance. Martin himself had of course a serious in-tention and must, for all his motley, be regarded as a heroic figure. Nor have I any sympathy with those who make prim mouths at him for introducing scurrility into a theological debate, for debate was precisely what the bishops had suppressed. Those who refuse to let their opponents dispute have no right to complain if they hear instead lewd catcalls in the streets; in a sense, it is what they have chosen. But Martin was speedily disowned by the graver members of his own party, and by his very choice of a weapon he was committed to methods which could hardly convert a critical inquirer. His importance as a controversial theologian is therefore small: his real place is in the history of prose.

The racy, fleering, cockney manner which Martin adopted was not, indeed, a complete novelty; we have seen something like it used, and used on the most serious subjects, by More, Latimer, and Poynet. What was new was, first, its sudden intro-duction into this particular controversy, and secondly, its continuous and exaggerated employment. Martin tells us quite clearly (in *Hay any Worke for Cooper*, 1589) why he adopted this manner. 'The most part of men could not be gotten to read anything in the defence of one and against the other. I bethought me therefore of a way whereby men might be drawn to do both.' He uses all the old devices and some new ones to draw atten-tion to himself; imitation of inarticulate noises (*Ha, ha, ha—Tse-tse-tse*), coinages or feigned mispronunciations (*Confocation house, Fickers General, Paltripolitans, fathermillerly, dissimblation*), interruptions or encouragements from voices in the margin ('Now I pray thee good Martin speake out') and again replies to these voices ('Why sauceboxes, must you be prating?'). He utters threats with a fine ogreish glee: 'I will watch you at euery half turne . . . I will place a young Martin in every diocese.' More maddeningly, he represents threats as promises. He will publish his other books; and 'Why, my masters of the clergy, did you neuer heare of my books indeede? Foh, then you neuer heard of good sport in your life.' Perhaps his best piece of sustained denigration is the long speech (*The Just Censure*, 1589) which he represents Whitgift as making to his dirty crew of pursuivants, the Mundays and their like.

Much of his invective falls on deaf ears today. We are not shocked that a bishop should swear 'like a lewd swag and say, By my faith'. We hardly believe that Lord Dumb John (the Bishop of London) stole cloth. We do not much care whether clergymen play bowls or even primero. Our sympathy goes all to the other side when Martin jeers at Whitgift because 'all the world knoweth him to haue been a poor scholler . . . so poore as he had not a napkin to wipe his mouth' and had to carry Dr. Perne's cloak-bag. Whitgift had the sense to reply that if it were true it would be no disgrace. But Martin's taunt was justified by the canons of that age: then, and long after, it was considered fair sport to expose your opponent's poverty. (In Lamb we see poverty turning from a topic of bitter, into one of tender and sympathetic, raillery.) What can hardly be excused by standards that Martin himself must have acknowledged is the passage (in *Oh Read Over*) where Whitgift is blamed for not truckling to worldly greatness. The Archbishop had apparently refused to put a parson into a benefice without subscription to the three special articles which had been made obligatory in 1583. That, of course, is a fair target for Martin: this subscription was a principal grievance to his party. But the point of the story in Martin's eyes, the aggravating circumstances which makes it worth telling, is that Whitgift had refused this non-subscriber despite a request in his favour from the Earl of Warwick. Martin quotes his words—'I would uery gladlie gratifie my lord, but surely there is a lord in heauen whom I feare'. Without the slightest perception that this redounds to the archbishop's credit, Martin continues 'I will tell you true, John of Canterbury, if I were a nobleman and a Councillor too, I should be sicke of the spleen, nay I could not beare this at your hands'. (It will be remembered that the puritans were accused of relying on great friends.)

The Martinist pamphlets were seven in all. *Oh read over D. John Bridges* in its two parts (the *Epistle* and the *Epitome*) appeared in 1588, *Certain Mineral and Metaphysical Schoolpoints*, *Hay any Worke for Cooper*, the *Theses Martinianae* (ostensibly by Martin's younger brother), the *Just Censure* (in which Martin senior affects to reprove Martin junior), and the *Protestation*, all in 1589. After that the printers were caught and the pamphlets ceased. Martin puts a bold face on it to the end though even in the *Epitome* he is already rejected by his own side—'I am fauoured of all estates (the Puritans only excepted)'. Later, in the *Theses*, he adds, 'I see my doings and my course misliked of many both the good and the bad'. It is possible that the bishops exaggerated the practical importance of the whole affair (slanders against oneself seldom seem trivial) and were ill advised to reply. Its literary importance I have already suggested. Martin certainly displayed a new manner in controversy and probably his successors learned from him. It can hardly be claimed that in this new kind he attained excellence. He seems at times a little tired of it himself. He is not best when he is rowdiest. I believe a quieter and more ironic prose, a prose closer to Swift's, would have been more congenial to him.

According to Strype it was Bancroft who first suggested among the bishops that the Martinists should be 'answered after their own vain writings'. Counter-attack by imitation was thus enjoined from above. This programme was partly carried out on the stage; in the *Theses* Martin junior taunts his brother with having been 'clean put out of countenance' by 'stage players, poore silly hunger starued wretches' who, having 'not so much as an honest calling' to live by, will be glad for a penny 'on open stage to play the ignominious fooles for an houre together'. (The other popular charge against the actors was that they were far too rich.) These vanished plays do not concern us. Of the literary anti-Martinist flytings we may mention, besides the three attributed to 'Pasquil', *Pappe with an hatchet* (in 1589) and an *Almond for a Parrot* (1590). Of these, *Pappe with an hatchet* is almost certainly by Lyly.

The Pasquils deserve more attention if only because the older scholars, from Collier to Sir Sidney Lee, attributed them to

Nashe. This claim has been overthrown, but one sees, nevertheless, how it seemed reasonable. The first of the three pieces by Pasquil, the *Countercuff*, is a little like Nashe, but very much weaker; such stuff as Nashe might have written before he came to his strength. The *Return of Pasquil of England* is much more formidable. The sympathy which might go to the puritans as the hunted and endangered party is skilfully diverted by the references to their influential backers: 'some of the cittie fauour' Martin, he 'hath great upholders', 'take heed . . . the faction of Martinisme hath mightie freends'. And perhaps there lurk among Martin's friends 'some few that are as readie as himselfe to rob the Church'. In the third pamphlet, the *First part of Pasquil's Apology*, Pasquil tells us, 'the sente of Church-robbers is in my nostrils'. All this is good tactics and not all of it is necessarily unjust. A higher note is struck when Pasquil exhorts the puritans to peace 'that the weake may not see vs runne at one another like furious Bulles foming and casting out those reproches which hereafter we shall neuer be able to wipe awaie'. The weakness of the pamphlet is that Pasquil often accuses his opponent of wresting scripture but does not very strongly substantiate the charge. It would not have been difficult.

Critics have always been reluctant to deny that Nashe wrote *An Almond for a Parrot* and an American scholar has produced external evidence to support his claim. It is certainly stronger meat than we find in Pasquil. Its main line of attack is that the puritans, by disturbing the Protestant settlement in the English Church, are really the Pope's best friends—a role which the puritans of course allotted to the bishops. The author narrates how, on inquiring one night at Bergamo why all the bells were ringing, he was told by his host that the town was rejoicing at news of 'a famous Schismatike, one Martin, newe sprung vp in England' who would soon fulfil the dearest wish of Rome and Spain by setting us all at odds and leaving us an easy prey to invasion. He also emphasizes the puritan threat to the universities: 'it were not two pins hurt if your Colledges were fired ouer your heades, and you turnde a begging forth your fellow-shippes like Fryers and Monkes'. All this might come from any fighting journalist with his wits about him; what is more like Nashe is such a vocative as 'good munckie face Machiuell' and the almost nightmare quality of certain passages. Such are the (quite serious) picture of Martin's damnation, 'swimming to hell' on the 'innocent bloude' of those who 'shall carrie the name of *Martine* on their foreheads to the vale of confusion' or the appalling humour about Penry—'Predestination, that foresaw how crooked he should proue in his waies, enioyned incest to spawne him splay-footed: Eternitie, that knew how awkward he shoulde looke to all honesty, consulted with conception to make him squint-eyed . . .', &c. We are driven to conclude *aut Nashius aut Diabolus*; and may even wonder if the second alternative is purely formal. This pamphlet is strong as sulphur. The unhappy Martin who first used gas in this war found at the same time that he was repudiated by his own higher command and that the enemy had gases much more deadly than his.

Thomas Lodge, the son of a bankrupt (who had once been Lord Mayor), the black sheep of his family, prodigal, imprudent in all things, and most honourably so in hardly at all disguising his adherence to the old religion, an adventurer to the Azores in 1586 and to Magellan in 1591, was driven by need to attempt almost every form of literature. Of his pamphlets, which alone concern us here, the *Honest Excuses* has already been noticed. He shows from the first a talent for realistic humour which, however, he did not venture to exploit fully until Martin Marprelate and Nashe had shown the way. In his *Alarm against Usurers* (1584) it peeps out but soon hides again behind rhetoric. We have vivid pictures of a typical gull, a typical 'heavy father', a typical broker, and a typical moneylender. But all these, except the broker whose speech rings fairly true, plunge us back into euphuism the moment they open their mouths. Those who hope to see in the father a portrait of the elder Lodge will be disappointed at his conversational style; 'Agree light and darknesse? Or the Icknewmon with the Aspis? Doeth the Weesell loue the Cockatrice?' At the very end Lodge rises into a strain of genuine and moving eloquence. The *Catharos Diogenes in his Singularity . . . a Nettle for Nice Noses* (1591?) is arrant bookmaking. Matter borrowed from the fifteenth-century *Dyalogus Creaturarum Moralisatus* and Jean Benedicti's *Somme des Pechez* (1584) is worked up into a sermon against usury and lechery, thinly veiled as a colloquy held at Athens between Diogenes and two worldlings; so thinly that these Athenians refer to Littleton's *Tenures*. The earlier part shows traces of euphuism: some of the railing dialogue anticipates Shakespeare's prose. The *Devil Conjured* (1596) is much the same kind of thing; a defence of the

o

ascetic life and an attack on magic and astrology, heavily indebted to Angles's *Flores in Librum Secundum Sententiarum* (Madrid,
1586) and presented as a dialogue between St. Anthony and
three visitors. It is seasoned, but only sporadically, with
euphuism. Lodge's Romanism is made very clear. Far better
than these, and possibly Lodge's best work, is *Wits Misery*
(also in 1596). Here, encouraged and perhaps assisted by Nashe's
Piers Penniless, he all but abandons his earlier rhetoric and
develops his racier vein. The structure is that of a medieval
sermon on the seven deadly sins. Each is subdivided and each
subdivision becomes a character, allegorical indeed, yet hailed
before us more vividly than those of Theophrastus—'But soft
who comes here with a leane face and hollow eyes biting his lips
for feare his tongue should leape out of his mouth.' Of Worldly
Fear we read 'if a butchers hook do but catch him by the sleeues,
he cries out, At whose suit?' The puritan is attacked under the
head of sedition as one lately 'flying under colour of religion
beyond the sea' and now on his return 'telling wonders of the
entertainment of good Wits in other countries' and whispering
to farmers that 'these rackt rents are the vtter ruine of the
yeomanry'. In the picture of the 'malecontent' it is interesting to
see how Lodge accepts motiveless malignity as a familiar fact
calling for no explanation. The 'right malecontent Deuill . . .
his hat without a band, his hose vngartered . . . if he walkes
Poules he sculks in the back Isles . . . hating his countrie of
meer innated and corrupt villanie'. This whole pamphlet is full
of interest, and not all the credit need go to the influence of
Nashe. An apostrophe such as 'Beelzebub the enuious, grand god
of flies, Archduke of Grecian fantacies and patron of the
Pharisies' is almost certainly learned from him; but in many of
his best passages Lodge is giving us simply more and better of
the sort we had in parts of the *Alarm*.

Thomas Nashe[1] (1567–1601) is undoubtedly the greatest of
the Elizabethan pamphleteers, the perfect literary showman,

[1] b. 1567 at Lowestoft. Sizar at St. John's, Cambridge, 1582. B.A., 1586.
Probably in London, 1588. Probably never in Italy. Patronized by Sir George
Carey. Stays with Carey at Carisbrooke Castle, 1592–3. Subjected to (undefined)
'persecution' by the City authorities, whom *Christ's Tears* had offended, 1594.
Lodges at the Dolphin in Cambridge, 1595. About this time appears to have lived
with John Danter the printer. His lodgings searched by the Privy Council on
suspicions aroused by his share in the *Isle of Dogs*, 1597. Visits Yarmouth. Mentioned
as dead in 1601. (Very little is known about Nashe's life.)

the juggler with words who can keep a crowd spell-bound by sheer virtuosity. The subject, in his sort of writing, is unimportant.

His highly individual style is still unformed in his earliest works. The *Anatomy of Absurdity* (1589) is a long, rambling, grumbling invective against women and (to adopt its own point of view) other evils. The style is embellished with rhymes and euphuistic similes, but beneath these decorations we often catch something not unlike the debased alliterative rhythm of Langland. The preface to Greene's *Menaphon* (also 1589) is somewhat rhetorical, and, what with tantalizing allusions and obscurity, has set scholars many problems. Nashe's views on contemporary literature are hidden somewhere in this preface if we could get at them. He clearly has something to tell us about English prose style but I have failed to understand him, except in that passage (significant in relation to Nashe's later work) where he cries 'but giue me the man whose extemporall vaine in anie humour will excell our greatest Art-masters deliberate thoughts'. There, and in one or two other places, he is beginning to achieve that style himself. The preface to Sidney's *Astrophel and Stella*, which followed in 1591, is better work; its opening sentence, irresistible. But it is in *Piers Penilesse his Supplication to the Divell* (1592) that he really found himself.

Nashe was later to tell us (in the Epistle to *Lenten Stuff*) that of all styles he most affected and strove to imitate that of Aretine. Pietro Aretino (1492–1556) was the yellow press of his day: his fame hung on the strong triple cord of flattery, libel, and pornography. The latter Nashe certainly never imitated in prose, and some doubt whether in claiming to follow Aretine's 'stile' he meant anything more definite than that he aimed at the greatest possible violence.

Wherever it came from, the style which appears in *Pierce Penilesse* offered the Elizabethan reader a new sort of pleasure. The core of the work is medieval, a satiric homily on the seven deadly sins in the grimly humorous temper of Langland or the *Ancren Riwle*. But this is enclosed in a petition to the Devil thus enabling Nashe to give a spirited account of his search for a suitable postman and to add some saleable Platonic daemonology from Georgius Pictorius. There are several digressions, including a defence of plays (especially chronicle plays) and an attack on

Richard Harvey, of which came afterwards a long and ludicrous paper war. It is very easy to see the faults of *Piers*; its shapeless garrulity, the reckless inconsistency of its attitudes, and the author's nasty pleasure in describing cruelty. It is more useful to try to see why it was once liked, for this was the most popular of Nashe's works and was even, if we can trust his own statement, translated into French. Its appeal is almost entirely to that taste for happy extravagance in language and triumphant impudence of tone, which the Elizabethans have, perhaps, bequeathed rather to their American than to their English descendants. The catchpenny lure of the title (carefully underlined by the printer's note to the reader) is characteristic of the whole thing. The opening words of the epistle, 'Faith, I am verie sorrie, Sir,' establish at once an intimacy between the performer and the audience: it is the same technique that Donne often uses in verse. Throughout the work Nashe's phrasing has the vividness of a clown's red nose. We read of old trots 'in the wrinkles of whose face ye may hide false dice and play at cherrypit in the dint of their cheekes'; the Devil is 'Master *Os foetidum*, Bedle of the Blackesmithes'; women have lips 'as lauishly red as if they vsed to kisse an okerman euery morning'; Nashe 'has tearmes (if he be vext) laid in steepe in *Aquafortis* and gunpowder, that shall rattle through the skyes and make an Earthquake in a Pesants eares'. He concludes his belabouring of Richard Harvey with a delightful *vos plaudite*—'Haue I not an indifferent prittye vayne in spurgalling an Asse? if you knew how extemporall it were at this instant and with what hast it is writ, you would say so.'

As this passage was the shoeing-horn to draw on the whole Nashe–Harvey quarrel, it will be convenient here to group together Nashe's other contributions to it, the *Strange News* of 1592 and *Have with you to Saffron Walden* (1596). The rights and wrongs of this great flyting must be sought in Dr. McKerrow's magnificent edition, and in fact they do not matter much. Nashe certainly, the Harveys not impossibly, were well aware that such stuff would sell. The example of great humanistic dog-fights like that between Poggio and Valla could hardly be absent from their minds. And whatever Nashe's extra-literary motives may have been, an enemy to bespatter was clearly an artistic necessity to one who had just discovered a style so suited for invective. The obscurity of the quarrel need deter no reader

from exploring these pamphlets, which are their author's liveliest works. You must come to them as to a ferocious game: if
you are looking for serious debate you will find them unreadable. The very qualities which we should blame in an ordinary
controversialist are the life and soul of Nashe. He is unfair,
illogical, violent, extravagant, coarse: but then that is the joke.
When a half drunk street-corner humorist decides to make a
respectable person (say, from Peebles) ridiculous, it is useless for
the respectable person to show that the charges brought against
him are untrue—that he does not beat his wife, is not a cinema
star in disguise, is not wearing a false nose. The more eagerly
he refutes them, the louder the spectators laugh. When the
butt is anyone so unamiable, so grotesque, as Gabriel Harvey,
we enjoy the fun with (almost) a clear conscience. The very
names that are flung at him confer a grievous immortality—
Gilgilis Hobberdehoy, Braggadochio Glorioso, Timothy Tiptoes, Gerboduck Huddleduddle. Nashe's satire, in other respects
the very reverse of Dryden's, always has Dryden's unanswerable
ease and gusto, seems to cost the writer nothing, kills with nonchalance. Poor Harvey may writhe at allusions to his father the
ropemaker; the more fool he, says Nashe, for 'had I a Ropemaker to my father and somebody had cast it in my teeth, I
would foorthwith haue writ in praise of Ropemakers and prou'd
it by sound sillogistry to be one of the 7 liberal sciences'. He
would have, too.

In *Christs Tears over Jerusalem* (1593) Nashe attempts a serious
theme with very little success. The bones of the work are, once
more, medieval. We begin with a long speech put into the
mouth of Christ, and of course Nashe fails as conspicuously as
More had failed in a similar audacity. We pass thence to a lurid
account of the siege and fall of Jerusalem in which we are
alternately nauseated by physical horrors and lulled asleep by
ineffective rhetoric. When we reach Schimeon's proclamation,
the author's irrepressible relish for roguery rather overwhelms
his (presumably) moral purpose. The book ends with a call
upon plague-stricken London to repent, set in a complicated
framework of eight vices which are the five sons and three
daughters of pride. This is a thoroughly bad piece of work: the
descriptions of the vices produce neither laughter nor compunc-
tion. Nashe's peculiar richness of phrase sometimes appears, as
in the description of the courtier whose 'backe bandieth colours

with the Sunne' and in many images of famine and corruption
which are veritably nightmares ten words long. But in the main
Nashe seems to be trying, and not very happily, to alter his
style—unless, indeed, the *Tears* is early work rehashed. The
Dedication, to Lady Elizabeth Carey, uses a heavy ink-horn
rhetoric foreign to his mature manner. In the speech given to
the Saviour he uses a strange artifice of which I do not know the
history (the 119th Psalm might be the ultimate model). A series
of keywords (*stones, gather, echo, would not,* and *desolate*) are used
in turn like *leitmotifs.*

The *Terrors of the Night,* published in 1594, is said to have
been written 'a long time since', but is more characteristic of
Nashe's developed manner than the *Anatomy of Absurdity* had
been. Perhaps it was re-worked and added to. It is a rambling
attack on demonology and oneiromancy. As usual, Nashe is
quite indifferent to consistency. He starts off by regarding night
as Spenser regarded it and dwells, movingly enough, on the
horrors of nocturnal conscience and solitude, when we are
'shut separately in our chambers' and Satan (who rules the
night, as God the day) 'reuealeth the whole astonishing treasurie
of his wonders'. Presently, however, night becomes the friend:
almost, as in Kipling's story, our kind protector against Police-
man Day. For 'he that dreames merily is like a boy new breetcht,
who leapes and daunceth for joy his paine is past', but soon 'his
master the day, seeing him so iocund and pleasant, comes and
dooes as much for him againe, whereby his hell is renued'.
Corda oblita laborum—who would have expected this Virgilian
pity from burly Nashe? Unless, having read our way so far into
his mind, we come to suspect—and I think every reader of
Nashe will—that the 'burliness' is by no means the whole story:
may indeed be only the 'manic' peak, balanced in private by
a 'depressive' trough. The *Terrors* is ostensibly a sceptical work
written to remove night-fears. And Nashe gets great fun out of
the minor devils of whom 'infinite millions wil hang swarming
about a worm-eaten nose' or 'entrench themselves' in the
wrinkles of a hag, or the Druids in Man who were positively
'lousie with familiars'. But these, like nearly all Nashe's comic
images, are comic only if you see them in a flash and from
exactly the right angle. Move a hair's breadth, dwell on them
a second too long, and they become disturbing.

The *Unfortunate Traveller* (1594) will be treated under the head of fiction. I mention it here only to notice that its long scene of torture deepens the impression of something in Nashe which is the reverse of comic, though also closely connected with his peculiar kind of comedy. The grotesque is a ridge from which one can descend into very different valleys.

On learning that *Lenten Stuff* (1599) is a panegyric on red herrings, the modern reader may feel inclined to yawn. Nashe was moved to adopt such a theme partly by the desire to repay some kindness shown him in the town of Yarmouth and partly by emulation of the great wits who had written paradoxes in praise of trifles or evils—Synesius of Baldness, Erasmus of Folly, de Mornay of Death, de la Noue of Imprisonment. His pamphlet is thus both a comic advertisement and a display of the skill that can talk on any subject. The latter task suited Nashe admirably. *Lenten Stuff* is one of his best works. The description of Yarmouth is a relief after the somewhat feverish unsubstantiality of his other pamphlets, in so far as it at last brings our minds to bear on real things like walls, sand, ships, and tides. The comic myths of the coronation of King Herring and the Pope's dinner are good, if not excellent. The first of them is prefaced with a serio-comic rehandling of the story of Hero and Leander, 'of whom Musaeus sang, and a diuiner Muse than him, Kit Marlow'. Our taste is a little offended by Nashe on this theme, as it is offended when we read Mark Twain on Arthur or Eloise. But his treatment has its own merits and works up to a vivid conclusion, when, as Hero stooped to kiss the dead Leander, 'boystrous woolpacks of ridged tides came rowling in and raught him from her'.

Though Nashe owed much to his predecessors he is one of our most original writers. The groundwork of his style comes to him, as I have indicated, through Martin, from the old, native tradition which we see in Latimer and More. He is the supreme master of literary *sansculottisme*. To these cheap-jack and guttersnipe elements (I use the words to define, not to dispraise, for these also require genius) he added, however, something quite different; comic ink-horn terms, burlesque rodomontade, gigantic hyperbole, Rabelaisian monstrosity. It is this second element which he himself refers to when he claims that his style 'is no otherwise puft vp than any mans should be that writes with any spirite' and prefers it to 'this demure soft *mediocre genus* that is like wine and water mixt together: but giue me pure wine of itself, and that begets blood and heates the brain thorowly'. The effect of this extravagance, most happily married to the colloquial, was new and strong. His predecessors had talked merely like Shakespeare's rogues: Nashe talked like Falstaff. Or, to put it the right way round, when Falstaff promises that his cudgel shall hang like a meteor over the horns of Mr. Ford, he owes something to Nashe.

Paradoxically, though Nashe's pamphlets are commercial literature, they come very close to being, in another way, 'pure' literature: literature which is, as nearly as possible, without a subject. In a certain sense of the verb 'say', if asked what Nashe 'says', we should have to reply, Nothing. He tells no story, expresses no thought, maintains no attitude. Even his angers seem to be part of his technique rather than real passions. In his exhilarating whirlwind of words we find not thought nor passion but simply images: images of ludicrous and sometimes frightful incoherence boiling up from a dark void. There is that in Nashe which connects him with artists like Bosch and the later Picasso. If he took himself seriously he would at once create horrors: he has all the material. In fact, however, in his pamphlets (as in the *Hunting of the Snark*) this material, if not quite controlled by, is usually exploited for, a comic purpose. In Chesterton's phrase he rides the nightmare, not the nightmare him, though his seat is not always secure. Hence he is closer to Mr. Thurber's pictures than to Picasso's. He is a great American humorist.

Within this century Nashe had no successor of stature comparable to his own. Henry Chettle in his *Kind-Heart's Dream* (1593) arraigns ballad-mongers, quack doctors, 'maligners of honest mirth', greedy landlords, magicians, and pettifoggers. He works his matter up into the form of a dream in which the ghosts of the actor Tarlton, Robert Greene, and others appear to him. The pamphlet is mainly remembered because it contains a defence of Chettle's integrity as transcriber and editor of the *Groatsworth*, an olive-branch to Shakespeare ('his demeanour no lesse ciuill than he excelent in the quality he professes'), and some information about contemporary balladry. It was probably readable while it was new. A more spirited work, published in the same year, was *Bacchus' Bounty* by 'Philip Foulface of Ale-foord', relating the adventures of one Tom Typsay who was invited to the gods' Whitsuntide party. There is some burlesque euphuism, and some burlesque 'poetical' prose; as when Bacchus 'from a muddie muse so cleered vp his cherry-like countenance that the majestie of his nose seemed as the beames of the sunne shining along the Coastes of Archadie'. The Bacchanalian spirit is well evoked but wearies us before the end. It is, however, a good book for a man who wants to enrich his vocabulary: here are the 'coppernosed crue, the knuckle-debunions of Rome' and 'that old Huddle and Twang, Aristodemus'.

In Sir John Harington's *Metamorphosis of Ajax* (1596) and its successor, the *Anatomy*, there is a quality (hard to describe) which makes us feel that we are emerging from the Elizabethan age. Coprological humour was no novelty; nor was the solemn praise of things that might seem least fit for eulogy. The style is modelled (in places closely) on that of Rabelais. Yet Harington is very unlike his master. Rabelais was a fighter, defending humanism and attacking the monks. He was also an inventor in the realm of Nonsense, a follower of Lucian, and a predecessor of Lewis Carroll. Harington lacks both qualities. That is why the *Water Babies*, also modelled on Rabelais, is, for all its propriety, more genuinely Rabelaisian. Nor is Harington very close to the earlier English humorists. He is too frivolous, too detached, to be as robustly comic as they. More had been a grave droll and Nashe a clown; Harington is only a wag.

William Kemp the actor (who almost certainly 'created' the part of Dogberry) has left us in the *Nine Days Wonder* (1600) an account of his great feat of endurance in dancing every yard of the way from London to Norwich, for a wager and doubtless also as what we should now call a 'publicity stunt'. This pamphlet has unexpected merits. At first we think we are in for one more exhibition in the cheap-jack manner ('myself, thats I, otherwise called Caualiero Kemp, high head-borough of heighs and only tricker of Trill-lilles', &c.). But very soon the narrative develops a quite different interest; the details of the exploit, the entertainment at each resting place, the behaviour of the crowds, and the adventures of the road, build up into something that shares the fascination of George Borrow. But Kemp, unlike Borrow, makes me believe every word he writes. The innkeeper of Rockland, clearly drawn from the life, is far funnier than anything in those earlier passages where Kemp had laboured harder to be funny. The prose is often such as, for its purpose, could not be bettered. Of the girl who undertook to dance with him for a mile (and did) Kemp writes, 'I lookt vpon her, saw mirth in her eyes, heard boldnes in her words, and beheld her ready to tuck vp her russet petticoate. I fitted her with bells which she, merily taking, garnisht her thick short legs and with a smooth brow bad the Tabrer begin.' In the *Wonder* we meet agreeable people of all social classes; the old century could not have gone out more sweetly.

It is saddening to think how much less convincingly, indeed how nauseatingly, an exploit like Kemp's would be 'written up' in the newspapers of our own time. It is a reflection which comes often to mind as we read the pamphlets of that age. I have concentrated, as (I think) reason was, on those that have some literary pretensions; but we should do grave injustice to the Elizabethans if we left the subject without noticing what good work there often was in its least literary productions. The *True Report of the lamentable Death of William of Nassawe* (1584) is, in a sense, merely the equivalent of our 'front page news'. But compare even our better journalism with this; 'two of those Bullets went through the Princes Body and the third remained in his Bellie, through which wicked strokes the Prince fell downe suddainly, crying out saying Lord have mercy vpon me and remember my little Flocke. Wherewith he changed his life. . . .' It is not enough (though it is doubtless true) to say that the author of this passage did not suppose himself to be writing 'literature' at all. That might secure him from affectation: but our reading of the Drab Age has shown us that it would not necessarily secure him from being clumsy or even unintelligible. Somehow or other during the latter part of the sixteenth century Englishmen learned to write.

II

The prose fiction[1] of this period—we invite misunderstanding if we call it 'the novel'—may be divided into three classes: the romantic, the realistic, and one other for which I can find no satisfactory name. Its characteristic is that it subordinates narrative to rhetoric. We are expected to be interested not in what the characters were or felt or did but in what they said, or (less often) in the fine things the authors say about them. Criticisms of such books on the assumption that they are unsuccessful

---

[1] For earlier references *v. supra*, pp. 276, 309-15.

attempts to tell a good story are out of court. The two earliest specimens of the kind are John Grange's *Golden Aphroditis* (1577) and Lyly's *Euphues* (1578). Scholars have disputed which of these should be called 'the first English novel'. In my opinion neither should be so called. The kind to which both belong is further from the true novel than medieval romance had been: its place in the history of fiction is that of a branch line going off to a different terminus. It is related about equally to the novel and to the colloquy: the individual specimens of course inclining now to the one and now to the other. *Euphues* I have already described. The *Golden Aphroditis* is equally rhetorical, but not usually euphuistic. Its rhetoric is more poetical and less sententious, florid, and loaded with mythology like the Latin *Kunstprosa* of the Middle Ages. What story there is, deals with the loves of Diana's and Endymion's daughter.

In 1580 came Austen Saker's *Narbonus* and Anthony Munday's *Zelauto*. Both are very closely modelled on *Euphues*, not only nor chiefly in their style but in their scanty story and their love of speechifying. Munday's literary ideal is amusingly displayed when he tells how Strabino's 'conceytes began to come so nimbly together that he now rolled in his Rethoricke like a Flea in a blanquet'. He is not often euphuistic for long at a stretch, and we find ink-horn terms and poetical passages where verse rhythms intrude. He is a jackdaw who will catch at any sort of finery. In 1582 we get a much better book, George Whetstone's *Heptameron of Civil Discourses*. This leans towards the colloquy, for though there are several inset stories, including *Promus and Cassandra* which he also dramatized, they make only a small part of the whole. None of them displays half so much novelistic talent as Whetstone's opening: the ride through the forest on Christmas Eve and the first sight of the palace might well be the beginning of an excellent story. Whetstone, however, is interested only in the gorgeous interior of the palace and the sophisticated courtesy of the debates (some of them quite serious) which he heard there. His aim is to re-create for a moment that world of high formalized flirtation and dispute which Castiglione had shown him. The tone is well exemplified by the scene in which the narrator, momentarily spell-bound by the richness of his surroundings, recovers himself with the thought that 'it belongeth vnto a gentleman to see and not to stare vpon the strangest Nouell that is; for base is his mynde whose spirit hourely beholdeth not greater matters then eyther beautie, buylding or braverie'.

In 1583 there appeared Brian Melbancke's *Philotimus* and Greene's first attempt, the *Mamillia*. The chief use of Melbancke is to reconcile us to the other euphuists; his heavier alliteration, his total lack of daintiness and melody, teach us that Lodge and Greene, in mastering the style, had done something not within everyone's reach. It is only against the background of this absurd book that *Mamillia* could seem tolerable. This is nearer to the novel than any of the works I have yet mentioned, but for that very reason all the worse: Greene teases us by seeming to offer a story and then frustrating us with endless digressions, tirades, and letters. His *Mirror of Modesty* (1584) is a rhetoricized version of Susanna and the Elders. Here his original inevitably forces some true narrative qualities upon him, but none of his additions were, I think, made for the purpose of enhancing them. Far better reading was provided by Barnaby Rich's *Second Tome of the Travels of Don Simonides*, published in the same year. The first 'tome', which will meet us in a few pages, is a romance: this is a quite different kind of book, a very pure specimen of the rhetorical *genre*. After a long debate between a divine, a lawyer, and a soldier we accompany Simonides to Athens with a letter of introduction to Euphues himself. By some extraordinary whim of fortune Simonides found him in a fit of taciturnity, but presently 'he broke off their unnecessary silence' and was himself again. In the dialogue that follows euphuism is, very properly, confined to the speeches of Euphues. The result is extremely funny, but I am not sure whether this was intended.

All the remaining specimens of this rhetorical *genre* are by Greene. The *Planetomachia* (1585) departs from pure colloquy only by having two inset 'tragedies'. *Morando the Tritameron of Love* (1587) is closer to Whetstone's work, a dialogue in a country house; and though Greene is no Plato nor even a Castiglione, not ungraceful. *Euphues his Censure* (also in 1587) uses the same method. There is a truce at Troy and the Greek lords and Trojan ladies exchange visits. Greene meets all the demands for pomp, ceremony, eloquence, and irony which his theme makes upon him. It is one of his happiest works. The play of passions and personalities underneath an exalted formality is well suggested. It is only when the inset stories begin that we lose interest: we are once more teased with a proffer of narrative and plunged back in the soliloquies and epistles of *Euphues*. *Ciceronis Amor* (1588) and *Orpharion* (licensed in 1589) show the vitality of medieval motifs. In the latter the hero speaks in the first person, presents a suit to Venus, visits an allegorical temple, meets Sloth as a porter, and is finally 'ledde alongst the galupin or silver paued way of heauen to the hie built house of Ioue', where he hears divine conversation and, unfortunately, stories. The *Farewell to Folly* (1591) is built on the same plan as *Morando*, but furnished with a lively, abusive preface that suggests the influence of Nashe. *Philomela* (1592) has most of the same characteristics as *Ciceronis Amor*.

I have now perhaps said all that modern ears can endure about this static and declamatory school of fiction. The taste which it gratified is long dead. If we hope even momentarily to recover it, we must carefully avoid reading these books for the story. Morality, eloquence, sometimes (but even this rarely) sentiment, are the things we must attend to. We must try to feel how bright, how civilized, how 'artificial' (then a term of praise) they all looked at the time. There is no direct line of descent from them to the genuine novel.

This is much less true of the romances: they, like the realistic stories, foreshadow later fiction. By separating these romances from the previous *genre* I do not imply that they are always less rhetorical, still less that their rhetoric is not often pure euphuism. The difference is that, beneath all the rhetoric, there is a genuine narrative interest. The authors aim at arousing curiosity, pity, terror, and admiration. There is often a complex plot, reminiscent of chivalric or Greek romance. High sentiment and florid descriptions of natural beauty are not uncommon.

Rich's original *Simonides*—his *Strange and wonderful adventures* (1581)—is the most rhetorical of them all, except at the end where the dialogue between Simonides and Anthonio is in a racier style. The more laboured passages are only at times euphuistic. The author prefers a slow and languorous piling up of images which is the very reverse of Lyly's manner. The story, which also moves slowly, is drenched in devout, rarefied, melancholy emotion. And it is not entirely a failure. The effect is like breathing in an air heavy with incense. These qualities set *Simonides* apart. Far more typical of the *genre*, though by no means a good specimen, is Lodge's *Forbonius and Prisceria* (1584).

The ingredients are lovers, cruel parents, a 'gymnosophical' magician, shepherds, and disguise. Lodge shows his literary allegiance by making his heroine the granddaughter of Heliodorus' Theagines. In the same year came Greene's *Arbasto*. It may be doubted whether Greene often enjoyed writing pure romances as he almost certainly enjoyed writing things like *Euphues his Censure*. *Arbasto* has all the appearance of being written for necessity by a man who took very little interest in his own story. Arbasto, while narrating his adventures in the first person, nevertheless gives detailed accounts of other people's thoughts as though he were the omniscient author. Then in mid-stream Greene forgets who is speaking and lapses into the third person. Doralice's change from hate to love is wholly unconvincing and the treason of Egerio too obviously dragged in to cobble up an unhappy ending. Worst of all in a story which cannot be regarded as realistic, there is not one really sympathetic character. Greene's sub-title was the *Anatomy of Fortune*; the anatomy of villainy would have been more accurate. He followed this with the *Card of Fancy* in 1587. I classify this as a romance because it has a fairly complex plot and adventures that ought to have excited our interest: it even ends with a combat between father and son. Yet as we read we can hardly keep our minds on the events. Characters are placed in situations only that they may talk. The youthful profligacy of Guydonius serves as a peg for moral lectures and as a pretext for reducing him to poverty: when it has served its turn, Greene seems to forget all about it.

In these books we see Greene still hankering after the pattern of *Euphues* and treating the narrative element as task work. In *Pandosto* (1588) a great change has come over him. Here at last the story is the thing. Dialogue and soliloquy, though still mostly euphuistic, have been reduced to reasonable proportions, and there is even some attempt to distinguish between courtly and rustic speakers. The narrative portions are often written without rhetoric in a plain, factual style; sometimes, indeed, too plain and factual to kindle our imagination. A consciousness that their plain prose tended to be low and dry (except in vituperation) may well have been one of the reasons why the minor Elizabethans welcomed so eagerly a ready-made recipe for beauty such as euphuism. *Pandosto* is thus a far more efficient piece of work than *Arbasto* or the *Card*, but it is unattractive.

A story so improbable needs to be transfigured by high sentiment and enthusiasm. In Greene it is bleached bare of any
moral feeling whatever. Pandosto, unlike Leontes, remains at
the end what he was at the beginning, a bloody and treacherous
tyrant; and though we meet shepherds there is no pastoral softness. There is a coldness, even a brutality, about Greene's mind,
which unfits him for telling this sort of tale. *Menaphon* (1589)
marks an advance, though it repeats devices which Greene had
already used in *Pandosto*. Here again we have an infant abandoned to the mercy of the waves, and here again disguise leads
to the threat of incest. This time, indeed, Greene goes one better:
the lady is wooed simultaneously by her father and her son.
The real interest of *Menaphon* is that it carries further that
escape from rhetorical rigidity which was beginning in *Pandosto*. We have here at times a different rhetoric that can really
convey emotion: 'I tell thee he made the chamber bright with
his beautie whan he was born.' Sometimes in the dialogue
there is a sparkle of wit. Elsewhere Greene's new freedom leads
him astray, Olympia becomes a mere scold in a scene where (I
believe) that effect was not intended, and Pleusidippus replies
to her in the manner of Pistol. There are some admirable poems,
and more feeling for external nature than Greene had yet
displayed.

Pandosto deserves to be remembered, as it is, chiefly in connexion with the *Winter's Tale*: but the celebrity of Lodge's
Rosalynde (1590) is not entirely due to our modern interest in
Shakespeare's sources; it had run through nine editions by
1624. It is generally supposed to be based on the fourteenth-
century *Gamelyn*. If Lodge read this he must have read it in
manuscript. The thing is not impossible, though the extensive
medieval reading which a modern scholar has traced in Lodge
seems to have been directed to useful compendiums ('Mirrors'
of this, and 'Flowers' of that) rather than to ballads and
romances. There may well be some intermediate version still
undiscovered. If Lodge worked directly from *Gamelyn* he must
be given credit for considerable invention, for *Rosalynde* is further
from it than *As You Like It* from *Rosalynde*.

Gamelyn is a simple, fierce tale addressed to all who have
reasons for hating elder brothers, abbots, sheriffs, and top-dogs
in general. Lodge had plenty of reasons for disliking his own
elder brother: but if it was this that first attracted him to the

story, the compensatory element in his imagination was soon subordinated to the disinterested. He softens, lightens, sentimentalizes the whole thing. Once we reach the forest, as in Shakespeare, no one has any further business than to make love and poetry and play at the pastoral life. This poverty of action in the book's second half is doubtless a fault; but the poems, and a certain freshness that comes through all the literary pastoralism, carry it off.

After *Rosalynde* it is a disappointment to turn to Lodge's *Robert Duke of Normandy* (1591). He here spoils the old tale of Robert the Devil by omitting the Devil's share in it. *Euphues Shadow* (1592) only just slips across the frontier between our previous category and that of the romances. *William Longbeard* (1593) is a piece of mere book-making.

The last of Lodge's romances, *A Margarite of America* (1596) is his best: if indeed it is his at all. Lodge himself tells us that he found the story written in Spanish, in the library of the Jesuits at Santos 'some four yeares since, being at sea with M. Candish'. Of course this tale of a Spanish book may be untrue. On the other hand, the commercial writers of Elizabeth's time were not inclined to waste their own invention if another man's would serve. Melbancke's *Philotimus*, Lodge's own *Catharos* and *Devil Conjured*, are full of borrowed stuff. And *Margarite* is suspiciously above Lodge's usual level. There are, to be sure, passages that could not have occurred in any Spanish original, but these could easily have been interpolated. What seems to me the strongest argument for Lodge's authorship will be thought paradoxical by some. I disbelieve his debt to the Spanish precisely because he acknowledges it. In *Catharos* and the *Devil* he pilfers silently. I think that a writer who hides his real debts would be quite likely to boast a false one if it lent an exotic flavour to his work.

The *Margarite* is closer to Heliodorus and Sidney than any of the romances I have yet mentioned, but harsher and (in some ways) more splendid than either. The scene is laid in the empires of Mosco and Cusco, both conceived as high pagan civilizations in some undefined period of the past. Its haste *in medias res* is admirable. Rhetoric (for the dialogue is highly rhetorical) is raised to quite a new power. Far from being a mere external decoration, it becomes in the best passages at once an ironic contrast to, and a subtle expression of, the pride and passion of the speakers. If the book is not realistic, it is real; the compulsive imagination of a larger, brighter, bitterer, more dangerous world than ours. It is hard romance with gorgeous backgrounds provided for scenes of lavish bloodshed: it is rather like the romances of Eddison.

Before proceeding to the realistic stories, we must notice a few works which do not fit exactly into any of my three classes. One of these, Greene's *Mourning Garment* (1590) is in a way very close to the *Mirror of Modesty*: as that retold Susanna and the Elders, it retells (and spoils) the parable of the Prodigal Son, tricking it out with inset stories, a pastoral interlude, and euphuistic diatribes, yet at other times reproducing the exact words of scripture. It has just too much story to be grouped with the family of *Euphues*, and parts of that story are, in matter if not in style, too realistic—indeed too close to what we surmise of Greene's own life—to be called romantic. Only this possible biographical interest could cheat us for a moment into thinking it a good book. The virtuous Rabbi Bilessi has a disquieting resemblance to Polonius. The two other books which Greene brought out in the same year, *Never too Late* and *Francesco's Fortunes* are really a single story. In it we see Greene struggling towards, but not quite reaching, a purely realistic type of fiction. An abstract of the story might sound like that of a true novel but this would be a little deceptive. Only through a meeting with a mysterious palmer at Venice do we reach the main theme; we end with a pastoral tale; and there are euphuistic letters and soliloquies. In between these the style is fairly plain. Taken as an imagined satisfaction of the unavailing wishes which may have beset Greene in the wretchedness of his last years, the story of Francesco is deeply moving. Taken as a work of art in its own right, it will not stand very high. I cannot agree with an earlier critic that Francesco's passion for Infida is 'depicted with terrible intensity and vividness'.

The works of John Dickenson defy classification for rather different reasons. The two which date from 1594, *The Shepherd's Complaint* and *Arisbas* are heavily influenced by the *Arcadia*. The *Complaint* is almost as static as *Euphues* but it does not at all belong to the same type. The story (what there is of it) is essentially a frame for ornate prose and for some charming poems. All is melting, amorous, 'Golden' to the last degree.

Arisbas has stronger narrative elements. The style is poetic prose, not euphuistic: so poetic that it sometimes reads like a not very lucid translation from real poetry in some other language. Many of the poems are perfect in their kind, and Dickenson handles classical metres better than most of his contemporaries. His third work, *Greene in Conceit New raised from his grave to write the Tragic History of Fair Valeria of London* (1598) is of quite a different sort. Greene's ghost, risen from an afterworld which is neither Christian nor pagan but merely satirical, appears to the author and relates the story of a wicked wife. We begin with Dickenson's poetical prose but soon lapse into euphuism, and the debate between Giraldo in love and the sage old misogynist is exactly in Lyly's manner. The book improves when Jockie, 'a sillie boy borne in the north of Albion', comes on the scene. We now have some tolerable realism, and once a flash of fancy that suggests Dickens; a bankrupt's house 'growing queasie stomacht through a long consumption of the moueables, did in a generall vomit spewe out the master, the mystris, and all their traine'.

Chettle's *Piers Plainness* (1595) also mixes romance and realism, but far more artfully than Greene. Like the Victorian novelists who catered for family reading by combining many different kinds of interest, Chettle contrives a single complex story which will enable him to regale us now with lovers, forests, shipwrecks, and battles, now with gulls, brokers, and money-lenders. This is quite a different thing from the medieval inter-weaving, and I do not know of anyone who did it before Chettle. The more comic and sordid scenes will probably appeal most to the modern reader. They are certainly excellent in their own kind. Chettle has a gift for describing personal appearance: witness the Merchant who was a 'man of meane stature with a sulphurous face, his eyes sanguine, his breath strong, his gate stately'. But the romantic parts are equally well done. Queen Aeliana, except for one euphuistic soliloquy (no heroine could then fall in love without it) is more credible and likeable than any woman in Lyly, Greene, or Lodge. The political affairs are strangely convincing. And the whole is couched in a style that never gets between us and the matter. Why, then, we may ask, has everyone heard of *Euphues* and *Pandosto* while only students have heard of *Piers*? The real reason, I fear, is that even post-humous fame depends largely on accident. Catch-phrases about

our 'first novel', interest in euphuism itself, the link between
Pandosto and Shakespeare, are the real causes.

I now come to the realistic stories, and must at once confess
that the adjective is here used mainly in a negative sense. They
are 'realistic' only in so far they generally avoid rhetoric and
the supernatural, write their dialogue in 'language such as
men do use', and deal chiefly with the life of humble people.
They have their own idealism, but it is of a homely sort. They
have, too, their own improbabilities: but these are admitted for
the sake of farce or sensationalism.

Greene's *Groats-Worth of Wit bought with a million of Repentance* (1592) might almost be classed among pamphlets: but in
so far as it is fiction at all, it is realistic. Greene is anxious to
parade rather than to conceal the autobiographical element in
his story of Roberto and passes finally into direct confession.
The historical interest with which we follow Greene when he
paints the misery and conscious degradation of the first professional playwrights, and the famous attack on the 'vpstart'
Shakespeare, will always ensure readers for the *Groats-Worth*.
As a work of art it is a slight thing. The style, generally free from
euphuism, is lively enough, and the portrait of the old usurer is
effective coarse painting.

The ancestors of Elizabethan realistic fiction are the jest-
books and a short digression on these will be relevant. The last
specimen of this kind which I noticed was the *Hundred Merry
Tales* of 1526. Several works, which hardly belong to literature
more closely than the comic papers of our own time, fill up the
gap between it and the date we have now reached. Among
them are the *Tales and Quick Answers* (1535?), the *Sackful of News*
(entered 1557/8), *Gests of Scoggin* (entered 1565/6), the *Merry
Tales made by Master Skelton* (1567), with *Tarlton's Jests*, the
Mad Men of Gotam, and others. Their dates, authorship, and
bibliography are often obscure. This is the less to be regretted
because we must admit that they show no progress towards
connected fiction. Even when the jests are all attributed to a
single hero there is no attempt at chronological sequence, and
hardly any character: neither Skelton nor Skoggan comes so
near to being a character as Ally Sloper or Ruggles. The
transitional work between these and real comic fiction is the
Life and pranks of long Meg of Westminster (1590).[1] Despite its

---

[1] The date, 1582, sometimes given for this work, springs from a false title-page.

popularity (in versions that may differ from one another as widely as those of a ballad) it is not of much value: you will hear better jokes *ex tempore* in any third-class carriage today. Its importance lies in the fact that it has some faint sequaciousness: it begins with Meg's first arrival in London and marries her (unemphatically) somewhere near the end. To that extent there is some 'life' as well as 'pranks' and Meg's stature, if nothing else, makes her at least an image. It is possible to think of her existing in between her jokes: and it is made clear that her heart was in the right place. Skelton, Skoggan, and Tarlton had been mere names.

The approach to unity in *Long Meg* is still, however, so faint that it left Nashe and Deloney with almost everything still to do.

The *Unfortunate Traveller* (1593), whether or not indebted to *Lazarillo de Tormes* (a subject on which different views have been held), is a novelty in English literature in so far as it combines old elements in a new way. Yet it remains rather a medley with picaresque elements than a fully fledged picaresque novel. It begins with jest-book material which is, however, greatly improved by the continuity of the narrative and the liveliness of the dialogue. We pass thence into a digression on puritanism where Nashe seems to forget that he is not now writing a pamphlet. It is only in the latter part of the book that the blood-curdling stories begin to succeed one another with tolerable freedom from interruption: and even of these Heraclide's tragedy is mainly a peg for the heroine's speeches. Whether Nashe finds narrative invention a strain and gladly escapes from it, or whether the exuberance of his mind was uncontrollable, he does not drive on so steadily as we could wish. The characters, vividly particularized by a few ludicrous gestures or the like, are good in their way, which is the way of the better pamphleteers: hardly 'characters' in the later novelist's sense of the word. Perhaps an exception should be made in favour of Cutwolfe. That grandiose depravity momentarily captures the imagination. The *Traveller* is far from being Nashe's best book, and cannot in my opinion be rated as the best Elizabethan 'novel'. It yields to Chettle's work in construction, to *Margarite* in passion, and to the *Arcadia* in ordered harmony. But it has those qualities which to some tastes (not all) will compensate for everything: it is emphatically what those who like it call 'full-blooded'.

Compared with Nashe, Thomas Deloney (who died about 1600) may appear almost tame. *Jacke of Newbury* (1597) comes nearest of his works to the shape of a true novel; *The Gentle Craft* (1597 and 1598) and *Thomas of Reading* (1598?) are rather narrative medleys. All alike are written to please a coarse, kindly, thrifty, and ambitious society of urban tradesmen. There are occasional, and not very happy, digressions into romance and even patches of borrowed euphuism; but for the most part we are in a world of industrious apprentices who either turn out to be disguised noblemen or else marry their masters' widows and are soon happily affluent widowers. They run model factories and make prodigious fortunes while treating their workpeople with the greatest generosity. It is, no doubt, a wishful sort of imagination: but the wishes were good ones. The comic parts are often (not always) either too coprological or too violent for the tastes of my own generation; I can hardly regard burying a man alive (even if he was a 'massing priest') as a 'mad pranke'. The real excellence of Deloney is in his dialogue; he has a peculiar talent for reproducing the chatter of silly women.

With Deloney our account of Elizabethan fiction may end. When we consider the copious and varied production in all its three classes, the surprising thing is that so little came of it in the end. In Richard Johnson, whose *Seven Champions* appeared in 1596 and 1597, we return to what is substantially medieval romance, though of the feeblest, and smirched with rhetoric. Emmanuel Forde, whose *Ornatus and Artesia* (1595) and *Parismus* (1598) fall within our century, is likewise romantic and rhetorical and, though uninspired, less crude than Johnson. He and Deloney both continued to be reprinted within the eighteenth century.

III

Of those who attempted at this time to write about literature not all deserve the name of *critics*, and Sidney, who deserves it best, has already been mentioned. William Webbe is in a class by himself, uniquely bad. His *Discourse of English Poetry* (1586) displays an ignorance even then hardly credible. He is a perfect specimen of the literary 'hanger-on' who without knowledge, sensibility, or sense volunteers support for all that his betters are doing when they are least wise and praises all who are already popular. One need hardly add that he is very fierce against 'ryming Ballet makers' and 'unlearned Pamphlets'.

The *Arcadian Rhetoric* (1588) of Abraham Fraunce, who wrote also the *Lawyer's Logic* and a Latin comedy *Victoria*, is remembered chiefly because its author had the happy idea of illustrating each precept not only by Greek and Latin but by English, Italian, French, and Spanish examples. His English examples come chiefly from Sidney, then unprinted. From Spenser he quotes passages both of the printed *Calendar* and the still unprinted *Faerie Queene*. This little textbook thus provides evidence both for the prevalence of circulation in manuscript and for the growing fame of the two recent poets whom it cites side by side with Homer, Virgil, Tasso, and 'Sallust' (that is, Du Bartas). Fraunce also quotes Richard Willey (or Willes) and 'the booke called Pierce Plowman'.

Francis Meres (1565-1647) is accidentally more useful to posterity than Webbe, but has no more claim to be a critic. His *Palladis Tamia* or *Wits Treasury* (1598) is an anthology of apophthegms or wise saws from various sources, grouped according to their subject-matter. The sections on *Poetrie* and *Poets* draw on Plutarch, Cato, Sidney, Harington, and others. To these Meres adds a *Comparative Discourse of our English poets with the Greeke, Latine, and Italian poets*; and this, because it helps to date some of the works he mentions and also provides evidence for contemporary reputations, has given him a twilit immortality in prefaces and footnotes. His method may be represented by the formula 'As A among the Ancients or Italians, so B among the English'. The point of the comparison may be almost anything from mere chronology ('As Greece had three poets of great antiquity . . . so hath England three auncient poets, Chaucer, Gower and Lydgate') to a play upon words ('As Anacreon died by the pot: so George Peele by the pox'). Meres's patterned equivalences bear about the same relation to real criticism as Fluellen's comparison of Macedon and Monmouth bears to real geography.

So much for the lumber; we may now turn to two works of real, though limited, merit, the *Schort Treatise conteining some rewlis and cautelis . . . in Scottis Poesie* which was included in the *Essayes of a Prentise* (1584) by James, still Sixth and not yet also First, and the anonymous *Art of English Poesy* (1589). The early and traditional attribution of the latter to one Puttenham has been questioned, but the case for George Puttenham (born *c.* 1529) is strong and I shall assume that he was the author. King James's book might, no doubt, have been treated in our very first chapter, but he is more use to us here, for the Scotch king and the English courtier provide an interesting contrast. Puttenham was obviously ten times the man that James could ever be, yet on versification James shows himself master of his subject and Puttenham is fumbling. This would not be very important if, as some suppose, James were merely copying Gascoigne, but of that I find no evidence. Their common subject compels them to raise the same questions and where both answer correctly both must of course give the same answer. Of identity in error, in terminology, or in the choice of examples, which might really prove a debt, there is no trace. What keeps James right is not Gascoigne but the great Scotch tradition which he inherits. His use of *fute* for 'syllable' is curious, but, being consistent, does no harm. He recommends a more wooden regularity than his great models, or he himself, practised, but that is his only serious fault. A man could still be grounded, though not per- fected, in English prosody by studying the *Schort Treatise.* He could even learn from it something of poetics in general, some- thing about the use of 'wilfull reasons' in love poetry (how much better this is than Puttenham's book on rhetoric!) and the different style suitable to flytings. James is, in fact, a good *prentise* who has had good masters and attended to them. Put- tenham in comparison is only a bewildered pioneer; poetically, though not in other respects, a barbarian. He has indeed grasped the idea of stress, which he calls 'sharpe accent', 'shrill accent', or simply 'accent'; but he handles the concept with great diffi- culty; notice the astonishing passage (at the end of II. iv) about a line of Surrey's, where for a moment his metrical unit seems to be not the syllable but the word, though he perhaps knows better. I do not believe we can conclude from this that stress within the line was really ignored by poets or the better sort of readers in the Drab Age. Gascoigne's theory, and the thumping regu- larity of most Drab poets, tell quite an opposite tale. The fault was Puttenham's own. Yet even he dimly heard what he failed to analyse. He points out that the verse *God graunt this peace may long endure* would fall less 'tunably' if you tried to read it in what we now call trochaic or falling rhythm (*Gód graunt thís peace*) and

disarmingly admits that he can't think why (II. xviii). And
here we touch on one of his excellences: few critics are so
honest.

It cannot even be claimed that Puttenham's taste compensates for his lack of science. His work embodies the standards
of the Drab Age and most of it was probably written long before
it was printed. It was clearly much added to and revised. The
list of poets in I. xxxi and the discussion of classical metres in
II. xiii–xvi are almost certainly later work. But whatever may
have been added later, Puttenham's taste was formed in the
Drab Age: formed indeed principally on Tottel. Though he
lived to praise Raleigh and Spenser, there is no sign that he
perceived any difference between their poetry and that which
delighted his youth. He loved, though his own verses seldom
attained, ruthless regularity. He also liked what he called
'ocular proportion', by which he meant poems that present some
geometrical figure to the eye; a beauty, he had heard, very
common in China, Tartary, and Persia. His examples suggest
rather the court poetry of Lilliput in the age of Gulliver. It is
perhaps more interesting that he regards the poet as a 'pleader'
(III. vii, xix) who must use all the tricks of debate, anticipating
answers and 'making wise as if he set but light' by some points
which he has really no intention of conceding. It will be noticed
that ocular proportion was still dear to Herbert and that the
conception of the poet as 'pleader' was magnificently realized
by Donne. The methods have indeed something in common
(however they differ in value) both with one another and with
Gascoigne's Rule of Invention. All bear witness to a taste for
something curious and clever in poetry—as Puttenham says
'a certaine noueltie and strange maner' unlike 'our ordinarie
talke' (III. i). And Golden poetry did not in any new degree, or
any peculiar fashion, cater for it. We may therefore suspect that,
even before the Golden Age began, the impulse which was to
lead to the metaphysical already existed, and perhaps lived
through the Golden Age without exactly noticing it. That would
explain why Puttenham sees no particular novelty in Spenser
and Raleigh. They gave in fact more than the Drab poets,
but not much more of the thing he liked best. I suspect that he
would have welcomed Sylvester's Du Bartas much more warmly.
Certainly his own best (or least helpless) verses seem to me to
have a post-Elizabethan flavour:

> How swift the circle stirre aboue,
> His centre point doth neuer moue:
> All things that euer were or be
> Are closde in his concauitie (II. xii).

Without knowledge, without much poetic sensibility, Puttenham might be expected to have made a very bad book. Actually, it is a refreshment to turn to him. Along with the weaknesses, he has also the merits of a gentleman and an amateur. He addresses himself to taste, even if not the best taste, as hardly any of his rivals do. He writes for courtiers, for the 'courtly Maker', for the 'learned eare' indeed, but learned in 'courtly trifles' not 'scholastical toyes' (II. xii), for men (and ladies) to whom 'schollerly affectation' would be 'very irkesome' (III. xxv). With him poetry escapes from the lecture room, becomes again the gay science. Cheap moralizing and misogyny disappear: 'the first founder of all good affections is honest loue' (I. xxii). Slavish humanism disappears, though his classical erudition is far more reliable than Greene's or Lyly's. He does not believe that poetry need be didactic: trifles are freely admitted as 'conuenient solaces and recreations of man's wit' (II. xii), and even moderate wantonness (I. x). He is quite free from the snobbish or envious acrimony which the commercial authors usually show to the 'rakehelly rout' of popular rhymers. He sees no reason why metrical romances of Arthur and the rest should be put down, for there are 'sundry formes of poems and not all one' (I. xix). Nor is his theory of poetry at bottom less serious than anyone else's. In two places (I. xxii, III. xxv *ad fin.*) he comes astonishingly near the conception of poetry as expression; even more astonishing, for that age, is the passage on imagination (I. viii). This is the paradox of Puttenham, that though he could not scan a line nor tell a good poem from a bad, he wrote more sense about poetry than any man of his age. The explanation is to be found in the quality of his mind; small and poor though his poetical experience was, he reflected on it with a mind at ease, disinterested, candid, well stored with 'experience and observation of the world' (I. i). If barbarous as a critic, he is highly civilized as a man. His prose style is free both from rhetoric and from the clumsiness of much Drab prose; the bad sentence at the end of II. xiii being, I think, the only exception.

Thomas Campion's *Observations in the Art of English Poesie*

(1602) and Samuel Daniel's *Defence of Ryme* (1603), despite their dates, fall properly within our province since they conclude— for a time—the characteristically sixteenth-century controversy about classical metres in English. Each states its case better than it had been stated before. Campion's doctrine is far removed from the crudities of Harvey and Spenser: he knows that dactylic metres are unsuitable to our language and feels, with a musician's sensibility, that five feet in English are equivalent to six in Latin. He is not in the least deceived by spelling; 'we must esteeme our sillables as we speake, not as we write'. Yet when all is said his theory has very little to do with English practice, even his own. Thus in analysing the line

> Men that do fall to misery, quickly fall,

he explains that the syllables *to miser-* are a 'Tribrack'. So they are; but the stress-accent on the first of *misery* has been ignored as if it had nothing to do with the movement of the line. Yet his temporary concern with quantitative metres bore delightful fruit in 'Rose-cheekt Lawra come'. I suspect that a poetic impulse towards the unrhymed lyric came first and the theory was devised to mitigate the innovation. Campion (quite erroneously) thought he could not swim without these classical bladders. And they are not at all becoming. He adopts the humanistic attitude in all its boastful ignorance: everything before Erasmus, 'Rewcline', and More is to him 'illiterate Monks and Friers', and rhyme in its metrical use must be bad because it is listed as a mere figure in the books of rhetoric.

It was this negative side of Campion's essay that chiefly provoked Daniel to reply, and the merits of his *Defence* are quite different from those of the *Observations*. As an artist Daniel is completely overmatched by Campion; there is more poetry in one of Campion's *Airs* than in all Daniel's epic and epistles, and there are passages in the *Defence* which suggest that the author is very little concerned with poetry, as poetry, at all. 'It is matter', not form, he says, 'that satisfies the iudiciall.' New metres will not make our poems 'the wiser'. And his own preferences in verse (he modestly declines to set them up as rules) do not suggest so fine an ear as Campion's. The value of the *Defence* is that, quietly, soberly, and irresistibly, it refutes all that was arbitrary and ignorant in the humanist position. To the oft-repeated charge that rhyme is used by 'barbarous' nations, Daniel very sensibly replies that 'the vniuersallitie argues the generall power of it', sweeps aside the 'tyrannicall Rules of idle Rhetorique', and presently questions that whole estimate of the Middle Ages which most of his contemporaries assumed. He lacks the historical knowledge necessary for a full support of his position, but he has the historical sense. He knows (and this is very rare) that what we call 'history' is 'but a Mappe' and 'dooth no otherwise acquaint vs with the true Substance of Circumstances, than a superficiall Card dooth the Sea-man with a Coast neuer seene, which alwayes prooves other to the eye than the imagination forecast it'.

We have still left untreated a great body of translations and of prose written not to entertain but to instruct; and most of it, in a book of this length, must be omitted. I shall pass over translations in silence: they no longer have the literary importance they had earlier in the century. Among original writers two theologians claim the chief place. But first a few pages must be spared for Hakluyt and for two authors who, to their lasting credit, tried to stem the cruel fury of the witch-scare.

Reginald Scot, who had written on the hop garden in 1574, lives by his gigantic *Discovery of Witchcraft* (1584). *Discovery* here means what we should call 'refutation' or exposure: Scot addresses himself primarily to judges, and his work, according to Wood, 'did for a time make great impressions on the Magistracy and Clergy, tho afterwards condemned by James'. Genuine humanity was clearly his motive when he began. He is the champion of 'manie poor old women' against those 'vnnaturall people' who delight 'to pursue the poore, to accuse the simple, and to kill the innocent'. But I think he was also actuated, intermittently, by a quality of mind which, if it had come to dominate him completely, would have lifted him right out of his own century and made him more at home in the period of Sprat and Locke. At times he seems on the verge of rejecting the whole outlook which made witchcraft credible. He thinks that the Devil took Christ into the high mountain only 'in a vision' (v. vii). He doubts, with Calvin, whether the Book of Job is *res gesta* or *exempli gratia*. He takes for granted the cessation of all miracles and all prophecy (VIII. i, ii). Finally, in the 'Discourse upon Devils and Spirits', he reduces all that is said of such beings in scripture to something not much more than metaphor. 'This worde [*sc.* Spirit] doth signifie a secret force and power wherewith oure mindes are mooued and directed: if vnto holy things then is it the motion of the holie spirit . . . if vnto euill things then is it the suggestion of the wicked spirit.' The super-naturals are turning into abstract nouns. Against the dominant doctrine of aerial bodies he asserts that 'spirits and bodies are by antithesis opposed to one another': we are near the Car-tesian dualism. Such is the skeleton of Scot's thought: but in the book with its fat flesh about it, it makes a different impression. In the thirteenth book, on that 'naturall magike' which he thinks both real and lawful, he seems credulous not only to the same degree but in the very same way as his contemporaries. He is also very full of anecdotes: the unsavoury, but sometimes funny, stories in Book IV do not seem necessary to the argu-ment. Finally, when in XII we find whole chapters of spells, and in XV of Salomonic conjurations, set out verbatim till the brain reels, we begin to wonder what our author would be at. In effect Scot has begun to make his refutation of magic into a magician's handbook, and has really little right to complain when an anonymous writer adds to the 1665 edition of the *Discovery* more chapters of magical instruction which give no hint of either scepticism or disapproval. Scot fell a victim to that psychological law whereby disbelief, equally with belief, will fascinate. Something, too, must be allowed to his love of rambling. His vast book, with its stories, curiosities, anti-popery, and theology, ends by being good 'mixed reading' like Burton's *Anatomy*. His style, which never attempts eloquence, is clear, muscular, and often vivid; VII. xv on 'Bugs' is especially good.

George Giffard (ob. 1620), the puritan incumbent of Malden, wrote two books on this subject, the *Subtle Practices* (1587) and the *Dialogue concerning Witches* (1593). He believes that devils really consort with witches but not that they give or receive any real power by doing so: the juries who condemn witches are often, he thinks, more ensnared by the devil than those they condemn. Giffard's tone is manly, and the *Dialogue* has some dramatic merits. Samuel, the countryman in a neighbourhood poisoned with fear and cruelty, lives as a tragicomical character. He talks as Shallow might talk on the verge of a nervous break-down: 'truely we dwell here in a bad countrey, I think euen one of the worst in England . . . when I goe but into my closes I am afraide, for I see now and then an Hare . . . and there is a foule

great catte sometimes in my Barne, which I have no liking vnto'.
His wife at first promises to be equally good, but after a speech
or two relapses into highly improbable silence.

If we could allot Richard Hakluyt (1552?-1616) space pro-
portional to his deserts, he would have a chapter: but he is
hardly an author. To his scientific zeal, his patriotism, and his
'huge toile' as a collector and editor of travels, we are immensely indebted. The *Principal Navigations . . . of these 1500
years* (1589), which afterwards became the three-volume *Principal
Navigations . . . of these 1600 years* (1598, 1599, and 1600), was one
of the most useful and delightful publications of the century. The
first-hand narratives which Hakluyt used wherever he could are
of very various origin; reprinted from books already published,
translated, found in 'an old ligier book,' found in possession of
a captured 'Portugall', 'collected' out of Hakluyt's own 'notes
and examinations', or written at his request. At one end of the
scale we have reprints of Raleigh's *Report of the Fight about the
Azores* (1591) and *Discovery of Guiana* (1596), works by a courtier
and an accomplished writer. The second of these combines
almost every charm that a prose narrative could have—substantial truth, a quest for a fabulous city that might have come
out of Rider Haggard, a sound prose, pathos, chivalry, a gift
for description. Few things in fiction are more enchanting than
Raleigh's picture of the manless forests from which 'still as we
rowed, the deere came down feeding by the water side as if they
had been vsed to a keeper's call'. And he knows the secret; not
to tell too much, even when it clamours to be told, for many
details 'are more pleasing in describing than reading'. Below
Raleigh, but still with literary pretensions, comes a writer like
Laurence Keymis: no bad pen, but better in argument than in
narration. After these (and one or two other exceptions) come
the ordinary ships' officers who write only to be understood
and have perhaps never written before. It would be pleasant
(in a certain mood) to believe that the plain man of action need
only set down what he saw to be sure of beating the literary
men at their own game. But it is not true. Hakluyt's untaught
authors differ very widely in merit, and some are bad. The
narrator of the 1595 voyage on which Drake and Hawkins
both died often has matter which no one could make dull, but
he brings it nearer to dullness than one would have thought
possible. John Sparke, recording Hawkins's voyage in 1564, is

livelier—the Samboses 'doe jagge their flesh as workemanlike as a Jerkin-maker with us pricketh a jerkin'—but can sometimes sadly mar a good episode. Thomas Cates, who tells of Drake's West Indian voyage begun in 1585, brings off the feat (great writers have tried it in vain) of so describing a physical object, the coco-nut, that those who have not seen it would really know what it is like. Two of the narratives (Anthony Sherley's voyage in 1596 and James Lancaster's in 1594) are of great literary interest. Both the authors insert speeches in the classical manner, obviously not because they are imitating the ancients, but because mere nature has in them rediscovered this technique. The second of these two pieces is perhaps the best of all those in Hakluyt which seem to owe nothing to art. I make these distinctions not to obscure the fact that voyage after voyage is excellent reading but to separate out those in which our enjoyment owes something to the teller as well as to the thing told. Hakluyt himself, though he is usually behind the scenes, comes vividly before us in the epistle to the first edition where he records the day and hour which first kindled his lifelong passion for geography: it is a passage that warms the heart.

The two theologians who deserve most attention from a literary historian are Cardinal William Allen[1] (1532–94) on the Roman side and Richard Hooker (1554?–1600) on the Protestant. Much of Allen's work was, naturally, in Latin; but the *Defence and Declaration* (1565), edited by Fr. Bridgett under the title *Souls Departed* in 1886, the *Treatise in Defence of the Power of Priesthood* (1567), the *Apology of the English Seminaries* (1581), and the *True, Sincere and Modest Defence* (1584) give him a higher place as a vernacular writer than our older critical tradition recognized. Like Hooker, he rises above the usual controversial methods of the time; he neither carps nor snarls and trusts more to a steady exposition of what he believes to be the truth than to a fussy detection of errors. This makes him in the long

---

[1] b. 1532, at Rossall. Entered at Oriel, 1547. B.A. and fellow, 1550. Principal of St. Mary's Hall, Oxford, and Proctor, 1556. Retires to Louvain, 1561. Once more in England, 1562–5. Becomes priest. Journey to Rome, 1567. Founds the English College at Douai, 1568. D.D., 1571. Second journey to Rome, 1575. The College, expelled from Douai, takes refuge at Rheims, 1578. Third journey to Rome, 1579. Douai placed under control of the Jesuits. In bad health, leaves the College for Spa, 1585. Cardinal, 1587. Succeeded by Richard Barret as Resident Superior of College, 1588. Ob. 1594, at Rome.

run more formidable. The autobiographical method adopted in the *Treatise* (II. i) is especially effective. And he is always at the centre of the controversy, always defending that which, not by polemical accident but by deep cleavage of spirit, was most repellent to the adversary. To him, as to all the Roman writers, Protestants were the very reverse of 'puritans': they were 'soft physitions' (*Defence and Declaration*, I, Preface), against whom he must assert a doctrine admittedly sterner and darker, 'the behoulding whereof must neades ingender som sorowe and sadnesse of minde' and even (such is our 'frailetie') 'a certaine bitter taediousnesse' (ibid. II, Preface). Significantly, he writes not only to refute but also 'for the stirring vp of the feare of God in myself' (ibid. I, Preface). Purgatory is for him essentially a balancing of accounts, a 'satisfaction of Gods iustice' (ibid. I. i, *Treatise*, II. viii) where sin is 'recompensed' by 'payne' (*Defence and Declaration*, I. iv). There is light as well as gloom in his theology, as we see in his beautiful chapters on heaven (ibid. I. vi) and on the communion of saints (ibid. II. ii). But he is very deeply impressed with the fact that 'gods trueth, for terrour and bitternes it beareth', is not always followed even where it is known (*Treatise*, Preface).

Allen will appeal most easily to moderns in the *Apology* and *Modest Defence* when he pleads, with great feeling but with great restraint, the sufferings of his church at the hands of Elizabeth's government, and disputes the claim that his brethren were killed and tortured not for religion but for treason. Yet we have with him the same disturbing experience as with all sixteenth-century theologians: when they speak for the persecuted we feel that they are men we can understand, but next moment they speak as persecutors themselves and a gulf yawns between us. Allen's opponents twitted him with the Marian persecution of Protestants, and his withers were completely unwrung. That was quite different. The whole argument of the third chapter in the *Modest Defence* leads up to the conclusion 'that as no lawe of God or man can force vs to be protestantes, no more can any reason be alledged nor iust excuse made for either yong or old why, being baptized or brought vp amongst Arrians or Calvinists, they may not be forced to returne to the Catholique Church'.

The true quality of Allen's prose style has, in my opinion, been much obscured by a theory which Professor J. S. Phillimore

suggested in 1913. According to this theory Allen's style (and
that of some other Recusant authors) represents 'the true
main-stream' of English prose, 'dammed' at home and not
recovered till the time of Dryden. Now all that is really common
to the mature style of Allen and that which came in with Dryden
is a negation. I say Allen's mature style, because Allen in his
youth sometimes writes as an Ur-Euphuist. He knows all the
tricks of Drab Age rhetoric and has left us sentences that Lyly
might have envied; 'commit what you list, omit what you list,
your preachers shall praise it in their wordes and practice it in
their workes', or 'Feasting hathe wonne the fielde of fasting
and chambering allmost banished chastitye' (*Defence and
Declaration*, Preface). This kind of decoration, however, disappears in his later work. His style then, admittedly, shares with
Dryden's (or Sprat's or Swift's or Defoe's) the negative characteristic that both lack fantastical tropes and figures. But if that
lack is enough to identify the 'true main-stream', then this
stream was never 'dammed' in sixteenth-century England.
Hundreds, possibly thousands, of pages of unadorned prose
were produced at home in the age of Elizabeth: the plainness
which separates the later Allen so neatly from a Lodge or a
Sidney does not separate him from Knox, Bridges, Scot, Henry
Smith, or most of Hakluyt's voyagers. Nor does Allen in the
least anticipate the short and easily intelligible sentences of
Dryden. Fr. Bridgett, who knew him as only a transcriber can,
was under no such illusion. He feared that readers would find
the 'length and intricacy' of his sentences an obstacle, and tried
to sign-post them by a revised punctuation. The staple of Allen's
style is the long sentence, but not the long sentence braced (as
in Winzet or Hooker) with a latinized structure: rather the
long sentence spreading like a pool. This is a very dangerous
instrument, as previous quotations from the Drab authors have
shown. The real merit of Allen lies partly in the trenchancy of
the short sentences with which he varies his style and partly in
the fact that he came as near as any man could to succeeding
in that type of long sentence. Some of them are surprisingly
vigorous in rhythm. None, I believe, ever comes quite to grief.
The apparent exception in Fr. Bridgett's edition of the *Defence
and Declaration* (II. iii. 189) is corrupt: the editor has dropped
out an essential *if*. But many are jaw-breakers. Let anyone who
still holds Professor Phillimore's theory try to read aloud, in the

Apology, cap. ii, the 357-word sentence which begins 'And for vs of the schoole' and ends 'domesticals of faith'. Even if a man likes that way of writing, he must not call it 'the true mainstream'. However we may judge it aesthetically, we must admit as historians that the long sentence, unstiffened by foreign idiom, had no future before it. The path which Allen followed did not lead either to Dryden, Defoe, and Cobbett on the one hand, or to Browne, Taylor, Gibbon, De Quincey, and Ruskin on the other. It was a dead-end. In that dead-end Allen, I confess, did wonders. He is a virile, dignified, and abundantly interesting author. The trouble is not so much that he has been overpraised, as that he has been praised amiss.

In order to give the work of Hooker its proper setting we must now retrace our steps and make some mention, however slight and selective, of the controversy which occasioned it. Since our subject is not ecclesiastical history, it may suffice if we begin our story in the year 1572. During the earlier part of the queen's reign the dress of the clergy (both in and out of church) had been the chief question at issue among Protestants. The puritan clergy had from the outset disliked, and had at first disobeyed with impunity, the regulations on this matter. Their dislike, of course, sprang from a deeper disagreement between their conception of the Church and Elizabeth's. Much that she regarded as essential was to them only tolerable; much that she intended to be permanent would, they hoped, soon 'wither away' (like the State in the Marxist millennium) and leave a purer, a more radically Protestant, Church. During the Vestiarian controversy this divergence was 'a sleeping dog'. But it was not allowed to lie. In the sixties serious coercive action was taken. And when it was, the dog soon woke and began to bark: indeed it never ceased barking until the restoration of Charles II. Men who had been deprived or suspended for refusing to wear a surplice soon questioned loudly (what they had always more or less distrusted) the validity of that whole Elizabethan settlement under which they suffered. The year 1572 marks a turning-point because it saw the publication of the *Admonition to Parliament* by John Field and Thomas Wilcox. The title is significant. They do not petition but admonish. They address Parliament, not Convocation, because in Convocation they have already failed. But in Elizabeth's view they had no right to address Parliament.

Parliament might advise her on 'commonwealth matters': it was for Convocation to advise her as Head of the Church. The whole thing smelled of insubordination.

The controversy soon became copious. In the same year an unknown writer supplemented the *Admonition* with a *Second Admonition*: on the episcopal side John Whitgift produced an *Answer of a certain Libel entitled an Admonition*. This was directed against the original manifesto by Field and Wilcox, but the *Second Admonition* reached Whitgift in time to be briefly mentioned at the end of his own pamphlet. In 1573 Cartwright retaliated with *A Reply to an Answer to M. Doctor Whitgift*: in 1574 Whitgift published his *Defence of the Answer*. That same year came Walter Travers's *Ecclesiasticae Disciplinae Explicatio*, translated by Cartwright as *A Full and Plain Declaration of Ecclesiastical Discipline*. In 1575 Cartwright continued his assault on Whitgift with the *Second Reply*, which he followed up in 1577 with *The Rest of the Second Reply*. Whitgift at this point abandoned the fight. In 1584, perhaps by Dudley Fenner but more probably by William Fulke, came *A Brief and Plain Declaration*, commonly known (from its running title) as *The Learned Discourse*, on the puritan side. This was answered in 1587 by John Bridges in his enormous *Defence of the Government Established*. In 1588 John Udall, for the puritans, brought out both his *Diotrephes* and his *Demonstration of the Truth of that Discipline*. In 1589 Thomas Cooper, for the Anglicans, published *An Admonition to the People of England*. By that time, as the reader may remember, the guerrilla episode of Martin was already in full swing.

This list, which omits a great many works, will, I think, give us a sufficient acquaintance with the controversy. I may note that Cartwright's *Reply*, *Second Reply*, and *Rest of the Second Reply* are respectively the T. C. Lib. I, Lib. II, and Lib. III which may have puzzled some students in the footnotes to Hooker. I shall use these same symbols here.

The modern reader, to whichever side he leans, will misunderstand this whole affair if he thinks that either party was defending liberty as we now understand it. This often appears to be the case, but the appearance is deceptive. 'It is allowed and commaunded to Christian men', says the *Second Admonition*, 'to holde that which is good, whosoever forbidde without exception, Prince or other.' It sounds like a manly assertion of religious

freedom. But next moment we read that when proper ecclesiastical rules have been deduced from scripture it is the prince who
'should see euery one of these things put in practice and punish
those that neglect them'. How this would work we learn later.
The civil power must force Papists to attend sermons and 'cause
them to be examined, how they profit, and if they profit not, to
punish them' and gradually increase the punishment, and finally
'cut them off' (T. C. i. 34, 35). Similarly, when the *Learned Discourse* says that princes 'are seruauntes of the Lawes and of the
common wealth'(p. 143) we seem to hear the voice of Bracton:
and when Bridges (xvi. 1370) replies that princes make the laws,
he sounds like the spokesman of Tudor sovereignty treading out
the last sparks of medieval justice. But in their context both
passages have a rather different value. The *Learned Discourse* is
arguing that as the prince is guided by wise counsel in civil
matters, so he must be guided by a consistory, that is, by the
puritan party, in setting up an ecclesiastical regimen to which
he must then bind his people by law. Those who are ecclesias-
tically censured will be also 'punished in body' (p. 141). To be
sure, the Church is to be distinct from the State, not (as now)
'shuffled wyth the common wealth' (T. C. i, Ep.). She will
not punish any Papist, adulterer, or blasphemer 'in body':
she will only hand him over to the civil power—as the Inquisition did.

Neither side questions the medieval assumption that unortho-
doxy is sinful and that sin must be treated as crime. Their picture
of Christianity always includes that disastrous figure 'the Christian magistrate' or 'godly prince'. As a result of his presence the
puritan maxim 'that nothing be don' in the Church 'but that
which you haue the expresse warrant of Gods worde for' (*Admonition*) has very serious political consequences. 'Gods worde' means
the Bible as interpreted by a consistory. The prince, enforcing by
law what the consistory declares to be God's will, thus becomes
in effect merely the executive officer of the Church, and, as
Bridges complains (*Defence*, xvi. 1335), the Church will thus have
that very dominion over the State which the puritans blamed
the Pope for usurping. The Anglican position, on the other hand,
by freeing the prince from this strict dependence on scripture
and yet making adherence to the prince's church compulsory,
leaves the religious life of every individual in bondage to political
power. Whatever they say, even whatever they wish, the puri-

tans are driven to put the Church above the State, and the Anglicans to put the State above the Church. And until the confusion between sin and crime is cleared up, there is no escape. Prince and priest in the sixteenth century both still desire to ride the pale horse theocracy: and when two men ride a horse we know where one must sit.

I have used the word *Priest* advisedly, though the puritans violently rejected it as a name for their 'ministers'. But Milton was quite right. The belief that puritanism necessarily tended to leave the layman 'alone with God' by abolishing any caste of spiritual intermediaries, seems to me a strange delusion. In Bunyan the women who are finally entrusted to Greatheart are first reproved for not having craved a 'conductor'. The preacher is as necessary in the puritan system as the 'massing priest' and the confessor had been in the Roman. Apart from a miracle, a 'wonderful worke', faith comes only from hearing sermons (T. C. i. 126). And 'sermons' does not include private discourses from a man's parents or religious friends; they can be preached only by one who is sent (ibid. 114)—that is, by a duly 'called' Presbyterian minister. It is only when they hear such sermons that men will 'fal down. . . acknouledging the great power of *God in his ministers*' (*Learned Discourse*, p. 68). The words which I have ventured to italicize are significant. Until preached, the Bible is 'as it were shut and clasped'; that is why the preachers who 'open' it are said to 'have the keyes off the kingdome' (T. C. ii. 380). Yet in another sense the 'assembly' or consistory has received the key of heaven from Christ: it can shut the door by excommunication (*Full and Plain Declaration*, p. 161).

The original *Admonition* of 1572 is a work not without literary pretensions: there are traces in it of euphuistic antithesis and even of rhyme. At that period such embellishments would not have seemed to any reader inconsistent with its high, prophetic attitude. Isaiah does not speak with more confidence of his mission than Field and Wilcox. Accept our 'platfourme' of church discipline, they say, or else 'be without excuse before the maiestie of our God who. . . hath by vs reuealed vnto you at this present the sinceritie and simplicitie of his Gospel'. The Genevan scheme of deacons, elders, ministers, and 'Seignorie' is then advanced, with the usual claim that it is all laid down in the New Testament. One disquieting feature of the puritan temper appears when the authors tell us that 'then' (in Apostolic times) church discipline brought it about that 'the congregation by the wickednes of the offender grieued, was by his publique penance satisfied'. One had hardly supposed that the main object of penance was to satisfy one's fellow parishioners. But this vicarious or disinterested 'grief' was ever-present to the puritan's mind. The 'godly' or 'tender' or 'weak' brother (ancestor of Mr. Podsnap's 'young person') is never told to mind his own business: the agonies he endures if his next door neighbour plays tennis on Sunday must be most carefully considered.

The *Second Admonition* was formerly attributed to Cartwright but Mr. Scott Pearson has, I think, sufficiently disposed of that claim. His opponents never accuse him of having written it: he himself speaks of it as if it were another man's work: and its style differs from his widely, and for the worse. It has hardly any literary merit. The sentences are very long and, though not exactly obscure, heavy and sapless. It differs from its predecessor by being more detailed and practical. The author knows how the revolution could be carried out tomorrow. But he seems to have little hope of efficient popular support. The godly discipline must be imposed from above. The Church will never keep these orders in peace 'except the comfortable and blessed assistance of the states and gouernors linke in to see them accepted in their countray and vsed'.

John Whitgift (1530–1604), though more memorable as an archbishop than as an author, writes much better than the second Admonisher. He is the most severe of those who wrote on the Anglican side, but severe without either scurrility or humour; as if he followed Bacon's precept that 'reproofs from authority ought to be grave and not taunting'. He thinks that 'lacke of seueritie is the principall cause' of the puritans' 'licentious libertie'. The main importance of his *Answer* is that it lays down the lines on which the controversy will run in the three books of Cartwright.

Thomas Cartwright (1535–1603) is the most striking figure on the puritan side, unless, perhaps, we should give that position to 'Martin'. He was a stormy petrel from his early years. He had conscientious objections to nearly everything. He himself tells us that when he was made a D.D. only the importunity of his friends persuaded him to 'swalow the fond and idle ceremonies' of degree-giving. An enemy describes him as 'highly conceited of himself for learning and holiness and a great contemner of others'. He lived to be the 'patriarke' of the party. Mr. Pig writes to Mr. Field in 1586 to 'moue Mr. Cartwright or some other our reuerend brethren to deliver their iudgements whether all layinge out of hayre be forbidden to all women'. He found it necessary in later life to deny that he had miraculous powers: no one ever accused him of healing the sick but it had got about that he killed sinners with his rebuke, as St. Peter killed Ananias and Sapphira.

No one doubts Cartwright's sincerity and learning, but there are passages in his works which might at first lead us to question his intelligence. He argues that the Apocrypha and the Homilies must not be read in church because unsanctified pans and besoms were not allowed in the Temple at Jerusalem (i. 157). Asked by Whitgift how he can prove that intending communicants were examined in the Apostolic period, he replies (i. 130) 'after this sort'; all things necessary were done, this thing is necessary, therefore this thing was done. These occasional absurdities, however, illustrate, not imbecility of mind, but the desperate shifts to which a strong mind may be put when hagridden by a premiss which it will never allow itself to reconsider. Cartwright's thought is twisted from the outset by the dangerous certitude (we have met it elsewhere) that God 'must have done' certain things. God does what is best for the church, this is best for the church, therefore God 'must have' done this; so runs the argument. The kind of faith which might be legitimately given to the major then gets attached to the minor, and facts repugnant to the conclusion have to be distorted. There 'must be' a 'platfourme' of church government in the New Testament, even though no one outside the puritan party can find it there. Whitgift is quite mistaken in saying that you cannot argue negatively from scripture: because scripture is perfect, even the negative argument from it is valid (ii. 50). It is injurious to the sacred text to suppose that it teaches only 'the principal pointes' of religion, only a 'rude, vnfashioned matter'. The Word of God did not merely cover the Church's nakedness: it gave her also all her 'chains and bracelets and rings and other jewels' (i. 14). Indeed, being perfect, it went much further: it contains the rule not only 'of all things pertaining to the Church' but of all things that 'can fall into any parte of mans life' (ibid.). For we are told to glorify God in all our actions, even in eating and drinking, and we cannot glorify except by acting in faith and cannot have faith except in the Word (ibid.). Thus all human tradition, all doctrines of Natural Law, and (equally) the new theory of sovereignty, are swept away to make room for what may be called a bibliocracy, the rule of the Book.

This position, however, is limited—perhaps confused—partly by certain concessions which Cartwright is forced to make, and partly by a second principle which has no logical connexion with it. He cannot deny that some practices must vary with time and place and are therefore left to the Church's discretion: but these variables will still be determined by scripture because they will obey the Pauline 'decently and in order'. This line of thought, if pursued, would threaten to blunt the antithesis between the puritans and their opponents. But Cartwright's distinction between variables and invariables would not coincide with the Anglican distinction between things indifferent and things essential to salvation. To an Anglican the essential was the Gospel, and many things in Discipline were indifferent. Cartwright will allow no separation of that sort; the Discipline is 'a parte off the gospell' (ii), nay, is the Gospel itself (ibid. 5), necessary to salvation, and 'of faith' (i. 14). The second principle which really, though never admittedly, supplements for Cartwright the bare text of scripture is the necessity of receding as far as possible from Roman practice. When you have to straighten a bent stick, he says, you bend it as far as it will go in the opposite direction (i. 103). Hence it would be better, in our 'indifferent ceremonies', to resemble the Turks than the Papists (i. 103).

This last startling assertion must not be taken as a mere ebullition of the spleen. Cartwright never forgets himself, says nothing he will not stand to. The Papists' practices are more to be avoided than the Turks', 'they being heretics and so near about vs' (i. 102). There is, of course, hatred as well as policy in Cartwright's attitude to the Papists; there was a desire, by no means unconscious, for revenge. This vengeance appeared to him not as a sin but as a duty. The 'vnreuenged and vnpurified shedinge of giltlesse blood' in the Marian persecution, so long as they remained unrevenged, were a national danger. That blood cried, like Abel's, from the cobble-stones of Smithfield, and 'the least drop' of it 'might be the destruction off a great and most mighty kingdome'. (This comes in the preface to his translation of Travers's *Disciplinae Explicatio*.) It will of course be understood that this 'perfect hatred' is levelled against Papists as Papists: of the men as men he doubts not that many will in God's good time be called to 'the knowledge of hys truthe' (i. 133).

The Discipline which Cartwright wished to impose, though ecclesiastical in name, would certainly have covered all things that 'can falle into anie parte of mans life'. Already in the opening pages of his first *Reply* he had promised that, under his system, not only great crimes but 'the smaller faultes of lying and vncomely iesting, of harde and cholericke speaches' would be corrected. But it is in the *Second Reply* that we really discover what tasks the Consistory was to lay upon its obedient 'godly magistrate'. Christ abrogated the ceremonial, but not the moral, law; and the moral law, on Cartwright's view, includes not only the second table of the Commandments but much of the criminal law of the ancient Hebrews (ii. 95, 96). The criminal law of England must be altered accordingly. There must be capital punishment for every 'stubbern Idolater, blasphemer, murtherer, incestuous person and suchlike' (ibid.). The penitent idolater may be pardoned once: but after 'willing sliding backe and mouing others to do the same', a second repentance ought not to lead to mercy (ii. 115). (The principle of receding as far as possible from Roman practice seems here to be momentarily in abeyance.) Whitgift is blamed for the 'imagination of choice' which he leaves the civil magistrate. The magistrate is to God simply as the sheriff is to the magistrate: he must carry out the sentence prescribed in Scripture (ii. 99, 100). But a few pages later Cartwright relents. He will leave the magistrate a little more freedom: he will leave him free 'to appoint the maner of death sharper or softer' (ii. 103). He must not pardon those whom scripture (interpreted by the Consistory) condemns: but he may—Cartwright would fain be reasonable—he may add a few tortures. As for the common idea that the reign of Christ was to be more merciful than that of Moses, Cartwright turns it by an astonishing argument. God, we see, has rather given up His old practice of sending temporal 'judgements' on offenders. We no longer see the earth opening to swallow up the congregation of Abiram. But that is exactly why the magistrate must now 'kepe by so much a harder hande ouer the punishmente off synne' (ii. 111). As God docs less, obviously He means us to do more. Finally, 'if this be bloudie and extreme I am contente to be so counted withe the holie goste' (ibid.).

In Cartwright we meet at last the 'puritan' of popular tradition and satire. What is harder to determine is the degree in which he deserved Hooker's most characteristic criticism. To Hooker Cartwright was the opponent of reason, the light of Nature: it was in answer to that aspect of Cartwright's teaching that Hooker, to our endless joy, drew out all the tranquil beauty of the old philosophy. Certainly there is in Cartwright a core of what we may venture, very loosely, to call Barthianism: a flattening out of all things into common insignificance before the inscrutable Creator. He does once mention the Natural Law 'written in the tables off the hartes off all men'. Both the occasion and the manner of his doing so are characteristic. The law which he finds written in the heart (so, I think, did Othello) is that which pronounces death against adultery (ii. 102). And he introduces it as a piece of 'equitie' which is still discernible even to 'this glymmering sight which remaineth in the accursed nature off men' (ii. 101). I think this is his only concession to nature. In 'diuine matters' human authority is 'off no force at all' (ii. 19). Hence, while Cartwright will quote the practice of the early Church when it supports him, he has no hesitation in condemning it when it does not (i. 17, 136). Even in 'humane sciences' the authority of men is of little value (ii. 19); of so little that you cannot argue from it either positively or negatively (i. 13). He derides Whitgift for talking as if there were 'some star or light off reason' which could lead us to ordain rightly anything in the Church without the guidance of scripture (ii. 56). Such passages are, I think, sufficient to show that Cartwright, at any rate sometimes, held the anti-rational views of which Hooker accuses him. I do not think they interested Cartwright so much as a reader of Hooker might suppose. It does not follow that Hooker's emphasis was mistaken. A man may (rightly) diagnose as the radical evil in another man's thought something which that other does not parade or is not even fully aware of.

Cartwright's prose is sound, if not great, and the Ciceronian exordium of the first *Reply* has been lovingly laboured. He writes with great resentment, using direct insult, innuendo, taunts, and irony, but all these with hardly any humour. Hatred so massive as his, so completely reconciled to the conscience, leaves no room for fun.

In the round between the authors of the *Learned Discourse*
(1584) and Bridges the literary honours fall entirely to the
puritan side. A student who wishes to get an idea of the puritan
position without spending too much time on it would be well
advised to concentrate on the *Discourse*. It is clear, systematic,
and economical; there is even some humour in its sketch of 'old
Sir John lacke latine'. Bridges in his *Defence* (1587) adopted a
method which is almost unendurable. He first quotes a passage
from the enemy. He then proceeds to answer the first sentence of
that passage, using its own words as much as possible and
dribbling in his own objections five or six words at a time. He
then probably requotes the sentence for a fresh attack (we feel as
if we were reading the words of an oratorio by Handel), adding
quotations from the Fathers, Calvin, Beza, Gellius, Snecanus
and who not? Then we are ready for the next sentence from the
Learned Discourse. We thus hardly ever get a whole paragraph
of Bridges's own work or of anyone else's work free from Bridges's
interruptions. Few men at any period can have obeyed Martin's
light-hearted command to 'rede ouer Doctor Bridges'; I have
skipped some pages myself.

In John Udall we meet a more literary puritan than Cartwright. The *Diotrephes* (1588) is an Erasmian colloquy. The scene
is an inn; the persons, a melodramatically wicked bishop, a
Papist in league with him, a usurer, the innkeeper, and a
virtuous puritan preacher, modestly named Paul. (The wicked
bishop's name, Diotrephes, comes of course from 3 John ix.)
Paul is a guest as unwelcome to an innkeeper as Uncle Joseph in
the *Wrong Box*—'if I had euery night such a guest, within one
moneth all men would refraine from comming to my house'.
Paul's conversation at first is such that we rub our eyes and
wonder whether Udall is not intending a satire on puritans. But
Paul mends as the dialogue goes on and is in places impressive.
If *Diotrephes* would convince no hostile reader, Udall's other
piece, the *Demonstration* (also 1588), might positively alienate a
wavering adherent. The argument is developed in a series of
syllogisms, but they all prove nothing unless you are prepared to
take certain scriptural texts in the peculiar sense which the
party gave them. And here that element of democracy which the
party programme seemed to offer by the parish councils is
revealed as spurious. The people are, no doubt, to choose their
own ministers. But then black sheep, such as drunkards, being

no true part of the Church, will not be allowed to vote; and if the remaining 'people' make a bad choice, the 'eldershyppe' must just 'reforme' it. There is much vituperation; bishops continue in 'damnable and deuellish courses', parsons are 'ignorant and filthy swine. . . in league with hell'.

Thomas Cooper, Bishop of Winchester, brought out his *Admonition to the People of England* in 1589. It contains, though it was not probably designed as, a reply to Martin. This, though not a distinguished, is a reasonable, well written book, rising in one passage to something like eloquence. Much of his argument, perhaps unwisely, is based on political and cultural grounds. Cooper keeps his temper and his syntax and is still readable.

Up till now there had, however, been no work on the Anglican side which could be called a resounding success: but a far stronger champion was at hand. In 1585 Richard Hooker,[1] then newly appointed Master of the Temple, had seemed to the puritans to confirm their darkest suspicions by his sermon *Of Justification* in which he said of our popish ancestors, 'God, I doubt not, was merciful to save thousands of them'. He had bidden his hearers 'Beware lest we make too many ways of denying Christ'. As if this were not scandal enough, he had gone on to say that even a contemporary Papist, 'yea, a cardinal or pope', truly penitent, and erroneous only on the doctrine of 'merit', will not be rejected by 'a merciful God ready to make the best of that little which we hold well', no 'captious sophister which gathereth the worst out of everything wherein we err'. Those who find 'arrogance' in such a sermon, preached at such a date, hardly recognize that Hooker is going to the very limits of what his premisses allowed him and far beyond the limits of personal or controversial prudence. Nor, I think, do they do justice to the humility and the almost agonized charity which vibrates in sentence after sentence; 'Woe worth the hour wherein we were born except we might persuade ourselves better things', 'the hour may come when we shall think it a blessed thing to hear that if our sins

---

[1] b. Heavitree, Exeter, 1554? Ed. Exeter Grammar School. Patronized by Jewel and later by Edwin Sandys. Scholar, Corpus Christi, Oxford, 1573. B.A. 1574. M.A., 1577. Deputy prof. of Hebrew, 1579. Holy Orders, 1581. Sermon at Paul's Cross, 1581. Living of Drayton Beauchamp, 1584. Master of Temple, 1585. Controversy with Walter Travers, then afternoon lecturer in Temple. m. Joan Churchman, 1588. Loses a son, 1589. Vacates Mastership, becomes Rector of Boscombe and Prebendary of Netheravon, 1591. Vicar of Bishopsbourne, 1595. Loses a son, 1597. Ob. 1600.

were as the sins of the pope and cardinals, the bowels of the mercy of God are larger', and finally 'if it be an error . . . my greatest comfort is my error; were it not for the love I bear unto this error, I would neither wish to speak nor to live'. If this is arrogance, it might be wished that divines of all three camps had more often spoken arrogantly.

I have mentioned this passionate sermon because, if it were ignored, the wholly different tone of the *Laws of Ecclesiastical Polity* might give a false impression both of Hooker's personal, and of his literary, character. But his other minor works cannot be noticed here, and I must now turn at once to the *Polity*.

The adventures of this text are among the strangest in literary history. The first four books (as we now know, but Walton did not) were published in March 1593. The fifth followed in December 1597. Hooker died in 1600. In 1604 Dr. Spenser, President of Corpus Christi, Oxford, in a new edition of the *Polity*, stated that Hooker had finished the three further books he intended: that certain persons had rifled Hooker's study after his death, abstracted the fair copies and left only 'unperfect and mangled draughts'; from which draughts, nevertheless, 'there is a purpose' of publishing the best text now possible. After this, nearly forty years of silence. Then in 1648 we have an edition containing Books VI and VIII. In 1662 Bishop Gauden, a man suspect to the High Church party, brings out an edition which for the first time includes VII; its matter, unsatisfactory to high-flying episcopalians. In 1666 we have an edition which contains Walton's life, discrediting the three last books. Walton wrote at the request of Gilbert Sheldon, Archbishop of Canterbury.

What lies behind this mysterious story has been dug out by brilliant scholarship in our own time, but it is far too complicated to be retold here. Nor do the stolen fair copies concern the literary historian: if they ever existed, at least neither we nor our fathers have ever read them. What does concern us is the authenticity of Books VI to VIII as they exist, and of this, in a general sense, there is now no doubt. Book VI is only a fragment, and VII and VIII have not reached the perfection which Hooker would have exacted from himself before he published them. What is a little disquieting is that Dr. Spenser spoke of bringing his 'mangled' materials to 'a reasonable perfection', words which might imply a sort of editing frowned on by modern scholars. Certainly at one place (VII. v. 8) a gloss has 'crept into the text'.

The internal evidence, however, suggests that nearly all we read in these three books is pure Hooker: his style is not easily imitated. It is true that they sometimes differ, in one particular respect, from the manner of Books I to V: they are sharper, more sarcastic, less tranquil. But then so are Hooker's manuscript notes on the *Christian Letter* of 1599. He admits into them a tone which he hardly ever allowed himself in the *Polity*. It is reasonable to suppose that his first drafts often differed from his finished productions in that way: the last labour of the file removed the asperities. And this leads to a literary conclusion of some importance. The mellow gold of the *Polity* is not merely the natural overflow of a mild eupeptic who has good reason to be pleased with the *status quo*. It is the work of prudence, of art, of moral virtue, and (as Hooker would no doubt have said) of Grace. It is also an obedience to 'decorum'.

Though Hooker hardly ever wrote an obscure sentence, it would seem that he has left us a very difficult book, for doctrines of varying 'height' (in the ecclesiastical sense) have been read into it. I approach with fear a task in which I am not likely to avoid error; first drawing attention to two elements in Hooker's thought which must, I believe, be fully grasped before we can understand anything else about him.

1. Though Hooker is not writing to defend the freedom of the individual, he is certainly writing to defend the freedom of Man from what he believes to be a false conception of supernatural authority. He feels as his deepest enemy what I have called the 'Barthianism' of the puritans, the theology which set a God of inscrutable will 'over against' the 'accursed nature of Man' with all its arts, sciences, traditions, learning, and merely human virtues. In the light of that ruthless antithesis there was only one question to be asked about any institution. Is it 'of God?'; then fall down and worship: is it 'of Man?'; then destroy it. Hooker is always insisting that the real universe is much more complex than that. 'All things which are in the Church ought to be of God. But they may be two ways accounted such' (VII. xi. 10). For, often, 'the same thing which is of men may be also justly and truly said to be of God' (ibid.). Certain powers are given to princes 'altogether by human right', 'at men's discretion', and yet princes may hold these same powers 'by divine right'. 'Unto kings by human right, honour by very divine right is due' (VIII. ii. 5-6). For explicit divine injunction, embodied in scripture, is

but 'a part of that rule' which we were created to live by (VII. xi.
10). There is another part, no less God-given, which Hooker
calls 'nature' (Pref. vi. 1), 'law rational, which men commonly
use to call the Law of Nature' (I. viii. 9), 'the light of Reason' (I.
viii. 3). The most permanent value of Hooker's work lies in his
defence of that light. We must not therefore expect him to give us
clear answers if we constantly ask him what things are divine
and what things 'merely human'. The word *merely* conceals precisely the point of view which Hooker declines.

2. Hooker had never heard of a religion called Anglicanism.
He would never have dreamed of trying to 'convert' any foreigner
to the Church of England. It was to him obvious that a German
or Italian would not belong to the Church of England, just as an
Ephesian or Galatian would not have belonged to the Church of
Corinth. Hooker is never seeking for 'the true Church', never
crying, like Donne, 'Show me deare Christ, thy spouse'. For him
no such problem existed. If by 'the Church' you mean the mystical Church (which is partly in Heaven) then, of course, no man
can identify her. But if you mean the visible Church, then we all
know her. She is 'a sensibly known company' of all those throughout the world who profess one Lord, one Faith, and one Baptism
(III. i. 3). None who makes that profession is excluded from her.
Heretics, idolaters, and notoriously wicked persons may be excluded from the 'sound' part of her or from salvation, but they
are still members of the visible Church (III. i. 7, 13). That is why
baptism by heretics is valid (III. i. 9) and if a heretic is killed
'only for Christian professions sake' we cannot deny him 'the
honour of martyrdom' (III. i. 11). In this Church we always have
been and still are. We have not left her by reforming ourselves,
nor have the Papists left her by their corrupt 'indisposition' to
do likewise (III. i. 10). No doubt many of the questions which
Hooker treats are what we should now call questions between
'denominations'. But that is not how he envisages the matter. He
is not, save accidentally, preaching 'a religion'; he is discussing
the kind and degree of liberty proper to national churches within
the universal, visible Church.

The first of these two principles—the refusal to oppose *jus
divinum* to *jus humanum* as his opponents did—explains what would
otherwise appear to be vacillation or evasiveness in Hooker's
view of episcopacy. It is true, as he freely admits, that his opinion
on this subject had changed: he had once thought it 'more

probable' than he did when writing Book VII that episcopacy was post-Apostolic (VII. xi. 8). But we must not exaggerate the importance of the change in a system such as Hooker's. He can say much that will please a High Churchman; episcopacy is a 'thing most lawful, divine and holy', 'authorized from Heaven', 'the Holy Ghost was the author of it'. Bishops are the apostles' successors. But Hooker, in his own sense, could have said all this before he came to believe that bishops were of Apostolic institution. Holding his revised position, he can still warn bishops that they must not treat 'the absolute and everlasting continuance' of episcopacy as a thing that 'any commandment of Our Lord doth enjoin' (VII. vi. 8). Experience and the old custom of the Church sanction it (not even they immutably) and the actual date and mode of its institution are less important. Even if it were universally admitted to have arisen 'a long time after the Apostles were gone' it would not be thereby 'disanulled' (VII. xi. 2). Either way, it is a thing 'which to have been ordained of God, I am for my own part even as resolutely persuaded as that any other kind of government in the world whatsoever is of God' (VII. i. 4)—words which, in Hooker's mouth, need not make it any more (or less) divine than constitutional monarchy. For every good gift, whether by way of revelation or reason, comes from the same source.

This readiness to accept the old practice of the Church, even if she cannot claim scriptural or Apostolic injunction for what she does, separates Hooker from the puritans and might seem at first sight to bring him nearer to the Roman position. But the appearance is deceptive. In the first place, Hooker is speaking only of order, not doctrine, the one mutable, the other not, because truth does not change and convenience does (v. viii. 2). In the second place, his theory of the relation between national churches and the universal Church would not commend itself to any Papist. Such metaphors as mother and daughters, trunk and branches, or empire and provinces, are foreign to his thought. The churches are 'rather like diverse families than like divers servants of one family' (IV. xiii. 6). No 'one certain form' of ecclesiastical polity need be common to them all (III. ii. 1). In things which scripture does not expressly command or forbid each is free to go her own way simply because she thinks it 'fit and expedient' (IV. xiii. 3). Sovereignty over them has certainly not been granted to 'any one mortal man' (IV. xiii. 8). The

supreme rule to which all are subject is 'what Scripture plainly
doth deliver': lower than that come deductions from scripture
made by 'force of reason': lastly 'after these the voice of the
Church succeedeth' (v. vii. 2). This voice is expressed in General
Councils: but councils cannot 'let the Church from taking
away that thing which is hurtful' (IV. xiv. 5). The voice of the
Church is also expressed in tradition, and it is in Hooker's
nature to listen to this voice very lovingly—to 'uniform practice
throughout the whole world' (VII. ix. 2), 'the use of the people
of God' or 'ordinances of our fathers' (III. xi. 15) which it would
be 'heathenish petulancy' to 'trample under foot' (v. lxv. 9).
Yet antiquity has no absolute binding force: we are not 'bound
while the world standeth to put nothing in practice but only
that which was at the very first' (v. xx. 4). Even scripture, on
matters of order, turns out not to be an absolute sovereign.
Things there ordered by God Himself 'have been changed and
that for the better' (III. x. 5), not, of course, because we are wiser
than He but because circumstances have changed. The result of
Hooker's ecclesiology is to leave the universal Church very free
of scripture and her own past, and the local churches very free of
her. I think, too, that Hooker's 'faith' in the Church (in one sense
he had a great deal) is clearly something different from that
'faith' in the Church which a Papist demands, and quite different from Hooker's own faith in Christ, or in the Bible. He
accepts the decision of a council not as part of revelation but
because 'that which the Church by her ecclesiastical authority
shall *probably* think and define *must in congruity of reason overrule* all
other inferior judgements' (v. viii. 2). The words I have italicized
are surely significant. They suggest, not so much faith in the
theological or supernatural sense, as the faith of a modest historian and scholar in the consensus of properly qualified opinion.
But here again we are forcing upon Hooker an antithesis which
he would not have accepted without explanations and distinctions that would greatly blunt its force. For to yield, and maintain, a faith even of this kind may also be a duty imposed by the
Law of Nature and therefore by God. Nor can we obey the Law
of Nature, in this or any other duty, without grace (III. viii. 6).
Thus, on the one hand, Hooker feels nothing but disgust for the
raw, provincial arrogance which leads T. C. (iii. 171) to ask 'why
we should hang our judgment upon the Church's sleeve'. On the
other hand, he would be equally repelled by those modern

Papists who say, 'It is nothing to us how many of our doctrines you share, so long as you accept them only on the wholly irrelevant ground that you think them true.'

Hooker's conception of the local or national churches is, almost admittedly, not applicable to the situation in which we live today. He understands of course that the Jewish Church in Babylon or the Christian Church in Neronian Rome were necessarily distinct from the 'commonwealth' because the commonwealth was then pagan (VIII. i. 3). But he did not at all foresee that such conditions would recur. He never envisaged a secular State in which Christians, in schism with one another, would permanently live side by side with atheist fellow citizens. He still hopes that the divisions between Christians will be healed (IV. xiv. 6) and the basic assumption of his thought is the unitedly Christian nation in which Church and State, however defined, are in fact 'the selfsame multitude' (VIII. i. 2). Nations are churches organized for the conduct of their temporal affairs: churches are nations organized for the conduct of their spiritual affairs. The distinction between spiritual and temporal powers within such a Church-Nation is not to be pressed too far; those persons and things which we call 'spiritual' are so called only 'by an excellency'—κατ᾽ ἐξοχήν, *par excellence* (VIII. i. 4). The ecclesiastical 'supremacy' which the Church (or Nation) of England allows to the Crown, for Hooker simply expresses the right of that Church to govern herself. The 'true original subject' (i.e. possessor) 'of power to make Church laws is the whole entire body of that Church for which they are made' (VIII. vi. 1) and this power ultimately operates through the Crown. We must, of course, understand supremacy not as our opponents feign to understand it—as though the English Crown claimed 'Headship' in the same sense as Christ—but as our lawyers understand it (VIII. ii. 3). In a certain sense, no doubt, 'our Church hath dependency upon the chief of our commonwealth' (VIII. i. 7), but this sense must be carefully defined. She depends upon this 'chief' to embody her corporate will and therefore makes him supreme in order that 'no foreign state or potentate' (such as the Pope) and no 'state or potentate domestical' (such as a Presbyterian senate) can impair her freedom (VIII. ii. 3). For the prince envisaged is a wholly Bractonian prince *sub Deo et lege*: Hooker will have nothing to do with the new-fangled notions of sovereignty: 'who doubteth' that the king is under the law and,

though greater in power than any, not greater than all? (VIII. ii.
3). Absolute monarchy is for Hooker a prehistoric blunder, soon
retracted when society found 'that to live by one man's will
became the cause of all men's misery' (I. x. 5). He is 'Head' *intra
ecclesiam non supra ecclesiam*, exercising 'dominion' in ecclesiastical
causes 'but according to the laws of the Church' (VIII. ii. 17). He
does not 'make' laws for the Church in the sense of inventing or
devising them: he makes or causes to be law what the Church
invents or devises (VIII. vi. 12). The 'very essence of all government' in England lies not in the prince but in the prince with
Parliament and Convocation: for 'all are there present' either in
person or vicariously (VIII. vi. 11). Yet even this composite
ecclesiastical sovereign is hardly sovereign in Tyndale's or Austin's
sense. It would be 'scandalous and offensive' if it acted without
regard 'to that which of old hath been reverently thought of
throughout the world': unless, of course, some law of God (in
scripture) should force us into the unhappy position of being
contra mundum (VIII. ii. 17).

The prince as 'Supreme Head' of the Church is, in fact, the
bottle-neck through which the decisions of the local Church-
Nation pass in order to become law. And that Nation-Church
owes an allegiance to the universal Church: yet the universal
Church might swerve from scripture and we should then have to
disobey her. (That is, all parts of her, except ourselves, might
conceivably become 'unsound'.) Where then does ultimate
sovereignty lie? I think Hooker would answer, 'Nowhere except
in Heaven'. He allows no unambiguous sovereignty on earth
either civil or ecclesiastical. Judged by the standards of Austin
and of modern Catholicism, the church and state which Hooker
welds together are both headless. And I do not think this is an
oversight. Hooker felt no need either for omnicompetent prince
or for infallible Pope. He was much more afraid of tyrannies and
idolatries than of ambiguities and deadlocks.

It will, of course, be obvious that Hooker's system does not
extricate us from theocracy. If not exactly 'the Godly Prince',
yet, in the long run, the autonomous Church-Nation, is undoubtedly to coerce Anabaptists, Papist recusants, and puritans. To that extent he is at one with his puritan and Papist
opponents. If either of these complain that he is a forcer of conscience, he has an easy *argumentum ad hominem*. It was notorious
that the puritans looked to the prince to enforce the Godly Dis-

cipline (VIII. vi. 14). As for the Papists, had not Stapleton claimed for the prince the right *dogmata promulgandi, defendendi, et contra violatores vindicandi*? (VIII. ii. 14). It was, after all, a Parliament that had in Mary's days resubmitted all England to the Pope; Rome did not then complain that such dominion of Parliament over men's souls was abominable or invalid (VIII. vi. 11). Thus Hooker answers his own age: it is perhaps absurd to ask how he would answer ours. Usually, in past controversies, the premiss which neither side questioned, now seems the shakiest of all.

The permanent appeal of a great philosophical work, however, seldom depends entirely on its success in solving the problem which the author had set himself. We go back, and again back, to Hooker, but not because we accept his ecclesiology as final.

In the first place the *Polity* marks a revolution in the art of controversy. Hitherto, in England, that art had involved only tactics; Hooker added strategy. Long before the close fighting in Book III begins, the puritan position has been rendered desperate by the great flanking movements in Books I and II. Hooker has already asked and answered questions which Cartwright and Travers had never considered and which are fatal to their narrow scripturalism. He has also provided a model for all who in any age have to answer similar ready-made recipes for setting the world right in five weeks. (Travers is dead: the type is perennial.) And all this, though excellent strategy, never strikes us as merely strategical. Truths unfold themselves, quietly and in due order, as if Hooker were developing—nay, we are sure that he is developing—his own philosophy for its own sake, because 'the mind of man' is 'by nature speculative and delighted with contemplation... for mere knowledge and understanding's sake' (I. viii. 5). Thus the refutation of the enemy comes in the end to seem a very small thing, a by-product. There had been nothing like this in English polemics before. Of his predecessors, Allen, of his successors, Burke and Newman, come nearest to Hooker. But, of course, the two last show much greater excitement.

Every system offers us a model of the universe; Hooker's model has unsurpassed grace and majesty. From much that I have already said it might be inferred that the unconscious tendency of his mind was to secularize. There could be no deeper mistake. Few model universes are more filled—one might say, more drenched—with Deity than his. 'All things that are of God, (and only sin is not) 'have God in them and he them in himself likewise', yet 'their substance and his wholly differeth' (v. lvi. 5). God is unspeakably transcendent; but also unspeakably immanent. It is this conviction which enables Hooker, with no anxiety, to resist any inaccurate claim that is made for revelation against reason, Grace against Nature, the spiritual against the secular. We must not honour even heavenly things with compliments that are not quite true: 'though it seem an honour, it is an injury' (ii. viii. 7). All good things, reason as well as revelation, Nature as well as Grace, the commonwealth as well as the Church, are equally, though diversely, 'of God'. If 'nature hath need of grace', yet also 'grace hath use of nature' (iii. viii. 6). Laws merely human, if they are good, have all been 'copied out of the tables of that high everlasting law' which God made, the Law of Nature (i. xvi. 2). 'The general and perpetual voice of men is as the sentence of God himself', for it is taught by Nature whose 'voice is but his instrument' (i. viii. 3). 'Divine testimony' and 'demonstrative reasoning' are equally infallible (ii. vii. 5). Certainly, the Christian revelation is 'that principal truth in comparison whereof all other knowledge is vile'; but only in comparison. All kinds of knowledge, all good arts, sciences, and disciplines come from the Father of lights and are 'as so many sparkles resembling the bright fountain from which they rise' (iii. viii. 9). We must not think that we glorify God only in our specifically religious actions. 'We move, we sleep, we take the cup at the hand of our friend' and glorify Him unconsciously, as inanimate objects do, for 'every effect proceeding from the most concealed instincts of nature' manifests His power (ii. ii. 1). Not, of course, that our different modes of glorifying God are on a level. Equality is not a conception that has any charms for Hooker. The charm of inequality is, indeed, the mainspring of erotic love. Woman is 'inferior in excellency unto man, howbeit in so due and sweet proportion as being presented before our eyes, might be sooner perceived than defined'. Hence 'that kind of love which is the perfectest ground of wedlock is seldom able to yield any reason of itself' (v. lxxiii. 2). There is no equality within us; the first Law of Nature is the law of internal hierarchy: that 'the soul ought to conduct the body, and the spirit of our minds the soul' (i. viii. 6). But we must not so regard the highest in us as to forget that the lowest is still of God, nor so call some of our activities 'religious' as to make the rest profane. Highest of all in us are the supernatural operations of the Holy

Ghost, but we shall be ill advised to try to identify them by introspection (III. viii. 15). We do not always know when we pray, for 'every good and holy desire hath the substance and the force of prayer' (v. xlviii. 1). Our worldly desires (unless sinful) do not fall outside our religious life: the prayers which the Church teaches us to make for temporal blessings are indeed 'a kind of heavenly fraud' bringing the soul to God by petty 'baits' that she may remain to ask and receive what is better (v. xxxv. 2). There is 'natural intercourse between the highest and the lowest powers of man's mind' (v. lxv. 11). We meet on all levels the divine wisdom shining through 'the beautiful variety of all things' in their 'manifold and yet harmonious dissimilitude' (III. xi. 8).

In reading Hooker we are reminded sometimes of Tyndale, often of Traherne's *Centuries*. Sometimes a suspicion crosses our mind that the doctrine of the Fall did not loom quite large enough in his universe. Logically, we must grant, it was pivotal: it is only because Adam fell that supernatural laws have come in at all, replacing that natural path to beatitude which is now lost (I. xi. 5). It is only because Adam fell that we need 'public regiment' (I. x. 4, cf. v. i. 2). But Hooker's philosophy is 'Golden' philosophy, quite as unmistakably as the *Arcadia* and the *Faerie Queene* are Golden poesy. He writes of Man, if fallen, yet now redeemed and already partially glorified; of Man unified in 'the mystical communion of all faithful men' (v. xl. 3), because 'nature doth presume that how many men there are in the world, so many gods as it were there are' (I. x. 12); of Man the oracle whereby everlasting law 'readeth itself to the world' (I. xvi. 2). We hope, hereafter, to 'live as it were the life of God' (I. xi. 2) and enjoy already 'the honour which our flesh hath by being the flesh of the Son of God' (v. liv. 5). The whole *Polity* is a soberer, yet not less exultant, *De Dignitate Hominis*. The distress or 'anguish' which is now commonly demanded as an earnest of profundity will not be found in it. Yet there is sometimes a hint to show that he had known darker and less tranquil hours than he chose to express in the *Polity*: such a phrase as 'that which we tremble to do we do' or 'looking inward we are stricken dumb' (v. xlvii. 4), or such an unusual passage as that wherein he turns upon Cartwright (who would deny baptism by women even if he believed the unbaptized to be 'assuredly damned') with his 'O Sir, you that would spurn thus. . . ' (v. lxi. 4). But, as I have already said, trouble and passion are most apparent not in the

Polity but in the sermon *Of Justification*. Not everything that he thought or felt was qualified for admission into the great work; its serenity marks not the limitations of his temperament but the greatness of his achievement, and was probably paid for at the right price.

The style is, for its purpose, perhaps the most perfect in English. In general it is far removed from the colloquial, yet it does not strike one as a decorated style. Exceptions to both these statements can be found. Hooker can on occasion speak with the voice of the people; 'ifs or ands', 'corner-meetings', 'make saleable your cause in gross', 'the best stake in their hedge', 'truss up bag and baggage'. On occasion, too, he can write a paragraph so heightened that readers who have no taste for Hooker will enjoy it, detached, in an anthology. Such is the passage beginning 'Now if nature should intermit her course' in I. iii. 2, or that on church music in v. xxxviii. I. But this is very rare; the beauty of Hooker's prose is functional. His characteristic unit is the long, syntactically latinized, sentence, unobtrusively garnished with metaphor, anaphora, and chiasmus. The Latin syntax is there for use, not ornament; it enables him, as English syntax would not, to keep many ideas, as it were, in the air, limiting, enriching, and guiding one another, but not fully affirmed or denied until at last, with the weight of all that thought behind him, he slowly descends to the matured conclusion. The structure mirrors the real movement of his mind. When he is not thinking so sequaciously, when he is merely reminding, defining, or reproving, he uses short sentences, often with great effect; 'but wise men are men and the truth is truth,' 'they never use reason so willingly as to disgrace reason', 'there is nothing which is not someway excelled even by that which it doth excel', 'our answer therefore to their reasons is no; to their scoffs nothing'. He has plenty of humour, almost a mischievous humour, but not of the kind that could appear in quotation: the point depends not on the verbal but on the argumentative context. Indeed very few of Hooker's beauties can be picked like flowers and taken home: you must enjoy them where they grow—as you enjoy a twenty-acre field of ripe wheat. Always an artist, he is never merely an artist. He does not reject eloquence, but he has broken and bitted her and taught her the manage. She is perfectly subdued to his task; her high mettle shows through her obedience. The great periods move steadily forward without irrelevant beauties but not with-

out any beauties that can make 'the face of truth' more 'orient',
not without melody and proportion, nor without frequent vividness of phrase (woes 'perpendicularly hanging' over wicked
heads, Tertullian 'a sponge steeped in worm-wood and gall',
peers spiritual 'a courteous bridle' to peers temporal). And
always, drawn in by the very genius of his philosophy, there is a
sense of 'the beautiful variety of all things'.

VERSE IN THE 'GOLDEN' PERIOD

I HAVE named the 'Golden' Age from those of its productions which seem to us, looking back, the most characteristic; but of course much work of a different kind was being produced. There is poetry, like Warner's and much of Drayton's, which simply lags behind and remains Drab. There is poetry like Donne's which anticipates and indeed inaugurates the Metaphysical period. There is also poetry like Southwell's which is sometimes Drab and sometimes Metaphysical, but never Golden: the poet, as it were, ignores the Golden Age and tunnels straight through from the Drab to the seventeenth century. Both these kinds I reserve for my Epilogue. There is poetry like Chapman's which is partly Golden and partly Metaphysical: Shakespeare's ripest work, which falls outside our province, belongs to this class. Finally, there is satiric work which neither lags behind the Golden movement through mere incompetence like Warner, nor departs from it in obedience to a revolutionary impulse like Donne, but eschews it for reasons of *decorum*, just as Spenser generally eschews it in *Mother Hubberd's Tale*, because satire ought not to be mellifluous. I will deal first with the poets who simply lag behind the Golden Age: the belated, or vestigial, poetry.

I

It is noteworthy that this class includes not only Drab work but work which is unmistakably Late Medieval. Such is the *Fig for Fortune* (1596) of that ambiguous character Anthony Copley (1567–1607?). This is a recusant poem in which Doblessa, though equated in the 'Argument' with Fortune, obviously symbolizes the Protestant religion. Copley is poetically, no less than theologically, a recusant, who simply ignores the literary history of the last ninety years. He writes a continued dream allegory in the first person and shows a true Late Medieval uncertainty about metre and even about rhyme. His vocabulary is, however, his own and very curious: he deserves to be remembered for the delightful verb 'to cravin-cockadoodle it'. The poem is a curiosity—an absurdity, if you like—but has a kind of earnestness which is not easily evaded by the reader.

Copley, a poet who outrages all chronological schemes, has

dragged us for a moment to the end of the century: I now return to treat the Drab poets of the Golden Age in their proper order.

Humfrey Gifford's *Posie of Gillyflowers* (1580), which contained, as well as verse, some prose translations from the Italian and French, is almost more characteristically Drab than anything the Drab Age proper had produced. All the symptoms are present; octosyllabic stanzas of Tottelian woodenness, poulters, fourteeners, fustian ('When dreadfull death with dint of pearcing darte', &c.), tasteless stanzaic experiments, and one poem, 'A pleasant Jest' which is a little better because the poet there drops what he thought his courtly vein and gives us something more ballad-like. The poem 'For Soldiers', fantastically overpraised by Grosart, looks like straight fourteeners but has in fact a most intricate (and unsuccessful) pattern of variations and internal rhymes. I do not doubt that it was written with intense enjoyment.

The attorney William Warner (1558?–1609) has been kindly treated both by his contemporaries and by posterity. Meres's praise is, however, worthless, and Drayton, in his Epistle to Reynolds, is almost admittedly disarmed by kindness for an old friend. What Warner really deserves to be commended for is his conception. His work is separated from the main stream of the historical epic by a structural idea; that of dividing his matter into separate stories and arranging these not chronologically but by artful linking and inset narration after the manner of Ovid's *Metamorphoses*. This he carried out in the four books of his *Albion's England* (1586), successively enlarged in 1589, 1592, 1596, and 1602 till it reached sixteen books in 1606 and came down to the reign of King James. It was a spirited attempt to avoid the formlessness of the mere metrical chronicle, but Warner failed in the execution. His fourteeners are usually Drab at its worst. From so vast a poem good phrases can of course be picked out: 'her red disperst in shadowed white', 'she blusht out beauty', 'to pearce the pathlesse ayre with shaft'. There is some hideous vividness on the death of Hercules, and everyone has heard the line about the blow that Queen Eleanor gave to Rosamund. But no one should be deceived by these quotations into reading Warner. The good things in *Albion's England* are as far divided as the suns in space. Warner may also have translated the *Menaechmi* (1595) and had published in 1584 a prose romance, or a nest of romances, called *Pan his Syrinx or Pipe*.

Matthew Grove's *Pelops and Hippodamia*, published in 1587 but written (we are told) at least four years earlier, deserves mention only for two reasons: because these dismal fourteeners throw into even bolder relief the transcendent novelty of all the Golden *epyllia*—Lodge's and even Marston's as well as Marlowe's and Shakespeare's—and because, in one of the shorter pieces that follow the *Pelops*, Grove in a sense anticipates Donne by wishing that 'Jove would him convert' into a 'blacke flea' in his lady's bed. But in what a sense!

One of the best known Drab works produced in the Golden Age is *Willoby his Avisa* (1594), but its fame had from the first little connexion with its poetical quality. That a work so apparently edifying should have been 'called in' five years after its publication shows that it was in reality a scandalous *roman à clef*. In our own age it has excited the attention of Shakespearian scholars because one of its minor characters is called W. S. and W. S. gives Pandaric advice to his friend H. W. The literary historian, attempting to judge it on its own merits, will find that it is fairly good Drab. The style and metre of some of the better Tottelians are used to tell, chiefly in dialogue, how a virtuous woman of humble rank resisted various would-be seducers. Like the rhetorical prose fiction of the age, it clogs the story with letters and complaints. But it is not quite without dramatic life. There is a pretty contrast between the demure virtue of Avisa as a maid and the rounder language in which she belabours those who assail her after her marriage. The theme, the unadorned language, and the confined movement of some stanzas, oddly remind us of *Lyrical Ballads*, not at their best. The identity and even the existence of the Willoby to whom the first edition attributes this poem have been doubted. Some think it is by Chapman's friend Matthew Roydon the mathematician. On stylistic grounds this is not improbable, for Roydon's *Elegy or Friend's Passion on Astrophill* (printed in Spenser's *Astrophel*) is also Drab, and good Drab. Its octosyllabic stanzas have the true *staccato* effect, and its most famous lines, though far beyond anything in the *Avisa*, might have been written by the same man—

> A sweete attractiue kinde of grace
> A full assurance given by lookes,
> Continuall comfort in a face,
> The lineaments of Gospell bookes.

We shall also find in this period many Drab passages, or whole poems, by writers who also produced Golden work for which they are justly remembered. Drayton was hardly ever safe from relapses into the Drab. Certain metres and certain genres tend to be Drab whoever is writing. The *Mirror for Magistrates* continued to be a running sore in English poetry and no one could write a 'tragedie' on that model without losing his Golden powers. The only hint of a redemption for this execrable kind comes right at the end of the century in Thomas Storer's *Life and Death of Wolsey* (1599): and here, it is interesting to notice, it is being redeemed not into Golden poetry but into Metaphysical poetry with a strong infusion of the dramatic:

> Why some are gone already: looke about.
> Did no man meete part of my soule before?
> I had but three, one and a halfe are out.
> Nay had I more then one? . . .
>
> My mother Earth mine onely wife shall be
> And yet no incest.

The beneficent influence of the commercial theatre on non-dramatic poetry is a feature of the nineties. The necessity of drawing and holding an audience forbade the dramatists to indulge in certain kinds (not all kinds) of folly and falsity, and the results of this discipline spread by example to others.

As might be expected, the Drab has a social distribution as well as a distribution by kinds. The Golden poets are chiefly poets who write for their living and have to face frank criticism: courtiers who versified at odd moments tended to be Drab. They may not have perceived the difference between the two styles, or may have preferred the old. The Queen herself had been a minor (or minimal) Drab poetess. Puttenham's taste was for the Drab. *The Phoenix Nest* (1593), which boasts of presenting us with the 'rare and refined' work of 'Noble men, worthy Knights, gallant gentlemen', though it includes true gold by Lodge and others, is predominantly a Drab anthology. Some of the drab pieces are good, like Breton's 'Chess Play' or the anonymous 'The Brainsicke race': many of them are the old mechanical fustian—'by day I freeze, I frie, I wish, I wait'. It contains two beautiful lyrics by unknown authors: 'O night, O ielious night', where the alternate feminine rhymes improve the alexandrines almost out of recognition, and 'Sweete Violets' which has something of Campion's delicacy. But the character of the collection as a whole becomes clear if we contrast it with that genuinely Golden anthology *England's Helicon* (1600), which makes no similar boast on its title-page and, as the preface points out, ignores social position in arranging its poets. Raleigh, the most distinguished courtier poet of the period, wrote more Drab than anything else, though, for one or two pieces, I have placed him later among the Golden poets. Sir Edward Dyer (ob. 1607), when stripped of the pieces falsely attributed to him on the strength of the signature S. E. D. in *England's Helicon*, emerges as an almost purely Drab writer. He is best when least gnomic, in 'Amidst the fayrest mountayne toppes' or 'Amaryllis was full fayre'. The more famous 'My minde to me a Kyngdom is' does not quite live up to its opening lines. Modern research has brought home to him some very damning work; it is kind to emphasize the fact that he was no longer young in the nineties and most of his poetry may have been old when the great age began.

II

Satire as a literary kind must be distinguished from the satiric, an element which can occur (like the pathetic, or the heroic) in almost any composition. It had been frequent in our medieval literature. What is new in the nineties is the crop of satires imitated, on humanistic principles, from the satires of the Romans. Whether the Roman satire is a true literary kind at all may be questioned. It has no structural characteristics peculiar to it; by writing a 'satire' one is committed to nothing except to a continuous use of the satiric element, so that to have a book called 'a satire' is as odd, and as suspect, as it would be if we had a book called 'A pathos'. It will be noticed that the Roman model, though it has produced great couplets and great paragraphs, has produced no great poem, no poem in which the parts really gain by belonging to the whole. The great works in the modern vernaculars which we usually call 'satires' do not descend from the *Satira* of the Romans. *Animal Farm, Erewhon,* Voltaire's tales, *Gulliver,* the *Dunciad,* the *Rape, Absalom,* and *Hudibras,* belong to a different family. They are all fantastic or mock heroic narratives, and their true ancestors are Rabelais, Cervantes, the *Apocolocyntosis,* Lucian, and the *Frogs and Mice.* It was therefore, arguably, in an evil hour that the humanistic passion for reviving all ancient kinds led certain Elizabethans to express their satiric impulse in formal satire. It was much more fruitfully expressed in their comedies and pamphlets.

It is doubtful whether precedence in this enterprise should be given to Lodge or to Donne. Lodge's *Fig for Momus* appeared in 1595, and Donne's first two *Satyres* may well be assigned, on internal evidence, to an earlier date. But since it is clear that neither poet influenced the other, it matters little who wrote first. The interesting thing is that they display two different conceptions of satiric style and metre which were to contend until, in the hands of Dryden, Lodge's conception finally won the day. A smooth Jacob and a hairy Esau were apparently twin-born.

Lodge's book, which contains eclogues and epistles as well as satires, is of little interest to the general reader. All the pieces are clear, neat, and reasonable; they are also very tame and there is little trace of real satiric power. But to the literary historian this book is of fascinating interest. At a line like 'Wit shines in Vertue, Vertue shines in Wit' (Epistle V), he rubs his eyes. Have we blundered into the eighteenth century? He will find that Satires I and III are in almost perfectly end-stopped heroic couplets and that even the internal structure of the line often anticipates Augustan practice. He is, in fact, confronted with a manner which differs both from the harshness of some other sixteenth-century satirists and also from the richer manner of Lodge's own 'Golden' poetry. In this volume only, and for satire and epistle only, Lodge has somehow achieved at a stroke something very like the style and versification which English satire developed in the age of its supremacy.

Donne, on the contrary, writes under the influence of the old blunder which connected *satira* with *satyros* and concluded that the one should be as shaggy and 'salvage' as the other. Everything that might make his lines come smoothly off the tongue is deliberately avoided. Accents are violently misplaced (II. 7), extra syllables are thrust in (II. 49), and some lines defy scansion altogether (I. 13, II. 103). The thought develops in unexpected and even tormented fashion. There is a complete absence of that cheerful normality which in Horace, or that occasional grandeur which in Juvenal, relieves the monotony of vituperation. In Donne if any simile or allusion leads us away from the main theme, it leads us only to other objects of contempt and disgust—to coffins, 'itchie lust', catamites, dearth, pestilence, a condemned wretch 'at Barre', vomit, excrement, botches, pox, 'carted whores'. Instead of a norm against which the immediate object of satire stands out, we have vistas opening on corruption in every direction. This technique is chosen in obedience to an ideal of satire, and the apparent parallels in Donne's lyric work are, I believe, superficial. In the lyrics metrical audacities are attempts (often successful) to achieve a subtler music; those in the first two *Satyres* are, and are meant to be, ugly. Violent or disturbing images in the lyrics have a definite part to play in building up a concrete dramatic situation; here, they belong rather to an *ex officio* censoriousness, supposed proper to the kind. It is difficult to guess how these two pieces would affect us if we did not know the author's name; the second would not, perhaps, be much read save by specialists. The first, distantly related to Horace's I. ix, is very much better; once Donne and his companion are out in the street there is admirable vividness. But the vice of the genre appears in lines 36–40. In real life a tuft-hunter might, no doubt, be a lecher, just as he might be red-haired or a B.Litt.; but there is no exploitable connexion between the two vices. Indeed the graver fault makes the lighter less comic and less interesting. The formal satire invites this kind of thing because it demands, in Elizabethan eyes, a more or less continuous display of virtuous indignation. This, even when sincere, can become very tedious, and it provides the inferior writer with an excuse for dabbling in saleable dirt and slander without loss of self-approval.

Donne had taken a vigorous step on the lane that came to a dead-end in *Hudibras*, and Lodge a feeble one on the road that led to Dryden and Pope. The same contrast, in a very much lower degree, will be found between their successors, Hall and Marston. Joseph Hall (1574–1656) was in his early twenties when he brought out the first three books of his *Virgidemiae* or *Toothless Satires* (1597) with the ungrounded boast that he was the first English satirist. The three last books or *Biting Satires* followed in 1598. He has a good deal to tell us about his art and seems, at first, more interested in satire than in the things satirized. The 'ruder Satyre' should go 'rag'd and bare', displaying 'his hairy hide'. One of its proper characteristics is obscurity. In the Prologue to Book III we learn that the two previous books have been blamed for not being obscure enough, and Hall pleads that it is hard to make English as 'darksome' as Latin. But, like a persevering humanist, he does not despair and promises at the end of the third book that in future his meaning will be much harder to find. His pains were successful and IV. i. is, in places, a mere puzzle. Thus Hall's theory of satire is the same as Donne's. But his practice often inclines rather to that of Lodge. There are, indeed, some unmetrical lines, some half-lines (imitated absurdly, we must suppose, from Virgil), and some alexandrines: even two together (III. vii. 20) with a curiously disagreeable effect. But a great deal of his verse, though less of his than of Lodge's, is smooth and even end-stopped. We often catch the Augustan note:

> Giue him the numbred verse that Virgil sung,
> And Virgil selfe shall speake the English tongue . . .
> The nimble *Dactils* striving to out-goe
> The drawling *spondees* pacing it below,
> The lingring *spondees* labouring to delay
> The breath-lesse Dactils with a sudden stay (I. vi).

or in a higher strain:

> Fond foole, six feete shall serve for all thy store:
> And he that cares for most, shall finde no more (II. ii. 58).

It was this quality, presumably, which moved Pope to declare the *Virgidemiae* 'the best poetry and truest satire in the English tongue'.

He spoke, doubtless, in a moment of enthusiasm and cannot have meant exactly what he said. It was the first of Book VI that he especially admired. Here, instead of vituperation, we have an admirable ironic idea: Hall, in reply to his critic 'Labeo', recants, admits that 'in so righteous age' he ought never to have been a satirist, and proceeds to praise his contemporaries for all the virtues they notoriously lacked. The device is not Hall's own but borrowed; it remains, however, a judicious borrowing, and well illustrates the power of an organizing idea to make what might have been a mere heap of poetry into a poem. The short 'Advertisement for a Chaplain' (II. vi) is well known, and stings by its restraint: Nashe, or even Donne, would have spoiled it by exaggeration and made the advertiser a monster. In Hall he is, far more effectively, simply a mean, purse-proud, philistine. In III. vi, the story of a dead toper who, in true Rabelaisian fashion, first drains and then replenishes the

Styx, is good in its kind; Dunbar would have done it better. The longer pieces usually read best in quotation. Thus in II. iii (on the Law) the opening lines on Natural Law are moderately impressive and the concluding image of the sheep is good; in between we are reduced to

> Wo to the weale where manie lawiers bee,
> For there is sure much store of maladie.

v. ii (on the decay of hospitality) is more continuously pointed than most; here we have the 'faire glittering Hals to tempt the hopefull eye' which are as ill suited to the cold cheer within as 'A golden Periwig on a Black-mores brow', and the desolation of the unemployed chimneys is well imagined. Few of Hall's satires lack passages that cling to the memory, but he is in constant danger of relapsing into flat querulousness. His conception of the art was not one that encouraged a man to write his best; 'it is not for this kind to desire or hope to please', he says in his 'Postscript', and he is seldom strong enough to horrify or shock.

John Marston (1576–1634), it must be allowed, makes his *début* as the most odious of literary characters, the man who publishes work he is not prepared to stand by and then pretends that he has been writing 'with his tongue in his cheek'. *The Metamorphosis of Pygmalion's Image . . . and certain Satires* appeared in 1598, but there is some reason for believing that the *Pygmalion* had been either printed, or circulated in manuscript, before that date. It is an erotic epyllion which looks as if it had been fadged up in haste by a man who believed that anyone could follow Marlowe and Shakespeare in this vein. Marston relies too much on those facile and ineffective rhymes which the abstract termination *-ion* (then disyllabic) provided for lazy poets. He claims the medieval licence of treating proper names inconsistently and once accents *Pygmalion* on the first and third (121). Having told us in line 7 that the image was carved in ivory, he forgets this and tells us in line 42 that 'its breasts like polish'd ivory appear', and by line 137 it is made of stone. In reality, of course, Marston is not thinking of the things (stone, ivory) at all: the words float into his mind from other men's works. By the time this poor poem was published, along with the satires, in 1598, it had apparently been severely criticized and Marston appended 'The Author in praise of his precedent Poem', in which he claimed to have written *Pygmalion* as a parody of

contemporary erotic verse. He returned to the matter in his
Scourge of Villany (also 1598). By that time someone had pointed
out that *Pygmalion* ought not to have apostrophized Ovid (*Pygm.*
68), and of course we are now told that this too was part of the
joke (vi. 61). Few have believed the pitiful *alibi*, and even if we
did it would save only Marston's moral, not his literary, character. Read as serious, mildly pornographic, poetry, *Pygmalion*
is admittedly poor stuff: read as parody or irony, it would be
infantile. Authors in Marston's position do not always realize
that it is useless to say your work was a joke if your work is not,
in fact, at all funny.

After this unsuccessful attempt at Golden verse Marston
turned to satire. His sixteen pieces (five in the *Pygmalion* volume
and eleven in the *Scourge*) are of considerable interest. In versification they conform to the ideal of *satira-satyros*. Like Hall,
Marston uses half-lines and alexandrines: he has 'headless' or
'trochaic' lines such as we find in Chaucer (*Pygm.* Sat. I. 31,
III. 51); and lines hardly metrical at all (*Scourge*, v. 14), for
which he pleads 'Rude limping lines fits this lewd halting age'
(ibid. 18). The first satire in the *Scourge* combines metrical violence with extreme obscurity, but in the prose address 'To those
that seem iudicial Perusers' it appears that Marston has once
more had his tongue in his cheek. He tells us he wrote the first
satire, ironically, for those who think 'all satires bastard which
are not palpable dark', and intended it as a shocking example.
Whatever the truth may be about his motives in writing it,
Marston elsewhere appears (in theory, and usually in practice)
as an opponent of obscurity. He remarks with great good sense
that Persius and Juvenal are 'crabby' only because they are
ancient and 'had we then lived, the vnderstanding of them had
been nothing hard'. He ridicules 'modern Satire' for giving us
'Sphinxian riddles' wrapped in 'such pitchy clouds' as would
have amazed Oedipus (*Pygm.* Sat. II. 14 et seq.). He may be
referring to Donne as well as to Hall whom he regarded, for
reasons that cannot be discussed here, as his prime enemy. But
though Marston rejects the ideal of obscurity he has very little
of the Augustan quality that sometimes appears in Hall; the
general effect of his work is much closer to Donne's.

The chief merit of Marston's satire is his frequent success in
striking an attitude which (for the moment, while the poetical
illusion lasts) is convincing and even infectious. He does not

Q

always get it right. When he professes to be grieved, vicariously grieved, like the tender brethren in Cartwright, and exclaims

> O split my heart lest it do breake with rage
> To see th' immodest loosenesse of our age! (*Scourge*, II. 104)

we are merely embarrassed: nor does 'Fair Detestation of foul odious sin' (ibid. *Proem*. Lib. III. 13) impress us at all. It is when Marston more frankly, though still theatrically, presents himself simply as an enraged Timon that he is most effective. He ends a Satire with the couplet

> My pate was great with childe and here 'tis eas'd:
> Vexe all the world, so that thy selfe be pleas'd. (*Scourge*, VI. 111)

He addresses his work 'To Detraction'. 'Partial praise' cannot heighten, nor malignant criticism lower, his self-esteem—'I am my selfe, so is my poesie'. The *Scourge* is dedicated 'To his most esteemed and best beloued Self'. He begins by bidding 'mechanic slaues' and 'dung-hill peasants' avaunt, but then changes his mind. No: let them all come and read. They won't understand, but their railing will be the highest praise: 'no greater honour craues my poesie'. This change of mood is a dramatic device which Marston elsewhere uses with success. The *Reactio* (*Pygm.* Sat. IV), which is his chief attack on Hall, ends unexpectedly:

> Lets not maligne our kin. Then satirist,
> I do salute thee with an open fist.

Thus it is never safe to read only the first half of a satire by Marston; he often has a card up his sleeve. He has indeed serious faults. There is far too much mythology: the second in the *Scourge* is very dull and general. But we seldom go far without coming to some passage which is almost as spirited as Nashe's prose. The whole of the 'Cynic Satire' (*Scourge*, vii), and especially lines 8–17, is highly effective. Even the prurient meandering of *Scourge* III is sometimes redeemed by the vigour of the phrases.

This same prolific year, 1598, saw the appearance of two other satiric works; in which (though I protest I set out with no intention of so patterning my material) we can again distinguish Jacob and Esau. William Rankins's *Seven Satires* would hardly be worth mentioning but for the paradox that in them one misconception cancels another. Rankins connects *satira* with *satyros*: but then since the satyr is to him an idyllic figure out of Ronsard and Spenser, his satyr's song becomes smooth and gentle. The Satyr, the child of uncorrupted nature, comes forth from the woods to be shocked (like Goldsmith's Chinaman, the King of Brobdingnag, and others) by the vices of our society. Edward Guilpin's *Skialetheia* . . . *Epigrams and Satires* is a very different matter. The epigrams are beneath criticism, but the satires have some merit. The *Preludium* attacks the 'oyle-buttred lines', 'wimpring sonnets', and 'puling Elegies' of the Golden love poets on moral grounds, complains that even 'the heroicke Poeme' now admits 'Cupid's chivalrie', and asserts that only satire and epigram have remained pure. The fifth satire owes something to Donne's first (unless some common model still awaits discovery) but the two poems have different virtues: Guilpin is less concerned than Donne with an individual companion and gives us more of the general bustle in the streets. His sixth, on Opinion, has a certain genuine moral dignity and gives us an interesting echo of things that were being said about famous writers. Guilpin has openings full of promise: 'Heere comes a Coach (my lads) let's make a stand' (II. i.), or 'Mary and Gup! haue I then lost my cap?' (III. i), but he cannot follow them up.

'Satyre' is now becoming as fixed a type as the sonnet sequence. In 1599 'T. M. Gent', probably Thomas Middleton, who had published three years earlier his *Wisdom of Solomon* (a paraphrase which dilutes each verse of the original into two *Venus and Adonis* stanzas, not without a good line here and there) brought out *Micro-Cynicon, Six Snarling Satyres*. They exhibit in some places the usual half-lines and other metrical irregularities: elsewhere they are faintly Augustan. The familiar types are attacked. The fourth, on cony-catching, set beside Greene's prose, helps to reveal the feebleness of this genre: the verse is doing nothing that prose could not do equally well. Such good phrases or images as T. M. offers us sound as if they had floated in from some different kind of poem: notably, in the first,

> Into this hel sometimes an Angel falls
> Whose white aspect black forlorne soules appals.

There are many obscure passages. Within a convention which affects obscurity it is not always possible to say which are intended and which result from mere incompetence.

It is difficult to understand how the satires of Hall and

Marston have won such celebrity at the expense of Samuel
Rowlands's *Letting of Humours Blood in the Head Vein* (1600).
Rowlands, alone of the Elizabethan satirists, has grasped the
fact that it is useless to attack knaves unless you entertain readers,
that neither moral purpose nor personal malice will do instead
of comic power. With him satire ceases to shout and learns to
chuckle, and by dropping the shrill moral pretensions of his
predecessors he becomes far more amusing and certainly no less
moral. He also quietly drops the tradition of obscurity and of
metrical violence. His speech, learned perhaps from the new
theatres, is nearly always dramatic. His first is on an impostor.
Rowlands sees him a long way off and does not recognize him:
'Who haue we here? . . . some swaggring fellow. . . . Now, a
shame take the buzzard. . . . I know the ruffiane.' We have
some excellent Munchausen stuff:

> Heele tell you of a tree that he doth know
> Vpon the which rapiers and Daggers grow
> As good as Fleetstreete hath in any shoppe,
> Which being ripe doune into scabbards droppe.

In IV we see 'the age grown so picked that the toe of the peasant
comes near the heel of the courtier'. Rowlands complains that
our comedians are out of date in their picture of the countryman; the modern rustic is just as concerned with eloquence (we
are given specimens) as any townsman. The fifth attacks censorious moralists and is—perhaps unintentionally—a reproof to
the other satirists, the poachers turned gamekeepers. Rowlands
is never great, but he is sane, readable, and often funny.

There remains a freak. Cyril Tourneur's *Transformed Metamorphosis* (1600) stands wholly outside the Roman and humanistic tradition which we have been following. He may have
conceived himself as obedient to that tradition when he made
his poem impenetrably obscure, but in reality he is going back
to a different sort of obscurity, to the cryptographic obscurity of
the *Spider and the Fly* or *Speak Parrot*. He may have coined his
hard words in order to inspissate the darkness, but their literary
effect is very like that of aureation. These characteristics, combined with rhyme royal, give us the feeling of returning to the
Middle Ages. The poem deals (certainly) with popery, and
(probably) with Essex and King James. Its editor Churton
Collins speaks of 'two stanzas which I shall not make myself

ridiculous by trying to explain': I can only extend his principle
to the whole. At its cloudiest it can be like this;

> The vine's Aedonides: dead Murcianie:
> Smooth Philoxenus: murder's ground:
> Disquiet Eriphila: hel's syrenie:
> Philocrematus: the soule's deepe wound. . .

The coinages (or revivals) include such words as *errorie, lyco-
phosed, Israellize, egencie, minulise, fact* (as a past participle, meaning 'made') and *Endymionie* (which appears to mean 'sleep').
And yet there is a kind of pleasure, or at least a fascination, in
the thing; a surrealist mixture of horror and nonsense. We see
a hall whose foundations are in Phlegethon, compassed with
'birds, vines, and flowres and eu'ry sundry fruite', a bridge, and
on the bridge a serpent 'in female shape' who 'soothes with
Leucrocutanized sound'. This might for most of us as well be
runcible sound, but we are certainly reading a poet, though
perhaps a poet who takes opium. After the loud-mouthed self-
righteousness of the Marstons and Halls it may even be a relief.

For it must be confessed that the formal satires of the nineties
are, in the aggregate, a weariness. They have their happy
moments; but there is far too little irony and invention, and far
too much direct denunciation. The shapeless Roman model was
a fatal encouragement to the Elizabethan love of facile moral
ferocity. Nothing is easier, or less interesting, than to proclaim
with raucous conviction that whores are unchaste, misers un-
generous, and hypocrites insincere: and the raucous passes with
equal ease into the falsetto. The frequent attacks of the satirists
on Golden love poetry would be of considerable interest if we
could assure ourselves that they expressed a genuinely literary
reaction against the Golden style and were thus pioneer work
for a new poetry; but this is doubtful. The professed motive of
the satirists is ethical. The real motive is quite as likely to be
personal as literary. Their own style is fully accounted for by
decorum: everyone knew—Spenser himself knew—that satire
ought not to be sweet or sublime. Marston had tried very hard
to be Golden himself, and failed. I do not think we can make
much of these satirists as leaders in a stylistic revolt.

The epigram in this period is closely connected with satire—
Whitgift and Bancroft forbade both in 1599—but is of much less
interest. The chief collections were the Epigrams of Sir John

Davies (printed in one book with Marlowe's Ovid in 1590), Edward Guilpin's (prefixed to his Satires in 1598), Thomas Bastard's *Chrestoleros* in the same year, John Weever's in 1599, and Rowlands's, published with his Satires in 1600. None of them rise so high as mediocrity. This form demands a polish and a 'wit' (in the modern sense of the word) which the Elizabethans could not supply. Guilpin's are the most abysmal. Rowlands's are sometimes tolerable, but this is when they cease to be epigrams and become in effect short satires: not much shorter than some of Hall's. One of Davies's (never ask me which) moved me to smile—but it did so by the story it told and would have been just as good in prose. Bastard vaunted that he had 'taught Epigrams to speake chastlie', but he had not made them much more delectable. The epigram usually affects the same style as the satire and is sometimes in doggerel metre, but some of Bastard's complimentary pieces are Golden. In all the collections I have mentioned there is probably not a single epigram which displays as much talent as a good limerick in our own days.

III

We are now at last free to approach the Golden poetry proper. Two preliminary observations must be made.

1. Mellifluous though most of this poetry is, we shall find in it a metrical phenomenon distressing to the modern ear. I call it Simpsonian rhyme; as we name Bright's disease after him who diagnosed it. Simpsonian rhyme in its simplest form is a rhyme on the second syllable of a disyllabic word where metre forbids that syllable to carry the stress. The second condition of course distinguishes it from mere terminal inversion, as when a ballad line ends 'my fair bodíe'. Thus in a couplet like Chapman's

> Till our Leander that made Mars his Cupid,
> With soft loue-sutes for iron thunders chid
> > (*Hero and Leander*, III. 211)

an inverted stress on *Cupid* would ruin the first line. This may be called 'Simpsonian A'. We also have Simpsonian A2 where the same relation occurs between two pairs of monosyllables, as when Barnes (Sonnet IV) rhymes *fróm thee* with *to mé*: or between trisyllables (call it Simpsonian A3) when the same poet (XLIX) rhymes *inextricáble* with *impórtable*. We then go on to what may be called *Plusquam*-Simpsonian rhyme, or Simpsonian B where two unstressed syllables, again with no possibility of inversion, are rhymed together. Thus Abraham Fraunce calls the metre of his Nativity poem (*The Countess of Pembroke's Emanuel*, 1591) 'ryming hexameters' because consecutive lines end with such words as *abashed* and *saluted*: or Richard Linche in his *Diego and Ginevra* (a fairly brisk stanzaic *novella* published with his sonnet-sequence *Diella* in 1596) has such rhymes as *lády, húngry* (St. 17) and *lóve her, offénd her* (44). If Simpsonian rhyme occurred only in satires we could explain it as a deliberate harshness: but it occurs in *epyllia* like *Scylla's Metamorphosis*, and in sonnets. If only bad poets used it we could attribute it to incompetence: but it is used by Lodge, Shakespeare, and (excessively) by Chapman. We may indeed suppose that stress was a little less tyrannous, and the rights of unstressed syllables a little more respected, in Elizabethan than in modern English, but the greatest allowance we can make for such a change hardly explains the phenomenon. (When Keats used it, as in *Endymion*, I. 450, he was doubtless enjoying it as an archaism.)

2. The proper grouping of Golden poetry is by kinds, not by authors. Any poet's sonnet has more in common with other sonnets than with his own other works. Any poem written in the tradition of the *Mirror for Magistrates* will contain much Drab, whoever writes it. Any song might, for all we can see, have been written by any poet. Our modern critical tradition of concentrating on idiosyncrasies is here a handicap. The likeness between all the Golden poets is much more important than their differences in poetic character, as distinct from their different degrees of perfection. And even these latter are curiously evasive. Nothing is more remarkable in the nineties than the way in which excellence may suddenly flow from the meanest pen. Incredible as it may seem, all external evidence points to the wretched Munday as the author of the song in *England's Helicon* that begins

> Beautie sate bathing by a Spring
> Where fayrest shades did hide her.

Poetic power is spread in such 'commonalty' that if we were not on our guard we should come to take the 'Spirit of the Age' for more than a figure of speech and believe that poetry could really be 'in the air'. But that way all the chimeras lie. This

extension of poetry was possible because it was a poetry content
to express the emotions in which all men are alike. What was
new was a technique, a learnable technique, soon leading to a
standard of workmanship which earlier poets had hardly even
attempted. Masses of hitherto thwarted poetic impulse were released. The first Golden poets had not so much sown a seed as
burst a dam. And the resulting poetry was very homogeneous,
even impersonal. That is why it matters so little whether a given
song or sonnet is a translation or an original. If it is harmonious,
if it is sufficiently full of pathos, or sensuality, or pomp, or frolic,
it will do. There is no demand that each poet should have an
idiom of his own. In this chapter I shall yield to the modern
mode by treating some great or copious poets separately, but I
shall group much of the work by kinds.

This period begins with surprising suddenness. Apart from
Spenser himself, who never became 'all Gold', the only poet
who might show gradual aurification is Breton. In his *Flourish
upon Fancy* (1577) we saw him writing purest Drab. If we were
sure which pieces were his in *Britton's Bower of Delights* (1591)
we might catch him just at the turn; for here we have a Drab
elegy on Sidney and Drab poulter's, but a tinge of Gold in 'Let
me go seek' and 'Cupid's Complaint', and the truly Golden in
'Pastoral'.

> On a hill there growes a flower
> Faire befall the daintie sweete;
> By that flower there is a bower . . .

In the *Pilgrimage to Paradise* (1592) he is clearly established as a
minor Golden poet. He is so minor that the change might escape
notice unless you actually juxtapose the 1577 Breton and the
1592 Breton. The 1577 Breton writes:

> My hart it selfe is bitten so with frost
> That all my senses now are waxed nome,
> My tongue his tast of pleasant ioyes hath lost . . .

The 1592 Breton writes:

> The seconde calde, his charge was but to heare
> In sweetest sounds which was the soundest sweete,
> What graces might in Musickes ground appeare . . .

Both are unimportant. But in the one we have ruthless regularity of accent, end-stopped lines, colourless abstracts as keywords, the fatuous epithet 'pleasant', brutal alliteration; in the

other, the phantasmal or merely theoretical stress on *was* in line 2, enjambment, the richer keywords, 'sounds', 'graces', 'music', and chiasmic alliteration in the last line. Breton has exchanged his boots for pumps.

Breton, then, is such a poet as the historian (not the general reader) sighs for: a textbook case, a human thermometer. But this is not characteristic. In the eighties Watson, Marlowe, and Peele are already Golden when we first meet them, and we can only guess how they achieved it. The two last names warn us that the separation between drama and other poetry forced upon us by the plan of this series becomes at this point artificial. It is significant that it had not troubled us before: until the Golden Period an historian of poetry need take hardly any notice of the stage. But now, no Form was more suddenly charged with gold than the dramatic. Peele, though no one could class him with Breton as an instance of gradual transmutation, grew more Golden as he went on. The *Arraignment of Paris* (1584) has gaps, as it were, in the gold leaf, and yokel ugliness shows through. But Peele, as he came to be in *David and Bethsabe*, cannot be left out of any account of the Golden Age. That play (so ineptly compared with the old miracles) is ablaze with the new, luxuriant beauties; 'His thunder is entangled in my hair', 'Take but your lute and make the mountains dance', 'Unity infinite and innumerable', or that line about the thunder's spouse which has, quite rightly, been called Aeschylean. And Peele can go beyond mere gorgeousness. A common imagination, personifying sin, would offer us either a beautiful courtesan or a loathsome monster: but Peele's David knows far better—

> Sin with his seuenfold crowne and purple robe
> Begins his triumph.

In Marlowe Gold so bathes the drama that drama all but disappears. The little, and often odious, puppets are as dwarfed by their own poetry as a circus-master by his own elephant. We forget Tamburlaine and Mortimer and even (at times) Faustus, and think only of Rhodope and Persepolis and celestial spheres and spirits 'shadowing more beautie in their aery browes than haue the white breasts of the Queene of loue'. The trochaic in 'What is beautie' matters more than the whole pretence of drama which is crawling about, down on the stage, fathoms below this region: like a tragedy about beetles.

The history of the lyric at this period clearly forbids us to exclude the theatre. Indeed the old Drab or Tottelian lyric died harder among the literary poets than among the dramatists, who are pioneers and masters of Golden lyric. It differs from the old kind in three ways. First and most important is the formal difference. It abandons poulter's and fourteeners: uses sparingly even the simple octosyllabic stanzas or eights and sixes of the better Tottelians; and explores the resources of stanzaic variation and variation within the line. Thus in Byrd's *Psalms, Sonnets and Songs* (1588) the song 'Though Amaryllis daunce' contains very old ideas ('friendly foes', 'flames of yce', and 'freezing fire'): the important thing is the varying line lengths within the stanza, the chiasmic rhyme, and the unexpected movement of the refrain. So in 'Adieu Loue, untrue Loue' from the same Byrd's *Songs of Sundry Natures* (1589), take the second stanza (not the first, for a reason that will shortly appear), cut off the refrain, and you have a Tottelian effect. Then read the whole poem as it actually stands: you are in a different world. Sometimes a Golden lyric differs from the Tottelian only by a hair's breadth: Lady Pembroke's 'Alas, with what tormenting fyre' would be pure Gnomic Drab if you removed the third and sixth lines of each stanza with their feminine rhymes. The second distinction of the Golden lyric is that it does not disdain to learn from the 'rakehelly rhymers': popular phrases, even baby-talk and sheer nonsense, are welcomed. Nothing could be more innocent, closer to folk verse, than Peele's 'Fair and fair and twice so fair': yet its melodic structure would make the best of the Tottelians' work look 'innocent' in a very different sense. To the same class belong his 'Whenas the rye', Nashe's 'Spring, the sweet spring', and some of Shakespeare's songs. Let any man try to hit off in verse this note of almost idiotic happiness, and then bow to his betters. Very different is Nashe's 'Adieu, farewell earth's bliss', a subtle mixture of the immemorially popular and the extremely sophisticated. What it sounded like with the music I do not know: its peculiarity as verse is that it never allows you to accept any interpretation of its metre as final. There is an over-all impression of a triple iambic beat ('All things to end are made'). But then there are the dactyls of the fifth strophe, and the amphimacers of the third (who could give less than full value to *died young*?) and the last line of each. The third characteristic of Golden lyric is its delight in external nature.

This had never been absent from the lyric, but there had, I think, been more of it in the Middle Ages than in the Tottelians. When I asked the reader to try an experiment on the second stanza of 'Adieu loue, untrue loue', that was because the first contained mountain and valley, a crystal well, and the 'shadow of a green oak tree'. Of the three characteristics which I have attributed to the Golden lyric, this last is, however, the least certain guide.

Thomas Watson (1557?–1592) has the distinction of being the earliest of the poets who are Golden from their first word. He is also a very minor poet indeed, and I welcome the fact as a further safeguard against any tendency to make 'Golden' a eulogistic term. What poetry there is in Watson is of Golden type, but (save for historical interest) almost negligible. He is as pure an example as we can find of the 'Renaissance' poet. He is more of a scholar than most of his contemporaries and wrote neo-Latin works, including a translation of the *Antigone*. The medieval elements in his love poetry all come to him through the Italians: he did not know they were medieval. His first English volume, the *Hecatompathia* (1582), is almost as heavily weighted with 'adminicular gear' as the *Shepheards Calender* itself; with analyses after the manner of the *Vita Nuova*, condescensions to 'the vulgar sorte', and diligent acknowledgement of every debt to Sophocles, Theocritus, Horace, Seneca, Petrarch, Aeneas Sylvius, Politian, Seraphino, Strozza, Parabosco, and Ronsard. These notes are the most interesting part of the book. The poems consist of three *Venus and Adonis* stanzas each, very tame, very derivative but all having that graceful movement which was then so new and (I suspect) still so far from easy. In 1590 came the *Meliboeus*, a lament for Walsingham translated from Watson's own Latin: it is perhaps a little better than the *Hecatompathia*. His sonnets, *The Tears of Fancy*, were published in 1593. The thirtieth and fifty-first show traces of the *Faerie Queene*, but Watson is perhaps closer to Shakespeare than to any other sonneteer in his conception of the sonnet. One of the uses of Watson's work is to show that, as between a plain and a beautiful face, so between supreme and mediocre poetry, there can be a clear likeness. All the elements of Petrarch's beauty are present in the *Hecatompathia*, all those of *Lycidas* in *Meliboeus*, and nothing comes of them. Perhaps one line of Watson's deserves to be remembered, 'In all this world I think none loues but I'. There is also a song, pleasant enough, attributed to him in *England's Helicon* (1600).

George Peele (1558?–1597) outside his lyrical and dramatic work is a very minor poet. He writes pageant verses, graceful and dignified, but tame. They were of course written to order, but if that is a sufficient explanation of their coldness this fact itself marks a momentous revolution in the history of poetry: such conditions would not have made Dunbar or Pindar cold. In some of these pieces, notably in *Poly-hymnia* (1590) and the *Honour of the Garter* (1593) the artificial simplicity of the syntax and the handling of the decasyllabic oddly remind us of Tennyson in his quiet moments. In the former the image of the old knight's helmet used as a bee-hive is memorable.

Greene's non-dramatic poetry with the exception of the *Maiden's Dream* (1591), a dull allegorical elegy in Spenser's unhappiest vein, consists of the lyrics scattered through his prose works. A few of these, such as the two songs from *Arbasto*, are gnomic Drab: the majority, eminently Golden. The subject is nearly always love, not passionate but playful or voluptuous. Almost invariably the mistress is praised, as Hamlet praised his father, by mythological comparisons. Menaphon's eclogue—a catalogue of physical charms in the manner of the medieval Latin poets—is only an apparent exception, for it exists chiefly to be condemned by the answering eclogue of Melicertus which is both a defence and an example of Greene's favourite method. The right way to praise, says Melicertus, is like this:

> Apollo when my Mistresse first was born
> Cut off his locks and left them on her head

or this

> Once Venus dream'd vpon two prettie thinges . . .
> And when she wak'd they were my Mistress breastes.

This continual recourse to Olympus might be expected to be tedious, but as we read the poems we do not find it so. Greene is a great metrical inventor and nearly all his stanzas are happy. Eurymachus' 'Fancy' (in *Never too Late*) is interesting for the melody it achieves by a sparing use of rhyme; 'Fair fields' (in *Menaphon*), for variations in the shorter lines. Infida's song in *Never too Late* is an almost impudent work of illusion; we feel we have read a charming lyric, yet there is really nothing in it but the refrain. In his longer, octosyllabic pieces Greene often uses what would now be called sprung rhythm, perhaps having learned to like it from Chaucer misread, and the results are sometimes pleasant. He is a great manager; his resources in thought and feeling are very narrow, but he lays them out to such advantage that we enjoy him more than many richer men. Even in his hexameters he knows that monosyllables are the only source of true English spondees. 'Face rose-hued, cherry-red' is a better opening for a line than we shall easily find in Sidney. 'Weep not my wanton' is, and perhaps deserves to be, his best-known poem.

There is no external evidence for the date at which Christopher Marlowe[1] (1564–93) translated *All Ovid's Elegies*, but it seems likely that this is the earliest work we have from his hand. He did not know very much Latin when he made it and even where he sees the point of the original he can sadly blunt it. The *Amores*, despite the sensuality which may have attracted him to them, are not really a work very congenial to Marlowe. Their metallic perfection of form, the almost scientific objectivity with which they expose the whole amorist's life (impotence included), their cool gaiety, are foreign to his temperament. He could not reproduce their almost puerile cleverness: *cedere iussit aquam, jussa recedit aqua* turns to the jaw-breaking 'Flye back his stream chargd, the stream chargd gaue place'. Conversely, Marlowe's best lines are often far from the Latin in poetic quality. Ovid never wrote anything that sounds like

> With beautie of thy wings thy faire haire guilded,
> Ride golden love in chariots richly builded.

But the work is very interesting because we can here trace in little those varying effects of the Ovidian couplet upon English poetry which are writ large elsewhere. When Marlowe writes 'Love slackt my Muse and made my numbers soft' or 'A scarlet blush her guilty face arayed' we see Ovid the Master of the Augustans. Turn the page and we shall see Ovid the Master of Donne:

[1] b. at Canterbury, 1564. Of humble origin. Entered at Corpus Christi, Cambridge, 1581. B.A., 1583. M.A., 1587. Accused by the informer Richard Baines in 1593 of holding 'that Moyses was but a Iugler and that one Heriots being Sir W. Raleighs man, can do more than he', that the Jews were right in crucifying Christ, that 'all thei that loue not Tobacco were fooles', that he had as good a right to coin as the Queen, and various other damnable opinions. Fatally stabbed in a tavern, 1593.

Vngrate why feignest new feares? and doest refuse;
Well maiest thou one thing for thy Mistresse vse.
If thou deniest foole, Ile our deeds expresse
And as a traitour mine oune fault confesse . . .

This argumentative brutality Ovid bequeathed to Donne, as he bequeathed to the Augustans his closed couplet, his balance, his antithesis and ease.

Lucan's First Book, mentioned in 1593 but not known in print till 1600, bears Marlowe's name. If it were ever reasonable to reject a contemporary ascription on purely internal evidence, I should be tempted to deny this work to Marlowe. It is of very great merit. At what date Marlowe wrote such verse as this, I do not know;

>   young men left their beds
> And snatcht armes neer their houshold gods hung vp
> Such as peace yeelds; wormeaten leatherne targets
> Through which the wood peer'd, headles darts, olde swords . . .

I should be inclined to put it late and see in it not an early manner which he outgrew but a new manner inspired by a congenial model, which, had he lived, might greatly have enriched his original work.

But of course Marlowe's greatest poetical achievement is the two sestiads of his unfinished *Hero and Leander*. This is a more perfect work than any of his plays, not because their poetry is always inferior to it but because in it the poetry and the theme are at one. Here, and here only, he found matter to which his genius was entirely adequate. For Marlowe is our great master of the material imagination; he writes best about flesh, gold, gems, stone, fire, clothes, water, snow, and air. It is only in such concretes that his imagination can fix itself. Dramatic necessity, born of economic necessity, often drove him into alien fields and he failed to crystallize in passions proper to his characters the heady exuberance of his own emotion. The monotonous megalomania of his heroes argues as much penury as depravity in the poet. They utter screaming follies very largely because he cannot think of anything more relevant or probable for them to say. But what incapacitated him as a tragedian qualified him magnificently as a writer of erotic epyllion. This was the work he was born to do. In this form his sole business was to make holiday from all facts and all morals in a world of imagined deliciousness where all beauty was sensuous and all sensuality was beautiful. The honey-sweetness which appears as one element among many in the *Faerie Queene* or the *Arcadia* was to be the substance of the whole poem. Nothing could be simpler or more obvious than such a project, but this does not mean that it was easy to execute. Most attempts of the sort have been failures: Shakespeare himself, as I shall presently argue, largely failed in *Venus and Adonis*. For the poet has to be continuously sweet yet never cloy us. He must be realistic enough to keep us in touch with the senses (for his theme is the flesh) yet never so realistic as to awake disgust or incredulity. Nor our sense of humour: laughter at the wrong moment is as fatal in this kind as in tragedy. Sneers at 'a pretty piece of Paganism' are inadmissible. We may, no doubt, condemn the whole genre on moral grounds: but if it is to be written at all it demands powers which hardly any poet possesses.

Marlowe's success is particularly instructive because it depends on the continual presence of a quality which would at first sight appear to be wholly inappropriate to his design: the quality of hardness. Marlowe chose for his epyllion a ringing, predominantly end-stopped couplet. He also excluded all tenderness. Love, in this poem, is not 'full of pittie' but 'deafe and cruell'. Leander woos like 'a bold sharpe sophister'. The temple of Love is decorated not with scenes of pathos and gentleness but with insolent grotesques:

> the gods in sundry shapes
> Committing headdie ryots, incest, rapes.

A male and immortal lover tries first to ravish Leander and then to murder him. The effect of all this is to dehumanize the story and thus, in one sense, to disinfect it. The mawkishness which (as Keats knew) frequently disfigures *Endymion* can win no entry. We do not think of Hero and Leander as a girl and a boy who have fallen in love; they are nothing but lovers and have no existence apart from their desires. It is as if we were allowed to share in the erotic experience of two daemons or two wild animals. And the word 'share' is here important. We do not see their frenzy from outside as we see that of Shakespeare's Venus. We are at the centre and see the rest of the universe transfigured by the hard, brittle splendour of erotic vision. That is the real function of Marlowe's preposterous, yet wholly successful, hyperboles. Hero has been offered Apollo's throne. A necklace of pebbles shines like diamonds with the light reflected from her throat. When the ladies of Sestos walk in procession the street becomes a firmament of breathing stars. In that world there are boys so beautiful that they never dare to drink at a fountain: naiads would pull them under. These hyperboles are not, even if Marlowe thought they were, mere rhetoric. They build up something like the world as the world appears at a moment of wholly unrestrained passion. In *Venus and Adonis* we are the spectators of such a passion, and it sometimes sickens us. In Marlowe's poem we see not the passion but what the passion thinks it sees. His very limitations here come to his aid. Shakespeare was even in youth too full and ripe a man to keep all reality and humanity (one thing excepted) out of his poem. Marlowe had no such difficulty: his difficulty had always been to bring them in, and this time he did not need them. We bid goodbye to the world of sober experience at the very outset. Hence the integrity, in a sense one might almost say the purity, of his poem. There is no nonsense about it, no pitiful pretence that appetite is anything other than appetite. I do not know that any other poet has rivalled its peculiar excellence. Lachrymose or melodramatic sensualists like Swinburne are of course out of the running. Byron and Ovid keep their sensuality tolerable (when they do) by being comic and ironical and thus write a wholly different sort of poetry.

Marlowe's poem is best read with Chapman's conclusion, but in a literary history we must postpone consideration of that great neglected work. Another epyllion, the *Scylla's Metamorphosis* of Lodge demands our attention. It had not been Lodge's first poem: but *Truth's Complaint over England*, published with the *Alarm* in 1584, is of little value. It was in rhyme royal and conformed to the medieval pattern of vision poetry which had affected Lodge (probably) through Sackville's *Induction*. *Scylla's Metamorphosis* appeared in 1589, when Marlowe's poem may have been unwritten. Neither seems to be indebted to the other. Lodge's epyllion is set in a medieval frame; that is, it becomes a proper epyllion only after the poet, walking alone, has met Glaucus. Except for one passage in which the 'outward show' of comfort which Thetis offers her son is contrasted with her secret tears, the mingled complaints and narratives which form the body of the poem do not appeal strongly to our emotions. They were probably not intended to. Lodge's chief aim was to paint richly for the inner eye and to charm the ear with fine phrases and feminine rhymes. Considering the early date of the poem, his frequent success is remarkable. His stanzas are full of lines that we repeat to ourselves for sheer pleasure: 'a mortall wound is my immortall being', 'Daughter of Jove and sister to the Sunne'. Spenser had as yet published nothing that would give Lodge much help, and Sidney's verse (if we suppose Lodge to have seen manuscript copies of it) though far more serious and passionate has seldom this airy, seeming-artless grace. The poet of whom Lodge most often reminds us is Shakespeare. Not all that Shakespeare learned from him was good: we could wish he had never seen such a stanza as that beginning:

> Of loue (God wot) the louelie Nimph complained,
> But so of loue as forced Loue to loue her.

It was in a happier hour that his eyes fell upon:

> Mark how the morne in roseat colour shines
> And strait with cloudes the sunnie tract is clad.

With all its beauties *Scylla* is a rather unsatisfactory poem. It is too static and deals too much in tears. The single stanza in which Lodge uses a wholly different metre ('Wretched love let me die, end my love by my death') is perplexing. We want to have heard the poet read it himself. If rattled off, as it could be, in Shenstonian 'anapaests', it would be detestable; read slowly, with full stresses on *let* and *end*, it might please.

Of the other pieces published with *Scylla*, 'The Discontented Satire' has many medieval traits, and the 'Commendation of Solitary Life' is a grave, harmonious poem in which appreciation of natural beauty counts for something. Both these, like *Scylla*, are in the stanza which Shakespeare used for *Venus and Adonis*.

In 1593 with *Phillis*, which I postpone, came the *Complaint of Elstred*, woeful and worthless stuff in the vein of the *Mirror for Magistrates*, and in 1595 those satires which I have already considered. Far more important than any of these are the lyrics, whether included in *Phillis*, scattered through his prose works, or preserved in contemporary anthologies. On these much of his lasting fame depends. In one or two of them—in the Hamadryad's song 'Pluck the fruit' from *William of Normandy* or 'Happy Phoenix' from *Euphues' Shadow*—there is just a hint of that slightly glib, over-emphatic melody which we find in

Dryden's songs. Once, in Montana's 'second sonnet' ('When the dog') the metrical scheme seems to me, or has sometimes seemed, a little arbitrary. But with these few concessions unfavourable criticism must end; for those, at least, who are prepared to accept this kind of poetry on its own terms. Some, like Sir Sidney Lee, demand originality and consider a poem to be somehow discounted if you can find a foreign original. Others may want high seriousness, or irony, or social awareness. Lodge offers nothing of that kind. He hardly offers even passion; only gestures, delightfully graceful gestures, symbolical of it. By varying line-lengths and artful disposition of the rhymes each stanza is a delicate surprise: when the pattern has been repeated often enough to be familiar, the poem ends. But it seldom seems to end just for that reason. Each poem has shape in the sense that the thought, or rather the playing at thought, progresses and comes to a full close. All these virtues can be illustrated from Rosalynde's 'Loue in my bosom' alone. There is aural surprise in the mono-rhymed quatrain towards the end of each stanza and aural suspense, long but just not too long, while we wait for the feminine rhyme from one stanza's end to another's. There is a progression from complaint in the first two, through revolt in the third, to submission in the last. We are not left asking, as so often in a Drab lyric, why it ends where it does. In 'Phoebe sate' there is a wonderful minuet of rhymes. The freshness, the illusion of spontaneity which in all these lyrics so refreshes the reader, depends on filling the highly sophisticated form with all the silly-sooth of love-making, with flowers, birds, lips, sun, and shade. They are of course, as they were intended to be, trifles. That is one reason why only an artist could have made them. In large, serious works there are so many means besides poetic art with which to hold a reader's attention.

I have said nothing about the sonnet-sequence *Phillis* because I wish now to consider several specimens of this form together. This will have the advantage of separating the sequences as far as possible from their authors. When they are thus separated the modern reader is more likely to treat them fairly and to cease demanding of them what they were never intended to give. The sonneteers wrote not to tell their own love stories, not to express whatever in their own loves was local and peculiar, but to give us others, the inarticulate lovers, a voice. The reader was to seek in a sonnet not what the poet felt but what he himself felt, what all men felt. A good sonnet (*mutatis mutandis* and *salva reverentia*) was like a good public prayer: the test is whether the congregation can 'join' and make it their own, not whether it provides interesting materials for the spiritual biography of the compiler. If we use the litany, this is not necessarily because we are interested in Cranmer. In this respect the Elizabethan sonnet is comparable to the Elizabethan song. It does not matter who is speaking to whom in 'Since there's no helpe' any more than in 'Oh mistress mine'. Love poetry of this sort is transferable. For this reason, and for another which will appear presently, it matters very little which sonnets are translations. Here again the analogy of a public prayer holds good. The whole body of sonnet sequences is much more like an erotic liturgy than a series of erotic confidences.

I hope no reader will take this to mean that sonnets are 'literary exercises'. We are not assuming that the sonneteer was never in love any more than we are assuming that all who compose liturgies are infidels. It is perhaps always more probable that any young poet is in love than that he is not. As for 'literary exercises', I am not yet sure that any such things exist. There are exercises, properly so called, in other arts. A pianist plays scales; a painter makes a study of a foreshortened foot which is not intended ever to form part of a completed picture. But does any man write a verse without at least the momentary hope and intention of producing a poem which will be delightful, even immortal, for its own sake?

Watson's sonnets have already been mentioned. John Southern's *Pandora* (1584) was unmetrical rubbish, never praised by anyone (I think) except Puttenham. In 1591 we reach a sonneteer who matters. In that year Newman's edition of Sidney's *Astrophel* included twenty-eight sonnets by Samuel Daniel (1563–1631). In the following year Daniel published his sequence *Delia* which omitted a few of those printed by Newman and added many others, bringing the total up to fifty-five. *Delia* stands in a different class from the rest of Daniel's work: if he had written nothing else we might hear less of Daniel but we should certainly hear less of 'the prosaic Daniel'. For assuredly those who like their poetry 'not too darn poetical' should avoid *Delia*. It offers no ideas, no psychology, and of course no story: it is simply a masterpiece of phrasing and melody. To anyone who complains that it is a series of common-

places we can only reply, 'Yes, but listen'. Of course it is commonplace to tell your mistress that she is young and now's the
time for love: but he says, 'Now whilst thy May hath fill'd thy
lap with flowers'. Of course it is commonplace to say that she is
virtuous as well as young: but Daniel says she is a maid

> deck'd with a blush of honour
> Whose feet do treade green pathes of youth and loue.

Any man may complain that he grows old; but Daniel says

> My cares draw on mine everlasting night

and builds out of it a hyperbole which leaves us not astonished
(as the metaphysical hyperboles do) but bowed down before
the magnanimity of the attitude it implies. In him, as in Shakespeare, the most ordinary statement turns liquid and delicious:

> Still in the trace of one perplexed thought
> My ceasles cares continually run on,

or

> Shalt bend thy wrinkles homeward to the earth.

The truth is that while everything Daniel says would be commonplace in a prose abstract, nothing is commonplace as it
actually occurs in the poetry. In that medium all the Petrarchan
gestures become compulsive invitations to enormous sorrows
and delights. And it really matters very little that he is so heavily
indebted to Desportes. A poetic translation is always to some
extent a new work of art. In the large, objective kinds, in epic
or tragedy, the degree of novelty is limited, because situation,
characters, and architectonics are common to both handlings.
But in so small a poem as a sonnet a seemingly trivial change
may alter an image, or an implied image, in such a way as to
alter the lighting of the whole piece. Thus Desportes writes:

> La beauté qui, si douce, à présent vous inspire,
> Cédant aux lois du Tans, ses faveurs reprendra;
> L'hyver de vostre teint les fleurettes perdra,
> Et ne laissera rien des thresors que j'admire.
> Cest orgueil desdaigneux qui vous fait ne m'aimer,
> En regret et chagrin se verra transformer,
> Avec le changement d'une image si belle . . .

Daniel turns it:

> Her beauty now the burden of my song,
> Whose glorious blaze the world's eye doth admire,
> Must yield her praise to tyrant Times desire,
> Then fades the flower, which fed her pride so long;
> When, if she grieve to gaze her in her glasse
> Which then presents her winter wither'd hue . . .

Nothing in the French corresponds to Daniel's throbbing first line, nor, of course, to his alliterations and sub-alliterations throughout. *Beauté* in Desportes is a high abstraction which, in obedience to the *lois* of Time, resumes something it has lent to the lady: in Daniel, not beauty but 'her beauty' yields to Time conceived as a greedy tyrant. The two images almost imply two different and antagonistic myths; the one a vindication of law, the other, at least in part, a protest against tyranny. Then, in the French, another abstraction, *orgueil*, will see itself turning into regret: but out of *se verra* Daniel gets the concrete picture of a woman, not her pride, looking into a real mirror—a picture implied, if at all, very faintly in Desportes's *image*. Thus the connexion between Daniel's poem and Desportes', though real, is superficial. The theme which they have in common with each other ('She'll be sorry some day') they also have in common with countless other poems; they do different things with it and lead our imagination through different roads.

Henry Constable's *Diana*, printed in 1592 and again 'with divers Quatorzains of honourable and learned personages' in 1594 (though the volume bears the false date 1584) is on a far lower level. Constable relies on the conceits rather than on the emotive resources of the Petrarchan tradition, and many of his contemporaries wrote lines that are sweeter on the tongue. No better, but interesting for other reasons, is the anonymous collection *Licia*, attributed on the strength of a passage in Phineas Fletcher's 'Piscatory Eclogue' to his father Giles Fletcher the elder. It bears no date, but the Dedicatory Epistle ends 'from my chamber Sept. 4. 1593'. I cannot accept Sir Sidney Lee's view that either in this epistle or in the subsequent address 'To the Reader' Fletcher 'deprecates' the notion that he has, or ever had, a real love affair. What he actually does is to poke fun at critics who ask such irrelevant questions: perhaps (who knows?) Licia may be a personification of Travers's 'Discipline'. It is a just rebuke by which nineteenth-century critics might well have profited, but the main interest of Fletcher's introductory matter lies elsewhere. His anti-puritanism, his serious reverence for love as the only proper ground of marriage, and his demand that a scholar should have the accomplishments of a gentleman, anticipate attitudes which were to become characteristically English. His sonnets (to which he added an eclogue and a dull poem on Richard III in the vein of the *Mirror for Magistrates*) are not quite without merit. In the Golden Age we hardly notice lines like

> In tyme the strong and statelie turrets fall,
> In tyme the Rose and siluer Lillies die,

but we should praise them in a fifteenth- or eighteenth-century poet. Nor has anyone said better what all must feel about the hazards and adventures of their own ancestors than Fletcher in the line 'I might have dyed before my lyfe begunne'. The whole sonnet (XXII) is good. There is some feeling for nature in *Licia*, and some graceful fancy: no pathos and no exaltation.

Sir Sidney Lee can hardly find words strong enough for his dislike of Lodge's *Phillis* (1593). He might have picked out for blame the thirty-sixth and thirty-seventh, in alexandrines, which revert to the clownishly over-emphatic diction of the Drab Age and thus show how form may determine style. Actually, what enrages him is 'the mire of deceit and mystification', and he ridicules Minto for praising their 'seeming artlessness'. But to seem artless when you are in fact heavily indebted to Ronsard and Desportes is an offence, if at all, against morality, not against art. If a poem seems beautiful, it is beautiful. Lodge, though not great, is very often delightful. The tradition of lovers' humility was very old when he wrote, but it renews its youth in a line like 'And working wonders, yet say all is dutie'. We have heard before that swans sing against their death; but Lodge makes the myth local and immediate when he writes:

> The rumour runs that here in Isis swim
> Such statelie Swannes, so confident in dying,
> That when they feele themselves near Lethes brim . . .

The second line, psychologizing the thing, limiting it to certain swans, is admirable. Sonnet XXXIV is a lesson in the perfect use of mythology ('I would in rich and golden-colour'd rain'). Notice in the second quatrain, how he becomes—how we

become—the god Zeus transformed into Europa's bull and yet
remain, thanks to the word 'fineness', the simplest of human,
yokel lovers pleased to display his new clothes. In the original,
by Ronsard, we do not find this. But Lodge is not always thus
fanciful. Elsewhere we have the very note of work-day, unsuccessful passion, ever demanding

> Such things as are not, cannot, may not be,

or lines that sum up a far larger mass of common experience:

> So passe my ioyes as doth a new-plai'd storie,
> And one poore sigh breathes all delight to naught.

The twenty-fourth might be called sub-Shakespearian. None
of them is, perhaps, perfect; but, once more, the real test is to
ask ourselves what we should think of them if they had been
written in any other period. In his own, Lodge's gold is 'killed'
by even purer gold. Hector was killed; but by Achilles.

In the same year, 1593, appeared the *Parthenophil and
Parthenophe* of Barnaby Barnes, containing madrigals, elegies,
and odes as well as sonnets, and followed in 1595 by his *Divine
Century of Spiritual Sonnets*. In *Parthenophil* we find Simpsonian
rhymes, a sonnet in alexandrines, and even the 'broken-backed'
line of Lydgate ('He gan with vermil, gold, white and sable',
Madrigal 4). We also see a characteristically Golden conceit
losing its golden quality through lack of phonetic beauty ('Restes
mist with silver cloude had clos'd her sunne', Sonnet IV).
But 'meaningless doggerel' is no true estimate of his quality.
He often, for a line or two, sounds like a weaker Shakespeare.
The sixty-first sonnet ('Ah sweet Content, wher is thy milde
aboad'), even if its first line suggests the namby pamby of
Bowles or the young Coleridge, soon recovers; and the Ode 'On
the plains' (much influenced by Ronsard) is pretty enough. He
follows the tradition of Ovid and Propertius by including a
frankly sensual poem—Madrigal 13—and sometimes so links
his sonnets in thought that they become like stanzas of a single
poem. The Spiritual Sonnets are less good but have a certain
polished dignity. If he were our only English sonneteer we
should probably praise him.

The year 1594 produced three new sequences. Two of them,
William Percy's *Sonnets to Coelia* and the anonymous *Zepheria*,
were worthless; the third was Drayton's *Idea's Mirror*, which
grew by successive prunings and augmentations into the mag-

nificent *Idea* of 1619. In this first version Drayton is still mainly
the diligent apprentice, learning from other sonneteers both
native and foreign. He has still much to learn. His seventh
sonnet (the germ of his fine seventeenth in *Idea*) ends absurdly
with a fourteener. The alexandrines of *Mirror* X are removed in
Idea III. But already in the 1594 version we catch the voice of a
great poet, in such a line as 'How love begun, how love shall
never end'; in the contrast between Cupid and the lady—

> Thy Bowe halfe broke, is peec'd with olde desire,
> Her Bowe is beauty, with ten thousand strings—

or in that passage which redeems the old comparison between the
lover's soul and a ship, 'See where shee flotes, laden with purest
love'. And already, in the Eagle sonnet, or in the apostrophe
'O starre of starres, fayre Planet mildly mooving', there are
hints of that quality (by no means its only virtue) which sets
Drayton's final sequence apart from those of all his contemporaries—that exaltation, that wildness, which, as Mrs. Tillotson
says, sounds 'almost as if Marlowe were writing sonnets'. And
indeed the quality cannot be better described than in the words
which Drayton himself used of the real Marlowe's genius 'brave
translunary things that the first Poets had . . . all ayre and fire'.
And I think Drayton was aware of it himself. It is no doubt true
that protestations of originality, such as we find in *Idea* XXXI
and XLII, were themselves traditional: but 'Ravish'd a world
beyond the farthest Thought' sums up the essence of Drayton's
best poetry too well to be so discounted. The madness he professes in *Idea* IX is not inappropriate: a poetic, not an erotic,
madness. For though Drayton can be human and heartfelt
when he pleases, his imagery of voyage, phoenix, star, and river
(he was enamoured of rivers all his life) mediates something,
not inconsistent with human passion, but going beyond it. He is

> a Man that in some Trance hath seene
> More than his wond'ring utt'rance can unfold,

one who 'builds his Hopes a world above the Skie'. Yet when
he speaks simply as any lover he can sometimes outsoar all the
sonneteers except Shakespeare. 'Since ther's no helpe' has an
opening as direct, as dramatic, as anything in Donne. Very
few poems can live up to such an opening: but in Drayton it is a
true starting-point. The colloquial tone is preserved for the

first eight lines, but with a subtle change of feeling as the mind passes from the present parting to a ruefully calm acceptance of the future. Then the ascent begins. We have four lines of intensely moving allegory. The sonnet might have closed on that note and, even so, would have been superb: instead, like a spell that reverses the whole preceding structure, we have the utterly unforeseeable last couplet. One cannot ask more of fourteen lines. Yet again, and in quite a different vein, that of towering hyperbole, Drayton (this time with no rival at all, neither Shakespeare nor any other) sets up the seamark beyond which poetry in that kind has never gone nor could go:

> And Queens hereafter shall be glad to live
> Upon the almes of thy superfluous prayse.

If he had never written another verse, these two would secure him that praise which is due to men who have done some one thing to perfection.

In 1595 Richard Barnfield brought out *Certain Sonnets* in a volume which contained also *Cynthia* and *Cassandra*. This was not his first venture: in the *Affectionate Shepherd* (1594) he had shown how very bad 'bad Golden' can be, when the verse is too indiscreetly, as he says, 'bath'd in a melting sugar-candie streame'. *Cynthia* is the first imitation of the *Faerie Queene*. *Cassandra* gives a good many delights unintended by the poet; Apollo, wooing Cassandra, 'briefly t'her relates his pedigree', refers to her as 'my Cass', and no one 'seemed more fair' than this god on an occasion when he 'invisibly did glide'. His sonnets, like the *Affectionate Shepherd*, are pederastic, whether because Barnfield suffered in fact from the most uninteresting of all misfortunes or in a sheer humanist frenzy of imitation. They are better than the earlier poem: at least they keep to the point, whereas the Shepherd in the very article of wooing had somehow drifted into a lecture on the flavours of fish. Yet Barnfield is not always a fool. In his *Lady Pecunia* (1598) there are comic stanzas that almost anticipate Byron and even in *Cynthia* he could steal from Shakespeare and add something worth adding—a star

> Shootes suddenly from the beholders eye
> And leaves him looking there where she is not.

His lyric 'As it fell upon a day' is perhaps his most delightful production.

The Elizabethan sonnet was now past its prime: to follow its senility through the work of Smith, Griffin, and Linche (all in 1596) and Tofte (1597) would be wearisome, though the fifty-fourth in Griffin's *Fidessa* shows a stately use of existing English models. Enough has, I hope, been said, to guard the reader from supposing that the *corpus* of sonnets contains only frigid conceits. The truth is almost exactly the opposite. Critics reading them, as they were never meant to be read, hastily and in bulk, are gorged and satiated with beauty, as a fish can be choked by holding its head upstream. The water is good water but there is too much of it for the fish.

We must now turn back to the important year 1593 and attempt to see Shakespeare's *Venus and Adonis* as an epyllion among epyllions, a successor to *Scylla* and *Hero and Leander*. We notice at once that it has abandoned Lodge's medieval preliminaries and that it does not, like Marlowe's poem, begin with long descriptions. The characters are in action by line 3. This is promising. We get, too, but not so soon nor so often as we might wish, lines of the deliciousness which was expected in this type of poem; 'leading him prisoner in a red-rose chain', 'a lily prisoned in a gaol of snow'. But in that direction Shakespeare does not rival Marlowe. We get, with surprised pleasure, glimpses of real work-day nature, in the spirited courtship of Adonis's horse or the famous stanza about the hare. The account of Venus's growing uneasiness during the hunt and her meeting with the wounded hounds gives us a fairly strong hint that the poet has powers quite beyond the range which the epyllion requires. What is not so certain is that he has the powers it does require. For as we read on we become more and more doubtful how the work ought to be taken. Is it a poem by a young moralist, a poem against lust? There is a speech given to Adonis (769 et seq.) which might lend some colour to the idea. But the story does not point the moral at all well, and Shakespeare's Venus is a very ill-conceived temptress. She is made so much larger than her victim that she can throw his horse's reins over one arm and tuck him under the other, and knows her own art so badly that she threatens, almost in her first words, to 'smother' him with kisses. Certain horrible interviews with voluminous female relatives in one's early childhood inevitably recur to the mind. If, on the other hand, the poem is meant to be anything other than a 'cooling card', it fails egregiously. Words and images which, for any other purpose, ought to have been avoided keep on coming in and almost determine the dominant mood of the reader—'satiety', 'sweating', 'leaden appetite', 'gorge', 'stuff'd', 'glutton', 'gluttonlike'. Venus's 'face doth reek and smoke, her blood doth boil', and the wretched 'boy' (that word too was dangerous) only gets away 'hot, faint and weary with her hard embracing'. And this flushed, panting, perspiring, suffocating, loquacious creature is supposed to be the goddess of love herself, the golden Aphrodite. It will not do. If the poem is not meant to arouse disgust it was very foolishly written: if it is, then disgust (that barbarian mercenary) is not, either aesthetically or morally, the feeling on which a poet should rely in a moral poem. But of course Shakespeare may well have failed because he was embarrassed by powers, essential for drama, which he could not suspend while writing an epyllion. Perhaps even then he could not help knowing what the wooing of Adonis by Venus, supposing it to be a real event, would have looked like to a spectator.

Venus and Adonis, if it were his only work, might not now be highly praised; but his next poem might stand higher if it stood alone and were compared solely with other Elizabethan products, not with his own masterpieces. *The Rape of Lucrece* (1594) presumably discharges the promise made in the Epistle to *Venus and Adonis* of 'some graver labour'. It is heroic poetry as the heroic was understood before Virgil had been sufficiently distinguished from Lucan and Ovid; and it differs from its predecessor in merit as much as in kind. The theme would at that time have tempted almost any other poet to one more 'tragedy' modelled on the *Mirror for Magistrates*, and only those who have read many such 'tragedies' can adequately thank Shakespeare for rejecting that form. It is, however, very much a work of its own age. It contains prettinesses and puerilities which the later Shakespeare would have seen to be unsuitable to his heart-rending subject. The conceit which makes Lucrece's pillow 'angrie' at 388 would have been tolerable in *Hero and Leander* but is here repellent; and so is the aetiological myth at 1747, or the competitive laments of the husband and the father at Lucrece's death. There is some of Kyd's fustian in the apostrophe to Night (764–77). It is hard not to smile when Lucrece invites the nightingale to use her hair as a grove (1129), but Edward Lear may be partly to blame. The passage in which she becomes preoccupied, like Troilus or a lover in the *Arcadia*, about the style of her letter to her husband is more difficult to judge: perhaps it is not impossible that a woman of the nineties, brought up by a humanist tutor, might, even at such a moment, have remembered the claims of *eloquentia*. These are merely local imperfections. But there is also, whether we reckon it an imperfection or not, something in the structure of the whole poem which is not quite congenial to our taste. It starts indeed with twenty-one lines of purposeful narration, not rivalled in that age outside the *Faerie Queene*: then our sails flap in three stanzas of digression. And we must be prepared for this throughout. Shakespeare's version of the story is about twelve times as long as Ovid's in the *Fasti* and, even so, omits the earlier stages. Much of this length is accounted for by digression (131–54 or 1237–53), *exclamatio* (701–14), *sententiae* (131–54), and *descriptio* (1366–1526). The technique is in fact that of the medieval rhetoricians. Even in those passages which, taken as a whole, are narrative, a great deal of gnomic amplification is brought in. We have 'theme and variations'. Thus at 211 ('What win I if I gain the thing I seek?') Tarquin states the theme of the game not being worth the candle in two lines: it is then varied for five. At 1002 Lucrece states her theme (*noblesse oblige*) in two lines and then varies it for twelve. At 1107 we have theme in two lines and again twelve lines of variation. Minor instances occur throughout. We must not put this down too exclusively to the Age, for Shakespeare was in fact fonder of amplification than many other Elizabethans and used it, sometimes rather grossly, in his earlier plays. There is nothing in *Lucrece* quite so crude as Gaunt's successive variations on the theme 'His rash fierce blaze of riot cannot last' in *Richard II* (II. i. 33 et seq.). There is a free use of simple one-for-one parallelism, as in the Psalms;

> The shame that from them no device can take,
> The blemish that will never be forgot,

or

> Bearing away the wound that nothing healeth,
> The scarre that will despite of cure remaine.

Whether the method shall prove tedious or delightful depends on style, in the narrowest sense of the word: that is, on the volubility of phrase which makes the variant seem effortless, and on phonetic qualities. Thus in *shame*, *device*, and *blemish* we have long monosyllable, disyllable in rising rhythm, disyllable in falling rhythm. In the second example we have the alliteration of *away* and *wound* and the very subtle consonantal pattern of *scarre*, *despite*, and *cure*. The first consonant group (*sk*) is not repeated, but one of its elements recurs in -*spite* and the other in *cure*.

Another example is:

> To stamp the seal of time in aged things (941).

No one reads such a line without pleasure. Yet its emotional content is weak and its intellectual weaker still: to say that time stamps the seal of time on things that have existed a long time is near tautology. The charm depends partly, as before, on the distribution of a consonant group between the simple consonants of two later words (*st*, *s*, *t*), and partly on the fact that all the stressed syllables are long and all have different vowels.

But *Lucrece* has more than formal beauties to offer us. If not continuously, yet again and again, our sympathies are fully engaged. The rape itself, from the moment at which Tarquin strikes his falchion on the flint to the moment when he 'creeps sadly thence' is presented with a terror and horror unequalled in Elizabethan narrative verse. And here, certainly, the digression on 'drunken desire' before and after its 'vomit' is fully justified. 'The spotted princess' (Tarquin's soul) is admirable: still a princess, unable to abdicate, and there's the tragedy. Lucrece, too rhetorical in her agonies, is not quite so good as Tarquin, but she has her great moments: 'I sue for exil'd majestie's repeal', pleading 'in a wilderness where are no laws'. And of all the good things that Shakespeare said about Time he puts perhaps the best into her mouth:

> Why work'st thou mischief in thy pilgrimage
> Unless thou couldst returne to make amendes?

She should not have gone on (good though the line is) to add 'Thou ceaslesse lackeye to eternitie'. It matters nothing that the historical Lucretia would have known neither Plato nor Boethius: the Elizabethan Lucrece ought not to have displayed her learning at that moment. For of course the characters are to be judged as Elizabethans throughout: even Christianity creeps in at 624 and 1156-8.

This poem contains what is rare, though not unique, in

Shakespeare, a sort of Simpsonian rhyme at 352–4. To make 352 a decasyllable you must make *resolution* (as the Elizabethans often did) five syllables, and the rhyming syllable should then be *-on*. But in 354 you must make the third of *absolution* your last accented syllable: to which you could get a non-Simpsonian rhyme only by turning 352 into an octosyllabic.

Shakespeare would be a considerable non-dramatic poet if he had written only the *Lucrece*: but it sinks almost to nothing in comparison with his sonnets. The sonnets are the very heart of the Golden Age, the highest and purest achievement of the Golden way of writing. We do not know when they were composed. They were published in 1609 'by G. Eld for T. T.' together with 'A Lover's Complaint' (a still-born *chanson d'aventure* in rhyme royal, corrupt in text, poetically inconsiderable, and dialectally unlike Shakespeare). But at least two of them (CXXXVIII and CXLIV) existed as early as 1599, for these two were included in the poetical miscellany which William Jaggard published in that year under the title of *The Passionate Pilgrim*. A year earlier, in 1598, Meres had referred to 'sugred sonnets' by Shakespeare: how far these coincided with the sonnets we now have can only be conjectured. External evidence thus failing us, we look for internal, and find ourselves in a world of doubts. Even if an individual sonnet can be dated (and I think it much more likely that CVII refers to the queen's death or her climacteric than to the Spanish Armada) this would not enable us to date the collection as a whole. Many sonnets, such as LXVI, LXXI, XCVII, and CVI, would be appropriate to any lover at any time and might, so far as their matter goes, be divided by years from other sonnets in the same collection. The evidence from style produces strong convictions in all readers, but not always the same convictions. On my own view it helps us much more to a *terminus post quem* than to a *terminus ante quem*: that is, I can hardly conceive a poet moving from the style of the best sonnets (which means in effect nearly all the sonnets) to that of *Venus and Adonis*, but can easily conceive one who had achieved Shakespeare's mature dramatic technique still writing some of the sonnets we have. For in all ages, and especially in that, form affects style. If Shakespeare had taken an hour off from the composition of *Lear* to write a sonnet, the sonnet might not have been in the style of *Lear*. We cannot even be certain that Shakespeare wrote his sonnets when sonneteering was the vogue: there are expressions in XXXII, LXXVI, and LXXXII which can (though they need not) be interpreted to mean that he knew he was adopting a form no longer fashionable. But I am not arguing that the sonnets were later than is usually supposed. I am arguing for agnosticism. We do not know when, or at what different times, they were written.

Shakespeare's sequence differs in character as well as in excellence from those of the other Elizabethans. It is indeed the peculiarity of these sonnets which has led to a misreading of all the rest. For here at last we have a sequence which really hints a story, and so odd a story that we find a difficulty in regarding it as fiction. It is the story of a man torn between passionate affection for another man and reluctant passion for a woman whom he neither trusts nor respects. No reading of the sonnets can obscure that amount of 'plot' or 'situation'. Yet even this sequence is far from offering us the pleasure we expect from a good novel or a good autobiography. Treated that way, it becomes a mass of problems. I do not mean those problems which (rightly) attract students of Shakespeare's life. With those the literary historian has no concern; he would not give a farthing to know the identity of the 'man right fair' or the 'woman colour'd ill'. The difficulty which faces us if we try to read the sequence like a novel is that the precise mode of love which the poet declares for the Man remains obscure. His language is too lover-like for that of ordinary male friendship; and though the claims of friendship are sometimes put very high in, say, the *Arcadia*, I have found no real parallel to such language between friends in sixteenth-century literature. Yet, on the other hand, this does not seem to be the poetry of full-blown pederasty. Shakespeare, and indeed Shakespeare's age, did nothing by halves. If he had intended in these sonnets to be the poet of pederasty, I think he would have left us in no doubt; the lovely παιδικά, attended by a whole train of mythological perversities, would have blazed across the pages. The incessant demand that the Man should marry and found a family would seem to be inconsistent (or so I suppose—it is a question for psychologists) with a real homosexual passion. It is not even very obviously consistent with normal friendship. It is indeed hard to think of any real situation in which it would be natural. What man in the whole world, except a father or a potential father-in-law, cares whether any other man gets married? Thus the emotion expressed in the *Sonnets* refuses to fit into our pigeon-holes. And this, for two reasons, makes singularly little difference to our delight.

In the first place many individual sonnets, and some of the most prized, are very lightly attached to the theme of the sequence as a whole. CXLVI ('Poor soul, the centre of my sinful earth') is not attached at all; it is concerned with the tension between the temporal and the eternal and would be appropriate in the mouth of any Christian at any moment. XXX ('When to the sessions of sweet silent thought'), LXVI ('Tired with all these, for restful death I cry'), LXXIII ('That time of year thou mayst in me behold') are meditations respectively on bereavement, *taedium vitae*, and age, hooked on to the theme of love only by their concluding couplets. The effect of this 'hook' is twofold. On the one hand it makes richer and more poignant the emotion expressed in the preceding twelve lines, but not until that emotion has been allowed to develop itself fully; it converts retrospectively into a mode of love what nevertheless could be felt (and has been felt until we reach the couplet) on its own account. And, on the other hand, there is a formal or structural pleasure in watching each sonnet wind back through unexpected ways to its appointed goal, as if it said at the end *vos plaudite*. Even where the theme of love reaches farther back into the body of the sonnet it is often as universal, as suitable to every lover, as in a sonnet by Daniel or Lodge. Thus XXV ('Let those who are in favour with their stars') or XXIX ('When in disgrace with fortune and men's eyes') are poems that any man can walk into and make his own. And those must be few and fortunate who cannot do the same with XXXIII ('Full many a glorious morning have I seen') and XXXIV ('Why didst thou promise such a beauteous day').

Such is the effect of many individual sonnets. But when we read the whole sequence through at a sitting (as we ought sometimes to do) we have a different experience. From its total plot, however ambiguous, however particular, there emerges something not indeed common or general like the love expressed in many individual sonnets but yet, in a higher way, universal. The main contrast in the *Sonnets* is between the two loves, that 'of comfort' and that 'of despair'. The love 'of despair' demands all: the love 'of comfort' asks, and perhaps receives, nothing. Thus the whole sequence becomes an expanded version of Blake's 'The Clod and the Pebble'. And so it comes about that, however the thing began—in perversion, in convention, even (who knows?) in fiction—Shakespeare, celebrating the 'Clod' as no man has celebrated it before or since, ends by expressing simply love, the quintessence of all loves whether erotic, parental, filial, amicable, or feudal. Thus from extreme particularity there is a road to the highest universality. The love is, in the end, so simply and entirely love that our *cadres* are thrown away and we cease to ask what kind. However it may have been with Shakespeare in his daily life, the greatest of the sonnets are written from a region in which love abandons all claims and flowers into charity: after that it makes little odds what the root was like. They open a new world of love poetry; as new as Dante's and Petrarch's had been in their day. These had of course expressed humility, but it had been the humility of Eros, hungry to receive: kneeling, but kneeling to ask. They and their great successor Patmore sing a dutiful and submissive, but hardly a giving, love. They could have written, almost too easily, 'Being your slave, what should I do but tend?': they could hardly have written, 'I may not evermore acknowledge thee', or 'No longer mourn' or 'Although thou steal thee all my poverty'. The self-abnegation, the 'naughting', in the *Sonnets* never rings false. This patience, this anxiety (more like a parent's than a lover's) to find excuses for the beloved, this clear-sighted and wholly unembittered resignation, this transference of the whole self into another self without the demand for a return, have hardly a precedent in profane literature. In certain senses of the word 'love', Shakespeare is not so much our best as our only love poet.

This content is mediated to us through a masterpiece of Golden technique. On the metrical side all those wide departures from the norm which make the life of Donne's or Milton's work, or of Shakespeare's own later blank verse, are excluded. That sacrifice was essential to his *cantabile*. He has to avoid the stunning regularity of Drab, yet to avoid it only by a hair's breadth. There is a high percentage of lines in which every second syllable is not merely stressed but also long: 'So I, for fear of trust, forget to say', 'So you in Grecian tires are painted new', 'When beauty lived and died as flowers do now'. Most of the rhymes are strong and many of them rest on monosyllables. There is a great use of alliteration both in its obvious and its less

R

obtrusive forms. Thus in XV we have plain alliteration, 'Cheered and check'd' (6) and 'Sets' and 'sight' (10); gentler alliteration on unstressed syllables in 11 ('debateth with decay'); consonant groups linked with simple consonants, where one is unstressed (as 'perceive' and 'plants' in 5) or both as 'perfection' and 'presenteth', 2, 3). In XII we have the heavy alliteration 'Born', 'bier', 'bristly', 'beard' side by side with the much more artful pattern *s*, *gr*, *g*, *sh* in the previous line—groups linked with simples and arranged chiasmically. CXVI opens with a wonderful fantasia on the consonant *m*: full alliteration of initial stressed syllables in 'marriage' and 'minds', a stressed but not initial syllable in 'admit', and the unstressed 'me' and 'ments' in 'impediments'. Then follow 'love' and 'love', no less an alliteration to the ear because they are the same word, and in the next line, a device Shakespeare used well, the play upon kindred words, 'alters' and 'alteration' (compare 'beauty making beautiful' in CVI, 'the wardrobe which the robe doth hide' in LII). Most of these devices are as sweet to us as they were to our ancestors. But Shakespeare does not share our modern dislike of sibilants (he will 'summon' remembrance to 'sessions of sweet silent thought') and in XLV we find the Simpsonian rhyme of 'to thée' with 'melanchóly'.

In most of the sonnets there is a frank and innocent reliance on words which invite emotion and sensuous imagination. Thus in XII we have *time, day, night, violet, sable, silver, trees, leaves, summer, green, bier, wastes*: in XVIII, *summer* again, *day* again, *buds, winds, sun, gold, death, shades*; in XXI, *heaven, sun* again, *moon, earth, sea, gems, April, flowers, mother*; in XXX, *remembrance, past, waste* again, *death* again, *night* again, *moan*; in LXVIII *cheek, flowers* again, *brow, golden* again, *sepulchres, fleece, hours, summer* again, *green* again, and *Nature*. This differentia of the Golden style becomes tolerably clear if we notice, for contrast, the keywords in the first stanza of Herbert's 'Confession'; *quest, grief, heart, closets, chest, trade, boxes, a till.*

The rhetorical structure is often that of theme and variations, as in *Lucrece*. The variations more often than not precede the theme, and there is usually an application which connects the theme of the particular sonnet with what may be called the 'running' theme of that part of the sequence to which it belongs. There are exceptions to this. In CXLIV, for example, we have something like a continuous progression in which each line adds

to the thought. CXXIX ('The expense of spirit') starts as if it
were going to develop in that way, but progression almost ends
with line 5, 'Enjoy'd no sooner but despised straight'. The next
seven lines are largely, though not entirely, variations on the
fifth. To see the typical Shakespearian structure at its simplest
we may turn to LXVI ('Tired with all these'). The theme occupies the first line, the application, the final couplet: in between
we have eleven instances of the things which produce weariness
of life. This numerical equality between the different variations
is very uncommon, and chosen, no doubt, to give a special
effect of cumulative bitterness. More often it is contrived that
the variations should be either unequal simply, or, if they begin
by being equal, that they should presently grow longer. Thus
XII ('When I do count the clock') is built on the pattern
variations—theme—application. The theme ('You too will
pass') occupies the four lines beginning 'then of thy beauty do
I question make', and the application is in the final couplet.
The preceding variations have the numerical pattern 1, 1, 1, 1,
2, 2; a line each for the clock, the nightfall, the violet, and the
curls, then two lines each for the trees and the harvest. The effect
on the reader is one of liberation just at the moment when the
one-line *exempla* were about to produce a feeling of constraint. In
XXXIII ('Full many a glorious morning') we have only one
variation in the form of a continuous simile filling the first eight
lines. But then this simile contains its own pattern: one line
announcing the morning, three which catch each one aspect of
its beauty, and four to tell the sequel. XVIII ('Shall I compare
thee to a summer's day?') is exquisitely elaborated. As often,
the theme begins at line 9 ('But thy eternal summer shall
not fade'), occupying four lines, and the application is in the
couplet. Line 1 proposes a simile. Line 2 corrects it. Then we
have two one-line *exempla* justifying the correction: then a two-
line *exemplum* about the sun: then two more lines ('And every
fair') which do not, as we had expected, add a fourth *exemplum*
but generalize. Equality of length in the two last variations is
thus played off against difference of function. The same transition from variation by examples to variation by generalizing
is found in LXIV ('When I have seen by Time's fell hand
defaced'); theme in lines 1–2, first *exemplum* in line 3, second
exemplum in line 4, the third *exemplum* triumphantly expanding
to fill lines 5–8, generalization (9–10) passing into Application

which occupies the last four lines. To some, I am afraid, such analysis will seem trifling, and it is not contended that no man can enjoy the *Sonnets* without it any more than that no man can enjoy a tune without knowing its musical grammar. But unless we are content to talk simply about the 'magic' of Shakespeare's poetry (forgetting that magic was a highly formal art) something of the kind is inevitable. It serves at least to remind us what sort of excellence, and how different from some other poetic excellences, the *Sonnets* possess. They very seldom present or even feign to present passionate thought growing and changing in the heat of a situation; they are not dramatic. The end of each is clearly in view from the beginning, the theme already chosen. Instead of a single developing thought we get what musicians call an 'arrangement', what we might call a pattern or minuet, of thoughts and images. There are arithmetical elements in the beauty of this pattern as in all formal beauty, and its basic principle is *idem in alio*. Of course it affects those who have no notion what is affecting them. It is partly responsible for that immense pleasurableness which we find in the *Sonnets* even where their matter is most painful: and also for their curious stillness or tranquillity. Shakespeare is always standing back a little from the emotions he treats. He left it to his created persons, his Lears and Othellos, to pour out raw experience, scalding hot. In his own person he does not do so. He sings (always sings, never talks) of shame and degradation and the divided will, but it is as if he sang from above, moved and yet not moved; a Golden, Olympian poet.

The most secret of his poems remains. In 1601 there came out *Love's Martyr* by Robert Chester, a long, mysterious allegory about a male Turtle-dove and a female Phoenix, halting in metre, defective in rhyme, and almost to be classed with Copley's *Fig for Fortune* as Late Medieval. To this are appended, 'diverse poeticall Essaies' on the same subject, signed by *Vatum Chorus, Ignoto,* William Shakespeare, John Marston, George Chapman, and Ben Jonson. Shakespeare's piece is, of course, what we call 'The Phoenix and the Turtle', though it appears without title. Whatever the external occasion may have been, Shakespeare uses his poem to expound a philosophy of love; the last word, presumably, that he has given us in his own person on that subject. Its doctrine consummates that of the *Sonnets*. In them the 'naughting' had been one sided. He had, lost himself in another but that other had not lost himself in Shakespeare. Now Shakespeare celebrates the exchanged death, and life, of a fully mutual love. He is not writing 'metaphysical poetry' in the technical sense critics give to that term, but he is writing in the true sense, a metaphysical poem. Such a task leads some poets (Browning, for example) into a loose form and a style *sermoni proprior*. Shakespeare, on the other hand, gives us formality within formality, the *threnos* within the funeral poem, the conduct of his work ritualistic, his metres rigid, deliberately, hypnotically, monotonous. His supreme invention was the introduction of Reason as the principal speaker. The words which sum up Shakespeare's doctrine, 'Love hath reason, reason none' owe all their importance to the fact that it is Reason who utters them. In the mouth of a passionate lover or a passionate mourner they would be the stalest claptrap; one more expression of 'will' revolting against 'wit', one more confirmation of the assumption, traditional since Chrétien, that Love and Reason are adversaries. But it is Reason who here exalts love above reason. It is Reason who has seen rational categories overthrown: 'distincts' becoming indivisible, propriety (*proprium*) 'appalled' by the discovery that the self-same is yet not the same (for of course *the self* in 38 does not mean 'the ego'), and something brought into existence which cannot be called two or one. It is Reason who confesses that neither truth (which is Reason's natural goal) nor beauty is the highest good. For beauty is only a brag or a bravery, a sign or hint, of the true good: and truth 'cannot be', it is not being, but only 'about' being. Reason, in fact, rationally recognizes what is beyond reason. We could not have guessed, I think, from internal evidence that this poem was by Shakespeare. As an anonymous work it would command our highest admiration. The oracular, which of all styles is most contemptible when it fails, is here completely successful; the illusion that we have been in another world and heard the voices of gods is achieved. Approached, as we usually approach it, after long familiarity with the plays, 'The Phoenix and the Turtle' has, in addition, another interest. We feel that we have been admitted to the *natura naturans* from which the *natura naturata* of the plays proceeded: as though we had reached the garden of Adonis and seen where Imogens and Cordelias are made.

In a previous chapter we had to observe what I called

'unfinished causeways', the beginnings of techniques whereby poetry might have emerged from its Late Medieval condition, though in fact it emerged in a different way. We have now to consider another unfinished causeway: an incipient movement away from Golden poetics, distinct from that Bartasian or 'Metaphysical' movement which was actually going to prevail. It might be called poetry of the Cryptic school, and there are three monuments of it left. One, the latest in time has already been mentioned among satires; Tourneur's *Transformed Metamorphosis*. A resemblance (probably accidental) to medieval work, and a nightmare quality, not without flashes of poetry, were its chief characteristics. Earlier than this came the *Cephalus and Procris* and *Narcissus* of 1595, which purport to be by Thomas Edwards. Both the poems (*Cephalus* in couplets and *Narcissus* in rhyme royal) are so loaded with mythological decoration that it is almost impossible to follow the story, and the mythology itself is often abstruse. Some kind of poetry is, however, fermenting in the man: once—I think, only once— it gets out, in the couplet about Sidney:

> And thou Arcadian knight, earthes second Sunne
> Reapt ere half ripe, finisht ere half begunne.

His work is like a bad imitation of Chapman at his worst. And that is probably just what it is: for the earliest document of this Cryptic school, Chapman's *Shadow of Night*, had been published in 1594.

Much work has been done on the circle in which George Chapman[1] moved and on its relation to 'the school of Night' in *Love's Labour's Lost*. It included the 'damnable proud' Raleigh, the scandalous Marlowe, Roydon the mathematician, and Harriot the astronomer (both these, serious scientists). Suspicions of atheism hang about them. What is known of their opinions helps hardly at all to elucidate the *Shadow*, though some of its characteristics are those we expect in the poem of a *côterie*. There are degrees of silliness which the individual can hardly reach in isolation.

This literary curiosity consists of two long poems, the *Hymnus in*

---

[1] b. about 1559 near Hitchin. Thought by some to have seen active service in the Netherlands. Already an established dramatist by 1598. Imprisoned for satirizing the Scots, 1605: same year in prison with Ben Jonson, perhaps for the same offence. Suspected of, and perhaps thrashed for, libellous intentions in *Andromeda Liberata*, 1613. Ob. 1634.

Noctem and the *Hymnus in Cynthiam*, both bad but the *In Noctem* very clearly the worse. Chapman himself would have attributed our unfavourable verdict to ignorance: but, alas, it is just the passages we do understand that repel us. What remains obscure might, for all we know, hide something of value: it is the flat, stale moralizing of the intelligible patches that damns the poet. The *In Noctem* suffers from having that amorphous subject which never attracts a good writer and always exposes a bad one: the general state of the world today. It uses 'Night' in three senses which do not enrich but collide with one another. It is (*a*) the original Chaos, conceived as a friend, because it is a pity that Cosmos ever dispossessed her; (*b*) the 'stepdame' Night of ignorance, the enemy, which enfolds everyone except Chapman and his circle; (*c*) the ordinary Night which occurs every twenty-four hours: apparently a friend. On top of this, Chaos, besides being the kindly womb which we ought never to have quitted, is also the horrid destination for which we are now heading. Chapman's modest proposals for remedying things are all on the lines of 'Ye gods, annihilate but space and time'; why doesn't Night (I think Night in sense *c*) rouse the Eumenides, 'drowning the world in Blood'? or couldn't Hercules shoot the sun? Or how about Atlas letting the sky drop? Through all this black smoke there come, very rarely, flashes of Chapman's real genius. They are more frequent in the poem to *Cynthia*. The multiple significances of this goddess agree together much better than those of Night in the previous hymn. Queen Elizabeth and the moon (under whose sphere, as everyone knew, lies all contingence) can both very well be described as

> the powre of fate
> In perfect circle of whose sacred state
> The circles of our hopes are compassed,

and there is nothing in either to repel the ideas of virginity and contemplation, or to prevent our crying to the real moon 'Wash thy bright bodie in th' Atlanticke streames'. The long allegorical story of the creation and pursuit of Euthimya (who became a Panther and finally turned 'a Bore') is indeed bad; not because its *significatio* is obscure today—which might not be Chapman's fault—but because the *sensus literalis* is hard to follow and very languid. Yet anything that is picturable and moves is a relief after the mere sermonizing of the *In Noctem*. On the other hand, nothing in either hymn is quite so bad as *In Cynthiam*, 369 et seq., where England is

> pau'd with Dames select,
> On whom rich feete in fowlest bootes might treade
> And never fowle them.

Throughout both poems the obscurities are often of the least pardonable kind: mere manufactured puzzles (like the use of 'Cynthian' to mean not 'lunar' but 'solar') or slovenly tangles in the syntax. Simpsonian rhyme is used with tormenting frequency.

In Chapman's next volume (*Ovid's Banquet of Sense. A Coronet for his Mistress Philosophy and his amorous Zodiac*, 1595) the sunlight of his sultry genius is beginning to break through the fog. Chapman has now learned the Golden style but uses it in an original way: with more than Golden 'points' and with learned subtleties that bring him to the border of the metaphysical. *Ovid's Banquet* is erotic epyllion sophisticated, no longer 'once born'. It does not lack absurdities: Ovid lectures his mistress at the most inopportune moments and Chapman ruins the atmosphere he ought to be creating by such a line as 'With this digression wee will now returne'. There are many metrical licences which I do not think successful, including a 'Trochaic' or 'headless' line. The old, querulous moralizing breaks out at 35 and 53. The thin and vague pretence of some ultimate philosophical justification for the sensuality really introduces a tinge of nastiness from which Marlowe's more shameless ardours had been quite free. Yet the poem is full of beauties. We have, in the first place, some very pure Gold; 'The blisse of her sweet brests diuinitie', 'Me thinks her tunes flye guilt like *Attick* bees', and beauty as 'The curtesie that speakes before the tongue' and pours forth 'All Rhetorick's flowers in lesse then in a word'. Secondly, we have the Gold, still Golden, but sharpened with a new brightness of paradox, as in 'The downward-burning flame of her rich hayre'. Then we have the Golden style, expressing a conceit so subtle that the result is Golden and metaphysical in one, as when Ovid, wishing that his soul could migrate into the singing Corinna, says:

> Thus should I be her notes before they be
> While in her blood they sitte with fierye wings.

The whole of Stanza 30 illustrates this beautiful moment of

transition in the history of our poetry. The obscurities are worth
puzzling over in the *Banquet*, as they were not in the *Shadow*:
we are ready to believe that if we knew enough alchemy, optics,
and acoustics our reading of the poem would be really enriched. 'Beautie, loues cold fire' is well worth pausing on. The
triple analogy in 8—Corinna undressing and the sky casting off
night and the upper aether, the real day (see Lucan, *Phar-
salia*, IX. 13) casting off the sky as we know it—is in my opinion
delightful. Two passages point to a greater work which Chapman was presently to write. 'Riches in a little Roome' (49)
shows his allegiance to Marlowe, and at 51 he shows a sad
awareness of the transience of pleasure which rings far truer
than his supposedly philosophic apology for it;

> This beauties fayre is an enchantment made
> By natures witchcraft, tempting men to buy
> With endles showes what endlessly will fade,
> Yet promise chapmen all eternitie.

Of the other pieces in this volume the *Coronet* (ten sonnets)
shows Chapman in moralizing vein but more melodiously than
in the *Shadow*, the *Zodiac* is from the French of Gilles Durant,
and the *Amorous Contention*, when it appeared separately in 1598,
was attributed to R. S., presumably the Richard Stapleton
whose complimentary sonnet to Chapman appears in the
Banquet volume. It is a very free paraphrase of the *De Phyllide et
Flora*. Thus the first four lines swell to eight in Stapleton,
because *picto terrae gremio vario colore* becomes 'When Tellus'
herbals painted were With issue of disparant cheer', and so
forth.

In 1596 Chapman contributed to Lawrence Keymis's *Second
Voyage to Guiana* what he called a *Carmen Epicum*, though it
contains no narrative at all. This exclamatory poem in blank
verse (though with a rhyme to end each paragraph and a few
others thrown in) reads rather like Marlowe modified by
enjambments and intellectually sophisticated. Chapman here at
last successfully assumes that magnanimity which he had tried
vainly to assume before. It ends with some serious praise of
marriage, significant of the direction in which his thoughts were
moving. It is also one of his most melodious poems.

In 1598 Chapman achieved the work that he was born to do;
which was not, as he imagined, translating Homer but finishing

Hero and Leander. The very idea of a poem begun by one poet
and ended by another is repugnant to modern taste, and modern
taste is usually confirmed by the event. The *Roman de la Rose*
has to be treated as two poems. Not so the *Hero and Leander*;
for there it so happens that the very nature of the story utilizes
the differing excellences of its two narrators and gets told between them better than either could have told it alone. Chapman
has well described the central impression which any adequate
telling of it must produce:

> Loue is a golden bubble full of dreames
> Which waking breakes and fils us with extreames.

It is certain that Marlowe could not have done the tragic
'waking' very well. Hero in her first love (as he had conceived
love in his two Sestiads) is half an animal, half a goddess: Hero
in her grief would have to have been a woman and Marlowe's
women are uninteresting. Chapman, with the powers he had
acquired by 1598, would indeed have done Marlowe's part,
though not so well as Marlowe did it, yet better than Marlowe
could have done his. For though Chapman's theme is that 'Joy
grauen in sence, like snow in water wasts', he has both a keen
sensibility to that joy and no small mastery in expressing it. He
can be rapturous and delicious when he pleases: can speak of
'white skin softer than soundest sleep' (even Shakespeare did not
disdain sibilants), can tell how Leander, still wet with Helles-
pont, flew to his sister 'singing like a shower' and 'All the sweetned
shore as he did goe Was crownd with odrous roses', or say of
Music personified that 'Wanton Ayre in twentie sweet forms
danst After her fingers'. Again, passing beyond Marlowe and
becoming Golden and metaphysical at once, he can write (of
a girl yielding to a virtuous love):

> The bribde, but incorrupted garrison
> Sung *Io Hymen.*

Finally, in the lyric Epithalamion (*Sestiad* V), which is perhaps
the crown of all Chapman's poetry, he can say:

> O come soft rest of Cares, come night
> Come naked vertues only tire,
> The reaped haruest of the light
> Bound vp in sheaues of sacred fire.

Any notion that Chapman is merely the dull moralist, playing skeleton at the Marlovian feast because he cannot relish it, is utterly mistaken. He knew well how Golden the 'bubble' had been.

His business, however, was to tell how it broke. At the beginning of the Third Sestiad he rightly warns us (like Milton in *Paradise Lost*, IX. 5) that the poem here changes its style;

> More harsh (at lest more hard) more graue and hie
> Our subiect runs, and our sterne *Muse* must flie,
> Loues edge is taken off.

In the books that follow there are, it must be admitted, unwelcome traces of the old Chapman, digressive, cryptic, anxious to be wiser than nature allowed him. But there is also a real wisdom, a real psychological insight, and a grandeur of passion. Essentially Chapman's continuation is a eulogy of marriage. The lawless loves of Hero and Leander are contrasted with the solemn wedding of Hymen and Eucharis. Marriage has the omens on its side (that is the significance of Teras) and disposes for ever of the *losengier* (Adolesche) who had been love's troubler all through the Middle Ages. It is significant that Chapman's condemnation of lawless love is based neither on the Christian law nor on any admiration of virginity. Leander is rebuked (III) neither by Diana nor Juno but by *Ceremonie*. This goddess clearly fills the same place in Chapman's thought as Concord in Spenser's or Degree in Shakespeare's: 'From her bright eyes *Confusion* burnes to death.' She lends 'sightly figures' to *Morallitie* and *Comelinesse*. Her enemies are *Barbarisme* and *Auarice*, who, but for her, would storm the city of the gods, and who even now are always at her heels 'eating earth and excrement And humane lims'. Her ally is *Time* in the sense of timeliness (*opportunitas*), the choice of the right moment, patiently awaited, *Time* whose

> golden Thie
> Vpholds the flowrie bodie of the earth
> In sacred harmonie, and euery birth
> Of men and actions makes legitimate.

Ceremonie is in fact the specifically human, the ordered, the chosen, the civilized, as against the merely natural and instinctive. She is even, from one point of view, luxury, for that also is the mark of the human. 'What simply kils our hunger, quencheth thirst' is not good enough: Ceremonie demands 'delicious cheere'. In her eyes the loves of Hero and Leander had been simply a coarse meal snatched ravenously,

> And who like earth would spend that dower of heauen
> With ranke desire to ioy it all at first?

Whatever else this is, it is not ready-made moralizing. I do not know any passage more quintessentially Elizabethan. It is linked up with so much in Shakespeare and Spenser, in the *Arcadia*, in Hall's chronicle; in their emblems and gardening and the conduct of their public life: in their very cosmology and theology. Yet it is not in these passages but in his study of Hero that Chapman is at his greatest. He shows the whole tormenting process from her first despair and remorse:

> She was a mother straight and bore with paine
> Thoughts that spake straight and wisht their mother slaine,

through the pause when passion sleeps

> (And all this while the red sea of her blood
> Ebd with *Leander*)

into reawakening passion, when once more 'all her fleete of sprites came swelling in With childe of saile' till she idiotically believed that 'the logick of Leander's beautie' would eke out her defence before the tribunal of the gods, and so at last into settled hypocrisy. Nothing could be finer or truer than the moment at which, after Venus had appeared and the appalling portents had begun to render self-deception impossible, still

> Betwixt all this and *Hero*, *Hero* held
> *Leanders* picture as a Persian shield.

Except for academic purposes the two parts, Marlowe's and Chapman's, should always be read together. Between them a great story is greatly told; and an important chapter in the history of poetry is unconsciously told too.

In the same year, 1598, appeared the first instalment of his Homer, *Seven Books of the Iliads*. The history of the whole gigantic work would carry us far beyond our chronological limits, but it makes such an interesting pendant to Douglas's *Aeneid* and illustrates so well the nature of the humanistic revolution that a brief notice of 'Chapman's Homer' (in general) is relevant. Its absolute merits, which have perhaps been exaggerated ever since the time of the Romantics, need not be canvassed here;

our concern is with Chapman and Douglas as gauge-readings of our changing relation to the ancient poets. Both translators read their own philosophy into their originals. As Virgil's after-world became hell and purgatory in Douglas, so in Chapman the nod of Zeus (I. 525) is related to the doctrine of the first Mover. In an age with no real historic sense this was perhaps inevitable. Again, both read their own practical ideals into their authors: but here Chapman is far more disabled than Douglas. The Scot's knightly and Christian ideal is not, for poetical purposes, very far removed from Virgilian *pietas* and valour: but there is a yawning abyss between the despair and passion of Homer's warriors and Chapman's half-Stoical, half-Machia-vellian, idea of the Great Man. Chapman's Homer is always teaching lessons (not always very noble) of civil and domestic prudence which never crossed the real Homer's mind. We may say of Chapman, as he (gratuitously) makes Hecuba say of Hector, 'policy was his vndoing' (xxiv. 214). His Jove hardly ever addresses Juno without some comment by Chapman on the proper treatment of shrewish wives. When Agamemnon sacrifices (I. 315–19) we are told how 'the politick king made show respectes to heauen'. In VI. 160 et seq. Homer says that Anteia wanted Bellerophontes to lie with her in secret 'but did not at all persuade the right-minded and prudent Bellero-phontes': Chapman explains that his prudence led him to shun 'the danger of a princesse loue'. Later in the same book (325) we have twelve wholly original lines explaining Hector's reason for addressing Paris exactly as he did.

Such reckless interpolations are one of the features that dis-tinguish Chapman's work from that of Douglas. Yet we are sure that Douglas did not reverence Virgil more than Chapman reverenced Homer. The truth is almost the opposite. In this passage, I think, we can see how his mind worked. He was sur-prised (as we have all been) that Hector at that moment should accuse Paris of ill temper rather than cowardice. But Homer is to Chapman like a sacred text; whatever seems inconsequent must really conceal wisdom. Homer wrote for people so wise that they would see the real 'politic' motive of Hector's speech: Chapman interpolates to make explicit what (he feels sure) must have been implicit in Homer. Thus reverence for Homer leads to re-writing Homer: the more sacred a text is, the more subject it is to glosses and strained interpretations. Douglas's reverence for Virgil was not quite of this blinding sort. He knew that Virgil had hidden significations 'wnder the cluddes of dirk poetry' (I, Prol.): an allegorical sense under the literal. But he did not think that Virgil had left the literal narrative half-written or full of puzzles and pitfalls. He thought he had made it 'quik' and 'lusty',

> felable in all degre
> As quha the mater held to foir thar ee (I, Prol. 13).[1]

The difference of approach appears at once. Douglas begins with praise of Virgil for obvious virtues which all men agreed in praising—his 'dulce ornate fresch endite', his 'eloquence'. Chapman in the preface to his *Seven Books* begins 'I suppose you to be no meare reader, since you intend to reade Homer.' Thus the simplest and most direct poet in the world, the poet whom everyone can enjoy that can enjoy poetry at all, is from the outset erected into a cryptic wiseacre on the model of Chapman himself. Hence the real Homer has to be darkened and bedaubed to make him more like the idol Chapman has conceived; hence the knowingness of Chapman's incessant interpolations, so sophisticated and yet so much less sophisticated than he himself supposed: hence the sheer nastiness (who can give it a milder name?) which he foists upon one of the most beautiful passages in Greek literature (*Iliad*, III. 154–7).

It is true that the fault is shared between Chapman and his teachers: that is what makes it significant of the veil that had fallen between us and the ancient world. Chapman's conceits, though always very un-Homeric and sometimes mere puerile 'clenches', do less harm than his 'wisdom'. But his hyperboles are ruinous in scenes of heroic action. Any medieval metrical chronicler (let alone Layamon, or the authors of *Maldon* and *Roland*) can do a better battle piece than Chapman. In VI. 327 Homer says, 'The people are being killed fighting about the city and the high wall', and we believe; Chapman bombasts this out into

> our slaughter'd friendes
> Besiege Troy with their carcasses on whose heapes our high walles
> Are ouerlooked by enemies,

---

[1] 'Thoroughly perceptible as though you had seen the things yourself.' Lit. 'as those who held (*or* should hold) the matter before their eye.'

and at once every image of real war fades from our minds; we are back in the world of books and declamations.

Yet Chapman was a very great man. His plays, with all their dramatic faults, are full of exalted poetry, though perhaps exalted in a rather unbalanced, Wagnerian way. He was the sort of man to whom the restraints of commercial art were necessary.

Since Walter Raleigh (1552?–1618) was associated with Chapman in life, he may be dealt with here, though he might almost equally well have been included among the belated writers of Drab. Of the forty-odd poems attributed to him about seventeen are in that earlier style. 'Sweete were the sauce' and 'Many desire but few or none deserue', for example, show the Drab in its gnomic mood, so heavily represented in Tottel. 'Your face, your tongue, your wit' and 'Fayne would I, but I dare not', are Drab knick-knacks, 'dainty devices' such as we met in the *Paradise* of 1576. (The former may be by Breton: let us hope it is.) 'The prayse of meaner wits' is in poulter's. The Epitaph on Sidney (a good poem) reads very like the work of Surrey. The 'Excuse', which has shape and point, is good Drab; and the epitaph on himself 'Euen such is Time', in its quietness, clarity, and finality, shows the Drab poetics at their very best. It will be noticed that much of this eight-line poem (which appears alone in the *Prerogative of Parliaments*, 1628) is also found as the last stanza of a six-stanza poem attributed to Raleigh in Harleian MS. 6917: and that the isolation, as well as the variants, improve it enormously. That is characteristic: Raleigh has happy moments but seldom gets through a longer piece without disaster. Some of his best lines occur in the fragments of translation scattered through the *History of the World*. Side by side with his Drab poetry we find weak Gold: 'Methought I saw the graue' or 'Like truthles dreames', or even (in 'What is our life?') a groping towards the metaphysical. The truth is that Raleigh has no style of his own; he is an amateur, blown this way and that (and sometimes lifted into real poetry) by his reading. Thus we attribute to him the famous Walsingham poem because it is so attributed to him in the Rawlinson MS., but I should not like to do so on internal evidence. Indeed, when we examine the poem we find that it has no unity of style at all. The early stanzas are clearly modelled on a popular poem and owe all their beauty to that model. In Stanza 3 we begin to get into a different, anapaestic metre. By the end this has worked up to the fine stanza 'Butt loue is a durable fyre': in the preceding stanza we had flat Tottelian morality, and sub-Tottelian cacophony, in 'Of women kynde suche indeed is the loue'. Thus, in forty-four lines, we have several heterogeneous virtues and vices. 'Give me my Scallop shell' is poetry of a far higher order. It might indeed be argued that even this is three poems rather than one; an ode with varied line lengths and plenty of sensuous imagery, ending at line 34, a regular octosyllabic poem which depends on analogies addressed to the intellect, ending at line 50, and a concluding stanza differing from both these in manner and metre. But the differences are not violent enough to neutralize the over-all unity. Of his *magnum opus*, the *Book of the Ocean to Cynthia* only fragments survive. These are in the Hatfield MS. and written by the poet's own hand. The Simpsonian rhymes (including Simpsonian B) might well have contented Raleigh even in a finished work, but there are other indications that these fragments were not ready for the press. As often happens in the work of an amateur, what is unfinished is more impressive, certainly more exciting, than what is finished. The hypothesis of the *Cynthia* is that Raleigh is the deserted lover of the queen. This is uncongenial to modern taste; but the quatrains do in fact vibrate with sombre passion. The monotony, the insanity, and the rich, dark colours of an obsessive despair are powerfully expressed. This, like Gray's *Elegy*, is one of those few poems in which the decasyllabic quatrain is the right form. The imagery constantly directs our minds to things 'under dust', fallen blossoms, sapless trees, broken monuments, mud, fading light, frozen winter, 'a tale told out of time'; and the effect of all this is every now and then relieved, yet also aggravated, by short glimpses of a happier past or sudden lifts of anger or adoration. The best of these, 'Shee is gonn, Shee is lost, shee is found, shee is euer faire', suggests possibilities in Raleigh which were never realized. Poetry, after all, made a small part of his life.

Of the verse translators, other than Chapman, who worked at this time, three deserve to be mentioned. The earliest is the unknown author whose *Six Idyllia out of Theocritus* were published at Oxford in 1588. He is a sensitive and original metrist who deliberately uses the alexandrine without a medial break—

With louely Netehearde Daphnis on the hills, they say (VIII) and rids the fourteener also of its even more tyrannous 'cesure'—

> Vpon a rocke, and looking on the sea, he sung these rimes;
> O Galatea faire, why dost thou shun thy louer true? (XI).

Both modifications really create new metres, whose possibilities have not even yet been fully exploited. XXXI, in trimeters, is intended to be like *Philip Sparrow*. Elsewhere this version sounds far more like Greek poetry than anything that was to be written in English before the nineteenth century;

> O Iupiter, and thou Minerva fierce in fight,
> And thou Proserpina, who with thy mother hast renoune
> By Lysimelia streames in Ephyra that worthy towne,
> Out of our iland drive our enemies, our bitter foe . . .
>   (XVI. 82 et seq.)

All that I have said about humanism in this book would have to be retracted if there had been many such humanists.

The other two translations are Harington's *Orlando Furioso* (1591) and the *Godfrey of Bouloigne* (that is, Tasso's *Gierusalemme Liberata*) which Edward Fairfax brought out in 1600. Both provide an interesting contrast to Chapman's Homer. Neither Harington nor Fairfax was, like Chapman, a man of genius. You could search their pages in vain for splendours like his 'the ladie of the light, the rosie-fingerd Morne', or (of Iris) 'dewie and thin, footed with stormes', or for a line that goes to the heart like 'Neuer again to be restor'd, neuer receiu'd but so'. In a word, there are fewer 'plums' in Harington and Fairfax than in Chapman: but then the cake is incomparably better. Those, therefore, who read (as Homer, Ariosto, and Tasso wrote) for the story will be held hour after hour by Harington and Fairfax, whereas in Chapman they will soon founder. This is largely because Harington and Fairfax are translating what they really enjoy: Chapman, incapable of appreciating the real Homer, chases a chimera. Harington's failures are mostly in the more licentious parts of the *Furioso*. The great Italian, at his most wanton, is always elegant and civilized to his fingertips: Harington's waggishness is, by comparison, a little raw and provincial. The trisyllabic rhymes, which he imitated from the original, have a more farcical effect in English than in Italian. The *Furioso* is not quite so like *Don Juan* as it appears to be in Harington. As for Fairfax, everyone knows that Dryden made him Waller's father in versification. This may be right, but the matter, and the rhyme scheme of the *ottava*, protect his version from any alien 'Augustan' quality. I read the *Jerusalem* in Fairfax long before I knew Italian enough to read the original, and it held me to the end. That is not, of course, the only test, but it is the supreme one. A man who knows no language but English need not be entirely ignorant of Ariosto and Tasso: he can get, not all, but a great deal, of their real quality from Harington and Fairfax.

Harington's preface, in a good working prose, repeats the ordinary defence of poetry and shows an appreciation of Ariosto's structural virtues. He is justly proud of the pictures, 'cut in brass' at his own directions: it is of interest that he thinks it necessary to explain perspective to his readers.

Before proceeding to the four interesting poets who will close this chapter we must glance at the attractive crowd of minor lyrists who appear only, or to best advantage, in song books and anthologies. Breton, in bulk, is so wearisome that we hardly notice his few successes: but in *England's Helicon*, isolated, his 'In the merry merry moneth of May' and, still more, 'Shall we go dance the Hay, the Hay' are delightful. In the same collection *Ignoto's* 'Coridon, arise my Coridon' is an almost perfect poem of happy love: its rhythmical effects, subtle and delicate. 'Come away, come sweet loue', from Dowland's *First Book of Songs* (1597) on the same theme, is even fresher and more piercing: it owes something to the *Song of Songs*, and perhaps anticipates some of the quality of Blake. Both these have a certain austerity in their art, though not in their matter. At the opposite end of the scale, homely and obvious, but no less successful, is 'What pleasures haue great Princes' which first appeared in Byrd's *Psalms, Sonnets and Songs* (1588). Of the named authors in *England's Helicon*, Edmund Bolton (1575?-1633?) is perhaps the finest. In metrical and emotional structure his 'Palinode' is almost as naïve as a poem could be, but compels us by its unity of tone and by the elusiveness (this was perhaps an unforeseen effect) of its imperfect rhymes. It contains one of the loveliest of all Golden phrases—'The daliance of the undiscernèd winde'. His primrose, like Milton's, is 'rathe', and in his 'Canzon Pastorall' the 'Matron-like' earth, attiring herself 'in habite graue', owes something to Du Bartas and perhaps contributed something to the 'Ode on the Morning of Christ's Nativity'. The lively 'Bright shines the Sun, play

Beggars play' is attributed by Walton to Frank Davison only, I suppose, because it was printed in Davison's *Poetical Rhapsody* (1602). The sonnet 'Were I as base as is the lowly playne', in the same collection, shows how a theme and a manner are never so old that a good poet cannot rejuvenate them.

It would be wrong not to notice that Golden poetry also has its limitations, which become its vices when it attempts matter beyond its reach. That failure of reach is what distinguishes it from certain other great styles—the style of Homer, Dante, or Chaucer; for they could handle anything. The Golden style not only fails but becomes ludicrous, even odious, when it attempts to present heroic action occurring in the real world. *The Tragedy of Sir Richard Grenville* (1595) by Gervase Markham is a good illustration. This is an epic narrative in *ottava rima*. All the deities are brought in. On that fatal day the sun began to decline soon after noon (not, by the by, an unusual phenomenon) because he feared lest Thetis should suspect him of an *affaire* with Virgo. A subordinate officer, arriving in the greatest possible haste, to tell Grenville that the Spanish fleet is in sight, describes in thirty-nine stanzas the debate in Olympus which had brought this about; Grenville listens without pistolling him, knocking him down, or even interrupting. It is true that Markham is a poor poet—witness his *Poem of Poems or Sion's Muse* (1596) with its

> You Daughters of Ierusalem behold
> The sable tincture of my spotted face—

but the imbecility of his epic manner is in fact symptomatic of a defect in that whole age, a defect visible in the battle poetry of Drayton, Spenser, and even Shakespeare.

Fulke Greville (1554–1628), the first Lord Brooke, has a double interest. To the historian he is interesting as a poet who began by being, as far as his talent allowed, Golden, and then went on to develop a new manner which pointed neither to the metaphysical nor to the Augustan, though it had more in common with the latter. Except for a few pieces that found their way into anthologies and for *Mustapha*, printed without his authority in 1609, his works were all posthumously published and cannot be dated with confidence. His Golden phase is seen in the earlier parts of *Caelica*—which is not a sonnet-sequence but a collection of poems in different metres and on different themes. No. IV ('You little starres that liue in skyes') is a really remarkable interweaving of courtly compliment, Platonic renunciation, astrology, and Calvinism, all made to sound effortless, like a song. No. XLV ('*Absence*, the noble truce') is even better, though few would agree that

> Where Wonder rules the heart
> There Pleasure dyes—

a doctrine reiterated in LVI ('Wonder hinders loue and hate'). The later pieces, more often religious than erotic, are less Golden. In them, as indeed often in the earlier, there is a toughness of thought which saves them from ever being vapid, but we are sometimes tantalized by the spectacle of such an interesting writer failing so often, and only just failing, to bring off a success. There is good satire in LXXVIII on little *arrivistes* who 'moue easily vpward as all frailties doe': stately compliment in 'Vnder a throne I saw a Virgin sit' (LXXXI): and in LXXXVII three lines on death which make most sixteenth-century poetry on that subject seem a little facile and external: Greville represents the soul as having fled from the body

> To see it selfe in that eternall glasse
> Where time doth end and thoughts accuse the dead,
> Where all to come is one with all that was.

In his later non-dramatic poems which he called 'Treaties' (*Of Human Learning, of Wars*) and an 'Inquisition' (*Upon Fame and Honour*) he departed widely from the Golden norm and wrote genuinely didactic verse, verse utterly unadorned and dependent for interest almost exclusively on its intellectual content. It is this that brings him into line with Davies and (to a less degree) with his friend Daniel.

But Greville has an interest quite apart from literary history. He wrote as he thought, and, being a man of his age, he thought chiefly about religion and government. Being a logical man, he connected his thoughts on the two subjects. What this led to he finally succeeded in expressing in four lines of such precision and such sombre melody that nothing can ever be added to them. They are, of course, the opening of the *Chorus Sacerdotum* from the end of his Senecan closet drama *Mustapha*,

> Oh wearisome Condition of Humanity!
> Borne under one Law to another bound:
> Vainely begot, and yet forbidden vanity,
> Created sicke, commanded to be sound.

He did not know how good they were, for the rest of the chorus (except the sting in its tail) is quite unworthy of them and his other works are little more than an attempt to say the same thing. I had to say of Spenser (and I might have said of many others) that he was the reverse of an Existentialist. Not so Greville. His mind was like Kierkegaard's and even more like Pascal's. His scepticism in the *Treatie of Human Learning* is the scepticism of the *Pensées*: he demolishes human learning to make way for revelation. Of course he uses contemporary resources for doing so: Agrippa's *De Vanitate Scientiarum*, the humanistic attack on metaphysics, the new Baconian contempt for all knowledge that is not utilitarian. But his end is theological in the most alarmingly practical sense. Disobedience that wants to 'deale With hidden knowledge' is to be silenced by 'powerful *Councels*' not by arguments (St. 85.) And though the State (this is characteristic) can really care nothing for divine truth, which indeed she despises (88), she must set up 'the discipline And practice of Repentance, Piety, Loue' (89). The name 'Discipline' raises cold fear in the mind of all who have studied this period: it is immediately confirmed. The State 'must assist Church-censure, punish Error' (92), and 'to the wounds of Conscience adde her paines' (93). The voice of Greville is now hardly distinguishable from that of Cartwright. Only superficial readers of the *Arcadia* will be surprised that such a man was Sidney's bosom friend. On one side—the side that created Gynecia—Sidney was very close to him. You might say that Greville was a *Sidneius dimidiatus*, or half Sidney. That half, living on through the long years after Zutphen by itself, would easily become the Greville of the Treaties, the man who said 'I know the world and believe in God'. But the commonplace words are in his mouth terrible: for they primarily mean the perpetual consciousness of an absolute gulf between the two, the incurable 'oddes betweene the earth and skie'.

Sir John Davies (1569–1626), though a very different man from Greville, occupies a poetical position not dissimilar. His *Orchestra* (1596) and *Hymns of Astraea* (1599) are Golden, but his *Nosce Teipsum* (also 1599) is, like Greville's *Treaties*, an unadorned and genuinely didactic poem. In this versified essay on the nature of the soul there is no question of using science as a peg on which to hang poetry. It is a perfectly serious textbook in which the arguments are as lucid as prose could make them.

The writer's talent appears in the success with which, while keeping our noses to the grindstone, he yet gives us a sort of pleasure by the verse. Some passages, such as the close of the introduction or the (wholly relevant) simile of the water nymph, rise higher than this: but the work as a whole produces admiration rather than pleasure. Both, perhaps, can be aroused by the *Astraea* where the poet sets himself the task of writing twenty-two acrostics (all in the same metre) on the words *Elisabetha Regina*, and succeeds so well that some of them are songs of real, though minor, charm. In 'Earth now is Queen' or 'Earley, cheerfull, mounting Larke' we forget all about the capitals: but it is a silly *tour de force* that vanishes from consciousness in proportion as it is successful. Davies's real fame rests on *Orchestra, a poem of Dancing*. Saintsbury, justly praising this work, used it as an illustration of his theory that in poetry the subject is immaterial—surely a misunderstanding, for to those who understand our ancestors' genial and mythical conception of Nature, the true subject of *Orchestra* is 'all the choir of heaven and all the furniture of earth'. If there is no personal passion in the poem, there is delighted and passionate contemplation. It was as truly 'nature poetry' for the Elizabethans as Wordsworth was for the Romantics. The style is Golden, a little sharpened (as the theme demanded) in the Bartasian direction.

Samuel Daniel[1] (1563?–1619) has already been considered as a sonneteer. It is shocking to find that the same year (1592) which saw the production of his admirable *Delia* saw also the production (in its first form—he tinkered it a good deal afterwards) of his *Complaint of Rosamond*. But we have learned to expect the worst from any descendant of the *Mirror for Magistrates*, and Daniel is here not even trying to achieve the sweetness and finish of his

[1] b. 1563?, near Taunton. Commoner, Magdalen Hall, Oxford, 1581. Trans. Paulus Jovius's *Imprese*, 1585. Visits Italy. May have accompanied Lord Stafford's embassy to France, 1586. After 1590 takes up residence at Wilton as tutor to W. Herbert, son of the Earl of Pembroke. His tragedy *Cleopatra*, 1593. At Skipton, Yorkshire, as tutor to the Countess of Cumberland's 11-year-old daughter Anne, 1597, or 8? (As a tutor seems to have got on well with his employers but to have disliked the work.) Under the new reign is frequently at court. Receives office of 'allowing' all entertainments played by the Children of the Revels to the Queen, 1603. His Masque *Twelve Goddesses* played at court, 1604. His tragedy *Philotas*, 1604: supposed to have a seditious tendency: D. defends himself successfully: his *Queen's Arcadia* (after Guarini). His *Tethys Festival* played at Whitehall, 1610. His *Hymen's Triumph* played before the queen, 1615. His (prose) *Collection of History of England*, 1617: becomes a groom of the Queen's Privy Chamber. In later life rented a farm near Devizes. Ob. 1619.

sonnets. After the historical 'tragedie' came the full-blown historical epic. The *First Four Books* of his *Civil wars between Lancaster and York* appeared in 1595, and this work rose by gradual additions to the eight-book text of 1609. It belongs to the same (happily extinct) species as Drayton's *Mortimeriados*, a species separated by its epic pretensions from the metrical chronicle of the Middle Ages, but still catering for readers who are at least as much interested in history as in poetry. Authorities are quoted and Daniel piques himself on having added nothing to the facts except speeches—as Sallust and Livy did in prose. He does not expect his work to be judged as 'pure' literature. We must not therefore be surprised if it is often prosaic (as in I. i–xxxvi) or if what would have been excellent prose (like I. 94–98) makes very tame verse. What is less pardonable is the clumsiness with which some sentences are forced into the metre as in

> And so become more popular by this;
> Which he feares, too much he already is (I. 63).

Here, as often in Drayton, we see the need for critical standards. A practised versifier like Daniel could have improved such a passage by five minutes' work: he was content with it because his readers demanded nothing better.

Yet he has carried out his ill-chosen task better than Drayton. Both poets relieve their narrative with reflections, but whereas Drayton's reflections are usually gnomic platitude, Daniel's show real, and interesting, thought: witness the passages on Order (II. 96), on the mixed causes of good and evil (v. 38–39), on popular blame (ibid. 65), and on the substantial indifference, to the people, of the issues for which they fought (VIII. 7). In the aetiological myth at the beginning of Book VI he opens to us his whole mind about the age in which he lived, and traces its miseries to the growth of great nation states (28), the 'swelling sciences, the gifts of griefe' which have 'let in light That all may all things see, but what is right' (35), religious controversy (36), printing (37), and gunpowder, whereby 'basest cowards from afar shall wound' (40). The latter complaint may, but need not, owe something to *Orlando Furioso*, IX. 90. Such passages, which illustrate a very important side of Daniel's literary character, would be equally interesting in prose, but he has others of more poetical appeal. He has expressed better than any poet I know what a man feels at the moment of his first big success: Bolingbroke, entering London in triumph,

> Admiring what hee thought could neuer be
> Did feele his blood within salute his state (II. 64).

The river that 'glides on with pomp of waters unwithstood' (II. 7) fully deserved the honour of being borrowed by Wordsworth. Henry VI's words as he looks down on both armies before Towton, 'They must a People bee When we shall not be kings' (VIII. 24) are memorable. No one perhaps has said anything better about the great deeds of our ancestors than 'The eternall euidence of what we were'. Best of all is the scene (II. 68–71) in which Queen Isabel waits to see Richard entering London and mistakes Bolingbroke for him. Here for a few stanzas the narrative is worthy of Chaucer. And these beauties, though rarer than we could wish, are never mere purple patches inorganically added to the story (as the beauties in Drayton's epic sometimes are); they arise naturally where the poet is kindled by his matter.

In 1599 came *A Letter sent from Octavia to Marcus Antonius* written to the formula of the *Heroides*. It is more gracefully executed than the *Rosamond*. Octavia says the things that a deserted wife of noble character (yet not too noble—she can be sufficiently catlike about Cleopatra) might be expected to say, but the verse does not carry passion enough to stir us. Yet here, as often and henceforward increasingly in Daniel, the thought holds our attention. Octavia digresses in an interesting way on the exclusion of women from affairs;

> We, in this prison of our selues confin'd
> Must here shut vp with our owne passions liue
> Turn'd in vpon us (18)

The matter of the poem is better than the manner. Daniel is never silly.

The long verse-colloquy *Musophilus* belongs to the same year. Philocosmos attacks, and Musophilus defends, the literary life, but it is not at all like a medieval *conflictus* between *Miles* and *Clericus*. Daniel is in earnest: the arguments of Philocosmos were those that really troubled his own mind and his defence has nothing glib about it. It is costly and difficult as though he were fighting for his life. He knows that he is living in a great age in which 'Nature hath laid doune at last That mighty birth wherewith so long she went' (247). Yet, like Pope in the *Dunciad*, he sees the enemy ahead—Confusion 'that hath all in chace, To make of all an vniuersal pray' (245). He realizes (and it is the vocational disease of scholars to forget) how small a part literature, even at the best, plays in human life; 'how many thousands never heard the name' of Sidney or Spenser (440), how the real 'managing' of the world's affairs requires arts unknown to literary men, so that often

> While timorous knowledge stands considering
> Audacious ignorance hath done the deede (490).

There are too many books already. Fame is at all times uncertain; and what fame can be hoped by those who write in a 'barbarous language' confined to a minute island? To this, as all know, Daniel makes at one point the spirited reply that English may have a great future on 'strange shores' in the 'yet vnformed Occident' (955 et seq.). It is well that he did not rest his whole case on that promise which history has 'kept to the ear' and 'broken to the heart', for though Daniel is read in America today, he is read there (as here) only by professional scholars; not such an audience as poets dream. He is wiser, and more appealing, when he faces squarely the possibility of almost total, or total, failure. How if very few read books? 'That few is all the world' (556), the world's heart which feels and knows only in a small minority. But how, if none? Certainly (for Daniel is very honest) that will cut off the author's 'comfort'; it cannot annihilate his love for his art. He must continue to do the thing he feels himself born to do. I am not at all sure that these thoughts have proved healthy to literature. It may well be that the author who claims to write neither for patron nor public but for himself has done our art incalculable harm and bred up infinite charlatans by teaching us to emphasize the public's duty of 'recognition' instead of the artist's duty to teach and delight. Things may have been better when you could order your ode from Pindar as you ordered your wine from the wine merchant. But that does not alter the fact that in *Musophilus* we find a sort of intellectual intimacy that hardly any English poet had offered us before. There is no common measure between this and the formal, external poetry about poetry which we find in Spenser and others. We are with Daniel in his solitude, chewing the bitter questions which come to all of our trade. In this poem every reader who is also a writer finds himself. It has also many other merits, and beauties too numerous to quote. I allow myself only this, on Stonehenge,

> That huge dumbe heape that cannot tell us how,
> Nor what, nor whence it is (339).

Daniel's Senecan closet dramas hardly concern us. His lyrical gifts were small, though the *Pastorall* 'O happy golden Age', loosely translated from Guarini's *Pastor Fido* (IV. ix), combines with curious success wantonness of theme and stateliness of movement; perhaps not the best thing in the world to do. The *Epistles* (1603) carry us beyond our chronological boundary and have been dealt with excellently by another hand. They claim to be 'after the manner of Horace', but of course the stanzaic form and the loftiness of Daniel's mind preclude any real similarity. In them Daniel is moving out of the Golden Age not in the 'Metaphysical' direction but towards a greater severity and weight. That to Sir Thomas Egerton is an essay (in prose it would have been a good one) on Equity as 'the soul of law'. That to Lord Howard is even more prosaic. But that to the Countess of Cumberland, a Christian-Stoical appropriation of the theme *suave mari magno*, is almost a success. It is at any rate frequently moving; and it is here that we catch Seneca's *quam res est contempta homo nisi supra humana surrexerit* (*Nat. Quaest. Prolog.*) on its way through Daniel to its predestined home in *The Excursion* (IV. 330).[1]

Though Daniel's poetry is often uninspired, sometimes obscure, and not seldom simply bad, he has two strong claims on our respect. In the first place, he can at times achieve the same masculine and unstrained majesty which we find in Wordsworth's greater sonnets, and I believe that Wordsworth learned it from Daniel. (The two poets had much in common and Daniel would have liked *Laodamia*.) And secondly Daniel is, in the nineteenth-century sense of the words, a poet of ideas. There had of course been ideas in Chaucer, and Spenser: but I think those poets felt themselves to be simply transmitting an inherited and accepted wisdom. There are, again, plenty of ideas in Donne, but they are, in my opinion, treated merely as the tools of his peculiar rhetoric: he was not interested in their truth or falsehood. But Daniel actually thinks in verse: thinks deeply, ar-

---

[1] Daniel exhibits interesting metrical peculiarities which cannot be dealt with in the space at my disposal.

duously, and perhaps with some originality. This is something quite different from Dryden's power of neatly poetizing all the stock arguments for the side on which he is briefed. Dryden states: Daniel can doubt and wrestle. It is no necessary quality in a poet, and Daniel's thinking is not always poetical. But its result is that though Daniel is not one of our greatest poets, he is the most interesting man of letters whom that century produced in England.

Michael Drayton[1] (1563–1631) is also a poet only half Golden, but in quite a different way from Greville, Davies, and Daniel. They began with Gold and moved away from it; he began with Drab, constantly relapsed into it, and in his old age, when the Golden period was over, at last produced his perfect Golden work, so pure and fine that no English poet has rivalled it. His weakness is the very opposite of Daniel's; he was in a sense too poetical to be a sound poet. His sensibility responded almost too quickly to every kind of subject—myth, the heroic past, tragic story, and (most of all) the fruitful, sheep-dotted, river-veined, legend-haunted expanse of England. He had an unquenchable desire to write poetry about them all, and he always seemed to himself to be succeeding because he mistook the heat which they aroused in him for a heat he was communicating to the reader. He himself has told us (in the *Epistle To Henry Reynolds*) how at the age of ten he hugged his 'mild tutor' begging to be made into a poet, and how the good man granted his request, in typically sixteenth-century fashion, by starting him on Mantuan. In that scene we have what is essential in Drayton the man: a man with one aim, devoted for life to his art, like Milton or Pope. If the Muse regarded merit he would have been one of our greatest poets.

His career began inauspiciously with *The Harmony of the Church* (1591), drab scriptural paraphrases to which critics are too kind when they accuse them of 'wooden regularity' for they are in reality wooden without being regular. *Idea, The Shepherd's*

---

[1] b. 1563 at Hartshill, Warwickshire. Page in service of Henry Goodere, 1573. In service of Thomas Goodere, 1580. Returns to the service of Henry Goodere, 1585. A friend of Stow and Camden. Connected with Children of the King's Revels and the Whitefriars Playhouse, 1607. Said to have had a meeting with Jonson and Shakespeare in 1616 at which the latter is said to have drunk himself into a fever of which he is said to have died. Mentioned by Edmund Bolton along with Chapman, Jonson, Selden, and others as a founder of the proposed Royal Academy, c. 1617. Ob. 1631.

Garland (1593) might be the work of a different man. These 'eglogs' are much influenced by Spenser's pastoral poetry but wisely refrain from his attempts at rustic realism. They were republished later with so many alterations as to make them a new book. But even the 1593 version shows promise: the lyrics, as always in Drayton, are the best part.

Idea's Mirror (1594), which I have already noticed, makes us think that Drayton is now going on from strength to strength, but with *Endimion and Phoebe* (1595) there is another check. In this perplexing poem the style of the erotic epyllion jostles with that of Du Bartas, and there is a similar wavering in Drayton's conception of his theme. He has, rightly, a feeling that this myth demands something more than a sensuous treatment, but has not quite made up his mind what that something more should be. I think he would like to have depicted the Platonic ascent from carnal to intelligible love, but has really no idea of what one would find at the top of the ladder. He has to fill up with astronomy and the theory of numbers. When he re-wrote it eleven years later as *The Man in the Moon* the discrepancy remained and was aggravated by a syntax so contorted as to be almost unreadable. In the earlier version the descriptive passages often have the prettiness that was intended. The movement of the couplets is a little monotonous.

His continual rewritings set us a problem. Detailed comparisons between versions are impossible in a short account, and if these are abandoned it becomes difficult to keep any kind of chronology. The 'Legends' of *Matilda, Pierce Gaveston*, and *Robert of Normandy* were originally written between 1593 and 1596; that of *Cromwell* did not follow till 1607. All four reappeared in 1619, with much revision. The *Mortimeriados* of 1596, much altered, became the *Barons' Wars* of 1603. Drayton's second thoughts are often important, but cannot of course be more important than the poems in which they occur. The truth is that this enormous body of historical verse, including the *Agincourt* and *Miseries of Queen Margaret* (1627), adds very little to his reputation.

Of 'legends' and 'tragedies' the reader of this book has now, I hope, heard all that he ever wishes to hear. And the historical epic is, almost equally, a *genre* diseased at the heart. Drayton, like Daniel, takes his historical poetry seriously as history: his marginal notes are significant. At the same time he adopts all the rhetoric and (on occasion) the sensuous richness which his age considered proper to high poetry. But such purple patches, like the fig-leaf in sculpture, only emphasize what they are meant to hide. The whole layout of the poem remains that of prose history. We are told that public persons did this or that and for such and such reasons, but we are not shown them doing it. In the *Barons' Wars* we are well into the second canto before we reach anything like an epic scene with a concrete where and when. No 'historical estimate' should deter us from saying that this is bad, bad work: interesting only in so far as it shows us how necessary the introductory letter to the *Faerie Queene* still was. Drayton has learned no structural lessons from all the great narrative poets who preceded him. He has not advanced on the old rhyming chroniclers. If you are going to be as artless as they in *ordonnance* it would be better to be artless in style too. It offends less and gets over the ground more briskly. Comparison between Drayton's epic *Agincourt* and his ballad on the same subject is instructive. The epic panoply adds nothing and loses all the race and relish of the humbler poem. The attempts to produce greatness and terror by such slaughter-house details as 'There drops a cheeke and there falls off a nose' are pitiable. The only good things in *Agincourt* occur in the speeches; notably in Gam's rodomontade

> I tell thee Woodhouse, some in presence stand
> Dare prop the Sunne if it were falling down.

It was not till 1597, when the first version of *England's Heroical Epistles* appeared, that Drayton's historical interests found successful poetic expression; so successful that his revisions in the later editions were less drastic than usual. The *Epistles* are of course modelled on Ovid's *Heroides* and we get rid of the epic chimera. They show a mingling of three styles, the genuinely Ovidian, the Golden, and the early Metaphysical. Thus the description of the grove in *Surrey to Geraldine* is pure Golden, the passage on gold in *Edward the Fourth to Mrs. Shore* faintly suggests an Elegy by Donne, and *Rosamond* is so like Ovid that we catch ourselves trying to remember the Latin. These styles, however, melt into one another without producing any discomfort; nor are conceit and hyperbole (common to them all) so managed as to exclude nature. Real passions at that time expressed themselves flamboyantly. Queen Isabel's remark on the element of fear in all sorrows is true and, I think, original; Henry II on kingship has pathos; the haggish malice of Elinor Cobham and the chivalrous patience of her husband are well brought out; Mortimer sustains his character of Stoic magnanimity successfully. One great virtue of the whole collection is the sweetness and vigour of its verse. The heroic couplet is here in its early perfection, looser than the Augustan mode but far from the meandering of the seventeenth century or the Romantics. It can throw up every now and then a line of astonishing force—'And care takes vp her solitarie inne', or 'Where the disheuel'd gastly sea-nymph sings', or (of lipstick) 'On Beauties graue to set a crimson Hearse'.

With the exception of these *Epistles* nearly all Drayton's valuable work falls outside my period: accounts of the interesting though very uneven *Polyolbion* and of *Nimphidia* (dear to some who do not care for 'faerie' and hateful to all who do) must be sought elsewhere. I cannot thus surrender either the *Shepherd's Sirena*, which appeared in the 1627 volume, or the *Muses Elizium* (1630). No history of Golden poetry could possibly omit them. In these the unfashionable old poet who had long been fighting a rear-guard action against those who would

> exile
> All braue and ancient things foreuer from this Ile

and proclaiming in his solitude

> Antiquitie I loue nor by the worlds despight
> I cannot be remoou'd from that my dear delight,

received at last his reward and was allowed to conclude the Golden Age with something (as the poetess said) 'more gold than gold'. For in these last poems of his all that richness turns finer, more rarefied, more quintessential, than ever before. The *Shepherd's Sirena* is in one way like all Golden poetry: yet in another way there is no poem at all like it. A hundred and twenty lines in the lulling incantatory metre of the *Phoenix and the Turtle*, lines full of winter and heartbreak, provide the base. Against this, silvery, cascading, the song stands out with startling beauty. Its incomparable music—which would be rather like Mr. de la Mare's if it were not so passionless and so free from his undercurrent of misgiving—depends on taking a metre which, of itself, is always threatening to develop into a commonplace dactylic tumble, and then delicately, deftly,

variously holding it back from that development. The charm of
this song is its inhumanity. We are nominally praising a woman,
yet it is a river as much as a woman, or neither. It is almost
'about' nothing: as near to 'pure' poetry as the nature of
language will allow. This 'purity' continues in the best parts of
the *Muses Elizium*. Nothing more Golden had ever been produced. They teach nothing, assert nothing, depict almost
nothing; or, if anything, Scaliger's and Sidney's *naturam alteram*.
Their methods are those of Pastoral, but the last links with real
shepherd life have been severed. But not the last images from
actual nature. There is an exquisite mingling of impossible
beauties with things really observed, 'either other sweetly
gracing'. Thus on the one hand all seasons are blended so that
the fruits hang 'Some ripening, ready some to fall, Some
blossom'd, some to bloome'; the eyes of Lirope turn pebbles to
diamond and tempest to calm; it is not beyond hope

> To swerue up one of Cynthias beames
> And there to bath thee in the streames
> Discouer'd in the Moone,

or that all the pearls of all the seas and either India should dis-
solve into a lake,

> Thou therein bathing and I by to take
> Pleasure to see thee clearer than the Waue.

But then, on the other hand, the reflection of a girl's yellow hair
upon the lily wreath that surrounds it casts a light 'like the
sunnes vpon the snow'; the 'west winde stroakes the violet
leaues': an early morning sky is 'chequerd' with 'thin clouds
like scarfs of Cobweb lawne': bees stagger homeward 'vp in
hony rould More than their thighes can hould'. The power of
this Elizian poetry to transform its material is perhaps best seen
in the first 'Nimphall'. Taken in itself the subiect of that poem
is scarcely tolerable. Each nymph praises the other's beauty by
preferring it to her own. The perversity of the original Greek
models survives only in the fact that this preference is dissociated from all idea of envy or even of regret: we are left with
two inhuman, inexplicable voices uttering their passion for
beauty and, save for that, passionless. It is thus that real
fairies (not the bric-à-brac of *Nimphidia*) would speak if they
existed. It is the ultimate refinement of Golden poetry, Gold 'to
ayery thinnesse beate', without weight, ready to leave the earth.

EPILOGUE
New Tendencies

I

MY Epilogue falls naturally into three parts, one dealing
with prose and the others dealing, respectively, with the
two different directions in which verse passed out of its
Golden phase. And the first must, historically, be the least
interesting of the three. The end of the century does not even
approximately mark the end of a period in the history of our
prose. In 1600 nearly all the great triumphs of Golden verse
were behind: in prose, Browne and Taylor and Milton and
Traherne were still to come. The real break is later; when men
like Tillotson and Dryden taught English prose to live on a
sparer diet. It is only necessary here to mention two writers
who even by 1600, as may be thought, are already moving
towards that drier and more utilitarian manner: but I do not
so much claim that status for them as submit the matter to every
reader's consideration.

A modern may at first find it hard to understand why Henry
Smith (1550?–1591) was known in his own days as the 'silver
tongued' and continued to be reprinted throughout the first
half of the seventeenth century. There are, however, good
reasons why he should have pleased many pious households who
would not care for Donne or Taylor. His sermons are short and
therefore suitable for reading aloud. They are free from royalist
sentiment. They are, or at least seem to be, severely practical.
They are puritanical in their theology and make no parade of
profane learning: Smith hardly ever quotes except from the
Bible. He can be eloquent—notably in the *Godly Man's Request*
—but he is no rhetorician. He writes a plain prose; and though
some of his homely allegories (in *The Wedding Garment* or *Satan's
Compassing the Earth*) may remind us of Latimer, his plainness
is not that of Drab prose. I think it looks forward to Dryden or
even Swift, and that herein lies his historical importance. He
knew what he was doing and is at pains to point out that 'to
preach simply is not to preach rudely and unlearnedly nor
confusedly, but to preach plainly and perspicuously'. This ideal
he certainly achieved. As a spiritual guide he may be ungracious

and may too often substitute denunciation (which is easy) for counsel (which is hard). But he is clear, musical, and strong. Some of his short sentences could hardly be bettered: 'Sin is neuer compleat till it be excused', 'This is the time, when the Devil saith the time is not yet', 'No man can abide to be disgraced in his wit: we had rather seem wicked than simple.' His popularity may possibly be taken as evidence that many before Sprat sympathized with Sprat's taste in style: not, to be sure, that most of those who read Smith were thinking about English prose, but that, almost unconsciously, they found the swellings and digressions of other preachers an obstacle.

The work of Francis Bacon (1561–1626) falls almost entirely outside our period, but the little volume which he published in 1597 contains things worthy of notice. It consists of the ten earliest *Essays*, the *Meditationes Sacrae*, and the *Colours of Good and Evil*: in the second edition (1598) an English version, probably not by Bacon himself, was substituted for the Latin text of the *Meditationes*. This neglected work contains things very much more like 'essays' (in the ordinary sense of that word) than Bacon ever gave us again: the sections *Of Moderation of Cares* and *Of earthly Hope*, both on characteristically Johnsonian themes, are like the best *Ramblers*. The *Colours* is work of quite a different kind, a precursor almost of Miss Stebbing's *Thinking to Some Purpose*. By 'coulers' Bacon means not rhetorical colours but what we should call stock arguments: he is constructing a 'defence to the minde' by showing under what conditions such arguments are invalid. Here, as in the great passage about Idols in the *Novum Organum*, we see Bacon at his best: not as a discoverer of truths but as an exposer of fallacies. From these two works, diversely excellent, it is a shock to turn to the *Essays*. Even the completed *Essays* of 1625 is a book whose reputation curiously outweighs any real pleasure or profit that most people have found in it, a book (as my successor admirably says) which 'everyone has read but no one is ever found reading'. The truth is, it is a book for adolescents. It is they who underline (as I see from the copy before me) sentences like 'There is little friendshipe in the worlde, and least of all betweene equals': a man of 40 either disbelieves it or takes it for granted. No one, even if he wished, could really learn 'policie' from Bacon, for cunning, even more than virtue, lives in minute particulars. What makes young readers think they are learning is Bacon's manner; the dry, apophthegmatic sentences, in appearance so unrhetorical, so little concerned to produce an effect, fall on the ear like oracles and are thus in fact a most potent rhetoric. In that sense the *Essays* are a triumph of style, even of stylistic illusion. For the same reason they are better to quote than to re-read: they serve (in Bacon's own phrase) 'for ornaments'. But in these ten first essays, as they stand in the 1597 text, that style overshoots the mark: they are altogether too jejune, too atomic. And many good touches were left to be added to them in the later editions. Their connexion with Montaigne's work is quite unimportant. If Bacon took his title from Montaigne, he took nothing else. His earliest essays resemble essays by Montaigne about as much as a metallic-looking cactus raised on the edge of a desert resembles a whole country-side of forest, filled with light and shade, well stocked with game, and hard to get out of. It is only in the *Meditations* that Bacon is at all like his predecessor; and even there, of course, briefly. Nor had he any successors. The cactus remains unique; interesting, curious, striking, worth going to see once, but sterile, inedible, cold and hard to the touch.

II

The reader's attention has been drawn, at various stages, to indications of a taste existing in the Golden period and before it for which the Golden poetry itself did not cater in any unusual degree. We have seen that Churchyard (in his *Light Bundle*) thought rhyme by its very nature adapted to revive the spirits and move a smile. We have seen that Gascoigne (in his *Notes of Instruction*) emphasized 'Invention', the avoidance of things trite and obvious. Gabriel Harvey, commenting on Gascoigne's 'Invention' in his commonplace-book, says *in hoc genere Lucianus* (but he must have meant to write *Lucanus*) *excellebat*, and also that 'divine Homer', Sallustius Bartasius; whom he praises in the *New Letter of Notable Contents* for his 'colours of astonishing Rhetorique' and 'amazing deuises'. The same desire for something that would 'astonish' and 'amaze' can be seen in Puttenham's ocular 'proportion' and in some of the bric-à-brac poetry of the Drab anthologies. Many men probably wanted poetry not so rich as the Golden but more sparkling, less emotional and more intellectual, less sweet and more piquant. That some wanted obscurity, the satirists and the Cryptic poets have shown. These tastes were to be gratified, and simultaneously transformed, by what is now called 'Metaphysical' poetry. The name is inept—'Bartasian' or even 'Catachrestic' would be better— but it is now too late to try to dislodge it.

The novelty, like most literary novelties, consisted in doing more continuously or to a higher degree something that had been done before. The 'Metaphysical' conceit grows up gradually, like euphuism. Everyone sees that there is nothing 'Metaphysical' about Spenser's comparisons of two contesting knights to two contesting beasts; and everyone would describe as 'Metaphysical' Donne's comparison of a pair of lovers to a pair of compasses. Between the two there are many stages. As the resemblances become more recondite, more intellectual and less sensuous or emotional, they are moving farther in the Metaphysical direction: at what point we shall begin to give them that name does not very much matter, nor what frequency of such recondite comparisons we demand in a poet before we call him a Metaphysical. It is more important to note that their frequent use is necessarily accompanied with another change in style.

Where comparisons are to be very recondite the things compared must often be sought for in fields of experience very remote from one another. Being remote, they will have already acquired different associations, so that they cannot now be re-united without a clash or shock. The feeling for *Decorum* in ancient, medieval, and Golden poetry flows from a desire to avoid such clashes or shocks. The desire, in some form, goes back to prehistoric times. This will be obvious if we reflect on the fact that while ancient life (and ancient comic poetry) was full of obscenities, yet ancient epic (save for a very few passages which are, significantly, intended to be funny) could almost all have been read aloud to a mixed audience in the reign of Queen Victoria. Certain things, well known to every ancient poet and perhaps disapproved by none, are from the first kept out of the grave kinds of poetry. In the world of fact, and in the stream of consciousness, all sorts of things jostle together: but the organized sensibility which we call taste had put some things apart by the time the Homeric poems were composed. It continued to hold them apart. Douglas's ninth prologue states the rule of *decorum* as it existed by the end of the Middle Ages. The tendency of humanism was certainly not to relax this rule: it lies behind Scaliger's complaint that the Homeric

Andromache is 'low'. Dryden, writing when the rule was once more in full vigour, says that 'the metaphysics' have no place in love-poetry. Chaucer's Pandarus would have agreed with him: he had warned Troilus not to use 'termes of physike' in a love letter (*Troilus*, II. 1037). The desire for recondite comparisons lays a poet under the necessity of breaking such prohibitions.

But the new poets welcomed this necessity. The rule of decorum exists to avoid clashes or shocks to organized sensibility: but it was an early discovery that an occasional defiance of the rule, resulting in a shock, can give pleasure; a pleasure rich in tragic or comic possibilities. Indeed one of the purposes for which the rule exists is that it may sometimes be broken. Thus taking 'decorum' in its narrower sense to mean a standard of decency in our references to bodily functions, it is clear that all indecent humour depends on that standard of decency: the mention of certain things becomes funny only after we have agreed that they are unmentionable. Breaches of decorum in the wider, critical sense of the word work in the same way, though the shock need not be at all a comic one. The grimness of Aeschylus' χρυσαμοιβὸς δ' Ἄρης σωμάτων, War the body-broker (*Agamemnon* 437), depends on the fact that, in our organized sensibility, the ideas of heroic, legendary war and of small, contemporary business transactions lie so far apart. The *moenia mundi* in Lucretius are especially interesting, because there the comparison of something so vast and unimaginable as the universe to something so small and familiar as a walled town produces sublimity. A more flippant and whimsical use of the same method can be seen where Ovid describes Olympus (*Met.* I. 171 et seq.) in terms familiar to every Roman man about town—*atria, plebs, potentes, penates, palatia*. The Metaphysicals were making no absolute innovation when they deliberately produced poetic shocks by coupling what was sacred, august, remote, or inhuman with what was profane, hum-drum, familiar, and social, so that God is asked to 'batter' a heart, Christ's 'stretched sinews' become fiddlestrings, cherubs have breakfasts, stars are a patrol, and snow puts a periwig on bald woods. The novelty lay in doing this sort of thing more often, and perhaps more violently, than previous poets had done, and indeed making it almost the mainstay of their poetics. For I think it is this *discors concordia* (Ovid, *Met.* I. 433), far more than its learning, that gives Metaphysical poetry its essential flavour.

It will be understood, of course, that these poets were not abolishing or ignoring poetic decorum but exploiting it, so to speak, in reverse. We must never suppose that they are writing from a sensibility in which the 'decorous' dissociations of high from low or the strange from the familiar did not exist. If there ever were a sensibility so ingenuous as that it was certainly prehistoric and probably pre-human: at no period would it have been harder to achieve than in the fifteen-nineties. Decorum was in their bones. It is interesting to note that John Hoskyns (1566–1638), sometimes claimed, and not without reason, as an Ur-Metaphysical, in his *Directions for Speech and Style* lays it down that 'unless your purpose be to disgrace' your metaphor must 'be taken for a thinge of equall or greater dignity'. Metaphysical poetry is 'twice born'. No literature could begin with it. It uses discords on the assumption that your taste is sufficiently educated to recognize them. If the immemorial standard of decorum were not in your mind before you began reading, there would be no point, no 'wit'; only clownish insipidity. We may thus describe Metaphysical poetry either as being 'parasitic' (it lives on other, non-Metaphysical poetry) or as being of a 'higher' logical order (it presupposes other poetry).

Poetry which yokes the remote and the familiar suffers from the risk that what was familiar in the poet's time may cease to be so in later centuries. In that way the edge has been taken off some Metaphysical images. It has been taken off the line about the released soul who 'baits not at the Moone', in Donne's *Second Anniversary* (195) because to 'bait' is for us an archaic word with poetical associations: to get the effect which Donne intended we should now have to say that she does not stop for petrol or change trains. The full poignancy of 'If I lack'd anything' in Herbert's 'Loue bade me welcome' is lost because 'What d'ye lack?' and 'D'ye lack anything?' are no longer commonplace: to get the right effect we should now need something like 'Are you being attended to?' Hence no old poetry needs to be read with such a constant alertness of the historical imagination as that of the Metaphysicals.

From what has been said it will be clear that no one can point to a moment at which poetry began to be Metaphysical nor to a poet who made it so; but of all poets perhaps Guillaume de Salluste du Bartas (1544–90) comes nearest to that position. He was a Huguenot and all his important works are religious:

the *Judith* (1573), the *Sepmaine*, in its seven *Jours* (1578), and the *Seconde Sepmaine* (1584) in which only four *Jours* are completed but each *Jour* is divided into four parts running to seven hundred-odd lines each. Any idea of austerity or pious drudgery which this account may arouse must be banished from the mind at once. He was a Gascon as well as a Calvinist; a literary d'Artagnan who would fight the French language, and the whole range of human knowledge, single handed: a man of delighted piety, of vivid, darting, uncontrollable imagination. Whatever else the *Sepmaines* may be, they are tinglingly effervescent. Sometimes there even arises a doubt whether all his *discors concordia* is intended to be quaint, or whether it is ingenuous: whether he is to be compared to Ovid describing Olympus in terms of Rome or rather to a savage poet, in all simplicity, giving the gods a kraal just like that of his own chief. I feel pretty certain that some passages must be understood that way. When he puts into Paradise (II. i, *Eden* 457)

> Roses que chaque jour, comme on eust dit, les anges
> Rangeoient en laz d'amours, triangles, et lozanges,

I think he is being ingenuous. He would have liked such a garden. The spirit which led Milton to an explicit rejection of 'nice Art' (*Paradise Lost*, IV. 241) comes from a real change of taste. So, when the Bartasian Adam, first transported from the place of his creation into the Garden, behaves like a country bumpkin on his first visit to Paris (ibid. 301 et seq.) I think du Bartas feels no quaintness. He is simply expressing an older kind of sensibility. Milton, once more, stands on our side of the dividing line: his Paradise is not like town to a countryman but like country to a townsman (ibid. IX. 445 et seq.). A more doubtful passage is that where Adam is commanded

> Qu'il gardast le depost entre ses mains commis
> Et cultivast ce parc que Dieu sans aucun terme
> Soubs ces conditions luy bailloit comme à ferme (ibid. 260).

But if that is on the borderline, we have surely crossed it when God reserves the forbidden tree,

> Pour tout droict de champart, de censive, et d'entree (ibid. 406),

or, in creating Eden, Himself *tend le cordeau, alligne les allées* (41). Elsewhere we emerge from the region of doubt altogether. In

> Le ciel n'avoit encor sur nos chefs canoné
> Ny l'escrit de divorce à la terre donné (ibid. 299),

or in this, of the heaven (which may have suggested Donne's 'baits not at the Moone'),

> Il va tousjours d'un train, et meu d'un faix sans faix,
> Il ne scait point que c'est des chevaux de relais (i. ii. 907),

du Bartas certainly intended the clash of associations. When all allowances have been made for his real simplicities, much remains which is genuinely Metaphysical, dependent on a calculated breach of decorum.

It may also be asked whether the genial or animistic conception of Nature did not render all his anthropomorphic images less quaint, less 'witty', than they have since become. This is not disposed of by pointing out that du Bartas did not fully share that conception, denies that the stars are alive, and says they are carried round *bon gré, maugré* on their spheres *tel que les cloux d'un char* (i. iv. 89-120). For what had been intellectually rejected might still colour the sensibility. It would be reasonable to suppose that the animistic conception facilitated, both in du Bartas and in our own Metaphysicals, their peculiar kind of wit. But much of it, even against that background, would be quaint and *piquant*. Animism could not take all the edge off du Bartas's picture of the wet winds that brought the Deluge (*Chaque poil de leur barbe est une humide source*, i. ii. 1082), or the gate and porter of lost Paradise (*l'ange pour huissier, pour huis le cimeterre*, ii. i. 142), or the angelic *escrimeur* (i. i. 738) sent with his *espée à deux mains* against the Assyrians. These are in the same class as Milton's sun in bed and Marvell's patrol of stars.

Joshuah Sylvester (1563-1618), who had translated portions of du Bartas in 1590 and 1592, brought out his *Divine Weeks and Works* in 1605. He was a free translator who inserted digressions of his own (but not without warning) and substituted native equivalents for French allusions: his Adam is like a bumpkin in London, not in Paris. He sometimes exaggerates, and sometimes diminishes, the Metaphysical qualities of his original. Thus the famous line (ii. i. 4. 144) 'And perriwig with wooll the bald-pate woods' has in the original nothing more remarkable to correspond to it than *Et que de flocs de laine il orne les forêts*. On the other hand

> de qui la parole
> Serre et lasche la bride aux postillons d'Aeole (i. i. 3)

sinks in Sylvester to the less fanciful

> at whose only word
> Th' Eolian scouts are quickly still'd and stirr'd,

and they run neck to neck at

> Phoebus s'emparera du noir char de la lune (1. i. 364)
> The Sun shall seize the black coach of the Moon.

Thus, sometimes overshooting, sometimes falling short, often hitting the target, Sylvester, on balance, preserves the literary quality of the French pretty well. Perhaps he makes it a little more conceited, but not much.

Du Bartas has had a strange fate. In his own age he was a serious rival to Ronsard. In England his influence was profound. He was doubtless 'Sunday reading' in many Protestant homes and we need not wonder that those who read him in childhood surrendered to him completely. More attractive food for young imagination and young scientific curiosity could hardly be found. All the Metaphysicals sound as if they had been brought up on him, or on Sylvester's translation. But Milton no less. We feel du Bartas in all the quainter parts of *Paradise Lost*, where the universe is circumscribed with a pair of celestial compasses, or where the emergent beasts almost seem to have come from a film by Mr. Walt Disney. We should object less (or, at least, make a less bewildered objection) to 'no fear lest dinner cool' if we remembered that Milton was also a Bartasian. Then came the beginning of the Augustan age. Dryden, who confessed that he had admired Sylvester's du Bartas in his youth, dropped him, as he dropped Cowley, as all the Metaphysicals were dropped. But the curious thing is that when Donne and the rest were revived in modern times, and humanist standards of criticism abandoned, there was no reconsideration of du Bartas. It is long overdue.

The saintly and heroic Jesuit Robert Southwell (1561-95) modestly but firmly refused to take any notice, as a poet, of the period in which he was living. He was not in the least 'contemporary': his work sometimes recalls the past, sometimes anticipates the immediate future which he was unconsciously helping to create, and often seems to belong to no period at all.

> May neuer was the month of loue
> For May is full of floures—

who, without the spelling to guide him, could date that? His weakest poems are gnomic and recall weak gnomic poems in Tottel: such are 'Tymes goe by Turnes', 'From Fortune's Reach', and a few others. But many resemble the Tottelians where the Tottelians, as we saw, resemble eighteenth-century poetry. 'The Prodigall Chylds Soul Wracke' might have been written in the Drab Age, but also, with a very few alterations, might pass for Cowper or Watts. But it is as an early 'Metaphysical' that Southwell is of most historical interest and also, perhaps, at his best. He has not the metrical characteristics of the Metaphysicals, but his conceits have their subtlety. He loves, like Herbert, to play on the edge of bathos (triumphantly), comparing highest to lowest things or best to worst. Thus Grace 'in Vertue's key tunes Nature's string': the Holy Infant lies in the manger 'as haye the brutest sinner to refresh': Christ's falling on the *Via Dolorosa* is 'kissing the ground' on which His foe (Man) treads; the beauty which God sees in the human soul

> lul'd our heauenly Sampson fast asleepe
> And laid Him in our feeble nature's lapp.

Closer still to Herbert in its sharp homeliness is

> My grace is saide: O death! Come take awaye.

Sometimes, even without conceits, as in 'A Preparative to Prayer' he has exactly Herbert's prose-like, yet never prosaic, sobriety.

In content Southwell's poetry is always religious. It is natural to connect the more tragic pieces with the horrors of his imprisonment and repeated tortures, but the connexion is by no means certain. 'Dyer's Phancy' is clearly concerned with the pains of the spiritual life itself. Southwell writes much about the inner conflict, and here his poetic moral theology (as a confessor he may have talked differently) brings him close to Fisher. All sin seems to come from the senses, all beauty to belong to the soul—'A briefe wherein all marveyles summed lye'. Life is a perpetual conflict

> where halues must disagree
> Or truce of halues the whole betraye.

Death parts 'two ever-fighting foes'. I do not remember that he ever refers to the resurrection of the body. Hence long before he came into the rackmaster's hands, he may have wished that

'Sampson's leaue' (that is, Sampson's dispensation from the prohibition of suicide) 'a comon lawe were made'. Probably the sweetness of his own nature shielded him from a real knowledge of the *mala mentis gaudia*.

Southwell's work is too small and too little varied for greatness: but it is very choice, very winning, and highly original. We never read him without wondering why we do not read him more. He has (in some poems) certain metrical peculiarities which, if I dealt with at all, I should have to deal with more largely than they deserve. For they are not characteristic: at his best, and most typical, he writes with almost Augustan smoothness, relieved occasionally by an internal rhyme: the greatness of the matter and the masculine precision of phrase save him from dullness.

John Hoskyns (1566–1638) is a much smaller, indeed an infinitesimal, poet and his letters to his wife (with whom he seems to have been passionately and unhappily in love till she died) are much more interesting than his verses, most of which are *jeux d'esprit* in Latin. In his English pieces he aims more or less continuously at wit and to that extent anticipates the new manner. 'Absence, hear my protestation' has sometimes been attributed to Donne. The following epitaph on 'a young gentlewoman' is, I believe, his happiest effort:

> Nature in this small volume was about
> To perfect what in woman was left out:
> Yet carefull least a piece so well begun,
> Should want preseruatiues when she had done:
> Ere she could finish what she vndertook,
> Threw dust upon it, and shut vp the book.

With a few exceptions the poems which John Donne (1572?–1631)[1] wrote before the turn of the century cannot be accurately dated. They fall into three groups of very unequal value. We have, first, those pieces in which Donne is primarily an Ovidian. The 'Heroical Epistle' of *Sapho to Philaenis* is obviously modelled

---

[1] b. 1571 or 1572. Lost his father, an ironmonger, in childhood. Descended through his mother from More's brother-in-law, John Rastell. Brought up as a recusant. Admitted to Hart Hall, Oxford, 1584 (the Oath of Supremacy was not imposed on freshmen under the age of sixteen). Friendship with Sir Henry Wotton. Took no degree. Prob. travelled. At Thavies Inn, 1591. Enters Lincoln's Inn, 1592. His brother arrested for harbouring a seminary priest and dies in prison, 1593. Sails with Essex on the Cadiz voyage, 1596. Becomes secretary to Sir Thomas Egerton, 1597–8. Clandestine marriage with Anne More, 1601.

on the *Heroides*. It is, like Drayton's 'First Nimphal', an essay
in Lesbianism, but the theme which is in Drayton a pretext for
formal beauty becomes in Donne a pretext for wit. Since both
celebrate an obsession from which, in the nature of things, their
authors cannot have suffered, both raise the doubt whether
other Elizabethan poems of perversion may not embody merely
humanistic affectations. One couplet in Donne's Epistle has a
formal prettiness very alien to his mature manner:

> But thy right hand, and cheek, and eye, only
> Are like thy other hand, and cheek, and eye (23–24).

It will be noticed that 'only' is not Simpsonian rhyme but
mere inversion. This piece need not have been written after
Drayton's *Heroical Epistles*; if with Donne's editor we call it
'heroical' we mean only that it is in the manner of the *Heroides*'.
The twentieth *Elegy*, though it does not achieve, and probably
does not attempt, any English equivalent to the Popian neatness
of Ovid's couplets, constructs a pert, pseudo-logical argument
of the kind Ovid loved. This element, which reappears in
Donne's lyrics, is his most permanent debt to the Latin poet.

In the second class we have poems which, though not all
satiric, all use the violently contorted metre which one kind of
Elizabethan satirist favoured. This is a different thing from the
metrical audacities (which have sometimes been exaggerated)
in Donne's lyrics. There we have an interplay between the
ostensible metrical pattern and the speech rhythms that cross
it. In this group, which contains Elegy XI, Satires III, IV, and V,
the *Storm* and the *Calm* (1597) and the three epistles to Sir
Henry Wotton, the ostensible metre is sometimes bludgeoned
out of all but typographical existence. In parts of Satire IV,
though the dialogue is in itself lively, one wonders what Donne
could have supposed it would gain by being printed as verse.
Elegy XI is a satire in all but name, and has great comic strength.
Satire III is one of those poems which, like *Sleep and Poetry*, are
so interesting for their content that we are apt to overrate them
as poems. The thought is bold, honest, sequacious, and (what
we might least expect in Donne) temperate: a touchstone which
reveals the almost purely rhetorical and dramatic nature of the
paradoxical 'thought' in some of his erotic poems. But the gems
of this group are the *Storm* and *Calm*. They are of especial
interest as evidence that though most of Donne's poetry is

highly subjective, this proceeded from choice and not from any inability to paint the outer world. On the contrary he can do this better than most of the Golden poets, and as well as most medieval poets. Only once (in the lines beginning 'Compar'd to these', *Storm*, 65) does he grow shrill: the breeze that 'mildly kist our sailes', the 'rowling trench', the rags of sail dropping, and the famous couplet about feathers and dust, are wholly admirable.

But of course it is the third group, the lyrics, that really reveal Donne's greatness. Though I have spoken of his debts to Ovid and du Bartas, I do not at all mean to deny the astonishing novelty of the *Songs and Sonnets*. Without wasting time on any proclamation that this is 'the new poetry' or any denigration of his predecessors, Donne creates a kind of poem that had never been heard before. He does so by combining two qualities which, had he not combined them, we might still regard as incompatible. On the one hand, his lyrics are dramatic; they sound like *ex tempore* speech and imply a concrete situation. They rap out a hot answer to something already said ('For godsake hold your tongue' or "Tis true, 'tis day') or start a conversation by expressing some thought as if it had that moment come into his mind ('I wonder by my troth' or 'Now thou hast lov'd me one whole day'). To that extent they are like lyrics by Catullus: but even more immediate. On the other hand, he weaves into these seemingly casual utterances the recondite analogies and *discors concordia* which in du Bartas had had no lyric or dramatic function, being used rather to vivify matter the most remote from our daily life. These diverse excellences are usually held together by Donne's adoption of the role of pleader (which Puttenham had desired of poets)—by his argument. The argument may be on different levels; shameless and essentially preposterous as in 'Woman's Constancy', or fanciful as in 'The Flea'; or (within the mood of the poem) serious. Thus in 'Love's Growth' we seem to be finding, as we proceed, more and more adequate intellectual models for an experience which demands them. The famous image of the compasses is 'wit' in no sense that implies frivolity. Dante would have used it if he had thought of it. Its essential rectitude could be shown, if need were, by the fact that Omar Khayyam had anticipated it so closely. The 'Nocturnal upon St. Lucy's Day' is less perfect—the hyperbole about the squibs and the irrelevantly denigratory reference to the goat might be questioned—but here the models are emotional and intellectual at once. In Donne's most serious lyrics, which I suppose to be his best, we have a poetry which is almost exactly opposite to that of Shakespeare's *Sonnets*. In Shakespeare each experience of the lover becomes a window through which we look out on immense prospects—on nature, the seasons, life and death, time and eternity. In Donne it is more like a burning-glass; angelology, natural philosophy, law, institutions are all drawn together, narrowed and focused at this one place and moment where a particular man is mocking, flattering, browbeating, laughing at, or laughing with, or adoring, a particular woman. And they all have, for Donne in the poem, no value or even existence except as they articulate and render more fully self-conscious the passion of that moment. His imagination is centripetal. Hence, though I am still unable to agree with those who find a valuable 'philosophy' of love in 'The Ecstasy', I now think that I erred equally in the past by criticizing the supposed 'philosophy'. The real question is how that particular progression of thoughts works to make apprehensible the mood of that particular poem. Each of Donne's lyrics is a world in itself; or, if you prefer, is the whole world foreshortened and transformed by, and sacrificed to, some one precise shade of passion. Each would therefore be suffocating, monstrous, if it lasted too long. But this intense concentration within the individual lyric is, of course, balanced by a great versatility of mood in the collection as a whole. When we re-read the *Songs and Sonnets* they always seem to be fewer than we had remembered. It is remarkable that in such short space so many different modes of love—frivolous, petulant, embittered, tragic, 'Platonic', rapturous, or tranquil—have found such striking expression.

The antithesis between Shakespeare's Sonnets and Donne's lyrics holds for versification as well as for temper. In all syllabic verse (though not in *vers libre* or in the metre of *Beowulf*) there is some difference between the ostensible metre, the pattern (as it were) announced or advertised, and the actual phonetic facts that fill it. Thus, even in 'The daliance of the undiscerned winde' there is a theoretical stress on *of*, but no real stress. The practice of the Drab poets was to sail as close to the metre as they possibly could. The practice of the Golden poets was to sail as close to it as they prudently could; to make music and variety

by comparatively small and unobtrusive variations and with
frequent coincidence. Shakespeare in the *Sonnets* is the supreme
example. Donne, at his most characteristic, departed from the
ostensible metre more widely and more often. There is thus
what some would call a sort of counterpoint between the actual
rhythm of his sentences and the ostensible norm. As will be
seen in a moment, the word 'counterpoint' must be kept for a
different purpose. I should prefer to call Donne's usage *Sprechgesang*:[1] a speaking tone against a background of imagined
metrical pattern. Thus in the line 'Sweetnesse and wit, they are
but *Mummy*, possest' we hear the speech-rhythm 'They're but
Múmmy', with only one full stress, but are aware of the theoretical 'They're bút Mummý' somewhere in the background.
Similarly in 'Spirits, as like soules as it can', the word *soules* is
ostensibly unaccented but in reality must carry as strong a
stress as *like*. The 'Nocturnal' is perhaps the finest example.
A high percentage of the lines are so built that they have to be
read as if the syllables could hardly be dragged out of the
speaker's mouth; for he is freezing, dying, sinking into nothing-
ness. Thus 'Drown'd the whole world—vs two—oft did we grow'
lingers at the centre in four successive syllables which have
stress, length, and emotional weight. Compare 'some ends,
some means: yea plants, yea stones'. An opposite effect of
impatient speed is achieved in the line from 'The Canoniza-
tion', 'Take you a course, get you a place'. It would be merely
glib and metallic if the ostensible metre were—as the actual is
—choriambic: its value depends on our hearing it against the
norm of 'The Phoenix ridle hath more wit' (23). In the same
way a poem whose ostensible metre was as spondaic as certain
lines actually are in the 'Nocturnal' would be merely a literary
curiosity. Of course this element of *Sprechgesang* in Donne's
lyrics must not be exaggerated. Examples do not occur in every
line or even in every poem. 'The Undertaking', 'Sweetest Love',
the 'Valediction forbidding mourning', and the 'Ecstasy' use
simple melody. Sometimes what might be mistaken for a breach
of the ostensible metre is no such thing. If we took the line
'Weepe me not dead, in thine armes, but forbeare' (from 'A

---

[1] This word properly means 'recitative'. Readers will understand that I am
using it to mean mere speech with orchestral accompaniment, such as we hear from
some Alberichs. The abuse of an old word, if explained, may give less trouble than
the invention of a new.

Valediction of weeping') in isolation, we should think that the stress on *thine* which the ostensible rhythm demands had been crossed by a speech rhythm 'in thine ármes' where it had no existence; but in the context there is real, as well as ostensible, stress on *thine* because the lady's arms are being contrasted with the (implied) arms of the sea in the following line. But though not a ubiquitous, *Sprechgesang* is a genuine feature of Donne's poetry.

Much more could be said about this immensely influential poet, but he is in no present danger of neglect and my few remaining pages must be filled with some notice of two other departures from Golden technique.

III

The first of these two need be only briefly mentioned, since its great triumphs were in 1600 still far in the future and its character is very well known. This was the movement towards the Augustan mode. It imposed new restrictions on the couplet and even on the individual line, limiting its musical range but working insatiably towards perfection within those limits. We have seen it beginning in the satires of Lodge, and we can see it also in one passage from Donne, a surprising metrical 'sport' (Elegy XVII, 26–59).

The other, represented by Milton and Campion, extends and refines a technique which we have noticed in Nashe's 'Adieu, farewell earth's bliss' and Drayton's *Sirena*. Like Donne, Milton and Campion depart freely from the ostensible metre. The difference is that while Donne crosses it with conversational rhythms, they cross it with rhythms as poetic, as unabashedly artful, as itself. Donne, as it were, talks against the music: they play one melodic pattern off against another. That is why I reserve the word 'Counterpoint' for their structure and distinguish it from his *Sprechgesang*. An example or two will make this clear. In Donne's 'Good Morrow' what crosses the iambic pattern is the conversational rhythm of 'What thou and I *did* till we lov'd'. In *Paradise Lost*, I. 26 the line 'And justifie the wayes of God to men', where the real and the ostensible rhythms coincide, is thrown up into enormous prominence by the two preceding lines where the real and ostensible are far apart. But then the real rhythm of those two lines (predominantly dactylic, and almost hinting, from far off, the Alcaic) is no more con-

versational than the purest iambics and suggests not speech but
high-wrought choric song. Similarly at the beginning of III,
'Hail holy light'[1] departs from the iambic not in the direction
of speech rhythm but to become even more solemn, more chant-
like. Sometimes, again, Milton's variations seek a more boisterous, country-dancing music than that of the norm: as in
'Wallowing—unweildie—enormous in their gate'. Nearly
always, in one way or another, we get verse-rhythm played off
against verse-rhythm, not against speech. And what Milton
did with heroic verse Campion did with the lyric. It is not indeed
impossible that Milton's conception of the decasyllable was
consciously influenced by Campion's analysis of it in the
Observations.

Thomas Campion[2] has left us about a hundred and fifty
lyrics of which there is only one that any ten lovers of poetry
might be expected to agree in condemning: it is I. 14, a paraphrase of Psalm cxxxvii, in *Two Books of Airs* (*c.* 1613). With that
exception his poems can be divided only into the good and the
better, or else into the more and less characteristic. Sometimes
he wrote good Drab as in 'A daie, a night, an houre of sweete
content' or 'Lift vp to heau'n, sad wretch'. At other times he
wrote in the homely and rustic vein of 'Jacke and Jone they
thinke no ill' or 'I care not for these Ladies', but of course with
an artful homeliness, working his rusticity up into something
finer. He can also do a pure Golden lyric like 'There is a garden
in her face'. Sometimes, but this very rare, he will do a dramatic
lyric in which a passion seems to grow and change, as in 'Thou
are not faire for all thy red and white', and this is his nearest
approach to Donne. But it is a distant approach and few great

---

[1] Milton may well have remembered that the same rhythmical phrase opens the
Faithful Shepherdess. He would not have disdained that poetical association any
more than he disdained the association with Ariosto in line 16.

[2] b. 1567. Gentleman pensioner at Peterhouse, Cambridge, 1581. Admitted
Gray's Inn, 1586. Perhaps served in Essex's expedition to aid Henri IV, 1591. His
five 'Cantos' included in Newman's edition of *Astrophel*, 1591. *Poemata*, 1595. *A
Book of Airs* (1601), the second part being by Philip Rosseter. *Observations*, 1602.
By 1606 had become a Doctor of Physic. *Masque for Lord Hayes*, 1607. *Songs of
Mourning* (elegies for P. Henry), *Lords' Masque, Masque at Caversham*, and *Masque
for Lord Somerset's Marriage*, 1614. In the same year delivers a sum of money from
Sir Jervis Elwes to Sir Thomas Monson, thus (we may assume, unconsciously)
assisting in the murder of Sir Thomas Overbury. *Two Books of Airs*, n.d. but
probably about this time. *Third and Fourth Book of Airs*, 1617. *Airs at Brougham
Castle*, 1618. *New Way of Making Four Parts*, n.d. *Epigrammatum*, &c. (enlarged
edition of his Latin poems), 1619. Ob. 1620.

lyric poets are more unlike; a comparison between Donne's 'Apparition' and Campion's 'When thou must home to shades of vnder ground', where there is some community of idea, illustrates this. There are passages, again, in the *Masque at Brougham Castle*, where Campion faintly reminds us of the lyric Milton. But none of these excellences show the essential Campion, the poet whose loss would leave a chasm in our literature.

To approach Campion's poetic art without a consideration of his music is not so risky a proceeding as might be expected. The musical and the metrical pattern are often such that neither, of itself, would suggest the other. 'Followe thy faire sunne' (*Book of Airs*, 4) and 'seeke the Lord' (*Two Books*, 1. 18) are set to the same air but are written in slightly different stanzas. The threefold repetition of 'O come quickly' in 'Neuer weather-beaten Saile' when it is sung corresponds to nothing in the form of the poem. However happily married to their 'notes' in the end, the poems had a rhythmical life of their own before the marriage, and it is their 'music' in that sense that the literary critic is concerned with. Campion's immense originality and delicacy as a metrist appear in his earliest work, in the partly unsuccessful *Canto Secundo* of 1591. The basis is a line like Horace's *Ergo Quintilium perpetuus sopor* (spondee, two choriambics, iambus). Campion's lines 3 and 22 realize it completely, stresses coinciding with longs. His 8, 13, and 27 realize it quantitatively but not accentually, with stresses on shorts (hetherward, merry, sodaine), and one unstressed long (*is meete*). These are the most beautiful and probably truest to the Latin model. His 16 and 28 realize it accentually but not quantitatively, making the second of 'enamoured' and the first of 'amorous' do duty as longs. Some lines do not conform at all, such as 4, 11, 21, and 25. I think his hope was that the surrounding melody would carry us through them without a jar and with the added pleasure of relief from the strict norm. In line 11 (especially if we allow a vocalic R in 'feltred') I think he succeeds:

> Blacke: their feltred haire torne with wrathful hand.

The poem is not a complete success but it already introduces us to the subtle audacities of Campion's art, his counterpoint. Thus 'Sleepe, angry beauty' (*Third Book*, 25) is ostensibly in decasyllabics. Line 2 is really so; but a different, a more gravely lyrical, movement has been already suggested in the first line, with its opening spondee and its strong pause before the second *sleep*:

> Sleepe, angry beauty,
> Sleep and feare not me.

And the spondaic opening is picked up again in lines 10 and 11. The total effect is unlike that of any decasyllabic poem we have ever read. In 'Loue me or not' (*Fourth Book*, 10) we have decasyllabics in lines 4, 8, 11, and 12, but a majority of lines consist of two choriambics and an iambus:

> Loue me or not—loue her I must—or die . . .
> Her to enioy—her to unite—to mee,

while the third starts off as if it were going to go like that and ends unexpectedly with the heavier 'would my wish'd comforts giue'. There is also a free use of equivalence. In these lines from the *Lords' Masque*,

> Dance, dance, and visit now the shadowes of our ioy,
> All in height and pleasing state, your changing formes imploy,

'dance, dance' is the metrical equal of 'all in height': in 'Come, O come' (*Third Book*, 23), the two syllables 'Come, then' in line 11 are perhaps equivalent to 'As swift to me' in line 12. But Campion's greatest triumph is his handling of those 'falling' or 'trochaic' lines which, ordinarily carrying too much emotion ready-made in their very form, are deadly to minor poets. The long lines in 'Follow thy faire sunne' (*Book of Airs*, 1. 4) are built on the same pattern as the long lines in that unfortunate stanza which Arnold chose for the second part of his *Tristram*. If there now seems little in common between 'Raise the light, my page, that I may see her' and 'Follow those pure beames whose beautie burneth', this is because, in Campion's poem, each stanza ends with a 'rising' echo of its opening line, because the central lines are in a different pattern, because 'follow' is so much less ruthlessly trochaic than 'raise the', and finally because no dramatic urgency is admitted. Even more remarkably, in 'Neuer weather-beaten Saile' (*Two Books*, 1. 11) the longest lines are in the same metre as *Locksley Hall*—if it is worth calling it 'the same' when we have been led up to them by the headless fourteeners, and their coarse emphasis has been muted by Campion's refusal to allow a pause at the eighth syllable. Hence that peculiar hovering or floating effect which is so common in Campion's long lines and so rare in other poets (though Shelley once approached it in 'Ah, sister, Desolation is a delicate thing'). He can use even the line of *Ormulum* without deafening or wearying us: setting it in mono-rhymed triplets and varying rising with falling movement (*Third Book*, 14). He can make trochaic or 'headless' alex-andrines delectable by mixing them with decasyllables and avoiding the banal, the inviting, pause at the fifth syllable (*Two Books*, I. 3). He will so write a fourteener that no reader can turn it back to its natural jog-trot—'Attending as the starry flowre that the Suns noon-tide knowes' (*Two Books*, II. 17). His subtlest patterns cannot even be exhibited in the space at my disposal. A poem like 'Author of light' (*Two Books*, I. I) really has to be learned as we learn a strophe and antistrophe of Pindar, com-paring each metrical phrase with its fellow ('Sunne and Moone' with 'Sinne and Death', 'Starres and vnder-lights' with 'Hell and tempting Fiends') before its full beauty is apparent. But then, lest you should suppose that he was confined in his own subtlety, he will next moment offer you something so straight-forward as 'The man of life vpright' or 'Now winter nights enlarge'.

Two passages may help us to approach Campion's poetry in the right way. One is in the *Lords' Masque* where he makes Orpheus say to Entheus (who is 'Poeticke furie'),

> thy excelling rapture, eu'n through things
> That seems most light, is borne with sacred wings.

The other, from the preface of the *Fourth Book*, says: 'The Apothecaries haue Bookes of gold, whose leaues being opened are so light as that they are subiect to be shaken with the least breath, yet rightly handled, they serue both for ornament and vse: such are light Ayres.' The 'excelling rapture' works through what appears 'most light'. Poetry—at least, this sort of poetry—has no weight at all. One breath of misdirected solemnity would blow it away. There is seriousness in Campion's art, and sometimes in his matter—he did the best versified psalm we have, and it was the *De Profundis* (*Two Books*, I. 4). But he is the least tragic of the poets. The first song in the *Book of Airs* begins as a translation of Catullus's *Vivamus mea Lesbia*; its effect is exquisitely unlike that of the original. The poignancy of *soles occidere et redire possunt* vanishes into the vast image 'heau'ns great lampes doe diue Into their west and strait againe reuiue'. The speed, the brilliance, of their movements is what impresses us: we want to applaud rather than to weep. And when death appears in the last stanza, it is 'timely' death, and the tomb a 'happie' tomb, not to be vexed with mourning friends but graced with the pastimes of 'louers rich in triumph'. Something sunny like Ronsard and gentle like Tibullus has dissipated the passion. The next air is ostensibly (for Campion plays tricks with his ostensible themes as with his ostensible metres) the traditional warning, Horace's or Wyatt's warning, that the mistress's beauty will not last. Yet despite the last line our main impression is less that the girl will die than that Campion will live to a hale and trusty old age: his 'Oke' is so very 'sturdie'. The third is typical of Campion's attitude to sensuality. How wanton, yet also how seemingly innocent, how comical and sensible, the word 'comfort' is in this piece! There is no tension, no swooning, no ravening, in Campion's poetry of fruition: he sings jocund sensuality, 'country matters'. The fourth is, certainly, much graver. The explicit moral is the same as in the second; the mistress (the Sun) and the lover (the Shadow) will both die, 'the Sun still proud, the shadow still disdained'. But the metaphor becomes a myth. We hardly think of a human lover. His sorrow seems to be part of the order of nature—an occasion not for resentment or passion but for a composed and not disagreeable melancholy. The fifth has a subject that invites tragic handling: but the rhythm, the refrain, and the hopeful resolution in the last stanza, all make it sound rather like the short-lived sorrow of a child. And the reader who does not like this kind of thing should take warning at once that this is what is going to happen to every subject when it enters the world of Campion's imagination. His poetry is as nearly passionless as great poetry can be. There are passions somewhere in the background, but a passion, like a metre, is to Campion only a starting-point: not for moral or intellectual activity but for the creation of a new experience which could occur only in poetry. By the time he has finished, the original, the merely actual, passion hardly survives as such: it has all been used. This happens as much in his religious as in his erotic pieces. The Christian life becomes an idyll or a romance. He can make more use of 'paradice' than of 'heauen': a paradise 'with Christall streames and flowers' from which wicked beasts are excluded, or an enchanted garden on a mountain-top (for that is what the words 'euer blooming' and 'high' really effect in 'Neuer weather-beaten Saile'). God's 'steepe hill is high' and the world is a witch (*Two Books*, I. 18). The thirteenth of the same book may be compared with Lord Vaux's 'I lothe that I did loue' in Tottel, which has the same theme. The Tottelian poem is dark and grim; Campion with almost a white, Blake-like vision, sees in his backward glance an adventure-story comparable to Bunyan's. This is not the only passage where he reminds us of Blake. They are of course extremely different; it would be hard to find a poet less prophetic and, in some senses, less serious than Campion. But there is sometimes in both the same sense of remoteness from the common world, and the same impression of being in a place that has few colours but much brightness. Campion is fond of words like sun, beams, sun-like beauty, 'a streame that brightly flowes' and, for contrast, of groves and shadows. Yet perhaps aural experience means more to him than visual—'silent' days, the 'peacefull' western wind, 'musicke' which is the beloved's 'Eccho' and 'beauties simpathie' (*Book of Airs*, 10). In one place (IV. 6), if I have not misunderstood him, he suggests that light exists only in order that beauty's 'grac't words might better take', as if the visible woman were merely an accompaniment to the audible woman. Certainly, unlike many of his sex, he thinks it a pity that a woman should be silent: 'Awake, thou spring of speaking grace, mute rest becomes not thee' (III. 13). No further development along the same line was possible after Campion. Indeed, when we read the description of his masques, we may feel that civilization itself, soon after his time, lost some of the elements which made such art possible. He 'makes mouths at our speech'.

When we look back on the sixteenth century our main impression must be one of narrow escapes and unexpected recoveries. It looked as if our culture was going to be greatly impoverished. Yet somehow the 'upstart' Tudor aristocracy produced a Sidney and became fit to patronize a Spenser, an Inigo Jones, an early Milton. Somehow such an apparent makeshift as the Elizabethan church became the church of Hooker, Donne, Andrewes, Taylor, and Herbert. We stole most of the honey which the humanists were carrying without suffering very much from their stings. The occultism of the Renaissance, though not laid till the latter part of the seventeenth century, did much less permanent harm than might have been feared. Puritanism, though destined to a short triumph by 'apostolic blows and knocks', was intellectually defeated. One great loss had indeed been suffered by poetry. I have already noticed how the Golden style was limited in its range by its own extreme poeticalness. It must now be added that the Metaphysical style was equally, though diversely, limited. If the one was too rich, the other was too subtle and ebullient, to tell a plain tale. Hence, between the two, huge territories that had once flourished under the rule of poetry were in effect ceded to prose. They have not been recovered. The unadorned, but strictly formalized, archaism of Morris's best narrative poetry (now totally misunderstood) was a successful technique for recovering the ancient and medieval liberty, but successful at a heavy cost. I do not suppose that the sixteenth century differs in these respects from any other arbitrarily selected stretch of years. It illustrates well enough the usual complex, unpatterned historical process; in which, while men often throw away irreplaceable wealth, they not infrequently escape what seemed inevitable dangers, not knowing that they have done either nor how they did it.

INDEX

Main entries are indicated by figures in bold type. Asterisks indicate biographical footnotes. Passages where an author is alluded to (e.g. by the mention of one of his works) are indexed under his name whether that name occurs in them or not.